JOHN FOWLES

JOHN FOWLES

———

A Life in Two Worlds

Eileen Warburton

VIKING

VIKING
Published by the Penguin Group
Penguin Group (USA) Inc., 375 Hudson Street, New York, New York 10014, U.S.A
Penguin Books Ltd, 80 Strand, London WC2R 0RL, England
Penguin Books Australia Ltd, 250 Camberwell Road, Camberwell, Victoria 3124,
Australia
Penguin Books Canada Ltd, 10 Alcorn Avenue, Toronto, Ontario, Canada M4V 3B2
Penguin Books India (P) Ltd, 11 Community Centre, Panchsheel Park,
New Delhi—110 017, India
Penguin Books (N.Z.) Ltd, Cnr Rosedale and Airborne Roads, Albany, Auckland,
New Zealand
Penguin Books (South Africa) (Pty) Ltd, 24 Sturdee Avenue, Rosebank,
Johannesburg 2196, South Africa

Penguin Books Ltd, Registered Offices: 80 Strand, London WC2R 0RL, England

First published in 2004 by Viking Penguin, a member of Penguin Group (USA) Inc.

1   3   5   7   9   10   8   6   4   2

LIBRARY OF CONGRESS CATALOGING-IN-PUBLICATION DATA
Warburton, Eileen.
John Fowles : a life in two worlds / Eileen Warburton.
p. cm.
Includes bibliographical references and index.
ISBN 0-670-03283-2
1. Fowles, John 1926– 2. Novelists, English—20th century—Biography. I. Title.
PR6056.O85Z89 2004
823'.914—dc21   2003047963

This book is printed on acid-free paper. ∞

Printed in the United States of America

Designed by Nancy Resnick

To Roger

CONTENTS

viii   Contents

INTRODUCTION

The truth about any artist, however terrible, is better than the silence. . . . I know many writers fight fanatically to keep their published self separate from their private reality. . . . But I've always thought of that as something out of our social, time-serving side; not our true artistic ones. I don't see how the "lies" we write and the "lies" we live can or should be divided. They are seamless, one canvas, for me. While we live we can keep them apart, but not command the future to do the same. The outrage some Thomas Hardy fans have shown over all the revelations about the private man seems to me hypocritical in the extreme. They hugely enrich our understanding of him. . . . I have had to convince a number of friends and relatives that the kindest act to the [writer] is remembering them—and that all art comes from a human being, not out of mysterious thin air.

—JOHN FOWLES, LETTER TO JO JONES, SEPTEMBER 15, 1980
(ARGUING FOR THE PRESERVATION OF JOHN COLLIER'S
PERSONAL PAPERS)

By the early 1970s John Fowles, still in the midst of his active career as a writer, was already the subject of academic scrutiny. He was beginning, at this point, to critique the critics, wondering why they "devoted far too much . . . time to the analysis and exegesis of 'dead' literary product as against the investigation of living literary experience." He himself was fascinated by the interior process of mythmaking, the transmutation into art of his own life, past personal experiences, understanding of nature, and reading. He defined inspiration as the state "of extreme sensitivity to past biographical data." It baffled him that scholars and commentators should focus their attention on finished texts and overlook the obvious, the "dark world of self-experience inherent in myth-making, . . . the subjective *living* experience."[1]

I met him around this time, in January 1974. I was probably typical: a twenty-six-year-old American graduate student, very nervous, armed with three carefully crafted scholarly questions about John Fowles's published books, his intentions, and so forth. But the day was miserably wet and squally. My husband and I had walked for hours, fascinated and anxious, around a Lyme Regis we both "knew" from *The French Lieutenant's Woman*. When we knocked at Belmont House that afternoon, we were soaked and cold and must have looked like two bedraggled children to the woman who opened the door.

I was struck speechless. This was Elizabeth Fowles (she insisted on "Elizabeth" immediately) offering her hand. But I "knew" instantly that she was Alison, the character I most loved in *The Magus*. John Fowles hurried up behind her, kindly, welcoming, pressing our cold hands and hustling us to the fireside. What I overwhelmingly felt at that moment was the conviction that the books and the life I was briefly touching were connected at a profound, organic level. My academic interview questions seemed shallow and beside the point.

I stumbled through the questions, of course, although I can't remember either what I asked or what Fowles answered. We tried to hurry off but were urged to stay. Through a long afternoon of cups of tea and concern over wet shoes, we were enfolded in the tender ordinariness of John and Elizabeth's world. We heard of Elizabeth's daughter, marrying that summer; I must someday meet her. They asked of our families, our life as young marrieds. Fowles spoke of a new book of short stories to be published later that year.

It was nearly evening, though still daylight, when the rain stopped and John led me down the muddy, sloping pathways deep into his overgrown garden. There were no Latin names that day and little talking. He parted dripping branches to reveal winter blossoms. He crushed leaves and held them to my nose to sniff. He stopped at the deep center of the garden and smiled. The outside world was gone, and there was only wet green, damp earth, silence, and fading light. These were his real answers, I now know.

So, many years and many meetings later, I became John Fowles's biographer. As I think he wishes I have tried to focus on what Fowles calls the ethnology of the novelist, the study of living behavior in the artist. For me, this means simply telling the story of how this man's life resulted in the books he made. In large measure, it has also meant writing the biography of a marriage. Elizabeth is at the center of the books, as she was of John Fowles's life. There were no publishable novels before her coming. There were none after her going.

It was possible for me to observe this relationship between the books and a private existence over the writer's lifetime because, with staggering generosity, John Fowles made his diaries available to me before they were published or openly archived at the Harry Ransom Humanities Research Center at the University of Texas at Austin. I read them while they were still archived (and not open) at Exeter University in Devon. Fowles further supported my research by permitting me to use his own correspondence, that of his first wife, Elizabeth Fowles, and a very personal assortment of private papers, photographs, and other materials. He introduced me and vouched for me to his friends, family, and professional associates, almost all of whom consented to be interviewed and/or to release materials. He himself gave me many hours of interview and research time, occasions I shall always treasure. What Fowles did not do was interfere, censor, or collaborate. He did not read drafts of the manuscript or review the book before publication. Mistakes are entirely mine.

John Fowles and I seriously began our discussions about a biography when he was touring the United States in 1996. Sitting on my back porch in Newport, Rhode Island, on May 22, he advised me emphatically: "There's only one way that you could do it. Tell the truth. Tell the truth." Since then he has assured me repeatedly of his trust. I am honored by his trust and have tried to be worthy of it by following his advice, telling the truth, even in places where it was difficult.

For all his astonishing support, I acknowledge John Fowles with deepest gratitude.

Fowles's diaries, from 1947 to 1998, provided the chronological backbone for the biography. (Chapters 1 and 2, covering 1926 to 1947, are the exception.) These diaries, however, are the record of an interior journey over half a century and are confined to Fowles's powerful personal interpretations of exterior fact, the immediate impressions recorded in a single moment. To balance the diaries with other kinds of witness, I have used other written documents and interviews. I drew on John Fowles's and Elizabeth Fowles's letters and a wide range of interviews with family, friends, and associates of both JF and EF. I was given access to all of Fowles's surviving papers, both published and unpublished.

Because of the magnificent, overwhelming richness of these primary documents, I have included very, very little from the vast library of secondary sources about John Fowles, the books and articles about his works. The exception is James R. Aubrey's *John Fowles: A Reference Companion*. I have only rarely used any of Fowles's published interviews with scholars and journalists. Beyond the interests of brevity, I wanted Fowles to speak for himself from diaries and letters as much as possible. I wanted to include a direct sense of his "voice," along with those of the other major figures in the story. Furthermore, I have learned to be somewhat suspicious of taking the "John Fowles" who speaks in interviews for the "real" John Fowles. I came to this conclusion both from reading what he says about interviews in his diaries and, more important, from interviewing him myself over a lengthy period.

Fowles's interviews with me were filled with stories and "memories" in direct conflict with other sources, particularly his own diaries. Although to this day he has phenomenal recall for facts of natural history and geographical place, Fowles would be the first to say what a poor memory he has and has always had for biographical fact. Throughout his life he has forgotten the details of events, safely recording them in his diary, then letting go of them. In fact, the written diary record was in many ways the most "real" part of any experience for Fowles. In addition, most of my interviews were recorded when the man was over seventy and his memories were further blurring. However, if Fowles forgot an incident, he simply invented it or reinterpreted it to suit his purposes. After a lifetime of regarding his own biography as raw material for his fiction, a malleable substance to be shaped and reshaped in his imagination, many of the stories he presented as factual were obviously fictional. Sometimes he presented other people's experience, in perfect sincerity, as if it were his own. Although I suspect that Fowles sometimes does lie to interviewers, particularly when he is bored or the interviewer is especially irritating, I learned to regard his interview narratives as different from deliberate lying. They were the product of what I call fertile forgetting. The personal past is forgotten or suppressed but returns through imagination in the writer's fiction, often in a different shape. Throughout the narrative of Fowles's life there is a marked tendency for him to slip away into hiding of one sort or another, then to reappear in a mask or disguise, refashioning himself as a fiction.

I confess that I was annoyed when I first became aware of this tendency in his interviews with me. But when Anna Christy, Fowles's stepdaughter, wrote me that Fowles was "playing the god-game" with me, I had to laugh. I learned to feel rather honored to sit listening to the great novelist actually weaving his fictions in my presence. I use these interviews in the biography only with caution. But I'm very glad we did them.

The Harry Ransom Humanities Research Center (HRC) at the University of Texas at Austin, Texas, awarded me an Andrew W. Mellon Fellowship, 1998–1999. This enabled me to spend several months among the papers of the John Fowles Collection at the HRC, the major repository for Fowles's documents. I am very grateful to Director Thomas F. Staley and the Ransom Center for this support and for the time, energy, and interest of the exceptional staff there, particularly of Pat Fox. Likewise, I am grateful to University Librarian Alasdair T. Paterson and to Jill Pyne and other very helpful members of staff at the Exeter University Library and at Reed Hall, Exeter University, for their kindness and interest during my 1997 research stay. My warm appreciation goes to the entire staff of the Lyme Regis Philpot Museum over the past twenty-some years of visits and especially to Liz-Anne Bawden, Jo Draper, and John Howells for their kind assistance with collections and archives in 2000. I also wish to thank Head of Special Collections Lori N. Curtis, Sidney F. Huttner, and the Special Collections staff of the McFarlin Library at the University of Tulsa, in Tulsa, Oklahoma, for their help during my visit in 1999. I am grateful to John Fowles for permission to publish from these collections.

Except for the Mellon Fellowship, financial support for this project came from my family. Two generous colleagues made it possible for me to continue working with a highly flexible schedule at various stages of the research and writing. I sincerely wish to acknowledge my late friend and teaching partner Patrick J. Keeley, Head of the Humanities Program at Bryant College, and Michael Semenza, Vice-President for Institutional Advancement at Salve Regina University.

Many people made my work possible, but I must begin by thanking three special women. Anna Christy, Elizabeth Fowles's daughter, has been (after Fowles himself) the person who gave the greatest support to this project in England. Besides providing memories and documentation, she has smoothed introductions and eased misgivings about me, encouraged me in a thousand ways, rewarded me with her friendship, and occasionally helped me laugh at myself. There would simply be no biography without Anna. Monica Sharrocks (after spending a morning sizing me up) shook me to the core by sharing more than thirty years of letters preserved from Elizabeth Fowles's intimate correspondence with Monica and Denys Sharrocks. Monica saved Elizabeth's "voice" and perceptions, making it possible for her to be present in this biography. Karen Daw transcribed and retyped the early manuscript volumes of Fowles's diaries, working directly with John Fowles to make out his difficult handwriting. Karen's massive labor, carried out with discretion, sensitivity, and accuracy, gave me and future scholars a key for reading the original manuscript diaries.

John Fowles, I have believed throughout this project, has been exceptionally fortunate in his friends. His oldest friends have immeasurably enriched my understanding, not only of him but of the times they shared and the places and people they knew together. It has been a delight and privilege for me to know Denys Sharrocks, Ronnie Payne, Freddie Porter, and (at great distance) Angus McCallum. I am also grateful to John's sister, Hazel O'Sullivan, for a sense of the Fowles family at Leigh.

Technical support at critical moments was received from Charles Glass, Roger Warburton, Nye Warburton, Richard Benson, and William Mello.

I am grateful to Sarah Fowles, John Fowles's wife since 1998, for her hospitality and patience.

I acknowledge with thanks my fellow biographers in the Providence Biographers' Group: Jane Lancaster, Joan Richards, Adam Nelson, Hadassah Davis. With my husband, Roger, they have been my most scrupulous, faithful readers through every single draft of every chapter. Beyond their friendship, they have given me the priceless gift of colleagueship, trusting me with their work, while they supported mine. My generous friend Judith Rényi helped me tremendously as the painstaking first reader of the finished draft.

Two great mentors inspired my love of biography: the late Kurt Weber, Professor of English at the University of Maryland, and that exceptional biographer Deirdre Bair, my doctoral adviser at the University of Pennsylvania, 1976–1980.

I am grateful for the many years of enthusiastic support from John

Fowles's American editor, Ray A. Roberts, who became my editor at Viking Penguin and a good friend; for Tory Klose's thoughtful, careful attention to the manuscript; and for all the help of Clifford Corcoran and Nancy Resnick. I record here my heartfelt thanks for the wise counsel, thoroughness, and hard work of my agent, Melanie Jackson. Tom Maschler, Fowles's British editor, warmly encouraged and supported the project from the first, while his successor at Jonathan Cape, Daniel Franklin, has continued that interest.

In my travels and through correspondence I have been blessed with cooperation, enthusiasm, extraordinary kindness, and great hospitality from my contacts. I have heard personal tales from the hearts of the tellers and shared adventures and broken bread with people I shall never forget. Some of these people have become my friends. All of them have been exceedingly generous. Simply saying thanks doesn't seem enough. Yet, in alphabetical order, I wish to express my gratitude to:

James Aubrey, Sarah Ball and the Essex County Council Archives, Liz-Anne Bawden, Peter Benson, Lilette Botassi, Suzie Botassi, Sally Burwood, Eileen Cacace, Anna Christy and Charles Glass, Tess Christy, Joanne Collins, Nigel Cozens and Lymelight Books, James G. P. Crowden, Karen V. Daw, Nicos Dimou and Marianne Betitoubi, Jo Draper, Ann Dyer, Sam and Maydelle Fason, Helen Faulkner for Ashridge Management College, Sarah Smith Fowles, Pat Fox, James C. Gedney, Fay Godwin, Bob "Magusbob" Goosmann, Anne Greenshield, Stephen Hoar, Will Homoky, Sanchia Humphreys, Charlotte and Tony Jackson, Ann Jellicoe and Roger Mayne, Kirki Kefalea, Lily Kefalea, Jud and Monica Kinberg, Maury Klein, John Kohn, Rodney Legg, Tom Maschler, Andrew McCallum, Angus and Patricia McCallum, Heather McCallum, Anne Mitchell, Christopher Moulin, John and Lillian Munby, Hazel and Daniel O'Sullivan, Kevin Padian, Ronald S. Payne and Celia Haddon, Anna Ruszkowski Peebles, Reverend Peter Pickett, Fred Porter, Neil Reid, Jan Relf, Judith Rényi, Mary Scriven, Denys and Monica Sharrocks, Betty Slowinski, Leonora Smith, Thomas F. Staley, Judith Swift, John Sylvester and the Old Bedfordians, Katherine Tarbox, W. Thomas Taylor, Gareth and Elizabeth Thomas, David and Annette Tringham, Elena van Lieshout, Dianne Vipond, Hazel Warburton, Jean Wellings, John Wilcox, Phyllis Wilcox, William Wilcox, and Tom and Malou Wiseman. Thank you all for your trust. Please forgive me if I have omitted anyone. It is not deliberate, and I apologize.

My fondest gratitude goes to my parents, Ed and Ruth Hand, for their love, assistance, and pride and their extraordinary patience and support; to my parents-in-law, Ron and Margaret Warburton, and the extended Warburton family in England for so much kindness, hospitality, and help of many kinds; to my sons, Nye and Rhys, for putting up with this endless project and my absences and doubts, for love, listening, support, and understanding beyond their ages, and for taking JF to their baseball game; and to my friends, old and new, who were patient and wonderfully encouraging.

Most of all, with a full heart, I gratefully acknowledge my husband and best friend, Roger Warburton, who got me through it.

—Newport, Rhode Island
September 2002

JOHN FOWLES

CHAPTER ONE

Voices in the Garden

Leigh-on-Sea: 1926–1939

> *Voices in the garden. I half-hide in one of the bamboo-clumps.*
> *Down the path beside the Cobb Road march two young gentle-*
> *men, age about five each. I challenge them: "What are you doing*
> *here?" All such previous encounters have resulted in almost im-*
> *mediate panic-stricken flight. But these two stand smiling.*
> *"We're going for a walk." Then one asks, "Is it your garden?" The*
> *other, "Are you the famous writer?" Already winded by this en-*
> *gaging frankness, I make them take me to where they got in. . . .*
> *"It's to hide from the other boys, we don't want them to know."*
> *"It's the best garden in Lyme, this," one of them confided, "a wiz-*
> *ard place."*

> —JOHN FOWLES, DIARIES, DECEMBER 7, 1986

It was not a show garden, although its owner loved to show it to visitors. It was the secret place of a solitary, turned in upon itself, not facing the outside world at all. The single acre of the Belmont House garden spread over a steep slope, dense, walled and fenced, with a lone locked gate at the bottom, shut off even from the sea beyond. Entering from the terrace by the house, sixty-year-old John Fowles had passed the greenhouse and well-kept orchard and vegetable patches and descended by winding pathways into a green chaos, where outside sounds quickly diminished and the light was filtered through heavy leaf canopy. He had always needed wild places, and his wild places were always places to hide. His own garden, where on this wintry day he waited unseen amid the green for his childish visitors, had grown wild and secret, a mirror to the mind and spirit of its gardener, much like the books for which Fowles was famous the world over.[1,2]

This garden on the Dorset coast of England had a peculiar, semitropical miniclimate, catching the sun on its steep south face, so that the unique and unexpected flourished there. It was old, and Fowles delighted in discovering the works of his predecessors, the plants stocked by owners stretching back over 150 years and the odd ruins of buildings from earlier times. He himself had filled it with plants from all over the world, specimens dug up or cuttings stealthily nicked while traveling and smuggled home stuffed into the pockets of his raincoat or trousers. He knew each growing thing with the intimacy of a lover in a long relationship and murmured the words of their names tenderly. Relishing the rare, he always identified his plants by their Latin names to scholars and interviewers, making up the Latin when he had forgotten and delivering this fictional mischief in an avuncular deadpan. Fowles truly shared this domain only with a stone statue of the goddess Ceres and with the other wild creatures that came and went unmolested: owls, hawks, blackbirds, herring gulls, dormice, foxes, hedgehogs, deer.

In the garden's hidden interior clock time seemed arrested. Time moved imperceptibly by seasons and each plant's secret ways. Fowles cherished this sense and found that only children, like these little boys, experienced the garden quite the way he did. The realm was created by adult labor, but in it, Fowles was also free to see like a child. When he had drifted for hours, breathing damp earth and blossom, mesmerized by the bending of light and the bending of time, he would hear the sound of a bell, calling him, as Conchis was to call Nicholas Urfe, back to the other world of everyday reality. Climbing up the path, slower for his six decades, John Fowles would reemerge from the garden to see waiting for him the one woman he had loved for more than thirty years.

John Fowles's earliest memories were of another garden, his father's garden in the Essex suburban town of Leigh-on-Sea. Unlike the Belmont House sanctuary, however, the garden at 63 Fillebrook Avenue was not a wild thicket for hiding. It was controlled and exposed, two circumstances John Fowles spent the rest of his life escaping. The merest tenth of an acre abutting a tiny semidetached house, Rob Fowles's weekend orchard was an obsessively pruned and espaliered collection of prized apple and pear trees. While John Fowles would walk through his garden, pointing out the exotic species he had surreptitiously acquired on his foreign travels or crushing a pungent leaf to hold to the nose of a visitor, Robert Fowles would proudly tell of the prizes won by his Cox's Orange, the exact yield of his Lady Sudeley, and of how he had bought each as a sapling for only a few shillings.

The son's memories of his father's garden, however, were not of prizes and prices but of scent and taste. No fruit ever equaled in flavor his father's James Grieves or matched the succulence of his D'Arcy Spice. In this fragrant, sensuous place, John Fowles in his earliest days was an adored only child, attended by two young, pretty, affectionate women. In the novels he published decades later, the configuration is often similar: A young man is lost in wonder in a green, enclosed natural place, instructed by an authoritarian older male and teased, cherished, and tempted by a pair of lovely young women. In the suburban reality of the late 1920s the women were John's mother, Gladys, and his cousin Peggy, who lived with the Fowleses as the little boy's caregiver until he was ten.[3]

Gladys May Richards Fowles was nearly twenty-seven when John was born. She was a handsome, full-figured woman, with dark hair, eloquent eyes, and a shy smile. John looked like her, tall, with wistful hazel eyes, a bashful smile, and an unruly shock of dark brown hair that flopped over his forehead. Neither of her children could remember their mother with a book, and she was not an intellectual. She was, however, a great talker, who kept up a constant flow of chat and was keen at crosswords. While her ten-year-older husband revered his meticulously controlled garden and was suspicious of the wild and rural, Gladys was a country walker, with a sharp eye for the first green shoots of spring. She kept birds, dogs, and cats, crooning to them like babies. She was a churchgoer and devoted to her parents, brother, and sister-in-law, all of whom lived within half a mile. As a girl she had studied in an excellent secretarial school but had not been allowed to take a job and so, as her son-in-law thought years later, had poured her considerable energies into the domestic sphere.[4] She kept a serene household for her nervous husband, so ordered and quiet one could "hear a pin drop."[5] She was, by every account, a truly exceptional cook and an excellent seamstress, who also knitted and worked embroidery and tapestry. Late in life she took up watercolors and handicrafts.

Gladys had feared she would not have children, so John as a boy was "the apple of her eye" and mother and son were close companions. In all her memories as an old woman (and her memory was as prodigious as her cooking), she recalled times spent with John, walks in the country, planned outings, projects she helped him with. A few years after his birth she lost a baby either to miscarriage or stillbirth, leaving John the sole object of her deeply reconcentrated love and attention.[6]

Side by side with Gladys was pretty, freckled Peggy Fowles, the daughter of Robert Fowles's elder brother, Jack, who had been killed in the war. Eighteen when she came to be nursemaid to the infant John, Peggy was the little boy's caregiver, playmate, and close companion until John was ten and she twenty-eight. He always spoke affectionately of Peggy Fowles. But this beloved cousin disappeared from his life in 1936, when she emigrated to South Africa with her two younger brothers.

Both the Fowles and the Richards families were Londoners who had moved to the rapidly growing Essex suburbs just after the Great War. Gladys and her younger brother, Stanley, had grown up in material comfort in fashionable Chelsea, the children of John S. Richards, a lace merchant. As newlyweds J. S. Richards and his wife, Elizabeth Pascoe Whear Richards, had come up from Cornwall to London, where, exactly like Sam Farrow in *The French Lieutenant's Woman,* he had joined one of the new department stores of the modern Victorian age and risen to be chief buyer of lace for John Lewis Ltd. He was a "master draper" in 1899, when his daughter was born. In 1918, as the Spanish flu epidemic decimated Europe, the Richardses moved to Westcliff-on-Sea, Essex, the western residential suburb of Southend-on-Sea. Although connected to the capital city by rail, this seaside town was reputed to have "good air" and a healthy climate.

The Fowleses, Robert Fowles's large family, were also well-to-do middle-class London merchants, originally from the West of England. They lived in a spacious house overlooking Clapham Common, attended by servants and sending their many children to good schools. Reginald Allen Fowles, Robert's father, was a partner in Allen & Wright, the family's tobacco-importing firm, founded a generation earlier. Even his children called him "Pard." The company flourished in several London locations, notably Piccadilly Arcade, and Reginald also owned income-producing commercial properties. He provided a comfortable life for his first wife, Lilian Ellen Lawrence Fowles, mother of Robert John Fowles, born the third son and the sixth of seven children in 1889. Robert was only six when his mother died. Reginald eventually remarried to a

Gertrude Brown ("Lovey" to the family), who gave him five more boys and girls.

Robert John Fowles grew up in a happy crowd of siblings and friends, avidly playing cricket, golf, and tennis and enjoying the urban pleasures of London vaudeville and music halls. He enthusiastically prepared for a career in law, clerking and reading in a barrister's chambers. He heard most of the great Edwardian King's Counsels arguing in court and was ambitious to be one of them.

The Great War crushed his dreams and his future.

Twenty-six when he enlisted as an officer in the Honourable Artillery Company, Robert saw three years of action in the trenches of Flanders. Memories of comrades dying beside him in battle tormented him throughout his life. Friends of his boyhood were slain. His brother Jack was killed in action at Ypres in 1917, leaving a widow and three small children. Robert himself was not physically wounded, but his nerves were shot. In 1919 he was sent to occupied Cologne, Germany, where he enjoyed being a military prosecutor for a year. When, in 1920, Robert Fowles was demobilized, he was thirty-one years old and, in the medical terminology of the day, "neurasthenic." His daughter sadly reported that he was acknowledged by the family to be "a mess."[7] His sleep was poor, his nerves were bad, and his hands shook "so that he could not even hold a teacup."[8]

If Robert was changed, so were his family and his prospects. In 1920 his father, Reginald, died and (Frank Fowles, the surviving older brother, being skipped over) the legally trained Robert was made executor of his father's estate. Because Robert was responsible for the children of his dead brother, Jack, and for his five young half siblings from Reginald's second marriage, the career in law of which he had dreamed was out of the question. He had to "go into the family firm" of Allen & Wright,[9] and he carried the burden of fiscal obligation for his extended family until 1951. Although Robert Fowles seldom spoke of Reginald and his legacy of emotional tensions and financial woe, his son, John, came to think of his Fowles grandfather as "a monster . . . hatching children and the eggs of disaster and hatred all round the clock."[10]

Reginald's wealthy business partner and cousin J. T. L. Tucker may have helped relocate the entire fatherless family to Essex. Supportive and concerned, Tucker, godfather to Robert Fowles, already lived on Canvey

Island on the Essex coast. By 1924 the struggling young Fowles was living nearby in Westcliff-on-Sea, commuting daily to London by train. He continued to be in "an awful state," suffering debilitating anxiety and nervous symptoms, though he stoically suppressed speaking of his war-time experiences until very late in life.[11]

Robert Fowles spent the rest of his life responding to what must have been a harrowing sense of loss. John Fowles was surprised to learn in the early 1950s that his father had sought help through Freudian psycho-analysis in 1923. This was quite a radical act at that time, both intellectu-ally forward and, perhaps, desperate. Sigmund Freud's theories may have been known to Robert Fowles through his assignment in Germany and his readings in German, but they were only just beginning to be generally known in England. The psychoanalysis completely overlooked the obvi-ous causes of Robert's mental distress—the savage carnage of the war, the experience of helplessly watching friends perish, the deaths of his brother and father, the crushing financial family responsibilities, and the sacrifice of his hopes. Instead, "the Freudian explanation," wrote John Fowles nearly thirty years later, "was that he had lost his mother at the age of six and had never acclimatised himself to his young step-mother."[12] Robert Fowles never returned to therapy, but he continued to look for answers. He spent the rest of his life reading, studying, and ar-guing philosophy and religion, a discipline that his only son also adopted.

The real remedy for Robert's illness was of a more romantic variety. Sometime in 1924 Rob Fowles met Gladys Richards at the tennis club in Westcliff-on-Sea. He was thirty-five, and she ten years younger. The lively Gladys was attractive and popular, with many boyfriends. But her other admirers suddenly seemed immature next to this responsible for-mer officer, who had survived so much in the war. She was moved by his experiences and felt needed. Gladys's parents were a bit alarmed at her attraction to a man in fragile health, burdened with such a dependent, complicated family. He had even expressed a reluctance to have children of his own.[13] But Gladys, as her son would put it, "nursed him back to health. . . . She was the cure."[14]

Love prevailed. Robert Fowles and Gladys Richards were married on June 18, 1925, in the Anglican parish church of St. Saviour at Westcliff-on-Sea. Robert brought his bride home to the house they named "Way-gate," purchased a few months previously. Only nine months and two weeks later their son was born there on March 31, 1926. The little boy was given the reversed Christian names of his father, John Robert Fowles.

There were two Leighs at the time of John Fowles's birth, and he was a child of historical transition. There was Old Leigh, a cockling, shrimping, and seafaring port near the mouth of the River Thames, ancient enough to have been mentioned in the *Domesday Book* (1085). Old Leigh sent ships to the Spanish Armada, captains to Trafalgar, and mariners to the evacuation of Dunkirk. Old Leigh was bounded on the north by the rural Hadleigh Hills and on the southeast by the vast tidal mudflats that John Fowles was to explore and hunt in and grow to love. Eastward Old Leigh looked out past the garish seaside resort of Southend-on-Sea, toward the mouth of the great estuary and the North Sea.

The "other" Leigh, Leigh-on-Sea, was a rapidly growing dormitory town created by the commuter railway to London, thirty-five miles upriver to the west, past oil refineries, docks, and factories. In 1925, when Robert Fowles bought the first little semidetached house built on Fillebrook Avenue, a cul-de-sac cut through from the London Road only the year before, the property was still part of the Chalkwell section of Westcliff-on-Sea. The Fowleses' house and the neighborhood were reassigned to Leigh-on-Sea in 1930.[15] The house was conveniently close to the omnibus line and the railway station, and Robert Fowles never owned or drove an automobile.

The Fowleses of No. 63 were part of a tremendous postwar real estate development boom as Leigh exploded in population from a village of fewer than four thousand to nearly twenty thousand in less than twenty years. Building plots and houses were sold from marquee tents, and special trains brought buyers to the auctions from London's Fenchurch Street Station. Residents of new streets often endured months of wheel ruts and mud as they waited for paving, sewers, and lights. To the loss of Old Leigh, historic houses dating back to the time of the first Queen Elizabeth were demolished during the early 1920s, as main roads were rapidly widened or extended.

Yet for all the frantic construction Fillebrook Avenue retained some of its pastoral character. Prittle Brook ran four houses from the Fowleses' front door. Blooming with wildflowers, thick with "brambles, nettles and rusting detritus," bordered by a concrete runoff ditch, an open field made an irresistible playground for John and the other children, despite being declared off-limits by their parents.[16] Just across the street from No. 63 were the Garden Estate Tennis Courts, where Robert played avidly and taught John to play. Spacious Chalkwell Park, with its expansive green lawns, formal gardens, and views of the sea, was a mere quarter mile from the house. Below the seaside cliffs, there were beaches along the Thames, where the Fowles and Richards families hired a tent-like beach hut each summer and spent their weekend afternoons in a sandy, sociable congregation of parents, siblings, grandparents, children, babies, and dogs.

Robert and Gladys referred to each other as "Father" and "Mother." In these capacities, they acted parentally toward their extended clan with Robert managing everyone's finances and Gladys welcoming siblings and half siblings, nieces and nephews, neighboring maiden aunts and distant bachelor uncles for meals and cups of tea. As a child John Fowles was enfolded in family, all living in the Leigh area. The Richards grandmother and Gladys's younger brother, Stanley, and his wife, Eileen, lived a few streets over. On the Fowles side, there was Robert's stepmother, Lovey, his sisters Maud, Maggie, Gertie, and Tots, his surviving brother, Frank, and half siblings Alan, Dick, Joan, Pat, and Kate. Besides Peggy Fowles, who lived with them, other young Fowles cousins were around often enough to capture John's imagination as he grew. To No. 63 came a much-envied cousin who lived in Kenya, a tea planter, big-game shot, and fly fisherman. Another eccentric cousin, Lawrence Wetherill, nineteen years John's senior and an international authority on ants, would also turn up from some exotic African adventure, fascinating his small cousin with photographs and stories.[17] John was often taken to visit his father's relative and godfather, J. T. L. Tucker, on nearby Canvey Island. An eccentric, lusty fitness enthusiast who had helped to establish the London YMCA while he grew rich in the tobacco business, Tucker would cheerfully greet the little boy by knocking him flat with a medicine ball almost as big as he was.

To safeguard the security of this rosy family world, Robert Fowles bore the anxiety of a shaky commercial enterprise. Each morning he joined his commuting neighbors as he walked five minutes up the street to the London Road, then a quarter hour down the steep hill to the Westcliff-on-Sea railway station near the Thames to ride an hour to Fenchurch Street Station, then cross London to Piccadilly Circus. Each evening he retraced his journey after spending his workday as managing director of Allen & Wright, Ltd., maker of briar pipes and purveyor of fine tobaccos. John Fowles recalled growing up "in the scent really of rather nice tobacco," the imported Havana cigars, the "rare, expensive . . . scented" cigarettes from places like Russia and Egypt, "the English cigarettes like Richmond Gems, and the house mixtures rolled by Allen & Wright."[18] In truth, however, it was "a luxury trade in an age of slumps and restrictions."[19] So many people also depended on the profits that there was never much gain. Some of the finances sustaining the extended Fowles family came from rentals of the other London business properties. Additionally, Robert Fowles owned a small amount of stock, which he monitored carefully.

Both his children recalled Robert Fowles as a thin man of very nervous disposition who constantly worried about his business and the people dependent on him. In the mid-1930s he developed a debilitating duodenal ulcer. John Fowles would recall how as a little boy he "decided that London was synonymous with physical exhaustion and nervous anxiety, and that the one thing I would never be was a commuter."[20] His father also hoped for better for him. Robert was extremely tight with money for housekeeping, and Gladys Fowles did not have use of a checkbook until she was a widow. There were few luxuries, though she did have household help.

The elder Fowles valued the comradeship and shared memories of his fellow officers from the Honourable Artillery Company and kept up connections with these veterans. But the other regimental officers were "well-to-do men . . . with good connections," John Fowles remembered, and Robert Fowles was condemned to watch his own resources shrink while hankering after the ethos and aspirations of this officer class. John Fowles wrote in 1951 that his father "was brought up in a rich home, lived with well-to-do people, still has friends and connections in a richer stratum of life. He regrets all that and has now an obsession about other people's riches."[21] Robert was determined that John would not have those regrets. He wrote to John's headmaster in 1944 how he felt qualms about his son's future "not necessarily because of the hazards of war, but more because I have constantly in mind the example of my own career being wrecked in the last war."[22]

John Fowles grew up in an atmosphere of thwarted ambition, with a father resolved that his son would not be disappointed professionally and a mother who plied him with intense, self-sacrificing attention. A sensitive only child until he was sixteen, the boy must have been aware that he was the object of very high expectations. In all outward ways he complied. He was an attentive son, an outstanding student, a talented athlete. At considerable sacrifice to themselves, the parents directed the family's resources, financial and otherwise, toward the boy's success for many years.

John's school was only a slight extension of the closely caring familial world in which he prospered. His uncle Stanley Richards began teaching at Alleyn Court Preparatory School in 1928, and when eight-year-old John was sent there in 1934, he was eligible for reduced tuition. From his front door John's school was an easy half mile by bicycle, mostly through Chalkwell Park. Riding to No. 3, at the end of Imperial Avenue where the neo-Gothic brownstone school building was located, John passed by the houses of his uncle and aunt on one side of Imperial Avenue and of several teachers on the other. His grandmother's home was in the next street. He rode in the company of another lad from Fillebrook Avenue, the two-years-older Trevor Bailey, destined to be the legendary England Test cricketer. The reflected glory of the school's sports hero made Fowles the envy of the other pupils. All six hundred boys, mostly day students, were highly visible in school uniforms of navy blue, and pink—blue blazer with pink braiding, gray shirt with pink tie, pink cap, and short gray trousers.

Even for a local preparatory school, Alleyn Court Preparatory School was unusually familylike. It had been founded by Theodore Wilcox in 1904 and has thrived under four direct generations of Wilcox headmasters. The administration was so benignly patriarchal that when Stanley Richards first asked out his future wife, the infants' teacher, he was sternly warned by the headmaster that "Miss Kidgell is a lady" and that his behavior was being watched. Stanley Richards and Eileen Kidgell were married in 1937 and, between them, taught at Alleyn Court for a total of ninety-two years. John Fowles himself could recall the young headmaster of his day bringing home his bride in 1938.[23] Gladys and Robert Fowles often took tea with Alleyn Court teachers. They also supported athletic prizes, and Robert annually played cricket for the Paters against his son and his fellow pupils.

The teaching staff was small, but upper school pupils like John Fowles received close attention. By the time he left the school at thirteen and a half, Fowles was studying Scripture, English, Latin, French, mathematics, history, geography, drawing, and natural science. His teacher for English, Latin, French, and mathematics was the Senior Master, a gentle, elderly man named E. P. Noble, who considered Fowles hardworking and "very promising." Under his guidance, the boy began his lifelong love of French language and literature. In English class, where he was one of Noble's two best students, John's essays showed "power of imagery." He was first in his class in natural science, taught to a high standard by his uncle Stanley, who also instructed in geography and drawing.[24]

History was taught by the headmaster, Denys Wilcox. But the handsome young D. R. Wilcox was more locally famous as joint-captain of Essex County Cricket Club and the coach of Alleyn Court's cricket side. Fowles, who had inherited both ability and a passion for cricket from his father, shone in the Saturday afternoon matches played on school fields just across the Crowstone Road. Playing for Rankine's, his athletic house, John was one of the team's best, noted as both bowler and batsman. He regularly took prizes in cricket events competitions. He was a strong competitor who excelled at most sports, training in swimming and diving in 1938, for example, until he could edge out the reigning swimming champion and capture the School Challenge Cup.

Sport was central to the school and to John's boyhood. He remembered with pleasure how D. R. Wilcox coaxed distinguished cricketers to the school's nets for demonstrations and to give "cherished autographs." By the time Fowles left Alleyn Court he "had been given a batting point or two by Hendren and even 'faced' the formidable Essex fast bowler, Kenneth Farnes." Farnes would "deliver very gently against [the] small boys" and then would terrify them with "demonstrations of reality" as he bowled "a few at full run-up and speed to the empty net."[25]

Robert Fowles taught his son to play golf and tennis well, but cricket was a shared passion and lifelong bond between them. Before the war Robert had been quite a good amateur, playing at club level against many of the greats of the age. His son heard personal accounts of W. G. Grace, Ranji, and Trumper. In John's boyhood, father and son attended all the local Essex matches, played in Chalkwell Park, just around the corner, or at Victoria Park in nearby Southend. John Fowles recalled seeing "almost all the great players of the 1930s on those two grounds" and soon had eyewitness tales of his own of "Patsy" Hendren, Verity,

Larwood, Hammond, and Frank Woolley, his father's hero. John played cricket as a talented amateur until he left Oxford University at the age of twenty-four, and badminton and occasional tennis until well into his fifties. Even after learning to disdain what he regarded as the class-conscious trappings of cricket, golf, and tennis, he remained an avid fan.[26] This love of athletics and the fierce thrill of competition were among Robert Fowles's permanent legacies to his only son.

Not until he himself was past fifty and his father had been dead for some years was John prepared to acknowledge Robert's other legacies, and then, characteristically, emotional acknowledgment came in written form. In his most moving essay *The Tree* (1979), John Fowles came to see Robert's "cunningly stunted trees" as emblematic of a life "severely pruned by history and family circumstance." He was "one of the generation whose lives were determined once and for all by the 1914–18 War," which had savagely narrowed his professional options, burdened him with responsibilities, and impaired his health, while at the same time strengthening some of his tastes and skills. The suburban orchard was Robert Fowles's "answer, his reconciliation to his fate—his platonic ideal of the strictly controlled and safe, his Garden of Eden."[27]

Despite his passion for his fruit trees and gardening, Robert Fowles had no feeling for nature in the wild. Indeed, John Fowles believed, he showed toward it "a distinct hostility." His was an urban soul, tempered by the unthinkable experience of trench warfare. Robert regarded even short walks away from houses and roads as "incipiently dangerous" and would claim "he had seen enough open country and breathed enough open air in his three years in Flanders to last him his lifetime."[28]

John Fowles came to regard his father as an example of "ghetto mentality," as having a kind of "Jewishness." While he had a "total blindness to nature," Robert demonstrated, more positively, "a keen admiration of intellectual achievement and of financial acumen . . . a love of the emotional . . . in things like poetry and classical music, of brilliant virtuoso performances . . . of quintessentially city arts." Using examples like Einstein or Spinoza, Robert Fowles was also apt to defend the contributions of Jewish intellectuals to European history against the casual, prevalent anti-Semitism of the day. He was a formidable opponent in an argument, by training as a prosecutor as well as by temperament.[29] His daughter recalled that he "could be quite hard," with his "sharp tongue" and strong opinions.[30] Just as the father and son competed fiercely in sport, so John

Fowles grew up competing in argument with Robert Fowles. Perhaps without realizing it, he defined many of his beliefs by choosing to hold the opposite opinion from his father.

Robert Fowles had returned from Germany in 1920 with good German, in reading, if not in speaking, and a great fondness for German culture. A quarter of his reading, John Fowles estimated, was in German Romantic poetry. "He must have known many poems of Mörike, Droste-Hülshoff, the early Goethe," the son recalled, "almost by heart."[31] Both Hazel and Daniel O'Sullivan also remembered her father, surrounded by volumes of German literature, reading Heine.[32] His love of poetry, like his garden, was intense and private.

The other three-quarters of Robert Fowles's intellectual reading was in philosophy, with which he was fascinated.[33] He favored the seventeenth-century Continental Rationalists, like Baruch Spinoza (1632–1677) and Gottfried Wilhelm Leibnitz (1646–1716). Both philosophers adhered to a mechanical picture of the workings of the universe and held that comprehension was possible through mathematical methods and a rational understanding of principles. Both redefined the divine and its relationship to the human search for wisdom so that it accorded with this mathematically logical universe. Spinoza viewed the universe pantheistically as a single infinite substance, which he called God. This "God" differentiates itself into particular things or "modes," even while it all remains logically and timelessly interconnected. Leibnitz, an inventor of the calculus, was also a proponent of a system called monadism. For Leibnitz, physical reality was constituted of indivisible, impenetrable units of substance called monads. Unlike the atom, the monad lacks spatial substance, thus is immaterial. Each monad is unique and a spiritual, soullike entity, while collectively also making up the appearance of the physical world. Each is dynamic and a perceptor of the whole of the universe. All monads exist in a perfect, preestablished harmony, synchronized by God. In these ordered, rational philosophical universes there is little room for human free will.

Robert Fowles was drawn to these philosophies strongly enough to have come up with his own "particular brand of monadism."[34] John Fowles once wrote that in religion his father held "strange views, Victorian views, Huxleyan, a kind of out-dated Protestant free-thinker. Reform the creed, modernize the church, and so on."[35] Robert Fowles called himself a Christian, but his son thought him the next thing to an atheist.

Beyond studying these European rationalists, Robert Fowles was particularly interested in the American pragmatists, especially the nineteenth-century thinkers Charles Sanders Peirce and William James. Pragmatism was the dominant approach to philosophy in the United States during the first quarter of the twentieth century. It is a material, anti-ideal philosophy, according to which the test of the truth of a proposition is its practical utility, the purpose of thought is to guide action, and the effect of an idea is more important than its origin. It is based in experience. "Truth" is relative to the time, place, and purpose of investigation and is as inherent in means as in ends. In other words, the test of a theory is empirical: "Does it work? Is it useful?" Although not inherently an individualistic philosophy, like the postwar French existentialist philosophy that John Fowles was to embrace, American pragmatism recognizes that truth is measured by relevance to each individual situation, therefore must be defined by each individual.

As he read these pragmatists and the other philosophers, Robert Fowles faithfully kept a notebook, a small dark-covered stationer's journal, in which he recorded short critiques and evaluations of each philosopher. His son grew up aware of this philosophic journal, with these pithy summations written in his father's neat hand.[36] As John Fowles grew older, Robert Fowles argued philosophy with his son in his characteristically forceful, challenging way. The young man felt these occasions were less discussions in which his opinion was respected than painful cross-examinations, "far more forensic than Socratic."[37] In his twenties, John Fowles sighed in frustration: "He has read so much, and knows so many -isms and long words which he brandishes in conversation, mystifying, confounding or embarrassing as the case may be. With me usually the latter, as he uses long words to dazzle simple people, and it seems to me like an aggressive superiority complex."[38] He remembered arguments in which Robert was "arguing, hectoring, talking above everyone else," and never listening.[39] Other thinkers were mustered into Robert Fowles's arguments. He admired Bertrand Russell's philosophy, not his politics. He thought highly of Charles Darwin and of Thomas Hardy, both great nineteenth-century materialists who emphasized determinism and a fateful lack of free will. Both influenced John's later work.

However important some of Robert Fowles's philosophical heroes may have become to his son, the greatest influence on the boy was simply that his father made the philosophical quest. John Fowles grew up in a home where someone asked the great questions: What is the good? What is the moral human life? What is being and what is not being? Is free will possible? He accepted that a central activity of his much-admired father was asking those questions, reading the great thinkers, and then evaluating those readings in writing in his carefully kept journal. John Fowles was the child of a diary-keeping philosopher. He was also the son of a secret writer of stories.

Although aware of his father's reading in poetry and philosophy and of his journal keeping, John Fowles was a young adult before he learned to his surprise that his father wrote fiction. Robert had produced an entire novel on his experiences in the Great War that included eyewitness descriptions of "going over the top" in Flanders and of battles like Ypres in which he had lost his brother. Although technically naïve, "stiff and old-fashioned," and "dated in language," Robert's novel was a somewhat poignant love story in which an Englishman and his German friend who loved the same girl before the war met "face to face in no-man's land," where "death and reconciliation" took place.[40] In 1950–1951 Robert also wrote some short tales of village life in the manner of late-Victorian magazines.

Seen on the commuter train to London in his bowler hat and black coat, or in his cricket whites on the club pitch, the reserved Robert Fowles would have impressed as a dry, unromantic character. John could not recall his father ever embracing him. But in his garden, in his stories, in his memorized poetry, in his love of the emotional and virtuoso in music, Robert Fowles was a secret, suppressed romantic. His intellectual life, the philosophy, the writing, his intense horticultural pursuits, and his keen sports life were an accommodation to a life of diminished expectations. The daughter born to him late in life observed how he never seemed content. She wondered if perhaps he might have even "had a bit of resentment that he didn't have the opportunities that John had."[41]

As a boy John Fowles, the brilliant student, the competitive athlete, the son that embodied the family's ambitions, also had a secret life. When alone, the shy boy could put off his public face and allow a dreamy, solitary self to emerge as he slipped away into nature or into a book of romantic fantasy and adventure. The key figure who unlocked the door to the world of nature was his mother's younger brother, Stanley Richards.

Years after his death in July 1983, Stanley Richards was vividly remembered by former students and colleagues at Alleyn Court with sincere affection and admiration. Ultimately he succeeded E. P. Noble as Senior Master, a position like Deputy Head. John Wilcox, who was both Richards's student and later his colleague, described him as "an imposing figure, tall, slim, very dark, very physically fit, a watercolorist, a naturalist, a handy cricketer, a talented all-rounder, and, above all, a gentleman." He recalled that Richards had a rich sense of humor and loved to tell jokes to the boys, although he could "look severe" when required. He was an exceptional teacher who loved the out-of-doors and was a fine athlete. Both he and his wife, Eileen Kidgell Richards, were ardent naturalists who spent their weekends on bicycle trips into the surrounding countryside. Richards could identify all the wildlife and often sketched the plants and birds they saw. He was especially talented in watercolor landscape and pen-and-ink drawing and found a ready market for his pictures.[42] He taught John, who was to paint and draw regularly, if very privately, for the next thirty years.

This magical uncle took his sister's son under his wing at a very early age, long before his own children were born. He was more than a dozen years younger than John's father and was merry and enthusiastic where Robert Fowles was reserved and dry. John Fowles later wrote of Uncle Stan, "I associate him with almost all my early red-letter days."[43] Together with his friend Mackie, another master from the school, Stanley made regular entomological expeditions into the unspoiled Essex countryside. Mackie had a little Jowett, a popular car in the thirties. With Stan's nephew John bouncing in the dickey, the open-air backseat, they motored off to spend the day searching for caterpillars and netting butterflies.[44] To Uncle Stanley John "owed the thrill of hunting for lappet caterpillars among the sloe thickets of the Essex seawalls near where we lived." Expeditions for moths, especially the beautiful hawk moth, were nocturnal, and on these trips Stanley taught John the art of sugaring, "the practice of creeping round Leigh-on-Sea and Westcliff, torch in hand, patrolling at his side various wooden fences and tree trunks anointed with the sweet gunge he concocted for attracting moths."[45] In his first published piece of writing, "Entomology for the Schoolboy"

(1938), "J. R. Fowles" revealed that the recipe for this entrapping bait was to "mix honey and beer together to form a paste and then smear it on a fence or tree. The moths, attracted by the honey, will sip it up and the beer will intoxicate them so that they will be unable to fly." The same essay describes how John was taught to kill his specimens using "a bottle containing a small quantity of cyanide" or crushed laurel leaves.[46] Uncle Stan also showed the boy how to set his collection, patiently and with an artist's flair.

As a child John longed to escape alone into the natural green world introduced to him by his uncle and probably by his mother. Reading by this time had become an escape as well. He was an early and avid reader—a "greedy" reader, he said—with a distinct taste for heroic adventure. Two of his favorite authors were Talbot Baines Reed and George Alfred Henty, the creators of popular late-Victorian "boys' books." Reed wrote tales of bold youths off upon exotic, fantastic adventures. "Huge, menacing anacondas, gorillas as big as Kong, man-eating tigers and enormous squids and tarantulas," Fowles recalled. "I largely swallowed them whole."[47] The endless supply of stories and books by G. A. Henty (more than ninety of them) was likewise delicious escapist fiction. Henty's just-out-of-school Kiplingesque heroes were deliberately fashioned to inculcate patriotism and model a code of behavior as they set out to fight injustice and establish order throughout the far-flung reaches of the British Empire.

Because it was a tale of adventure, full of hair-raising escapes, kidnapping, rescues, and true love triumphant, John also read and reread R. D. Blackmore's *Lorna Doone* (1869), a novel universally assigned to British schoolboys. Except for *Robin Hood,* he missed reading other classics of children's and youthful literature, however, until he was an Oxford undergraduate or older, when he documented each discovery in his diary. As a celebrated writer in his forties and fifties he would "remember" reading as a schoolboy such books as Kenneth Grahame's *The Wind in the Willows* and Alain-Fournier's *Le Grand Meaulnes*.[48] But Fowles's factual memory was poor as an adult, while his associative memory was abundantly fertile and plastic. He so constantly fictionalized his past that he often convinced himself. Read in adulthood, the classic stories of youth with their adolescent idealism and their tender appreciation of the rural world seeped into his soul like a potent green dye, permeating his earlier memories and perceptions until his *recalled* youth (if not his *factual* youth) was completely colored by them.

In reading, John created an alternative world in his mind. He once wrote that when confronted with a situation that made him uncomfortable or afraid, he treated himself "as a character in a novel. This must all be happening to someone else, it can't be me . . . or not quite me."[49] When he was ten years old he discovered the literary boy that he really wanted to be and in whom he recognized his own deepest self. The book was Richard Jeffries's evocation of a country boyhood, *Bevis: The Story of a Boy*.[50] This mythic adventure resonated through Fowles's life and work.

It may be coincidental, of course, that John entered Bevis's fictional world at the very time when he was experiencing the sorrow of being abandoned by his cousin and lifelong caregiver, Peggy Fowles, who left for faraway South Africa. Retreat into a private, imaginary domain through printed words and romantic fantasy became a coping pattern for Fowles when faced with loss, guilt, or sadness. *Bevis* is a deeply escapist book, and it would not be surprising if the boy, feeling the loss of this beloved woman, had first slipped away into its pages to ease his confusion.

Richard Jeffries (1848–1887) was one of the most intensely poetic naturalist writers of the nineteenth century, possessed by a kind of Wordsworthian vision into nature's transcendent and poignant immediacy. He drew on his own childhood in Wiltshire to create Bevis, a bright, sensitive, imperious boy vaguely between ten and fourteen, who has adventures on his father's farm during a long, sunlit summer. Bevis and his friend, Mark, explore, learn to swim, and build a sailing boat. They organize a full-scale Roman battle with other boys. They build a raft, make their own guns, and secretly camp out on an island in a lake for several weeks. The natural world is sharply observed and poetically rendered. The pace of the book is lazy, as the reader is a participant in the detailed, even laborious, thought processes of this young boy.

Competent and knowledgeable, Bevis has an easy familiarity with each plant, insect, bird, tree, or bend of the brook. His youthful adventures in his private rural domain are charming. What is key, however, is that Bevis is not content merely to know the prosaic landscape that actually exists. He mentally reshapes it. His imagination controls this kingdom, his perception and his will transform it, and his will and superior imagination ensure that his more practical friend, Mark, and all the other boys will accept as "reality" Bevis's imaginative projections on the land-scape. When Bevis decides that the lake is the New Sea, the island New Formosa, the entering stream the Nile, and the pasture the Battlefield of Pharsalia, no one ever contradicts him. Bevis's romantic and geographic reading, his hand-drawn maps, and, most of all, his boyish powers of narrative description compel the others not only to agree but to enter into his projected vision of the natural landscape. The boy is in fact a power-ful creator of fiction.

In Jeffries's rural world, boys John's age had absolute freedom to ex-plore, to know with complete authority every tree, every bird, every in-sect that they encountered. It was a world where a boy might reimagine a familiar landscape in heroic patterns and master himself as swimmer, builder, sailor, warrior, and even romantic lover, shyly falling for distant beautiful maidens. It was a world that words could reshape according to a child's will.

Bevis is also a tale of escape. In the woodlands and fields, on the lake, and especially on his small secret island, Bevis slips away from parents, from supervising adults, tempting girls, and, sometimes, even his closest friend. *Bevis* is the story of a child-man who craves solitude and the free-dom of a private natural world in which his imagination may work unen-cumbered by the presence of other people. Ten-year-old John, in his small suburban house in a predictable 1930s English town, loyally living up to his parents' expectations for conventional excellence, yearned with his whole hidden self to be that boy. Only in his imagination could he be. So as a child John Fowles "lived" *Bevis,* he would remember, reading and rereading it, sometimes turning back immediately from the final page to the first and starting over.

In July 1939, John Fowles's childhood in the bosom of his family drew to a close. In the greater world, war with Germany began to seem in-evitable as Fowles prepared for the next stage of his education. Encour-aged by his Alleyn Court teachers, he took the examination for a House Exhibition for Bedford School and was successful. The award gave partial tuition relief, making it possible, again with sacrifice, for Robert and Gladys Fowles to meet the annual costs of a Bedford boarding school ed-ucation. Their contribution for the five years of John's residence would be a hundred pounds a year, plus books, uniforms, and personal expenses.

The school, in the town of Bedford in Bedfordshire, was only fifty miles north of London, two hours' rail journey. Still, Gladys Fowles was reluctant to let John go. Added to the normal anxiety of separation from an adored only child who was close to her were the deep dread and uncertainty of sending that son away to an unknown environment just as hostilities seemed about to erupt. However, Gladys submitted to the male authorities around her. Robert Fowles wanted to seize the opportunity for his son's education. The staff at Alleyn Court encouraged the move. Finally, the Headmaster of Bedford School made direct contact with the hesitant parents, and his interest resolved the matter. The decision was made for John Fowles to begin boarding school at the Christmas term, late September 1939.

CHAPTER TWO

The Greenness at the Heart of Our Growth

Bedford, Devon: 1939–1944
Royal Marines: 1944–1946

The truth is, of course, that the Green England is far more an emotional than an intellectual concept. Deep, deep in those trees of the mind the mysteries still take place; the green men dance, hunt, and run . . . more than all other races, we live two emotional lives: one under the Sheriff of Nottingham's eyes, and the other with Robin under the greenwood tree.

—JOHN FOWLES, "ON BEING ENGLISH BUT NOT BRITISH," 1964

John Fowles's adolescence, easily the most formative period of his life, coincided almost exactly with the years of World War II in Europe, 1939–1945. Not yet old enough to join the fighting, he and his friends lived in its shadow, their lives shaped by its encroachments and conformist demands. Green in years, John spent his teenaged years in a duality of green, on the green playing fields of Bedford School and in the wild green world of rural Devon. At Bedford, his good citizen public self was part of a collective life, forged by tradition, strengthened by the war. Fowles came to embody and, indeed, enforce the best of Bedford's expectations and social morality. From the playing fields and classrooms, however, he moved in a kind of rhythm to discover a private self in Devon, a young man deeply secretive, profoundly alone, ecstatic in his intimacy with green nature, and a beginning writer.

Bedford School was chartered in 1552, and its legacy stretches back to a twelfth-century priory. In 1939 its 1891 campus combined monumental Victorian buildings with modern science and sports facilities and residences for six hundred of its nine hundred male students, ages six to eighteen. The imposing brick architecture was unified by rolling green lawns, well-kept cricket pitches, fields for rugby and other team sports, a parade ground, and paved walkways under overarching trees. Modernization of the school and its curriculum over the preceding decade was largely due to Headmaster Humfrey Grose-Hodge, a vigorous man in his late forties, as known for his dedicated encouragement of students as for strict traditional standards. An energetic Cambridge classics scholar who had served with the Guides Regiment on the Northwest Frontier of India, Grose-Hodge had come from a position at Charterhouse as headmaster to Bedford when only thirty-six years old. His 1928–1951 tenure was remarkable for its renewal of the school's academic mission and finances, as well as for its successful management through the Depression and World War II.[1]

The war had come to Bedford three weeks before Fowles arrived on September 21, 1939. On September 1, Germany had invaded Poland, and Great Britain and France had declared war. Until spring 1940, however, the nation waited in the so-called "phony war," a lull in which Hitler's aggressions seemed far away and Britain seemed more prepared and secure than was the actual case. Bedford School at the beginning of the Christmas term 1939 reflected both the bustle of war preparation and the illusion of security. The ground-floor exterior walls of all buildings were barricaded with stacked sandbags, and bunk rooms in each residential house had been fortified as refuge rooms with iron girders, timber props, and galvanized steel ceilings. Timetables for classes, theatricals, clubs, and athletics had been altered to facilitate the blackout. Yet for all these preparations, a cheery confidence prevailed that the war was a faraway adventure. "Business as usual," declared the school's magazine, the *Ousel,* but from neither complacency nor denial, rather "because we believe that steady nerves and smiling faces are the best contribution which we can make while the war lasts and that the chief war-work of a school is the building up of a generation fitted by their education for the task of healing and reconstruction when it is over."[2]

Away from his family for the first time at age thirteen, John Fowles was very homesick. He was assigned to Burnaby House with sixty other boys, all dressed alike in a uniform of dark gray trousers, blue jacket, black shoes, black tie, and school cap. He didn't like the food, the bitter cold, the lack of privacy in a dormitory for forty, or the roughness of rugby. He was taken in by "whopping great lies" told by the older boys to frighten the new.[3] He was scornfully teased as a sissy for not stealing chocolates on a dare.

The house system ran on the ancient practice of "fagging," whereby each junior boy was for a year the personal servant of a senior boy. Fowles loathed, as he wrote to the son of friends decades later, "having to clean a prefect's shoes and press his trousers and cook his tea and run his messages—and every time you made a mistake you got the cane or the slipper." He hated serving, taking orders, and living at the bottom of the hierarchy.[4] Other boys, more eager to belong, participated willingly. In contrast with Fowles's attitude, his friend and contemporary Angus McCallum took immense pride in polishing the shoes and bicycle of an important senior boy and fetching him fish-and-chips, considering himself generously paid and well treated.[5]

It was so easy, Fowles found, to make mistakes when there were rules for everything: school rules, house rules, and arbitrary rules imposed by the older boys. Even wearing the uniform correctly was difficult, and the often untidy Fowles was stuck with the nickname "Cheesy." There were rules about deportment at prayers and in class and rules about behavior in the town of Bedford. Rules were enforced by about twenty-five school prefects, or "monitors," assisted by sixty or seventy junior and senior "options." Part of their responsibility was to mete out punishments, mostly by denial of privileges, but also in the form of canings and slipperings.[6] Smacking with a slipper was intended as a less painful punishment for the younger boys. But skillfully used, the special slippers with hard heels and flexible leathery soles could hurt more than the cane. Fowles was proud by nature and, at five feet nine and 133 pounds, was big for his age. The humiliation of being called a sissy for avoiding punishment was as odious to him as the sting of being punished. He was dismayed by the sneaking atmosphere of boys who constantly told on one another.[7] In his isolation from his fellows, his natural reticence deepened. H. Boys-Stone, the warmly perceptive housemaster of Burnaby House, noted that John was "an extremely sensitive boy" but careless, untidy, overgrown, and very reserved.[8] The form master worried that he was withdrawn and often appeared "sleepy."[9]

In the way of traditional boarding schools, however, Fowles was made to participate. He was assigned to the JTC, the Junior Officers Training

Corps, attended chapel, and played cricket and rugby in his house teams. He joined PT exercises in the middle of each morning, led by the snapping ex-military bark of one Sergeant Jackson: "And don't forget, every morning of your life: a warm-up, a leg, a neck, trunk, lateral, dorsal, abdominal, jumping and vaulting, balancing. Dismiss! Work hard, play hard, then you'll be able to love hard—but don't tell that to the young 'uns."[10] Academically, as a first-term junior in the fourth form of the Lower School, he did well in French, managed in mathematics, struggled in Latin, plodded along in German, and was surprisingly indifferent in English. There were no sciences in his course. The masters thought him intelligent but careless.

This shaky start at Bedford worsened in the Easter 1940 term, when John succumbed to a major ear infection, the first of many illnesses he experienced while he was at school. His father had to travel up to visit him in the infirmary. Discouraged, sick, and unhappy, John missed so many lessons that it was "impossible to estimate his work," and his subject reports were universally poor.[11] His health improved in the summer term, but his studies were distinctly lackluster. In September 1940 he did not return to Bedford.

Later in life, when Fowles had become the subject of scholarship and speculation, he mythologized his absence from Bedford School as "a sort of nervous breakdown at the age of 15." Boarding school was brutal, and the students were worked savagely hard, he explained in a 1974 article (to the consternation of his classmates). In that version, his mother had rescued him, removing him from the school because of his fragile emotional health.[12] Fowles had had no breakdown, however. He reshaped the events in his mind, perhaps unconsciously, by remembering being sick and unhappy at the time of his leaving and by needing to think always of his own story as unique. But he was simply one of thousands.

For, in the spring of 1940, as John lay nursing his throbbing ear in the newly fortified infirmary, the phony war ceased, and the real one began. The Germans invaded Scandinavia, then the Netherlands and Belgium. Neville Chamberlain resigned, and Winston Churchill became prime minister, promising the nation "blood, toil, tears, and sweat."[13] In late May, as John was beginning the summer term, the attention of the world was riveted on the evacuation of Dunkirk. He must have been aware that Leigh fishermen were part of the rescue fleet. Indeed, wounded men straight from the beaches in France were soon quartered in every house in Bedford and "weary battle-stained Tommies . . . in a state of shock and bewilderment" were encamped on part of the school campus.[14]

Fowles, trying unsuccessfully to make up lost studies that summer, had genuine cause to be anxious and distracted. On June 22, France fell. In mid-July, as the term was finishing, the Battle of Britain was beginning. Hitler's Luftwaffe prepared for a German sea invasion of England. Day after day, night after night—as many as eighteen hundred in a single attack—German bombers and fighter escorts streamed across the Channel to bomb and strafe British ports, airfields, and factories. Outnumbered four to one, British RAF resistance was so intense that the planned invasion never came. For months, however, London was a primary target. Leigh-on-Sea, John's family, and his home lay within what came to be called Bomb Alley, the southeastern towns and villages of Essex and Kent along the Thames. The Fowleses received official letters warning them to evacuate.[15]

At that moment families all over Britain were evacuating, but children, especially, were being hurriedly gathered up by the thousands and sent off to remote or rural areas. At Bedford School, in the very same term as John's removal, more than 150 boys left the school suddenly, exactly as Fowles did, pulled out by anxious parents. Over the entire year 220 boys left, more than twice as many as in any previous year, with the *Ousel* reporting that they "chiefly went to homes overseas."[16] One boy was killed as his outbound ship to Canada was torpedoed by a German submarine. He was only the first Bedford School victim of the war. During that term alone, 4 Old Boys were killed, 6 were wounded, 6 became prisoners of war (1 of them wounded), and 2 were listed as missing. Five members of staff received orders, and 4 more were awaiting orders. Ultimately, 274 Old Bedfordians died in the service of their country during World War II.[17]

In August 1940 the entire Alleyn Court Preparatory School, including Stanley and Eileen Richards, left Westcliff-on-Sea for Bigadon House, at Buckfastleigh, on the edge of Dartmoor, deep in rural Devon. The grand, romantic, gaslit country house, occupied through the war as a boarding school, was unusually full of small children since many Southport-area families had enrolled their youngest sons to send them to safety. Quite a number of babies were born to staff families as well, including the Richardses' daughters, Jane and Ann.[18]

Robert and Gladys Fowles, with fourteen-year-old John and Gladys's widowed mother, Elizabeth Richards, followed the Richardses within weeks, evacuating to the village of Ipplepen, where relatives of J. T. L. Tucker had a chicken farm, and Stanley and their friends were only a bicycle ride away. They may have boarded for a few weeks at Altoona with Mrs. Turner, the farm's owner. By the autumn they had rented Ashleigh, a detached cottage on Croft Road belonging to Mrs. Turner, where they remained for the duration of the war. After being absent for the Christmas term 1940, John returned to Bedford School in January 1941 but spent all his holidays at Ipplepen through 1945.

No longer the safe routine of the prewar years in Leigh, life in Ipplepen for John's parents was a struggle. Robert's duodenal ulcer flared, and he was often incapacitated. When he could, he made the dangerous rail journey to London once or twice a week to look after the shrinking returns of Alleyn & Wright and his leased properties. Money was extremely tight. Gladys Fowles struggled to manage, grateful for her mother's three-pounds-a-week lodging, which paid for their food and for Queenie Hellyer, the maid. After her mother's death in 1941, Gladys took in paying boarders and kept a vegetable garden.[19] Yet while the Battle of Britain raged and the German blitzkrieg destroyed British cities and lives, fourteen-year-old John Fowles found himself living his sweetest dreams in a landscape he was to love for the rest of his life.

When he read *Bevis* as a child, John had fantasized a rural, wild landscape over which he, like the young Bevis, was acknowledged master. Not only a domain known intimately, this would also be one that might be mentally transfigured through his imagination. When he explored the marshes and farm country of Essex in the patient, knowledgeable company of Uncle Stanley, John had learned how to observe the natural world, discovering, collecting, and recording its seasons and secrets. Now, in the sunny, fragrant fields and leafy woodlands of Devon, down hedge-lined lanes and around water-filled quarries, in the shadow of the war, John entered fully into a boy's Eden, a green landscape that endured in his imagination and the writings of his manhood.

Worried by the war, the evacuation, and a failing business, Robert Fowles, age fifty-one, was also nearly prostrate with ulcer pain. In the autumn of 1940 he underwent a radically new surgical treatment at Plymouth that "gave him a second lease of life" and another thirty years.[20] While his father recovered, John and his mother explored Ipplepen and the countryside.[21] Though she surely did not know it then, this was to be

Gladys's last golden time with her son, when he was still willing to love her as unconditionally as she loved him. Together they walked the "narrow road between the ferny, greystone walls" to "the fine old high church, the red stone glinting through the old grey plaster" that stood on the site of an old Norman church, "the capitals and the roodscreen with its crude Byzantine figures and the Devil's door," surmounted by "a red sandstone block with a swan and a Maltese cross a lovely relic of the earlier Norman church." They listened to the fine peals of bells, "elegant, sprightly cascades of bronze . . . the two tenor bells beating a great deep pulse into the air." Walking the country lanes, they peeked into "those deep, rich Devonshire hedges . . . like zoos, botanical gardens." Gladys bought honey from Dornafield Farm at nearby Two Mile Oak, and John caught tantalizing glimpses of the farmhouse kitchen. He was allowed to select a spaniel puppy from a farm litter, finally settling on a little female he called Sheila. He and his mother discovered "an ideal field," the quarry field of the neighboring Majors' Croker Farm, "with outcrops of old rock, constellations of flowers, slopes, views, copses, the sudden, hidden, secret quarry . . ." and in the "interstices in the quarry-faces . . . white splashes . . . restharrow there, the oxeye daisies there."[22]

Even in this bucolic place, the war could intrude. Ipplepen and neighboring villages were occasional targets of cross-Channel hit-and-run raids by German bombers, who swooped down to machine-gun or drop incendiary bombs. John and his family would hear the muffled "crump, crump" and murmur, "Just Totnes," or, "Newton Abbot." Robert Fowles, an experienced former officer, became second-in-command of the Ipplepen Home Guard. On his holidays John was assigned the job of cleaning all the unit's rifles, by pulling a rag through the barrels with a string. During the 1942 Easter holidays the boy and his family watched the entire eastern sky grow red and were deafened by the overhead drone of planes as the Germans began the devastating firebombing of Exeter.[23]

By January 1941, when John Fowles returned to Bedford, the war had transformed the school. The honor roll of casualties steadily lengthened, staff members were called up, and participation in the Junior Training Corps was compulsory. Rationing, instituted nationally that year, affected food, school uniforms, and even the permitted page length of the *Ousel*. School fees were raised, economies imposed. Two female teachers were appointed for the first time in school history, replacing some of the fifteen staff men at the front. Eventually squads of students maintained the school grounds and buildings. Sheep were grazed to save fuel from mowers, and Victory gardens dotted the lawns. Everyone was required to contribute to the defense effort as the boys joined ambulance services, collected newspapers and other salvage, and labored as agricultural help on Bedfordshire farms. Soon the few remaining boys of Victoria College on the Isle of Jersey were evacuated into Bedford classrooms.

Fowles and his schoolmates were aware of the bombing as they studied at night behind blacked-out windows. Angus McCallum recalled "bursts of gunfire, the beams of searchlights and the glow of fires over London." He remembered lying awake "on the nights when the Cathedral City of Coventry was laid waste . . . listening to the unmistakable throb of the engines of dozens of German bombers flying overhead. Later, towards dawn, the sound of them returning to their bases in Europe woke us again." He recalled "window-shaking explosions" from mines dropped by parachute, German bombers pursued by RAF fighters through the daylit skies over Bedford, and bicycle expeditions to survey the wreckage of a German plane crash north of town. Toward the end of summer 1941, on the very morning of the School Certificate examinations, an enemy plane swooped low over the school property while its entire populace was assembled for prayers on the parade ground.[24]

The roof of Bedford's Great Hall, six hundred square feet, was judged a potential target for German bombers, so fire-watching teams were rotated, eleven boys and three staff, each paid half a crown a night. For boys like John, sitting hushed on the dark rooftop, these were enchanted nights. Bombed out of their Bristol wartime studios, the BBC Symphony Orchestra, the Theatre Orchestra, and the Singers and Choir were secretly in residence from January 1941 until 1944. From the blacked-out Great Hall of Bedford School, conductors like Sir Henry Wood, Clarence Raybould, Sir Malcolm Sargent, Sir John Barbirolli, and Sir Adrian Boult led the orchestra in clandestine broadcasting, as it was announced over the wireless, from "somewhere in England." As the orchestra rehearsed until dawn, the boys on the roof, who swapped their duty nights according to the announced program, were enveloped in the sounds of the symphonic repertoire. Some of the older, advanced pupils were also allowed to listen quietly from the inside galleries.[25] From his perch on the roof of the Great Hall or standing silently in gym shoes in the gallery, Fowles eagerly drank in Mozart, Bach, Purcell, Britten,

Chopin, Handel, Mendelssohn, Rossini, Dvořák and Beethoven, his touchstone for divinity.[26]

He worked hard at his studies now, and his teachers were pleased and encouraging. However, John's health, never an issue while in Devon, remained a problem. Characteristic of all the teachers' comments are remarks by the form master O. V. Bevan, who wrote that Fowles "deserves credit for maintaining his efforts in spite of frequent illnesses."[27] Headmaster Grose-Hodge picked up his red pen and underlined "deserves credit," adding sympathetically, "Creditable. He struggles well against adversity."[28] In term reports for 1941 through 1944, this is the pattern of John Fowles's career at Bedford: absence caused by frequent illness— scarlet fever, pneumonia, severe stomach pains, and ear infections—and a mixed classroom performance, encouraged by generally understanding teachers, who clearly respected Fowles's intellectual gifts as they manifested themselves in essays, translations, and exams.

Despite illness, despite the distractions of the war, fifteen-year-old John Fowles sat his School Certificate in summer 1941. His pass, which elated his teachers and delighted his parents, was impressive enough to advance him directly from R2 (second remove) to Modern Language Sixth Form. He had gained his matriculation in one leap.

His new form master evaluated the boy with insight. "A quiet, not showy worker," he wrote. "I hope that in his case we shall find that still waters run deep."[29] John Fowles was tremendously fortunate in this man, who was to oversee his work for the next three years. Nicknamed "Agah" by generations of Bedford boys from 1927 to 1954, A. Goderic A. Hodges was one of those extraordinary teachers who not only help youth to master a subject but introduce them to a wider view of humanity. They all thought of him as an old man, but when Fowles become his pupil, Agah was forty-eight years old, the age of the headmaster and several years younger than John's own father. He had a lifetime's experience behind him, however. Himself an Old Bedfordian, Hodges had left theological studies at Cambridge at the start of the First World War. He had learned to fly in Egypt, seen his two best schoolfriends die in action beside him at Gallipoli, and been recruited for the dangerous new balloon corps in Belgium. In May 1917 he barely survived an artillery attack. Bleeding profusely, his ankle and part of his left leg shot away, he was carried through the firing on the back of a New Zealander to a makeshift dressing station, where his leg was hastily amputated without anesthetic. He had served behind the lines until the war ended but at the age of twenty-five had "to face the world with one leg, and a knowledge of balloons and Hebrew." He had studied at the Sorbonne and Hamburg University, then returned to teach French language and literature and German literature at Bedford School.[30]

The history and generous personality of this "plump old man, with a gaunt leg, a quiff, and intelligent, smiling eyes in a chubby face" made him a legend at Bedford.[31] "A bit rocky" on his artificial leg, he was vulnerable to the pranks of his sixth formers. Fowles and the other boys learned to tie his academic gown to the chair so that when he stood up, teacher and chair rose entangled together.[32] Known as eccentric, Agah believed that the German master at Bedford was a Nazi spy and regularly lectured his pupils against trusting him. He could never resist a classroom "hate Nazism" session and could be easily distracted by clever students.[33] Fowles recalled that "'Tell us how you lost your leg, sir' was an unqualified ploy with him."[34]

Though "a hopeless disciplinarian," Agah Hodges was a superb teacher, teaching the French language with "method, discipline, and skill of presentation" and both German and French literature "with great sympathy and insight."[35] It was in the wider way of education, however, that his students came to revere him. Agah was a "tough, gutsy sort of intellectual" whose mesmerizing talk of the world beyond the Channel took their breath away.[36] John Fowles, writing when he himself was a teacher, remembered the sound of Agah's voice as "moving." In the classroom with a dozen adolescent boys, Agah showed photographs and spoke unforgettably "about the places he had seen and the people he had met." Locked in beleaguered England and yearning for adventure, these boys hungered for his stories. "For us, who had never travelled," Fowles wrote, it was possible to forget that "this was mid-England in war, not Aix."[37]

While John Fowles successfully adjusted to fitting in with the Bedford School community, he was beginning to enjoy a true sense of belonging in Ipplepen, Devon, where he spent each April, August to mid-September, and the Christmas to mid-January holidays. While characterized by a neighbor as a "deep-thinking boy," hard to know, and with "no particular friends," John "always wanted to be with the farmers in the field."[38] By his first summer he was a valued and accepted hand who joined in the harvest and threshing. Years before he re-created in *Daniel*

Martin this pastoral world and the boy he had been, Fowles wrote his memories to young Michael Sharrocks. At harvest the corn was cut until only "one little square in the middle was left and that would be full of rabbits," and everyone, even "ancient old women," set on them with sticks. There were swarms of rats at threshing and rat-hunting lurchers; "not a breed, they were half greyhound and half sheepdog. Very badtempered, but very fast and intelligent at catching."[39] Elsewhere he recalled the hard cider drunk in Devon harvest fields, its taste an "old fresh innocence, a sort of sleepy applejuice, treacherous as Circe."[40]

That summer, 1941, Fowles was absorbing an unexpected change in his family. In the aftermath of Robert Fowles's successful surgery and "new lease on life," Gladys Fowles had become pregnant. She was very surprised and even frightened. She was forty-two years old, and Robert was fifty-two. With the baby due in early January, John must have known of the pregnancy by the time he returned to Bedford in September. Such news and, to a middle-class English boy of nearly sixteen, such embarrassing circumstances may have deepened the normal adolescent divide between mother and son. Her attention was necessarily focused on the expected new child, his on the absorbing masculine responsibilities of the Upper School at Bedford and his rural explorations in Devon, where Gladys could no longer be his companion.

The very moment in John Fowles's life when he was displaced in the complete attention of his adoring mother by another child is the moment when he began his diary and became "John Fowles, the writer." Later Fowles insisted that the habit of keeping journals was begun at Oxford with the fragmentary intellectual notes he called the disjoints. Yet on Monday, December 22, 1941, he turned, in an ever-deepening pattern of personal solitude, to pouring his life onto the page. He began keeping nature journals. Unlike the early disjoints, these are not forays into art, literature, and the meaning of existence. Yet the mind and the personality of the writer—the young boy in the harvest field of *Daniel Martin*—are concretely, even poignantly present in these slim books. The nature journals, with their close observations and vivid sense of place, precede the disjoints by a good five years and are the first instance in which John Fowles's intense observations are made "real" by being written down.

He had returned to Ashleigh cottage on December 18, to an atmosphere of welcome mixed with anticipation and anxiety, for the new baby was due within that fortnight. By the end of the first weekend he had block-printed "NOTA NATURA RES, Ipplepen" on a school composition book, carefully divided the book into charts for sightings of wildlife by counts and seasons, and escaped. For the next three weeks John was out walking and writing observations every day except Christmas Day. Bored at that family celebration, he noted: "Nothing. Good weather." Every other day, in weather from "wet, windy storm" to "champagny," he listened to the rooks and jackdaws calling, noted that magpies were abundant, watched a buzzard being mobbed and a sparrow with a piece of hay in its beak, and searched for early primroses and young leaves in bud. "Eager and painstaking detail—sublimation," he later called the entries in this journal, "a love affaire."[41] So absorbed was he in his explorations that he did not make note, on January 3, 1942, of his mother's long labor at Ashleigh or of the birth of his sister, Hazel Mary Fowles.

At Ipplepen, through the next few years, John Fowles, the new writer, roamed joyful and solitary every day from dawn until after dark, often failing to turn up for meals. In the spring, he noted missel thrushes and goldfinches, watched blackbirds pair up, and puzzled out mating calls. In April there were bluebells, in summer blackberries. In September he kept watch on a "martin's nest with still fed young under Major's south eaves in the middle" and found an orchid with "a sweet sickly honey-like smell." On a "starlit night" he saw "swallows and martins still about in big quantities." By day he watched a pair of ravens wheeling over the woods and harked to their snoring caws. His observations grew increasingly detailed, and the notes were often interspersed with little roughly drawn maps of the area: a simple sketch of a lane with adjoining fields, a hayrack, a village, a hill, a crossroads. Here, he wrote, there were rabbits and field mice. Here he heard the cuckoos. There he marked a pair of daws. Wood pigeons were there, in "Buzzards Wood." He noted grasshoppers, dragonflies, bats. He was stung catching "a Humble bee (the pain went away after 10 minutes)" and marked his map accordingly.[42]

Knowledge of the natural world went much deeper than reason and observation for John Fowles as he grew into young manhood. It was a profoundly felt experience, a nearly mystical identification. An early diary entry from 1950 expresses some of what happened to him as a wandering youth and what he continued to feel each time he entered the natural world of woods and fields. ". . . The wood is deserted and I walk quietly down the paths, listening to birds, feeling so content to be in the real country again and alone, after so long. I still feel the old pantheistic sympathy, the feeling that I know everything that's going on, the delight in little things, little scenes, in the ever changing atmosphere of each second. A great tit's cap, brilliantly glossy and iridescent in the day's brightness. Jays screeching, a missel-thrush, robins, singing. Fragrant blossoms, clumps of primroses, and the sweet taste of violets."[43] He began to feel that he had a special "touch" with wild things. "The secret is slow, very slow movement, and the cultivation of an intuitive sense; and developing the continuity of awareness in observation. Not just at odd times, but always."[44] He returned over and over to the same places, exulting in "the pleasure of knowing a place intimately," and listed, among other pleasures and details, "the places to hide."[45]

He was well past the onset of puberty by the time of his rural explorations in the early 1940s. He had fallen in love for the first time at twelve or thirteen, when he had met a girl on a family holiday in Norfolk. Back at Leigh he had sat bewildered "in my bedroom . . . with an intolerable, because it seemed at that age irrational and inexpressible, melancholy in my heart."[46] But the life of a shy teenager at a boys' boarding school and in an isolated village in Devon was hardly conducive to meeting girls socially. If a real farmer's daughter corresponded to Nancy Reed in *Daniel Martin,* she is not documented. Fowles recalled that in his adolescence he was very lonely and had a "wild imagination" and indulged in "conscious fantasies, or nocturnal day-dreams." His favorite fantasy, which he enjoyed well past adolescence and which he wrote about several times in his diaries, was the one "about imprisoning women underground." They "rarely had a perverse feature," Fowles recalled, "in their commonest and to me most pleasurable form they always constituted a sort of wooing—that is, the girl kidnapped gradually fell in love with me, sometimes because she admired me, sometimes because she was so bored." Sometimes the daydreams were masturbatory; often the girl "knew me . . . only psychologically—not carnally."[47] These romantic daydreams sometimes included a real princess, as Fowles "day-dreamed of seducing Princess Margaret," which he later analyzed as "an extreme example of the tendency to imagine a future in the most aristocratic (aesthetically and socially and artistically) of worlds."[48] In any case, young Fowles was "excited" and satisfied by these daydreams of being with a girl in "isolating extreme situations." He was to say that his richly imagined inner life—both the excursions into the natural world and the erotic fantasies—"finally made me self-sufficient . . . as Crusoe-like as could be." He needed the outer world less and less, he believed, "because my inner world conquered me before I could begin to think independently."[49] The wraith girl imprisoned, adored, and seduced in his imagination would come to have her greatest creative power when she was intimately associated in Fowles's later work with the natural green world he loved so passionately.

Self-taught in the ways of nature by constant observation, by the age sixteen John had been taken under the wing of several of the older men of the area. Foremost was B. W. Brealey, or B.B., an expert hunter and former gamekeeper, who lived at Kingsteignton. B.B., recalled as "stern and willful and playful, all at the same time," taught John to shoot.[50] He was an exacting taskmaster. John was not allowed to shoot at a bird until B.B. was satisfied by the boy's skill on cans and bottles. Some months were spent in these tests until, on August 4, 1942, John made his first kill, a rabbit shot at Two Mile Oak. He memorialized the event by starting a new journal, *Up-Shot*, a hunting diary and kill record.[51] He carefully kept a running log for all expeditions, classifying the kill, the time, and the number of cartridges. A master chart designated columns for rabbits, lapwings, ducks, gulls, wigums, pheasant, partridges, pigeons, jays, rooks, crows, and doves. It is therefore possible to reconstruct, for example, that in August 1944 he killed seventeen rabbits, nine pigeons, one stoat, one albino rook, and two jays on twenty trips using fifty-three cartridges. John Fowles had become a passionate hunter. On school holidays he was out with his gun at dawn or after dark at least two or three times a week, often every day for a week.

For the most part he hunted with B.B. and was content to abide by the code of that punctilious man. John was allowed to shoot only at legitimate and edible game and only if he could reasonably expect to kill it at the range. B.B.'s notion of a "sporting chance" limited the hunter to two shots, "not above 30 yards with number six shot, above 40 with number four, above 50 with number two." Firing blindly into a pack, or browning, was as uncivilized as using an automatic shotgun. One never gave up searching for a wounded bird. In less legitimate forays Fowles dodged the letter of B.B.'s laws.[52] He was introduced to night poaching and fly fishing by the gentleman squire of the village, Major Lawrence. Once the English salmon-catching champion, the major was a wily fisherman and an expert shot. Fowles also made private mischief, shooting even ravens for pleasure, a destruction he deeply regretted in later years.

On a scrupulously daily basis, Fowles kept *Nota Natura Res, Up-Shot,* and other nature journals going until he left for Greece the second time in 1952. Apart from yielding information about his interests, these invaluable records track Fowles's whereabouts on particular dates until the early 1950s. The journal was restricted to Ipplepen at first but traveled with him to Bedford by 1943. Although the school's science club, the Alchemists, was keen that year for ornithology, John's explorations and journal continued to be a solitary enterprise. He never joined that club or shared his nature observations. Indeed, he never willingly joined any school organization other than an athletic team or the school monitors.

In contrast with his unfortunate start in 1939 and despite recurring illnesses, Fowles had emerged as one of the leaders of Bedford's Upper School, an excellent athlete and a fine student. In the classroom he remained quiet, self-absorbed, and dreamy. He progressed steadily, but his subject masters often noted that "he does not err on the side of enthusiasm." Agah sighed that "he continues to plod," but he often praised Fowles's translations of French and German verse.[53] The young man had grown into his 141 pounds (or ten stone one pound in the British system), standing slim, dark, and self-possessed at almost six feet tall. There is, even in photographs, a marked reserve about him.

Cheesy Fowles's schoolmates, however, thought of him as "outgoing" and "well liked."[54, 55] The key to this success was his athletic prowess. Always a cricketer, Fowles still played in Devon for Newton Abbot. At Bedford his abilities were coached to a new level by Jack "Taggy" Webster, recently a fast bowler at Cambridge University, and Ben Bellamy, former professional wicket keeper for Northamptonshire. Between them, Taggy and Ben turned John, previously only a batsman, into a formidable "swerve" bowler. By the time he was sixteen, he was the opening bowler on the school's First Eleven. Reviews in his first season were mixed, but Fowles was soon earning the notice of masters, the headmaster, Old Bedfordians, and his father. By the summer term of 1943 seventeen-year old Fowles was a school hero. The *Ousel* sang his praises, and at season's end he was written up as "easily the most successful of the bowlers."[56] Besides playing for the school, John led the Burnaby House team to victory, to the elated congratulations of Mr. Boys-Stone. Headmaster Grose-Hodge proudly wrote to Robert Fowles that John combined "an interested and cultivated mind . . . with the best bowling average in the School!"[57]

His star grew ever brighter through his time at Bedford. By 1944, in spite of unspecified injuries and intermittent ill health, Fowles was Captain of the First Eleven and best bowler. He was celebrated throughout the school for having "taken the wickets of a total of six Test Match players," including Gubby Allen and R. E. S. Wyatt. He faced Learie Constantine at a crowded charity match, delivering "a short and wide outswinger . . . for him to practise on." But Constantine, tired from his journey, changed his mind mid-swing and was caught. In the "horrified silence" around the pitch, the exasperated but secretly proud Grose-Hodge informed Fowles that as "the most hated young man in Bedfordshire," he was condemned to "buying Mr. Constantine all the Guinness he chooses to drink" while awaiting his train. Fast bowler Learie Constantine, then in the Lancashire League, had been a mighty Captain of the West Indies and spent his career and life working for racial equality in sport. An hour in his company "comprehensively destroyed" the remnants of schoolboy color prejudice for eighteen-year-old Fowles.[58]

When new arrival Ronnie Payne first set eyes on his future friend in 1942, Fowles struck him as a commanding schoolboy figure out of a boys' adventure novel. Tall and prominent at the center of a group of admiring boys setting out from a boardinghouse, Fowles appeared in "a cricketing white sweater with hair sort of slightly swept forward . . . and a rather diffident look on his face." Impressed, Payne marveled, " 'Wow! This is the real English aristocrat! I'm meeting a real English aristo.' "[59]

Ronnie and John were each the hidden wish of the other. Perhaps this drew them together. The sons of an impoverished Evangelical Methodist minister, Ronnie and his younger brother, Derek, had been bombed out of Hull by the Germans. Ronnie was overawed by Bedford and a latecomer to the established social structure of the Modern Language Sixth Form. A day boy, he was an outsider for at least a year. Just as John had established his place at Bedford by dominating the system, so Ronnie created a niche by affecting a rebellious attitude. Although he eventually shone in drama, debate, and languages, the tall, glib-spoken boy was constantly being called down for "looking sarcastic," for wearing his cap and uniform rakishly, or, worst of all, for "being a slacker at games." In a whiskey-soaked exchange of confidences years after the war, Ronnie admitted that he had envied John as "the nice conventional public schoolboy" who belonged. John confessed to having been jealous of Ronnie, "because everyone had you down as a rebel, as a trouble-maker. What I wanted to be."[60]

John had other friends who shared his station in the hierarchy of the school and were his rivals as much as his mates. One was J. A. L. Auden, known as "Auntie," who took much ragging on behalf of his cousin Wystan Hugh Auden, because the great poet had taken refuge from the war in the United States. Another was Angus Bruce McCallum. The blond "Mac" was warm, sociable, and completely devoted to Bedford. In Agah's Modern Language Sixth Form, Auden was first, Fowles second, McCallum third. Both other boys were also student leaders and talented athletes. Auden bowled with Fowles on the First Eleven, while McCallum kept wicket. The *Ousel* consistently wrote them up together: "Rain, plus Fowles and Auden, saved the school from defeat. . . ."; "Fowles bowled really well, taking six wickets for 22 runs, while McCallum kept wicket well, claiming four victims. . . ."[61] Auden captained the Fives team, headed the Chapel Choir, and was vice-captain, then captain of cricket, while Fowles was secretary and then captain. Mac and Auntie played rugby together in the Second XV (John was in the Third XV), while Mac was also a hurdler for the athletic team. They all played in their house teams for cricket and rugby. They all rose to become options, then monitors, with Mac, then Fowles serving as Head of School. They trained together in what was then called the Army Training Corps. Together they also sat examinations for the Higher Certificate of the Oxford and Cambridge Examination Board.

It galled John Fowles that Agah did not support his taking the Higher Certificate in July 1942. Agah, Fowles believed, favored the "scholars" in his class (Auden was a particular favorite), and John was labeled "the athlete." John was "jealous" of Agah's attention to other students. Proud and competitive under his reserve and diffidence, Fowles sat the Higher Certificate examination anyway. He passed (though missing a "distinction"), while some of Agah's favorites (notably McCallum) did not. Agah was surprised, and John smugly enjoyed feeling "contempt on the failure of his judgment." For more than a year after the examination, the stiff-necked adolescent held himself apart from Agah. "Our relationship was not a very satisfactory one," he wrote in 1954; "the fault was almost all mine." [62]

A model helpful student for the younger boys to emulate, John Fowles was made Head of House for Burnaby in September 1943. Angus McCallum was tapped by the headmaster to be Head of School, and Mac in turn promoted John with several others into the Monitorial Body. Thus, Fowles became one of the most elite members of the school's leadership, those with special privileges and responsibilities, responsible for scheduling and handling events and enforcing discipline. As a mark of his new status, John wore a different uniform from that of most other students: pale gray trousers, brown shoes, blue tie, and blue jacket. Moreover, he was given a cane, both a symbol of his authority and a functional instrument of discipline. By January 1944 he was Mac's deputy head.

To be Head of School by the time Angus McCallum assumed the role, was "a full time job." The war meant that the older boys left school early and more younger staff were called up. Even the headmaster was often in London providing the government with his specialist's knowledge of India. "In short," McCallum recalled, "as the boys were getting less mature, the staff were getting older and so somewhat less able to cope."[63] The monitors essentially ran the school.

There was a general tightening of discipline when Mac became Head of School, a strategy in response to the erosion of standards during four years of war. It was "not a punitive discipline," however, "but a return to the normal way the school was run before the disruptions of the war."[64] McCallum, in agreement with the headmaster and other monitors, believed that "the general behaviour of the school, particularly outside the grounds and in the town, had deteriorated."[65] He was credited by the headmaster and his own deputy head, Fowles, with restoring "the smooth running of every branch of the School's activity . . . by vigorous, sometimes even drastic action."[66] These reforms and all forms of correction had to be approved by the headmaster and discussed with the deputy head and other monitors.

Beatings were considered a serious punishment and a last resort. McCallum refuted Fowles's memory that the school had a brutal disciplinary system. Beatings, he wrote to me in 1999, were "very, very few . . . rare occurrences and not severe" in his experience.[67] Only the Head of School and his deputy were authorized to administer a beating and then only with the knowledge of the headmaster. Usually the withholding of privileges was enough correction. In Easter term 1944, for example, the popular Bedford Dujon Café was "put out of bounds for a week" after some of the boys had misbehaved there. This solution was first discussed with the deputy head, John Fowles, and "it worked." McCallum did recall administering a beating to four "miscreants" who disrupted with a barrage of paper airplanes the 1943 Carol Service in the Great Hall when it was "filled to capacity with dignitaries, parents, staff and pupils." These boys were caned only after McCallum, as an extremely annoyed Head of School, consulted with the headmaster, who agreed "that a beating was called for."[68]

Fowles, however, remembered disciplinary beatings as frequent, a more or less daily matter. "You held court every morning," he told a 1974 interviewer, "and flogged the guilty. Terrible."[69] He recalled beating boys in the large upstairs room of the old library, under the memorial tablets of the fallen Bedfordians of World War I. He recalled running the length of the room to strike sobbing boys with his cane, "normally two or three strokes, very rarely more than three or four." He recalled always operating with another monitor "just to make sure it didn't get out of hand."[70] He kept a notebook to keep track of his own duties and of the offenses of the Bedford pupils for whose behavior he was responsible. In its methodical way, this record is curiously similar to the nature journals and hunting journal, as Fowles carefully recorded names and infractions, adding a check mark to indicate a punishment delivered. The notebook indicates that during that single term in 1944, Fowles imposed some sort of penalty on more than three hundred boys for such crimes as "slacking," "late for prayers," "not looking on house notice board," "bathing in river," "out after lock-up," and "wrong name in cap." Fowles called this record of boys and punishments his Beating Book, but it did not formally have that title until 1992, when he added the annotation: "We heads of school called this a beating book. . . . I have kept this as a memento of the wrong path on which I was forced at Bedford."[71] Yet it is likely that while receiving some sort of discipline for their misbehavior, not all of these proscribed mischief-makers were caned. Fowles's frequent illnesses would have precluded daily court and daily enforcing in any case.

Fowles, for some reason, needed to remember Bedford discipline as more draconian than it was. He may also have been disturbed by what discipline he did mete out. During the Christmas term 1943 he was so visibly unsettled that both Agah and Grose-Hodge remarked on it. John was "a thoughtful person" for whom the times were "difficult," noted the headmaster, who then stressed that he had confidence in him.[72] More penetratingly, the form master wrote: "He is going through a difficult stage of growing up, reserved, shy, he is struggling with things inside himself, hesitating and a little bewildered. He will find his path, even if it be neither obvious nor straight, and it will be neither dull nor selfish."[73]

There was more to distress Fowles than the disciplining of boys, however. As a monitor, Head of House, and deputy head he bore the burden of listening to and consoling "boys grieving over the loss of relatives and friends in the war." McCallum's memoir recalls poignantly how much of his time and that of other monitors was devoted to "counselling," as Bedford boys wrestled with the terrible losses and insecurities wrought by the hostilities. Fathers and older brothers were killed, wounded, missing, or taken prisoner. Parents were stationed overseas for years at a time. School friends, as McCallum put it, "someone who just months before had sat beside you in class, or in the monitor's room; or who had rowed behind you in the eight, or played beside you in some team," were killed or missing. For Mac, by the war's end, "the names of some forty-eight boys, with whom I had had at least a nodding acquaintance, appeared on the lists of those Killed in Action." As Head of School McCallum may have enforced the rules with renewed disciplinary vigor, but what he most recalled was this counseling, "listening to some fresh 'casuality' of such a situation."[74] The outgoing Mac may have been a more naturally sympathetic listener than his reserved friend, but McCallum recalled that Fowles was not exempt from this sad duty and "did his full share."[75]

About to turn eighteen, Fowles was also facing direct military participation in this war. As they approached their eighteenth birthdays, all his friends were eagerly leaving school to serve. McCallum, the senior NCO in the Army Training Corps, was extremely keen to go. He and Auden left at the end of the Easter term and were inducted into the army together on May 4, 1944. John Fowles remained a full term past his eighteenth birthday.

He was suffering a monthlong bout of pneumonia when the headmaster visited him in the Easter term 1944. On Mac's recommendation, Grose-Hodge offered Fowles the position of Head of School for the summer term. Agah also influenced John's acceptance when he twice visited the infirmary to discuss Fowles's declared intention to read French at university. Aware of Fowles's sulky self-pity that the teacher had "lost interest in me," Agah brought the sick boy an anthology of Céline's poetry. John liked only some of the poems, but Agah's gift meant a great deal to him. "I knew then," he wrote later, "that he was trying to retain my soul; that he had come to the conclusion that I had a soul worth retaining."[76]

Both teachers were conscious that John Fowles needed a push into maturity. Under his reserve, he remained proud and judgmental. While recording all the boy's excellent qualities ("gentle, but firm, nature, and a refined, sensitive taste . . ."), both headmaster and form master observed his less forgiving side.[77] Grose-Hodge noted that John's sensitivity and high personal standards often made him find fault with others. "I hope he will never lower his standards, but perhaps widen his sympathies!"[78] Agah recommended: "If he can suffer fools with patience—and I believe he can—he may live to be a valuable servant of the community."[79] No amount of school responsibility would erase this character trait, however.

As Head of School Fowles was completely dedicated. The farewell written by his successor, C. W. Edwards, noted how "he was able to deal in a cool and certain manner with the most difficult situations . . . one of those born leaders who inevitably retain the respect even of those with whom they have to deal most hardly." The *Ousel* reported how "Cheesy . . . was endowed with an unusually attractive personality and a natural dignity . . . (and) was liked throughout the School."[80] During that term Fowles worked in close partnership with Humfrey Grose-Hodge, and the headmaster came to take a personal, mentoring interest in Fowles and his future. He wrote warmly to John's gratified father that beyond recording the respect and thanks of the school for the boy's exceptional service, he wanted to record his own pleasure at working with "someone of his mental caliber . . . who understands and cares for the things which I myself feel to be most important." Grose-Hodge pledged to see John Fowles attend Oxford, even to promising a grant for him from Bedford School.[81] "My son is not a demonstrative fellow," Robert Fowles responded, "but he has more than once given me evidence of his admiration of you."[82]

The headmaster's interest in Fowles extended to placing him in an officers' training program when he left Bedford School in July 1944. When John chose the Royal Marines over the Royal Armoured Corps, Grose-Hodge's influence helped him into a Naval University Short Course at the University of Edinburgh from October 1944 to April 1945.

Fowles's duty at Edinburgh was comfortable, companionable, and far removed from the continuing hostilities on the continent. He studied languages, primarily German, finishing with distinction and "a standard equivalent to a pass for the Degree of Master of Arts in the Class of German (First Ordinary Course)," for which he received a Certificate of Merit.[83] He also attended lectures in French literature, given in an old medical theater of the university. Off duty, he connected with a charming uncle by marriage, Charles Wetherill, father of ant-loving Cousin Lawrence. Wetherill, former Secretary of State for Agriculture for Scotland, introduced his wife's nephew to Gilbert and Sullivan productions (toward which Fowles was lukewarm) and the pleasures of Scottish malt whiskey (toward which he was more enthusiastic). No longer the model Head Boy of Bedford School, Fowles also took up cigarettes and the occasional cigar or pipe. By the end of the war he had become a heavy smoker.[84]

He underwent basic training at Deal, on the coast of Kent. Then, after a highly selective process, Fowles was one of thirty (out of eighty) chosen for Officer Cadet Training Unit, OCTU. He was sent to Thurlestone, near the Devon coast, "where I spent a miserable time learning to be a Marine officer." He lived in a "big posh hotel," converted to officers' quarters. Revisiting in 1973, all he could remember were the "humiliations: falling off a horse, being told by a Captain Bradley . . . that I was in his opinion not officer material, but he had to pass me because Grose-Hodge had recommended me personally to the Commandant-General; the hateful business of 'milling' (boxing all out for three minutes in the ring they set up in the ballroom)."[85] He liked to tell later interviewers that the war ended on the day he completed his training. Fowles always loved stories with synchronous connections, and this is an exaggeration. He finished his training in June 1945, while the war in Europe ended on May 8, 1945. When the news came, John thought immediately of Agah Hodges and he fancied himself walking up the stairs and into his room at Bedford to ask, "Tell us how you lost your leg, sir."[86]

In July, nineteen-year-old Lieutenant Fowles was posted to Portsmouth (Pompey to the Royal Marines), where he was hit with the full force of all he came to deem pompous about the Marines. The corps was code-bound, he thought, taking pride in silly rituals and traditions, like regimental silver, snuff at table, and port.[87] Not only was he less than an enthusiastic officer, but he was even unable to master driving a motor vehicle. After a minor accident he was restricted to a motorbike. Fowles never drove an automobile again. For all his duties, Fowles was able to go shooting at least once or twice a week, play golf, and visit home frequently.[88] To his anger and dismay, his parents left Devon to return to Leigh-on-Sea in autumn 1945.

In a piece of good luck, however, Fowles was assigned the training of new commandos on Dartmoor, not twenty-five miles from his old haunts at Ipplepen. The northern extreme of Dartmoor, where the Okehampton camp was located, is a bleak granite upland, dotted with massive outcroppings of stone, called tors, sculpted into grotesque shapes by wind and rain. Deep bogs threaten the unwary traveler on this rainy, windswept, foggy landscape. Roadless and unmarked, such a vast, empty tract was ideal for training recruits in the basics of navigation and survival. From his years of hunting and exploring through all kinds of wild terrain, Fowles was well suited to teach these vital skills. His job was to put the commando trainees through "the kind of roughness" that would simulate their future assignments. A group could be put out on a bare part of the moor without food or water, for example, and ordered to find sustenance and march several miles to a new location. It seemed simple, but fog and confusing conditions could make it fiendishly difficult.[89] Searching for lost recruits, Fowles himself was once frightened by some threatening shape, a "pure atavistic terror" that turned out to be a moor pony. He was also set upon by hounds seeking fugitives from Dartmoor Prison. He was lost once or twice.[90]

The men Fowles trained were what he called "very rough diamonds," semiliterate working-class youths from the North of England. Tracking them on Dartmoor was not nearly as challenging as keeping track of them when on leave in Plymouth, which was one of Fowles's other responsibilities. In the pubs of Plymouth, with his fellow officer and friend, a Lieutenant Hardy, and one or two other officers, he had to round up his charges, always warily looking out for the "matelots," their slang for sailors who relished a fight with his "leathernecks."[91]

It was not a time for introspection or intellectual maturity, a fact that embarrassed Fowles later on. He kept a regular diary while serving with the Royal Marines, just as he kept his nature and hunting notebooks. When a fragment from 1946 turned up in October 1953, Fowles read of wet marches in the rain, drinking at an "Officers piss-up," milling with other young officers, and being upbraided during inspection. He was shocked at his "naif and puerile" entries, "as inarticulate as a dummy."

He wondered if he would "ever overcome my past."[92] As years went on, Fowles tried to suppress the commando-training, Royal Marine officer part of his character, destroying the diaries that embarrassed him and casting aspersions on his time in the corps. But "the commando" as a character and as a thinly disguised mask of John Fowles made comeback appearances in several unpublished pieces of his fiction. Although this character never saw print, his author usually presented him in a positive light and sometimes with considerable pride.

Being posted to Dartmoor and Plymouth had distinct advantages when Fowles was not on duty. The moor, he later wrote, had "flashes of beauty." He loved exploring this lonely tract with its archaeological remains and unusual plants and insects. He hunted most mornings. He played golf. His chief companion on his forays was another officer, Bob Paine, who shared his nature interests. On at least one occasion they went down the River Exe together. Looking back eight years later, Fowles had to admit that he had "enjoyed being in the Marines." He had been inspired by the values of military service that Agah Hodges had taught him, indeed was frequently sustained by thinking of him: "[W]hen I was exhausted, . . . afraid, indifferent: he would come to mind."[93]

It was not a bad life, and when, in the fall of 1946, Fowles was offered a regular commission as an officer in the Royal Marines, he was tempted. While acting as aide-de-camp escorting the Lord Mayor of Plymouth, Isaac Foot, around the training camp, Fowles mentioned being torn between accepting a commission and attending Oxford. Mayor Foot, a Quaker and the patriarch of a famously leftist family, snorted in disbelief. He declared, "Well, only a total and utter fool and idiot would even consider a career in the military, if he had the opportunity to attend Oxford University!"

As Fowles repeated this favorite story through the years, he emphasized being shocked by Foot's outburst into making a hasty application to Oxford the very next day. This oft-quoted anecdote, characterized by "suddenness," a quick and decisive change in a life's path, has all the earmarks of years of Fowles's imaginative cultivation. It presents Fowles (to himself as well as to interviewers) as isolated, independent, and decisive in the existential manner of making an *acte gratuit*, a free gesture. But however much Foot's incredulous intervention shook Fowles's romantic notions about a career in the Marines, Oxford had long been his destiny.

Both Robert Fowles and Humfrey Grose-Hodge had ambitions for John Fowles's future, and Oxford University was their shared goal for him.

On December 30, 1946, Fowles was "demobbed with honour and a brown suit," with an official release date of February 28, 1947.[94] The rail trip to Leigh was, he wrote, a "rotten journey back." He spent a frigid winter in Essex, living with his parents and five-year-old sister, enduring rationing, frequent power cuts, and unemployment. His days passed on Leigh marsh, shooting wigum, shelback, and curlew. In the spring he joined his family on a fortnight's holiday in the French Pyrenees, his first extended trip abroad and probably the first time Robert and Gladys had been out of England since John's birth. His sole record of the holiday, April 2 to 20, is a list of the birds he saw as they traveled.[95]

Fowles taught at Bedford School for the summer term of 1947 (May, June, July), taking a class of fifth form boys. He helped coach the cricket teams and taught a French class. Because he had just been an officer in the Royal Marines, Grose-Hodge also assigned him to train the Junior Training Corps of the Army Cadets. At twenty-one John Fowles was still a Bedford boy, who depended on the guidance of his headmaster and willingly embodied the ambitions of his father.

But when he went up to Oxford, Fowles turned on his previous life and the people who shaped it. In his new way of looking at the world, his past was deficient. He did his best to leave it behind.

CHAPTER THREE

A Larger World

Oxford and Early Travels: 1947–1950

But at the time it was being up in the mountains; everything was clear, the clouds had dispersed, and the world was cold, bare, dangerous, but magnificent. Reputations based on rhetoric, emotionalisms evaporated; only the rock-giants, the anti-romantics, anti-metaphysicalists, the anti-establishmentarians, gained our interest. Now, the period reeks of self-interest; I can see that clearly. We had won the war, we were being educated free, at Oxford, university of universities, we were the temporary chosen of the gods. We hid our self-interest behind the masks of socialism and unpretentiousness—the former because of the latter— and we voted in the Welfare State, fair shares for all and even fairer ones for us. It was all a chauvinism of self.

—JOHN FOWLES, "OXFORD IN THE LATE 40S,"
THE MAGOS, DRAFT (SUPPRESSED)

They were often called, a little ironically, the Conquering Heroes. They were the qualified veterans who could now afford an Oxford education through the government subsidies offered by a grateful nation. When they arrived after the war, still wearing Army greatcoats and camouflage jackets, the remnants of military uniforms, seven hundred years of university traditions quaked. Older by years than the traditional undergraduates and often of middle- or even working-class backgrounds, these veterans transformed the social structure of the ancient institution simply by their presence and numbers.[1]

The mix of years was exciting. Mature students who had served through the entire war and older men who had returned to interrupted studies rubbed shoulders with youngsters straight out of school. Young women, surrounded by eager men of all ages, may have had the best time of all. Despite austere living conditions, strict rationing, power cuts, and shortages of all essentials, the entire undergraduate population seemed effervescent with the energy of ambition and youthful possibility. The war was over.

Under the onslaught of these Conquering Heroes, the old protective rules of undergraduate Oxford crumbled. The turning point came in 1947 when one of the veterans bought himself a pint in a local pub and was arrested by a university "bulldog" (a campus cop). The offending undergraduate was revealed to have been a distinguished lieutenant colonel decorated with the Military Cross. Thus ended rules and restrictions against undergraduates drinking in pubs, keeping their own hours, or entertaining friends of the opposite sex in their rooms. The ex-servicemen were even excused from all examinations until Schools, the final examinations at the end of the entire course of study. Ronnie Payne, who read Modern History at Jesus College from 1947, recalled happily that "it was like one big Officers' Mess . . . we were thoroughly feckless."[2]

John Fowles joined his generation at Oxford in October 1947, enrolling at New College to read Modern Languages. Though he was a twenty-one-year-old veteran, his fresh, boyish face made him appear much younger. He was assigned a room in Halls at the top of a stairwell facing across the quadrangle from the New College chapel. It was a narrow, poky room with neo-Gothic windows. It had its own bathroom, however, and was far more comfortable than officers' quarters in the military. Most of all, it was private, his own. After twenty years of growing up in conformance to the expectations of his family and society, of supporting the values of the group at school and in the Royal Marines, he had come to a place "where the individual was paramount, not the nation."[3] John painted the walls of his new home himself with the "weird shapes and figures" that he then regarded as avant-garde interior decoration.[4]

New College had a reputation, Fowles wrote later, for "a sort of Socratic skepticism . . . a sincere belief in the virtues of doubt," an attitude congenial to his nature and one that affected him deeply. Enrolled in the Honours School of Languages and Literature, he began by reading both French and German. Unimpressed with the German faculty and content with his certificate from Edinburgh, at the end of the first year Fowles elected to drop the German and exclusively concentrate on French. He was assigned the distinguished Isaiah Berlin for his traditional "moral tutor." "I know absolutely nothing about morals," Berlin was apt to joke. Perhaps half a dozen times while an undergraduate John paid a formal call and sipped a glass of sherry, while the great man asked pleasantly, "Well, how are you getting on, Mr. Fowles?" He developed a more intellectually influential relationship with his French tutor, the first ever appointed by New College. Merlin Thomas, fresh from studies on Céline at the Sorbonne, was a charming and learned young man. His students were envied their good fortune for Thomas's scholarly gifts as well as for his risqué sense of humor and collection of daring French postcards.[5]

The fixed point of John Fowles's week was his tutorial with Merlin Thomas, when he presented an essay for the tutor's comments. The academic bias of these discussions was traditionally humanistic, with more emphasis on the student's individual response to the reading than on critical analysis. In support of the weekly essay, the tutor suggested readings and lectures to attend. Not as stimulated by the other Oxford dons, Fowles sat bored through lectures by Alfred Ewert and Enid Starkie, among the university experts in French literature of his day. Fowles was also consistently offended and embarrassed by the esteemed faculty's "failure to pay any attention to the spoken language."[6]

Under the direction of Merlin Thomas, however, Fowles covered the full range of French literature from the medieval to the early modern. Here he first experienced those writers whose sensibilities were to echo in his own work: the courtly lyric poetry of the twelfth century and the romances of Marie de France; the intensely focused moments of Villon; the love poems of Ronsard, the earthy humor of Rabelais, and the self-exploring essays of Montaigne in the Renaissance; the witty wordplay and psychological probing of seventeenth-century masters such as Honoré d'Urfe and the enigmatic *Pensées* of Pascal; the romantic bandying and delicate psychology of the eighteenth-century plays of Marivaux; the naturalistic sensibilities of Rousseau; and the psychological realism of writers as diverse as Baudelaire, Flaubert, and Proust.

Through these French studies, Fowles discovered his vocation as a writer. In his first year at Oxford he began translating sixteenth-century French poetry, particularly Ronsard, du Bellay, and Louise Labé. Until satisfied with his own version, Fowles was haunted by Ronsard's evocative ode on love, youth, and mutability, which begins *"Mignonne, allons voir si la rose . . .* " (which Fowles was to recall as "My love, let's go and see if the rose has bloomed . . .").[7] The day was a "turning point . . . the seed from which this new egotistic me grew. The sense of mission, the chosen."[8] Once the floodgates of poetry had opened through translation, Fowles began to write his own poems, and continued throughout his Oxford years. One cold, clear night in 1947 on Magdalene Bridge, for example, he wrote, "Ecstatic static/ I fill the world with myself. Stop," one of his first efforts.[9] Only a few fragments like this survive, however, for he judged these early poems "all bad . . . like seeing oneself in a film walk naked through a crowded street."[10] His sense of vocation rapidly expanded beyond poetry, and he tried plays and short stories, all of which are lost.

Lecture attendance was optional, and Fowles sometimes skipped. He spent hours in isolated dreaming, sitting in an old wickerwork chaise longue in his narrow room at the top of the stairs, fiddling with the tassel at the end of the curtain cord and staring "up out of the mock gothic windows at the sky over the New College buildings." He cultivated silence and passivity, composing poems in which he imaged himself as Solomon's lilies of the field or as simulating a block of stone. "He also lives who only waits; and watches . . ." he wrote. "That was my philosophy of the moment."[11]

Although in these aesthetically passive moods, Fowles may have been the not-toiling, neither-spinning lily or the stolidly observant, silent block of stone, this certainly was not the whole picture of his undergraduate life at Oxford. He didn't bother to turn up when invited to trials for the Blues, the university cricket team, but he played for the Nomads, a "casual New College cricket team made up of 'good' players and enthusiastic rabbits." With their ties "emblazoned with a duck, with as many eggs below as the member had merited," they played village teams where the bowler might be a bone-cracking blacksmith on a pitch otherwise used as a cow pasture.[12]

He discovered a kindred spirit in his neighbor just across the stair landing. Roger Hendry, reading Greats, shared with Fowles a similar sense of humor, a love of nature, and a passion for late Beethoven. The two spent evenings listening to records cranked loud on the gramophone and many days searching for orchids in the fields around Oxford, usually ending with drinking in a country pub. Sharing their pub life as well as many natural history expeditions was Basil Beeston, another student.

Part of Basil's charm was his car, which allowed John to travel farther afield on bird-watching trips than by bicycle. Basil was quite a fair jazz pianist, and John sang to his playing in many a country pub. Captain of Shooting for the Revolver Club and, like John, an amateur painter, Basil was "immensely *correct* in all his nuances of . . . behaviour, like a skilful fencer with life and personalities."[13] Their mutual friend Guy Hardy shared their passionate interest in birds and nature. Hardy was an ex-flier, still in the Officer Reserve, and so likable and self-possessed that John envied his assurance. Hardy and Fowles became involved together with the Severn Wildfowl Trust, a tide-covered grass salting sanctuary at Slimbridge, Gloucestershire, maintained by the painting profits of the wildlife and landscape artist Peter Scott.

While accepting veterans from all backgrounds on intellectual merits, Oxford still retained class consciousness and, for a future novelist, was a superb vantage point from which to observe the uneasy postwar shifting of British class structure. Just as he made ornithological observations, John sorted his own friends into categories by their language and behavior. There were bourgeois, like Basil, "sophisticated . . . not rich, sometimes well-off . . . jazz-loving . . . fairly hard-drinking," frank about women, and "contemptuous of grammar school and snob types." There were "snob-Etonian types," like Guy, "amiable, tolerant to intruders, but only friendly to each other" and identified by "exaggerated mannerisms," loud drawling ("Exactlay . . . Indiah"), name-dropping of double-barreled monikers, and an unconscious self-assurance bordering on arrogance.[14] Then there were the insecure newcomers he thought of as "the New People": "mostly ex-Grammar School" and "excellent" until they began "wanting to be taken for Public School." These "coarse misfits . . . the over-drawly, over-slangy, over-line-shooting persons . . . are the image of what one might have been."[15] Fowles himself, aware of the veneer provided by his Bedford and Marine officer's background, was conscious of his suburban upbringing, small-business dependence, and middle-class family. Innately competitive, he always prickled at being less than one of the best. He could be deeply "jealous" of the Honorable John Grigg, "so much richer and more of a gentleman than I was, who tolerated me, and paid for many entertainments."[16] He could experience a "slight attack of class inferiority complex," lunching with the generous Michael Ferrar, assuring himself all the while "that I see through them and further than they do."[17]

The girl closest to Fowles at Oxford was Michael Ferrar's girlfriend. Fowles fell in and out of love with breathtaking ease at Oxford but, beyond some wild kissing, had no sexual experience there. Girls to whom he was attracted whirl quickly through his journal after 1948, most identified only by initials. Thinking of the twinned actresses in Fowles's later fiction, his friend Ronnie Payne remembered two "stunningly beautiful" sisters ("the big game at Oxford at the time") named Scatchard, both involved in dramatics, who may have fascinated John.[18]

But Constance Morganstern was different. Sullenly handsome, with dark-ringed green eyes and moody silences, she was unhappily married to the pianist at the Playhouse Theatre. She fell for country squire Ferrar, a tall, fair member of the landed gentry who read Agriculture at New College and struggled relentlessly to return his family's ancestral home, Cold Brayfield, to its prewar condition and prosperity. Because of Michael, John suppressed his own considerable "magnetic attraction" for Connie,[19] "never slept with her," and "kissed her only in affection." Yet his friendship with her is the first recorded instance of Fowles's recurring attraction to dark, enigmatic women onto whom he projected a romantic mystery and wisdom. While Fowles thought of her as "'deep,' both erotically and psychologically moving," she may not have been so. Indeed, she was "almost inarticulate." Silent and secretive, Connie inspired a combination of both sexual excitement and creative thought, "a benign *femme fatale* . . . who constantly excited one . . . and made one think."[20] The very presence of this type of woman called forth in Fowles's life and later work an erotically charged artistic response, rather than ordinary sexual consummation. This type of woman became in his fiction a silent, mysterious guardian of some larger personal truth that the protagonist is moved to discover. Fowles visited Cold Brayfield several times with Michael and Constance and spent Easter 1949 alone with her, innocently touring Paris as mutual friends, at the time her marriage was dissolving.

Although Fowles enjoyed socializing with his handpicked friends, the sensitive, thoughtful Bedford boy with his solitary reserve, isolated by recurrent illness, was still ever present. Throughout his Oxford career (and, indeed, off and on for years afterward), Fowles suffered from what was eventually diagnosed as chronic amebic dysentery. The disease, undiagnosed until January 1950, caused painful and embarrassing symptoms. During an attack he could be prostrate with severe abdominal pain, nausea, diarrhea, fever, and cold sweats. Fred Porter, who knew him well in his last two years at university, recalled that Fowles was frequently very ill, often unable to work or even to leave his room.[21] As they had at Bedford, these episodes of illness deepened Fowles's sense of isolation, threw him back on his own resources, and often made him cranky and judgmental.

As a bout of illness developed one spring weekend, for example, he was conscious of withdrawing into solitude as a result of both basic temperament and physical sickness. Fowles wrote of a "feeling of isolation . . . cannot integrate myself with other people. . . . Hostile aloofness within one's heart. Too much observing, not enough participating. Unease and recoil of pride in being different. Inability to descend from my own highbrow level, the return of nuances and sensitivity."[22] When the chronic condition was upon him two days later, he wrote: "Depressed by the body. . . . Ill-health is curious; feeling of frustration . . . a hate of movement of all externals; a sharper vision—the faults of people become uncovered. Feeling of isolation and corollary need for comfort; isolation because everyone else is well, and because there is a withdrawal out of the body so that one hardly participates in what is going on around it. Withdrawal comes through dreaming, and the watching of others."[23]

Fowles's sense of detachment also became sharper and more poignant as he began to grow apart from his parents, both intellectually and emotionally. At Leigh on his long vacations, confined in the tiny house with his family, he was conscious of "the unspoken gaps . . . the awkwardnesses . . . the strains in the air." He was painfully aware of his own "cold bloody-mindedness [in] a relationship which will not expand or blossom" and felt "unwelcome, unmeant contempt, equivalent to panic in a shipwreck."[24]

As he measured it by the standards of Oxford University, Fowles was growing to despise Leigh-on-Sea and to see it as representative of all he held in contempt. "I feel violent with 'hate' against this bloody town," he wrote, ". . . against the way of life, and then the people who allow it to sap all the beauty of life out of them. . . . This town can have as much horror mentally for a sensitive person as a blitzed city may have, physically, for a turnip." Leigh, thought Fowles, was unsociable, colorless, insincere. "Niceness" was the standard of conduct. "God," he howled, "how I hate that word!"[25] As he longed for a life of meaning and intensity, of beauty, culture, adventure, and fame, Fowles's loathing of Leigh-on-

Sea was in direct proportion to his own ambitions and to his fears that he too would turn out to be merely ordinary, "a turnip."

His parents' life was embedded in this much-maligned suburb. The house and rooms of 63 Fillebrook Avenue seemed so small, with "the nursery stuffed full of things, always untidy; the dining-room dark and gloomy." It was a very sore point for John that his parents had chosen to return to Leigh after the war ended rather than remain in rural Devon. Nearly sixty years old, Robert Fowles had sought a return to his familiar suburban security and the beloved trees he himself had planted. Savagely, John characterized Robert as "a rabbit Victorian pater familias with . . . the great weight of 19th century middle class morality and semi-puritanical initiative outlook on life . . . stagnation . . . appalling emptiness and greyness."[26]

However, he felt more sympathy toward his "passive" father than toward his loquacious mother. While leaving the Devon countryside had been "a great wrench," Gladys had acquiesced to Robert's wishes to return to suburban Essex and there had immersed herself in domestic duties and pleasures and the community life of her neighborhood.[27] John labeled her "bovaryste" and was deeply irritated by her constant worry over the house and its "nice" appearance. He was irritated that she cleaned, irritated that she didn't read, irritated that she talked constantly of trivial things. In her perpetual flood of talk John felt he could not speak about the things that he had really come to value and love. Any discussion of modern art or literature caused embarrassment and the accusation of being "highbrow. . . . No mention of art can ever be developed in case we are 'highbrow'—God, how I hate that word!"[28] He resented what he interpreted as his mother's ignorance and domination of conversation.

Most unforgivable to Fowles was his parents' insensitivity to his ecstatic love of classical music. As John listened raptly to the broadcast of a Beethoven symphony, Gladys counted her stitches aloud or rattled the newspaper, while Robert went to sleep. "I feel sick and sad," he mourned, "that something which penetrates right to the heart of me runs off their backs like water off a duck's."[29] At twenty-three Fowles thought his seven-year-old sister seemed "like a small pet." While admitting that they seemed younger for being parents of a child—and Hazel remembered them as good parents to her in every respect—John was annoyed that she swallowed up their energy and affection at a time of life that should have been free of such responsibility. The occasional presence of a much-older brother who stopped her parents from arguing but "hardly knew I existed" confused the shy, quiet little girl.[30] Was Robert, so much older than her friends' fathers, really her grandfather, and this youth her father? When she asked this question, John felt she twisted "a dagger in the wound."[31]

Fowles escaped. Indoors he spent his time reading, writing, and listening to the wireless. Outdoors he tramped all day over the Leigh marshes with his guns, a twelve-bore and a .410. Despite his increasing estrangement from his birthplace and his family, he returned repeatedly for months at a time. He felt guilty knowing that he was "financially . . . a passenger in a leaking ship," completely dependent on his father and the foundering family business and contributing nothing.[32] Trying to discover an intellectual destiny so different from his parents', Fowles could only feel their way of life as imprisoning him, undermining his resolve, and threatening his new, hard-won values. He had now a craving for new faces, new meetings, new places.

His New College friend John Griggs organized a monthlong April 1948 visit to Aix-en-Provence for a small party of Oxford undergraduates. John Fowles and Ronnie Payne took few clothes but stuffed their worn military rucksacks with tins and tins of coffee beans ("like gold dust in war battered France") that they traded to the patron of the Deux Garçons café on the Cours Mirabeau. They lived "lordly" on their black-market profits, staying well past the official visit.[33] Though grown-up, they were still Agah Hodges's boys on their first French adventure. "We were young, exuberant, étrangers," John wrote in an unpublished poem.[34]

Hosted by the city of Aix and the University of Aix-Marseilles, the visit was a novelty when travel was still restricted by currency control. The Britons were welcomed as liberators and were offered first-class accommodation and entertainment as well as lectures and research facilities. John and Ronnie, however, with only a single lecture attendance between them, were "the black sheep of the party." As the others, like John Bayley, Faith Falconbridge, Desmond Dunphy, and Kenneth Rose, diligently passed by en route to museums, Ronnie and John systematically sampled every aperitif in the café. Fowles not only missed the museums, the cathedral, and the fountains that give Aix its name, he even missed the poet T. S. Eliot for the chance of chatting up a girl. Excited by rumors of planned Communist riots, they did visit Marseilles to hear Charles de Gaulle speak. Frisked for weapons, they heard "the great

man, gaunt and gesturing," but were disappointed that there was no assassination attempt, only a "youth hit by half a brick."

Aix was sensuous and social, not academic, for Fowles. He dropped
his reserve and entered into the spirit of the group, swimming, eating,
drinking, and experiencing no illness. He took part in bread fights and
was smuggled with other men into the girls' wing of the Cité Universitaire. He drank with fiery Corsicans and danced the samba with French-
women whose bodies made him feel hot and clumsy. He fell in love
forever with the Côte d'Azur in spring, the color of the Mediterranean,
the pastels and burnt ocher of the countryside, the butterflies, and the
croaking of frogs at night.

John was smoking and drinking with Ronnie in the Deux Garçons
when Fred Porter entered their lives. Always called Podge by his closest
friends, Porter was an Army veteran, older by twelve years, reading
French at St. Catherine's College. The three remained friends, off and
on, for the rest of their lives. Podge was a passionate, committed Marxist
and a gifted pianist and cellist. Although he traveled alone, he was married, with an infant daughter. As they shared their Gauloises, Porter
began needling them in his "questing voice (everything Podge says is in
quotation marks . . . mocking himself as he does it)."[35] Disturbed, John
found the older man "dark" and "cynical" and disliked him at first, but
Ronnie took up Podge with enthusiasm. Together the two homed in on
fellow student Faith Falconbridge, becoming an inseparable threesome,
with John "a fluctuating member of the quartet." Fowles found Porter to
be deliberately shocking about sex and, with Faith in particular, "cynical,
frank, gross." Yet with his constant challenging questions, Fred benefited
John "by his lack of pretence; he helped cut away the shreds of romance
still in me." Fowles later called him "the Socrates in my life . . . whose
doubts and queries eternally nag."[36]

Fowles was bereft at leaving his new French friends. As the train
rocked through the night on its way back to Paris, he tried to capture his
sadness by scribbling poetry "feverishly" on the back of his demobiliza-
tion orders. Leaning across the crowded third-class compartment, Ronnie asked gently, "What are you doing, John?" and John murmured
"something evasive, too shy to say 'poetry.'"

A sweltering heat wave in July found him playing exchange host to
twenty-eight Aix undergraduates visiting Oxford. Besides the bus tours of
Windsor and evening garden parties with classical concerts, they danced

and drank, singing their way home arm in arm down the Broad. When Fowles tried to climb a group of Marseilles medical students over the New College walls after hours, they clattered noisily onto a pile of slates and roused the neighborhood. No less a dean than Alan Bullock slipped Fowles the key to the Fellows Hall to avoid future detection. Every day for a month John went punting on the river with the French students, spending each sultry day "hedonist, repressed . . . just sex-starved" as he flirted with laughing girls dressed in bikinis, the first such costumes he had ever seen. He fell clumsily, ostentatiously, and unrequitedly in love with the red-gold hair, green eyes, and perfect figure of the "maliciously roguish" Georgette, the worst tease of all.[37]

As soon as the Aix group departed, John Fowles and Ronnie Payne returned alone to the far southwest of France, meandering by rail to the Catalan village of Collioure. It was an enchanting place, whose lush Mediterranean light had inspired Matisse's fauvism, and the young travelers could hear Pablo Casals playing his cello from his balcony in the evening to the streets below. The twenty-two-year-olds put up in a "hellish uncomfortable" hostel in an old harborside fortress that swarmed with mosquitoes and Marxists. John was often convulsed with laughter by Ronnie's keen imitations of one fiercely left-wing resident they called La Passionara. They found temporary work picking grapes in the surrounding Roussillon and at the port of Banyuls. With the lunatic bravado of youth (and to impress two Catalan girls), they entered the local bullring, daring (and failing) to snatch a rosette from the bull's horns and gain the big cash prize.[38]

When Payne was called back to England at the end of August 1948, Fowles stayed on, hired for two weeks as harvest help. The vineyard at Banyuls-sur-Mer produced a cheap, sweet aperitif, made from vintage trucked in from all over the region. Fowles later wrote that it was "quite the hardest and most unromantic work I have ever done."[39] The exhausted workers had to receive the rumbling lorries at all hours of day and night, then press the wine with their feet, while being constantly stung by swarming wasps. The powerful chemical fumes in the huge mixing vats made John and the others woozy, leery of being sent inside to clean unless someone was in earshot. His fellow workers were rough-tongued convinced Communists, bitterly contemptuous of the operation.

In mid-September 1948, John Fowles stood alone at the side of the road outside Banyuls-sur-Mer, his small earnings in his pocket. He looked and felt like the scruffy student: unshaved, needing a haircut, clothes worn by travel and several weeks of dirty, exhausting physical labor, a battered military rucksack at his feet. But the approaching automobile, a Citroën, stopped when Fowles put his thumb out, and he climbed in to meet the driver and his passenger. The driver was M. Jullié, "an unusual millionaire from Lyons, a gentle elderly man with heart trouble. . . . With him was his friend." The "friend," Micheline Gilbert, became in this fortuitous fashion, one of John Fowles's most important mentors, "a different kind of education." The two travelers recruited Fowles on the spot as crew for the *Sinbad*, M. Jullié's ten-ton ketch on which they summered at Collioure. Fowles lived alone with the pair for several enchanted weeks, sailing *Sinbad* along the coast.[40] Like Nicholas Urfe on mythical Phraxos in *The Magus*, he was briefly and blessedly the hazard-brought guest of a rich and unusual old man and the young, beautiful woman who was his mistress.

Fowles was completely smitten by this mesmerizing "older" woman with her worldly ways. Micheline Gilbert was probably in her late twenties and, in a "very French arrangement," had a beloved husband in Paris while also being the mistress of her rich Lyons jeweler. She had enormous feminine charm without sentimentality, "superb good looks and a very fine intellect . . . dual virtue of domesticity and mondaineness." Micheline had been with the French maquis during the war, smuggling over the Pyrenees into Spain British airmen who had been shot down over France. On her leg she bore a brand from a Gestapo interrogation. She had profound leftist political convictions and contempt for any French person who had not been involved in the Resistance. The sincerity of her passion made her admirable to John. "Biased but not unintelligent," he wrote, "attractive because of the vehemence with which she *feels* her ideas."[41]

She could be "scorchingly funny" about sex. Micheline knew at once that Fowles was both inexperienced and smitten and she taunted him endlessly, teasing him "about the silliness of the English in all sexual matters." More important, she took John under her left wing intellectually, insisting that he must read Camus, Sartre, St. Exupéry, Aragon and providing "a kind of reading list of all the people I'd heard of, but knew nothing about." Although he knew her only a few weeks of his life, John's friendship with Micheline Gilbert came at a profoundly impressionable moment. Forever afterward he credited her teasing and tutoring with deepening his knowledge of France and challenging him to learn about existentialism. He one day repaid her wise affection by creating the character of Mrs. Lily de Seitas in *The Magus*.[42]

As in the novels, there were two women in this adventure of initiation. John stayed with *Sinbad* as the boat's designer joined them in late September to sail the yacht to its winter berth at Le Grau du Roi. The cook for the journey was a young Danish woman, Kaja Juhl, who took virginal John Fowles for her lover. Kaja was slim, blond, pretty, and several years older than John. She was also sexually experienced; indeed, a letter from some years later indicates that she had a son from an earlier relationship.[43] Kaja, "so no-nonsense about sex," realized that twenty-two-year-old John Fowles was a "totally English naïf." She was "very gentle," and he was "wildly in love with her." Yet at the journey's end they parted with scarcely a pang.[44] They saw each other at least once more and exchanged letters off and on, but there was little lingering emotional dependence between Fowles and this generous free spirit.

The alchemical effects of Collioure lingered that autumn at Oxford as Fowles ached with "nostalgia . . . for the heat and vividness of Provence, the sun and shade and dust."[45] As in an emotional and intellectual crucible, Micheline Gilbert's teaching combined with the ongoing influence of Merlin Thomas.

In the autumn of 1948 Fowles began intense reading in the existentialist authors Micheline had recommended. French existentialism was just emerging in the British postwar world. Jean Paul Sartre's *Being and Nothingness* had been published in 1943 and was yet to be translated into English (1953). Sartre and Simone de Beauvoir had launched *Les Temps Moderne* in 1945, only three years before Fowles read these works. Of them all, he was most attracted to Albert Camus, whose novel *The Stranger* (1942) had appeared in English in 1946. *The Myth of Sisyphus* (1942), however, would not be available in English translation until 1955, and it was here, in the original French, that Fowles was most affected by Camus's arguments for stoicism and atheism.

But as Fowles read the French existentialists, he was also reading the *Pensées* (1670) of Blaise Pascal, probably on assignment from Merlin Thomas. Pascal, the great mathematician who laid foundations for the theory of probabilities and the digital calculator, was also an eloquent apologist for Christianity. Believing that man has a contradictory nature, aspiring to supreme good but incapable of reaching it in his fallen state, Pascal taught the doctrine of salvation by grace rather than works, by emotional apprehension (or the principle of intuitionism) rather than the rigorous rationalism of contemporaries like Descartes. Pascal's own ec- static, mystical conversion experience came in what he called the night of fire (*la nuit de feu*) that opened him to religious certainty. Later the ex- istentialists claimed Pascal as their precursor because of this very rejec- tion of rationalism. As the cure for human skepticism, Pascal proposed the "wager": If God does not exist, the skeptic loses nothing by believing in Him; but if God does exist, the skeptic gains eternal life by believing in Him. Pascal's wager is a call to hope.

Himself a skeptic, struggling uncomfortably toward atheism, Fowles rejected Pascal's wager solution to the question of mortality and mean- ing, saying this kind of Christianity was "a white lie." Fowles looked in- stead to Camus's existentialist testimony for a life that recognizes no illusory escape into imagined immortality. He was strengthened by Camus's call to a life "without appeal" in which man's dignity is defined by living in "revolt . . . constant confrontation between man and his ob- scurity . . . awareness to the whole of experience . . . devoid of hope, . . . that revolt is the certainty of a crushing fate, without the resignation that ought to accompany it."[46]

As his father had done before him, John Fowles began arguing these philosophical matters in journals kept in simple composition books. Be- cause of their fragmentary nature, he called these notebooks "disjoints." They show marks of the wildlife and hunting journals and the sketchy di- aries kept for years before Oxford, but Robert Fowles's philosophical notebooks seem the greatest influence.

In the disjoints Fowles wrestled with the leap of faith to God of Pas- cal and Camus's irrational faith in man lost in an absurd universe. Fowles came down on the side of Camus's "bet" that there is only this mortal life and the individual must define his own values in the face of that absurd- ity. Ironically, Fowles found this argument to be hope-full, a call to the creation of an authentic self. However, he was less inclined to agree with Camus that all of an individual's life is composed of choices that are re- sponsible acts of free will. Fowles, who had grown up believing in a rough sort of biological determinism, wondered if freedom of choice was as absolute as Camus thought. Freedom was perhaps restricted by fac- tors beyond the individual's control. "However absurd," he wrote, "life is destiny self-created, the sum of all past memory. The moving time-point of the present can be directed (But only within the bounds of hereditary and environmental factors governing character, will-power, imagination, etc.?)." From this point on, throughout his life and his work, John Fowles struggled to define the fluctuating boundaries of genuine personal freedom, identifying the moments in which choice was possible or impossible and laboring to create imaginative space for the free play of his own relatively free will.

His disjoints of 1948–1949 show Fowles preoccupied with religious issues and the question of his own mortality. In the journal's pages he grappled with Pascal and Kierkegaard, rejecting their acceptance of Christian faith. He even tried on various Christian poses as a test. On Whit Sunday in 1949 he attended Church of England services for the first time in the New College chapel a few steps from his door. Uncharitably, he wrote of the "complete futility . . . irrelevance . . . sterility . . . only an excuse for inaction" of the Anglican service. The symbolism and aesthetic qualities of Catholicism's "clever lie" also attracted him, but he dismissed "the mystery and impracticability . . . the guilty feeling of escape, of not facing up to reality."

But accepting religious and moral relativity was very difficult for Fowles and made him "feel like a prisoner in a cage, searching for . . . escape into some absolute." Unfortunately, "death seems to be the only absolute, and . . . doesn't help with life." Thoughts of his own death caused him great mental anguish. He was full of "horror in becoming nothing . . . in being aware that one is only a speck that will leave no trace on the blankness of infinity." Yet if the soul had no immortality, Fowles believed one's achievements might compensate. To die without fame was "a wasted crucifixion," and immortality was "the highest ambition." Already an ambitious, proud young man with dreams of future greatness as a writer, the newly atheistic, existentialist John Fowles now was fired with a vision of artistic immortality as the only possible way of overcoming personal oblivion.

Although calling himself an atheist, Fowles could not easily abandon the divine, but rejected common understanding of God. Even as he applauded Camus's conclusions, he exulted in pagan pantheism about nature, while cycling under a full moon and experiencing "jubilation. Being one with nature . . . full of happiness. . . . Everything related by love within the whole, a pantheistic joy."[47] More intellectually, he began to identify the concept of God with the infinite potentialities of life. "God," in the pages of the disjoints, becomes the freedom that makes all other freedoms possible. "God as a selector of potentialities," Fowles noted. There was some free will in the choice of potentialities, although environmental circumstances would be influential.

"The existence of potentialities is, in itself, no proof of God, but the choice of them is. God is a series of potentialities which is in continuous progression," Fowles wrote as he groped for a definition. He concluded that "God" was the ultimate negative, an absence of being, which allowed all possibilities of being to come forth. "The necessary nature of God is that he does not exist, and that therefore the happiness of humanity depends on material self-reliance and an acceptance of all that a godless cosmos and existence implies—briefly . . . love and respect for fellowman—benevolent egotism, controlled hedonism." He adopted Sartre's term *néant* to indicate this absence that fosters potentiality. By the mid-1950s, while writing and rewriting *The Aristos*, Fowles clarified this word to *nemo* to describe both the nothingness from which everything comes and the individual's sense of obliterating personal nullity.

Although he personally elected to wager on the side of Albert Camus and existential atheism, Fowles retained a deep, affectionate admiration for Pascal and the *Pensées*, keeping a copy with him for many years after Oxford and adapting the pithy clarity of its aphoristic form to *The Aristos*. Even as he rejected the conclusions of Pascal's religious logic, Fowles was very moved by the *experience* that led Pascal to his position. Pascal's famous night of fire on November 23, 1654, remained for Fowles the model of an inexplicable conversion experience, a moment of transformation and emotional comprehension of the possibilities of all life. Some sort of similar mystical, deeply irrational, highly personal confrontation with the mystery of the universe became an experience common to many of Fowles's protagonists.

John Fowles himself had such an experience in the summer of 1949. He and his friend Guy Hardy were selected by the Severn Wildfowl Trust for an expedition of four ornithologists traveling north through Sweden, crossing into Norway, and across the Finnmark. Headed by Basil Morson, a London physician, the group was to confirm postwar sightings of the rare Steller's eider duck and to net some lesser white-fronted geese for Peter Scott and the trust's sanctuary. They failed on both assignments, after weeks of searching, although they managed to bring home two nestling bean geese.[48]

Alta, Vardo, Vadso, Kirkenes, and down the Pasvik River: the austere northern landscape of the Finnmark thrilled and moved Fowles. The towns "sparkling with simplicity" under the midnight sun, "the steep, stern faces of the fjords," and "the black loomings, lowerings and glowerings over the water when the rain is near" all impressed him with a sense of the remote and unapproachable, something still and nonhuman. At last, seeking their elusive birds, they came to Noatun, a farm at the edge of the world about ninety miles south of Kirkenes near the Russian border. Fowles renamed it Seidevarre (the hill of the holy stone) when he began writing The Magus around this episode seven years later. The farmer was a moody, intelligent, retired engineer named Schaaning, "slightly embittered . . . cynical," with failing eyesight. His was not a peaceful family, with a nephew jealous of the property, a repressed niece, and a wife, speechless and cast down. In the isolation and utter silence, Fowles saw them teetering between madness or sainthood, a "setting for real tragedy, with something fixed and inevitable in it, like the ancient Greek."

It was the eerie serenity of Noatun itself, however, that corresponded with his philosophic observations about the nothingness from which all possibility could be created. The forest lake was a dark, cold mirror rimmed with silent firs, occasionally rippled by ducks swimming or swans landing. It was a kind of quiet "that can be traced back to the eternal absence of man—noone has even been here since the beginning." It was, he wrote, "the world minus man." One August dusk, as Fowles waded ashore from fishing, he was filled with "the uncanniness of all the absence welling up into the personification of loneliness and inhumanity." His philosophical readings of the past year, his struggles with concepts of being and nothingness, his nontraditional definitions of the divine all fused intuitively into a personal faith.

When he came to re-create this episode in The Magus, Fowles used it to dramatize the moment in which the young Maurice Conchis moves beyond intellectual knowledge and rationalism to an intuitive, emotional apprehension of the incomprehensible divine moving in the universe. Specifically, reference is made to "the intensity of Pascal's famous Memorial—those two crucial hours in his life that he could afterwards describe by only one word: *feu*."[49] John Fowles could certainly grasp and analyze information and theories through study and thought, but for him, for his characters, the conversion to new knowledge was always accomplished through emotional, intuitive encounter, through *feu*. This insight lies at the very heart of his books. In December 1949, following his year of philosophical study and his experience at Noatun, twenty-three-year-old John Fowles began the first of them. After fifteen years of being reworked, this philosophical volume was published as *The Aristos*.

The one Oxford friend with whom Fowles felt he could openly argue existentialist issues was Fred "Podge" Porter. Both agreed that "the existentialists—whether they were Camusars or Sartrists—offered . . . a view of one's personal responsibility in life and in society generally." Fowles much preferred Camus to Sartre, while Porter deeply admired Sartre and scorned Camus. The difference, as Porter recalled they had understood it, was "between Camus' use of the word *revolt* which—when you strip away the wordage and so on—really means rejecting present-day values and improving current society. And Sartre, as opposed to *revolt*, was for *revolution*. Seeing the ills of society as being inherent in the economic-political set-up and which is ultimately unreformable."[50] By emphasizing the individualistic and by regarding the creation of a personal identity as a valid act of moral commitment, Camus appealed to the lone ego of Fowles. Sartre, by the late forties, was insisting that *engagement* required collective political action, a stance that would have appealed to the deep-dyed Marxist activism of Porter.

An argument with Podge, usually over supper in the Porters' small North Oxford house, combined "intelligence and bitterness and a sense of humour" with "cosmological reflections of the absurd in trivial things." Podge's method, introduced "with an amusing mock air of showmanship," was to pretend "faint ignorance" and follow it with "positive destructive criticism." Fowles thought him lacking "the touch of heart" but wonderfully "astringent" and valued these scourging intellectual examinations.[51]

He was equally attached to Eileen Porter. As politically radical as her husband, Eileen was a whip-smart Irishwoman whose devastating wit was delivered in a droll brogue. When she simply read the newspaper aloud, John thought she was the funniest woman he had ever met. Their conversation fulfilled Fowles's longing for serious engagement. They had a "facility for plunging quickly into metaphysics and philosophy and life and art." Although the Porters were invariably "cynical and gaily, absurdly pessimistic," their kindness touched Fowles, who felt "in complete—in the best sense—sympathy with them." He thought of them as "the Podges," "one personality . . . a perfect duo; in harmony or perfect discord."[52, 53] Indeed, their marriage did exist in both states, since they lived a pattern of quarreling and separating, then reconciling. They had more in common than not, for both were activists for the Oxford Labour Party and devoted parents to their daughter, Catherine.

The Porters came to be a substitute family for John Fowles, though it took him many years to realize it. As he grew apart from his own parents and retreated into dutiful silence rather than discuss things he thought they could not understand, he increasingly relied on his friendship with this invigorating, older married couple. At one time he had argued philosophy with his sharp-tongued, opinionated father. At one time he had depended on the attentive affection of his mother. By his second year at Oxford, sadly, there was an "immense gap . . . ridiculous and tragic, unnecessary and inevitable. . . . No common ground at all. I too proud and abstracted to want to talk trivialities, to discuss the deep, loved things . . . they too absorbed . . . in the minute details and facets of the *vie quotidienne*."[54] Escaping all he associated with the "bourgeois" life of his suburban parents—the conventional, too clean, dull, unemotional, "nice"—he found refuge in the Communist chaos of the Porter household, unconventional, untidy, explosive, politically committed, sexually frank. Once more he argued with a sharp-minded older man and laughed with an outrageous and interested older woman. The tiny daughter, Cathy, completed the mirror image of the rejected bourgeois Fowles family.

In his final undergraduate year at Oxford, October 1949 to July 1950, John Fowles lived at the Maison Français, at 72 Woodstock Road, where conversation among the residents was in French. He and Porter partnered up for lectures, attending together or taking notes for each other. He kept up his friendships with Basil Beeston, Roger Hendry, and Guy Hardy but was content to be more observer than participant. On Guy Fawkes Night, for example, he watched his friends throw themselves into the "crowds, fireworks, general rowdyism," while he had "absolutely no desire to do anything but watch, wanting to be everywhere and see everything, observing people's faces."[55] As Fowles had become more articulate about his philosophy and assured in his ambitions to be an artist, he had grown to value his role as the withdrawn observer. By "balancing" himself between his own need for introspection and "the intention of creating beauty for others," he began to believe that he would find self-fulfillment.[56]

By the end of 1949, however, this balance crumbled as ever-worsening attacks of his chronic illness weakened him and eroded his confidence. He was besieged by doubts about his literary abilities and overwhelmed and depressed by Oxford's rivalries. Characteristically, he came to feel an acute sense of doubleness, of being both an assured public person and a vulnerable private one, just as he had been as a boy at Bedford School. "Two mes," he wrote: "Ego, thinking with and at tangents from the others, full of the right words, curious ideas and so on; and the alter ego, not being able to break into the discussions, anxiety, fade, unwanted."[57] The pattern of Fowles's illnesses charted through his diaries shows that symptoms recurred when he was under stress and feeling vulnerable and challenged to perform. If he indeed suffered amebic dysentery, as he was diagnosed in January 1950, the condition was at least aggravated, if not caused, by emotional and psychological factors. It is remarkable that Fowles could travel light, live rough, and move rapidly through France and Scandinavia with no signs of sickness. With Michael Ferrar at Cold Brayfield, Fowles could match his friend's fourteen- to sixteen-hour workdays of feeding animals, hoeing, haymaking, digging, and sheep-dipping with no worse than blisters and a yawn. Yet formal meals at the Maison Français were "a torture" of nausea and no appetite. "I haven't sat down and enjoyed a meal for two years," he mourned, "they must think me wholly heavy and stupid. But I wanted violently to be sick, and it was all I could do to sit at the table, let alone smile and make witty conversation."[58]

Fowles's symptoms were very real, however, as were his pain and isolation, especially as he was confronted with his last university term and the prospect of Schools, Oxford's rigorous final examinations. In January 1950 he was admitted to a London nursing home, a "quiet, drily inhabited little house in a grey and bourgeois suburb." During the five extraordinary weeks he spent there as a patient his diary, hitherto a notebook on philosophy, exploded into lengthy narrative and self-analysis. Indeed, there is correlation between enforced isolation or illness and Fowle's rapidly developing narrative imagination.[59]

He had looked hopefully to the nursing home stay, longing for a cure.

He saw his confinement as a gift of work time, and he read voraciously. However, the weeks stretched bleakly on in "absolute friendlessness." He had no visitors except his parents and felt guilty at his indifference to them. Little by little, Fowles's spirits sank. There was no cure. He was depressed by his own "withdrawal from life, from reality, from responsibility, like a toad in his flower-pot by a busy walk."

In the "extraordinary inversion of sickness," Fowles's private dream life intensified and spilled onto the expanding pages of his journal. "Because I feel myself no better," he observed of the process, "a kind of compensatory masochism, not so much a psychologically whining self-pity as a tight-lipped stoic self-dramatization, arises." A fantasy of self in a dangerous adventure became "real, and the sense of difference, the growing away from the normal world is universal." He felt guilty that his fantasies substituted for reality and responsibility, calling them "pernicious . . . [but] cannot be willed away." He tried to remain focused on reality, resisting temptation "by an effort of will, by concentration on externals," but the compensatory fantasies won, opening "doors into gardens and storeyards of self-realization."

Illness, isolation, and introversion all obstructed Fowles's return to his normal life at Oxford. At the Maison Français he found it difficult to resume a camaraderie when the old role "of reserved coldness still clings, an old shell." His symptoms recurred through March, and Fowles, trying to cope with pain and disgust at his situation, fell back on his growing ability to detach himself: "I can return out of my body, separating myself from it objectively, and I would like to do the same thing with my mind. Could I leave my mind as well?"[60]

Fowles had returned from his nursing home stay to face an enormous amount of postponed work. Feeling useless, and will-less, he did none of it. Instead, he raged against the futility of Oxford and its values, writing long, scathing—unsent—letters to the *Times* protesting "the disgracefully antiquated syllabus imposed on undergraduates." He invented a new, reformist curriculum for Modern Languages based on "the spirit of rapprochement, a humane spirit and the power to intercommunicate freely. . . . Literature should be regarded as the basis."[61]

His fellow third years now spoke of little except the forthcoming Schools. Fowles felt increasingly panicky, surrounded by earnest, studious colleagues who put in their ten to twelve hours a day. In the Maison Français the residents quizzed one another and debated the critical questions. Fowles's characteristic response to the anxiety provoked by this peer group pressure was to create a bolt-hole of superiority, then justify his rejection of that which the others took seriously. "I hate people who are academically sound," he wrote scornfully of a brilliant, hardworking friend, "who accept the futility instead of resenting and rejecting it."[62]

He could not bring himself, however, to resent and reject outright an offer by Merlin Thomas, who recommended Fowles for a teaching appointment as *lecteur* at the University of Poitiers in France in the coming year. Fowles felt both grateful and trapped, fearing that the year would simply extend "the *détente*" in which his youth slipped away and he was threatened with "an existence of mediocrity."

His distress came to crisis after an April weekend spent at Cold Brayfield. While Michael Ferrar, determined to be the "dutiful churchwarden," scuttled between services in his two parishes, Fowles rambled in happy solitude down country lanes and through the woodlands. On his return to Oxford, however, he was felled by a major anxiety attack, with vertigo, breathlessness, and the audible pounding of his heart.[63] A few days later Fowles had decided what to do. He would fail.

He reasoned that since he had done no work for weeks, "a Third or fourth, and probably a fail, is bound to ensue." A second, however unlikely, "would certainly mean oblivion." Rather than confront this feared outcome as a looming disaster, Fowles decided failure was his only "ideally honest and sincere" course. "I keep on saying, I must fail, to keep free, to give my real self a chance." He would reject examinations leading to safety and stagnation. He "would be as free as possible, in order to give the artist in me elbow-room." He entertained a noble new vision of himself as laborer and writer: "I see myself now failing, being penniless and getting work somewhere on a farm, a ship—I don't know. And fortunately don't much care."[64]

Dreading his tutor's disappointment, John went to see Merlin Thomas, feeling "guilty and ashamed and a little bit resentful that I have *chosen* to do badly." Thomas laughed at his pupil's "great bout of denial," saying, "I put you between 1 and 2, on the borderline."[65] The Podges were less charming and even more unsympathetic. Their refusal to believe that John "could become a farm labourer without falling into intellectual malaise" only strengthened his stubborn resolve. Fowles "felt violently convinced of free-will." By deciding to fail and dressing up the decision in the quasi-existentialist costume of freedom, sincerity, and giving "my real self a chance,"[66] John Fowles relieved himself of the anticipatory anxiety of trying to compete and possibly doing poorly. With a reasonably good conscience, he could simply give up and pursue distractions.

His health improved. Through the green and sunny spring Fowles avoided all academic matters. He bought himself a big notebook and dedicated it to his diary keeping. He began to record the minutiae of his observations about his friends, his interests, and the natural landscape. Although he called it "a monument to . . . wasted time," it reflected his growing compulsion to write narrative, rather than only poetry and philosophy.[67] He read stacks of fiction and went to films starring Alan Ladd or Humphrey Bogart. He visited the Severn Wildfowl Trust and went bird-watching at night. He played cricket, rejoicing in "the relaxation of not having to think."[68] He and his friends lay about in the evenings listening to Duke Ellington records. He spent days in the country with Basil Beeston and his half-grown red setter, fishing, painting watercolors, and pub crawling. They went to the Trout (their favorite), the Doghouse, the George, the Bablock Hythe, a tiny pub at Appleton, the Eight Bells at Eaton, the Fox over Boar's Hill Way, the Sandford, and the Rose Revived. They returned repeatedly, sometimes to three or four small village pubs a night, where Basil played the piano and John sang with the locals in the back.

As June arrived and examinations began, John suddenly found motivation to study. It was all just a game![69] Thinking of Schools as being like bullfighting or cricket, the competitive Fowles found it "impossible to resist the excitement of beating the examiners." Each night was spent "cramming frantically for the morrow." Each day, wearing "sub-jusc and white tie, . . . gown and mortar-board," he spent in "the great room with the bent figures . . . writing, writing, writing." Fowles surprised himself by the amount of material he had mastered and chided himself that he would be considered "intelligent, but lazy."[70] He particularly feared the examination on sixteenth-century French grammar, a subject he had scorned. Having crammed Fred Porter's well-kept notes the night before the exam, Fowles sailed through. In a spirit of "relief . . . and smug jubilation," he noted: "Noone could have done less work than I have, or deserved less credit."[71]

Fowles was still resolved, however, to live the potentially free writing life of a farm laborer or sailor. Accordingly, in June 1950, he returned to

North Buckinghamshire to work for Michael Ferrar. Cold Brayfield, overlooking the river Ouse and the small village of Newton Blossomvilles,
was, Fowles wrote, "a large house on a large estate, a kind of Brideshead,
ruined by the army in the war, now derelict, useless, the house of another
age." Ugly huts of corrugated iron and brick were scattered over the park;
the weather-beaten house was locked up; the remnants of the gardens
were in ruins. Michael Ferrar, heir to all this, was determined to bring
the farming estate back up to productivity. A "long-legged, thin, upright
bundle of energy, continually on the go," he rose at five-thirty in the
morning and collapsed in exhaustion at eleven at night. His determination to rescue his land cost him his Oxford degree, for he failed his examinations. But Fowles would remember Ferrar's relentless devotion to
his estate when he created Compton and the character of Andrew Ran-
dall in *Daniel Martin*. John plunged into work alongside Michael, leaving
blistered skin from his soft hands on the pitchfork handle, feeling the
"pleasure of doing hard work again, sensing the strain and the rhythm of
manual labour," "recontact with the country, the feel of closeness to the
true life. The animals dying and being born, the sense of a continuity, beneath all the incidents."[72]

In his five weeks at Cold Brayfield, Fowles's noble notion of working
as a farm laborer while continuing to write was put to the acid test. Certainly, there was ample material: upstairs gossip in the eccentric, aristocratic Ferrar family (distant relatives of the famous Mitfords) and rural
pastoral in the farmhands, blacksmiths, and family retainers. Fowles's diaries sketch reams of verbal portraits, right down to the dogs and cart
horses. But laboring on the land was not the writing life that he had
imagined. Within a few weeks Fowles had been sucked into "the hard
deadening routine at Brayfield." The days merged, and "work and tiredness drug all the finer side. . . . One notices things, remembers them a
few moments, how to transmit and write them down, then they go. The
veins of all this are dirt and strain. Constant muck and constant labour."
Fowles's class sensitivities also began to be irritated by the local fox-
hunting set, and he resented following Ferrar's orders or being judged on
his farm-laboring skills.

On July 26 he was dabbing Stockholm tar on the wing of a gosling
that had been attacked by a rat in the night when a letter arrived from
Fred and Eileen Porter. While "the gosling trailed off dripping pine
scent," Fowles learned that he had earned a second at Oxford and stood

laughing, joyful and relieved, at "the triumph of absurdity."[73, 74] At the end of July he left and returned to Leigh-on-Sea. In the house on Fillebrook Avenue a letter was waiting for him confirming his appointment to teach at the University of Poitiers in November. "Poitiers is open," Fowles noted in his diary. "Future smiles."[75]

CHAPTER FOUR

In the Land of *Illusions Infantiles*

Poitiers: 1950–1951

The truth was that I was not a cynic by nature; only by revolt. I had got away from what I hated, but I hadn't found where I loved, and so I pretended there was nowhere to love.

—JOHN FOWLES, *THE MAGUS*

Out walking on Leigh's London Road in September 1950, John Fowles spied across the street his father's half brother Alan Fowles, walking— John thought scornfully—"like a poor dog too starved, too whipped . . . stunned by the poverty and monotony of his existence." Ashamed to have a relative whose life was "so feeble and without colour, so flat, dull, drab, grey," the young Oxford graduate ducked back and pretended not to see his uncle. Alan Fowles was the vision of all that twenty-four-year-old Fowles feared that his own life could become, for Uncle Alan's dismal life was not his fault but "an appallingly *pure* hereditary one." All male Fowleses were cursed, John thought, with a "dull miserable powerless-ness to act . . . a kind of timidity and sensitivity about change, about try-ing to climb . . . an abnormal contentment with lot." This was the legacy of the grandfather, Reginald, "self-indulgent and self-righteous," who had "spent all his money and spawned like a rabbit."[1]

His own father, Robert, had been snared by this curse of biology, John thought, and living at No. 63 while waiting to depart for Poitiers, he could observe the result. Robert Fowles was deeply depressed by the dis-covery that his manager at Allen & Wright (a Mr. Wood) was embezzling from the company. Since the struggling business and its aging owner depended on Wood's skill and contacts, dismissing him was out of the question. Robert, almost completely retired, spent "funereal" days "groaning and mumbling and sniffing and coughing, in a kind of dreadful psychological hypochondria . . . assuming the very worst about everything," his life reduced to "a tissue of suburban conventions." His son could not argue him into a changed life or a move to a different house or village. He saw his father trapped by genetic inheritance and the circumstances of his life into "complete nullity."[2]

Watching his father staring listlessly out the window and jingling his pocket change, or listening painfully to his mother's forced cheerfulness and trivial chat, Fowles felt sucked into their "dwarfed existence" and drifted, jobless, broke, and dependent on them ("I sponge") through the months before his departure for France.[3] He felt passive, saw no friends, had no company. He barely talked to his parents but was most baffled by "the complete lack of any sign of affection or family love." He himself was "emotional and dreamy and sensitive below and dry and cold and reserved on the surface" and wondered what had "put that crust there . . . hardened me." John felt unspoken pressures to sink "back into the rut. Get a job, and become a Fowles, an ordinary mortal." He feared the oblivion of ordinariness that he associated with Leigh and his family.[4]

Given these constraints of biological inheritance and background, Fowles wondered how he could summon the free will to make the life he longed for. Given his sense of entrapment, he tried to escape into places of his own created freedom. First, there was the retreat into words. He read, in a short two-month stay, Henry James, Sherwood Anderson, Samuel Butler, Homer, Oliver Goldsmith, Graham Greene, Herodotus, Marivaux, E. M. Forster, D. H. Lawrence, Shakespeare, Dante, Villon, T. S. Eliot, and volumes of commentary on Eliot. He wrote. The diaries grew enormously. He also began what he regarded as his first serious attempt at literature, a play he titled *Pandoras,* intended for submission to a competition in the autumn. Through three frantically typed drafts Fowles wrote, knowing "I never write well enough," that it was "too topical . . . too wordy . . . too sentimental . . . too highflown" and that he was incapable of objectivity.[5] He distrusted his abilities because his words were "not creating in themselves" but a means to regain his own fantasy world: "they are only stepping-stones to the other shore." He did not meet the contest deadline but lived in the hope of one day writing well. This hope kept him "rebellious."[6]

Fowles also escaped the oppression he felt living on Fillebrook Avenue through his immersion in nature. He collected butterflies again, removing their delicate, iridescent wings and preserving them in cellophane envelopes.[7] He continued to shoot wildfowl on the Leigh marshes, delighting in the hunt and the isolation. His keenest pleasure in hunting was "at having outwitted and caught a very wild creature," but he was slowly beginning to have conflicting emotions about the ethics of this sport.[8] He thrilled to the "clipped grace" and beautiful plumage of a flight of plovers, even as he repeatedly fired into the flock. Bringing down a curlew, he felt uneasy at having killed it.[9]

In the 1970s, Fowles was to promulgate, and probably accept himself, a dramatic personal fiction, illustrating what he wanted to believe (and wanted others to believe) was a sudden renunciation of killing wildlife. In the many versions of this story, Fowles, usually at the age of twenty-one, wounds a curlew on the Essex marshes and, trying to finish it, nearly blows off his own foot with his gun. "The next day I sold my gun," he wrote in 1971. "I have not intentionally killed a bird or an animal since."[10] This compelling cautionary tale of wounded nature, sudden insight, and morally reformed hunter is, alas, not factual. Neither in the diaries nor in his scrupulously kept hunting and nature logs is there evidence of the incident. To the contrary, Fowles did not sell the gun, but continued to hunt with it even after his eyesight had become so poor that he could no longer hit anything. He stopped wildfowling only in late 1954 at age twenty-eight, when he moved to London.

Like many of Fowles's personal anecdotes, the "how I stopped hunting" tale is an improved version of pale biographical circumstance, a "good story" that is sharper and more dramatic than mundane fact and delivers a comic sting or neat moral lesson. These stories are usually distinguished by "suddenness." It was important to Fowles that he come to some moral resolution or vital insight in a flash of inspiration, by suddenness. As an existentialist he valued the decisiveness of emotional lightning, the *acte gratuit*. In actuality, however, Fowles's beliefs and decisions were arrived at through slow change, in ways that seem more organic and subterranean than swift and superficial. On the surface he often appeared indecisive, even confused. Beneath the surface of his daily life, his ideas slowly evolved like the powerful, mostly hidden root system of a forest. He arrived at what he knew by telling himself stories. Fowles's unconscious capacity for reshaping his past into metaphorical,

condensed fictions was remarkable, a process we might call fertile forgetting.

He planned that his year in France would also be a year of lightning,
in which he would write publishable work that would launch his talent
on a waiting world. He chafed at news of any professional success by his
friends,[11] impatiently agonizing over his own inability to be "fighting, entering the world."[12] France, however, was only the beginning of his long,
arduous apprenticeship as a writer, as a thinker, and as a mature adult.

At some level he may have known this. On the eve of his departure
Fowles had an "extremely vivid . . . allegorical" dream. In it, an old
woman showed him a map, labeled in French, "a normal enough map except for a huge area in the centre which was absolutely without a mark."
Printed on this dark, blank area were the words *illusions infantiles*. "I
went there a long time ago," said the old woman, looking at John, "when I
was very young."[13]

The dream was prophetic. The year 1950–1951 was for Fowles a journey both into an unknown, but geographically real, country and into a
place where his childish illusions were displayed and tested. He fell in
love with France but failed in his first professional position. He acquired
friends and lovers but emerged more hardened in his emotional isolation.
He committed himself to his artistic ambitions but produced nothing on
which to launch a writing career. He was transformed by the year, and
those changes and memories ultimately found their way into his later fictions.

Located in the west of France not far from Brittany, Poitiers was in
1950 an unexceptional provincial city of perhaps sixty thousand people. It
had been badly bombed during the war. Even in 1951 John and his
friends occasionally turned off a main street by mistake and found themselves amid uncleared rubble. Fowles, arriving on November 2 to take up
his first postgraduate job as *lecteur d'anglais à la Faculté des Lettres* at the
University of Poitiers, found it a "grey, *closed* town. One feels there is a
secret, but it is hidden."[14]

He had anticipated France with eagerness, but the first two months
found him bitterly lonely and desperately homesick. His severe shyness
prevented him from even speaking to anyone for the first three days.
Only slowly, over many weeks, did he become acquainted with other
people, mostly undergraduates. His tiny third-floor room was bare and
unattractive, with an unreliable toilet and washing limited to a jug of

cold water and a bowl. He looked out over a steep sloop of roofs and the marshaling yard. In the new, bright Cité Universitaire restaurant the food was "adequate, but always cold," but Fowles could not afford to go elsewhere. His pay, thirty thousand francs a month, kept him on a short financial string. His landlords, the Malaports, he suspected of overcharging him at five thousand francs a month.[15] He began to feel "far more psychologically than physically ill" with returning colitis symptoms, and he terrified himself with self-doubt about why he had come. He felt he was losing his "grip on self-faith . . . frightened by the world . . . with only my hopes of becoming a writer to cling to."[16]

Fowles was also completely at sea as a lecturer. What disciplined critical analysis he had learned to apply to literature was grounded in the French he had read at Oxford. Now he was in a French institution where he was required to teach the English language and English literature. To judge by his diaries, Fowles had read, indeed had analyzed an astonishing cross section of English literature. However, he had not approached the canon academically or systematically. He had precious little pedagogy, and knowing the literature, as every novice teacher has discovered, is not the same thing as knowing how to teach it. His first presentation, lecturing to French students in a language foreign to them, was given on *The Waste Land* by T. S. Eliot. Although Fowles was more prepared to discuss this "brilliant analysis of a decadent civilization" than he later admitted, the poem would be daunting for most beginning teachers.[17]

Moreover, at this stage of his career, Fowles wasn't much of a teacher. A shy, self-absorbed young man, he was also lazy and easily distracted. "I am not doing this job properly," he admitted. "I can't be bothered to prepare lectures minutely. I just know enough to bluff my way past."[18] He talked in a loud, slow voice, writing names on the board with chalk. His students sat mute, not comprehending. No one responded, and Fowles often found himself laughing awkwardly at his own jokes.[19] Nevertheless, with only seven hours a week of required contact time, there was no excuse, he thought, for not producing significant, publishable work. Yet Fowles was unable to write at first, except for his ever-lengthening diaries.

The narrative voice of the Poitiers diary is startling, recognizably the early voice of Nicholas Urfe, protagonist of *The Magus*. Fowles, in 1950–1951, regarded himself as certain of his vocation as a poet and writer and of his intellectual and perceptive superiority over virtually everyone else with whom he came into contact. His diaries pour vinegar on his friends, his family, his colleagues, and even perfect strangers. He himself was aware of this attitude and began labeling himself a "prig," which he defined as "knowing one is superior to everyone else." The obverse of his elitism and cynicism, however, was his scathing criticism of himself. His self-consciousness was a two-edged blade. Every confident assumption of superiority was matched by weeks of agonized depression and self-accusations of mediocrity, egotism, coldness, cruel objectivity, isolationism, intellectual snobbishness, laziness. Like Nicholas, Fowles had not found where he loved, so defensively he pretended there was "nowhere to love."[20]

In the depths of *his* self-delusion, Nicholas Urfe met the wise and instructive Maurice Conchis, who offered lessons in deeper humanity and brought him to a rededicated resolve. At Poitiers, unfortunately, no magus appeared to help confused John Fowles find his true path. However, the experiences and characters of Fowles's stay in Poitiers are embedded in the narrative layers of *The Magus*. Although the events were transposed and fused to Fowles's experiences on a Greek island and in England in the six following years, Poitiers, France, was one of the principal biographical inspirations for much of the novel. The John Fowles of Spetsai, Greece, was a more mature, more secure young man, neither lonely nor lacking affectionate companionship. The John Fowles of Poitiers, France, sounds like Nicholas Urfe and shares with him the searing sense of isolation and the pain of exile, by geography, by language, and by temperament that makes Nicholas so vulnerable to Conchis's experiment.

Indeed, what rescued John Fowles from the sadness and self-absorption of the first two months in Poitiers was an experience worthy of *The Magus*. At 3:00 A.M. on a bitterly cold late December night Fowles left a café and crossed the freezing, empty Square of the Préfecture in darkness. Suddenly "everywhere. In the sky. On the rooves of the houses," there were "countless thin voices, the unmistakable whistle of redwings" crying their "thin, high-pitched, glistening whistle. . . . Like a sudden small gleam of old silver in a dark room. Strange, remote, beautiful sounds." This was followed by the "wild, romantic whistle" of a cock wigeon. Fowles, standing still and cold and completely alone in darkness in "the middle of a grey, silent, inland city," was transfixed to realize slowly that "the sky was full . . . a huge migration rush was going on." For half an hour he was spellbound, surrounded in the dark by the cries and whistles of vast numbers of plovers, redwings, wigeons filling the night. "So absolutely unexpected, and so full of special meaning for me; that I of all the 60,000 people here, should have heard them," wrote Fowles in wonder. Exactly as Nicholas Urfe was to declare when initiated into the mysteries of Bourani, John Fowles "felt profoundly that I was a link between two worlds. That I, standing . . . and listening to the wigeon whistling, belonged to a wilder, more mysterious world than anyone else in this whole city, that I understood faintly the ways and the impulse that was hidden away out there in the night, that I was immeasurably privileged."[21]

Although by daylight he was filled with frustration and sadness that he "could never transmute the intensity and the magic of such an experience,"[22] this sense of privileged, transcendental awe before the otherness of a mysterious universe melted the despair Fowles had felt, and he was able to write again. "Writing all the time," he noted eagerly. "Creation is a period of complete happiness." As in his encounter with the invisible migration, in writing Fowles experienced himself as the link between two worlds: "Everything disappears in the present world except the pen or the typewriter, the things on the table, and I am standing at a doorway between two rooms, the one dark, the other full of light, and fascinating conversation, and fascinating people. And the miracle is—in all objectivity—how they do actually live and talk in other ways from those which one had planned. And sometimes they get excited, and I am left behind, so that I can't remember all that they have said, and feel disappointed when I have to sit and try and remember."[23]

As the months went by, Fowles's sense of being able to connect imaginatively two opposing worlds became articulated in his aesthetic. He became determined to fuse the bleak existential vision of Camus and Franz Kafka, whose work he was reading, with the fantasy world of Pierre Carlet de Chamblain de Marivaux, whose plays he had come to admire at Oxford. Kafka and Camus, he thought, had "laid bare the one truth. The absurdity and hopelessness of things. The end of immortality. Whatever we do is only temporary." Hope and consolation were possible, however, through the realm of romantic enchantment, for which the eighteenth-century French playwright Marivaux was Fowles's model.[24]

Characteristically, Marivaux's gentle comedies depict the stages by which men and women fall in and out of love and the false social perceptions that create obstacles to their coming together. The characters are developed with exceptional psychological insight and delicacy of feeling. The clever, romantically charged dialogue is considered so subtle that the French use the term *marivaudage* to describe witty and suggestive banter between lovers. For Fowles, Marivaux's plays were an aesthetic island, an "art completely isolated from any other except pleasure. Hermetic, individual, a world of gentle fantasy into which one can plunge." Over many years Fowles was never without his volume of Marivaux as he traveled through France, Austria, Spain, England, and, especially, Greece. He observed how "M. can declare a deep and lasting love in ten lines. There are daring abridgements of time and the development of emotion . . . the immense speed of emotional development." He repeatedly admired the "effortless removal onto another plane . . . a strange hermetic world." How, Fowles pondered, could he reconcile this hermetic romantic fantasy with the unblinking acceptance of absurdity of the modern existentialists?[25]

After he experienced the invisible migration, Fowles also became more open to new human relationships. The postwar University of Poitiers had attracted many students from abroad. There were sophisticated Iranians and Iraqis, at least one black man from the Ivory Coast of Africa, and even two Germans whom Fowles was surprised to see treated well in France. The most numerous contingent, however, consisted of American Fulbright scholars. They spoke English, and John took to them. He regularly criticized them in his diary as shallow, naïve, and lacking in aesthetic sense, but he was constantly, and apparently happily, in their company at cafés, cinemas, dances, and on sightseeing tours of the surrounding area. His particular companion was Charles Gaisser, a recent Harvard graduate in history, who hailed from Oxford, Mississippi.

Charles Gaisser was John Fowles's first real experience of an American of his own generation, and characteristically Fowles began the relationship feeling smug and superior. The humorous self-deprecation of an educated Southern gentleman Fowles mistook for ignorant gaucherie. The deep Mississippi drawl John heard as "slowness and imperfection of . . . expression," revealing an inability to feel.[26] Within two weeks, however, Fowles was brimming with praise and inseparable from Charles, who exemplified for him the best in American writing, "toughness, efficiency, a dominating attitude to drink and women," a rare "sweet inner tenderness," yet "not devoid of culture nor of ethics."[27] It was typical of Fowles, as of his first protagonists, that in these early days he measured people by literary types. He was also impressed that

Charles's family was acquainted with William Faulkner. While at Poitiers and friendly with these young Americans, Fowles chose classic and modern American authors for most of his personal reading.

Among the French undergraduates he made one great friend with whom he shared a mutual passion for wild birds, the countryside, and the arts. André Brosset was a student from Thouars, almost exactly John's age. A shrewd, intellectual, deeply reserved young man, with a surprisingly Rabelaisian sense of humor, André commanded considerable authority when he chose to speak or comment. His friends as an affectionate joke called him *le président*. André was an avid naturalist and widely read, and he reminded Fowles of a bear or a badger, "massive, reserved . . . sagacious, tolerant, but very well able to maul."[28] In his company Fowles was introduced to the deeper and more intimate France that he came to call *la Sauvage,* the wild country of France. The two went on wildfowling expeditions with other French friends and on painting excursions in the countryside. At Brosset's suggestion, Fowles took up oil painting for the first time.

Through his friend's "vast" family at Thouars, Fowles was introduced to the warmth of French bourgeois family virtues: displayed affections, abundant rich food and excellent wines, shared adventures, passionate talk of politics, and unashamed loyalties. The Brossets were a well-to-do family risen from the craft workshop level to factory owners. All ten lived in an untidy, noisy, welcoming house with a complex, mysterious kitchen, making Fowles feel poignantly the contrast with his own upbringing.[29]

André Brosset does not appear in *The Magus* or any of Fowles's fictions, but his influence was lasting. Through André's expertise on bats and birds, for example, Fowles met the prototype of Alfonse de Deukans, the pornographic count whose fortune and motto are inherited by Maurice Conchis in *The Magus.* This elderly Marquis d'Abadie was a shockingly salacious collector of women, pornography, and wildlife ("thousands of birds, eggs, fossils, reptiles"), a "rich aristo" of old family, with a heavy, pompous face, a white mane of hair, and carious teeth.[30] André's ornithological reputation earned them a repellent visit to the marquis's château near Magnac-Luvac. On a perfect spring day the young men drove the fifty-three miles in a prewar Opal of "very imperfect condition" that shed pieces as they traveled. Their hilarity and high spirits were quelled by the dark, disintegrating château, filled with the marquis's collections of stuffed dead animals and pornographic materials, all neatly indexed and cross-referenced.[31] Pornography and collecting remained linked in Fowles's attitude forever afterward. Likewise, the cavernous underground quarries of Thouars, and the tales of German occupation John heard while exploring them with André and his brothers and uncles, led Fowles to create "the earth," the underground hiding place of the disappearing characters of Conchis's masque.[32]

Fowles's immediate senior on the faculty, M. Leaud, was his only friend on the staff. Leaud was lonely, intellectual, and enigmatic. He initiated Fowles into what became a year-long exploration of religious ritual that helped structure *The Magus*. A devout Catholic, Leaud briskly hiked Fowles, breathless and foot-blistered, the five miles to the monastery at Liguge. Fowles was enchanted by the plainchant, "sexlessly, quietly, millifluously pouring out of another world," and fascinated and a little shocked by the "complete mystery" of the monastic life and the "oriental preoccupation" with ceremony in the ritual of the high mass.[33] Alone and in Leaud's company, Fowles returned to Liguge and to other churches, where he analyzed the "ludicrously profane . . . stage management" of the mass. Indeed, the more emotionally affected he was during the service, the more his defenses were aroused. "It seems incredible to me that all this staginess is not penetrated by the intelligent Catholic," he wondered. "That it is all only a masque, a glorious sham, and that behind the altar there is only empty darkness. As if the spectators refused to admit the unreality of the theatre."[34] During Easter vespers at Liguge he was quite unsettled by the strength of his own response to the power and authority of the abbot during the formal procession of officiants in their gold and white ceremonial robes. The abbot seemed magnificent, with "eyes of great weight . . . the very image of the power temporal and celestial personified." Fowles had the sensation of being "completely crushed by another personality."[35] This awakening sense of the power of mystery, the sense of being awed by a ritual's celebrants, and Fowles's defensive cynicism about religious ritual as a masque, a sham, or a staged theatrical eventually echoed in the narrative of *The Magus*.

Fowles's most important relationship, also formed in the days following the invisible migration, was with twenty-year-old Ginette Marcailloux, one of his own language pupils and the favorite of the Professor of the Faculty. In a pattern that was to become typical, his interest in her was roused when another man, his friend Charles Gaisser, began paying her serious attention.[36] Ginette and John were soon a couple, joining the Fulbright Americans and other students for drinks and meals, going dancing or walking together. She was the daughter of a bourgeois family of Limoges, vivacious, bright, and well read. To Fowles's delight, she was even an amateur entomologist interested in moths and butterflies. He thought her one of the few pretty girls at Poitiers, "a meridional beauty . . . with black hair, a finely-shaped mouth, brilliant red in a pale face." She had large, expressive dark brown eyes and an alabaster complexion.[37]

Ginette was expert in the verbal teasing and taunting that Fowles loved, flirting hot and cold in a modern *marivaudage*.[38] She was warm and affectionate and a good listener. In a "rather self-dramatized representation . . . in the main sincere," John poured out to her, with "the incredible relief of a confession," his sense of destiny as a writer and of "solitude, the abyss between myself and my parents."[39] He credited Ginette with restoring his balance. As a couple they were hardly discreet as they spent long hours in John's tiny room, kissing, embracing, caressing, progressing to ever-greater physical intimacy, yet refraining from intercourse. It was 1951 in provincial, bourgeois France; the restrained behavior was not unusual, and Fowles respected Ginette's attitude. "I would sleep with G. tomorrow, if she offered herself," Fowles wrote. "But I admire her refusal more than I could have welcomed her acceptance . . . I admire her virtue."[40] Nonetheless, he often felt ill with frustration.

Ginette was a perceptive girl, who grew disturbed by the way her English lover changed "from private hot to public cold." She argued with John that his "duality" was a dishonesty, "a hypocrisy." She accused him of always isolating himself, of escaping even during intimacy. "I suppose," he wrote, "she senses my cruel objectivity to all experience, even though I try and conceal it from her."[41] She could characterize John cuttingly as a *prêtre sans foi,* a priest without a faith,[42] while his ironic pet term for her was *une caniche,* a pet dog or a poodle.[43]

Ginette was obviously falling deeply in love with him, and Fowles constantly mulled the question of marriage. Sometimes he was certain that she would make him an excellent wife, measuring her by "the D. H. Lawrence qualities . . . heart and soul and heat, humanity, intelligence and simplicity when it is needed." He could speak openly with her on any subject, and she was "warm, nubile." Yet each time he acknowledged Ginette's assets, Fowles argued himself out of a permanent relationship.

She had, he sniffed, "no aristocratic traits." She made him aware of his class sensitivities. He imagined her in various situations, "whenever they entail 'chic,' she disappoints me . . . aesthetically I need a little aristocracy, a little carriage, manner, fine-bred beauty."[44] Worst of all, Ginette was assertive and refused "to accept the inferior role of woman."[45]

By spring 1951 Fowles was feeling restless with the affair and depressed about his writing. An inventory of his literary output to date made him unhappy: four plays; one written, one half written, two in "fragments"; four "ideas" for filmscripts; eighteen short stories in need of rewriting; about fifty poems "not Juvenile," plus his disjoints (the diaries) and a fragment from Collioure.[46] At twenty-five he had written nothing publishable, finding it all "mediocre . . . a series of pastiches . . . derivative, or faulty in technique or conception."[47] He accused himself of wasting his life. He was cheered by a letter from his father, confessing that he himself wrote for his own amusement, wryly recognizing that his stories were far from professional quality. It encouraged John to know that his father was writing stories. He had the "sense of someone else building behind me," hidden in "the blood-link.[48]

Fowles's future was murky once more. The Head of the Faculty of Letters, Professor Martin, informed Fowles that he would not be reappointed after the spring term. Despite a positive start the relationship between John and his superior had deteriorated. Professor Martin was shocked when Fowles had taken on a second, very part-time position, practicing English conversation with the boys at the local Jesuit college. The two systems never mixed. Martin also had a reputation for overfamiliarity with women students, and Fowles always suspected that his blatant romantic involvement with Ginette Marcailloux, the professor's favorite, had cost him his job. However, Fowles's teaching was most of the reason. He despised lecturing, saying, "How I bore people. Churning out the facts. Regurgitating. I hate it."[49] His students must have agreed. At one of his principal lectures, not a single one had attended. Fowles had "virtually no pupils; not more than a dozen a week except at the one big lecture." Leaud, to the younger man's embarrassment, had had to advertise Fowles's lectures to try to draw an audience. Fowles felt both guilty and slighted. "I am much too ego-centred to be a good educator," he admitted.[50] He wondered if he could return to teach at Bedford and visited an employment agency in brief hopes of becoming an agent for a cognac firm.[51]

In this atmosphere of change, he treated Ginette disdainfully. As spring turned to summer, she wept often, wishing she had never met John and accusing him of loving her less than she loved him. Fowles admitted it. "I explained that I did not think I was capable of completely loving any woman. . . . I loved myself, above all my future, uncreated self, too much ever to be able to give myself completely. I explained egoism was not a quality I enjoyed having." Even as he sought to console her, he was aware of being "only partly involved. . . . Always the rest of me withholds and watches."[52] Yet he could not break off the relationship, was stunned with regret whenever separated from her, and still thought occasionally of marriage.

In a psychologically revealing strategy, John Fowles managed Ginette's sincere distress and his own troubled feelings by withdrawing into his private aesthetic domain where real events were refashioned into art. While she begged for his commitment, he began "to plan and formulate a nouvelle about her." While she wept, he treated her "more as the character in the novel than as her real self" and observed dryly how "we are no longer (for me) real, but characters in an unwritten novel." For the sake of this unwritten novel, he played the heartbroken girl psychologically "like a tired ball, experimenting, risking, showing off." He could see that the ending would be sad, but his own feelings were not in jeopardy, for "sadness is a romantic hypocrisy." So he prepared and indulged "in melancholy for our departure." As Ginette sobbed, "But what is the point . . . ?" John said, "You must try and forget me. But I don't need to forget you. For me you will be past experience."[53]

To some extent, she indeed became part of a novel. Like so much of his year at Poitiers, Fowles's affair with Ginette Marcailloux echoed in *The Magus*. The relationship between Nicholas Urfe and Alison Kelly was modeled on that of Fowles and his future wife, Elizabeth Christy. However, some of Ginette must have been folded into Alison's character. Many years after their youthful love, the provincial literature teacher Mme. Marcailloux wrote to the world-famous novelist John Fowles, saying she "got the impression after having read *The Magus* that perhaps we are as we once were. You were the reader, the *lecteur* at the Faculty of Letters of Poitiers, and I was one of your students." Fowles wrote back warmly, confirming her influence on *The Magus*, to which Ginette Marcailloux replied: "My dear John, Well then, so I wasn't mistaken. All those literary references were good indications or clues."[54]

Receiving her letters in 1983, Fowles felt sad and guilty. But in 1951, fascinated with his own actions, he wondered: Was he a "hypocrite"? "A monster"? Was this "Schizophrenia. Or priggishness of an esoteric kind?" Whatever it was, he was prepared to embrace it. "I am beginning to realize," he mused, "that I have become faintly detached from real life, in my efforts to observe it objectively, to *solve* it. I don't believe I wish to regain terra firma; and the drift in this sea of complex self-analysis is away from the terrestrial contact . . . the relationship with my fellow man or woman."[55] "The strongest part of me," he confessed to the diary, "is the part I never divulge; a mixture of the ego of my ambitions and my best capability, ruthlessly determined to achieve its own fulfillment."[56]

Fowles spent part of June with his family, meeting them on their holiday in Brittany. They were undemonstrative; he was judgmental. He was scornful of their delight in small tourist pleasures, complaining of the "stifling platitudes" that passed for conversation among English middle-class people on holiday. He was acutely embarrassed when people expressed curiosity about the relationship between him and his nine-and-a-half-year-old sister and so critical of her speaking accent that she was glad to get away from him.[57] Despite his sincere joy when he had learned by letter of his father's literary attempts, John was mortified when his father remarked aloud before others, "I wrote some short stories last winter," Hazel asked, "What did you call them?" and nearby people smiled.[58]

Yet in surprising contrast with this chilly, awkward visit with his family in June 1951, and in contrast with the surly self-absorption of his months as a lecturer, was Fowles's August fortnight on a student camping tour organized by André Brosset. It was one of the rare interludes—always, before his marriage, brief and separated from his ordinary life—in which Fowles's intellectual defenses were conquered by gaiety and affection. As in some of his own short stories, as in Alain-Fournier's *Le Grand Meaulnes* (the book that Fowles later so passionately admired), there is a straying off the path of the ordinary into an enchanted domain and being received into the sweet simplicity and love of a party of innocents. On this particular journey, a boyish, tender, and seldom seen young man emerged.

From August 3 to 19 a charabanc, or tour bus, filled with young campers between ages eighteen and twenty-five toured across Switzerland, the Austrian Tyrol, and Bavaria. Fowles was one of the oldest in the group, though he realized that psychologically he was one of the youngest. Knowing only André and expecting disappointment, John was completely enthralled.

Most of the group had known one another from childhood, some were siblings or cousins, and they related like a family. John was touched and astonished as they enfolded him in a "kind of corporate, inclusive love." There were a dozen or so young men, some with military background, all capable and comradely. There were about sixteen young women, *les jeunes*, who sang and giggled and teased and flirted all across the Alps. Fowles was borne along by the "freshness and the gaiety, the simplicity and the sentimentality, the spontaneity" of these companions. The journey seemed magical. "From time to time," he recalled, "there was a kind of sparkling surge which lifted us all into a kind of momentarily eternal youth."[59] The group camped in the open and were soaked with rain, but "the girls went on singing . . . indefatigable harmony" in songs like "La Chanson des Marais," "Les Maries de Notre Ville," and "Froufrou, Froufrou." To tease him, the girls took to chanting his so-English name at odd moments: "*John Fowles . . . John Fowles . . .* with a kind of mock sanctity and prolongation of the syllables."[60] When a piano could be found in a café, someone played and they danced. In some towns they were offered civic halls or ballrooms to camp indoors, with much fooling of the dividing curtain between the sexes and many suggestive comments. At first the lack of inhibition embarrassed Fowles, but he soon understood its innocence. He realized that he "was thawing out under the charm of *les jeunes*. A kind of second adolescence . . . an essence my own adolescence never gave me."[61]

The travelers delighted in amusing one another, and John, who had never before tried to entertain, took up telling card fortunes. He pleased his new friends with a newly discovered gift for flamboyance and wit. Accepted into the "family," John felt he had been "simplified, ironed . . . out." They took him from the lonely, disdainful Poitiers lecturer, "too involved, reticent . . . intellectual, back into an old, more natural self." They "performed a sort of miracle," he later wrote wistfully, "made me believe I was charming. I knew myself well enough to know that I am anything but that."[62]

On the journey John began a tentative *affaire de coeur* with freckle-faced Ginette Poinot, an "aloof, inscrutable little person, with an enigmatic and slightly ironic smile." This Ginette was very timid and inexperienced and completely "without intellect, culture, and co-quetry."[63] Their short relationship was confined to wandering out of the group and stealing kisses. Fowles felt proud of having beaten out the other men for the attentions of one of the girls.

Among *les jeunes* he thought the graceful, demure Nanni Baraton was the most beautiful. Fowles was reading Freud at the time and was shocked at the implications of his admiration when he recognized Nanni's resemblance to his own mother as a girl.[64] His favorite, however, was the youngest and most exuberant traveler, Monique Baudouin. Still a schoolgirl, Monique alternated between "flashes of *enfant terrible*" and self-contained repose. She had a hoarse, husky voice and "a genius for singing in discords, for the deliberate *gaffe*, for the timing of her bricks and *bons mots*." With her "dark, alive eyes, a mischievous smile, pigtails tied in string, a round, tanned face," Monique stood "on the brink of womanhood . . . the wit and the tomboy, but always the woman."[65]

Little Monique wept, Ginette Poinot smiled faintly, and the other girls sang "Auld Lang Syne" as they said farewell to John Fowles at Poitiers on August 19. In his terribly silent room he was aware of the lack of friends in his life. It was "like the abrupt cessation of a music" in which he had been "completely lost."[66]

Though he tried to cling to the evanescent magic of the journey, the memories rapidly became distant and faded. Fowles's defensive reserve quickly grew back, closing over the approachable traveler of days earlier. Ginette Marcailloux came to spend a last day with him before his return to England. She threw herself at John, sadly repeating her love and desire to marry him. "The woman's interior theatre," he observed. "I took it all coolly." They parted at the railway station, "dryly, apologising to each other, tenderly cold." He pressed Ginette's hand, turned his back, and yawned. "It felt good to be free again," he wrote caddishly, "and not obliged to imagine myself a cynical brute."[67] Four days later he was back in Leigh-on-Sea.

Leigh was unchanged. In Fowles's view, it was futile, ugly, and nurtured genteel hypocrisy. No. 63 Fillebrook Avenue was unchanged. His father was depressed and greatly aged, his mother "indefatigably trivial," and for the first time they quarreled in front of him.[68] John Fowles, however, was changed, hardened by his months in Poitiers. He felt aloof and uninterested. He was broke and "shameless" about his financial dependence on his parents.[69] Despising family gatherings, however, he embarrassed them and offended the Fowles family by refusing to attend the October wedding of his father's half sister. He welcomed solitude, playing golf alone, hunting alone, the costs borne by his father. He went on solitary wildfowling excursions on the Leigh marshes as if testing his emotional response to shooting. In stark contrast with his misgivings of the previous year, he held a wounded curlew under his foot in a creek to drown it, watching its death struggles "dispassionately."[70]

Able to withdraw into his imagination, content to dwell inside himself, he was "virtually monastic."[71] Fowles occupied himself with work on a Camus-inspired novel, *The Design for a Gateway,* with its "Suicide Appendix." He wrote poems and short stories and started several plays. He discovered he could commit his stories to the page "almost at full writing speed, without pauses," but the creation of his diary, fleshed out from daily notes, was a slower effort, requiring deliberation between every sentence.[72]

He searched for his next job. The Organization for European Economic Cooperation in Paris was seeking translators, and Fowles took the preliminary examination with three hundred other candidates but failed, to his surprise. He did better in the civil service competitive selection process. He looked at jobs in the British Museum and the BBC and had an unpleasant interview at Unilever. He considered a post teaching apprentices in the Dockyard School at Rosyth. Yet throughout the process Fowles could not imagine working in a routine position and yearned for the exotic and uncertain. He admitted that his ambition for enduring fame as a writer dictated his attitude to life, his "lack of interest in ordinary people; . . . interest for the famous; . . . contempt for contemporary artists; . . . fear of growing stale, . . . sacrifice of any careerist future; . . . miserable dependence on . . . parents; . . . withdrawal from society and its kindred comforts."[73]

In early October 1951, shortly after he had penned a wish "to go abroad again, to live in a solitary place, an island,"[74] Fowles was interviewed by the British Council. The people were helpful; the atmosphere was cordial. He looked at openings in Brazil and in Baghdad but was fascinated by a vacancy at a school on a Greek island, Spetsai, south of Athens. It would be "madness," of course. It offered no future "except lotus-eating."[75] A fortnight later, however, John Fowles was offered the position of English master at the Anargyrios and Korgialenios School on Spetsai, to commence at the new year. He accepted immediately.

Straightaway Fowles was certain he had acted foolishly. He had imagined Greece romantic; now it loomed ominously. A letter from Kenneth Pringle, the master he was replacing, added to his unease. The pedagogical and political conditions of the school were far worse than Fowles could imagine, wrote his predecessor. Morale at the school was terrible. The English section was in turmoil, with three masters leaving. There was constant interference from important parents and politicians and constant intrigue between the masters for popularity with the headmaster and the boys. The boys were undisciplined, uninhibited in their curiosity, their affection, or their hate. The school was a kind of laboratory, with a hothouse atmosphere, where eccentricities were enormously exaggerated.[76] Fowles, nervously packing clothes, wireless, typewriter, books, and a supply of his favorite powders and pills for recurring stomach troubles, told himself that his duty as a poet was to "refuse the safe and the obvious." He decided to abandon all his previous writing as "immature . . . rubbish" and make a fresh beginning.[77]

He left Leigh two days after Christmas 1951 and kept New Year's 1952 aboard the Adriatic steamer *Campidoglio*, waiting for dense fog to lift in the harbor at Venice. The two-day cruise down the Adriatic was passed in playing canasta with an odd assortment of international passengers: a slippery Marxist Syrian, a family of arrogant Americans on the grand tour, a hysterical Austrian woman, and an inoffensive Egyptian. Somehow the political positions and the social expectations among the group became mixed into the increasingly confrontational—and dishonest—card game. Fowles, as he watched the Greek coast materialize in the dawn of January 3, felt grateful to be an Englishman. The episode set him thinking, however. Some months later he began a new novel exploring these feelings. He called it *Journey to Athens: A Fragment of Growth*, but the journey this book began was to take him beyond Athens and out into the wide world.

CHAPTER FIVE

An Island and Greece

Spetsai and Spain: 1952

Phraxos was beautiful. There was no other adjective; it was not just pretty, picturesque, charming—it was simply and effortlessly beautiful. It took my breath away when I first saw it, floating under Venus like a majestic black whale in an amethyst evening sea, and it still takes my breath away when I shut my eyes now and remember it. Its beauty was rare even in the Aegean, because its hills were covered with pine trees, Mediterranean pines as light as greenfinch feathers. Nine-tenths of the island was uninhabited and uncultivated; nothing but pines, coves, silence, sea. Herded into one corner, the northwest, lay a spectacular agglomeration of snow-white houses around a couple of small harbors.

—JOHN FOWLES, *THE MAGUS*

In the bright afternoon sunlight of January 3, 1952, two of the English masters from the Anargyrios and Korgialenios School entered Ommonia Square in Athens, Greece. The older man, in his forties, fleshy, choleric, with filthy hair and fingernails, was Fowles's predecessor, Kenneth Pringle, author of two disappointing novels, embittered teacher, and alcoholic. Pringle's acid disposition had estranged him from the staff, and he had just been fired for writing homosexual love letters to a student. The other man was thirty, tall and fair, with pale good looks, a wide smile, and an ironic eye. He wrote poetry. Denys Sharrocks had watched masters come and go for three years, having survived on staff longer than anyone else since the war. People often went "rather to pieces" on the island. But Sharrocks had a reputation for balance, for staying above petty intrigue, and for effortlessly eliciting the classroom cooperation of his otherwise undisciplined pupils. He had come to escort the new English master to Spetsai. "That must be Fowles," he said, noting the boyish appearance of the man waiting for them at a café table. "Ah!" murmured Pringle cynically, "Saint Sebastian."[1]

Beyond Aegina, beyond Poros, beyond Hydra, a four-and-a-half-hour ferry journey from Piraeus lay Spetsai, the outermost of the Saronic Gulf islands. More recently called Spetses, Fowles named it Phraxos in *The Magus*. In 1952 it seemed to lie on the far rim of the world. About four miles long, two miles across at its broadest point, the island is roughly pear-shaped. On the northwest side Spetses town, with a sparse population of a few thousand, clustered around the harbor and sprawled partway up the hill and around a central square called the Dapia. The school was on the outskirts of this town. On the south side of the central ridge of the island, rising to eight hundred feet, were a few scattered villas. The island, once denuded of trees by the robust shipping and shipbuilding population (some twenty thousand) of the seventeenth and eighteenth centuries, had been thickly replanted in Aleppo pine forests by Sotirios Anargyrios, the same philanthropist who had founded the school in which Fowles was now employed.

In the school's lovely park by the sea, the sound of the waves lapping the shingle could be heard from the classrooms. The grounds were planted with olives, cypresses, and pines, through which the veronica blue sea was visible. Hibiscus bloomed scarlet in the garden, and vivid citrus yellow oxalis grew wild by the thousands. Fowles was given a furnished thirty-by-thirty-foot high-ceilinged room on a hallway two or three doors from Denys Sharrocks, with windows overlooking a grove of olive trees. But the five monstrous multistory blocks of school buildings were a shock to the newly arrived English master. Voices echoed on bare stone floors and down unfurnished wide corridors. The place was superbly equipped for 400 boys, with a fine gymnasium, tennis courts, a football pitch, and two fives courts, but enrollment had dipped to 150. In the hills behind the buildings was an outdoor amphitheater with a two-thousand-seat capacity.[2]

From Pringle's warnings, Fowles had expected worse. The school was "grim, but not terrible." The twenty-three hours a week were easy, with four daily teaching periods and two duties. He found the students

charming, "ebullient, spontaneous, and eager; more feminine than English boys." Surprised, he watched boys returning from holiday kiss on
the cheek and saw the seniors showing more affection to younger boys
than English boys would dare.[3] In class their constant whispering, laughter, waving of hands, and jumping up to ask questions made discipline
difficult. Fowles was a far better teacher to these ebullient boys, however, than he had been to the French university students at Poitiers. He
ventured beyond the dry prescriptions of *Eckersley's Essential English* to
engage them with thoughtfully designed lessons. Like Nicholas Urfe, he
sometimes substituted teaching the parts of an automobile engine for a
lesson on Byron's poetry. He gave creative assignments ("describe the
end of the world"), to which his pupils responded with imagination and
zeal, if not with accurate grammar and spelling.[4] The boys liked Fowles
and, for his large-boned, shambling movements, nicknamed him "Ark-
oudi" or "the bear."[5]

From almost his first day in the classroom, Fowles was frustrated by
the school's system. He thought the teaching methods were antiquated
and the boys' schedule of seven daily class periods and two and three-
quarter hours of homework excessive. They were allowed off school
grounds only on Sunday afternoons, when they marched into town in a
snaky line. He thought they should have the run of the island, with more
time for themselves for games and hobbies. Examinations made him especially angry, since the tough work routine shut the boys in from six in
the morning until nine at night with only two short breaks. Glassy-eyed,
yawning, and restless, they were not even allowed to swim except on al-
ternate days, in case they became too exhausted to study. Looking out
over the wind-tossed, sun-sparkling waves of the strait from a classroom
window, Fowles commiserated with the boys cramming in the room behind him as "poor imprisoned innocents."[6]

Despite grinding classroom hours, discipline was all but impossible.
The declining enrollment meant a scramble for fees. The school could
not afford to fail or dismiss any pupil, a situation the more cunning boys
exploited to their advantage. A master who gave his students "help" with
answers during examinations was commended by the headmaster.[7] Another, who had failed the son of the Minister of Education, was forced to
apologize before the entire school for being a poor teacher. The only organized discipline was a weekly "court" of the entire faculty, where students' misdemeanors were debated among the masters and demerit

points assigned, but no real punishments meted out. Fowles believed a much stricter system of marking was necessary and, above all, "a harsh system of punishment. Punishment is fresh air;" wrote the former Bedford Head Boy, "without it the school will always remain stifled, a hothouse of compromises, intrigues, despised by the boys and hated by the masters."[8]

The masters knew nothing but their subjects and had nothing in common but gossip. The headmaster was Gerandopoulos, "a shriveled, scholarly man, with a passion for Shakespeare," but the school was run by his assistant, a tough Maniot named Anagnostopoulos, who bore grudges against those who crossed him.[9] Leader of the archconservative faculty faction was the theology master, Timaigenis ("a reeking Tartuffe"). The old French master was a stuttering Romanian Greek, Abdelides, whom Fowles once watched beating a boy for the wrong answer. One-eyed, sulky, muscle-bound Papyreiou, at one time the champion hammer thrower of Greece, was the pugnacious games master. Dokos, the clownish music master, played with such thumping brio that Fowles suspected him of formerly working the crowds in busy restaurants. Distant, secretive, and enigmatic was old Notokos, the maths master.

On the English faculty, besides Denys Sharrocks, there were two Greek English teachers with whom Fowles spent social time. Because of his name, Fowles (an inveterate nicknamer) always referred to Potamianos as "the Hippo," though this was hardly a physical or psychological description. Smug and self-interested, the young Potamianos looked like "the pride of the seminary" with his downy cheeks, protuberant lips, and backswept curly hair. But he was thick-skinned and sensuous. The prototype of the character called Meli in *The Magus,* the Hippo had a store of smutty stories, an unstoppably salacious imagination, contempt for women, and enthusiastic schemes to divide among his friends the cost of bringing an Athenian prostitute to the island. Fowles could satisfy Potamianos's disbelieving curiosity about his solitary explorations on the island only by lying that he hiked into the hills to use the goats, since no women were available.[10]

The Hippo's opposite was sad-eyed, "parsonical" Egyptiadis. With his massive, swollen torso, bull neck, and shaved head, he looked like an ex-wrestler, but he had lived a life of renunciation, "more ascetic than many monks, abstemious, thrifty, moral, a tremendous worker." After working nineteen years in the United States, Egyptiadis had returned to wed and raise a family who lived in an Athenian suburb.[11] He was an autodidact who had taught himself seven languages, but who knew them only as words divorced from the world around him. He constantly confronted the two Englishmen with his dictionary and demands for meanings.[12] It took only a glass of brandy for him, above all a quoter, to begin imitating an owl or an American train, breaking into the Eton College boating song, or "thundering out an endless variety of hymns, Turkish and Greek songs, novelty numbers, national anthems and lines from the *Iliad*" in a deep bass voice loud enough to shake the building. His attitude of abject humility made Egyptiadis the butt of cruel jokes from the other masters and the boys. Fowles engaged him to teach him Greek.[13]

Even a year earlier, dealing with this gallery of grotesques might have triggered in Fowles a priggish sense of superiority and a smoldering moral indignation. The other masters were "so uncultured, so childish and transparent and insular in their motives." Yet in this first year of teaching at Anargyrios School, Fowles's annoyance usually dissolved in laughter, simply because he had Denys Sharrocks to share his perceptions, point out the ridiculous, and give way to hilarity. In Denys's company, John could find the notion of "this ridiculous great mock-British school on a gem-like Aegean island . . . intrinsically absurd. One has to laugh."[14]

Although they came from differing backgrounds, Denys Sharrocks's education, wide reading, and military experience had made them comfortably similar to each other. From the King George V Grammar School in Southport, Lancashire, Sharrocks had read English literature at the University of Liverpool, interrupting his studies during the war and returning to finish his degree after service in the RAF. While assigned to the Second Tactical Air Force, he had been a navigator on Mosquitoes on more than thirty night missions attacking German communications in France and Holland. After leaving operational flying, he was assigned to the Allied Control Commission in Austria and was, while in his early twenties, placed in charge of a camp for German prisoners of war. After the war, degree in hand, Sharrocks found himself his first teaching appointment at the Anargyrios School in Greece. When Fowles met him in 1952, both knew it was his last year on Spetsai. In March 1953, Denys was to marry Monica Perry, an aspiring young actress whom he had met on one of his holiday returns to England. He had promised the headmaster that he would help find his own replacement.

Sharrocks's ironic perspective was tempered by "a sense of wonderful freedom and privilege at actually going to Greece to a Greek island and being paid, however modestly, for it." Although he claimed to be "a callow . . . extremely innocent creature" on his first teaching experience, he had realistic expectations about the school that were not disappointed. For three years he had survived the comings and goings of even odder characters than the present faculty: a *soi-distant* Norman baron, a Royalist of Franco-British origin with dangerously violent mood swings, a headmaster who washed the legs of boys he was attracted to, a Swiss who made such enemies locally that his cat was decapitated and left as a warning, various "moonstruck" colleagues entangled in love affairs, and an assortment of would-be writers. But Denys Sharrocks went on teaching English effectively, coaching sport, making friends, and traveling widely. He loved Greece and got on well with the staff and the boys.[15] His capacity for accepting things as they were with philosophic good humor seems to have rubbed off on Fowles in his first year in Greece.

They were friends immediately and friends for life. They were the only two fluent English-speaking people on Spetsai, and they found it easy to be together ("insofar as it was easy for John to share confidences with anyone"). Not only were they similar in experience and beliefs, but they were both "*private* English," close without being intrusive. Each surmised that the other was writing and spoke of it, on extremely rare occasions, "glancingly." They shared values, believing in books, art, and ideas. They shared an "ironical perception" and many private jokes. They traveled together comfortably at a time when travel was not always convenient or easy.[16]

After several years on the small island, Sharrocks knew everyone. He had been welcomed into the villas of the wealthy back in the hills. In town he was friendly with fishermen, local officials, and taverna owners. He immediately introduced John to the limited nightlife of Spetsai. They spent free evenings at Lambrou's taverna or on Georgio's terrace shaded by eucalyptus and pine trees, overlooking the sea. They ate octopus and fat olives, fried cuttlefish, bread and tzatziki, lamb chops and cabbage, and drank retsina and beer. Sometimes they were joined by the Hippo or Egyptiadis. Sometimes they drank alone, speaking passionately of writers and writing. Fowles found his new friend to be very skilled socially, "un-ruffled, diplomatic, amused and amusing; socially supple." Sharrocks's most irritating fault, Fowles grumbled, was being unaffected by drink on the morning after, always turning up fresh, pleasant, and bright-eyed. "I said last night," Fowles wrote painfully one morning in late January, "that two more evenings like that, and I could die for Greece. Two more hang-overs like this, and I shall."[17]

Wherever a social group gathered in the evenings, the guitarist Evan-gelakis turned up to play. John came to love and appreciate his extraordi-nary musical gifts and repertoire of songs, "bawdy, melancholy, sentimental." "Sekina mia Psarapoula," "Thelo krasi poly na pio," "Der-biderissa," "Opou anthropos kakia," "E morphi Athena," "Athena kai pal-lis Athena," "Harouni," "Trabarifa"[18]: Evangelakis sang them all with his "whole spirit, intensely, absorbedly . . . with closed eyes and a serene, al-most ecstatic kind of force, bursting the words out, prolonging them, quavering." Fowles was as deeply moved by these performances as by the broken rhythms of Catalan music. Evangelakis's most distinctive talent was his phenomenal ability to improvise comically, with a speed of versi-fying and barbed humor that reduced his taverna audiences to fits of laughter.[19]

In the tavernas and the common room of the school Fowles also lis-tened to hair-raising tales of the German 1941–1944 occupation and the 1944–1946 civil war. He was to adapt to his future novel Spetsai's three World War II occupation stories. In one, two sisters caught clandestinely supplying Communist guerrillas were shot and crucified by the Germans, their bodies disemboweled on the doors of the Hotel Poseidonian. In an-other, the mayor was ordered to execute two captured guerrillas. Handed an empty weapon, he "was obliged, under the eyes of his whole village, to club the guerillas to death with a light sub-machinegun." In the third, a German storeship was bombed and sank, its contents rapidly salvaged in "a redletter day for the starving islanders."[20] Fowles's older pupils actually recalled the civil war and, being ferociously anti-Communist, regaled their teacher with accounts of the Communists' executing prisoners by chopping off their limbs or digging out their eyeballs and sending them in tins to Moscow.[21]

The rest of the world faded into unreality as Fowles went weeks with-out even reading a newspaper. When he and Sharrocks paid some distant attention to a broadcast of the funeral of King George VI, they both felt detached from an England that seemed "minute, twisted, pettily inflated."[22] Fowles's favorite publication, the *New Statesman*, seemed affected, an intellectual world now "a minor planet, and faintly grotesque, a narrow small heart of a small faction who live in North London and Oxford and Cambridge—and nowhere else."[23] An old common room copy of Bedford School's the *Ousel* bewildered him with its illusory, frowsty, Victorian old-tie sentimentality.[24] On a rare trip to Athens to meet poet Stephen Spender, Fowles nervously felt himself "a rustic . . . bewildered, tossed about by all the people. . . . My road sense . . . atrophied."[25] Denys Sharrocks recalled that their vocabulary became so "shrunken" that they sometimes groped for English words and came up with a sort of "pidgin." Once women were picking olives in the grove beneath Fowles's window. Watching them, John searched at a loss for a word. "Ah," Sharrocks remembered him saying, "woman-noise."[26]

Realizing he was being transformed by traveling and living in Greece, Fowles began to write about it. He admired travel books that described the exterior journey through a place and its people while mapping an interior, psychological journey. Like Patrick Leigh Fermor's *The Traveller's Tree* and Laurens Van Der Post's *Venture to the Interior,* books Fowles admired that had both appeared to great acclaim in 1951, these books went beyond Baedeker to being bildungsroman, novels of a young man's maturation. In winter 1952, on Spetsai, Fowles began a travel book in which the narrating traveler is changed by the experience of the journey.

A Journey to Athens: A Fragment of Growth[27] is a barely fictionalized version of Fowles's voyage down the Adriatic, January 1 to 3, 1952, journalistically faithful to the real chronology, characters, and appearances of the passengers on the *Campidoglio.* "John," a twenty-five-year-old Englishman en route to Greece, feels "in exile from my country . . . [and] from the person I wanted to be." He disowns the "four deficiencies" of his background: being born into the middle classes, having attended public school, having been an officer, having gone to Oxford. These "deficiencies" remain his mask, however, for his hidden true self is unformed and vulnerable. Between Venice and Athens, he spends two days playing canasta in a small company of international passengers. In the card game he is partnered with a crafty English-speaking Iraqi Kurd whose vehement leftist politics and hatred of the United States exemplify a defined personal "self" for the envious (and unnerved) narrator. Their stereotypically drawn American opponents include a well-to-do middle-aged California woman escorting her bored, selfish teenaged daughter and her naïve, clean-cut college-age nephew on a European tour. A nasty, sexually tinged incident between the American girl and the Iraqi reveals hidden prejudices, and the game becomes the arena for the tensions. As "John" observes, "A game of cards is a kind of intense microscopic parody of the real world; a world of masks and symbols . . . the world in miniature, with all its vices, crimes, its patina of selfish emotion . . . reduced to a few dozen scraps of printed card with man-imposed unreal values, and . . . man-made unreal rules." Acting out their hatreds, their politics, and their personalities, both the Iraqi and the American matron begin to cheat ruthlessly. "John" examines the national traits of the others as though they were biological specimens and weighs his identity as an Englishman against their poor character and weak integrity. Disembarking at Athens, he is reconciled to the virtues of his own Englishness ("fair play . . . hatred of conformity . . . of cant and rhetoric . . . a supple-hearted neutrality") and to the mask of conventional Britishness that protects him and allows him, hidden inside beneath the surface, the freedom to become the person he wants to be.

Fowles had not yet learned how to dramatize his ideas within a narrative, so this slim traveler's novella is extremely uneven, with long, stodgy, overwrought disquisitions alternating with vivid, nuanced character scenes like the canasta game itself. He was to revise the twenty-three-chapter, 136-page manuscript for ten years, but mine its contents even longer. Condensed and packed into the short chapters like seeds of literary-genetic information waiting for the right conditions are many of the great themes of Fowles's future work. Besides the obvious relationship of the card-playing narrator to Nicholas Urfe in *The Magus*, the genesis of *Daniel Martin* appears in a chapter analyzing "my generation," those nineteen when the war ended, who had "spent our green years in a world of official hatred, national duty . . . the individual and individuality were unimportant . . . were bad. Being was to conform, to obey." This "trauma of our teens" created a generation of individualistic young people intent on personal survival. They are educated and perceptive, critically sophisticated, fairly tolerant, and politically lukewarm but also politically powerless, uncreative, religiously indifferent, and emotionally guarded. Exiled from other generations, Fowles calls them "ghosts."[28]

From the beginning of Fowles's sojourn on Spetsai, he often escaped the school and his new friends by exploring the island alone. As he walked, the school dwindled in the distance and disappeared. He soon gained the central ridge and was received into the silence of the pine forests and surrounding sea. On his first walk on January 8, 1952, only three days after his arrival, he arrived at a "supreme level of awareness of existence, an all-embracing euphoria" induced by the Mediterranean light and the pregnant stillness of place. He wrote how "a purity and simplicity of emotion, a kind of quintessential mediterranean ecstasy, pervaded the air, the air infused with pine resin and winter sharpness and the brine from far below." He sat on a rock, facing westward, "and the world was at my feet. I have never had so vividly the sense of standing *on* the world; the world below me." In this perfect landscape, "a compound of exquisitely blue sky, brilliant sunlight, miles of rock and pine, and the sea," he found the elements "at such a pitch of purity that I was spellbound." He was lifted up and out of himself: in the fragrant wind "I was suspended in bright air, timeless, motionless, floating on a sublime synthesis of the elements." The effect was "weird," he continued, "and for a few minutes I felt incomprehensibly excited, as if I were experiencing something infinitely rare. . . . Landscapes like this, on such days, advance men immeasurably. Perhaps ancient Greece was only the effect of a landscape and a light on a sensitive people."[29] Looking back, he believed this moment was the "genesis of *The Magus*."[30]

Throughout his months on the island, Fowles opened himself to the enchantment of this powerfully evocative landscape. The peculiar silence and emptiness affected him, stimulating his imagination to call up something that was not there. Roaming for hours in solitude, he occasionally had a "flash of vivid perception of the marvellous, the poetic—a tissue of the legendary, the enchanted forest, the spirits of places, nymphs in groves—partly French and medieval, partly Greek and classical, partly my own dream-world."[31] He also began to experience a kind of sixth sense of presences in the strange noonday silence, hearing "rushing . . . sometimes when there is no wind."[32] Occasionally, dreaming by the sea, he felt the place "imperceptibly haunted," having the "momentary impression of a chase, a swift passage of—I don't know what—bare feet, a shadow in the shade, a stir in the air, lost before I could turn . . . always in brilliant sunshine . . . never frightening."[33] Like the Pasvik River at twilight, like the nocturnal migration over Poitiers, the perfect isolation and noontime peace of Spetsai stimulated a heightened awareness of the otherness in the universe and evoked in Fowles the sense that he was a link between two realities. On these walks he began to understand how the two planes fused, as his world of imaginary marvels was embedded in the ordinary: the bells of sheep, the minor-key songs of women floating disembodied through the air, even the sudden, unexpected appearance of a visiting film company in the midst of this sun-baked, isolated landscape.

A reason for the profound silence, particularly in the middle of the island, was the lack of standing or flowing water. Each house had a cistern, stocked with a few eels to clean the water. There were no springs, and wild bird and animal life could be found only near a drinking source. Nonetheless, there were flowers everywhere, and abundant birds, mostly close to the shore. Fowles, tramping the hills and coves alone for hours, was excited by the variety. In his meticulously kept, carefully organized nature logs, he recorded eighty-six different birds and eighty-seven kinds of flowers, with notes on dates, circumstances of sightings, appearances, and numbers, and sketches illustrating his discoveries. He watched peregrine falcons, kingfishers, ravens, and storks, listened to warblers, thrushes, finches, wood larks, and shrikes, and flushed scops owls from the treetops. He was thrilled to discover spider orchids scattered all over the island and small colonies of bee orchids, weirdly resembling human faces.[34] He believed that being a natural historian gave him an advantage over others. The birds, flowers, and insects of a new country meant as much to him as "artificial" human society and gave him "a kind of ubiquitous sanctuary."[35]

Fowles was aghast to learn that Denys Sharrocks did not share his rapture for the natural world and was "blind" to the natural history of the island he had lived on for several years.[36] Since Denys spoke better Greek, was a more seasoned teacher, and was socially more adept than John, this area of superiority may have leveled the playing field of their friendship. Both on and off Spetsai, they were often walking and traveling companions. They were together the first time Fowles visited Agia Paraskevi (Good Friday Bay in *The Magus*), and it was Denys who took him for the first time to the villa called Yiasemine (or Jasmine), which Fowles used as Bourani in the same novel. Situated on the headlands just above the bay, he thought it "the most wonderful situation in the world, poised as it is on a bluff between two beautiful coves, with the pines plunging into the sea below, the whole Parnon range opposite and the sunny wooded hills of Spetsai behind. One could not dream of a more perfect site—a sublime blend of wood, sea, sun, wind and mountain. Not a romantic, but a classical perfection."[37] The villa belonged to the Botassi family, whose ancestor had distinguished himself in the fight for Greek freedom from the Ottoman Turks. Denys had been the invited guest of Mme. Botassi on earlier occasions, and he took John over the ridge to introduce him. Approaching the house, they heard the sound of someone playing a harmonium, "the most incongruous sound imaginable in such a divine landscape."[38] On this occasion, in the perfection of such a poetic landscape, Sharrocks remarked that he had written his own final poem at Yiasemine and was now retiring his dreams of being a poet.

At the Easter holiday in the last two weeks of April, the pair traveled to Crete, where they toured by bus and on foot, staying in hostels. The ancient Minoan sites of Knossos, Phaestos, and Agia Triada were absolutely deserted, breathtakingly solitary in those days before jumbo jet tourism. The two men dug for shards and took naps in the ruins. Everywhere they encountered the ancient Cretan rituals of Easter: festivals and fairs, men with bleating lambs slung around their necks, and processions of chanting people carrying banners and flowers. On Resurrection Night near Phaestos they were part of the candlelit crowd of chanting worshipers parading the sacred bier around the tiny village church at midnight. At Knossos they wandered in awe through mazes of time-ravaged rooms and desolate gardens until it was too dark to see. In the night, as the frogs began singing by the river, Knossos seemed "haunted, full of ghosts." Watching lights spring on in distant cottages, Fowles was emotionally harrowed by a sense of the lost past.[39]

As soon as Cretan villagers knew they were English, not German, the travelers were taken up by schoolmasters, former maquis, shepherds, and farmers. Their simple generosity melted Fowles's poor opinion of modern Greeks, based largely on his colleagues at the school. In one incident in a dingy café, a tough mountain maquis wearing a massive cartridge belt across his chest appeared with two henchmen in the doorway. "My friend," said John, pointing at the startled Denys, "he speaks Greek." After a long hour of fierce political discussion that stretched Sharrocks's Greek "to the absolute limit," the headman extended his hospitality, including an invitation "to help in the castration of his sheep. An offer we politely declined."[40] Fowles was less affable when they were guests of their bourgeois students' families, who were anxious to impress with what he considered a stifling hospitality. Forced to sit through indigestible meals with all the village relatives or visit "grotesque" local mausoleums displaying artificial wreaths and bullet-ridden skulls from German or Turkish massacres, John even lost patience with the ever-courteous Denys and rudely stalked out. "Thank God being English allows you to be queer," he wrote in annoyance.[41]

Fowles was touched and humbled, however, by the hospitality of the monastery at Arkadi, a major center of the Resistance during the war. As they had hoped, they met the former abbot, tiny, white-bearded Father Dionysus, in a cell filled with books, a crucifix, and guns on the walls. The old abbot's gentle humility made Fowles feel honored to be called *"paidi mou*, my child." During the war Father Dionysus had hidden hundreds of Englishmen in the monastery and kept records for a huge Resistance group. Beaten, tortured by the Germans, he continued his activities. Once, in an incident Fowles adapted to *The Magus,* "as he was carrying some papers to a hiding place outside the monastery, the Germans machine-gunned him. He pretended to fall, and lay still, believing him dead, they went away."[42]

John and Denys returned to the blistering heat of the summer term, when end-of-year examinations and festivities put constant pressure on students and masters. Pompous, ill-organized ceremonies honoring the school's founder reduced Fowles and Sharrocks to tears of hysterical laughter. But there were also delightful excursions of masters and their families to jewellike Spetsopoula, a mile to the southeast, and across the straits to Porto Heli for picnics with the boys. School met from eight to one. Each afternoon, though deeply fearful of sharks and leery of octopuses, Fowles swam from the beach in front of the school, using a mask to glimpse the marine world. For the rest of the afternoon he slept. He was brown and healthy. For the first time since 1948 his diary never mentions illness.

But heat, isolation, and lack of feminine companionship led Fowles to find the boys more and more sensually attractive. With troubled honesty he noted "the dormant homosexual in me. I enjoy being with certain boys, have too many eyes for them, speak to them too often." Among them, he sometimes felt as if he were "in a river of tenderness dangerously near to overflooding." He believed he would never try to seduce them, but he loved to watch the young boys, "caught in that last budding year when their sexlessness only makes them more feminine . . . very beautiful. Mischievous and exuberant and full of a green innocence like spring birdsong or fruit-trees in blossom." Precocious, cynical, they exhibited "a slightly *faisandé* quality; something corrupt in even the most innocent."[43] Fowles sat for dinner each day with his English-speaking favorite, an "attractively sophisticated, blasé little siren of 13. . . . A tall, slim boy, very dusky . . . his face has perfect Arab female beauty. Very dark expressive eyes, a soft, full red mouth, warm brown skin, eyelashes of incredible length and curve and a general air of Arabian Nights allurement."[44]

The issue of homosexuality at the school was very complicated, and the administration was very sensitive to any public notoriety about it. In 1934 a former English master named Kenneth Matthews had published *Aleko,* a love story about his affair with a pupil at Anargyrios School, and the reputation raised by this novel flared up now and again.[45] There were constant rumors of affairs during Fowles's time as a master, and he became aware of cases reported to the headmaster that were "hushed up" quickly. "Some small boys have quite prostitutional reputations," Fowles wrote, "and the name for the junior block among the senior boys is the 'brothel.'" The senior boys in the Eighth class explained in a worldly way that there was "a good deal of active homosexuality in the school, that . . . the house-master knows it, and shrugs his shoulders." They claimed to be able to "smell a homosexual master a hundred miles off," exploiting their knowledge for better marks or for the fun of embarrassing a teacher. But, these older boys tried to assure Fowles, their *own* love for the small boys "was quite platonic and pure." Scoffed Fowles: "Pure nonsense, but I believe they do see it like that. The Greeks have an immense capacity for deceiving themselves."[46]

This hypocrisy over sexuality drove Fowles to distraction. In preparation for the summer term program, he and the bawdy-minded Potamianos were given the assignment of translating into Greek the dramatis personae of Shakespeare's *A Midsummer Night's Dream.* When Fowles explained the anatomical meaning of "Bottom," his shocked colleague said the only Greek word was very coarse. This provoked hours of vehement protest from all the other Greek staff members, ending with a unanimous declaration that "Bottom was a filthy and obscene term." Suddenly all the other names of Shakespeare's Athenian herdsmen were doubtful. A boy's father, said the deputy head, was not going to like his son being called "Pig-faced" (Snout). The names were left in English, while the worried headmaster cautioned nervously, "We mustn't make the play seem funny."[47]

The same evening as the "highly (and typically) puritanical teacup storm about the abominable name 'Bottom,'" Fowles was disturbed to watch the dancing at the sixth form end-of-term party. As the headmaster smiled in approval, the tall boys took out the "pretty ones," to dance sambas, tangos, fox-trots, "close and with every sign of pleasure . . . some, it seemed to me, abnormally." The day confirmed Fowles's opinions about modern Greece, where "the drinking water and sewage pipes run side-by-side; their mental sanitation, disinfected one minute, and stinking the next, is bewilderingly naif. Every Greek seems to possess two quite unrelated persons inside him."[48]

With examinations over, parents and dignitaries arrived for end-of-term festivities, and the Shakespearean play with its offensively named cast of characters was presented on a warm June night. Fowles managed a cast of twenty boys in A Midsummer Night's Dream, and the production went off well with a full crowd of two thousand in the amphitheater and "plenty of laughter at the clowning."[49] A few days later the boys left for the summer. Fowles watched in wonder as the older ones stood on the jetty, kissing, sobbing, waving off the weeping junior boys. July 1 was the end of the term, and Fowles walked into the Eighth classroom to fetch Denys Sharrocks, who was returning to England. Denys, full of hidden emotions of his own, spit vehemently on the floor before leaving. They drank through the night at Georgio's with the Hippo and Egyptiadis, with Evangelakis to sing them farewell. Then they caught the dawn boat to Athens.

Once more alone, Fowles set out from Athens on a fortnight's "homage to the past," visiting the ancient sites of Greece: Mycenae, Delphi, Parnassus, Tiryns, Argos, Nauplion, Epidauros, Corinth, and back to Athens.[50] Except for Delphi, he experienced all these classical ruins in nearly total solitude. Dropped off by buses, he walked alone into each site, carrying his luggage, asking directions from taverna keepers and herdsmen. Of all these experiences, two stood out for him as a kind of "test." At Mycenae, he was morbidly "hynotized by that massive sphinx-like door" at the Tombs of Atreus and Agamemnon. Feeling oppressed, he entered, "daring the supernatural to manifest itself. Here if anywhere, at night, in the most ancient, inner death-tomb, surely the dead would stir." But there was nothing but quiet emptiness, and Fowles declared:

"Death was as I had always believed it to be . . . an all-possessing silent oblivion."[51]

Two evenings later he was scrawling on a piece of paper, "John Fowles, 4 July 1952, clear evening sky, superb visibility, violets in bloom on the southern slope—alone with the Alpine swifts and the Muses," folding it into a tin, and placing the message on the top of Mount Parnassus. He had spent the day arduously ascending Mount Parnassus alone. He was aching, footsore, and hungry. He was growing cold. The sun was going down. He had become lost at least once on the ascent and was to injure himself stepping into a wolf trap (untoothed, fortunately) on the descent in the dark. Yet, in this personally defining moment, John Fowles entered "a central point in the universe . . . a natural monasterey of the spirit." He stood "spellbound by the height, the absence of earth, mundanity, the majestic, divine solitude," feeling himself "rise out of time . . . absorbed into nature . . . completely existing among existence, as godlike as mortality can imagine." Parnassus was a symbolic landscape, and his solitary journey was for Fowles a spiritual test, a pilgrim's progress. There could be no companion, no guide, no maps, he wrote. "One has to pass through the dangers by oneself—the fatigue, the strange country, the silence—it is all part of the sense of victory won in the end."[52]

After only a few days at home in the "small grey universe" of England and his family,[53] Fowles was off to join André Brosset and the *famille* on a three-week charabanc tour through Spain and across the Strait of Gibraltar into Morocco. At Thouars, he rushed through the railway ticket barrier, "impatient, eager as a lover," to find them all waiting, André, the girls, his campmates, as if he had never left them.[54] But, alas, the wonder of being like a child among other free spirits had vanished. Fowles had "lost his novelty." André was engaged, and his fiancée was part of the group. Fowles often felt "outside their circle, . . . bitterly alone, unloved, out of the game."[55] As failure of the old enchantment disappointed him, however, he fell under a different sort of spell. Within three days of his arrival, he had distanced himself from the group into a private realm by becoming bewitched by Monique Baudouin.

Monique, the charming, funny, wild child of the 1951 Alpine journey, had grown up into a lovely young woman of nineteen. She still showed the exuberant mood swings that always captivated Fowles, moving in a mercurial instant from gaiety, witty teasing, and boisterous singing to a complete inner withdrawal into distant silence. Fowles became obsessed. For three weeks he watched her in abject adoration, devoting the nearly thirty-six thousand words of his fifty manuscript diary pages to describing her against the ill-defined, burning hot August landscape of Spain. His obsession with Monique, however, had qualities new to Fowles's passions for women. It was idealizing, chaste, distant, and transcendent, the love of a troubadour for his lady. It was the love of a poet for his muse. It was also an affair of observations, not interactions, and reads, as he watched her "secretly," like the love of a hunter for his prey. A collector's love.

The diary is reminiscent of Fowles's written nature observations, as though he were stalking Monique like a bird or butterfly, noting his sightings. In contrast with his descriptions of landscape and fellow travelers, his observations of Monique are detailed studies in color and aesthetic sensuality. "Morning swim," he wrote. "Icy-cold and wonderful. Monique in a yellow woollen costume, a thin, lithe body, breasts like apples." . . . "Monique in the briefest of geranium-red corduroy shorts, and an unbuttoned sleeveless blouse; but something boyish, virginal in her . . ." . . . Monique. "Her supple willowy walk, a classical movement, upright but full of grace; her chignon floating behind her, balancing, giving her individual, unique outline . . ." . . . Monique "combing out her long hair, down to the middle of her back, almost black, luxuriant, silky. It framed her face . . . a beautiful wild deer look, her eyes and brown face under the frame of her hair." . . . "Monique coming up from the beach with her blanket draped round her shoulders, her hair down. . . . A divinity, even at that hour." . . . Monique, "her small piquant face with its pale brown skin, its sleeping eyes, the little mole above her lip like a strangely placed beauty spot. . . ." . . . Monique, "that fresh simplicity, that green—something flows out of her for me, blesses me, loses me."[56]

Fowles was most powerfully affected when Monique appeared to him as a work of art, an object that expressed the ideal. She was a "caryatid" on the Erechtheion. She was "April." She was "all of Ronsard, Ausonius."[57] Most compellingly, she was "my Gioconda," a "Madonna," the "da Vinci head of Saint Anne." The "utter peace and love of da Vinci's great heads (above all that of Saint Anne)" Fowles ranked "with the Beethoven last quartets and one or two of the late Cézanne landscapes—supreme visions of humanity and beauty." St. Anne, in the Leonardo *Holy Family*, "is the essence of woman—all that is best in mother, sister, wife, even mistress.

The great mother, the great compassion, nature herself."[58] When the girl napped against him on the coach trip, Fowles swore that he had now known true love. In wanting to prolong that night journey, he believed he understood Romantic suicide, the desire for time to cease at a moment of perfection.[59]

They were not a couple in any way whatsoever, and Fowles had but one serious conversation with Monique, in which he learned with astonishment that she was a laboratory assistant. He had only a bantering, teasing relationship with her, the *marivaudage* of the previous summer. As he clowned and teased, Fowles felt "grotesque, a Caliban to her Miranda."[60] Constantly anxious, he was jealous of almost every other man on the trip. His attentions sometimes made her nervous, and occasionally, it seemed to John, Monique avoided him or spoke dryly. "Whenever that happens," he wrote, "I see myself distorted—a grotesque master fawning on a fairy princess."[61]

Fowles's feelings read like a schoolboy crush, even comically like calf love as he wallowed in melancholy idealization, feeling "all the bittersweetness in the beautiful transient."[62] Yet Fowles's *experience* of being affected by Monique's presence was a key to poetic creativity. When in the presence of this nineteen-year-old girl, Fowles wrote. He wrote reams of diaries, poem after poem, an entire series of sonnets. "A sonnet in fifteen minutes," he noted after the gardens of the Alcazar. "I felt happy."[63]

It was important to Monique's role as muse that his feelings were unconsummated and unconsummatable. Fowles was actually aware of not being very interested in her mundane reality. Starved for female companionship for the previous eight months and lusting after every girl he since had encountered on English streets, he yet had virtually no physical desire for Monique. "Often I try to imagine her beside me, smiling at me, talking to me," he wrote. "I fall into daydreams. But it is not a thing of the flesh; I cannot imagine myself even kissing her. A profound conviction that she is of my spirit, *in* my spirit. Almost a romantic, platonic idealization, unlike anything I have experienced before." Weeks afterward he wrote, "I loved not so much what she was, as an ideal I could easily build from her reality. I saw in her a shadow of the perfect woman, and in her youth an image of all the tenderness and spontaneous gaiety my own youth has gone without."[64]

Remarkably for a budding philosopher so wedded to the existential notion of there being no previously defined essence before existence, John Fowles was easily seduced into adoring this platonic idealization of woman, this universal essence of the feminine. In years to come, he would require some explanation for this deep yearning and would satisfy this discrepancy between philosophy and desire with psychological theories.

Leaving Monique and the others at Thouars, Fowles wept in misery and self-pity in the train on the way to Paris. At Gare Austerlitz, however, by previous appointment, Ginette Marcailloux was waiting for him. He spent a week in Paris with this devoted lover from Poitiers, finding her prettier and more seductive than he had remembered.[65] He was "sexually excited" to be with her, though still frustrated by "so many inconclusive caresses." Yet Ginette's real presence had little chance against the idealized memory of Monique. Fowles saw his muse's face at the Louvre in every painting by Leonardo da Vinci. He found her again in the Rodin Museum in the "ideal head . . . the lovely head of Mrs. Sackville-West, dreaming in marble."[66] Fowles was to make this head and the da Vinci smile into sacred artifacts in The Magus. For Ginette, with whom he had reestablished an easy conversational and sexual chemistry, Fowles had only a quick kiss at parting.

Spending September in England and unable to forget his romantic dreams of Monique, Fowles rearranged his travel back to Greece in order to revisit Thouars by rail. So in early October, Fowles saw André, the Brosset family, and several of his friends from the two charabanc adventures. Before he left Thouars, they accompanied him to visit Monique at the laboratory where she worked. For five minutes the two talked banalities on the doorstep, while Monique, in her lab coat, fiddled with a ballpoint pen and eyed John with "mischevous obliqueness." Ecstatically, Fowles traveled on, writing how he would "travel around the world for five such impersonal minutes on a daylit street doorstep," pledging that she would be his "Beatrice," inspiring him to write for her.[67]

He never saw Monique, or any of the others, again.

The reason lay in two new acquaintances. As he had promised, Denys Sharrocks had recommended a replacement for the vacant teaching post at Anargyrios School, his old friend from Lancashire and the University of Liverpool Roy Christy. In September, while staying at Leigh, Fowles had gone twice to Hampton Court to meet Christy where he lived with his wife and infant daughter in a mews flat. In his brief first impression,

Fowles felt superior. Christy was a lower middle-class intellectual, though seriously a writer with two works written. But he had, thought Fowles, "no holy fire," just unimaginative industry.[68] Yet, as was so often the case, Fowles revised his opinion after spending more time with the new candidate. Fowles was impressed by the sincerity of Roy Christy's literary ambitions. He had been an architect, and Fowles admired his courage at changing careers to pursue writing novels. The "bearded, shrewd, jovial personality" reminded Fowles of D. H. Lawrence, "the Lawrence of *Sons and Lovers*, the industrial North." He liked him.

Fowles also envied him. Roy Christy had a wife, "a matter-of-fact classless modern girl, tall, pretty and well-dressed," who had stuck by him as he changed careers and followed his dream, who had encouraged him to find himself.[69] So it was that on September 2, 1952, peripherally and unnamed, Elizabeth entered John Fowles's life.

CHAPTER SIX

Elizabeth and Roy

Greece: 1952–1953

This year has been a kind of slow moral crack-up.

—JOHN FOWLES, *DIARIES*, JUNE 15, 1953

Elizabeth. Liz. Eliz. These were the names by which her friends, her daughter, her grandchildren, both her husbands, and the world knew her. Growing up, she was none of them. She was born plain Betty Whitton, and to her parents, Edgar and Doris Whitton, she was always Betty. She was Betty Whitton as a high-strung, imaginative child, Betty Whitton as a footloose, independent teenager, and Betty Whitton as a WRAF sergeant stationed in Scotland and around England during the war. She remained Betty on every legal document she signed for the rest of her life. She was born in Walsall, outside Birmingham, in a district called the Pleck, on October 7, 1925, the elder child, and for fifteen years the only child, of a theater electrician (aged twenty-eight) and his wife (aged twenty-three).[1]

Edgar Bradley Whitton, her father, had wanted better for himself. His family had once had a large house in Yorkshire, with live-in servants, a horse and carriage, and a summer house in Redcot. His successful accountant father, J. Bradley Whitton, had been an accomplished organist who composed church music and pantomime songs and also wrote light fiction for Yorkshire weekly newspapers. As a boy with artistic ability Edgar was promised education as a draftsman, though his real ambition was to become a newspaper cartoonist. But, so the family story went, the father "got in with the wrong people" and lost his money in drink. With changed fortunes, the family moved to Birmingham, where Edgar, at seventeen, was apprenticed to an electrician. After serving in the First World War, he worked as a theater electrician in Birmingham in the theater management enterprise of his elder stepbrother Percy. In the 1940s he was an electrician for several nontheatrical firms.[2]

Doris Culm Whitton, Betty's mother, had come from a reasonably prosperous working-class environment. Although her mother, Annie, had started "in service," Doris's father, William, once owned a thriving business until changing times eroded demand for Culm's ivory shaving brushes. Early family portrait photographs show the Culm family, gathered in a pleasant drawing room, the children well dressed, and servants standing by. Betty/Elizabeth, however, could remember her beloved maternal grandmother living in a crowded working-class neighborhood of tiny back-to-back houses. Years later she recalled happily listening—"always with piece of bread and jam in my hand"—as this grandmother made endless, vague "plans." Once she simply got up and moved from one address to another in the same block, leaving her husband a note pinned to the door: "Moved to number 16."[3]

Although lacking in confidence, Doris Culm was bright, especially with numbers. When she left school at thirteen, she assisted in the school afterward. She trained as a bookkeeper and was encouraged by admiring teachers to try accountancy but was too shy to pursue it. Doris remained a bookkeeper and was good with figures well into her eighties.[4] She was a "noisy, jolly girl," in her daughter's memory; "if she wasn't laughing, she was singing." Her long black hair made Betty imagine that her mother was a witch, a notion reinforced when the black hair developed dramatic white streaks.[5]

Edgar Whitton was tall and lanky, and his little girl inherited his long legs and good looks, blond hair, wide, engaging smile, and direct gray-green eyes. Father and daughter doted on each other. Holding hands, they went for silent walks in the afternoons. Edgar was "a soft, gentle, quiet man" who seldom laughed. Betty too was called quiet. She was shy, afraid of being noticed or laughed at. She had few childhood playmates. She was afraid of dogs and, for a long time, of the dark, crying unless her mother sat by her until she was sleepy.[6]

In Betty's earliest years, Edgar worked at the theater in the evenings, and Doris often attended the box office. His steady work evaporated in the Great Depression, however, and he was basically jobless from 1932 to

1936. To a protected seven- or eight-year-old, these were happy years. Both parents were always home, Betty liked school, and she was allowed 1/2d (halfpenny, old money) pocket money a week to spend on "always a lemon Orchard Fruit, good suck for hours and hours." Her parents' view was different. The family was on the dole, and after the rent was paid, ten shillings a week remained to live on. Edgar was often depressed. Doris allowed him a shilling a week pocket money, which went for tobacco. He spent evenings unrolling old cigarette ends, picking out bits of tobacco, and rolling new "cigs." Each Friday Betty was sent on a weekly "mission" to buy Edgar's tobacco, and one summer evening in 1933 she dropped her father's shilling, and it rolled down a drain. Angry and appalled when told, Edgar rushed down the street, lifted the cover, and groped about in the muck, covering his shirt with filth, while his seven-year old-daughter cried, blaming herself bitterly for her "stupidity." She never forgot her feelings of "pity, anguish, and shame" at having failed her adored father.[7]

In 1935 the Whittons had to leave their Walsall home in the Pleck and move into Birmingham. While the parents sought work, ten-year-old Betty lived for a year with Sid and Doll Barber, friends with no children of their own who kept an off-license. The girl never knew if support came from the Barbers, her own parents, or the Walsall grandmother, who died in this same period. Betty Whitton was lonely, disoriented, and proud. She woke screaming from terrible nightmares. She "borrowed" money from adults she liked. She lied to other children about her parents and circumstances, often insisting that when her father worked as an electrician in the theater, she herself was acting there. She played by herself in a vacant garage or in the empty pub, where the smell of the beer became a vivid memory. Her sole emotional comfort was a "lady teacher" who praised Betty because she was so "good at writing imaginative compositions."[8]

Before moving to Birmingham, she had been the favorite of the Walsall primary school master, Mr. Gibbs, and was, she believed, envied by the other children. When, in 1936, the Whittons were able to return to Walsall, Betty was falsely accused of cheating by her new, "less sympathetic" teacher. She was sent in tears to see beloved Mr. Gibbs, who accepted the accusation and didn't seem to care for her any longer. The child felt doubly rejected in that she also felt "deeply ashamed" of her "disintegration in character"—that is, her family's fall from prosperity.

They now lived in a house with "various other people" who could come and go through the family's rooms. Her parents worked at the theater every evening, and nervous in the dark, Betty was alone until late.[9]

Shy and full of eager curiosity, she became a great reader. The Victorian Gothic splendor of the Birmingham Public Library was her refuge, and she pulled heavily bound novels off the shelf in excitement. She seldom had, she later recalled, "the faintest idea of what those bloody novels were about . . . but they transported me into something I understood or half realized, expected to be educated into eventually."[10] She never lost her love of the theater. As she grew older, she bicycled to Stratford-on-Avon, alone or with other teenagers, to see the plays performed there. Around thirteen or fourteen, she left school to work as a shop assistant.

Doris's late pregnancy, when Betty was fifteen years old, embarrassed her to the point where she told lies about it. When her sister, Joanne, was born, Betty first enjoyed the new family closeness. Then, asked to wash and cook or stay home as an "unpaid nursemaid," she resented her new responsibilities. She moved in part-time with the family of her best friend, Betty Pace, and her own boyfriend, Betty P.'s brother, Alan. Though she always had plenty of boyfriends, Alan stayed in her life well into her twenties. In Stratford one afternoon the group of teenagers picnicked and went swimming in the river. Determined to show Alan she was as brave as his sisters, Betty got in trouble beyond her depth. Alan pulled her out, then slapped her out of hysteria. For the rest of her life she never swam out of her depth or put her head under the water.[11]

Around 1943–1944 she joined the Women's Royal Air Force (WRAF) and was assigned to the Coastal Command at Tain on the eastern coast of Scotland. In 1947 she was at RAF Benson near Oxford and in 1948 Boscombe, Hampshire, after demobbing. Her duties were clerical, and her self-esteem rose when she was promoted to sergeant.[12] Sparkling with life, even in old snapshots, Betty learned to love American jazz and to dance with easy grace. On weekend passes she took the train back to Birmingham to see her family or went off with Alan, who was also in the RAF. She occasionally camped out with him, pillowing her head on a stack of Henry James novels. Alan's letters over four years, full of love poems, jokes, and endearments, are also enthusiastically rich with shared talk of theater and radio plays, discussions of novels like *Don Quixote,* and comments on jazz and classical music.[13] They were lovers, and Edgar Whitton expected his daughter eventually to marry Alan. However, Betty said to her mother, "We are like brother and sister."[14]

Other men also fell for Betty, and she had flirtations and several affairs during the war. In the mid-1940s she was wild about an Anglicized Czech pilot named Peter. Like the well-read, critically perceptive Alan, Peter was literary, a translator of his father's plays.[15] Betty agreed to marry him and even visited Czechoslovakia briefly. When Edgar Whitton learned of the proposed engagement, he was furious. He absolutely forbade it, said his daughter Joanne Collins; and "in those days, you simply did what your father told you."[16] By 1947 Peter was writing Betty letters from Prague, regretting not marrying her when he had the chance. But despite her ardent boyfriends, friends thought Betty had never really been in love. She looked to her men for education and guidance, as her first husband was to note, schooling herself in understanding through attachments to educated or brilliant men.[17] Her friend Anne Manning (later Mitchell) thought that for all her verve and independence, Betty was compliant with her first husband.[18]

Betty Whitton became "inseparable friends" with Anne Manning in 1948, when both entered the City of Birmingham Training College in a tutorial program for primary school teachers. Anne still grieved for a fiancé who had died on D-Day. Betty offered emotional support, smiles, and laughter as a "tonic" to her new friend. Her sense of humor was "delicious." She was always generous, never envious or jealous, and encouraged Mitch, the new boyfriend whom Anne eventually married. Anne was touched to be singled out by such "an aloof personality. I felt very special knowing that she valued my friendship."

Anne thought her friend "the most beautiful girl I had ever seen. Her skin, hair, bone structure and figure were perfection." Betty was very tall by feminine standards of the day, nearly five feet eleven inches—with long, long legs and a casual, lopey walk. A natural blonde who was apt to change hair color on a whim in the London years, she had cool gray-green eyes and a long, mobile mouth, which could be distant or break suddenly into a broad, all-embracing grin. She was a stylish dresser who loved funny hats. Her voice was unforgettably low and throaty, made sensuously husky by cigarette smoking. Small wonder the two young women had "loads of admirers" among the returning servicemen who studied at the college and "were eager to make up for their loss of female company." Betty and Anne would "rock with laughter," comparing notes the morning after their dates.[19]

Alan, who had both a job and a car, came around often with his sister, Betty P. Anne thought them unimpressive "dull people" and noticed that Betty Whitton "treated Alan in very imperious fashion" if she paid attention to him at all.[20] In the summer of 1949 Betty underwent an emergency appendectomy. Afterward she joined her parents and sister at the seaside resort of Boscombe, the only family holiday that Joanne Whitton Collins could remember.[21] With illness, Betty's attitude toward Alan softened, and her parents believed she would marry him.

However, when recovered, she bolted, leaving her teacher training course uncompleted. Betty left for London in 1949, without a job lined up, and took a flat in Bayswater with some other women. In later years she explained that she had been restless and full of vague dreams of the London stage or perhaps modeling. Yet it is just as likely that she left to escape pressure from Alan, who continued to write sad, increasingly desperate letters to her from Birmingham. Betty took odd jobs, working in a canteen and a secretarial office and indeed looking into modeling. She was "very lonely and hated her job."[22] She fell into a complicated and extremely messy romantic involvement with "Tex," the husband of Alan's sister, her friend Betty P., who tolerated it. John Fowles later referred to her life in this period as "a mess . . . reacting rather violently from the bohemian sex and chaos you'd got into."[23] At the very least, it was an unhappy, emotionally confused interlude.

Anne Mitchell had given her a contact. In autumn 1949 Betty looked him up. Roy Christy was a successful architect and teacher who lived in Thames Ditton. Five years older than Betty, he was good-looking, brilliant, accomplished, and established. He had a compellingly powerful personality and firm philosophic and spiritual beliefs. He was a writer, with manuscripts in progress and hopes of publication. He was an artist, a painter. In her obstructed circumstances, Roy seemed very romantic and very secure. He seemed to have all the answers. Indeed, she thought he *was* the answer.

It was Roy Christy who renamed Betty "Elizabeth" in November 1949. Anne Mitchell recalled her accepting this new identity "as a rather fun thing."[24] In the same month Elizabeth broke off the last of her relationship with the shattered, sorrowing Alan. In February 1950 she moved in with Roy Christy and on March 4, 1950, they were married in the Registry Office of Surrey Northern. He was twenty-nine; she was twenty-four. She was already a month pregnant with a child that Roy had persuaded her to conceive.

Roy Thompson Christy came from Southport in Lancashire, where his father, John Edward Christy, was an engineer's turner, journeyman in the works for a shipyard. His parents were close to forty when Roy was born in August 1920, and his brother, Stan, and sister, Sylvia, were his elders by sixteen and twelve years. The family were strict evangelical Protestants. Young Roy was recalled as "having a strange upbringing" in "a very spartan, bleak northern Methodist family environment."[25] A very bright child driven by a dominant, ambitious mother, Lillie Thompson Christy, he was constantly under severe family pressure "to be the *best* at everything." Roy won scholarships as a boy and attended the King George V Grammar School in Southport, excelling in academics and athletics. At the University of Liverpool he studied architecture, driving himself hard and distinguishing himself as a brilliant student. Under the pressure, however, his shadow side occasionally emerged. There were stories of Roy's being found "totally out" on a park bench in his student days, and a "slight sort of breakdown" was hinted at. Beyond the academic pressure, however, these blackouts seem related to Roy's heavy drinking. The child of a religiously severe, teetotal family, Roy had begun drinking in his teens and, by the time he went to Liverpool, was certainly a problem drinker, if not completely alcoholic.[26]

Roy's was an intensely volatile personality. Dark, dapper, and handsome, he was, by all accounts, "charismatic," "flamboyant," and very "creative." He could be immensely charming in a social situation and loved a party where there was dancing or singing. He could be frighteningly moody and withdrawn. He was a dominating character, articulate, with a powerful will and a need to excel in everything he did. Yet he was personable enough to attract many women and have many men friends, including the two-years-younger Denys Sharrocks, who had viewed Roy "with awe and respect" from the time they were grammar school pupils together.[27]

Roy's relationships were characterized by twisted emotional extremes. Anne Manning's fiancé, Dennis Hargreaves, was Roy's close friend from childhood to university, who left his studies for service in the RAF. Unknown to all, he and his Australian pilot were working in top security areas for the French Resistance. Just before D-Day, Hargreaves, certain he was going to his death, came home to say his farewells. Roy Christy, his dearest friend, refused to see Denny Hargreaves because he was taking his university finals. "The week after Dennis went missing," remembered Anne Manning Mitchell, "Roy was hysterical with grief because of the way he had treated Dennis. Tears, sobbing, hysterics and guilt. A pattern repeated over and over again throughout his life."[28]

Unlike Sharrocks, Hargreaves, and other friends, Roy was exempted from military service during the 1939–1945 war for a minor heart condition. Instead, after completing his studies, he won travel scholarships and went off to exciting postwar architectural work in northern Europe, Czechoslovakia, and Scandinavia. He also married, in 1945, Marie Wright, a fellow Liverpool graduate from a prominent Marshside, Southport, family. Marie traveled with Roy, but, as recalled by Anne Mitchell, he "was an absolute beast to Marie. Unfaithful, completely selfish. Always able to find her most vulnerable spot and use it in the most cruel way." Marie divorced him after three years, and once again Roy was emotionally repentant. He poured out his regrets in letters to Anne, Marie's friend, who "stupidly began to feel sorry for Roy," believing that he had "learnt a lot from his unhappy past."[29]

However, unknown to his friends, Roy married again almost immediately to "someone quite rich, possibly American." But the union was annulled after the bride refused to consummate the marriage on the wedding night. Around 1948, in England once more, Roy joined the staff of the Kingston College of Art and Architecture, where he was the friend and colleague of such distinguished designers as Eric Lyons.[30] Roy had considerable talent as an architect, won several competitions, and was able to purchase his own mews flat.

While living in London, Roy Christy came under the influence of Frederick Lohr, a Roman Catholic of "a strong, mystical, religious turn of mind" who had gathered a little group around him. Denys Sharrocks, who met him while visiting Roy in London in 1951, remembered Lohr as someone who actually preached from a soapbox in Hyde Park and was "a man of tremendous charisma," but "a dangerous person" with cultlike tendencies.[31] Lohr preached a kind of Nietzschean Catholicism that recognized a mystical power of "Will" in the affairs of the world and a sort of Manichaean battle in the universe between the forces of evil and the forces of good. Historical Action (always in capital letters) was a necessary part of God's intentional fulfillment of Himself.[32] A group called the

Forum possibly helped support Lohr's activities. Several followers, including Roy Christy and his closest friend, John Liddell, had aspirations of becoming writers. Roy was falling under Lohr's "spell" around the time that he met and fell in love with Betty Whitton and gave her a new name, Elizabeth Christy.

Immediately after their wedding Roy and Elizabeth visited Anne Mitchell in Birmingham. Elizabeth, in early pregnancy, looked "gorgeous," and "Roy was exceedingly happy, especially over the pregnancy."[33] Edgar and Doris Whitton learned of their daughter's marriage after it had been solemnized. Perhaps Elizabeth feared a repetition of her father's anger over the Czech pilot affair. Edgar was indeed angry and expressed suspicion over Roy's beard. "Why is he disguised? What has he done to be wearing a beard?" he demanded. Doris sighed that she had always suspected that Betty wouldn't be "a white bride" ("I can read between lines," she wrote) but wished her daughter happiness.[34] Elizabeth, however, was already apprehensive about her future with Roy. He "had 'religion' and was pleading with the local priest for conversion."[35] Indeed, Roy's desire for a child seems connected to his desire for conversion, for a kind of spiritual rebirth for himself.

On November 11, 1950, Elizabeth Christy gave birth to her daughter, Anna, at Bearstead Memorial Hospital. Anna was a chubby baby with sparkling blue eyes and spiky dark hair. Overjoyed, Roy was, for his day, an unusually devoted father, who fed, bathed, and enjoyed the baby.[36] Elizabeth was very ill postpartum ("a physical wreck," she once wrote).[37] At the baby's Catholic christening the priest kept "hissing" at Anne Mitchell, the godmother, "You must tell Mr. Christy there is no way he can become a catholic." Roy was converted, however, and Anne suspected he had "worked away at the Jesuits . . . until he broke them down."[38]

Home from Spetsai in summer 1951 to look for future employment, Denys Sharrocks stayed a few days with Roy, his wife, and the baby daughter, still in swaddling clothes. Elizabeth looked the guest over warily because she was suspicious of some of Roy's "bohemian" drinking friends. With Denys, however, she quickly formed a lasting and "pretty close mutual sympathy." Denys was puzzled to hear that Roy wanted to "chuck architecture and become a writer." Indeed, he was openly envious of Denys. To Roy, it seemed ideal to be teaching on a Greek island and writing in one's ample free time.[39]

In 1952 Roy's teaching job at Kingston College of Art and Architecture went sour. He was part of a group, including Eric Lyons and another close friend, Canadian architect Charles Greenberg, that pressed for the formation of a staff association. The group, of which Roy was probably secretary, innocuously hoped "to encourage contact between teachers of different departments . . . to increase understanding of each others problems, with the school . . . [and] to improve the relationship between the assistant staff, the Heads of Departments and the Principal and remove the feeling of friction and frustration which has grown up over the last year."[40] The principal was not sympathetic, and the members of this proto-union were branded "communist." Christy, Lyons, Greenberg, and others all were fired in early April.[41] Roy "had a furious row with his College Principal" before walking out.

Elizabeth was beside herself, Anne Mitchell recalled. "A small baby, an unhappy husband. No money. Roy was ghastly to her at the time. Very cruel." Poor Anne tormented herself with regret over her "utter stupidity" that she had "brought them together."[42] After a few weeks Roy went to his family's Southport home to try to work on his novel, writing loving letters from a distance, full of missing his wife and baby. Elizabeth took Anna home to Birmingham, where Edgar took his daughter to the horse races to cheer her up.

When Denys Sharrocks returned from Spetsai in July 1952, Roy contacted him. On Denys's recommendation and with John Fowles's active support, Roy was offered Denys's vacant teaching post at the Anargyios School. Roy was tremendously excited at his good fortune and turned tender and loving with his wife. Elizabeth worried privately "about her baby's health" but "went along." She shopped for vitamins with Anne Mitchell and "hoped for the best."[43]

On November 11, 1952, John Fowles stuffed Marivaux's plays into his pocket and took the ferry from Spetsai to Piraeus to fetch the Christys. He was eager to welcome the newcomers, for he had been a month without adequate teaching support in the English department. Moreover, without Denys Sharrocks, Fowles felt much more "outside, something strange" on the staff. He was bored and lonely, and sad over Monique. His amusements were solitary and withdrawn: teaching himself the guitar and reading. Marivaux was now a remote, beautiful world ("a sunlit glade in a French royal forest") read with wistful escapism. Even his solitary walks in the hills sometimes "oppressed" Fowles, as he sat on the rocky slope overlooking the sea, pondering that a future on the island and traveling meant "never a chance of a wife and home." His feeling of "doomed bachelordom" was exacerbated by house hunting for the Christys, accompanied by the melancholy Egyptiades as translator.[44] When finally he selected the whitewashed house of the Korkondilas family just outside the school gates, Fowles wrote to Roy Christy with advice on what to expect and what to bring.

Some of his collegial hopes were dashed, however, as soon as Fowles met "Roy Christy and wife." He found them "very . . . British abroad . . . more naif than I had anticipated." They wandered "coolly" around the Parthenon, where Roy was disappointed there was so little by which to judge the architectural worth and Fowles was offended that he "did not seem to feel any of the romantic, symbolic side of it at all, the ruins, the ghosts, the wonderful situation." On the boat to Spetsai, the couple slept in the saloon, seemingly impervious to the "wonderful voyage into light. The ship slipping through the blue water, past Salamis towards Aegina. A warm breeze, dazzling light, dancing waves." Roy's enthusiasm was "atrophied," Fowles thought in bewilderment. He saw "nothing miraculous" in his first sight of Poros or a hibiscus. How could he be a writer "if he takes things so prosaically"? Elizabeth was the same, "tall, drooping, walking like a lanky dog, a rather distant person, happy-go-lucky, but self-willed and as unamazed as her husband by Greece." He felt Roy's reaction was "obtuseness," but Elizabeth's was a "modern . . . defensive pose . . . that it would be stupid to be amazed." Fowles pitied them, for they knew "nothing of nature . . . will not let the world without man exalt them."[45]

In one of her few early memories of Greece, Anna Christy could recall her arrival: "lights, and boats, and a port."[46] Four days and nights of rail and sea foreign travel with a two-year-old must have affected Elizabeth and Roy Christy. Surely, they were weary and had extra luggage. Someone must have carried the toddler up and down the steep steps of the Propylaea of the Acropolis and held her hand constantly. Someone must have worried about meals and naps. In fact the day was Anna's second birthday. Yet in John Fowles's reactions to the newcomers this child is invisible, going entirely unnoticed and unmentioned.

Willy-nilly, John Fowles was now almost constantly in the company of

Roy and Elizabeth Christy. They were colleagues, drinking partners, traveling companions, and in all these roles Roy and John rubbed each other the wrong way even as they liked and fascinated each other. Roy filled Denys's place on the staff, but Roy Christy was no Denys Sharrocks. Indeed, it is tempting to speculate that in the presence of the responsible, diplomatic Denys, Fowles might not have been sucked into the vortex of the maelstrom that followed the Christys' arrival.

"The Christys," as John Fowles lumped them at first, struck him as "vaguely earthy, coarse, uncontrolled . . . ego-centric."[47] "They clamour and squabble and whine about the slightest and most trivial wants," he observed, "as if they are too Bohemian, too emancipated, 'too much themselves' to brook any restriction."[48] They drank excessively, smoked a great deal, borrowed money, and complained if they were deprived of any comfort or small pleasure. John soon realized that Roy was wildly irresponsible, "addicted" to alcohol and argument,[49] imagining himself "strong-willed because he expresses himself violently, and follows his whims."[50] Within days of their arrival "the Christys" became invasive presences, eroding Fowles's sense of balance and privacy.

One of his last recorded solitary walks evokes the magic of the island that was increasingly spoiled for Fowles by these newcomers. In late November 1952 he escaped after a night of heavy drinking with the Christys to a day swimming alone at Good Friday Bay (Agia Paraskevi), "the most lovely and most lonely bay in the Mediterranean. A wide beach with a spacious pine-grove behind, a little chapel—and absolute peace. In its arms and beyond, the sea and the distant mountains of the Peloponnesus." He was surprised by a visitor, "bald but for a wisp, in shorts and a green shirt, brown-faced, freckled, with pleasant, amiable eyes; an old scout master, one would have said . . . the famous Mr. Botassi, who owns the nearby villa Jasmine. He asked me up for coffee after my swim and faun-like disappeared."[51]

When he joined Mr. Botassi (in whose appearance readers of *The Magus* will recognize *one* of the manifestations of Maurice Conchis), the "strange little man, childish, charming, full of vitality and enthusiasm; attractively vain, warm and hospitable," showed Fowles "all around the house, as thoroughly as if I were a prospective buyer. He planned and built it himself; not a beautiful house, but pleasant, with many round arches, and the most wonderful situation in the world." Botassi "took me into a comfortable salon, left me to stare at his pictures, his harmonium—he told me he had sung in opera professionally—to read his guestbook." John warmed to the hospitable gentleman with his fund of stories about his life and characters on Spetsai. As they stood on the roof terrace, "far away below a girl sang in a lonely valley, her voice wild, untrammelled, singing some Turkish song which drifted up to us in snatches, without reality. Then we saw a little boy running up a path to the house. 'A telegram' Botassi said. As unexpected as Hermes." His host walked halfway to the school with John, leaving him to make his way "Back along the sea home. A wonderful moon, glittering paths of light, and brilliant enough to read by. Black pine-branches, shadows of cypress, and blisters on my feet."[52]

Such interludes were precious because back at the school Fowles could not avoid the chaos the Christys wreaked in his life. Indeed, the deteriorating condition of his nature diaries is the most telling evidence of Fowles's emotional turmoil. Scrupulously kept and immaculately organized since he was fourteen, these journals from the turn of 1953 abruptly went to hell, becoming scanty pencil jottings or unreadable notations if they were kept at all.[53] Fowles's attention had been diverted.

Alcohol was the center of Roy's life, John discovered in dismay, and essential to any joy the man could feel. Neither was he a quiet drunk. Drink pumped him up, made him "excitable." A "model for young Silenus,"[54] Roy took on "his quizzical, drug-eyed drunken look—a devil in him coming grinning and somnolent to the surface—and then the trouble began . . . [with] glazed eyes and faintly frenetic gestures. His voice gets loud, he sings at the top of his voice, and argues violently about nothing at all."[55] Under the influence of alcohol, Roy's ordinary need to be the center of attention became voracious. In restaurant after restaurant, bar after bar, he spent hours at a stretch singing loudly, dancing, forcing his attentions on the other patrons. Typically, "the other people in the restaurant looked disgusted, bored, hostile. Most of all . . . the owner, who had a frown like thunder all the evening."[56] The couple's dancing at parties attended by stiff, conservative Greek families earned polite applause until Roy began sweeping the virginal daughters of locals onto the dance floor. The shocked silence at the "exhibitionism" mortified Fowles and aroused class tensions between himself and Elizabeth.[57]

Also, as in most other things, Roy was competitive about the boozing, contemptuous of those who did not share his capacity. John, whose sense of competition was easily roused, found his evenings drowned in bouts of "forced drinking," "a heavy night with the Christys. A waste of time . . . ," "another weary drinking-bout with the Christys." John was so troubled by his response to Roy's drinking that for several weeks he tried "mild abstinance," saying "they drive me into puritanity."[58]

Roy also constantly cadged money from his new friend, which he never repaid, ignoring his obligations with a "Bohemian" attitude. Roy and, indeed, Elizabeth as well helped themselves to John's books, his liquor, his cigarettes, the dinners he had ordered in restaurants, even his newspaper before he had read it. He was always left with the lion's share of any bill, was forever slipping money to Roy under the table. "On a desert island such trivial things assume magnitude," Fowles confided to his diary.[59]

Fueled by alcohol, masculine rivalry, and—we must suspect—the silent presence of Elizabeth Christy, Roy and John were also locked in philosophical argument and intellectual one-upmanship. John, only son of Robert Fowles, had been a debater from his cradle, but Roy's contentiousness could become overwhelming. A quarrel about something trivial was "the almost inevitable end to a harmonious day with the Cs," as Roy spoiled for an argument, "itching to be in the right." Like "a cockerel," he was "inclined to shout, to crow, to get pugnacious," or "like a bantam cock," he danced up and down, crying, " 'You're wrong, you're absolutely wrong' . . . as het up as if we were discussing some urgent matter of life and death."[60]

Roy's extreme views drove John into engaging in public shouting matches. Roy ranted about the "polarity" between "Teutonic romanticism–Christianity–the North versus classicism–paganism–the South." He expressed a bitter "bias against classicism, Greece, France" and described "Mediterranean culture and philosophy as a 'phoney, false hedonism.' " For John, however, the "classical side . . . is the only side a crusader, a progressive can adhere to . . . a little clearing of light in a forest of darkness."[61]

World War II was the subject of one of their most ferocious battles, "a ridiculous, heated argument about Nazi guilt." John had lent Roy a book by Hugh Trevor-Roper on the death of Hitler. Roy "worked himself into a white heat about its anti-Teutonic bias . . . seemed actually to find the

Nazi leader maligned and innocent." The Nuremberg trials were "wrong; violently wrong," shouted Roy; "the Nazis should not have been punished . . . the Allies were equally guilty when they raided the German cities."

The quarrel, pursued publicly in a Spetsai taverna, got uglier. "'Well,' shouted Roy, what about the charge that they were preparing for war? Of all the bloody hypocrisies!'" John Fowles "got wild when [Roy] started talking about the mental conduct of the Allies towards the Nazi prisoners at Nuremberg."

"*What* mental conduct?"

"'It was outrageous,' said Roy. 'They were made to wear prison clothes. They were interrogated for hours without food. They were treated abominably.'" This charge was too much for Fowles, who began shouting "about Dauchau and Belsen and the S.S. and the scar on Micheline Gilbert's leg where the Gestapo branded her." Roy, seethed John, took "no account of intentions, of the difference between the heat of battle and cold-blooded racial extermination."

Roy Christy's defensive mysticism about the superiority of Teutonic-Nordic Christian civilization made his other great philosophical passion all the more bizarre. For the Jews were "the beginning and end of everything for Roy. The only homogeneous people, the core, the heart of the world, the only race with a mission, a sense of destiny, a 'historical sense.'" Roy taunted John with a perverse compliment: "'You're a Jew, John,' he said. 'You think like a Jew, and don't know it. You think you're French and ancient Greek, but you're a Jew.'" John answered with the equally perverse compliment that Roy was "a hedonist, an existentialist" who lived only in the present for his own pleasure. Shouting indignantly, John called him "a reactionary . . . a barbarian; and when I asked him why he wrote, he could not answer."[62]

Rather amazingly, within weeks of the Christys' arrival the two men were also sharing their works in progress, predictably, disliking each other's work. John found Roy Christy's novel "contrived," "phoney" and "very impalatable": "The style crude, violent, over-emphatic, over-violent, with his *idées fixes* (Semitism, historical will and so on) dragged in."[63] Roy did have "a flair for vivid landscape descriptions," but most of the book was "philosophical discussions; and the characters more viewpoints than anything else, mouthpieces, puppets. The atmosphere is so gloomy, and the psychology of the people so weird, that the effect at times is almost comical. Very sincere. But he mixes up Catholicism, anti-anti-semitism, conscientious objection, theology, metaphysics and a dense, incomprehensible theory of the Will (capital W) as history, or History in the Will."[64]

With uncharacteristic self-assurance, John Fowles typed out *A Journey to Athens, 1952* to try on Roy Christy. He felt certain of "its weight and worth . . . though conscious still of the wrong, too self-conscious, too derivative style." Not surprisingly, Roy disliked John's work as much as John had disliked his. Fowles comforted himself by realizing that Roy's peculiar opinions were violent and personal. He was more worried about the style: "Where is the style? It must begin to appear soon, or never. All the dross still, the inaccuracies, the inconsistencies, the imitations."[65]

Why would the guarded, self-conscious John Fowles allow another writer—and such a writer—to read and critique his unfinished novel? Only a year before Fowles had written how he and Denys Sharrocks were "both shy of our literary ambitions . . . show each other nothing, never discuss our own work; and to write in the other's presence would be tantamount to inviting an almost . . . obscene intimacy." Indeed, Fowles had been so "paralytically shy" about his literary activities that he was incapable of even making notes for his diary while traveling with Denys.[66] Yet in early 1953 Fowles was swapping off manuscripts with a less perceptive and far less congenial man than Denys Sharrocks. But Sharrocks had avoided personal competition, respecting his friend's privacy and keeping his own. Roy goaded John into open competition, constantly and openly bragging "of himself as a writer, 'my books,' 'my agent,' 'my work'—with all the confidence of a firmly established novelist."[67]

The more important answer, however, must be Elizabeth. Seldom mentioned in these long drink-soaked arguments, she was a palpable presence, the quietly provocative third party between two rival men. Elizabeth was always with them in the evenings. Anna, the baby, was regularly cared for by the generous and loving Korkondilas family. "Anna was doted upon by all the villagers," Elizabeth wrote to Anne, who added, "She hardly mentioned Roy."[68]

In Fowles's diaries from November 1952 through March 1953, Elizabeth slowly, slowly emerges as an individual distinct from "the Christys." While annoyed, infuriated, or disgusted by Roy, Fowles gradually became less critical of Elizabeth. He began to note grudgingly that "Elizabeth sang best of all, in a soft, husky voice,"[69] that she danced with "willowy" grace,[70] that she was pretty. Writing angrily of Roy's behavior, he was apt to exempt Roy's wife from censure, saying, "I like Elizabeth better—laconic, with a style, unimpressed, untouched by anything except the present, and much more thoughtful and gracious than he is in the minute everyday affairs of life."[71] When an attractive Americanized Greek flirted with Elizabeth one drunken, volcanic evening in February after Roy had crashed them into a private party, John felt jealous and possessive and began to wake up to his own friendlier interest in Elizabeth. Carefully reviewing in his diary all the reasons why any relationship with her on the tiny island would cause a disastrous scandal, he resolved "to keep as distant from her as possible."[72]

While John Fowles struggled with the challenges of the Christys' presence, his relationship to the school changed. In December 1952 one of the school waiters, "a moronic-looking boy of 18 or so," was caught stealing. Fowles entered the common room, where the boy was being starved and questioned, to see the police beating him with heavy sticks. Fowles's own pupils were permitted by the other masters to watch this interrogation and thought it all a joke. Angry and sickened, Fowles protested and was further dismayed to find himself censured for criticizing the brutality of the police.[73]

About six weeks later there appeared a new teacher, a published educational theorist brought in as an outside adviser to "reorganize" the school. Smooth, cultured, and multilingual, Papadakis delighted and impressed Fowles because he had known the poet Cavafy in Alexandria and spoke excellent French. It does not seem to have occurred to Fowles that this influential adviser's arrival signaled danger to his own position, that in fact he was being observed. In truth, Fowles was becoming indifferent to the school. He had become a better English teacher, yet played fewer sports with the boys and scarcely mentioned them in his diary. Increasingly an outsider, he was determined to leave the island after the academic year ended.

Fowles did not keep his resolution to remain distant from Elizabeth Christy. Indeed, to his own surprise, John offered to "loan" Roy the fares to join him on an Easter tour of Crete. He regretted his "charity" immediately. The money was never repaid, and John had to go "back over old ground," revisiting all the places where he had happily traveled with

Denys the year before. Worse, in the Christys' irritating company he could not reenter the magical solitude of places like Knossos and Phaestos. Roy and Elizabeth quarreled and sulked. Roy's wild carousing was such an embarrassment to their Cretan hosts that John was several times asked to intervene or remove him. Set on his "good time," Roy often sang loudly and long, standing in the road outside someone's cottage or on the veranda of the hotel.[74]

Although Roy's drinking was a constant annoyance in Crete, it also pushed John and Elizabeth together. Roy frequently left them to sleep it off, so John and Elizabeth were alone attending a Cretan wedding, alone sitting in the lamplight talking, alone exploring a village. Eyes often met or hands brushed. Fowles was happiest when Roy was not with them and "less aware that Elizabeth was married."[75] A day sunbathing on a gypsum beach "was the kind of day a Proust should describe, or a Mallarmé derive a poem from—full of nuances, the vaguest hints of sensuality, adultery . . . Elizabeth in a swimming costume, or at least the bottom part of one, and a dazzlingly white brassiere . . . very long legs, well-shaped, a good body. . . . Exotic among the ruins, and faintly troubling for me."[76] In the bedroom the three shared, John was occasionally, and unhappily, aware of rhythmic heavy breathing and the creaking of bedsprings. At Phaestos one night with Roy sleeping heavily, Elizabeth, clad only in a shirt, met John "in midroom for a moment to light cigarettes." For him, the brief moment in which "Love did not materialize" blossomed into a poem that finished: "Only a second/Of infinite inner suspense,/A swift yes of hypothesis/Before the no that never ended."[77]

After ten days Fowles broke away to travel on his own. Traveling rough, moving quickly, he met many interesting characters and even climbed Mount Dikta alone. Classes at the school had already begun when he returned several days late. The headmaster, his deputy, and Papadakis were waiting for him. John and Roy were roundly criticized for low standards in teaching and lack of interest. Angry recriminations were exchanged.

John Fowles and Roy Christy were clearly being watched. Besides the late return to classes and the signs of Fowles's professional indifference, in a tiny, enclosed community like Spetsai, the school's administrators were surely aware of the public drunkenness, the angry shouting in the streets and tavernas, the party crashing, the "exhibitionism." They may have already been alarmed at the growing friendship between the bachelor English teacher and the wife of another master. If not, they soon would be. Fowles, however, blamed the "corrupt" system of the school, since "the atmosphere it engenders obliges me to be irresponsible."[78]

In 1953 the school's end-of-year production was *The Tempest*. As he had the year before, Fowles directed this annual Shakespearean play, sharing the production credit with Roy Christy. Roy, however, preferred to slip off to his house and type on his novel; therefore his involvement was minimal. So Fowles recruited the stagestruck Elizabeth Christy. Together, through May and June, they rehearsed the boys for Shakespeare's last comedy of thwarted vengeance and redeeming love on an enchanted island ruled by a powerful magician. For the role of Miranda, Elizabeth coached one of the village girls, teaching her the words by rote and to respond in English to such speeches as Ferdinand's pledge of "Here's my hand" with the promise "And mine, with my heart in't."[79]

Alone in the night after evening rehearsals, John and Elizabeth would share a bottle of brandy, talk in the darkness, smoke, and listen to the wireless. "I can sense a growing tenderness between us," John wrote, adding, "I scrupulously avoid touching her, but our conversation is so open, and other actions so unhidden, that lack of contact isn't a sufficient check." On one such occasion Roy joined them later in the town and became overbearingly "roaring drunk." He ended a riotous evening in the town square by "getting people to push him around in a handcart. (The news was all round town the next day.)" After helping him home to sleep, John and Elizabeth lay side by side in the darkened living room till dawn, not touching, not looking at each other. "We have got as near as one can to the danger-line," John wrote.[80]

As the hot weather intensified, John admitted his desire to himself, sensing his resistance to Elizabeth weakening. He assured himself, however, that he "couldn't tolerate the faintest eternal triangle here" and that by not touching her or kissing her when she seemed to offer it, he was not transgressing. He reasoned that his desire was "only a result of the isolation, of the constant nearness." It was not, he thought, "real love," that chaste, transcendental state he had experienced with Monique, but "a more physical lust, a loneliness that needs soothing."[81] Elizabeth herself watched him, "enigmatically, a little contemptuously, sometimes a little pityingly, as if the situation now amused her, then distressed her. . . . It hangs over us, is implicit in her every gesture, is almost palpable at times."[82] They drifted together constantly, going to the cinema while Roy drank alone or worked, sitting on a rock by the sea, paddling "our feet together in the water, silent, touching." On a school visit to Monemvasia, Fowles "was hyper-conscious of E., each small touch, look, intonation." On a night fishing party they dozed in the darkness, "E's hand on my arm; the stars above, the lap of the oars, the two girls crooning Greek songs softly." Elizabeth invaded his sleep, and his dreams became "strange . . . erotic . . . real, as real as weight."[83] Invited to the Christys' house for coffee while Roy slept, John several times remained with her until dawn, "silent, awkward, but not unhappy . . . mostly leaning, shoulder to shoulder, out of the window over the sea."[84]

By May 21 a rumor was circulating that the two were deceiving Roy. Elizabeth seemed unworried. Roy laughed at the idea. A wild fluctuation of the drachma had effectively doubled their salaries, so on the day the rumor surfaced, Roy proposed traveling to the nearby island of Poros to celebrate. On Poros, apparently oblivious of the attraction between his friend and his wife, Roy left them alone while he drank or slept. Insisting on riding a mule on a visit to the monastery, Roy left them to walk. John and Elizabeth "lingered, loitered . . . strolled down through the lemongrass. It was very hot, the road dusty, the tree-shade dark, the earth shimmering, very Greek." They sat resting "under a carob-tree, talked literature, literary projects, touched shoulders, came near the frontier." Later, in "a troubling atmosphere" under a waning silver moon, John told Elizabeth the myths of Hippolytus, Phaedra, Theseus. Sharing sleeping quarters, John claimed they lived "in a kind of intimacy absolutely devoid of sex. We dress and undress before each other, say, do, exactly what we like. But never touch." When they touched, however slightly, he yearned; and "the air becomes quickly charged." An unannounced schedule change meant they missed their boat to Spetsai, and to "the headmaster's disapproval," the three once again arrived back a day late.[85]

Anna Christy, the two-and-a-half-year-old daughter, fell very ill on June 9, a Tuesday spent by John, Roy, and Elizabeth swimming and sunbathing at Good Friday Bay. The child's temperature reached 104 degrees Fahrenheit, and there "was something of a panic." Anna "lay swaddled on a bed, still, silent, mummified, only her blue eyes twitching about, fixing people in a strange, other-worldly, hostile stare." She allowed

John, for the first time, to touch her, and he sat stroking her hair while Elizabeth watched, "a little worried, motherly in her absent-minded way." They deemed the child well enough by Friday to be left with the Korkondilases while the three adults took the dawn ferry to Athens.[86]

"The gathering heat, the summer solstice creeping up," the June 13–14 weekend in Athens was, as John Fowles wrote in wonder, "an entry into a long-desired, long dreamed-of new world."[87] Flush with cash, the three "spent money madly . . . completely abandoned," shopping, eating, drinking. Roy, blacked out at two in the morning, was put to bed, and then John and Elizabeth decided to visit the Acropolis.

After being turned away by the watchman at the Acropolis, they wandered in bright moonlight, hand in hand through the silent streets, until they reached the Areopagus, "the rock-hewn steps that lead to the little bluff where Saint Paul stood. And we stood, poised, between the first faint dawn and the full moon." Sitting against a rock, "she leant back against me, a thin, grave body, silent, and I was silent. It was warm, 'pregnant with silence' as she said afterwards, the light creeping greyly in against the moonlight through the trees." Elizabeth whispered, "Don't you think we should kiss or something?" and so, at last, they did. "Her face soft, transfigured, a new woman." Afterward they lay in the grass for hours, "kissing, caressing, whispering, drunk, and astounded, exploring, discovering that we had both thought the same." When "the first sunlight came through the trees, and a white hen came and pecked through the grass around us." Elizabeth stood and cried "because things are so sad."[88]

Like enchanted children, they made their way through the predawn streets where waiters and shopkeepers slept at their posts. The first to wake stared strangely at "tall E. with her mannequin figure and short hair, and I, rubbing arms, like adolescents." They walked back up the hill, into the theater of Dionysius. In a shady, bushy corner up under the walls of the Acropolis, they "kissed again, and again, and again. The way a dam breaks, a swift sweet catastrophe."

As the morning advanced, they "remembered R. and the beginning of deception." Returned to the hotel, "E. went to sit by him and kiss him, while I peeped through the door at his upturned troubled face and lied."[89]

When, after a weekend of dodging and fevered, stolen kisses, the three returned to Spetsai, they were greeted with the news that John

Fowles and Roy Christy had been fired. The reason cited for John Fowles was that he was "unqualified in the fulfilment of your duties, not participating in the School life, as your contract clearly fixes."[90]

It "irked" John Fowles's pride "to be kicked out of such a corrupt place," but the dismissal seemed "irrelevant to the astounding natural warmth and harmony we have reached in three or four days." With the end of term the room across the corridor from John's fell vacant and, incredibly, the Christys moved into it until their mid-July departure. It was a "nightmare situation," John and Elizabeth "suddenly violently in love, and the three of us living in the school, almost in adjacent rooms . . . living on dynamite." Their days were spent "snatching kisses behind his back, touching feet beneath the table, exchanging swift looks, caught in all the corruption of adultery."[91]

Their affair was consuming, but unconsummated. They wanted to be lovers, sexually complete, but "that, here, would be complete madness."[92] Fowles also worried that Elizabeth thought him "far more experienced than I am." Even when she argued that "the betrayal might just as well be complete," John remained "determined not to copulate with E. before we had reached England."[93] Instead, there was the piquancy of romance: "kissing every moment when Roy was away, once only by a miracle avoiding being caught by him. . . . Kissing in the water, when R. has his back turned. Kissing on the roof, when R. is typing below. Kissing, touching, caressing." They spent stolen afternoons "lying together on the hill, under a pine-tree in sun-dappled shade; kissing, talking, over the blue sea, facing Argolia for hours." They met to swim at midnight, Elizabeth "sylph-like . . . in her white costume, me in mine, in moonlight," spent days on the beach with Anna, "close, touching, forgetting Anna." They seized moments of "lust" although the child ran about near them and John worried that "she knows."[94]

They both were aghast at their capacity for deceit. Fowles felt like a "monster," "crushed with guilt" in moments that seared his conscience. The strain on Elizabeth was "appalling." While his best friend and his wife disappeared for hours, Roy wrote his book and seemed "not to notice the affaire going on under his nose." As Roy, increasingly estranged from his wife, grew more bitter and silent, Fowles wondered if he knew the depth of the betrayal. Did Roy, the veteran of so many affairs himself, consider it "at the most a flirtation" that would run its course? Living together, dining together, drinking together, they were "caught in a rigid society of three, inextricably entangled." Roy seemed to trust John "so absolutely" yet went about looking haggard, "alone, haunted, full of un-spoken reproach."[95] Roy's daughter, Anna, remembered "my father crying in the kitchen of the house . . . on the beach, the Korkondilas' house," her only memory of 1953.[96]

Fowles was captive, however, to Elizabeth's "strange, wayward charm. . . . Her sadness, tender eyes, tiredness. Her teasing, playfulness, smiles. Her hardness, indifference, callousness. She changes like the sea." Daily she grew on him: "gay, mysterious, sad, frank, tender, sensi-tive, she is all one could want in a woman. Sometimes she is silent, inar-ticulate, unable to think or speak . . . irksome to a quick-talking introvert like myself. But she has so many steady, earthy, common-sense qualities beneath the waywardness and the feminine will." In the intense warmth of John's love and fascination, she "bloomed" for him, melting into a younger, sweeter girl than the subdued matron Fowles had met with Roy.[97] She had, he thought, "the kind of looks that would keep forever. Green eyes that can go cold and melt with softness, perfect shoulders, tiny breasts, and the slimmest of tall bodies. A gangling, elegant, crea-ture."[98]

Living "from hour to hour, from escape to escape, from pleasure to pleasure," they passed the last days on Spetsai "feverishly, in the brilliant heat." Roy, "to the very end, seemed not to understand what was going on." They spoke of divorce and being together in England, but Eliza-beth was "still in [Roy's] power, since she pities him." She feared leav-ing him would shatter Roy's life. So, in "a delightful, fatal onward glide," they did not look ahead, spending "wonderful days, gay, full of laughter, kisses . . . as if we were adolescents. And terrible days, guilt-ridden, neu-rotic, tense. . . ." Prophetically Fowles glimpsed the future: "The plunge into reality will be appalling."[99]

They ignored time to the end, "until the last hour, when it suddenly towered beside us, a shadow become giant." They left Spetsai "in a rush," packing wildly and flinging away the detritus of the year to the school staff, which gathered, "like vultures, eager for all the remains from our packing feast."[100]

The five-day journey home was surreal, marked by tension and anger. Fowles grudgingly paid most of the travel expenses. Throughout the arrangements in Athens, the voyage back up the Adriatic, the rail journey north through Europe, and the ferry and rail journey from the continent to London, there was no privacy, with Anna to think of during the day, and Roy at night. Roy still clung to his pretense "that our closeness was no more than a friendship," although he displayed "sudden bouts of fatherly solicitude for Anna" that John considered "unfair domestic pressure."[101] As they slipped off at every opportunity to steal embraces, Fowles thought the "theatrical" situation was "out of this century . . . the impudent young lover seducing the young wife before the old cuckold's very eyes."[102] Finally, they occupied the compartment with Roy and Anna. Elizabeth slept with her head on John's lap; John stroked her hair. "R. was awake," wrote Fowles. "We had all lost all sense of perspective." By Paris, John and Elizabeth were "so flagrantly in love" that Roy stared at them puzzled, "as if he had previously pigeon-holed me, and only just seen that it was a mistake, and now felt lost, at sea, betrayed as much by his own first judgement of me as by me myself." Roy became "triumphant" as they approached England. On the deck of the ferry crossing from Calais, the three stood in the cold spray of the English Channel: John desperate and inarticulate, Elizabeth openly weeping, and Roy "gay as a lark" as they approached Dover.

We can only imagine the thoughts of the "shrewd, very English, very cosmopolitan, very polite Englishman of middle age" who walked into their London-bound railway compartment and withdrew hurriedly after he had "sized up the situation at a glance." In this desperately tense atmosphere, as the train approached London, little Anna began to wail uncontrollably. She was fevered and terribly ill, her leg covered in boils that made her scream when touched. Bundled into a taxi, the travelers rushed to the nearest hospital. There John last saw Elizabeth, "sitting in a bare waiting-room, clasping the sobbing Anna." She looked up at him with "eyes infinitely sad and remote," and John quickly kissed her and left. "It was not a final parting," he said. "But it seemed to constitute a frontier."[103]

CHAPTER SEVEN

Anna

London, Oxford,
Birmingham, Ashridge: 1953–1954

"They call her the French Lieutenant's . . . Woman."

"Indeed. And is she so ostracized that she has to spend her days out here?"

"She is . . . a little mad. Let us turn. I don't like to go near her."

They stopped. He stared at the black figure.

"But I'm intrigued. Who is this French lieutenant?"

"A man she is said to have . . ."

"Fallen in love with?"

"Worse than that."

"And he abandoned her? There is a child?"

"No. I think no child . . ."

—JOHN FOWLES, *THE FRENCH LIEUTENANT'S WOMAN*

Anna Christy was diagnosed with septicemia and remained in Brompton Children's Hospital for more than a fortnight. Elizabeth was on her way to visit her when she met with John at the lion house at the zoo in Regent's Park. "Spell-bound . . . swept away by romantic love," the couple wandered through the park as Elizabeth explained that she and Roy were discussing separation.[1] A day later, August 1, 1953, Roy threw her out, forbidding her to use their flat or to visit Anna again. Penniless and desperate, Elizabeth moved in with her longtime friend Betty Pace, whose brother Alan had been her own lover during the war years. Betty P. and her husband, Tex (another of Elizabeth's past lovers), were separating, leaving her with a baby son in "the same state of disintegration" as

Elizabeth.[2] Indeed, Elizabeth was back in the very situation of bohemian drift and financial dependency that she had married Roy to escape, although now, with a crumbling marriage and responsibilities for her own child, she was worse off than before.

For the first time Fowles worried about the problem of his beloved's child. He considered both Elizabeth and Roy unsuited to be parents, "largely children themselves, morally." He predicted "if they separate, neither of them will want Anna." However, while John considered himself "morally adult," he "would not take E. with Anna. I don't like, don't want children of my own, let alone anybody else's." He longed for Elizabeth, however, as "the ideal partner . . . as near the ideal woman as I shall find."[3]

Fowles invited Elizabeth to Leigh for the August bank holiday weekend, inventing a transparent tale of being "the friend go-between" comforting his separating friends. This story duped neither Robert nor Gladys Fowles, and they surprised him. John's mother, so often the object of her son's contempt for being so "normally conventional," was "extraordinarily understanding." His father was, "for all his reading, violent and conventional." Robert suspiciously regarded this married woman from Birmingham as "a gold-digger," "no stability," "out for what she can get." The two men quarreled savagely, with Robert shouting, "Dirty, filthy. . . . You haven't the courage to break it off!" and John defending himself with cold fury. Later Elizabeth pointed out accusingly that he was "scared . . . so bound up with your parents," and John recognized that he had unconsciously tried "to precipitate a crisis" and "must break away."[4]

It took a further crisis over Anna to force commitment, however. While the little girl remained in the hospital, John and Elizabeth continued in an uneasy false peace, meeting on the Fenchurch Station platform to go out in London. Then, with Anna's release from the hospital imminent, the situation exploded. Roy determined that if Elizabeth left him, she must also take Anna and leave John. He telephoned Doris and Edgar Whitton and threatened them with never seeing their granddaughter again, if they did not insist on Elizabeth's return to Birmingham. It was the first that the anguished Whittons, innocently awaiting the Christys' homecoming from Greece, knew of their daughter's situation. Roy also arrived furious and unannounced at Betty Pace's flat to demand that Elizabeth take their daughter and live apart from John Fowles. Elizabeth was "torn, but determined that she must look after Anna."[5]

As Elizabeth swayed toward Anna, Fowles came to a crisis of resolution and consummated their love affair. Near Paddington Station they were beckoned by an illuminated sign, ACROPOLIS HOTEL. Hearing Greek music, speaking Greek to the proprietors, they took "a sordid little backroom looking down the rears of a dozen bleak tenements" and, "eager and afraid," spent the night feeling "as happy as two foreigners finding their fellow-countrymen."[6]

The following day John met with Roy alone, at Roy's request. They sat drinking beer ("Roy pints to my half-pints") at a table outside the Scarsdale Arms in Edward Square. Roy did most of the talking: "about himself, his guilt, nature; how he had gone through life hectoring people, indulging his own ego, wrecking every happy situation he had found himself in." Although Roy spoke in terms of a Catholic confession, John was "reminded of a Communist self-criticism. The criticisms were severe, but there was an unbearable complacency about them." To John, who had, "only the night before, possessed his wife," Roy pledged his friendship. Of Elizabeth, with whom he acknowledged mutual antipathy, Roy stressed "the Catholic conception of a marriage in eternity." Listening, John Fowles began to see his own rivalry with Roy Christy in symbolically cosmic terms. He and Roy were, he wrote, "such fundamentally opposed characters that I should feel eternally bound to fight against him and his influence." They both were, "in widely differing ways—Catholic and Puritan—religious people." John was "morally religious," Roy "metaphysically so." Elizabeth was "a kind of ordinary human, a figure-in-the-street, torn between the two of us, the light and the darkness, the black and the white." They both were "priests, struggling for her soul—or really, in the end, for our own."[7]

Yet while battle raged over Elizabeth's soul, she herself was not allowed to be present. She was also absent as the two men decided Anna's fate. John Fowles "suggested that [Roy] put Anna into a convent and he agreed that it would be the best idea. He would go that same afternoon."[8] To Roy's unbridled fury, the Catholic nuns refused after asking Anna's age (two years, nine months). A convent of Anglican nuns admitted her, however. Relieved, Roy telephoned and, "calm and practical," asked John to take Elizabeth shopping for new clothes in Anna's size. So Elizabeth was able to select her daughter's dresses, rompers, socks, underwear, nightclothes, and shoes, though she was not allowed to deliver these clothes with John. Nor was she permitted to see her daughter again before Roy retrieved Anna from the hospital and placed her directly in the care of the Anglican nuns. Then John and Elizabeth boarded the train for Oxford.[9]

They stayed in Oxford from mid-August until early October, living on John's money from Greece, in a flat located by Fred Porter. John had returned eagerly, "with affection," as if to his true home and family, to "a place I could live in." He was dismayed instead to find the North Oxford of his warm memories "a rather unpleasant world when one plunges into it; cold, and only exhilarating when it is left." This shallow world glittered "with all the stored-up maliciousness of frustrated creation." Conversation took the place of card games elsewhere, "and people tot up their conversational scores at the end of each evening." The conversational fencing was "full of subtleties, implications. Upsmanship all the time," distinguished by such cattiness that everyone was "prepared to sacrifice a good deal for a witty remark or an outrageous maliciousness." Even the Porters, for all their hospitality, were steeped in this world.

In this society Elizabeth was shocked into silence. "Although none of these people were snobs," John observed, she "knew herself not of their class. She hadn't quite the right accent, or quite the slickness—and nowhere near the quickness—of expression." How keenly she must have sensed her lover's worry that she would embarrass him, that "the others would sneer." John admired Elizabeth's silence and reserve and, when he "sometimes did reply in their key and style," was aware that it seemed to anger her.[10]

People intruded very little on their isolation, however. John and Elizabeth, as they were to do at intervals for the rest of their lives, withdrew into a private world. Their life was "bohemian." With no clock, they "lived by desires; slept, ate, made love when we wanted. Took no exercize, went to parks, cinemas, read papers, argued, kissed, wrote letters." John applied for jobs without interest in getting them. He was constantly "seduced" by Elizabeth's simple presence. He was very happy.

They quarreled a great deal, in a complicated dynamic response to the situation. While being sexually educated by this sensuous and more experienced partner, John saw himself "reeducating her, gradually pulling her out of the quagmire of religiose immorality and metaphysical nonsense R. had dragged her into." Days of happiness were followed by predictable, vehement clashes, invariably about artistic opinions. In the speedy reconciliations, full of "tears, tender embracings," Elizabeth had her "catharsis," John his "superiority complex." She was painfully self-conscious of "that gap in learning between us, that educational abyss which irks her," surely made more distressing by the North Oxford society surrounding them. The difficulty, Fowles believed, was that "she is so inarticulate, and really, for all her intuition and innate taste, and all her belated attempts to educate herself, ignorant." When he "started to give names and 'talk-isms,'" Elizabeth became furious, but, thought Fowles, "the fury was really with herself and her lack of articulation." He believed her intelligence was organic and intuitive, "a slow, cautious, mental digestion: the only peasant thing about her." But John was growing to love this "feminine" quality in her. "She would be intolerable if she was quick-witted," he declared. He baited her, pretending to misunderstand what he privately conceded was often "a perfectly legitimate point of view." Choking, she would fall back—"like a woman"—on the "personal." Elizabeth threw an arsenal of adjectives at him: "'ridiculous,' 'stupid,' 'suburban,' 'middle-class,' 'public-school,' 'slick,' which were all 'I hate you' expressions, aimed to hurt, especially the latter four." An argument about realism in the theater became so heated that in response to John's sarcastic sneer "Have you ever *heard* of Strindberg?" Elizabeth hauled off and smacked him across the ear. "A quite extra-ordinary thing!" he gasped.[11]

They argued about literature and art, "never about our real selves, or our predicament, or our past actions with regard to one another."[12] It was safer for Elizabeth Christy to risk feeling intellectually inferior or to disagree violently about whether Australia would ever produce a significant body of art than to speak her heart. She could not decide what to do about Roy and Anna. Fred Porter, believing that leaving her child deeply "grieved" her, remembered her at this time as "obviously . . . extremely depressed and distressed."[13]

Elizabeth lost herself in the day-to-day love affair and avoided discussing her situation with Fowles. But she shared her distress and guilt with her friends and family by letter from her arrival in Oxford. "My dear Betty," wrote Doris Whitton in sad dismay. "What *is* the matter with you? Of course *we* want to see you . . . *you* have not failed at all either as wife or mother. Roy is the failure. . . . To think is to torture yourself."[14]

Friends from her London days replied very sympathetically as she mourned her separation from Anna. As this postwar generation of young adults had lost jobs, searched for employment, moved from bed-sit to bed-sit, separated, divorced, and reunited, several had experienced lengthy separations from their own children. The most astonishing correspondence is from Betty Pace, who had taken up with Roy Christy within two weeks of Elizabeth's departure from her London flat. It was mutual interest, she pleaded, since both had been deserted by their spouses and each had a young child temporarily living elsewhere. Roy had made her realize how trivial, lacking, and confused her values were, and now, as Roy talked of new values, she was beginning to find answers. How powerful, persuasive, and sincere in the moment Roy must have been to be able to sweep away Elizabeth's closest childhood friend.

Roy also wrote to his estranged wife, waiting in suspense for her decision. He blamed himself, admitting he had treated her so badly that she had turned to John Fowles as to a rescuer, just as she had done with him in 1949. He was desperately looking for work, blacklisted ("and as a communist, if you please!") in the London schools of architecture because of the staff blowup at Kingston College in 1952.[15] He sold off his flat and applied, fruitlessly, for "a million jobs."[16] He found temporary work teaching English to foreign students for seven pounds a week. A month later he earned four pounds a week tutoring, while his weekly room rent was two pounds.

When John and Elizabeth moved to a claustrophobic single room in London's Notting Hill Gate in mid-October, Roy's presence hung over them like an "uneasy conscience dogging our footsteps."[17] They deliberately kept their whereabouts secret from Roy, yet using mutual friends and real estate agents, he tracked them down. His message was terrible: "Anna, it seemed, was very ill; she had become a baby again, receded psychologically back to the beginning. E. must go back to look after her." If Elizabeth refused, Roy would divorce her, and she would never see her daughter again.[18]

She was pulled between the two men, each of whom argued relentlessly for the role he insisted she play. Finally, Elizabeth agreed to stay with John, although "she seemed a little despairing under her air" of acceptance. Roy prepared to take Anna north to his sister.

At the very last moment—"so swiftly, terribly, as if on a stage . . .

timed, a part of the plan"—there was a telephone call from Betty P., "full of Anna, how ill she was, how changed." Elizabeth capitulated. Numbly John and Elizabeth said their farewells walking through Kensington Park on a late October afternoon. In years to come, he remembered the details in the controversial ending to *The Magus*: "Fallen leaves, smouldering bonfires, winter coats, a pale sun . . . a taxi, tears."[19] Hours later he wrote despairingly from Leigh the first of many wildly romantic, passionate letters in their complicated correspondence. "O Liz," he said, "we've killed each other. . . . I feel so frighteningly and absolutely alone again, as I was before I knew you. . . . These last few hours have been a terrible moment of truth for me, a vision of my own complete solitude."[20]

Jobless and desperate, Elizabeth took Anna home to Birmingham. Although her parents welcomed her, her return created financial and domestic pressure for the Whittons. The single living room was always crowded, and Elizabeth and Anna shared a bed in a corner of twelve-year-old Joanne's bedroom.[21] The working parents had limited income, and Elizabeth had no means of support. Roy, at one point, sent her two pounds. John sent her nothing.

Roy had claimed that Anna had regressed into infantile behavior and mental instability, which John incorrectly termed "psychopathic." Heartrendingly, Anna's condition was the opposite. Barely three, Anna behaved with the unnatural self-control and precocious false maturity characteristic of an emotionally abused or abandoned child. Silent, polite, she kept to herself and kept still. She did not play. Her grandmother Doris Whitton was shocked to see this tiny girl eating, hands in her lap, taking a small bite of bread and placing the slice carefully on her plate while she chewed. She was obsessively tidy, carefully folding her clothes in a precise pile and arranging her little shoes just so. Doubtless the nuns had been kind to this sad little girl, but a convent had hardly been the place for a child so young and so vulnerable. In the convent she had never mentioned her mother. Yet when reunited with Elizabeth, who wept uncontrollably, Anna recognized her immediately and ran eagerly, calling her name. Anna also cried often but never made a sound—her "silent cries," Roy called them.[22] Anne Mitchell was disturbed to see her little goddaughter "suffering . . . so confused and emotionally scarred."[23] Living with her mother and grandparents, Anna slowly improved, becoming livelier and more confident.

Elizabeth was determined that Anna would not be abandoned again but felt she lacked what she assumed were the natural maternal feelings of her mother's generation. Fowles wrote her that she was "not, obviously, the maternal type," that she hadn't "motherliness." He defined "maternal" by his perception of his own mother. "Nothing is more harmful to a child," he wrote, thinking of Gladys, "than an over-affectionate and mothering mother. Having one myself, I know all about that." He offered Elizabeth the cold comfort of saying that she "could make as good a mother as the next" by providing "a more cool, practical, unbinding relationship."[24]

At Leigh, where John was again living, his own mother laundered and pressed without comment the woman's handkerchiefs left in his pajama pockets and silently placed on the hall table the daily letters from "Mrs. Christy."

Trapped in Birmingham, Elizabeth poured herself into correspondence with John Fowles as if clinging to a lifeline. She feared he would laugh at her use of English. But he was happily surprised at the richness of her letters ("Woman, you can write. . . . Really, why don't you try a bit more seriously?"). He encouraged her to carry on with her "chattyways" descriptions to become "a second Eudora Welty." They would live together, "both writing, criticizing." Fowles's encouragement had its limits, however, since Elizabeth's talent was "obviously not philosophical— literary women's very rarely is." Her strength lay in "giving glimpses of things—purely woman's-eye views on incidents." He urged her to "write as you think and talk." He would correct her "trivial mistakes."[25]

The correspondence in fact stimulated *both* of them as writers. Fowles found that he was able to write "better letters to her than I have written before," full of passion, longing, and humorous observation.[26] Delightfully, he drew cartoons in the margins: lovelorn swains, waiting beds, punnish jokes. He even constructed a rescue fantasy in which he would win the football pool, "creep up to your house . . . a bit of a miner's slum," and save her just as she was about to drown herself ("and the prince and the princess live happily ever after").[27]

Fowles was also working feverishly on a book about his Greek experience that he had begun in September at Oxford. Called *An Island and Greece,* it was an extension of his *Journey to Athens,* which itself became the first of three sections (or "volumes").[28] Produced at a clip of five thousand words a day, the three-volume whole ran to 368 typed pages.

Like everything else Fowles had written to this point, the 124-page second volume is a straightforward, thinly veiled account of his own experiences. The very faintly fictionalized version of the factual events is derived from Fowles's diary of his initial six months (January through June 1952) spent in Greece. Denys Sharrocks appears as "Pirett," an older, more experienced friend at the school who shows the ropes to "John," the narrating protagonist. The plot picks up from the end of volume 1 (the *Journey to Athens*), as Fowles describes the arrival of "John" in Athens, the school, the students, the town on the island, his walks alone in the hills, a visit to an island villa with Pirett, their Easter holiday on Crete, and his own solitary tour of Parnassus, Delphi, and Mycenae. All the masters make recognizable appearances (the Hippo being designated "'the Pig"). The volume concludes with the departure of Pirett and "John" facing the coming academic year alone.

In late October, broke and hunting a job, Fowles was interviewed at a place called the Ashridge College of Citizenship, at Berkhamsted, deep in rural Hertfordshire, thirty miles outside London. Ashridge proved to be an immense, breathtaking stately home, on a historical estate of 235 acres of sun-dappled beech forest and legendary formal gardens. The present house, claimed as the longest in England, had been built in the Gothic revival style between 1808 and 1814 on the foundations and ruins of the 1283 monastery manor in which Elizabeth I had spent much of her girlhood in the 1540s and 1550s. Parts of the early gardens had been laid out by a colleague and student of Capability Brown.[29]

The Ashridge College of Citizenship was first established in 1929 as a short course training college strictly for the Conservative Party. Operation was suspended during the war, when the buildings served as a hospital, and when the institution reopened in 1947, financial considerations and postwar social changes urged its evolution into a nonpartisan adult training college. Its mission was to bring together business and government leaders with working people, union men, and others to examine (in the words of Lord Davidson, head of the Board of Governors) "moral values, culture, and the duties and rights of citizenship for those engaged in advancing British industry." The short, modular courses were facilitated by a small staff of young, educated single men who moderated sessions, entertained guests, and assured a smooth operation.

Along with redefining the College of Citizenship at Ashridge, postwar financial pressure had led to the establishment of a girls' residential finishing school, which shared the great manor house with the college. Opening in January 1950 under the direction of Miss Dorothy Neville-Rolfe, the Ashridge House of Citizenship for Girls offered young women between seventeen and twenty-five a general course in civics and the choice of secretarial training or study in French, history, literature, and art. This controversial move led several members of the board and the principal to resign. The new principal, or Head of the College, was Admiral Sir Denis Boyd, K.C.B., C.B.E., D.S.C., who had been captain of the aircraft carrier *Illustrious* in 1940 and had retired from the British Royal Navy as Commander in Chief of the British Pacific Fleet in 1949.

Fowles and the Admiral liked each other immediately. "A small, wiry, charming but steely man, keen about chapel and industrial relationships, but shrewd, not conventionally naval,"[30] John recorded of the interview. "A first-class man, ruthless, a rapier, but clean and straight."[31] Disarmingly, Fowles told the Admiral that he was "a socialist, a non-believer, unqualified for the job, indifferent." "Fine, Fowles," said the Admiral, "you're the first man here who's said what he thinks. Can't stand hypocrites. The job's yours."[32] Hired on the spot over forty applicants, Fowles protested that he didn't want the job and had not tried to impress. "I looked sincere. Marines, cricket . . . Public Schoolboy, gentleman, so on."[33]

He spent his last few pounds on a visit to Elizabeth in Birmingham and found her "old, hag-ridden, exhausted nervously," although she remained physically "vastly and infinitely attractive." She was in a "paralysis of despair," and John argued with her, using "the existensialist (Camus-Sartre) credo, minus free-will," trying to "force her to make a clean break with the past." But although Elizabeth increasingly despised Roy, she was haunted by worries about her little daughter and determined not to "send Anna back to him when she knows that he will not look after her." Fowles thought her weak-willed, lacking courage, and wondered how long he could "go on forgiving" her attitude. He loved her, however, as "an enigma, slow, hesitant, but profound and true. A child groping her way towards the sun." With his middle-class prejudices, Fowles also condemned her family and background on a mere hour's acquaintance. Edgar Whitton was a violent drunkard, "a man with a sense of failure," with sparks of a better man extinguished by "drudgery." Doris was "a tired, will-less mouse of a woman, with no courage, no fibre, no backbone left in her." He was resentful that Doris was reluctant to lose a day

Robert John Fowles, father of John Fowles, in the uniform of the Honourable Artillery Company, about 1915.
Collection of John Fowles, by permission.

John Fowles's mother, Gladys May Richards, about 1917.
Collection of John Fowles, by permission.

John Robert Fowles, 1927.
Collection of John Fowles, by permission.

Stanley Richards (1905–1983),
John Fowles's maternal uncle and
earliest instructor in the ways of
nature, early 1930s.
Collection of Ann Dyer, by permission.

John and Gladys Fowles at
Stonehenge, about 1935.
Photograph by Robert Fowles.
Collection of John Fowles, by permission.

White Horse Inn, East Runton:
John Fowles, Gladys Fowles,
Eileen and Stanley Richards,
about 1935.
Photograph by Robert Fowles.
Collection of Ann Dyer, by permission.

Bedford School, Modern Language Sixth Form, 1942. Back row (*left to right*): J. A. L. Auden, D. G. Parren, J. R. Fowles, A. B. McCallum, G. E. Bowyer, A. D. Smith. Front row (*left to right*): J. M. Richards, C. I. Mantle, form master A. G. A. Hodges, G. W. Walker, P. H. Hailstone.

Collection of Angus McCallum, by permission.

John Fowles in the uniform of the Royal Marines, about 1944.

Collection of John Fowles, by permission.

(Left) Ronnie Payne at Aix, April 1948. *(Right)* Ronnie Payne, Desmond Dunphy, John Fowles, Fred Porter at Aix, France, Easter 1948.

Left: *Collection of Fred Porter, by permission.* Right: *Collections of John Fowles, Fred Porter, and R. S. Payne; by permission of Fred Porter and John Fowles.*

John Fowles and the crew of *Sinbad*, September 1948. The woman with her arm around John is Kaja Juhl.

Collection of John Fowles, by permission.

Betty Whitton in WRAF uniform, about 1943.
Collection of John Fowles, by permission.

John Fowles outside
the Maison Français
at Oxford University
with Cathy Porter,
1949.

*Collection of Fred Porter,
by permission.*

Edgar Whitton, Elizabeth Christy, Doris Whitton, baby Anna Christy, and Joanne Whitton, late 1950.

Photograph by Roy Christy. Collections of John Fowles and Anna Christy, by permission.

Yiasemine, the model for Bourani in *The Magus*, 1996.

Photograph by the author.

John Fowles's room at the Anargyrios and Korgialenios School on Spetses, Greece, c. 1952. School buildings and an olive grove are visible through the window while Fowles's notebooks and bird-watching binoculars are on the desk.

Collection of John Fowles, by permission.

John Fowles and members of the staff of Anargyrios School: Fowles stands on a bollard by the harbor, surrounded by the other English masters. To the immediate left is Potamianos; to the right are Denys Sharrocks and Egyptiadis.

Collections of Denys and Monica Sharrocks and John Fowles, by permission.

John Fowles, Headmaster
Gerandopoulos, and Denys
Sharrocks, Spetses, Greece,
1952.

*Collection of Denys and Monica
Sharrocks, by permission.*

John Fowles and Father Dionysus, legendary former abbot of the monastery at
Arkadi in Crete, 1952.

Photograph by Denys Sharrocks. Collection of Denys and Monica Sharrocks, by permission.

Elizabeth Christy, Anna Christy, Roy Christy, John Fowles, and students of the Anargyrios School, shortly after the Christys' arrival on Spetses, winter 1952–1953.
Collections of John Fowles and Anna Christy, by permission.

Anna Christy, Roy Christy, Elizabeth Christy, and John Fowles after a few months on the island, spring 1953.
Collections of John Fowles and Anna Christy, by permission.

Elizabeth Christy and John Fowles, summer 1953.
Collections of John Fowles and Anna Christy, by permission.

John Fowles and Elizabeth Christy, summer 1953, holding hands on the beach in front of the Anargyrios School. Their love is acknowledged. Fowles loved this photograph and wrote on the copy he sent Elizabeth: "Think of this . . . not only as where we were/not only as what we were/ But as a place/What we are/and will be/. . . as *our* place."

Collection of John Fowles, by permission.

Sanchia Humphreys, Fowles's romantic interest at the Ashridge College of Citizenship and the inspiration for the character of Lily Montgomery in *The Magus*, about 1956.

Collection of Sanchia Humphreys, by permission.

Sanchia Humphreys, 1954, at the time she first knew John Fowles.

Collection of Sanchia Humphreys, by permission.

John Fowles as a teacher at St. Godric's College, Hampstead, London, about 1956.
Collection of John Fowles, by permission.

Elizabeth Christy is welcomed into the Fowles family amid the apple trees of 63 Fillebrook Avenue, Leigh-on-Sea, Essex, March 31, 1957, two days before marrying John Fowles. *Left to right:* Hazel Fowles, Gladys Fowles, Elizabeth Christy, and Robert Fowles.
Photograph by John Fowles. Collection of John Fowles, by permission.

Liz and Anna on the rooftop of 28 Church Row, Hampstead, about 1959. Elizabeth is wearing her late father's watch on a ribbon around her neck.

Photograph by John Fowles. Collection of Anna Christy, by her permission and permission of John Fowles.

Cheltenham Literary Festival, October 1963, John Fowles's first public literary appearance. *Left to right:* John Bayley, John Fowles, Iris Murdoch, J. B. Priestley, Anne Scott, Frederic Raphael, and Gabriel Fielding.

Collection of John Fowles, by permission.

Terence Stamp as Clegg and Samantha Eggar as Miranda in the film of *The Collector*.

Elizabeth Fowles poses with Denys and Monica Sharrocks on a holiday in the Black Mountains of Wales, 1964.

John and Elizabeth Fowles at home in Highgate, 1965.
Photograph by Jerry Bauer, by permission.

of work to stay with Anna while Elizabeth went out with John. The lovers wandered "hopelessly" through the streets of Birmingham ("dull, vast . . . the ugliest of cities . . . I hated it"), sat through a matinee, went to a pub, and spent the night "sordidly, feverishly, in a hotel."[34]

The reunion confirmed their passion for each other but stripped away any lingering romantic glamour from the relationship. John was shocked by Elizabeth's homelife, her city, and her parents. For the first time he was directly confronted with her unvarnished emotional worst: despair, depression, confusion, leaden passivity. Also, he now understood that she wanted to keep Anna. The visit shook them both.

The "existensialist (Camus-Sartre) credo, minus free-will" with which Fowles tried to convince Elizabeth to leave Roy and Anna behind and start fresh with him was emerging as the active core of a personal philosophy that accompanied him to Ashridge. By 1953 the French philosophers Fowles had read at Oxford were being discussed and interpreted by English writers. His recent reading of E. L. Allen's *Existentialism from Within* had given coherent structure to many of Fowles's own conclusions, although he dismissed the author's Christian perspective. Fowles agreed with "the de Beauvoir–Camus view of man conquering the absurdity of his condition." However, the issue of free will was "the main snag in existentialist theory." John Fowles had been a believer in biological determinism all his life. Since reading and admiring Freud's writings, he had also become a believer in psychological determinism, declaring that the existentialists' complete schism from Freud was "dangerous." Life choices might well depend upon "pre-established cell-patterns of will" in the brain, just as a man was "at the disposal of the past factors, hereditary and acquired, which have made that man what he is, and wills, in the present moment." Fowles could not "see any way out of determinism," though it was good "to *presume* free-will; to imagine free-will." Yet if human life was truly determined by biology, psychology, and environment, how could the moral individual *exercise* free will? Could one create freedom? Fowles speculated that one genuine area of real choice was the "conscious creation of fidelity" in loving. "Love," he declared as he wrote about existentialism, "is an act of creative fidelity. Fidelity has to be created."[35]

Fowles took up his new position on November 9, 1953. Fred Porter, drolly congratulating his friend, wrote: "It certainly amuses me to wonder how long they'll go on with a viper in their bosom."[36] The air at Ashridge, John wrote Elizabeth, was "full of earnest Christianity and the Tory view of life."[37] One or two short courses might be offered per week for more than one hundred participants. Tightly scheduled from Friday evening through Sunday evening or from Monday through Thursday, they followed conference format: opening address, four or five lecture cycles, then small group discussions or "management exercises," general discussions, and a final plenary session. Courses typically addressed subjects like "Town and Country Planning," "Structure of Industry," "Industrial Leadership," "Problems of Training for Industry," "Selling in a Buyer's Market," "Foreign Affairs," "Effective Speaking," or "The Economics of Industry." Yet there were also lively "Society and the Arts" courses on film and television, theater, opera and ballet, and spirituality. Even the standard business courses were laced with cultural aspects. Special arrangements were often made for schoolteachers and students ("Education and the Great Ages of England"), and there was even a monthlong session for visiting teachers from western Michigan during the 1954 summer. The standard fee was £17.10, including meals and local transportation.[38]

Featured celebrities lent glamour and gravitas to the proceedings, and Fowles met famous speakers, journalists, filmmakers, politicians, well-known leaders of particular industries, and "assorted bores and twits." Most daily lectures, especially on industry and management, were given by the regular staff, with Admiral Sir Denis Boyd invariably lecturing on "Leadership." Fowles's £24.2.2-a-month position as a staff "tutor" involved no teaching until April 1954. His job was to play hospitable host to assigned celebrities, keep the ample bar stocked, run the film projector, and "chair" discussion groups, acting as moderator. His first assignment was to moderate a discussion featuring Mary Adams, head of BBC-TV ("brilliant brain for a woman—frighteningly so").[39] He had never seen a single television program. Two years on a remote island had made him nervous, awkward, and overly formal before the large audience, especially when his group erupted in furious argument. He was soon able, however, to find his feet in these sessions.

For the industrialists and working people taking the course, the celebrity speakers and a "good boozy weekend" were part of the appeal, but they were also impressed by the sense of being at an elegant "continuous country-house party."[40] Elizabeth's judgments (shaped by Roy and his friends) had made Fowles more sensitive to architecture. Ashridge, he pointed out, was a "mock Gothic monster in a lovely park . . . like something out of 'Citizen Kane'—vast baronial halls, Venetian ceilings, battlements." But he became fond of its "grotesque charm," which reminded him of "an oldfashioned ocean liner."[41] Meals were formal, with a high table hosted by the Admiral and staff for the current celebrities.

The other side of daily life at Ashridge was the finishing school. While the staff there was "Girl Guidey," the seventy debutantes were anything but. Rich and spoiled, sophisticated and bored, they came from around the world. Two were train bearers from the coronation of Elizabeth II only five months earlier. The others were daughters of earls, daughters of ambassadors, daughters of wellborn English families and newly wealthy English families, Greek girls, Spanish girls, "two glorious sultanas, doll-girls not four feet high," who were Malayan princesses, Indian princesses, "a charming Swiss. . . . A delicious Persian, with superb gazelle's eyes and auburn black hair and a sex-rich figure, a tall sinuous Belgian," and Danes with bobbed ash blond hair.[42] "Really they are dingers," wrote John, teasing Elizabeth into jealousy, "but o my God, so unapproachable—not just in this situation, but anywhere. So pure, society-bound."[43] The girls seemed "an integral part of the architecture, like fountains in Spain."[44] They talked about fashion, holidays, and their parents' divorces, flirted innocently with the course participants or shocked them with feigned sexual worldliness. John, dining with them alone for the first time, was conscious of their eyes on him, "sizing me up." To Elizabeth, he wrote that an affair would be too dangerous—"like chasing a boy at Spetsai"—and anyway, he felt "no inclination *at all*."[45] To his diary, he confided that he was tempted. With all his existential belief in love as "creative fidelity," Fowles was "constantly tested sexually— aware of the damnable masculine promiscuity that makes a man ashamed of himself every time a new pretty woman passes."[46]

Each Saturday evening the finishing school girls joined the visiting industrialists for dances that ended promptly at midnight. The hugely popular square dances and reels were "all very innocent and English," and a girl caught dancing cheek to cheek was sent straight to bed. It was part of a tutor's duties to make these dances a success. John's shy, earnest, "Boy Scouty" colleague John Cross was transformed on the dance floor into "an ace jollier-up," who shouted, clapped, led dances, and made people laugh.[47] Fowles, who had sniffed of "exhibitionism" at Roy and Elizabeth when they danced in Spetsai, taught tangos, waltzes, and even an exhibition samba with a "buxom and Rubenesque" Greek girl. He loved the dancing, admitting that he had been "so long a sort of recluse" who criticized others, "that this sudden entrance into the crowd has stimulated me . . . made me aware of . . . short-comings."[48]

The whole setup reminded John of Spetsai somehow, with its remoteness, its odd staff divided between old hangers-on and bright youngsters eager for change, its "mad direction," its hugeness, its old-fashioned formalities and out-of-date qualities.[49] Even today Ashridge impresses as something of an enchanted island. It was then a sequestered domain; a long gray stone mansion with a crenellated tower and a spired chapel, riding high on a ridge six hundred feet above sea level, set like a jewel in the wide green lawns and exquisite formal gardens and surrounded, as in some fairy tale, by hundreds of silent acres of magnificent beech forest full of mist, slanting sunlight, and deep fernbrakes.

Ashridge was also populated by a peculiar mix of people. On the one side, besides the small staff, large groups of strangers, many of them the most important, celebrated public figures of the day, suddenly appeared and disappeared. Fowles came to believe that all of them, and he himself as well, were wearing masks and playing a role. Individually they were often relieved to drop the pretense and be themselves, but "once back in the ruck again, they put on their masks."[50] "An elaborate masque of dead people," he called these gatherings of celebrities, "rooms of little worlds that spin around each other, mute, beseeching, passing away."[51] On the other side were the seventy debutantes, young, nubile, beautiful, bored, and rich. They danced and flirted and dined with him. *Houris,* he called them, likening them to the seductive, soulless female beings of Arabian legend.

Elizabeth called it "phoney." It was a "cocktail-bar existence," she wrote.[52] Abashed at his own enthusiasm, Fowles admitted that in "such an atmosphere of Oxford accents, doing the right thing, playing the conventions," he was shocked into being unnatural.[53] On a superficial level he had to be "the public school boy and the ex-officer and so on" and feared losing "the real individual." He would need Elizabeth more than ever, he begged, "to keep sane and whole."[54]

Fowles was given a private room in "a glorified pre-fab" that had been used[55] first as part of the wartime hospital, then as part of Geddesden Training College for Teachers and was still in use by the Public Record Office as a repository. Nonetheless, he had central heating, cleanliness, his own bathroom, all his meals, and plenty of privacy. He had ample free time for writing when courses were not scheduled. He often had a week to himself and weekends more frequently still. He sometimes rose at dawn, took his gun, and went shooting squirrels in the beech forests in which Edward VII, George V, and almost all the royal dukes had hunted in the past. However, he was becoming "so short-sighted . . . that it's a wonder I can hit anything."[56] He enjoyed the formal gardens and orangerie and had free mornings or afternoons for the woodlands and fern-brakes.

In November and early December 1953 he was happy at Ashridge. He liked the physical surroundings, the house, the country, and even enjoyed "the faintly formal atmosphere—always wearing a suit for dinner, bathing every day, living inside the upper middle-class conventions—as a change for the last few years when I have lived largely outside them." He liked his cotutors and relished "meeting new 'celebrities' every day, and getting them to let their hair down in private." In these early days Fowles felt his job was valuable. In the industrial courses, "the machine-minded men, the profit-men, the productivity-lunatics" could be reeducated. "They are dehumanizing industry, and we are trying to get some of the humanity back."[57]

Elizabeth's life was a harsh contrast. Roy saw her twice in Birmingham in early November, meeting his wife and daughter on the station platform to pass them a suitcase of clothes. He wrote long, heart-wringing letters, expressing remorse, love, and forgiveness, setting forth his Catholic commitment to marriage as a sacrament for eternity, begging her to return to him. Why, he asked, had Fowles never offered to take Anna with Elizabeth? "There may be very complex reasons for this (as usual)," declared Roy, "but most ordinary people would call it spinelessness—and I would agree with them."[58] Perhaps weighing John's awkward visit and subsequent absence against her poverty, sense of failure, and deep worry about Anna's welfare, Elizabeth reluctantly agreed to go back to Roy. On the verge of reconciliation, Elizabeth burst out that John Fowles would always be her lover even if she never saw him again. Infuriated, Roy demanded a divorce and insisted that Anna be sent to his older sister in Yorkshire. The sister refused, saying responsibility for the child would be good for Roy's character. So, at the beginning of December 1953, Roy and Elizabeth reached a compromise. No divorce for the present. Roy would find a room in London for his wife and daughter. Elizabeth would work and keep Anna while he tried to help financially.

The fascinating correspondence reflecting these messy fluctuations is often extraordinarily painful to read. Roy Christy's and John Fowles's letters survive. Elizabeth's voice is silent, since in May 1982 she destroyed her letters from this period. But her anguish fairly screams from between the lines of the letters written by her husband and her lover. When Fowles believed from her "sad and hopeless" tone that Elizabeth would return to Roy, he alternated between desperate declarations of love and snide defensiveness: "I think the sooner you go back to Roy now the better . . . you still have a deep, subconscious affection for Roy. . . . I felt that your letter was full of a hidden desire to go back to Roy . . . as far as Anna's concerned, the responsibility, since you are such a *very* scrupulous person in that respect, must be met." He continued to see the triangle as some sort of grim morality play, a metaphysical battle waged for Elizabeth's "soul" between the false religious authoritarianism of the fallen Catholic husband and the courageous, if uncomfortable, atheistic existential truth of the puritanical lover. John couched his accusations in the language of existentialism, angrily telling Elizabeth that she was not "capable of accepting the terrible non-continuity of existence," wasn't "adaptable" in terms of commitments and duties, and was incapable of acting to "conquer your own destiny by some swift, complete decision."[59] Days later he desperately apologized. "You were a bitch and I was a prig—they are our natural faults, I suppose. . . . I always blame people for not living according to my moral and aesthetic theories—and don't even live up to them myself, so it is entirely ridiculous."[60]

Yet when a divorce looked likely, John hesitated. An innocent letter from Denys Sharrocks, awaiting the birth of his own son, flushed Fowles out. It was so simple, wrote Denys. Why didn't he and Elizabeth and Anna go live somewhere together? Caught, Fowles had to admit to Denys as well as to Elizabeth "that I didn't in fact want to live with you and Anna. . . . I want you more and more, but alone, unencumbered—I know that you would always have . . . the guilt of Anna, but not her physical presence. Always reminding me of Roy. I could never love Anna . . . could you ever give up Anna for me?"[61]

Despite Fowles's increasingly desperate pleas (including a telegram) to hear from her, Elizabeth was silent for several days and threatened to take sleeping tablets in a subsequent letter.[62] How, Elizabeth must have written, could he "visit the sins of the father on the child"? John could not conquer his distaste: "I don't want any other man's child, and least of all the child of someone I despise as much as R." While admitting that he wanted freedom to travel and freedom to write ("not the intolerable burden of a menage"), he defended his position intellectually. "I know too much about biology," he wrote, "not to believe that the sins of the father do in fact continue in the child. It is not the child's fault, but the sins remain. Put in other words, I should always hate Roy in Anna."[63]

Still in love with Fowles, Elizabeth returned with her three-year-old daughter to London in the first week of December. Staying less than a week in the room Roy had found for her, she moved to the house Betty Pace lived in. In prefeminist 1953 London, lacking child care or support services for working mothers, this was an extraordinary establishment. The large, architecturally fine Regency house at No. 35 Edwardes Square was run for single mothers and their small children by a beautiful Irish-woman, Sybil. There was a nursery of sorts, and the women took turns with the children as well as paid small fees. Elizabeth, called "Beth," was billed £2.10 for two weeks' rent, £3 for nursery, and £2.4.3 for gas and electricity. Fowles called it "a madhouse." In his view, Sybil was "a congenital liar . . . [with] a weakness for living in a charitable mess." She had created a "little mad Irish world in the middle of London . . . dirty, carnal, friendly, neurotic; noone quite sure where tomorrow will come from; enjoying and rueing."[64]

Elizabeth and Anna Christy lived at 35 Edwardes Square for two gallant months. Elizabeth took a seasonal job in a London department store from nine to six each day. She sold handbags, then perfume. "The child"—Fowles clucked in disapproval—"is looked after in the mad Irish house."[65] Roy was jobless and broke again. John, making less than twenty-two pounds a month after taxes and insurance, spent his money on the typing of his manuscript, was overdrawn, and gave Elizabeth nothing. She had barely enough for necessities but was elated to be back in London and supporting her child. She often went hungry; Anna was always fed. The department store job ended on Christmas Eve and a surveying job that was to have kept her through January never materialized. She borrowed Betty P.'s winter coat for job interviews. She sold her wedding ring and her one good piece of jewelry for three pounds. Since she was unable to pay her rent, she and Anna first had to share their room with another paying resident, then were moved from room to room. Finally, at the end of January 1954, she was evicted.

While she lived there, Fowles found the Edwardes Square situation repellently bohemian. Elizabeth was once more involved with "the sordid group" she had known for years. Betty P. lived there with her four-year-old son. Her brother Alan came around and tried to make love to his old girlfriend. Roy Christy was a regular presence. They ran into him in pubs in the company of other women. Roy was also still seeing Betty P. and once, when he had been drinking with her, blundered into the room where John was with Elizabeth.[66] Each weekend in December and January and for a fortnight after Christmas, Fowles left the luxuries of Ashridge and lived here, "on the fringe of existence," with Elizabeth. They were herded from room to room, eventually "camping out" in a basement scullery for privacy and being nearly trampled by the morning rush of women and children struggling to get breakfast.[67] Occasionally they took a cheap hotel room.

As "bleak" and "grim" as these visits were, their love seemed untouched by the desperate conditions. There was always "a perfect harmony, affection, love and lust between us, for all the misery roundabout." They no longer argued, living in "an almost perfect and strangely beautiful inner harmony." They spent hours daydreaming themselves elsewhere, yearning for sunshine and the south.[68] They spent unwisely on cinemas, coffee, cigarettes, and sandwiches. Elizabeth lived "so near the fringe of breakdown, so constantly without money, food, hope" that Fowles felt guilty that he did not help her.[69] His money was spent on typing his manuscript, and he confessed that he was such "a complete egocentric. . . . I should find work and help her; but I must get the writing done."[70]

He also felt guilty about three-year-old Anna. Fowles (nearly twenty-eight years old) "detested" the child; she "haunted" him. He often fancied she stared at him "in a strange hostile way."[71] He stared back, making "no move to put it at ease. . . . It is an 'it,' not a 'she,'" he complained. "It moans, cries, whines, loses its temper; is thoroughly spoilt by its parents and its past. It needs a year under a strict nanny, an old-fashioned regularity of routine, cleanliness, order. Not the present chaos of a mad rooming-house." He thought the little girl had "the ugly egocentric face of R. already; will be wild, spoilt, a mess all its life." He felt guilt, but no pity, he said. Anna was "an abstract something . . . to be pushed aside."[72]

John Fowles did not hide his feelings about her daughter from Elizabeth. Indeed, through the months of December 1953 and January 1954, when Elizabeth's sole refuge was John's love and esteem, he repeatedly urged her to give up the child, to choose between him and Anna. Typically he wrote: "It's the old mother or lover issue. You know as well as I that you can't have both. . . . Liz, there is no hope for us until you are prepared to commit a brutal act, a sin, a burning of boats, and start again, totally without Roy and Anna, or as totally as you can achieve."[73] The choice was: "Whether to be a good mother or a good lover. And an emotional rush from mother to lover is no use. You did that in Oxford, and we both suffered for it continually, as you know. When you made the choice between me and Anna in London," he continued relentlessly, "I made up my mind that you would have to reverse that entirely before it would be possible for us to live together again. It would not even be enough to leave Anna. You would have to leave the guilt behind as well."[74] Yet through the end of January 1954 Elizabeth Christy hung on.

In this passionate, contradictory time, fraught with guilt and desperation, John Fowles wrote the final volume of *An Island and Greece,* finishing it on December 16, 1953 (although there were future revisions).[75] In this badly told 124-page volume, he tried to write the story of 1952–1953, the year in which his life on Spetsai was overwhelmed by his relationships with Roy and Elizabeth Christy. Yet he must have felt that he could not reveal the characters and incidents in the near-factual manner of the first two volumes and all his earlier writing. He needed to hide the facts yet tell the truth. So for the first time in his life, John Fowles wrote true fiction, inventing a tale to present the essence of his experience as if it had happened to someone else.

For Elizabeth, out of guilt, love, and secrecy, Fowles learned to write fiction. Guilt, love, and secrecy—and Elizabeth—are also the elements of the story. It concerns a love affair between a young English master at the island school and the desperate woman with a past who betrays her loveless marriage to another teacher. The adulterous couple awaken to passion, youth, and the life force of the natural world of Greece, only to have the affair end tragically, with a bitterly melodramatic ending. The tale has an obvious relationship to the triangular John-Elizabeth-Roy situation on Spetsai in 1952–1953. Astonishingly, however, this story of volume 3 that Fowles wrote to disguise the factual situation was not the forerunner of his famous "Greek novel," *The Magus* but the ancestral prototype of *The French Lieutenant's Woman*.

Volume 3 opens as "John," now the sole English master at the island school, awaits a replacement for Pirett. But the new man, Kenneth Wilson, is not a fictionalized version of the Roy Christy who actually replaced Denys Sharrocks in 1952. He is a John Fowles double or doppelgänger, with Fowles's looks, mannerisms, school and military background, and Oxford accent. He is a twenty-one-year-old writer, "struggling to free himself from the dimly apprehended chains of his class and his education," who recognizes his own snobbery "and is ashamed of it." A decent, if conventional, sort, Wilson is an unawakened soul, trailing an irritating assortment of public school attitudes and having no feeling for nature or natural history. Thus Fowles created *two* doubles for himself. One, the "John" character of volumes 1 and 2, is older and established, a kind of moral center or superego who acts as both friend to Wilson and judge of the action. The other is Wilson, an immature Fowlesian protagonist, who is transformed by the love affair with the dangerous woman and then punished for it.

The woman is twenty-eight-year-old Maria, a darkly beautiful, mysterious "older" woman. She is the second wife of Keratos, the teacher of ancient Greek, who was a notable Resistance fighter during the war. Middle-aged and aloof, Keratos blames himself for the death of his beloved first wife, killed by the occupying Nazis in reprisal for his actions with the Resistance group EDES (the National Republican Greek League).

The elusive, sad Maria also has a terrible war secret. To feed and protect her aged parents during the occupation, she became the mistress of an enemy Austrian but fell in love with him. Maria, in essence, is the "Austrian Officer's Woman." Like Sarah Woodruff of *The French Lieutenant's Woman*, Maria had traveled to join her lover—in this case to postwar Austria—only to learn that he was married with three children. This "betrayal" was to her "worse than the cruellest atrocities." The experience of love and betrayal exiles Maria, like Sarah, from her own society, even while she lives within it, "betraying Greece as well." She, also like Sarah Woodruff, is set apart, identifying with her shame.

Maria and Keratos expiate their guilts in a platonic marriage. In their arrangement, she is not to reveal her past or speak German, and he will not insist on a sexual relationship. Wilson, when he and Maria have begun their affair, protests in his own defense: "But they're dead, they're dead. And when one of them reawakens to life . . . if one can make her live again. . . ." Falling in love, beginning a secret, forbidden relationship, Maria and Wilson both are awakened to sincere, sensuous life in the natural world, on lonely, sunny hills overlooking the Aegean or hidden in the pine forests of the Greek island. Just as Sarah Woodruff's and Charles Smithson's passion for each other is quickened in the wild woodlands and abandoned tracts of the Undercliff in *The French Lieutenant's Woman,* so this couple—transparently John Fowles and Elizabeth Christy—are transformed through the place in which their love blossoms, the isolated natural world of Greece.

When "John" discovers Wilson and Maria are lovers, he—very like Dr. Grogan with Charles Smithson in *The French Lieutenant's Woman*—confronts his errant alter ego, wrings a confession from him, and makes him promise to cease the dangerous relationship and the betrayal of someone who does not deserve it. Like Charles Smithson, Wilson breaks his promise, precipitating a flight through the wild forest, pursued by the mad, murderous Keratos. "John" helps Wilson escape to Athens. Reflecting Elizabeth's indecision over returning to Roy while still loving John, Maria self-sacrificingly elicits from Keratos a guarantee of Wilson's safety as the price for returning to her husband and never seeing her lover again.

The "John" of *An Island and Greece* goes to Athens to look for his friend, who has been missing for several days. In a hospital Wilson lies comatose, stripped of all signs of identity, the victim of a terrible traffic accident . . . and the Greek Furies. Although he lives, his legs are amputated, and his phallus is "mutilated." In the melodramatic and fatalistic Greek ending, Fowles essentially punishes the adulterous version of himself with castration and also, as in *The French Lieutenant's Woman,* with eternal separation from the beloved.

Whence came this cryptic Austrian officer? As a "good" Austrian, "not a Nazi type at all," he is undoubtedly the original of Anton Kluber, the "good Austrian" occupying officer of *The Magus*. As the lover of the suffering heroine who betrays her to shame with lies about his past, he is the ancestor of the mysterious "French lieutenant" of Fowles's 1968 novel. As the heroine's abandoning seducer, the shades of both Roy, who "rescued" Elizabeth in 1949 and then let her down, and of Fowles himself haunt this absent character. But the Austrian derivation may have been influenced by a personal story shared with Fowles by Denys Sharrocks when they were together on Spetsai. Toward the end of World War II, Lieutenant Sharrocks was put in charge of a POW camp near Spittal in Austria. He was no more than twenty-three years old, "terribly young . . . very callow," and the accommodation was a "most magnificent Austrian schloss" with servants, a fleet of German cars, and a stable of horses. He had "freedom to wander around Austria" without hindrance or tourists. When the nonfraternization regulations were relaxed, Sharrocks had a relationship with a mysterious Austrian woman with a past. Years later, looking back, he suspected she might have been spying, taking advantage of his youth and naïvete.[76] It is the kind of enchanted kingdom wonder tale, all love and lies and betrayal, that would have sunk into Fowles's unconscious mind, even if he had consciously forgotten it.

At the end of January 1954 Elizabeth Christy was evicted from the mad Irish house in Edwardes Square. Five pounds would have saved her, but she was penniless. Roy Christy, however, had found temporary work in an architect's office in Penzance, Cornwall. The job drawing plans for a school was a great humbling from the kind of design work Roy had been accustomed to do at Kingston College, but it was his first salaried architectural work in more than eighteen months. He hired a German girl, Inga, as a nanny, and Elizabeth agreed to let Anna go with him. Perhaps she knew it was more or less permanent. On February 1, 1954, in one of the rare scraps of sadness that slipped through her later destruction of her letters, she wrote for Inga: "Anna likes the hall light on and the bedroom door quite a little ajar when she goes to bed. Also likes a lot of things to sleep with. . . . 7 or before, is a reasonable bed time for her. . . . She likes to dress and undress herself and can wash too, after a fashion. . . . She'd eat sweets and chocolate all day, but . . . I give her very little. This annoys her. . . . She seems more determined than most three year olds to get her own way. . . . She is a very bossy little person quite often. But very independent and placid and pleasant most of the time. Lots of energy—will walk for miles."[77]

Years later Elizabeth described to her friend Monica Sharrocks the scene at the railway station as she parted from Anna. She instructed Roy in three things: "Don't drink too much, work hard, and don't get entangled." Crouching down, she fumbled to tie the ribbons at the neck of Anna's little coat. Weeping, she said to Roy, "It should be me going away with her." To Monica, she recalled ruefully, "Silly man, if ever there was the moment when he could have had me back just by asking it was that one." But Roy had sighed in exasperation. "Oh, Elizabeth, you know the tickets are already purchased. It's all arranged." And, taking Anna by the hand, Roy boarded the train.[78]

CHAPTER EIGHT

The Lily and the Rose

Ashridge and London: 1953–1954

> *No correlative whatever of my fiction . . . took place on Spet-*
> *sai. . . . What ground the events of the book have in reality came*
> *after I had returned to England. . . . This unresolved sense of a*
> *lack . . . led me to graft certain dilemmas of a private situation*
> *in England on the memory of the island and its solitudes. . . .*

> —JOHN FOWLES, *THE MAGUS: A REVISED VERSION*

As Elizabeth struggled in bohemian poverty in London to retain custody
of her daughter and keep John Fowles as her lover, Fowles himself led a
secret double life in the aristocratic isolation of Ashridge. Within six
weeks of his arrival there he came to chafe at the institution, challenging
the system in the manner characteristic of his personality and past history. He escaped into private flouting of the rules and became two people: the mask of respected tutor and the contemptuous "outlaw" of his
own imagination. He liked the place and the Ashridge life very much.
Out of the physical reality of the estate—the luxurious great house with
its orangerie, crypts, wondrous gardens, and celebrity visitors—and the
realm surrounding it—a nearby manor house and the solitary natural
world of the forest—Fowles created a private world, to which the symbolic key was two young women.

He had not been long at Ashridge before his relationship with Admiral Boyd began to deteriorate. The Admiral's deep, commanding voice
and assured presence made Fowles "revert to type" as a public schoolboy
and junior officer.[1] He seethed with resentment. He began to show his
scorn for such rituals as high table ("a froth of foolish chatter, fairly

bright, but so superficial") and for the Admiral's "snobby family." He despised Mrs. Boyd, calling her "the Admiral's Barge," then "the Dinosaur" ("a tiny brain in a huge body").[2] Most threateningly, he made mockery of daily chapel, which the Admiral, a devout Roman Catholic, took seriously. A mere ten minutes a day, this service was mostly a lesson read by one of the tutors, the part of the liturgy Fowles liked best, with a hymn thrown in. Fowles read his lessons to the debutante girls with theatrical solemnity: "the soul of Christianity, with lots of dramatic pauses and meaningful intonations . . . deathly hush so that they could all hear my voice . . . full of religiosity so that those who could hear could understand that I thought it was all nonsense." To his annoyance, the girls were so conventional and lacking in irony that they misunderstood Fowles's sarcasm and thought him "seriously a very earnest Christian . . . a churchy bastard," but the Admiral was not deceived.[3] From early December, when Fowles read with relish "a juicy old Testament passage" to the assembled girls, Admiral Boyd regarded Fowles with suspicion and, increasingly, with dislike.[4]

In 1951 in Poitiers, when he resented the head of the faculty, Fowles had taken up with M. Martin's favorite student, Ginette. Feeling excluded from the group on the 1952 Spanish charabanc adventure, Fowles had fallen madly for Monique. On Spetsai in 1953 he had become involved with Elizabeth partly out of competition with Roy Christy. In 1953–1954, at the moment when John Fowles began to feel defensively irritated at the Admiral's authority and the system he represented, he began a forbidden relationship with first one and then two of the debutante girls.

Fowles also felt anxious and confused about his relationship with Elizabeth Christy. He loved her. But he felt guilty for betraying Roy and Anna, and responsible, although he took no responsible action. He daily expected Elizabeth to return to Roy. Instead she stuck it out, taking Anna to London while remaining faithful to John. Characterized by "a certain foreigness . . . youth . . . freshness . . . simplicity . . . upperclassiness," the romantic involvements Fowles pursued at Ashridge were an escape, a psychological refuge from the too-complicated reality represented by Elizabeth.[5] That the first romance began only a day or two after Fowles completed the guilt-drenched volume 3 of *An Island and Greece* is surely not a coincidence. He emerged in relief, and Sally was there. "One slips so easily when one welcomes experience," he wrote.[6]

Sally Simpson was a twenty-year-old South African girl, "very smooth, snobbish, sharp, pert, quick, intelligent—comparatively, at Ashridge. Smart, compact, small and with a full, tempting body. Carrying herself well, always well-dressed; aloof, not enthusiastic about Ashridge. With dark, very dark, indigo washed grey eyes, alive, penetrating, expressive, in a sophisticated, plump little very pretty face. And the most perfect complexion I have ever wanted to touch." Sally, with her upper-class accent and "plunging neckline," was very much "a rich man's daughter, knowing all the social and sexual answers" and "an untouchable." Surely, that was part of her attraction for Fowles. By December 20 he was lost in "all the joy-miseries of young love" and found his letters to Elizabeth "a duty."[7]

Just outside the forest of Ashridge lay the village of Little Gaddesden, where musical evenings were often held in a superb Elizabethan manor house. The hostess was Miss Dorothy Schart, "the lover of antique instruments," who played her clavichord and spinet-harpsichord and invited other musicians to perform. The concerts sometimes disturbed "Jarman," the resident ghost, with whom Miss Schart would plead from her keyboard, "Just five minutes more, Jarman, just to the end of this movement, please."[8] Days before Christmas 1953 John Fowles escorted Sally Simpson to the manor house to hear an exquisite concert by the young, then unknown Julian Bream. "An old carved mantelpiece," he wrote in delight, "panelling, the soft lute and guitar, a handful of musical people. Then a walk home . . . S. by the hand."[9] Otherwise, they flirted but scarcely touched. It was two months before he kissed her.

He still wrote daily to Elizabeth and visited her often at Edwardes Square. However, his attraction to the rich, spoiled Ashridge debutante allowed him distance and a new, contradictory perspective on his working-class lover. Elizabeth was "at times . . . beautiful . . . poised, warm, so easy to be with; sensual, casual, undemanding yet affectionate . . . her fine figure, so very young." At other times he thought her "ugly, vulgar . . . a kind of cheap shop-girl that . . . clashes with me. Her face becomes lined, a shade prostitutional."[10] The distance also allowed him to consider "two moral problems." First, Fowles resolved "not to have E. if it means taking Anna." Second, he began to doubt he was capable "of a separated fidelity; even living conjugally" and wondered "How much of this is existentialist will?"[11]

He surprised himself by the ease with which he passed back and forth between Elizabeth's world and Sally's. In the week before Christmas 1953, Elizabeth sold handbags at the London department store, ate little, and spent her evenings with Anna. Fowles escorted Sally to the Little Gaddesden manor house, played Buttons in the finishing school pantomime, and sang himself hoarse in the carol service. He hobnobbed with the Archbishop of Canterbury on a "rather ginny weekend" with 220 people ("so many titles around, too") filling the great house to capacity.[12] From December 26 until January 20, 1954, he stayed with Elizabeth for days at a time, even taking her to the Severn Wildfowl Trust, "a new world for her."[13] They ate nothing but bread and cheese but laughed and made love. "I do feel now, Liz," he wrote afterward, "that a healthy certainty exists between us."[14]

At Ashridge after the holidays, Fowles slipped back easily into the flirtation with Sally, justifying it by saying how "slim, mature, sincere" Elizabeth was proved by contrast.[15] He sent Elizabeth job postings from the *TLS* and the *New Statesman*, insisted she was "much too sensitive and self-indulgent" about prospective employment, and suggested she consider returning to Birmingham.[16] As Elizabeth was evicted at the beginning of February, as she watched Roy take Anna away, as she ratcheted around London, staying with friends and looking for a job, Fowles walked out with Sally and remarked on their "growing tenderness." They enjoyed what he considered "the best period of love, the constant walking in danger, the not-quite certainty . . . tense with the delicious danger of contact." In the teasing atmosphere of Marivaux, they savored "an XVIIIth century love of the nuances," the temptations, coy refusals, and postponing of kisses.[17] When Sally was sternly warned by Miss Neville-Rolfe and Mrs. Boyd and John was watched with "muted suspicion," the piquancy of the affair increased.[18]

In the horrific February week when Elizabeth lost custody of Anna and became homeless, Fowles realized uneasily that "a divorce will presumably follow" and he would be expected to make a commitment. On a chilly evening he sat romantically by the fireplace with Sally while yet another Ashridge girl "told us ghost stories which she invented on the spur of the moment. Telling them in her rich young voice, acting the parts, staring into the fire." In that moment Fowles was overwhelmed with "an incommunicable sense of love and respect for her." This fiction maker was Sanchia Humphreys, nineteen, "another south African . . . grave, enigmatic, moody. . . . A statuesque face, and a self-dramatizing power which is remarkable; a silent girl, shy, but deep . . . a mime, a dry wit, very cool, sane, balanced, yet able to be her age as well as strangely mature." Sanchia always wore "a strange South African scent, sweet yet elusive, some exotic flower." Fowles thought her beautiful, intelligent, cultured, and mysterious, of "the da Vinci breed, the Kore smile" he had worshiped in Monique. Above all, Sanchia had "what E. lacks, a virgin freshness, a something not yet moulded. The beauty of a snow-white page waiting to be written on."[19]

He was appalled at himself when he next saw Elizabeth and realized that he had "dallied with Sally" during the time Elizabeth most desperately needed him. At the "sort of brothel-cum-rooming house" in Bayswater where she temporarily lived, she greeted him coldly and distantly, but her frostiness soon dissolved in the "curious unworldly passion that invades us." Society, Fowles wrote wonderingly, must think he was "a callous prig and her an immoral neurotic . . . but to each other, we are perfect, sanctuary." Their illogical love "ought to have died long ago, been defiled; but it burns on with a clear brilliance and purity."[20] Fowles had become "the sinning Catholic" who believed in the creation of fidelity and of Elizabeth "as the personification of that belief." But he felt "no violent necessity to choose" between the two women; rather, they were "complementary." He was reading Carl Jung's psychology and decided he must be "hunting the woman archetype." He suspected he had found it in Elizabeth ("the one woman I have known whom I cannot imagine losing") but needed to test it against other women.[21]

From February through April 1954 Fowles slipped back and forth between Sally's world at Ashridge and Elizabeth's London world—with the same ease that Nicholas Urfe glides between the romantic fascination of the masque on Phraxos and the powerful emotional demands of Alison Kelly in *The Magus*. The transference of interest and affection was "surprisingly, dismayingly easy . . . almost disgusting."[22] In his mind the two women and his relationship with each were so different, so extreme that he betrayed neither. By the end of February Fowles was meeting Sally (who now bored him) to kiss and caress in secret rendezvous around Ashridge—in "a tangle of undergrowth," in the badminton court[23]—then ("like returning to a nest"[24]) spending urban weekends with Elizabeth, loving, arguing, and defending himself from her suspicions. Sally became the key to his perception of the natural world of the Ashridge estate. John walked with her through the beech forests on wintry mornings ("a breathless blue sky, scintillating drops of thawed ice") as snow fell off

the branches onto their heads and shoulders "in icy douches of powder."[25] As spring arrived, he met Sally each morning for a walk before
chapel. "Spring, green, juvenile, sappy is here," he exulted, "grey and
powder-yellow catkins against a bright blue sky; daffodils, the first chiff-
chaffs, cawing of rooks, warmth of sunshine, dew." In the afternoons
sometimes they walked on the heath, found "a glade in the gorse and lay
there." In the evenings, after dinner, they met in the twelfth-century
crypt that survived beneath the nineteenth-century mansion to walk with
arms entwined and kiss "in the shadows of the old columns."[26] Returning, he waited by the telephone to hear Elizabeth's "soft, sad voice, full of
wisdom, astringent in a way that no other woman can be," murmuring
down the wire.[27]

John Fowles's obvious, if subconscious, need to hold on to his passionate, guilt-ridden, poverty-stricken, overwhelmingly complex relationship with Elizabeth Christy while creating a romantic fantasy zone of
distance from her was further complicated by his growing dependence
on her regarding his writing. By January 1954, just at the point where
Fowles was beginning his double life, Elizabeth was reading *An Island
and Greece* in draft and telling John what he himself knew: that it wasn't
good enough. The period of Fowles's revision of this manuscript and his
earliest negotiations with an agent precisely correlates with his escapist
romance with Sally Simpson (December 1953–April 1954). During this
same period he was nakedly frank about his creative doubts, fears, and
anguish with Elizabeth Christy, an exposure he did not risk with the
"mostly superficial," twenty-year-old South African heiress.[28] He had,
and shared with Elizabeth, "doubt about my writing; a deep, all-
pervading doubt. The agonizingly slow process I make towards coherence
and grace; the constant misuse, semantic and euphoric, of words. The
effort to achieve something more than platitudes seems wasted, in
vain. . . . I have no ease, no aptitude for writing. It is almost always an
act of will." Elizabeth insisted he must revise. He agreed but could not
"bear to think what that involves."[29] As Elizabeth was separated from
Anna and Fowles romanced Sally and grew fascinated with Sanchia, he
simultaneously bewailed the lost impetus of his book. During her next
brief office job Elizabeth filched paper at his request and typed his revisions. When he visited Elizabeth in London, Fowles made contact with
an interested agent, interviewed with him, and left his manuscript, returning each time, nervous and needy, to her.

Elizabeth was not only part of the subject of *An Island and Greece* (so obviously the model for Maria in volume 3) but an integral part of the process, an advising reader and, as time went on, an editor. Fowles's repeated references to her as "stupid" or "inarticulate" fail to tell the real story. Elizabeth was certainly uneducated in the academic sense. In the early 1950s she lacked a polished vocabulary to describe what she experienced or read in the intellectual manner to which Fowles was accustomed. The vitriolic, showoff banter of North Oxford that had shocked her into silence, however, would never be her forte. She remained fairly scornful of academic categories all her life and forever treated spelling and punctuation rules with cavalier indifference. But uneducated is not synonymous with unintelligent. Elizabeth read a great deal, frequented museums, and often went hungry to buy a theater ticket. Her intuition awed Fowles even then, and her taste was to become a benchmark among her friends.

From the beginning of their emotional and physical intimacy, Fowles also made Elizabeth the intimate of his writing. Elizabeth and Fowles's texts became wrapped around each other, in substance and in style. He had joked that he would correct the "trivial errors" of her writing. She instead became the supporter, tester, and editorial adviser of his. She believed in him, but she was a harsh and demanding critic. She tore apart his stories and plays, insisting that he could be better. She accused him of writing in a *Woman's Own* style. "By which she means sentimentality, triviality, banality, the cheap poignancy and hackneyed language of the women's magazine stories," admitted Fowles, and "I know that by the standards and tastes of the age, that is true."[30] While he swallowed the unpleasant truth of her criticisms and needed her emotional and pragmatic support, Fowles felt exposed, ambivalent, and hurt. As Elizabeth spit *Woman's Own* at him, Sally coyly teased him with an offer to spend her twenty-first-birthday inheritance driving him from Tangier to Johannesburg.[31] Fowles didn't love Sally, but she offered a fantasy that was a relief.

The two women, Sally and Elizabeth, also inspired revealingly contrasting literature. While Fowles tried to immortalize his transformation by Elizabeth's love on Spetsai in the impassioned, implausible manuscript of *An Island and Greece*, he also wrote poems about the Sally affair. A surviving example, written the day before the girl left Ashridge, is a carefully constructed, stress-marked, repetitious, unimaginative pastoral, in which John and Sally are cast, conventionally, as shepherd and shepherdess shivering "under the black but budded bough." The poem has all the charm and conviction of a run of scales on the piano.[32]

Fowles felt little regret as separation from Sally neared ("as if I were losing a pet dog"), but he valued their affair. She was the "revenge" that had "made Ashridge tolerable." Breaking rules with Sally was his "secret consolation . . . the card up my sleeve" against a system that had "crushed me, tried to dwarf me, ignored me. Infuriated and tyrannized me."[33] Fowles was filled with rage and frustration in a position so undemanding that "an office-boy could do it."[34] He poured scorn on "the conventional, public, old-fashioned standard whale of society here" and hated, self-righteously, "the wordy, self-important international affairs courses" taught by people he regarded as "small" and "blind."[35] His war with Admiral Boyd grew hotter as the Head demanded that all tutors read from the Passion in chapel and Fowles refused to read any more lessons at all. The Boyds came to represent "all the faults of the upper-class British," and Fowles heaped censure on their snobbery, their conservative social framework, and their religious creed.[36]

In his clearest moments, however, Fowles realized that the Boyds were not the problem. Fowles was "incapable of working *under* anybody at all . . . born a hopeless insubordinate."[37] He blamed his parents for so instilling in him "the Victorian virtues," especially his father's "subservience" and "subconscious respect for authority." He blamed his own "unforgiveness . . . ingratitude and mockery of them" for causing his parents pain. His "fear of disobeying their way of life" had caused him to "overuse" a "persona . . . so elaborate, yet so artificial, that subconsciously people must realize that it is a mask." At Ashridge, particularly, he felt "I still hide what I truly am."[38]

Fowles and Sally Simpson flouted the conventions they despised in a carefully planned adventure for her final night at Ashridge. At midnight she climbed out of a ground-floor window, and they slept together in an empty room off the garden walk, like "children, shameful, cocksure, crowing against the adult universe." Though they undressed and caressed, they "did not make love." Like a scene from Casanova or Defoe, there was "a special pleasure in . . . having all liberties but the last." Someday it would appear "shameful," Fowles mused; "now it is still warm, exciting, a rose in the night." Sally would be remembered as

Rose/June, the sensual twin of Conchis's masque. In the morning ("grey crowing of rooks in the first light"), Fowles caught the train for London, where he slipped happily into Elizabeth's bed.[39]

Elizabeth was living in Hampstead in a "small, dark room with nothing in it" at 8 Holly Hill, just up the hill from the tube station.[40] She shared this tiny two-bedroom flat with another Edwardes Square woman from February until mid-July. Elizabeth's courage and optimism had vanished with Anna's departure. She was deeply depressed, and her life was chaotic. She had virtually no money, and Fowles chided her in letters to eat regular meals. She had no coat, and her shoes were thin. She supported a friend through an illegal abortion. Betty Pace's ex-husband, Tex, appeared and hung around for several weeks, begging Elizabeth to go live with him, "another of the moths round the candle of her."[41]

She could not keep a job. On a day when she was sacked again, Elizabeth wrote: "Feel terrible really, sick, sick at heart. There seems nothing at all, no one to trust nothing to trust, a worthless battle always to be fought. I could cry if tears were at all worthy of the bottomless depression I feel today." In a keenly clinical description of depression, she complained that she couldn't wake up and her responses to both good and bad had faded. "I think I haven't felt alive for more than a few hours here and there for so long now." And she asked, "Is that what it means . . . is it all one can expect? I am really very low. I'm sorry. John . . ."[42]

Fowles lectured her on having too much fastidiousness over jobs. "You won't even try and do a job you dislike efficiently," he wrote to Elizabeth the week after she lost Anna; "the creative jobs are one in a million, and for someone totally unqualified they are astronomically difficult to find."[43] He was bewildered by her emotional change. Roy was "earning more than enough money to look after Anna," so worrying about the child was perverse, "a determination to sink right to the bottom."[44] He regretted not being sympathetic enough, but wasn't she "a little in love with misery at the moment?"[45] Part of her trouble, he told her, was her "own lack of control, Liz . . . even in the allowance of feminine mood, sometimes you are a BITCH!"[46] Yet while urging her to brighten up, to be practical, to find work and accept it, he also told her that it was her "feminine," impractical qualities that made her attractive to him: "Your flair is for personal relationships with the opposite sex, you are brilliantly a woman, a mistress in the flat, a hostess in the home, alone and aloof. I don't believe you're capable of earning a living. I almost certainly wouldn't love you if you were."[47] Significantly, in this definition of "brilliantly a woman," the word *mother* does not appear.

Roy Christy wrote Elizabeth often from Cornwall, detailing Anna's progress at considerable length. Which of his reports was the most painful and difficult to read? How Anna cried for days and nights at the hotel in Penzance, until they settled in a cottage in the nearby fishing village of Newlyn? How Anna talked of Elizabeth constantly, cried when Roy left for work, and asked and begged for her mother? How, in Roy's absence she screamed hysterically, kicking and lashing out? Or how good and patient was the German girl, Inga? How quickly Anna had become attached to her, had ceased to be difficult and became sweet, outgoing, and—reminiscent of the child's reaction when left in the convent—"terribly well behaved"?[48]

Roy's letters from Cornwall are articulate and poignant and sound sincere. He begged Elizabeth to have him back, swearing that he would love her better if she gave him the chance. Her answer made him sad.[49] He told her he was lonely but observing her instructions. He sent her a little money when he could and a pack of Gauloises for the "nostalgic" aroma of the continent.[50] In mid-March the nanny returned to Germany, and Roy arranged to board with a family while entering competitions and applying for jobs. He made a real effort with Anna, taking her for walks and to a country fair, buying her clothes, bathing her and reading to her at bedtime. In late April the two spent a Sunday afternoon picking primroses and decided to send a boxful of the flowers to Elizabeth from Anna.[51] When the flowers arrived withered and dead, Elizabeth became hysterical with grief. John Fowles, with her on that day, observed the incident and eventually adapted it to *The Magus,* where "a tangle of clumsily pressed flowers" sent by post is the symbol of Alison's presumed suicide.[52]

Yet together John and Elizabeth were happy. Her depression lifted; his scolding tone vanished. For three weeks of spring holiday they lived at 8 Holly Hill, absorbed in each other. "Happy times on a Sunday lunch," Fowles wrote, "steak, wine, raspberries, sunlight and the Schubert great ninth on the wireless; the trees alight with green flames, the buildings soft slate-blue, spring and spring-music. We made love most of the afternoon, in the warm sunlight, crisscross shadows across our naked bodies." They wandered hand in hand on Hampstead Heath in the chilly evenings, "the trees dancing, St Elmo's fire, with green shoots.

Willowwarblers sung liquidly from each small copse," and ended at their favored "noisy trippers pub," Jack's Straw's Castle.[53] They had pet names for each other. She, probably for her political passions, was "Lizbushka"; he was "Lubushka" or sometimes "J. Papotsi."

They both read a great deal and went to art exhibitions, and Elizabeth took John to visit the British Museum for the first time. They went to cinemas and bought cheap tickets to plays. Their quarrels, frequent and quickly made up, generally focused on conflicts of values and were often ignited by arguments about art, particularly the theater. Elizabeth was angry, for instance, when John liked plays about wealthy, socially upper-class people, the standard West End fare in those pre–*Look Back in Anger* days. Seeing Clifford Odets's *The Big Knife* caused a battle that lasted until dawn, because it spurred her to criticize Fowles's "disinterest, my refusal to argue, to take up positions, positive stands." In her world, wrote Fowles, people had to hold "violent views . . . have, not ideas, but faith." If they did not "burn," they were "suburban." John Fowles, however, did not want to burn, admitting he was "too much the spectator. . . . I watch." He had "no public spirit at all" and wanted nothing more than to write.[54] Elizabeth's was a "close, warm, intensely real sincere world of individual pleasures, constant probing experiences, constant sincerity in personal relationships." One second of it was "worth a thousand years of Ashridge," where one lied continually "to one's beliefs and inclinations."[55] To live in Elizabeth's world, Fowles had to measure up to her standards of absolute sincerity without compromise, critically examining "every single thing, thought and being that crosses her path."[56] Loving Elizabeth was exhausting. Life with her demanded such "a courage and an effort" that he sometimes longed to leave her, but there were other times, "most times, when any such thought is impossible."[57] To return to Ashridge on Sunday, May 9, was "agony." He felt "stranded, out of place."[58]

The day after John Fowles left Hampstead, Roy and Anna Christy returned to London. Roy had found a good architectural job, and father and daughter boarded with a French family that Elizabeth had scouted out for them. Elizabeth was greeted with wild three-year-old enthusiasm by her little girl. Roy had "plenty of money" now and began entering, and winning, architectural competitions.[59] He never allowed Anna to visit alone with her mother, so Elizabeth saw Roy every day. Occasionally she allowed him to buy her drinks or take her to the cinema. Fowles was very jealous and—groundlessly—daily expected her to return to Roy. "I still don't like this love-lorn-look-and-milky-kindness relationship with R.," he wrote.[60]

While Roy's presence in London was disturbing him, Fowles also came to a crisis over his manuscript. In mid-March 1954 Fowles had interviewed with an agent from Perm, Pollinger & Highams. "A tired, smooth, vague, judging man," Paul Scott, later a successful novelist himself, encouraged Fowles with the opinion that he would one day be published.[61] Fowles left *An Island and Greece* with Scott when he returned to Ashridge. He was aware that the book still fell short, wrote that it bored him, but he remained hoping "too much against hope," even "cocksure" that the book would be praised.[62]

PP&H reported promptly, fully, and unfavorably on May 15. On the "debit side" it called the book "a series of chapters, rather than a book, with a sprinkling of pleasant but not very original comments. . . . A procession of places, irrelevant meals and chance encounter . . . too messy a book to find a publisher." Fowles's prose lacked "the power of compelling unresisting attention." On the "credit side," Scott wrote that when "John" (the book's protagonist) became "more than an intelligent tourist . . . part of the landscape," the book improved "in flavour, individuality and confidence." Scott worried about being unfair to Fowles "because he is so close to writing a good book." However, Fowles lacked "that touch of magic which would have brought real life and sparkle to his fervent admiration for beauty, his feeling for the past, his sense of the drama in strange places." The book was structurally unsound. The factual travel elements did "not cohere into a pattern of recreation sufficiently fresh and stimulating." Fowles needed to "force a design on, discipline material that might well be saleable."[63]

Fowles called it "a fair report," but he was nevertheless shocked and chastened. Sally had left Ashridge, but he sought Sanchia Humphreys's company immediately, though never mentioning the book. He telephoned Elizabeth, feeling "nauseated."[64] He wrote her how furious he was "that I'd been so cocksure with myself. And I wanted, like a little boy, to come running to you."[65]

From mid-May, the time of Roy Christy's return to London and the PP&H report on *An Island and Greece*, Fowles was insecure, resentful, jealous, and easily hurt. His financial situation was precarious, while Roy had a good income. Elizabeth saw Roy and Anna every day, and Fowles worried that Roy had "only to wait and economic circumstances alone will drive you back." He felt "increasingly dependent" on Elizabeth's love, while imagining she needed him "less and less." Elizabeth's whole attention was on Anna; as she admitted, "she is as much in love with Anna as anything else."[66] Fowles swallowed his pride and wrote to PP&H, agreeing to cut and rewrite some of the manuscript. Elizabeth tore one of his stories "to shreds" and continued her "harsh criticisms of me and my work."[67] Fowles's passionate, lonely love letters from Ashridge complain of the difficulty of "living with you when you're so stripped of hope, and so impossible to comfort, so hostile to sympathy. . . . Why I allow you to say and behave to me in a way that I could tolerate from noone else."[68]

At Ashridge he was adrift. A party of American schoolteachers from western Michigan were in residence for an educational exchange. The more the Ashridge staff delighted in "all this international bonhomie business," the more Fowles displayed his scorn. These "dull slabs of Michigan turnip" were "a bore," their language "crawling with clichés, like maggots on bad meat,"[69] and "naïf, methodical, stereotyped in their responses."[70] The Ashridge staff, notably the Admiral, "frowned on" him "as an anti-American." Eventually one of the American women had a "showdown" with him: "I haven't been so savagely attacked for quite sometime. How contemptuous I was, how rude to women, how rude especially to American women, how arrogant, how supercilious." He was upset by the "element of truth in it."[71] Moreover, Ashridge, he thought, had humiliated him once again. In early June 1954 the Admiral refused to allow Fowles to lecture on existentialism. This situation festered for about six weeks. John's colleagues vehemently protested their indignation, and on August 1, with the Admiral sitting in "stony silence," Fowles gave his existentialism lecture to "plenty of bouquets."[72] The initial refusal was "like an earthquake or a fever," however, and he felt himself strange and excluded, "as if I do not belong."[73]

In characteristic fashion, John Fowles reacted to the stress and uncertainty of this period by beginning another, very serious, escapist romance. On June 27, 1954, Fowles "suddenly" found himself "indifferent to E." and "completely in love" with Sanchia Humphreys.[74] His obsessive relationship with nineteen-year-old Sanchia took up the month of July, so one of the names of the character she inspired was Julie. Her other name in the masque of *The Magus* was Lily, indicating her purity, chastity, and aloof, otherworldly innocence. Although in the novel Fowles made Lily the twin sister of Rose, Sanchia was similar to Sally Simpson only in age, background, and nationality and in being designated as an "S" in Fowles's diaries.

Fowles resumed the romantic rhythm he had enjoyed with Sally. With Sanchia, there were more afternoons of stolen forest walks, more harpsichord and clavichord concerts at the Little Gaddesden manor house, more forbidden walks at midnight, more soul-searching conversations lasting till dawn, followed by fierce, passionate weekends in the city with Elizabeth. Yet the relationship with Sanchia went deeper than the one with Sally and was far more threatening to Elizabeth.

John called Sanchia "Curio," because of her rarity and strangeness.[75] She was a "fairy-like, fantasizing, childish, sage, charming, infinitely charming person." She often teased and had a gift for the witty remark or the apt word. She wrote poetry, told stories, was full of "fantasy, feyness, whimsicality." When she told him about her life and family in Johannesburg, Fowles did not know whether to believe her. She had none of Elizabeth's mature, arresting beauty, was "a white face under black hair, a red bud of a mouth under her ridiculously retroussé nose."[76] Her "constantly changing series of expressions," however, indicated that mercurial quality that so attracted Fowles, "a kaleidoscope, a procession of women."[77] Sanchia was "as evanescent as thistledown . . . impossible to pin her down to any sustained mood. Shy and girlish where emotion crops up; very inexperienced, green; but subtle, as attractive as a will-o-the-wisp. So hard to catch."[78]

Fowles associated Sanchia, like Monique, to whom he favorably compared her, with a romantic natural context or with works of art. They walked for hours past midnight along the long, deserted beech ride on "a cool grey night with high swathes of vapour veiling the stars," never touching, "not even finger tips."[79] They sat on a gate in brilliant moonlight, cold in the heavy dew, while a badger came snuffling around their feet, then lumbered off.[80] They discovered a "see-saw tree" among the beeches, "a tree with a low springy bough" that became their private play place.[81] As Monique had been in 1952, Sanchia was consistently described by color. In her "sky-blue macintosh with brass bobbles"[82] at a harpsichord concert at the beautiful Elizabethan manor house, "Sanchia stood like a blue flame, and I was entranced." The morning after their first kiss, "she walks about in a magenta dress; laughs at me, looks coy."[83] She appeared in the school-leavers' play "in a sea-green dress, very blue jade, a deep harmonious colour for her black hair and her white face and her red mouth. Elegant, very abrupt, elusive."[84] Even while acknowledging Elizabeth's "strong pull, as slow and sure as gravity" within himself, he was mesmerized by Sanchia's likeness to "a world-famous painting," as she appeared "in a flower-dotted dress with a schoolgirl top and a gay straw hat; something from Renoir. She sat in a branch of a chestnut tree, dappled with sun and wind, black mop of hair, violet eyes in the pale face, soft smile, her female presence perfect in the summer scene." She had "the chameleon's trick of changing to blend with her environment. Like a flower, and I feel powerless near her."[85]

Fowles loved the forbidden quality and sense of secrecy in his romance with Curio. The girl was a games player of his own kind, and he relished her ability to slip out with him at midnight and pass him in the corridor like a stranger the next day. After a nocturnal walk on July 10, they returned at 1:00 A.M. to find the doors locked. An approaching car caught them in its headlights, and John "walked away hastily, guiltily, in the full glare of the headlights, furious, frightened, caught with my trousers down." The returnees were three of the American teachers, who, as he fled, giggled: "He sure is an immoral character, that John."[86]

For all his obsession with her, John Fowles was not physically attracted to Sanchia at all. He found her "very unapproachable, virginal, armoured." He wondered whether it was "frigidity" or if she was simply "inexperienced."[87] He thought of her, and his relationship with her, "in hunter-prey terms." Recalling his butterfly collecting, his hunting of birds and animals, Fowles wrote, "she of all women . . . needs careful stalking, delicate playing."[88] Sanchia provoked "no physical desire, she doesn't excite, except by her feyness," yet he longed to kiss her "because she is so unkissable."[89] This powerful longing wasn't sex or love, "but just the satisfaction of achieving something difficult to attain."[90]

Yet from the first moment that he acknowledged his attraction to Sanchia, Fowles wanted to marry her, had "never wanted to marry anyone so much before."[91] She would be "such a wife," he wrote. "There exists (or rather the potentialities exist) between us an accord of unusual natures, a harmony."[92] Without feeling sexual desire, Fowles walked about "in a permanent state of electricity; pent-up till she appears."[93] He was "enchanted," "possessed by her," "haunted," "lost in her." She was "an enchantress, in the vast sense; more than a touch of the sea about her."[94]

He wanted to marry a woman who offered him his most valued quality: mystery. Sanchia "looks as if she might have an enduring mystery."

Elizabeth had mystery "but no fantasy."[95] Fowles longed "for a more formal, more fantastic relationship," and confessed feeling a class bond
with the nineteen-year-old debutante. Sanchia also had, as John did, a
need to withdraw into solitude, for "sanctuary in herself." He thought
Elizabeth (constantly compared with Sanchia in the diaries) demanded a
"sincerity," a "transparency" that was "exhausting," a "total love" in which
lovers behaved "naturally . . . as naked animals, and naked souls, in each
other's presence." Sanchia held back, saying, "I must have something hidden . . . one must allow the other certain secrets."[96] Elizabeth was also
"an equal striving to be a superior, too close," while "S. is distant, junior,
not an equal because she does not combat ideas."[97] In working-class Elizabeth, he noted "a certain prolixity, vulgarity" that contrasted with
Sanchia's "reserve . . . careful choice," although he admitted, "It may
merely be the difference between a primary-school and Roedean education and the lack of it."[98]

Looming over all his other justifications, however, was guilt, "the guilt
between E. and I for what we have done to R. and A. It haunts our lives,
it is waiting around each corner, at the end of each day."[99] Loving
Sanchia was a fantasy of escape from that reality for Fowles. He felt
soiled and ashamed, thinking that Sanchia was "what I no longer deserve
to know. Innocent intelligence, virginity, a whole unadulterated bud." He
longed to "be loved by her; act out the part; and start a new life. . . . As if
in my cult of love I needed something fresh and gleaming to worship; an
infantile drive? Something untarnished."[100] When walking out with
Sanchia in the forests around Ashridge, Fowles felt "free of E. in a sense,
lightened, released into the liberty of my own world again."[101] When he
finally kissed Sanchia, an entire month after falling in love with her, he
rejoiced that he felt "so free from guilt; innocent."[102]

Part of Sanchia's appeal was her impossibility. Scheduled to leave
Ashridge at the end of July, she was returning to South Africa in late August. The closer her departure date drew, the wilder grew Fowles's possession. She was so young, so distant, so inexperienced, so unformed,
and she was about to pass out of his life forever. "Sanchia," like
Monique, he wrote, "touches the unattainable. With them both I sense
all kinds of worlds I can never achieve."[103] As with Monique, Fowles's
idealization and sense of impending loss of Sanchia filled him with inspiration and spurred him to poetry.

In one of his earliest letters to Elizabeth, Fowles sent her the poem he had written about her at Phaestos, Crete. It had been inspired by the April night that Roy slept and Elizabeth, dressed only in a shirt, had met John to light a cigarette in the middle of a dark bedroom. It had been one of Fowles's poetic moments, entered by a trivial experience that took on "a kind of symbolic key value." As it was for the symbolist poets, these undeclared moments held "a subtle, complex, ambiguous and delicate charm, an almost undiluted *poetic* quality." Fowles explained to Elizabeth that "my relationship with you is . . . much more profound, self-revealing and satisfactory—adult, if you like. You are to me as much a companion as a mistress." Yet, he admitted, since the first day of their adultery he could no longer think of her in this "poetic" manner.[104] Despite this claim, there would be many other Elizabeth poems. Indeed, on June 13, the anniversary of their dawn on Areopagus (just two weeks before falling madly for Sanchia), John wrote Elizabeth a revealing poem "so full of highly charged emotion" that he couldn't bring himself to show it to her.[105] However, in Fowles's mind, Elizabeth had descended from the poetic pedestal by becoming "real," manifesting herself as sexual, attainable, knowable, and a person in her own right.

On the other hand, Sanchia Humphreys, like Monique Baudouin, was the quintessential girl muse for John Fowles. Whatever and whoever she actually was, he cast her in his imagination as asexual, unattainable, and mysterious. She was infinite potential, an invitation, a virgin, blank page for his poetry. In the wee hours of July 2, for example, they searched a starry sky, looking southwest past Mars, and John pointed out Cygnus and the other classical constellations. Sanchia resisted his set definitions, protesting, "I can see shapes everywhere." Fowles "suddenly saw the sky as a kaleidoscope for her, infinitely deep and changing, as it really was, incoherent beautiful chaos, and for me, a man's set of arbitrary patterns; man and woman views."[106] He set this insight into a poem in which "she endorsed the great sedition,/Saw the monsters where she would,/Inventing strange new bestiaries/To prove her womanhood." The unnamed girl of the poem reveals the universe as it is, irrationally, as "incoherent beautiful chaos" and the poet's rationalist definitions as arbitrary and limiting. The poet becomes "the learner from her sex," who banishes "systems from my skies/Until my mind can form her myths/And sense the same sad mysteries."[107] Both the Elizabeth poem and the Sanchia poem are predicated on a sense of lost possibility. The "Phaestos, April" poem hangs on "a swift yes of hypothesis/Before the no that never ended."[108] The Ashridge poem ends by wondering if the girl knew "that our two stars/Could never be a constellation/Except in my imagination?" For John Fowles, it was the unattainable and undefined that held poetic power.

Within days of becoming enchanted with Sanchia, Fowles began to fantasize about leaving Elizabeth. She knew something was wrong immediately, even suspected that it might be Sanchia. Her circumstances could not have been much worse. Roy had begun an affair with a model and asked his wife for a divorce. He again asked his sister to take Anna, and Elizabeth, again, frantically tried to regain custody of her daughter. She hated her job and was facing a move from 8 Holly Hill. A close friend had become accidentally pregnant and was threatening suicide. The worse Elizabeth's situation became, the deeper Fowles retreated into his romance with Sanchia.

Yet it is clear from his revealingly conflicted behavior that John Fowles was so deeply in love with Elizabeth that it was nearly unbearable. Throughout the period of his romance with Sanchia (including his marriage fantasy), he searched for a job that would allow him to live with Elizabeth. He spent every July weekend with her in London and snatched at least three midweek nights with her as well. They wrote or telephoned every day, sometimes both. He could talk with Sanchia until four in the morning and then wake, to phone Elizabeth "urgently, just to hear her voice; reality; not dreams, idealizations, classical myths. An equal love."[109] Arriving at Holly Hill, John would remark of Elizabeth with happy surprise, "I forget what a strange, beautiful creature she is."

Fowles painfully attempted to convince himself that he was not in love with Elizabeth and was capable of leaving her. Reminiscent of his 1950 Oxford decision to fail deliberately and take on manual labor "to keep free, to give my real self a chance" because he feared a poor degree, in July 1954 he constructed an elaborate escapist daydream of retreating into a monastic writer's existence. Complaining how he never had time to write, he declared that he required "solitude, celibacy, in order to indulge the process of self-love that writing is."[110] He would have two years "free of all female contact," with Sanchia "as a remote Beatrice to prevent the desert from being absolute."[111] When she was a little older, he would try to marry her. Without revealing the Beatrice role he had assigned to

Sanchia, he tried to convince Elizabeth that it would be wise for them to separate. It would be better for her, he pleaded, since his prospects "as a bread-earner" were so poor. There was such tension between them that he could not write and needed solitude. And there was the "true test" of her past: "If Roy and Anna did not exist, then I cannot imagine not loving you." How could they "live together until you quite definitely feel—in the deepest sense—married to me"? He held up the specter of Frieda Lawrence (not the last time Elizabeth was measured by the shadow of the wife of D. H. Lawrence), saying, "She had all her guilt and remorse, but she knew who she was married to, who she wanted to be married to."[112]

In mid-July Fowles wrote Elizabeth about Sanchia, describing her as "young, enthusiastic, a poetess, and I think . . . rather in love with me." He, he claimed, was "not, Liz, in love with her, but I am in love with what she represents . . . innocence, I suppose, greenness, freedom from guilt, all that we can never be now." He assured Elizabeth she should feel no jealousy, for he felt no physical desire for the girl, even found her "physically refrigerating."[113] However, he confessed, he had discovered in himself "this capacity for dual loving, which I hate." He was untrustworthy and unable to "love you as you should be loved."[114] Elizabeth wrote him back "a very good letter about discipline . . . about the capacity for two loves and its control."[115]

During July 1954 John Fowles wrote at least four long letters of farewell to Elizabeth and sent none of them. On a July 15 visit he talked all night about separation. "I was dry and cool and remote, classically sad, frozen," he recalled. Elizabeth clung to him, and he "left her standing in the middle of the room, weeping." But on the train back to Berkhamsted, he was overwhelmed to think of never seeing her again. He wrote to her immediately; he telephoned; he returned.[116] Again and again, through July, Fowles determined "I must see her once more; then no more," then could not stay away.[117] He simply could not leave her.

Miraculously, at the end of July, Fowles found a job in Hampstead, a poorly paid post teaching English at a secretarial college for young women. He and Elizabeth made plans for living together.

"But," as he wrote, "the two places, the two women, don't live in the same world."[118] So at Ashridge, Fowles desperately continued his fantasy of marrying Sanchia. She left the debutante school for Denmark on July 28 but briefly returned to London before departing for South Africa. In a

Lily-like gesture, Sanchia left on John's desk "a dead rosebud slashed in half, as if by scissors. And a piece of paper underneath, with the one word 'John!' scrawled on it. Typical of her, ambiguous, mystifying, delightful. . . . Nipped in the bud?"[119] For days he poured out love letters full of melancholy longing and whimsy. He begged Sanchia to meet him in London, choosing for the rendezvous the zoo in Regent's Park, where he had met Elizabeth exactly one year before.

They met on Friday, August 6, and it was not a success. "The zoo was crowded, the weather wet, our nerves frayed." John was terrified of meeting Elizabeth. Sanchia wanted a gay farewell, to be happy and amused. Fowles wanted intense conversation. After they left a little pub off Piccadilly, a storm arose: "sheets of rain, lightning." As they stood against a shopwindow, dodging the rain, it was on the tip of his tongue to ask her to marry him. But he kept silent. They went to a cinema, ate sandwiches in a café, walked hand in hand around Leiceister Square. Then, before putting Sanchia on the underground, Fowles asked, "Shall we meet again?" "No," said Sanchia, "I don't think so." And Fowles was "sad and relieved."[120]

He went home to Elizabeth. In later years John Fowles remembered his parting with Sanchia as an *acte gratuit,* a sudden existential decision to choose Elizabeth and reality. Indeed, the choice worked out that way, but there was nothing sudden about it. Fowles brooded for days and wrote Sanchia letters and love poems for another two weeks. He complained of Hampstead's "same tired routine of cinema and pubs," of how Elizabeth looked "old at times, lacking for all [her] beauty, the qualities of S."[121] Elizabeth was not fooled. In one of her rare surviving letters she wrote how, at the beginning of August, John was "totally disinterested, all tied and bound with the past-filled—Sanchia, no *me* anywhere much." She hung on, ironically calling herself "the perfect mistress."[122]

Toward the end of August, Fowles woke up. What had happened with Sanchia seemed "unreal, a fever, an illness, something abnormal."[123] He read what he had written in July and thought it written by "a total stranger." He felt "amused" by the idea of marrying Sanchia.[124] Elizabeth was astonished and happy. "Now you have a job and all your shirts are here," she wrote in amazement, "I can't cope, sometimes, with the quick breeze change in you. . . . I *do* love you back more than a little. I kiss your dirty shirt in the bathroom. Love Love Liz."[125] Fowles returned to Ashridge for his final leave-taking, thinking, "Only a madman would throw up this job, objectively."[126] On September 3 he wrote a farewell letter to Curio, told her she had touched "not my skin, but my soul . . . mind and heart, me," and wished her well.[127]

Three years later the Ashridge of John Fowles's time was gone. Beset by financial problems and social and educational changes, the College of Citizenship closed in 1957. It reopened in 1959 as the Ashridge Management College, a specialized school for longer residential business courses. The institution enjoys this identity, and a fine reputation, to this day. The change was total. Admiral Sir Denis Boyd retired, and the College of Citizenship ceased to operate. The young ladies also departed, with Miss Neville-Rolfe amicably moving her House of Citizenship to Hartwell House, near Aylesbury. But the Ashridge of Fowles's particular experience—the constant visitors with their masks of celebrity, the two seductive girls, the authoritarian master of the revels, the remote, extraordinary house isolated in the forest, the harpsichord music in an exquisite manor—all this would endure, transformed, in his novel *The Magus,* even as the reality vanished into thin air.

Fowles left Ashridge, as he put it, "in a calm whimper," prepared to settle down in Hampstead with Elizabeth. Her life was not so easily arranged, however. At the end of August she was fired from yet another job. In early September Roy Christy, who was having an affair with another woman, forbade Elizabeth from seeing Anna. Elizabeth went to pieces. Ten days later, September 14, 1954, she left John to go back to Roy.

John Fowles, waiting in anguish in Elizabeth's tiny Hampstead cottage, faced the terrible reasons for her desertion by writing, writing, writing through the long evening. It was "the result of the S. affaire in no small part," he agonized, and "her feeling of loss with regard to Anna." Seeing Roy and Anna detach themselves as Roy pursued another woman and having "no certainty of me" had been too much. Fowles admitted to himself at last that he could never compensate Elizabeth for the loss of her little girl. He felt sick and frightened contemplating living without her, even going to a cinema, walking down a street, or having a meal without her. He "felt the bottom of the world falling out." Before she left, he had begged her over and over to marry him. He had even written to Roy, insisting that he wanted to marry Elizabeth. He "at last realized how profound my love for her" had become and that he wanted her "for life."[128]

He looked up from his many diary pages when it was nearly midnight.

Elizabeth opened the door, having returned from Roy's flat in Bayswater on the last tube. She was drawn, weeping, despairing. She couldn't go back to Roy; she couldn't leave John.

In the ending of Fowles's novel *The Magus,* Alison, the character based on Elizabeth, is given a choice, administered with a slap across the face. "Pain!" says the narrator. "Her turn to know."[129] Elizabeth was to struggle forever with the heartbreaking consequences of staying with John and thereby losing her daughter. But for John Fowles, the harrowing evening he spent believing he had lost Elizabeth was the beginning of a decisive change. He was now certain of whom he belonged to. He remained certain for the next thirty-six years.

CHAPTER NINE

The Waiting Room

Apprenticeship in Hampstead: 1954–1957

You stuck to me through sin and sin,
Through self-deception, thick and thin.

You stuck to me through sun and snow,
But I was always the one below.

You clung like harrow to my earth.
You cleaved, you tore.
As roller rolls the new green wheat,
The more I fell the more.

So I must love, I must love you,
But not till late, till late in May
When rich green acres rule the day;
And then, in quite another way.

—JOHN FOWLES, "POEM, MAY 1956"

Hampstead in 1954 was an unusual part of North London. Largely because of its proximity to Hampstead Heath, 802 acres of untamed, legally protected open land, Hampstead retained much more of its village character than the other villages and towns that had been absorbed by the outward sprawl of Greater London over the centuries. Hampstead was still a borough unto itself, politically independent of nearby Highgate or Camden Town. The London underground connected Hampstead High Street to the urban heart of the capital in minutes, but the heath gave many of the side streets a semirural flavor. It was a place of émigrés, a postwar haven for the likes of Elias Canetti and Anna Freud, for Middle Europeans, Jews, intellectuals, and artists who had fled from the Germans in the mid-thirties and early forties. John Fowles barely brushed these circles in his early Hampstead years. The village had odd divisions of class. Expensive, "snobbish" areas, increasingly gentrified by the rising London professionals who lived in them, were close by the down-at-the-heel quarters of the bohemians and the working and lower middle classes. In these constricted, shabby places John Fowles and Elizabeth Christy lived for several years.

For the first ten months of their life together, Elizabeth, in an agony of guilt, tried to decide if she could ever be Roy Christy's wife again in order to reclaim her child. For the following two years Roy dangled and withdrew the prospect of divorce, as he dangled and withdrew Elizabeth's time with her daughter. For John Fowles himself this was a time of humbling, when he served an impoverished apprenticeship as a serious writer, learned to work among ordinary people, and embraced the commitment of his daily relationship with Elizabeth. This period—waiting for Elizabeth to decide to stay with him, waiting for Roy to let her go, waiting for something he had written to be publishable, waiting for better days when there would be more money and a little respectability, while being ground down with poverty, a job he despised, and uncertainty over the woman he loved—he called the waiting room. In the "desert" of this waiting room John Fowles came of age at last.[1]

Characteristically, however, he began by hiding. In late September 1954, Fowles went home to borrow money from his parents. His father, unasked, had a check ready, but Fowles "couldn't bring himself" to accept, much to Elizabeth's later annoyance. He could not speak of Elizabeth to his parents and felt a "great gulf" separating them. Loath "to confess my departure from their straight and narrow path," he was very conscious of "all in the past that I shall never repay them for; not being anything like what they wished me to be." Robert and Gladys seemed "to have guessed the nature of things," but Fowles projected his own feelings of shame and embarrassment on to them, keeping them ignorant of the details of his life.[2] Until 1957 he and Elizabeth, in their late twenties and early thirties, spent Christmas and Easter with their respective families. Fowles yearned to speak of Elizabeth but never did, creating awkwardness at these family gatherings. Elizabeth was more forthcoming to her parents, and Edgar told her gruffly that she might well have been "happier married to a Walsall policeman," a phrase she cherished later in life.³ John's sister, Hazel, recalled that although their father had been "quite hard" in his initial judgment of Elizabeth, "he later softened." John's mother "always wrote to him, although he seldom replied, because she said, 'You never know . . . ' Because the worst thing would be to lose John . . . and, of course, she did."⁴

In Hampstead, in the mid-1950s, John and Elizabeth had "the effort of 'living in sin.'"⁵ To rent their various flats, they had to pretend to be married. Some socializing was necessary for Fowles's job, and Elizabeth came to be friendly with some of his colleagues. He kept a low profile about his marital status, however. With few exceptions, Fowles avoided friends from his days at Oxford, although this may have been as much from financial embarrassment as from awkwardness over his adulterous relationship with a working-class woman. In Fowles's view, Elizabeth herself was socially impossible, very unsure, and terribly self-conscious about her lack of education and their bohemian lifestyle. "There was never a woman less self-sufficient psychologically . . ." he wrote, "She is so pathetically ill-at-ease in any company, because of her lack of education, of savoir-faire. She can't pass off anything, can't stand up on her own with strangers of our own class and type."⁶ "She doesn't fit in anywhere socially," he wrote, adding, "but that is precisely her charm, outside society."⁷ They lived, at least in the beginning, a "very inturned pattern of life" with "only the powerful attraction that binds us" keeping them from separating.⁸ Fowles had accepted the necessity of living outside the values and expectations of his middle-class upbringing, but he was not comfortable with it. He continued, at least in part, to judge himself by the standards by which he was raised and to assume that others judged him that way as well.

They both were employed from the beginning of October 1954, he teaching at the secretarial college, a job he found "repugnant,"⁹ she working seasonally at Gamages toy shop selling little lead Knights of the Round Table, the leading Christmas item inspired by an MGM film. Her job, wrote Fowles, was "tiring, noisy, airless, and the people she works with cheap, garish, out-of-work actors, film extras, a tinselly scum."¹⁰ The hours were long, the pay was poor, and Elizabeth developed bronchitis, grew thin, and was will-less and fatigued. Between them, they brought home about thirteen pounds a week, of which five pounds went straight to the rent. Yet their love was warm. They danced together, "absurd dances," in the little cottage at the end of Prince Arthur Road. On "gay, crisp, sapphire" afternoons, amid "whirling leaves, flower gardens all tawny and mature colours," they walked on the heath "hand in hand; almost tramps, with the tramp's sour-sweet freedom."[11]

St. Godric's Secretarial College, named for the patron saint of business, was a far cry from Ashridge and the debutante school that had so seduced Fowles the year before. Classes were taught in three bleak-looking Victorian houses along Arkwright Road, while students boarded in six similar houses on adjacent streets. There were normally about two hundred full-time students, though part-time, nonboarding enrollment could double that. Fowles called St. G.'s "a seedy, mediocre institution" for "the mere cramming of 16–18 year-old girls who are not intelligent enough to aim higher than a secretarial career." It was not pretentious, however, offering "strictly practical" courses in a factorylike atmosphere. The "pale, plump young" director, John Loveridge, was a Tory town councillor, the staff was largely female ("a mixture of failures and mice"), the staff room was the "pale ghost" of a proper common room, while the real power was wielded by the secretary. When he began, Fowles taught "small classes of foreign girls—temperamental Greeks, noisy, lively French, silent, aloof Icelanders, and mixture of all the other nations; never the English girls."[12] The college offered diplomas in typing, short-hand, and other specific business skills, as well as preparation in the Cambridge Lower and the Cambridge Proficiency Examinations, the Chamber of Commerce examination, the Royal Society of Arts examination, The Institute of Linguists examinations, and the General Certificate of Education (GCE). Fowles's starting pay was £550 a year.

He prospered at St. Godric's, almost in spite of himself. In the early days he raged about wasted time in "the work I have to do at the college—the futile teaching, lecturing, fiddling; correcting the grammar of pseudo-morons, future shopgirls, typists, female riff-raff" and the "stupidity" that surrounded him.[13] But slowly he came to think better of some of his students. He thought the Turks "the best of the nationalities at St. G's" and became the encouraging mentor of a Turkish girl who wrote "vivid and evocative" compositions.[14] He found the European students hardworking. He discovered "historically very explicable" reasons to judge less harshly the arrogant behavior of the Israelis that offended the other students. He was sympathetic to groups like the Thais; "far and away the best mannered and often the hardest working . . . they put all the other nations to shame."[15] Fowles also stood up for his students in matters of curriculum, arguing successfully against those who wanted to replace the "set books" of great literature and serious English composition with strictly commercial English. As time went on, he influenced curricular development. After his arrival, the French and Secretarial Course placed emphasis on those twentieth-century French writers whom Fowles admired: Anouilh, Giraudoux, Pagnol, Sartre, Cocteau, Aragon, Giono, Proust, Malraux, Apollinaire, Mauriac, St.-Exupéry, Valéry, Camus. The survey course came to include lectures on existentialism and "the essentials of philosophical theories as expressed in present-day French literature." Fowles's readings and interests are also evident in everything from examinations to typing tests.[16]

Life took on a predictable routine. Each weekday morning Fowles taught from nine-fifteen to ten and again from eleven to one. By 1955 he was teaching the advanced beginners ("a French girl, a Czech, a Swede, a Cypriot, a Norwegian, a Turk, a Greek, an Italian . . . all eager, moderately intelligent").[17] He taught a literature class of set books, two or three modern books, and one "older" from authors like Charles Dickens, Jane Austen, or Anthony Trollope. His afternoons were varied: on Tuesdays a Greek translation class, on Wednesdays a French translation class, and on Fridays a class in psychology.

The break from ten to eleven every morning gave Fowles his chance to walk from Arkwright Road, down Fitzjohn's Avenue, crossing the bridge into the village in his threadbare wartime duffle coat to do the daily shopping. He liked the routine of it, buying his papers here, his cigarettes there, fruit or vegetables, cheese or sausage from shops on Pennies Walk, bread from the baker's opposite Church Row.[18] On Saturday mornings, while Elizabeth worked, he went to the launderette. He still had "to steel myself to go in," he wrote with chagrin. "So much snobbishness I still have; and fear to be seen by my pupils."[19]

John Fowles, former Head Boy of Bedford School, former lieutenant Royal Marines, Oxford graduate, university lecturer, stopped thinking beyond a week and learned to live "paypacket to paypacket." Friday payday was the "climax."[20] Like the crowds of working people surrounding them on Saturday afternoons, John and Elizabeth lived in "the wage-packet rhythm . . . Fridays, Saturdays bathed in light; a kind of continual progression to breaking-point, a dive, a nadir; then, at the last moment, the kick up to light."[21] During the week their staple diet was baked potatoes. As colder evenings drew in, they shivered and went early to bed since gas was too expensive for anything but cooking. They both needed winter clothes, coats, and shoes. Yet on the weekends there was respite. On Fridays John began meeting "Fletcher," one of his few male colleagues, for lunch. Friday evenings he and Elizabeth met at the Guinness pub after work. They went to films at the Everyman Cinema in Hampstead. On Sundays John himself made stews rich with meat, root vegetables, and spices, slow-cooked to a recipe of his own invention, calling them "the best stews I have ever eaten."[22] Together they lay on their single bed, reading, loving, and listening to serials and BBC plays on the wireless.[23]

Although living with John Fowles and loving him, Elizabeth Christy was ambivalent, "tormented by guilt still" over her child and also over Roy, whose legal wife she remained.[24] Alternating with periods of intense, self-sufficient happiness with Fowles, Elizabeth's despair could bear down on her like an "avalanche" of misery, burying her alive.[25] Roy wanted her back and used their daughter to manipulate her.

He had placed Anna with his religious mentor and his wife, Frederick and Mollie Lohr. To see her daughter, Elizabeth had to rely on Roy, thereby feeling the sadness and guilt of interacting as a family, or she had to go through the frightening Mollie Lohr, who thought Elizabeth sinful and a failed mother. It is unclear if Roy himself was living with the Lohrs, but he was certainly under Frederick Lohr's baleful influence. By November 1954 Roy was feeling so spiritually wretched that he threatened to enter a monastery, leaving the world and Anna. But this proposed solution was brief. Soon he was boasting of his genius as a writer once more, "his face . . . absolutely grave and self-convinced."[26] His notion of "Jewish Will" was now called "the will to universality" and applied to definitions of futuristic architecture.[27] John began to notice how talking with Roy was sometimes "a clinical occupation. . . . His mind was on with a shocking inconsequence; denying himself, hardly listening to what I say, seizing isolated words and running after them."[28] Denys Sharrocks, visiting John and Elizabeth while interviewing for a job, agreed with John that Roy was a "schizo" and would someday be a clinical case.[29]

Since Anna was not allowed to come to her, Elizabeth had to meet Roy frequently, traveling by bus to Bayswater. Often he canceled arrangements at the last minute, and Elizabeth was denied her time with the little girl. Each time she saw Roy, the emotional consequences were harrowing. He played her emotions, Fowles wrote, and had some "Svengalic . . . malignant charm over her." She thought of Roy as a "gigantic person" who humiliated and destroyed her.[30]

Himself under the influence of Frederick Lohr's strange Nietzschean Catholicism, Roy still exercised a moralistic authority over his wife, for "he is in black and white, where the rest are in grey. What he believes and disbelieves, he does absolutely."[31] However liberated Elizabeth claimed to be, John believed that he could see Roy's views "still there in her eyes."[32] Leaving Roy meant discarding this moral anchor, and this, for Elizabeth, was very difficult to do. She continually asked John for "authority, for guidance from me, as if I could, if I was only clever or profound enough, make the sea smooth."[33] She craved meaning, but Fowles could only offer existentialism: "I tell her that there is no order; that one can only get it at the expense of reality; that happiness, in an absurd world, is only possible by self-deception or by what consolation can be drawn from seeing more or less in perspective—ie that reality is chaos, and our own value a combination of our recognition of that fact and of our attempts to remedy it. But she, of course, wants a faith, an explanation, a panacea."[34] Fowles complained that she was "incapable of seeing life in humanist terms of expediencies, compromises, golden means."[35] She complained that he had failed her by not giving her "guidance, purpose—she constantly accuses me of not telling her 'where I'm going, what's the point of all this, of what the hell there is to live by.'"[36]

Roy also argued that Elizabeth's sexually passionate relationship with Fowles was mere "animal lust" compared with their own spiritually eternal marriage. Fowles, he told her, wanted only her "animality and a gay, trivial companionship."[37] She herself was disturbed by John's intellectual self-sufficiency, his tendency to "never tell her anything of what goes on inside me."[38] She also remained jealous of his idealization of Sanchia, which he occasionally discussed with her, for several years. When Fowles left his diaries or Sanchia's letters out where she would find them, she became too depressed to get out of bed.[39]

Roiled by Roy and her own uncertainties, Elizabeth's "guilt and shame and confusion," particularly over Anna, provoked a pattern of agonizing depressions and battles that alternated with the periods of sweet harmony. Life with her, said Fowles, was to ride on an "oceanic swell . . . troughs and mountains; easy, rolling glides in air and light and vertiginous plunges into the troughs."[40] He could usually predict the onset of what he came to call the *nuit blanche*, terrible all-night battles after a happy day, "during which we examined everything, said most of the unforgivable things, and decided nothing."[41] Elizabeth's self-accusing voice during one savagely bitter *nuit blanche* in September 1955 was to be echoed by Alison in *The Magus*. "'You don't know,' she sobbed, 'what it's like to wake up hating yourself and not knowing how to get through the day with that hate. You're noble and perfect, you prig, you . . .' etc." Fowles was fascinated. "Very true. I have never woken like that. I've never been able to *loathe* myself," he wrote, "I disapprove of myself, but I never cease to interest myself. I examine myself closely, but I never blame myself. . . . My superego is an admiring, indulgent censor. E's is harsh and tyrannical."[42]

The most astonishing aspect of the ongoing crisis was the congenial understanding—one hesitates to call it a friendship—that continued between John Fowles and Roy Christy. When Elizabeth was lost in anger and depression, John often turned to the one person who had also experienced the power of her emotional turbulence. He rang up Roy and met him for lunch or evening drinks. They talked about Elizabeth: "Six pints of beer for him; we both agreed on all E's faults; both said we were profoundly in love with her."[43] "I met R. last night and we both felt united against E.—that she had abused us too long, deceived us, dangled us. . . . R. says he does not really want her back; and I don't really want to keep her; both of us are, of course, chained to her. . . . But it gave us a feeling of freedom—this being in agreement about her."[44] When things went well between John and Elizabeth, Roy turned to John for conversation and comfort. "'Why should I suffer, why should I still love E., and let she love you, and you her, and be happy?'" Roy demanded as they drank together, repeating over and over, "'I don't see why I should be the one left out. . . . It's time you thought of me.'"[45] Fowles ruefully pondered how "suburban morality" would judge this *Huis Clos*. But there was "a sort of sad nobility" in the way the two men could meet sympathetically. "He can't take E. back, I can't let her go. . . . I feel, perhaps for the first time, genuinely and continually sorry for him."[46]

The dance dragged on until 1957. In the spring of 1955, for example, Roy set an ultimatum for Elizabeth's return, using Anna as the threat. Elizabeth spent an agonizing April and May trying to agree and to convince Fowles of the necessity, only to choose John once more. By May 19, 1955, Elizabeth had made up her mind to stay with Fowles and told

Roy to "go ahead with a divorce."[47] But it took Roy to February 8, 1956 to start proceedings, and then only under the condition that from his meager wages Fowles would supply the sixty pounds "to set the ball rolling."[48] Three months later, May 8, 1956, a private detective called with adultery statements for John and Elizabeth to sign. At the end of the following month, June 30, 1956, Roy refused to proceed, saying he needed Elizabeth and Fowles did not. The divorce case bumped along, however, and a decree was handed down during the first week of December 1956. The ruling hit Roy hard "where it hurts most; in the judgement of authority." The court costs were symbolic for Roy, who was shocked when the judge ruled that they be shared. Independently Roy decided that since Fowles was "morally guilty," he must pay all costs or Roy would delay the decree absolute for another eighteen months, also exacting Anna's maintenance costs from Elizabeth.[49] Fowles struggled to find the money, while Roy tried once more to seduce Elizabeth.[50] Not until February 1957 did John and Elizabeth (hearing "nothing from the lawyers") begin to believe that the divorce was final.[51]

Daily life in "the waiting room" went on against this stormy emotional background. Elizabeth had taken a new job by February 1955, working for Heal's of London, retailer of fashionable domestic furnishings on Tottenham Court Road. The interesting Heal's staff was "a crowd of the proletariat liberally sprinkled with the curious Heal's intelligensia; people difficult to place, a kind of pool formed by the backwash from more creative corners—artists manqués. All quite elegant, quite sophisticated, but displaced."[52] Elizabeth had only one Saturday off each month and, at first, was exasperated by the work. Eventually, however, she was assigned to the china department, where her taste was noticed, and she rose to be a buyer. While small, her Heal's salary helped the couple achieve the stability of a predictable income.

Also in February 1955, they found respite from six months of dingy rooms and prying landladies, moving to a top-floor one-room flat at 55 Frognal, close to Arkwright Road and St. Godric's. Though cold in winter, the tiny flat had French doors that opened onto a little roof balcony. In spring they slept with the doors open. "Sometimes, at first dawn, four-five in the morning," wrote Fowles, "a blackbird sings on the rail. As if it was in the room. A dazzling pure cascade of song, put over with tremendous force—quite different from the flirty, melodious old evening-song. An explosion of pristine, beginning of the world joie-de-vivre...

Extraordinarily beautiful, to wake up, the two of us, like that, stunned by the very roots of wildness in the tame labyrinth of London."[53]

Living day to day with Elizabeth Christy was a tremendous catalyst for change in John Fowles. Just as his Greek diaries of 1952 had reflected greater ease, humor, and social connection while he was in the steady company of a friend like Denys Sharrocks, so from his Hampstead years on Fowles's diaries present a man more comfortable with himself and with his community than before he lived with Elizabeth. For all her social discomfort in early years, Elizabeth became John's bridge to other people. He felt emotionally secure as her lover, her friend, and eventually her husband. He needed the domestic base she provided him, and he trusted her insight about other people as well as about art.

From Elizabeth he "learned the values outside intellect."[54] She had, he believed, an intuitive directness, a hatred of "fussiness, elaboration, ornaments," and loved "simplicity . . . the simplicity of the one chosen from thousands, not the one picked up at random."[55] She also had a powerful ability to live in the moment and "an intuitive, immediate power of appreciation and pleasure and enthusiasm . . . which I do not so strongly possess." She (and Roy, growled Fowles) "despise in me . . . the name-hunter, the spines-collector, the number complex," the tendency to list species of birds or kinds of music "not for the birds or for the music, but for . . . collections."[56] He was touched, even a little envious, at how deeply Elizabeth could be affected by books.[57] He grew to be patient and "amused" by her "half-dazzled, half-disgusted" silences in the company of his North Oxford friends. There the "clouds of perfumed talk . . . poses, dialectics" made him feel "lumpish, clumsy as an ox in a rococo salon," but stealing a glance at Elizabeth sitting in silence, John thought with pride how she had "an apprehension of essentials; they a mastery of superficials."[58]

The "Podges," Freddie and Eileen Porter, were among the few Oxford friends Fowles kept in touch with. Significantly, they remained rebels against the establishment, outspoken Marxists and "a thorn in the Oxford Labour party's side."[59] Fred Porter, like Fowles, was a teacher and paid far more attention to his language pupils and his music than to climbing in a career. John and Elizabeth saw them regularly in Oxford and London and joined them on cheap holidays at the seaside or in the north of France. Porter also reviewed books for the *Glasgow Herald* during the fifties, and Fowles continued to send his short stories to his old friend, the only person besides Elizabeth who was allowed to read and criticize John's works in progress. Porter, who remembered making remarks like "Well, it's at least as good as most of the novels I've read,"[60] offered "very detailed and cool and detached criticism,"[61] more measured than Elizabeth, who could still savage one of John's efforts as "so bad there is no reason for him to go on with it . . . 'people unreal, style bad, lending library.'" Fowles groaned: "Criticisms could help . . . but . . . annihilation"?[62]

With one important exception, Fowles avoided those friends of his Oxford days who were achieving traditional professional success. After a visit to the Severn Wildlife Trust with Basil Beeston, for example, Fowles dropped him as conventional and well-to-do. On a London street Fowles all but fled when he ran into the delighted Roger Hendry, just returned from Brazil. Pressed to dine with Roger and his family, Fowles felt painfully that this great friend of his student days had remained mired in the past while he had grown and changed. He saw Roger no more.[63]

The cheerful survivor of this weeding out of Oxford successes was Ronnie Payne. By the time Fowles became reacquainted with him in the summer of 1956, Payne was an established journalist with the *Daily Telegraph*, a job that Fowles and Fred Porter considered a writer's sellout for a politically right-wing newspaper. Payne led an exciting life, covering wars and military confrontations overseas. His fluent French later helped make him correspondent at the Paris bureau of the *Telegraph*. Fowles found Ronnie "successful, steady, greatly set in the world" and expected to envy him. Instead Ronnie and his "rather silent, soulful second wife," Betsa, were "the first people E. and I have met and liked for years." Perhaps because they had been schoolboys together and Fowles knew his modest background, he felt a greenness about Ronnie, "that he was much older than me in worldly things, and much younger at the core."[64] Payne remained a superlative raconteur, overflowing with perfectly timed funny stories and insider gossip, and a devastating mimic with scores of voices and accents. Over many years Fowles and Porter often clucked their tongues over what they assumed was Payne's cynicism or conservative politics, yet neither ever really disapproved of him. He remained all their lives the good-natured, companionable exception to all their social pronouncements and a window on the fast-paced world on which they had turned their backs.

Since leaving Greece in 1953, Denys Sharrocks had remained Fowles's friend and confidant through correspondence. He taught English to the apprentices at a Huddersfield technical college. In 1955 Denys accepted a teaching post in Indonesia through the Columbo Plan, taking with him his wife, Monica, and year-old son, Michael. Despite his own unsuccessful interviewing for positions abroad, Fowles argued with Sharrocks that "the current picaresque, the restlessness" that took him overseas was "foolish . . . all part of the great post-war emancipation of the individual."[65] Nonetheless, John Fowles carried his friend's heavy suitcase and enviously saw him off on his journey to Malang.[66]

John and Elizabeth were slower to warm to Monica Sharrocks on first acquaintance. In May 1955 she was only twenty-four, to Denys's thirty-three and the others' twenty-nine, a mother for one year, a wife for two. A former actress from the provinces with a working-class background, Monica was "ambitious," then a difficult thing for a talented young woman to be. Fowles called her "wilful . . . sensitive . . . easily hurt; full of suppressed and repressed drive towards self-expression. One of those persons struggling to be better than she is, yet up in arms at any attack" (a description easily applied to Fowles himself). She offended Fowles's traditional notions of femininity by disagreeing with his opinions. There was also tension between Monica and Elizabeth, who treated the younger woman with "a kind of mother-in-law jealousy, full of sneers and cutting remarks."[67] In Monica Sharrocks Elizabeth was confronted with a woman who shared many of her own insecurities about class, education, and the future. Yet despite the upheaval of an overseas move and uneasiness over career ambitions, this determined girl was packing up a child and following her husband into an unknown place at the very moment Elizabeth was racked with guilt and indecision over returning to Roy and Anna. In a relationship that later blossomed into a profound, even sisterly friendship, Monica and Elizabeth started badly.

Elizabeth had no close women friends at this time, beyond cordial relations with coworkers. She had dropped the old Birmingham cronies and fallen out of touch with Anne Mitchell. Alone among her old London circle, she and Fowles saw Alan and Jean Kemp, as John liked playing his recorder at their musical evenings. Besides staff gatherings for St. G.'s and the annual dance for Heal's, the couple kept their social distance. Fowles spoke of his job "as an absurd joke" at private parties with "people who are on the climb," where conversation was "built round the question of 'What do you do?'—with implications. 'Are you any use to me? Are you worth impressing? Is your job better than mine?'"[68] Watching associates and coworkers enter into affairs out of boredom, John and Elizabeth felt grateful for their own relationship. Dining in the homes of married friends, they often felt depressed by their vision of the conventional dullness they associated with "normal," bourgeois marriage. Fowles thought matrimony would have no effect on them but wished to marry legally for Elizabeth's sake.

While adhering to his time-consuming teaching schedule and living with Elizabeth in a single room, Fowles still struggled to write. His years in the "waiting room" were an intensely resolute apprenticeship. By the end of summer 1955 he had revised *An Island and Greece* and delivered it to Paul Scott. Though the agent's reader criticized it as "shapeless, discursive," Scott himself thought it worth trying with publishers, and Fowles revised once more.[69] By January 1956 three publishers had turned it down. Fowles's concern for the fate of *An Island and Greece* became a nagging constant of his emotional life, alongside the other personal pressures.

The "discursive" style remained a problem, for Fowles was determined to write engaging works presenting the existentialist issues he had so labored to define. He had little respect for writers who wrote with facile elegance but had nothing to say. Style without substance, he thought, was "the modern rococo." The characters of Kingsley Amis, for example, were "profoundly unreal," ugly, lacking in "moral depth."[70] Americans like Philip Roth, Truman Capote, and John Barth wrote "quite cleverly . . . economical, professional. They say nothing." Fowles, with his vision of a literature of philosophic ideas, believed that "slick competent writing for writing's sake . . . is very trivial. Rococo."[71]

He struggled to put his ideas into dramatic form, writing plays based on his own experience and personality. He worked on *The Passenger* from December 1954 to February 1955, finished *Theseus* in September 1955, and began a play titled *The Explorer*. By mid-November 1955, he had completed a second draft of *The Young Man*. In 1956 he was working on *The Deceiver*. Spoken style was very difficult, he complained. When his characters dealt in ideas and abstractions, it was hard to make them "something more than epigrammatists or mere sock intellectual-play characters. To endear them to the spectator."[72] *The Passenger* he abandoned after Elizabeth had read it and hated it. "She used all her adjectives . . . worthless, cheap, nauseating." Sadly, he agreed. He himself found *The Explorer* "polemic, heavy." He was tormented by doubts, felt "inarticulate . . . blind groping," while "style, any kind of style eludes me."[73]

While the Hampstead plays do not survive, Fowles's obsession with convincing conversation is evident in the masterful dialogue of his later fictions, filmscripts, and stage translations. At the time it was also apparent in the dialogue-rich stories scribbled in a hasty, nearly illegible hand in St. Godric's exercise books. He typed the best of them on the reverse of college assignment sheets and examinations, energetically editing with black crayon and by cutting apart and repasting.

The long short story, "For a Casebook" (1955), for instance, reflected Fowles's philosophic beliefs, as well as his artistic doubts, sense of insignificance, and the grinding material circumstances of his daily life.[74] An unsuccessful writer (like Fowles) is a voyeur who watches a younger, struggling writer and his "bohemian" lover (like Fowles and Elizabeth Christy) in the adjacent building through opera glasses. He writes the young man a letter of advice and observations on the state of society and literature, which he never sends. His horror of his own sense of nothingness, or *nemo*, at last moves him to self-annihilation, first obliterating his physical identity, then committing suicide. Like *The Collector,* which was to follow it by some years, this is a case study of someone mentally in extremis who commits a deranged act. The piece was rejected by *Encounter* and the *London Magazine*, but Fowles thought it important enough to preserve.

Fowles reacted enthusiastically when just such a trapped, destructive character appeared on the London stage in August 1956. He responded to Jimmy Porter, the protagonist of John Osborne's *Look Back in Anger,* as "a seriously democratic personality" who sees "the futility and mess of life" and protests his entrapment, "walled in by shoddy brick buildings." The play was a "warning notice . . . demolitions about to begin . . . and death to all the old verbal and mental clichés of the London stage."[75] But while *Look Back in Anger* gave voice to what Fowles thought was the legitimate resentment of a marginalized, hopeless generation, it also celebrated an uneducated, inarticulate antihero. Fowles himself, by the time he wrote *The Collector* five years later, was thoroughly fed up with "the 'good' inarticulate hero . . . whose inarticulateness is presented as a kind of crowning glory." Fowles's monstrous protagonist, Clegg, would be "inarticulate and nasty."[76]

In this way frequent visits to live theater influenced Fowles's education in dialogue and ideas. But Fowles was even more moved by the cinema he and Elizabeth took in each week at the Everyman in Hampstead. Fowles's experience was made more immediate and direct because he was now so shortsighted that he had to sit in front in the cheap seats. The screen took all his vision, and he had "to live the film." All around him, the groundlings reacted, gasping aloud at every action: " 'E's fallen over the bannisters!' . . . 'E's killed her!' "[77] Fowles tried to analyze the power of cinema to move so easily, raising more emotion than some of the greatest written art. Even more than at a stage play, the audience became engaged in an immediate participation. "One plunges, in a film," he wrote, "into a past dream-scream." Perhaps the physical situation of cinema going was part of the reason: "Size of figures on screen . . . Looking up, not down . . . In-escapability of screen." More important were the range and mobility of the camera eye, "the sudden power to change subject or the angle; so that one's attention can't stray," the emotional revelation made possible by the close-up, the demands for subtlety and realism in the acting. "The camera-eye," he mused, "means that the cinema-actor must be realistic, since a film cannot be anything but uneasily fantastic."[78] Fowles would welcome the day when his books were translated into film, but he also longed to write directly for the screen.

The "waiting room" of "this interminable desert" also educated the apprentice writer intellectually through his always voluminous reading.[79] It was as seminally rich a reading period as Fowles's three years at Oxford. In the Hampstead years, however, Fowles was guided not by any authority like Merlin Thomas but only by his own taste, which he now began to discover. There was, first, a renewal of his deep love of words in and of themselves. He read his way methodically through the *OED*, "missing nothing." Reading old books and pamphlets, he often copied an archaic word or phrase into his diary, turning it over and over like a solitary shiny stone in the beak of a magpie. *The Greek Myths*, by Robert Graves, was his first organized encounter with classical mythology, and he found "each myth and its explanation like a poem."[80] He read Freud, Jung, Adler, Karen Horney, and other classic psychologists. He read Albert Einstein, though the mathematics was a struggle. "I can just distinguish the huge shadow, like a mountain in mist, of his theories," Fowles wrote, "but continually, one is face to face with the incredible."[81]

The most influential source for Fowles's reading in this period, and so for his future novels, was Norman's bookshop, just off Heath Street in

Hampstead. Francis Norman was "a bluff, awkward, friendly second-hand bookseller with a mind like a jackdaw's nest and a shop which must rank as one of the dirtiest, most disorganized and lovable in North London."[82] Fowles later remembered him as, "behind his shyness, a very distinguished scholar, a delightful man, a prince of booksellers."[83] Norman's prices varied according to his mood. He practically gave his wares away to this local teacher, John Fowles, whose quirky tastes and voracious appetite for books must have impressed him and who was, by this point, nearly as shabby as some of the secondhand volumes in the shop. Fowles loved to lose himself in Norman's almost windowless back room where the more interesting books were kept, retreating there to be completely isolated and to make discoveries among the strange, oddly as-sorted books from the past. In Norman's Fowles began to learn his own tastes and desires, beyond the set texts of his university education. He began to savor books as "documents," writing, "More and more it is psy-chological, sociological, anthropological, historical value that I seek . . . bad books are often more 'valuable' and amusing than good books. A bad novel of 1857 tells one much more about 1857 than a good one."[84] He treasured "prayerbooks smelling of incense and paper"[85] and volumes of French history riddled with bookworms ("nothing could be cleaner than the holes they make").[86] He bought, for extremely low prices, copies of eighteenth-century and nineteenth-century journals like the *Tatler* and the *Edinburgh Review*, volumes of third-rate poetry, the sanctimonious biography of an American child poet, sensationalistic eyewitness ac-counts of the French Revolution, a forgotten French novel titled *Ourika*, chapbooks of music for stage plays of the late eighteenth century, collec-tions of long-forgotten plays, a monograph on the painter Rossetti, or-phaned volumes of encyclopedias, masses of tattered novels . . . an endless list of historical and literary detritus. He felt, when the generous Francis Norman let these things go for pocket change, that the book-seller was "mad to let such a book leave him so cheap. As if he sold Lon-don, 1709, for 6d,"[87] or that he had "the year 1815 for 3/6, this time."[88]

Part of Fowles's joy was his sense of wandering, as the sole initiate, in lost worlds, imagining and experiencing those books that had been neg-lected, forgotten, buried by time. Through these strange, vivid books he discovered in himself "this power of plunging back into the past; but not in the usual sense—this is a stepping out of one line into another parallel line." Pastness was "only an illusion." Experience in time, actually, was simultaneous, "all parallel." He felt that he did not merely read the biographies and hagiographies, but "relive[d]" them. He felt himself "growing out of time," finding his pleasure in "old books about realities" both "very beautiful" and "terrible." In his imagination, these reading pleasures were also "smashingly cinematic." "One recreates," he wrote, "according to the visual media of one's time. I . . . cinematize these past disciplines, words, words, I swim in the film of them."[89]

By the end of 1955 John Fowles had reached a kind of crisis of despair in waiting. It was a particularly bad midwinter. He and Elizabeth fought. There was no money. They both were ill for weeks with flu. At Christmas he felt estranged from his family and mean because he could not afford decent gifts. *An Island and Greece* was rejected by another publisher. Approaching his thirtieth birthday, Fowles was sick at heart—from the strained relationship with his parents, from the endless difficulties of his love for a married woman, from the "poverty I have condemned myself to," from the "badness of my writing," from "the meaningless of life."[90] He entered a curious state of will-lessness that lasted about six months, into the summer of 1956. He complained constantly of having no energy, of being passive and paralyzed. Though he actually wrote a great deal, he accused himself of being lazy and unproductive. He felt "exiled" from himself.[91]

In January 1956 one of his old pupils from the Anargyrios School passed through. Kokolakis was full of gossip and memories, and after his departure, Fowles felt a violent nostalgia for Greece, like a squall hitting him, a mood "of memory and desire."[92] For weeks afterward in "bitterly cold weather: grey skies and a continual scruf of falling snow," Fowles dreamed every night of "green islands and South."[93] Roy Christy allowed divorce proceedings to begin. The detective visited them for adultery statements. Fowles spent his thirtieth birthday with his parents, sad and silent, unable to speak about his life with Elizabeth. Elizabeth herself got "more and more neurotic at Heal's" while John bought a guitar they could ill afford and spent his time playing his recorder and composing "little Bartoky pieces of music." She called him a "dilettante." He ignored her, yet abandoned both a novel and a play he was writing. He drifted, feeling depressed and lost.[94]

Yet for all his sense of will-lessness and heartsickness in the late winter and spring of 1956, Fowles was writing something entirely new. It was a new Greek book, although it began with an incident in Norway. By the time he finished it, more than seven years would have passed and the alchemical process of writing would have absorbed and transformed into universal narrative the characters and events of the last five years of Fowles's life. He changed the title at least three times, rewrote it over and over, but the world read it as *The Magus*.

By late March 1956 Fowles was typing up a polished eight-page untitled fiction based on his own experience at Noatun, Norway, in 1949.[95] Overall, the episode is similar to the published form that appears in *The Magus*. Maurice Conchis, young and steeped in rational materialism, goes to Noatun to study bird calls and, like Fowles, is deeply affected by the mystical qualities of the silence and solitude. There is a literal vision of "pillars of fire," corresponding to Pascal's *feu*, that saves the life of Renoen, the warden facing blindness, and transforms Conchis's life. Conchis tells this story a quarter century later to the young visitor to his villa on a Greek island. The "ghosts" of Renoen and others appear, and "Lily Montgomery" is romantically present. An emotionally overwhelming vision of the pillars of fire appears to them all as they look out over the Aegean Sea, accompanied by an unearthly, hypnotizing music until the "inhuman power and strangeness" made "the night . . . dense, ringing, shimmering with sound. The sky, the sea, the earth, the pine-forests were rich, pervaded."

Even as Fowles was progressing with this narrative, he continued to complain about his "chronically will-less state," his "kind of paralysis," which held him a psychological prisoner. He abandoned work. He saw a "bad film about Ulysses" and "found the Circe sequence oddly powerful." It described his current state, he thought, writing afterward that he felt "completely incapable of leaving the shore of this enchanted island." But by mid-May of 1956 Elizabeth had had quite enough of John's psychological will-lessness. She picked a stormy fight with him that, "like all storms," cleared the air. For the first time "objectively," Fowles became conscious and self-aware of his repeating pattern of withdrawal from emotional commitment and self-induced failure just at the point of achievement.[96]

Fowles was surprised that he had "never seen this great Freudian truth about myself before" and recalled his solitary, lonely adolescence, when he had become "self-sufficient . . . as Crusoe-like as could be. I don't need to make contact with the outside world, because my inner world conquered me before I could begin to think independently." He decided that he had "to break out of that fortress . . . leave the island."

But, he continued, he had to do it in terms of "the inner enchanted-island me," his own unique psychology. "I could only escape on a raft of island materials; it is the island which must help me to escape from it. One cannot escape from Circe without Circe's help."[97] The metaphors Fowles used to describe his psychology—the island, Circe enchanting Ulysses, the lonely, self-sufficient man trapped in himself, the fortress—all adhered to the narrative he was writing, forming its structure, shaping its meaning.

It is just as true to say, however, that Fowles was consciously able to realize an important truth about himself because he was creating metaphors that yielded up that truth. Because he was writing about isolation on an island, he was able to see clearly, perhaps for the first time, how the metaphor applied to his own psychology and his own behavior. This surprised recognition often repeated itself as Fowles wrote his new book. He had been working on the manuscript nearly nine months before he recognized the deep parallels with *The Tempest*.[98] It was September 1964 when he at last saw, through writing another draft of *The Magus,* his own oedipal pattern of rebellion against the male authority figures of his life. "As I write now I realize that the whole theme is strongly Oedipal," he said in surprise. "I never saw this before."[99]

More than Fowles telling the story, the story told Fowles who he was. This sense of discovery through the workings of an active imagination in the story itself was Fowles's experience in writing the book. This self-discovery and transformation are also the experience of Nicholas, the protagonist of the novel, as he more and more actively becomes aware of his own psychology and the consequences of his own behavior through their reflection in Conchis's stories. Shortly after the May 1956 quarrel with Elizabeth and his first conscious experience of this self-discovery, Fowles changed the title of his manuscript from *The Joker* to *The Magus* (at first *The Magos*). While the joker in the pack is the unpredictable wild card, "the magus" in the tarot deck is the sign of the great alchemist of the soul, the card of personal transformation. Elizabeth, always such a severe critic, loved this book from the first, feeling from the beginning that it was "a great novel."[100]

To Elizabeth and her difficult, demanding love, John Fowles gave the credit for what must have felt like an emergence from despair and stagnation. He ceased to talk about being in a desert or a waiting room. Instead he wrote her love poems in which he sees himself as earth made green and fertile by being turned violently, plowed by the harrow of Elizabeth's persistence and loyalty.[101]

The divorce decree freeing Elizabeth Christy from her marriage to Roy Christy was handed down at the end of 1956. Fowles immediately wrote to his parents about Elizabeth but then was afraid to send the letter. He passed another Christmas at Leigh in silence. But at the end of February 1957 he returned to tell Robert and Gladys Fowles of his plans to marry Elizabeth Christy. To his surprise, "they were as mild and pleased as kittens." He wondered if he "had been silly to hesitate so long."[102]

To the couple's joy, the flat immediately next door to their bed-sitter at No. 55 Frognal fell vacant. There was a large sunny room facing west and a little bedroom with a double bed. "A separate bedroom," Fowles exulted. "And the doubleness of the bed." They redecorated, staining the floor and painting the walls white, pale gray, and frost green. They framed reproductions of paintings and ransacked the junk shops of Camden Town and Kentish Town. Beginning a lifelong avocation of rescuing and refinishing old furniture, Elizabeth showed a keen eye for orphaned but beautiful objects. She also selectively picked up Heal's "seconds." They moved on March 2, 1957. Typically, "the upheaval" made Fowles ill. Elizabeth, thrilled, excited, happy, handled the move.[103]

The night before Fowles's thirty-first birthday Roy Christy tried to break them apart for the final time. He insisted that Elizabeth must talk to his new psychoanalyst, and Elizabeth, feeling guilty and upset, thought she should. She and Fowles quarreled through the night, making up just in time to catch the morning train to Leigh. So, on March 31, 1957, John's birthday, Elizabeth met Robert and Gladys Fowles again. John's father was "nervous," almost comically gallant. His mother, John sighed, "talking, talking . . . meals, meals, meals. . . ." He felt "a kind of retrospective guilt" because his parents were "very kind; excited, planful, inexhaustibly planful." They were "like greedy children . . . try to swallow E. whole."[104] They gave the couple fifty pounds as a wedding gift, more than a whole month's salary for John Fowles.

The elder Fowleses were not at the ceremony late on Tuesday morning, April 2, 1957. Nor were Elizabeth's parents, her daughter, her sister, or John's sister present. The wedding was as solitary and secret an act as John Fowles could make it. The only witnesses were Alan and Jean Kemp. No one at Fowles's college was informed. Indeed, the original registry office appointment was for April the first, but since that was All

Fools' Day, Fowles feared publicity and changed the appointment to the next day.

The wedding day was "a grey day, a grey day, but mist-grey; and the mist cleared when we went off." Elizabeth had dressed with care "in a pale yellow-green suit, olive shoes, an eggcustard-yellow hat." Fowles was relieved that "noone saw us; we slipped in." The registry office was "a sort of board-room with canvas and steel tube pile-chairs; a large gilt basket of faded flowers; two men, one rather bored and beery, the other suave. . . . Outside a tired little garden, and the chimney of the hospital furnace gently smoking in the pale blue sky."

The ceremony was a "silly little ritual, so short, so empty." Fowles paid the 11/3 fee, and then the newlyweds took the Kemps to the nearest pub for a drink. It was all "fundamentally unnecessary," he thought, because "marriage won't alter our relationship." And yet, and yet . . . when they had hurried "home to our nice new flat, and a nice good lunch, and Asti Spumante, and the sun in the room," Fowles had the "feeling that it is good to be married," that it was "a sort of symbol, a crowned, sealed look-wehavecomethroughness."[105] John and Elizabeth Fowles had no wedding gifts for each other. That evening, however, he wrote and gave her a poem:

> *There were six yellow tulips*
> *By the new green wall.*
>
> *That was not all;*
> *The sun did shine.*
>
> *The day was yours, was mine;*
> *Was ours.*
>
> *The unexpected sun,*
> *Six yellow flowers.*[106]

He called it "Epithalamion," which is the traditional wedding poem for a bride.

CHAPTER TEN

A Writer Unpublished

Hampstead: 1957–1962

ENGLISH TEST

Punctuation

ghosts are not the misty ethereal things of popular imagina-
tion said Conchis they look like real people they feel like them
smell talk and even as youve just heard walk like them I cant ex-
plain now but I think youll understand forget the footsteps I
know she's here I dont have to hear her pass shes here I think
that at this point I began to be frightened I shifted my chair as
silently as possible so that I could see the door onto the terrace
Conchis lit his pipe in the flare of matchlight his face seemed
masklike ominous he smiled
shall I go on
I cant understand about the steps
you think its a thief perhaps
how could but I was not able to finish my sentence

—ST. GODRIC'S PAPERS, 1962

On an afternoon in early August 1958 John Fowles stood gazing at the
Ashridge manor house once more. Beside him were Elizabeth, his wife of
sixteen months, and Fletcher, his colleague from St. Godric's who had
driven them on this outing. Ashridge was silent and deserted, the College
of Citizenship dead, the School of Management not yet born. The three
walked through the peaceful, well-kept gardens and the enormous, empty
house. There was "not a soul . . . a terrible soullessness in everything." But

the silence of the uninhabited estate was haunted, for Fowles, "by those girls; Sally and Sanchia, and the rest of them; all the noise of a big evening there, two or three hundred people—and the gardens." The gardens and the girls were "a sort of love labyrinth; a labyrinth like the Minoan ones, like the maze-dances—it is impossible to say what their real significance was." Fowles felt acutely "a kind of deep myth . . . still there, still living . . . as if it had only happened yesterday, as if it was still to come."[1]

Through months and years after his wedding, Fowles wove this myth into the oft-revised manuscript titled *The Magos*. Although he labored on other projects, the characters from this book curled invisibly around him like smoke. This story was the shadow sliding alongside his ordinary round of work and home. In all his writing he had continued to live "on those two years in Greece . . . an incredibly rich meal."[2] Now he combined them with the "deep myth" of the Ashridge year to tell of the transformation of a man called Robert Urfe, his own middle name, his father's first name.

The swelling text was also shaped by the events and objects of Fowles's daily life, by people he met and, especially, by books he read. Books about masked dance, ancient ritual, and Paleolithic man all adhered to the tale. He reread Robert Graves's *The Greek Myths*. Conchis's memories of Ypres were partly derived from a "staggering" description of that 1915 battle in Henry Williamson's *How Dear Is Life*.[3] The powerful effect of Robert Foulkes's *An Alarm for Sinners*, a 1679 pamphlet lent him by Francis Norman, inspired an entire episode.[4] Fowles continued reading deeply in modern psychology, particularly Freud, Jung, and Adler, while recording and analyzing his own dreams. He was stirred by major London exhibitions of Picasso, Braque, and Modigliano during 1956 and 1957. A carving of an Indonesian fertility goddess given Fowles by Denys Sharrocks on a visit from the Far East became a disguise for one of the novel's masquers.[5] Only Elizabeth was not reflected in the early manuscript, for as yet there was no Alison Kelly.

Heracleitos, the sixth century B.C. Greek philosopher, influenced Fowles more than anything else he read. ("The power of his philosophy stuns me.") Heracleitos's theories of universal continuous change (expressed metaphorically by the element of fire), the tension of polar opposites (the war between and the underlying unity of pairs like love-hate, pleasure-pain, life-death), and the seeking of universal answers through self-knowledge all corresponded to what Fowles was trying to say in *The Magos*. However, to reflect the philosophy, he changed the title to *The Aristos*. By late 1957 *The Aristos* was to be an appendix, "Conchis's commentary on Heracleitos."[6] In August 1959, Fowles was still referring to the yoked text as *The Magaristos*. Fortunately, by April 1960 the two books were separate entities: *The Magus*, a narrative fiction, and *The Aristos*, a philosophical manifesto. These works made up the imaginative world in which Fowles dwelt, even as he maintained an outward life of unexceptionable, increasingly happy ordinariness. His two worlds were mutually dependent but operated separately, since Fowles could not yet bring himself to join his imaginative private world with his daily public self by the act of publishing.

Fowles's life was transformed by contentment within a few months of his marriage to Elizabeth. Though there were worries about money and sadness over Anna, life was "smooth now, rutted, placid, domestic. No sin, and not much guilt." John and Elizabeth were "grafted, indispensable to one another . . . with a curious equality."[7] By their first wedding anniversary Fowles marveled at how Elizabeth had acquired "a firm balance I never thought possible—an ability to accept, to shift the ballast, take the blows."[8]

The security of his marriage helped Fowles to partly repair the damaged relations with his family. He was more open with his parents, less secretive, and saw them more frequently. More important, however, Elizabeth's presence changed the chemistry among them all. Robert and Gladys liked her, and with them, no matter how John behaved, she kept up "a sort of sweet dutiful reasonableness."[9] She accompanied Robert Fowles on his shopping errands, holding his hand, as she had with her own father. She listened politely to Gladys's "floodgates of talk" till she felt "brainwashed."[10] She moderated John's behavior toward his mother by emphasizing her positive qualities. Toward Hazel, now a young woman, Elizabeth was friendly and interested.

Within two months of his marriage to Elizabeth, John found "a curious shift in my attitude" to his family. He still thought Leigh-on-Sea a "foul little town" and Fillebrook Avenue "a dreadful, monstrous cul-de-sac."[11] However, he looked anew at his sister and found her "refreshingly nonconformist," with interesting opinions and a likable personality. He worried lest she be swayed by the Young Conservativism of Leigh.

Fowles now liked, tolerated, and pitied his father. He enjoyed Robert's company, walking and occasionally playing golf with him. He laughed affectionately at his father's "worlds. . . . The world of high finance, jeremiads against Labour and anything that is likely to bring his shares down in price. The old officers' world."[12] While their conclusions mostly differed, the two men shared a common intellectual drive, philosophical commitment, materialistic logic, personal scholarship, secretive habits, a dry public persona, and a passion for gardening. Even as John competed with Robert, he identified with him intellectually.

John Fowles could not forgive his mother, however, still regarding her as "the great enemy of my adult self—the great vegetable mother—ignorer of arts, thoughts, realities, trampler-down of all my father's best qualities."[13] Gladys Fowles was "still the tyrant of any conversation," and John was sulky and "morose" around her, often refusing to meet her eyes.[14] Sometimes, as he observed her growing "bitter," he felt sorry for her. He knew his mother was innocent of ill intent ("She is not malicious, witty, evil, inconsiderate, catty, steely—she has the morals of a convent sister"[15]). Unlike her husband, however, Gladys was not intellectual. She wanted to reclaim her son's emotional attachment, and he resisted with all his passive might. She "slaved" when he visited Leigh. She cooked magnificent meals that dominated the schedule ("Chicken in aspic, wonderful pressed ham, beef hung as it never is today, till it is very, very faintly gamey, melting like butter"[16]). She delighted in reminding John of "trivial incidents from my childhood—she knows I hate this." He felt "retarded" by her intellectually, and in his diary accused her of standing, in his youth, "between me and girls, then . . . between me and ideas."[17]

In the Fowles family story, John was cast as a Richards, who looked like his mother's Cornish family and shared their obstinacy. John Fowles refused to recognize Gladys Richards's other gifts, but Elizabeth was more observant. In December 1961 she stayed alone with her parents-in-law while recovering from surgery. She wrote John of "incredible" afternoons by the dining room hearth, as his mother began to weave "a terrible void. . . . It is Family History—hers, or any ones. She weaves herself into a kind of spell. Words which express nothing, subject covered—no less than—Birth marriage, and death and remarriage." With her extraordinary memory for people's lives, Gladys Fowles, weaving herself "into a kind of spell," spun a web of words: "The whole complex pattern of generation upon generation."[18] She spoke words, unstoppably. John Fowles, whose most real life was lived on the page, wrote words unstoppably. His writings, as he relentlessly revised, took on force and shape and intellectual power. But in some sense, at least, his mother's verbal memory and unintellectualized emotions were a kind of wellspring for the verbal richness of John Fowles's imaginative fictions.

Fowles could not consciously accept that Gladys's gifts were a positive influence on his work, and to the end of his mother's life his relationship to her continued to be guilty, resentful, and confused. Within only a few years of this time, however, Fowles was formulating a psychological theory that male writers of fiction were motivated by a recurring obsession to recover the lost mother of infancy. Gladys Richards Fowles, speaking her floods of unstoppable words, burbling with unedited memories, adoring her son in spite of his growing distance, was this lost beloved mother. Only disguised and on the written page could Fowles acknowledge his love for her.

In his diary, Fowles often accused her of being "narrow." Gladys Fowles's life must have felt very narrow indeed. After years of semiretirement, her husband had fully retired from his London business and was, according to his daughter, "always there . . . always an old man . . . seemed old for years." Gladys's daughter soon entered a teachers' training college in London and was terribly missed. Hazel tried to encourage her mother's interest in painting, tapestry, basketmaking, and craft classes. Gladys complained that Robert resented things she did without him, "was possessive of her . . . would 'watch and wait.'" His constant, dependent presence was "quite restrictive." The couple argued. Whereas Robert had been the dominant partner, with his "sharp tongue" and set ways, Gladys became "harder" and "got the ascendancy in the relationship" as he aged. Robert never relinquished the purse strings, however, and kept his wife "on a very tight rein."[19]

The placid, predictable daily life Fowles enjoyed with Elizabeth extended to his workday. At St. Godric's Secretarial College he had achieved his own kind of balance. The school was "really a sausage-machine for exam results," and its lack of academic standing dismayed him. He realized, however, that while he might have found another more respectable and better-paid teaching post, the conditions at St. Godric's were the best to be had for the purpose of nurturing himself as a writer. Fowles had learned "the minimum of time I can devote to my present job without letting down the students or my employer." He had established a modus vivendi with Mr. Loveridge: "[H]e underpays me, but he doesn't drive me at all." So Fowles nurtured his "split personality," teaching to a satisfactory but not exceptional standard, then shutting out his work "when I shut the front-door coming home." He actually feared "more integration of my two selves," resisting any job that could "dominate one's life . . . turn means into ends."[20]

Moreover, Fowles had come to genuinely enjoy teaching. He liked his students, the "flocks of Greeks, the usual strange hybrids; Persian-Germans, French-Chinese," and all the other foreign girls.[21] They confided in him about their parents, their lives at home, and even their religious beliefs. They came to his office to talk about music, and some gave him gifts of recordings. Fowles liked the relationships but could be tough. In September 1958, he expelled from his classroom several girls caught shoplifting. At St. G.'s, Fowles was his "own master, I can teach as I like. I have no interference at all on the academic side."[22]

Both the Fowleses enjoyed John's congenial St. G.'s colleague Fletcher, as he drove them into the countryside in his car on weekends, shared pints with John, and made Elizabeth laugh. They also became friends with Lorraine Robertson, Head of the English Department. Lorraine was a warm, vivid, though often misguided, personality, an alcoholic, and very emotional. In 1958 she fell in love with one Cyril Charles, a "self-destructive relationship," Fowles thought. He recorded his own attempts to comfort her emotional distress in the 1958 poem "An Academic Moment."[23] In late summer 1959, Lorraine Robertson quit her job at St. Godric's to follow this lover to France. Calling at her cottage to say good-bye at the end of September, Fowles and Fletcher found her frantically packing in "a welter of whiskey, chaos, paper" and escorted her to the ferry.[24]

With Lorraine's departure, John Fowles found himself "Head, as they call it, of the English Department, as they call it,"[25] a promotion that loaded him with time-consuming petty details ("listmaking, timetable-twisting, reportwriting . . . dreadful organizing, everything-must-function-smoothly that I thought I kicked off after Bedford"[26]) for only a pound a week more after taxes. Still, his father congratulated him, and he himself felt pleased, chuckling at the thought that "Pretention lurks in me."[27] In May 1961 the salary scale was revised, and Fowles, raised to twice his former salary (now £1,445 annually), received a decent wage for his job.

For someone who claimed a minimal commitment to teaching, Fowles worked hard as Head. Between 1959 and 1962 he first evaluated the English department, then reorganized it. By the early 1960s he had ranked the examinations offered and recommended discontinuing some and expanding attention to others. He fought a temporarily successful battle to retain the set books of the literary canon, over objections from some colleagues. He also invented an elaborate system of four "streams" of student curricula—set out complete with charts and an appendix—that promoted and managed the regular intake of pupils on the basis of abilities and the passing or failure of the set exams. "This admittedly complicated system allows me to fit any kind of student, of any capacity, into the right group," he wrote to the staff in *Functioning of the English Department,* an in-house booklet he produced. Fowles also grouped the girls by their nationalities. Like a field naturalist making biological observations, he described each species and subspecies in his collection, generalizing and assigning categories of *"The types of foreigners we have to deal with."* Israelis were "noisy, undisciplined . . . and especially bad spellers." Europeans liked taking examinations, and the French and Greeks were domineering. All West Indians and Africans were interested only in secretarial work and "should always be on the Basic Course." Spanish-speaking South Americans were lazy, bad linguists, and of "low general culture."[28] As Head Fowles also was not afraid be unpopular. In the 1961 summer term he pressed for the firing of an unsatisfactory teacher. He accurately predicted his action would cause repercussions among the staff but acted on his conviction nonetheless.[29] When he left St. Godric's in 1963, he was a respected colleague. Another staff member told Elizabeth that what she would most miss on leaving the college was "J. Fowles and his lovely sense of humor!"[30]

When he shut the door of their flat behind him at the end of the day, however, John Fowles wrote. Much of his time was devoted to poetry, of which multiple revisions were an integral part of the process. He gathered the poems into three "sequences." There was the Greek sequence that was "ready," the Robin Hood sequence ("still shadowy . . . shaky . . . incomplete"), and "the rest, all lumped together, good and bad."[31] He revised these endlessly. In poetry, Fowles aimed "to find a way through to the heart," by which he implied that meaning was "as important as the words in which it is expressed." Treatment and technical issues were distinctly secondary, as Fowles looked for ways "to put pressure on words" by breaking up meter, suppressing "functionwords," and experimenting with punctuation.[32] He had no time, he declared, "for obscure verse; nor for the over-imaged and over-metaphored verse . . . nor . . . intellectual curlicues." He wanted his meaning and his feelings to be plain. He wanted "the real mystery, not the cheap mystery anyone can summon up . . . by evoking private symbols in a private world." When at last in 1962 he prepared the poems for publication, they carried the personal motto "Mystery enough at noon."[33]

He prepared the manuscript, but he did not seek publication. Fowles was now aware of this pattern in his life and alternatively chastised and defended himself to his diary. He admitted that his personality was reserved and withholding, that he was afraid of publication, public scrutiny, and possible criticism. He acknowledged fearing the "shame" of failure in front of his friends, his parents, even his wife. Everything he wrote was a "laying-bare of myself . . . because . . . my self is the only thing I really know. I think of my self almost as an 'it'—something separate from me." He also confessed to having "too much ambition," wanting only the best and being willing to wait for it. Most of all, he couldn't face the "climb to Parnassos"; he couldn't bear "the humble slog." Fowles wanted to write a significant book "immediately recognized as worthwhile," so that he could move in one jump from safe anonymity to public celebrity. Fame would bring him immediate "ecstasy at the top."[34] Years passed as Fowles continued "to live in the illusion of greatness." Sometimes, he admitted, he was afraid to look in the mirror.[35]

So semiautobiographical drafts like *The Adulterer,* a novel begun after his April 1957 wedding, and a 1959 "play about the young officer" stayed on the shelf.[36] One valued unpublished manuscript, begun in January 1959, was revised over many years. The theme of this novel, first called *Tobias,* was the *nemo* operating in the flawed relationship of Lorraine Robertson with Cyril Charles. Calling the novel, structurally "a kind of cubist assembly of fragments,"[37] in spring 1959 he renamed it *Tesserae,* Latin for the small glass or stone squares used in mosaics.[38] Conceived as a mosaic deliberately constructed of narrative fragments, *Tesserae* evolved from analysis of a friend's destructive love affair into a novel of his own early married life in Hampstead. Fowles kept the manuscript with him until at least the year 2000, exempting it from his archived papers in the 1990s, always contemplating its publication, and often dangling its title before interviewers who asked him about works in progress.

Meanwhile, after years of awkward unmarried isolation, "Mr. and Mrs. J. R. Fowles" were finally a socially acceptable couple. The gauche, unpolished woman of whom Fowles had despaired grew increasingly sophisticated at Hampstead parties and dinners. She must have worked hard at her accent, for she passed as educated, though it probably helped that tall, blond Elizabeth was beautiful and possessed a natural elegance. Yet there always lurked an irreverent, mischievous girl beneath the cool, careful exterior. The wide grin and sparkling green eyes, the slyly ironic comment, and the husky rich laugh rewarded those whom Elizabeth Fowles trusted. With others she had learned to beware. At a formal dinner given by the Loveridges, for example, she held her own seated between Sir Edward Crowe and the "wife of a power Fraser tory." However, when banished with the other ladies, "I did have an impulse to be Red, when the daughter of Crowe remarked in that ghastly cloying English . . . but you see in those days before the war I mean everyone throughout the whole of England had domestics. I mean there was the cook-general and two maids plus the daily, of course children were no problem . . . I felt like saying coldly, Madame my Father, before the war was actually one of the unemployed millions and picked his, rather other people's fag ends out of the gutter and I lived on a strict diet of bread and margarine, with the odd potato here and there for a hot lunch. However I sat and hugged at my brandy in a casual way and wore what I imagined was the correct expression."[39]

Elizabeth was now the bridge in relationships with others, for John Fowles was seldom one to enjoy idle conversation. Indeed, he dismissed random "pass-time occupations, such as work, play" as "sublimation," activities "harmful, or neutral, to our attempts at building a valuable, durable self." With such an attitude, social occasions could turn into clashing philosophical arguments. A hapless dinner partner who voiced the belief that there were "other-forms of knowing" beyond the ordinary apprehension of the senses put Fowles into a towering rage. "People who insist that there is something in every experience which is not apprehensible by physical means—that this 'other' experience is the important one, really do, now, infuriate me. The world is still so stupid, and has such dangerous toys to play with, that I feel violently about these things." Only the "enduring mystery," an elusive first-cause "external mystery at the beginning of the universe," could be respected as "the essential force in the otherwise static, lifeless mechanism of evolution."[40] After such arguments,

Fowles pitied the "provinciality" of people who could not overlook his faults, speculating that they were misled by "the voice" of his Oxford accent. Elizabeth exclaimed in exasperation, "They think you're arrogant and pontifical."[41]

Though politically left-leaning and vehemently anti-Tory, Fowles was little impressed with the material gains of the postwar world, either economically or technologically. When salaries were raised for his colleagues at St. Godric's, he observed how an inconsistent application of the new scale had created "jealousy, all the money-snobbism and hysteria of this 1961 world."[42] Television, which he and Elizabeth only watched to escape his parents' conversation when visiting Leigh-on-Sea, Fowles thought "unimaginably low in its standards, even in the socalled highbrow programmes." He despaired over "the printed word and the spoken word and the whole range of public word utterers from every field, and from Left to Right," who seemed to him "to be more and more double-talkers and vacuum-fillers." In all the media, everything, he chided, was "turned into a woman's page" by the "gimmick-craze, the new angle, the explain-craze."[43] Cellophane packaging became a symbol for everything dissociated from sincere reality in the modern world. Television, newspapers, ordinary language, "every bloody thing in subtopia" was cellophane ("the great God of this modern world—the window between man and externality").[44] Fowles longed in his own writing to "work to change the nation's psyche" with a "new simplicity, reality and sincerity in place of all this awful highbrow behindface-talk, this modishness, being up with the latest analysis."[45]

Fowles had few kind words for the "masses," ordinary people empowered by material rise in the 1950s to buy houses, cars, and other goods. He often spoke of "New People . . . lower middle-class at best . . . rankers risen in the war, shopkeepers and so on."[46] At one point, as he wrote and revised The Aristos, he toyed with suggesting that the voting age be raised to thirty and enfranchisement tests imposed, requiring certain levels of education to vote and a checking system of electoral colleges. He refused to blame individuals, however, since he believed that society had reneged on its obligation to truly educate. As a juror at the Old Bailey sitting on cases of rape, murder, assault, arson, theft, attempted murder, and manslaughter in May 1961, he thought the prosecution of those on trial "barbaric." The defendants were, he believed, "sick . . . mad" and would have been better served by "a panel of doctors . . . [than by] the high priest in a red robe with the terrible sacrificial knife of society-must-be-revenged in his hand."[47] In the chapter 61 trial scene of *The Magus*, he revealed the judges as just that, a panel of doctors.

The Fowleses most liked their own company. Because he knew the area from his days at Ashridge, John and Elizabeth often traveled by train or bus to Buckinghamshire villages and spent Sundays walking in the country. Their favorite walk was through woods and over fields around the town of Wendover. Having mastered English plants, butterflies, birds, and trees, Fowles became enthralled by spiders and the challenging "new world" their pursuit opened to him. It was, he wrote, "the very small world of the small insect—under bushes, deep in the undergrowth, beneath the mat, the green outer skin of plants. Where beauty is rarely more than five millimeters long."[48] When not exploring the countryside, they explored London. With Pevsner's *Buildings of London* and a street map, they rode the tube to a far section of the capital city to guide themselves on architectural tours. From Holborn to Islington, Bloomsbury to Clerkenwell, they examined churches, poked into tea shops, and delighted in streetscapes whether Regency or Victorian.

Fowles's other explorations were his substitute for hunting, a pastime deeply regretted, though left behind since the 1954 move to London. He had become a fanatic collector of New Hall china, first produced in 1810. New Hall appealed to Fowles as part of "the old green England," for the earliest issues were "never pretentious" and played "so many variations on the spring and bouquet . . . theme." New Hall craft was a "blend between peasant art and bourgeois elegance." But the thrill of the hunt outweighed his admiration. From his earliest days in London, Fowles went on scrounging expeditions to junk shops and antiques dealers. New Hall was, he decided, "the only pottery (porcelain) of its date that dealers still don't always recognize" and was "underrated aesthetically by all the experts."[49] Fowles loved the sense of hotly pursuing a specialized object and outfoxing the dealers. He speculated that "the exercise of catching" was "an archetypal thing with me."[50] A shop loaded with mostly undervalued cups and saucers, teapots, and milk jugs could send him into a mania, "a buying fever."[51]

New Hall china, treasured old books, rooted cuttings, jars of spiders, and a collection of cactus and succulents held pride of place in the new flat they took in the spring of 1959. Sensibly looking for cheaper lodgings after a rent increase at 55 Frognal, they found instead a flat not only more expensive, but in derelict condition. On Church Row, the oldest street in the village, No. 28 was a long rooftop flat in the canon house facing the approach to St. John's Church. The building was in appalling condition. The Fowleses' entrance was at the southeast Heath Street corner over a restaurant and required climbing three floors of dark interior stairway. But John and Elizabeth were excited. "To live in a 1720 house," he exulted, "and up in the sky, surrounded by roofs, gardens, vistas."[52] Borrowing ninety pounds from Elizabeth's mother, they gleefully moved into the "sty" in April. For months they stripped layers of paint and wallpaper, restored the boarded-up chimneypiece, tore out sagging shelves, and refitted doors and windows. They put in a coke-burning fireplace against the severe winter cold of the rooftop. They daily dealt with plumbers, electricians, and gas board inspectors and spent well beyond their budget. But No. 28 became, in Fowles's words, an "enviable flat."[53]

This was the Hampstead flat fondly recalled by those who knew the couple in the early 1960s. The Porters and the Paynes were regular visitors. The Sharrockses stayed there on returns from various overseas postings. Anna was occasionally allowed to visit, even—on rare weekends after 1961—to stay the night. John's sister, Hazel, often spent Sundays there while a college student in London. Elizabeth's sister Joanne and her widowed mother, Doris, visited. Joanne was awed to see the electric heating fires they had added in every room. The rooftop location was their particular joy. John and Elizabeth never tired of sitting out on the little terrace high above the street, enjoying the open sky and the treetops and roofs. In the distance lay the cityscape of London; closer was the open land of Hampstead Heath; nearer still the attractive prospect of St. John's Church. Fowles set up his telescope by the window, and Monica Sharrocks remembered how he used the clock on the church tower as his timepiece, checking it through the telescope. He also scanned the neighborhood with this telescope, watching the street life and occasional roof life. The "girl watching" incidents he documents in his diary led sometimes to angry words from his wife.[54] She was no longer made jealous by her husband's roving eye but could still be irritated by such behavior.

Like her husband, Elizabeth Fowles had also advanced in position and salary. She had changed jobs in the spring of 1958, taking a position in the records-keeping section of the Medical Research Council, conveniently located on Holly Hill in Hampstead. By September 1959, Elizabeth was supervising thirty-two other women. Allowed to choose her own staff, she said, tongue in cheek, "I must have a fringe of fringe-like intellectuals," and picked RADA-trained repertory actresses and university graduates (a sad commentary on the work available to educated women in 1959). Writing to the Sharrockses, she said, "O it has made a great deal of difference. I have little Jane Austen chats at one side of the room and then cosy ones with the old crew about ironing or their plastic curtains."[55] Overall, however, the work was dull. Fowles, as he approached his mid-thirties, was privately embarrassed that his wife still had to work. He tried to get her into a position at St. G.'s but was unsuccessful.

Resigning herself to her job, Elizabeth pursued other interests. She studied pottery making at the studio of a German émigré artist.[56] She wrote poetry, mostly for her own amusement or John's. Loving the theater, she thought briefly to take drama classes and become an actress. Reading Mary McCarthy's *Memories of a Catholic Girlhood,* she began a personal "collection of essays . . . on similar lines."[57] Lack of time, work weariness, and the absence of her husband's ruthless determination to write at all costs ended the project. What she really wanted was a family of her own.

Elizabeth had, of course, a child, whom she treasured but whose company she was often denied. Anna herself was old enough to form memories of the time.[58] She remembered her unhappiness living with the Berrys, her foster family after the Lohrs. Herbert Berry was a furniture maker who taught with Roy Christy at the Hammersmith School of Art and Design. He was kind to Anna, but Betty Berry was "horrid." There was a son, a little older than Anna. He had a huge room, the biggest in the house, filled with electric trains and toys. But when Roy gave Anna a dollhouse, Betty Berry made Anna give it to the poor girl who lived in the house opposite.

Until she was nearly nine, Anna attended a Catholic convent school. The nuns were kind and caring, and she always had the feeling that the sisters were watching over her. When Roy gave Anna a doll, Betty Berry made Anna donate it to the school's charity fete. A nun drew Anna out of class and said kindly, "Oh, Anna, do you really want to give this doll away?" Anna nodded yes but wanted to cry. Betty Berry did not take away a little book Roy gave to Anna, and Anna slept with it at night. Betty Berry, Anna said years later, "disapproved of my father and the whole situation."

Roy himself lived in his own flat on Cheyne Walk on the Chelsea Embankment, a "funny, little triangular building on the end," across from the boats, with a pub next door. When Anna was six, seven, and eight years old, she spent a lot of time sitting on the pub doorstep while her father was inside. When Anna pleased him with her studies or artwork, Roy was "*incredibly* proud of his little girl." But if she was not "quick and fast and sharp," able to do math problems in her head, for example, she was told she was stupid. When he was angry, Roy said things that were so "solid and fixed and set," so full of "terribly fixed disapproval," that she was "terrified." Roy often told his daughter how hard it was to have all the responsibility for her. Anna felt herself to be a burden.

Glowing in Anna's memory of the time was a very pretty lady, someone very, very special. Her name was Liz. She was not called Mummy, and it never occurred to Anna that Liz was her mother. Liz came to take her out several weekends a month, riding buses for an hour and a half to come from north London to see Anna in southeast London at Forest Hill. These were Anna's favorite days. Together they rode buses to catch a riverboat to Kew Gardens or Greenwich. They had picnics with sandwiches Liz had brought and tea from a flask. Sometimes they stopped for an ice cream or ate an omelet in a coffee bar. Once Liz brought a camera, and they took turns taking pictures of each other, sitting on the grass of a London park. They saw *The Red Shoes* in the cinema and *Peter Pan* onstage every year. Once in 1960, John Fowles joined them to see *Oliver!*, much to Anna's annoyance, for she hardly knew John and didn't want to share her time with Liz with anyone. The two walked a lot, and Liz listened to what Anna had to say. Then Liz would take Anna home, and Anna would wave her off on the bus. Sometimes Liz didn't come to see Anna. This was because Roy told her she couldn't and Liz obeyed.[59]

Elizabeth's anguish over the loss of her daughter continued. Fowles remarked to his diary that the guilt over Anna was "comfortably . . . suppressed," and perhaps Elizabeth did suppress it at home.[60] However, Roy's frequent refusals to grant her access to her daughter and the partings after a day's outing produced feelings of "disintegration." In April 1958, when John and Elizabeth had been married just a year, Roy "disappeared" for a while, moving without telling them where.[61] In desperation, since Elizabeth could not see Anna without Roy's permission, the Fowleses sought out Roy's German psychiatrist, Catherine Guinsberg, at "a horrid . . . seedy . . . brick block off the Edgware Road . . . icons, wood-carvings, a gilt crucifix; like a town priest's study." In a bizarre and upsetting interview, the psychiatrist accused Fowles of being "the obstacle" to Elizabeth's reconciliation with Anna and the cause of Roy's reluctance to part with his daughter. Why, she demanded to know, "hadn't we got custody of Anna? Didn't we want Anna as a tool to cement our marriage? Were we happy (surely not)? She would say nothing. It was not my concern. She must see E. Neither of us was to see Roy." But when Guinsberg asked if John and Elizabeth would take Anna, they both replied yes. Did they want her "for love or conscience sake"? "For love," said Elizabeth. "Conscience," thought John.[62] Yet he had reached a point where he would have willingly supported custody for Elizabeth's sake.

The following July, in 1959, Roy Christy married Judy Boydell. He brought her to meet Elizabeth beforehand, and the three spent "a somewhat strained but pleasant and amicable time" at a pub one evening. Elizabeth was "taken aback by the nice simplicity of the girl and really did feel she was a nice easy kind of person." Anticipating the incredulity of Roy's old friend Denys Sharrocks, to whom she was writing, she described her former husband as "so altered . . . I feel he is an elder brother of R. Christy of ten years ago. The nonintellectual, rather naïve, kindly thinking elder brother." Yet Roy's narrow, moralistic side was intensified by his new relationship, and he was judgmental about any "single offbeat . . . remark." Elizabeth watched him grow "hurt and worried" when she spoke lightly or irreverently and found him "not very easy for me to be with."[63]

On a summer's evening Roy took Elizabeth and eight-and-a-half-year-old Anna to see the cottage in Putney that he was converting before the wedding. Anna was "madly keen," exploring the weedy garden and picking a posy of golden rod. "I love these sorts of places," she said. "She was as complete a creature as one could ever imagine," Elizabeth wrote of her child, "All innocence and wholeness, surrounded by the derelict garden and what must be one of the most derelict of childhoods. I am sure it was not illusion, and I hope it wasn't, that at least she had so far come through. She was quite delighted with the whole business of Roy getting married and saw it as an end only to a baby. This will be useful for the baby, she said, and dragged up an old tin bath from beneath some tattered golden rod." Afterward Anna escorted her "special friend" Liz to the bus stop, cheerfully singing "a tuneless rendering of various catholic songs" and enthusiastically waved her off. "And I sit on the top of the bus," wrote Elizabeth later, "in a kind of breathless choking despair, for a time I feel I shall never reach reality. I stay suspended and discon-nected."[64]

Roy's wedding, his fourth, was, Elizabeth informed the Sharrockses, "a grand 'do' at the bride's home." Elizabeth was not present but tele-phoned later to offer congratulations: "And my golly I meant every word . . . Roy settled at last and long may it be so."[65] Her absence was felt by Anna, who was "made a fuss of" by the wedding guests, but kept having "this feeling that I know there's someone missing." It never oc-curred to the child that it would be inappropriate for "Liz" to be at her fa-ther's wedding, and she recalled "searching through the crowds for that other figure, that beautiful woman, not being able to understand why she wasn't there."[66]

Roy's marriage did provide Anna with a settled family life for the first time, and the new stepmother was a blessing for the child. Anna, who as an adult remained close to Judy, described her as "very warm-hearted."[67] When her own two children were born, Adam in 1962 and Rachel in 1965, Judy Christy included Anna in her love and attention. The new Catholic school to which Anna transferred in Putney was the opposite of the gentle, caring place the girl had attended while living with the Berrys. Anna was unhappy and frightened, and it was Judy who intervened and insisted that her stepdaughter be moved to a "normal primary school . . . a relief." Judy was herself a painter and a potter and she encouraged Anna's emerging interests in drawing and sewing.

Yet Judy also had, in Anna's words, "been painted the blackest picture of Liz and John . . . and she had to support Roy."[68] She was often placed in the position of making the excuses for Roy's refusals to let Elizabeth see Anna. John Fowles would intervene when, for example, a "distraught" Elizabeth was forbidden to see Anna before Christmas in 1960. "Drunk!" Fowles raged after he had spoken to Roy, "at his diabolic worst; a sort of cosmic meanmindedness."[69] By the following year the Fowleses were reg-ularly begging for Anna (now eleven) to be allowed to come stay with them for a few days or a weekend. Roy and Judy refused, John character-izing the meeting as "they were the Russians and we were the Americans. White-faced 'niet' on one side and indignation on the other." John Fowles thought Judy "a bit of wax for Roy to put his Victorian seal on."[70]

Roy's jealousy and disapproval also made his attitude to Anna's rela-tionship with Elizabeth "pretty brutal." The girl learned to suppress her elation after seeing Liz, especially after Anna had worked out that her 'friend' was her mother. Roy was "moody," angry. He was the one, he would tell her, "given the burden and the responsibility of bringing me up . . . *she* left." Now, he complained aloud "it was all treats, it was all going to the theatre and the cinema. Eating out." Yet meals "out" were picnics or an omelet in a coffee bar. Liz could not afford to give her daughter presents. "Still," Anna recalled, "she had a way of making it special. Just her presence and her attitude and the simplest things we did." At these homecomings, Judy was nervous and shy and found Roy's anger difficult to cope with. Anna "felt incredibly uncomfortable."[71]

It is probably not coincidental that within days of Roy's marriage, John and Elizabeth began to try to start a family of their own. In 1959 Elizabeth was thirty-four years old. The death of her father in February 1958 had affected her, leaving her feeling "closed up as if a telescope had rammed together, my 33 years in it" for a year after Edgar's speedy passing from cancer.[72] By August 1959 the Fowleses were living in the new, larger flat at 28 Church Row, and John was about to become Head of the English Department with a little more pay. Now Roy had married, settling Anna in a nuclear family that did not include Elizabeth and denying her more visitation time. Elizabeth brooded and sighed. It was time for a baby.

They were "dubious and semi-comical" about it at first. Fowles mused that in a "novelist's view of the business . . . you decide to have a child and go headlong into it—perhaps headlong is not the right word—also with calculation, financial and physical. But we have left it in hazard . . . begetting . . . half by accident, perhapsing a child." Fowles himself wanted a baby for Elizabeth's sake; she so longed for a baby. He also wanted to please his father (not his mother), feeling strongly that Robert Fowles "wants us to have a child," though the elder Fowles never spoke of it.[73]

Eighteen months later, however, Elizabeth had not conceived. Sad and desperate, she visited a fertility clinic in March 1961 and was told that "the fault (anatomically) is with her."[74] Two months later her condition was diagnosed. "We've looked it up in a gruesome book: 'Diseases of Women' from the library," wrote John. Postpartum infection after Anna's birth in 1950 had left the fallopian tubes obstructed and the fimbriae damaged. Elizabeth was informed that the condition might be corrected by a salpingostomy, which would reopen the fallopian tubes, but there was "only a 1 in 4 or 1 in 6 chance at the end of it."[75]

Fowles supported her decision to have the operation, though he wrote that if children were impossible, he would not mind. "It's all one with the greater exile; and a love that has to be nourished by children is not my sort."[76] Sometimes, he admitted, he lay sleepless at night, thinking about it. "But I'd swap the paternity of all the children in the world for five years' freedom from earning bread and butter."[77]

Frightened but determined, from November 22 to December 8, 1961, Elizabeth was a patient at a run-down National Health hospital near the Angel pub in Liverpool Road. She was thirty-seven. She went almost eagerly to surgery. Fowles meanwhile was ill with sympathetic pains, could not sleep or concentrate, lost the thread in conversations, and read through the night "like a drug."[78] Two days later a young Church of England curate appeared in the hospital to preach a sermon on sin. He thundered at a ward filled with women who had had hysterectomies, fibroid tumors, a tubal pregnancy, Elizabeth's salpingostomy, "and several other delightful complications of female reproductions area." Saddest was a cancer-stricken former governess of ninety-one, who softly repeated, "God, help me to die," over and over in her "cultured voice," wringing Elizabeth's heart.[79] The curate admonished these "sinners" to ask for forgiveness, then charged them to sing hymns. Wrote Elizabeth many years later: "If anyone of us had had the strength—we, or one of us, should have kicked him in the balls . . . since which time I have a total horror of all things Surgical and religious."[80]

John saw the surgeon's report two days later. "Virtually hopeless," it read. "Bitter sadness," he wrote, "because the operation was apparently not successful—the Fallopian tubes are too heavily encrusted to be made patent." Elizabeth cried. John returned to Church Row that night to drink "too much whiskey" and write letters to their friends. Characteristically, Fowles put his grief on paper. "UnEnglish letters, too revealing," he wrote curtly on rereading them the next morning, and tore them all up.[81] He tried to be philosophical and found it worked "ominously well." He felt angry against fate for a few days, then decided he didn't really care about children. Perhaps, he thought, what he really felt was "relief."[82]

It was typical of Fowles first to pour out his unspoken feelings on paper and then to deny his emotions to himself as well as to the world. In later years he spoke positively to interviewers of being "free of the responsibility of children."[83] He always acknowledged Elizabeth's infertility as a tragedy *for her*. However, his own denied sorrow went underground, into his work, reappearing in his writing in ways of which he himself was not always conscious.

Fowles was writing two novels, virtually simultaneously, at the time of Elizabeth's operation in 1961. The first was a failure. Bearing the working title *Poitiers Novel*,[84] this unfinished semiautobiographical work was Fowles's last attempt to use his diaries nearly verbatim to tell a story, as he had done with past manuscripts like *An Island and Greece*. The widow of a novelist accidentally killed quite young has discovered the missing diary (or disjoints) of her husband's year as a teacher in a provincial French university. This novelist (another Fowles double, variously called John Twinny, John Temple-Jones, and John Corcoran-Jones) had published a series of minor, forgettable novels in a passé movement called new classicism. Like a reverse mirror image of John Fowles, Twinny had elected to pursue the logical and dispassionate in art and the "lack of lyricism" in love, rather than the "warmth of heart . . . more spontaneity" that would have made him a great writer. His widow's description in her extended prologue of those "rigid and elaborate novels of his, where every character seems like a puppet brilliantly near to life—but not living—and every situation is petrified" recalls Fowles's contemptuous references to modern literature's "new rococo." The missing diary of 1951 supposedly reveals why a talented young man of feeling and sensibility had evolved into a writer of "arid precision and . . . intellectual remoteness." He had betrayed the passion and trust of his French lover from his teaching days, and with the guilt and loss, the heart had gone out of him.

The diaries themselves made this novel unworkable. With mere name changes, Fowles used his own Poitiers diary from 1951 and the affair with Ginette Marcailloux for John Twinny's lost disjoints. Unfortunately, of all of Fowles's personal journals, that of 1951 shows the diarist at his most "priggish": selfish, shy, icily reserved, self-absorbed, stiffly superior, harshly judgmental toward others, although Fowles's unwritten memories of Poitiers may have been much more tender. Through these diaries, the novel's theme of discovering the hidden, lost life of a once warmhearted, passionate young man is completely unconvincing.

Furthermore, the voice of the unappealing young man of the diary section of the *Poitiers Novel* is completely overshadowed by the voice of his widow added as the prologue ten years later. Penelope is an engaging narrator—wistful, ambivalent, ironic, and complex. She is simply much more interesting than the putative protagonist, because by 1961 Fowles had become a much better writer (not to mention, a better human being) than he had been in 1951.

After the failure of this experiment Fowles never again used his undigested diaries in a novel. Although it is clear from these attempts that he had originally thought of the diaries as grist for the mill of his fiction, in the future he always presented his diary keeping as no more than the writer's exercise, "great practice for the novelist . . . like a barre exercise for the writer."[85] Indeed, when he came to read back through his diaries in 1961 and 1962, Fowles was shocked. "Fantastic outbursts of priggishness, of vanity, of expectations," he groaned. "The temptation is to suppress such blemishes. But that defeats the diary. This is, and always will be, what one was." He was glad he had kept them so long but wished that he had paid more attention to people and events and had spent less time recording thoughts and ideas.[86]

However, at the same time that Fowles was incorporating his own diaries into the failed novel, he was successfully writing a journal-based narration using entirely fictional diaries. This new work, *The Collector*,[87] is structured identically to the *Poitiers Novel*. Frederick Clegg, the narrating kidnapper, directly addresses the reader and claims to have discovered Miranda Grey's diary. This is followed by the captive girl's diary, which is, among other things, a record of personal transformation. For Fowles, the diary format was supple and familiar. He had, after all, been telling a story in diary fashion for many years.

Fowles had begun *The Collector* at the end of November 1960 in a time that felt claustrophobic, "stale . . . too safe." Elizabeth could not conceive. Roy withheld visits with Anna. Only days earlier John had once more seen off Denys Sharrocks and his family to another overseas posting. He was annoyed with Denys for avoiding England by leaving for Laos. But Denys remained "the one male person who never bores or irritates me, and with whom I actually like being," and Fowles missed him. Elizabeth, now better friends with both Sharrockses, was "envious" of the "new world" they were going to.[88] Fowles began writing about a feeling of being trapped and fell into his story.

Fowles's story of Frederick Clegg, butterfly collector, lottery winner, psychopathically repressed romantic, who becomes obsessed with an art student, Miranda Grey, kidnaps her, and holds her prisoner in the underground cellar of a rural cottage until she dies immediately excited him.

He felt from the first that this was the book that would finally make it into print. For some time Fowles had searched for the right vehicle for the theme of his social convictions, the predicament identified by Heracleitos: "the intelligent trapped in the world of the stupid." The collector himself, he wrote, "is to symbolize the mediocrity of our present society; the girl he kidnaps stands for its hope and its vitality, pointlessly and maliciously crushed."[89] Clegg was to be one of the "New People," given money and power in postwar England, but not the education or morality to do anything but destroy the best of an older tradition. Fowles declared that Clegg would be "inarticulate and nasty, as opposed to the 'good' inarticulate hero." Miranda would be "articulate and intelligent . . . clearly a better person because she has had a better education. The story would "attack the money-minus-morality society (the affluent, the acquisitive) we have lived in since 1951."[90]

Several sources inspired this disturbing novel. Béla Bartók's opera *Bluebeard's Castle* had impressed Fowles deeply when he saw it a few years earlier. A highly publicized late-fifties news incident had remained in his mind "in which a young man kidnapped a girl and kept her for several weeks in an air-raid shelter at the bottom of his garden. He forced her to dig a pointless hole in the ground inside the shelter; he made her work in her underclothes, but there was no sexual intercourse."[91] However, such "sources" as these that he was willing to acknowledge publicly only reverberated powerfully in Fowles's imagination because they echoed his own erotic fantasy life. He wrote, but suppressed from publication, how "From puberty until recently I frequently had conscious fantasies, or noctural day-dreams, about imprisoning women underground," imaginings not stopped by his "very happy marriage." The "girl kidnapped" always fell in love with her captor, and the imprisoning was always "a forcing of my personality as well as my penis on the girl concerned." He analyzed many situational variations, including: famous women, such as real princesses and film stars; the harem; the threat, but not execution, of flagellation with a whip; the selection board, where he chose several girls from a crowd of candidates; and the kidnapper-as-fellow-victim scam.[92] Fowles generalized that what aroused him in all of these was "the dramatic psycho-sexual implications of isolating extreme situations." For other writers and for filmmakers from Bergman to Antonioni, Fowles noted that "imprisonment was only the most extreme of a whole group of allied situations."[93] Despite recognizing the extent to which his longtime sexual fantasies inspired the story, Fowles regarded *The Collector* as very much "an exterior book, with nothing of us in it, except in a few superficial details." It was "refreshing," he thought, "not to write of oneself."[94]

Fowles wrote the first draft at top speed, getting down five or ten thousand words on Saturdays or Sundays or late on a workday's night. He wrote in "great gobbets, scene by scene," afraid to stop. When alone in the flat, he paced about, "whispering conversations, even acting them in a muted way." He was embarrassed by this self-dramatization and tried "to conceal it even from my wife." For the surface realism he so valued, he drew on Daniel Defoe, "that supreme master of the fake biography." He felt Sartre's and Camus's influence in "countless things." For Miranda, he consciously drew on the psychological evolution of Jane Austen's heroines and on the girls in novels by Thomas Love Peacock.[95] But "the most fertile source" for the appearance and personality of his twenty-one-year-old art student heroine was his own students from St. G.'s and Ashridge, a twist to the Bluebeard fantasy he only acknowledged in the diary. "Once I used to 'kidnap and imprison' 'generalized' girls— archetypes," he wrote. "But for many years it has had to be someone I know—students."[96] He finished the first draft in less than three months.

He showed this version to Elizabeth in March 1961. Reading, she took "the attack on the uneducated to her heart . . . and resented it." Fowles groaned. "I can't get her to realize how symbolical it is intended to be. Platonic. Gold against lead. Of course, like everyone else today, all her sympathies are for the leaden-souled." He saw the book in Heracleitean terms: "the Aristos is in Miranda, the Polloi in Clegg; and the Polloi are . . . stifling, murdering by not . . . striving to keep alive, the Aristoi."[97] But Elizabeth saw in John's character Clegg people from a background like her own. Despite his confidence in the novel, Fowles let the book rest for nearly a year.

Elizabeth was recovering in Leigh under Gladys's care from the November 1961 surgery when Fowles, alone in the Hampstead flat, wrote a revised second draft. He made two significant changes. First, he rendered Clegg, "the monster," impotent. In the earlier draft, Clegg had had sex with Miranda, but now he was depicted as unable. "It makes for better symbolism," wrote Fowles; "now even his evil is passive, seedless." Second, Fowles "much elaborated" Miranda's death, drawing out the details of her pneumonia, writing with "a medical dictionary at my elbow."[98]

He found both changes very "difficult to write," and they demonstrate how Fowles's fiction grew out of his emotional life. Written within a month of Elizabeth's operation for infertility, the revisions reflect John Fowles's struggle to absorb the recognition of his own childlessness (his "seedless"-ness) and to recover from his fear that his beloved wife would die during the surgery. Outwardly Fowles seemed to have adjusted to his sadness over Elizabeth's infertility. Characteristically, however, he had internalized and suppressed his feelings, only to have them pour into his work, reshaping his fiction. In the experience of writing, it was the characters themselves who demanded the changes. Clegg and Miranda had become "intensely real," existing "independently of me." Fowles found that they would "reject" some of the things he tried to make them say and do. "I have to search and search," he wrote wonderingly, "until I find exactly what they would do and say" as if they were playing the children's game hide-and-seek. Now it was these characters, not the longed-for child, who emerged from "the womb" and were "born."[99]

Elizabeth put aside her misgivings about the book, but Fowles was wounded by another opinion. In March 1962, as he prepared a third draft of *The Collector* for the typist, he allowed Fred Porter to read it. "Up to standard. Publishable," snapped Podge curtly, and said no more. "Plainly his silence means 'it is bad, but I'm not going to say so,'" Fowles noted with hurt feelings, musing that his old friend did not like "to think of me as doing something well. To think differently from him." While his personal friendship with Porter continued, Fowles never again showed him unpublished work. Not that he blamed Podge. Not even "publishers, readers, or contemporary critics" could like this book, thought Fowles. But he brimmed with "inexplicable confidence." It was "complete, it says what I want to say . . . could be improved, no doubt; but it's like a poem. I *know* the backbone is right."[100]

Paul Scott had given up being a literary agent in 1960 to begin writing his brilliant *Raj Quartet*. Mrs. Shirley, Fowles's typist at twenty-one pounds for the manuscript, recommended James Kinross, of Anthony Sheil Ltd., and on May 4, 1962, Elizabeth delivered the typed manuscript to its Grafton Street offices. Less than a fortnight later Kinross wrote to congratulate Fowles on "an extremely well accomplished feat of characterisation" that was "extraordinarily promising, in a spine-chilling sort of way."[101] Kinross sent the book to the prestigious literary publishing house of Jonathan Cape. He spoke of "film possibilities." Fowles, basking in Kinross's praise and compliments at their May 18 meeting, "couldn't help smiling with pleasure."[102] Yet even as his hopes soared, Fowles was suddenly anxious about public exposure. He wrote to Kinross immediately after their meeting to request that *The Collector* make the rounds under a pseudonym. The mask John Fowles chose was a compound of the maiden names of his wife and his mother, "Richard Whitton."[103]

It was John Fowles's last moment of pure anonymity. On July 4, 1962, Kinross wrote excitedly that *The Collector* had been sold to Jonathan Cape Ltd., enthusing on the distinction of becoming a Cape author and its exceptional list and reputation. Fowles pasted the letter in his diary and scrawled below it, "One doesn't quite believe it when it comes."[104] Two days later he went to meet his future, in the person of publisher Tom Maschler.

CHAPTER ELEVEN

Straight to the Top of Parnassus

London, Greece, New York: 1962–1963

I too have felt like Cinderella all this week. A play could be written on Cinderella at the ball; and not have a child's line in it. But all glitter and anxiety.

—JOHN FOWLES, *DIARIES*, SEPTEMBER 21, 1963

He was something of the wunderkind of British publishing, this Tom Maschler. His earliest memory was of the Nazis confiscating his family's home in Germany. After escape to England, his father had made a name in British publishing. Tom Maschler's own star had risen from age twenty-one, when he joined Andre Deutsch. From an editor at MacGibbon & Kee, he was tapped by Allen Lane in 1958 as fiction editor for the young, innovative paperback reprint house Penguin Books. In 1960, still in his twenties, he became literary director at Jonathan Cape, one of Great Britain's most respected imprints. Although he already published talents like Doris Lessing and Joseph Heller, John Fowles would be the first English writer Tom Maschler would publish throughout his entire career from the very first book.

The Collector arrived virtually unheralded, and Maschler was electrified. He had never read such a well-written first novel. He found it "moving," "extraordinary," and "amazingly written for a first novel."[1] He and James Kinross agreed on terms immediately. Cape would pay an advance of £150 against royalties of 10 percent to 3,500 copies, 12.5 percent from 3,500 to 7,000, and 15 percent from 7,000 to 15,000, a handsome sale for a first novel in 1962 Britain. Given the book's plot, Maschler harbored concern that public libraries would hesitate to buy it, so Cape was granted 10 percent interest in any stage or film rights.[2]

To the "grand premises" of Maschler's richly paneled Bedford Square offices came John Fowles on July 6, 1962, wearing "a rather dirty macintosh, quite shabby-looking . . . a slight shambles." The young editor was so impressed with Fowles's manuscript that he asked straight off, "Is this the first book you've written?" "Oh, no, I've written others," Fowles replied, admitting to nine or ten other novels. "What?" exclaimed Maschler, "Cover to cover? What did you do with them?" Fowles said he had sent one out to two publishers and shelved the others. Maschler reeled. It confirmed his sense while he reread *The Collector* that this was a writer who would probably go on to write "*totally* other things . . . completely different. And much more ambitious."[3]

Fowles was usually guarded at first meetings. But he found Maschler "an intelligent frank tall Jew," not as charming as Kinross, but more trustworthy and with sharper instincts.[4] Whereas he had resisted Kinross's suggestions for his manuscript, Fowles listened carefully to Maschler. Unusually for a first novel, they "hardly changed a word in the whole book."[5] But Maschler urged Fowles to increase the suspense by shuffling a mere four pages so that Miranda's diary was "cut . . . into the monster's narrative . . . when she is just clearly beginning to be very ill."[6]

Maschler coaxed Fowles out of his recently acquired pseudonym, "Richard Whitton," by encouraging him with his own optimism for *The Collector* and Fowles's future work.[7] He assured the soon-to-be-signed author that he was likely to be published in the United States and should hope for film and even stage prospects. Excited, Fowles moved swiftly. In less than two days he had turned around the requested changes. When Maschler assured him by return post that indeed, he was serious regarding film opportunities, Fowles sent him, that very day, a film treatment, including notes about camera angles, sound track, narration voice-overs, and potential problems.

Success had its disappointments, however. On the July day the contract with Cape was being drawn up, Fowles told his father that a novel he had written had been accepted for publication. All of Robert Fowles's "petit bourgeois fears came tumbling out. . . . I must 'get a good lawyer,' would it affect my job? Was it wise? . . . not one word of congratulation or pleasure." For the rest of the weekend neither father nor son mentioned the book.[8] When Robert actually read *The Collector* six months later and tried hard to encourage and offer good wishes, his response must have wounded his son. After disclaimers about his inability to judge modern novels and a fair compliment about the "very good plot," John's father turned to the characters. He admired the psychology of the "unhappy" Clegg. He was bewildered by the girl and doubted that he should ever understand women like her. Most painfully, however, "the artist fellow"— George Paston, whose opinions transform the captive Miranda and is John Fowles's mouthpiece—Robert called "a type of historical nastiness, and I despise him to the extent of failing in lavatory language to express my views." Without comment, John Fowles pasted his father's criticism into his diary.[9]

By July 21, when the contract was signed, Fowles was "jumpy, anxious, can't concentrate, can't write, can't sleep."[10] In August his alternations between euphoria and anxiety continued on holiday with Denys and Monica Sharrocks. John had a month's use of a colleague's flat in Rome, while Denys was willing to drive his Ford across Europe and around Italy, on condition of a rest and a beer every two hundred miles.[11] The others took immediately to Italy, while Fowles found it "soft" and "too warm," criticizing Italian colors, Italian taste, and "over-decorated" Italian cathedrals.[12] Rome disappointed him ("vulgar," "brutal"). St. Peter's was "ugly, lying there like a monstrous lobster with its colonnade always waiting to clutch one into the black maw of the Great Catholic Lie. . . . It brings out Dissent like a rash."[13] Fowles had sudden attacks of anxiety that fire would destroy his manuscripts during his absence from London.[14] On one occasion he so roughly refused to shop for sandals with Elizabeth that she was left shaking, weeping to Monica, "Half an hour, that's all it would have cost him to make me happy!"[15]

Yet Fowles wrote several tender, evocative poems in Rome at this time, happily returned for future visits, and even considered living there. Episodes of irritation with his companions were balanced by delightful shared times, for the Sharrockses were eager to see and try all, churches, museums, restaurants, gardens, and woodlands. They toured Florence, Piacenza, Siena, Montepulciano. Besides a memorable day spent at Horace's Sabine farm at Tivoli, the best of the shared journey was a drive to Tarquinia, where the Etruscan tombs touched them all with "the simplicity, the absolute freedom with form . . . art flowed direct out of their fingers' ends, continuously, a sort of invisible umbilical chord [sic] between artist and artefact."[16] On the way to Tarquinia, they swam at a deserted beach.[17] Years later Fowles recalled the friendship and harmony of this incident in the chapter "Tarquinia," an epiphany among Daniel Martin, Anthony Mallory, and the two sisters who love them.

In England that fall Elizabeth and John Fowles worked together to cut and revise *A Journey to Athens* once more, emphasizing the melancholy portrait of the narrator's too-knowing generation, victimized by the forced conformity of the war during their teen years and, as adults, "ghosts" cast adrift from belief and optimism into a kind of individualistic exile. Retitled *Between*,[18] it was quickly rejected by Tom Maschler as a "young man's book" that would spoil the effect of *The Collector*.[19] Kinross agreed that publishing it would be "disastrous" and damaging to his new reputation but that Fowles should save the characterizations "for something much stronger."[20] Fowles confessed to "the second-work shakes" over the rejection.[21]

Fowles had spent the previous fifteen years dreaming of his own literary celebrity. Now that *The Collector* was about to become public, however, he felt "stripped naked before a crowd."[22] He was mortified by the first slick jacket blurb, presenting him as a reformed butterfly collector amid his "old books and china."[23] He needlessly worried that the cover of *The Collector* would look like an Ian Fleming novel and was relieved and excited by Cape artist Tom Adams's trompe-l'oeil design. He was also alarmed and confused to find himself a valuable commodity pulled between his agent and his editor.

Maschler had thrown himself into promoting *The Collector*, essentially shouldering Kinross aside. He brought the book back from the printers to show it to a producer from the British Lion film company. He upped the size of the first British edition twice, eventually to an unprecedented eight thousand copies. By January 1963 he had sold the British paperback rights to Pan Books for an English first novel record of thirty-five hundred pounds. In October 1962, Maschler and Kinross raced to send the book across the Atlantic, with Maschler hoping to offer it to Simon & Schuster, and Kinross getting it to Little, Brown first. ("It's in New York, that's all we know," wrote Fowles uneasily.) Eventually, Little, Brown bought the book for a hefty thirty-five hundred dollars, "apparently well above the average." To Fowles, his agent and his editor competed in "a no-holds-barred."[24] Elizabeth called it a "slanging match," adding slyly, "They think up such lovely names for each other these dealers in literature."[25] Kinross sniffed that Maschler was "a bagman, he ought to be flogging cigarettes round the Brandenburger Tor." Maschler urged Fowles to let Cape act directly as agents, for a smaller percentage of American deals. Kinross didn't understand the book, said Maschler, and "doesn't know who the hell you are."[26] To Elizabeth, this was all "killingly funny."[27] But Fowles scrawled alongside one of these diary entries: "like a man with a cut leg in a sea of sharks."[28]

Fowles was also dealing with the deeply personal matter of their childlessness. Just before Elizabeth's thirty-seventh birthday a new surgeon at the fertility clinic told her the previous operation had been "wrongly done . . . all might have been well if *she'd* done it in the first place." *This* was what came of expecting successful surgery through the National Health Service. The chance of favorable outcome was now "minute," and Fowles tried to dissuade Elizabeth from a second attempt. However, Elizabeth needed to know for "certain that a child is forever impossible," and Fowles bowed to her insistence as "an existential . . . brave decision . . . as real and almost as valuable as a child."[29]

Elizabeth's October 5, 1962, operation at the private Florence Nightingale Hospital in Lisson Grove must have been the first major expense the Fowleses incurred after the sale of *The Collector*. "Eliz," wrote Fowles wistfully, after helping her register, "in her Chanel suit and red glass beads, looking so fit." It was October 4, the day of a major rail strike, and between visiting hours, Fowles wandered heartsick through empty, silent streets, in and out of art galleries—where the pictures seemed to have no structural coherence—and cinemas—where he caught random snatches of newsreels and cartoons. The operation was no more successful than the first. [30]

Some months later, John wrote his own disappointed sorrow into a poem, "The Rain Took the Road This Winter," in which, guiltily, he traces the "living stem" of his ancestors, which "stops in me." His forebears "do not understand . . . this dying of their hope." The poem ends:

> *Twice from a window in my heart*
> *I have heard gatherings in the street*
> *And seen mysterious faces stand*
> *Grim witness to the house's hurt.* [31]

By the time Elizabeth was recuperating at 38 Church Row, the world at large was also grim witness to the Cuban missile crisis of October 1962.

On the surface, all London joked about it, tossing off what Elizabeth called "sick humour . . . typical of the particular brand of schizo behaviour of the English." "At St. Godric's Fowles explained how this part of Hampstead was tilted to receive the maximum blast. . . . I suggested a notice to be put up: 'Owing to the end of the world today, there will be no classes tomorrow.'" John's jokes, Elizabeth reported nervously, "almost cleared the college single-handed."[32] Yet he was deeply conscious of "the hysterical anxiety that underlies everything." Walking home along Fitzjohn's Avenue on a calm afternoon, he felt momentary panic that "at any moment the huge heat-blast would come, all the houses fall . . . the end of the world has seemed close these last few hours." Night after night he stayed late at the college, helping his frightened students put telephone calls through to their parents in Asia, Africa, Europe, and South America. Privately he raged over "the vileness of this world . . . the rottenness of all present political theories and philosophies and religions."[33]

During these autumn months of 1962—months of underlying anxiety about his book, publication, and public exposure, about the rejection of A Journey to Athens, about Elizabeth's second operation and the acceptance of their childlessness, and about the pervasive social terror generated by the missile crisis—Fowles expressed through his writing his sense of things gone awry. He was working hard on The Magos and revising The Aristos again. However, he also produced, through October and November 1962, a new poetry sequence in a "minor key." Sequence Four focused on "the macabre . . . the artistic employment of the morbid complex of images and ideas surrounding death." Fowles was fascinated by the "polar tension" between life and death, believed an attentive consciousness of death was what defined life, and had begun exploring violent death through his stories. Now, in these twenty poems, he used the grave to symbolize mental sickness, "from the unhealthy room to the perverted or narrowed mind and the totalitarian or otherwise pressuring society." The common theme was "the breakdown of love and of humanity," inspired by news items and murders of the day as well as by the Bible and the Roman poets Catullus and Martial.[34]

The disquieting images of Sequence Four have an eerie nightmare quality. Prostitutes slip out of clothes, then their skin and "black blood," to couple with clients as white bones. Little girls disappear. Disturbed, narrow-minded men (like Clegg) justify their savage murders of women by saying, "She asked for it." Predatory men lure girls home, murder them, and fold the bodies into cupboards, into trunks in the loft, or under the floorboards. Young women shudder as they marry rich old men. Unable to endure a breakup, a man murders his lover, then commits suicide in "the red wet bed." At the solstice, a pack of ten career girls hunt and murder a man in the orgiastic manner of the Bacchae. A swimmer, meeting mermaids in the moonlight, is pulled down to a shark attack. A man slips his hand under his lover's dress and plunges his arm into ashes and nothingness. The poems were rejected in February 1963 by both Tom Maschler and the Sheil agency.

Fowles, however, continued this exploration of the tension between the macabre and the life force in a short story. "Totentanz" (or "the dance of death") was eventually published in 1964 as "The Woman in the Reeds."[35] Two postwar Oxford students, a lower-middle-class boy and girl ("New People"), are punting on the river on a summer afternoon. They discover in the reeds a murdered prostitute, strangled with her own stocking and drowned, the body rotting and teeming with maggots. Alone later, the couple is changed, liberated by shock. Confiding her dreams of becoming a dancer, the girl dances before the boy. When she wraps a stocking around her neck, they are aroused to have sex for the first time. Although Fowles would later be embarrassed by the "amateurish effort," this image of the corpse in the reeds was the genesis of *Daniel Martin*.[36]

The Collector felt "real" when Fowles held the proof copies on November 20, 1962, and he wondered if he could afford to leave his job. His dilemma was resolved by the sale of the film option for *The Collector* to Blazer Films, a subsidiary of Columbia Pictures, working on British films.

Blazer Films was a producing partnership between two "Yanks," Jud Kinberg and John Kohn. Both veterans of films and live dramatic production for television in the United States and Britain, they had teamed up to produce English films under the aegis of a British–Columbia Pictures agreement. Their first film, *Reach for Glory,* about wartime tensions among boys in an English village in 1939, won both a British Academy Award and the Silver Sail at Locarno, Switzerland. The partners were seeking the second project of a three-film contract when Tom Maschler sent them the galleys of *The Collector*. "Read this quick!" exclaimed Kohn, bursting into Kinberg's office. The two producers saw the suspenseful tale as a tightly made "little black and white" film, both a thriller and a story with philosophical substance.[37]

John and Elizabeth Fowles met them at their Wigmore Street offices just after New Year's 1963. The producers were "taken aback." Fowles was nothing like the "don" they expected, a teacher at a Hampstead girls' school. Elizabeth, beautiful, stylish, husky-voiced, was "startling." Fowles saw two foreigners in gray cardigans, "earnest, sincere, and slightly obtuse." John Kohn asked John Fowles where he had gotten the idea for his story, and Fowles replied, "Oh, of course, you know." Kinberg suddenly thought of the famous newspaper story of the girl kidnapped and made to dig in a bunker. "Oh God," he thought, "we've bought a pig in a poke." But Fowles smiled confidingly, "It's every man's dream." Completely bewildered at his meaning, Kohn and Kinberg "breathed a sigh of relief."[38] By January 24, 1963, all film rights to *The Collector* belonged to them. John Fowles gave notice at St. Godric's College a day later.

Characteristically, Fowles escaped from the confusion he felt over new wealth and sudden success by writing. In the unfinished comic play *The Temptation of Anthony,* he struggled to keep his balance by satirizing himself as a self-righteous hermit tempted by a suave, worldly Satan.[39] A fourth-century Egyptian hermit, St. Anthony spent twenty years in a desert tomb, loudly protesting as the devil tempted him with seductive, demonic visions. This medieval hagiographic favorite obviously appealed to Fowles, who named several of his published and unpublished Roman Catholic characters "Anthony."[40] The temptations to which this Anthony is susceptible, however, are those that most tempted Fowles himself: to be a good preacher, to be a great writer, to be loved by other men, to punish evil, and to be better than other men. This last, "priggishness," St. Anthony acknowledges as his "worst" sin. "I have despised other men for not being as I am." He prays, "I humbly ask your mercy . . . and your help." The characters are sharply drawn, the dialogue is funny and deft, and the philosophic arguments are insightful. But Fowles left it unfinished. For Fowles, starting this play after the July 1962 sale of *The Collector* and resuming it in January 1963, a week after meeting Kinberg and Kohn, *The Temptation of Anthony* was more psychological refuge than publishing opportunity. The play itself was his hermitage. More and more, Fowles's writing became his sanctuary, his retreat. The greater his celebrity grew, the deeper became his ambivalence about exposing his private place of safety to a waiting world.

Money was at the root of much of Fowles's anxiety. Months before publication, *The Collector* was already a success. In February, for example, Little, Brown informed the author that they were doing the biggest first American printing since *Goodbye, Mr. Chips* (twenty thousand copies) and that the American paperback figure now exceeded thirty-five thousand dollars. All the new wealth from British book rights, American book rights, paperback book rights, and film rights made it possible for Fowles to quit his teaching job and devote himself to writing as he had always dreamed. Many of the things he and Elizabeth had gone without were now within their reach. She had already left her job and was house hunting. They discussed buying a car. But, he wrote, "it is like too sudden a change to a warm climate from a cold one—we still wear the clothes of the winter of our discontent."[41] They worried and argued. John finally had an overcoat and a new suit. Elizabeth had a new suit. They purchased some secondhand chairs and a coffee table. John bought himself a long-desired secondhand camera. But when he paid sixteen pounds for New Hall pottery, Elizabeth was furious at the "waste . . . wicked . . . non-practical" collecting. They quarreled over "this bread-alone view of life . . . a hangover from our poorer days."[42] Concerned that his money would not last, Fowles scribbled worried pencil calculation down the margins of his diaries. The accountant he consulted advised "employing Eliz to dodge taxes; and to claim for expenses for ten years back."[43]

Besides money, Fowles worried constantly over the progress of *The Magos*. In his sleep, he was visited by the characters, their eyes carefully avoiding him, "as if I (the living) were the one who did not exist."[44] He was indecisive about what to write after *The Collector*. He felt certain that "the professionals think it's a freak, a flash-in-the-pan." He thought people hated him if they avoided talking to him about his book but was shy of bringing up the topic himself. He alternated between praising Elizabeth's tactful support and complaining that she "doesn't seem to understand what this is doing to me."[45] He complained he had no one he could trust in literary matters, that Kinross was useless and the other Sheil agents were silent. "I need someone to take me in hand," he confessed. "I feel like an engine with no driver."[46] Yet when Tom Maschler phoned a week later with advice on not being exploited, Fowles was "atrociously" insulted that Maschler would presume to guide him on "the ideals of writing." In his nightmares, Fowles dreamed he was "pissing blood, a thick red stream." He dreamed he was "being drowned in a writhing sea of entrails. Endless heaving bowels and guts, pinkish-brown."[47]

The *Evening News* of March 23, 1963, ran a small notice on John

Fowles's sale of the film rights to his first novel. When the telephone rang four nights later, Elizabeth answered, and a girl's voice quickly said, "Wrong number," and hung up. The following day a letter saluted him, "All hail, hatcher of plots!" "No, no, no!" cried Fowles, as he read a puzzle about "a flying shuttlecock, a pattern of stars, a see-saw tree, a zany zoo-ramble, and an irate Admiral . . . weekend culture-vultures, ceramic dogs (spotted as the minds that made them), ghost stories in crypts, 'Edward,' birthday strawberries & cream, lessons on wild flowers and an elusive badger seen at the witching hour."[48] There was a telephone number. The writer was Sanchia.

Since his memory for details was so poor, Fowles went back to his 1954 diary and read it aloud to Elizabeth. While he wrung his hands, his wife wrote a poem and handed it to him. "Why this sudden fear" on receiving a 1963 letter that "seems to bear a postmark/1954?" she asked in the poem. The rest of "There's a Sting in the Tail" indicates both Elizabeth's secure confidence in John's commitment to her and how deeply she had absorbed Fowles's philosophy into her own beliefs.

Life has its meaning
In the moment
Beyond the present nothing
Can exist.
Reality we hold—
Is here.
Not back in time
Or times that are not now.
Then why this sudden fear?

The figure on the skyline
Waits.
One day you'll doubt
Look up and see
That reality
Is never held
But only imagined when it's
Past.
So why this sudden fear?[49]

John Fowles's fear was of reentering the fertile past and somehow diminishing its fecundity. He didn't want to see the "real" Sanchia again. She was a "ghost," like the characters in his novel; indeed, she was part of *The Magos*. He wanted her to remain "back there, in that strange other world at Ashridge; as in a glade in a beech-forest that can never be returned to."[50] Yet, with Elizabeth's encouragement, he decided to see the girl he had so worshiped in 1954. In mid-April he met Sanchia Humphreys again. She was now twenty-nine, "still with a girl's face, but with grey hair among the black . . . with the same odd easy-formal manner as if we'd last met yesterday." They walked for hours up and down Tottenham Court Road while Sanchia dramatically told the story of her past ten years. Fowles found she had the same "princess lointaine charm," a "unique . . . approach to life and . . . her extraordinary mythomania." She was still oblique, ambiguous, elusive, and fey. She reminded John of "the sort of young woman one reads about in Peacock—a sort of late eighteenth century amalgam of shrewdness and snobbishness and femininity." He felt a kind of sad tenderness but decided that his whole feeling for Sanchia "was, is, and always will/would be literary. Not real." Elizabeth was reality. So committed was Fowles to his wife that he had not "the ghost of a shade of Kierkegaardian anxiety—there was no choice to be renewed."[51]

The meeting energized Fowles's work on *The Magos*, however. He decided that in addition to Sanchia's considerable influence on the character of Lily Montgomery, there was a touch of Micheline Gilbert in Lily. "The Conchis-Lily relationship is Jullié-Micheline at Collioure—my situation vis-à-vis them," he wrote bemusedly, "Alison = Kaja. Perhaps that summer at Collioure is inherent in the psychological situation. It is not Spetsai at all."[52] Nonetheless, when *The Collector* was published, Fowles sent one of his few personal copies to Sanchia, cryptically inscribed, "Dig the garden!," a reference to Miranda's burial beneath the apple tree at the end of the novel.[53] He later sent Sanchia a personal copy of *The Magus* as well.[54] Fowles's relationship with Sanchia at Ashridge in 1954 stood behind *both* books and *both* stories of a possessed protagonist and his obsessive pursuit of a twenty-year-old girl.

However, John Fowles's commitment to Elizabeth/reality was now reflected as much in the text of *The Magos* as in his daily life. In early 1963, a little before the reunion with Sanchia, he introduced into the novel the character of Alison Kelly, who was recognizably based on Elizabeth.

Around the same time he changed the name of his protagonist from Robert Urfe to Nicholas Urfe. Without the letters *ch,* Nicholas and Alison are anagrams. "'All mixed up, but the better part of Nicholas' . . . six letters," as Alison says. Although the Alison character became deeply symbolic for the writer, standing for "reality" in opposition to "imagination," represented by the Lily character, Fowles did not put her into the book originally for symbolic reasons. He had "just a feeling that another girl character, sex interest, was needed in the first part." He was discovering, however, that fictional characters developed in an "organic" fashion—that is, "from outside my own invention." Alison "herself built herself up . . . into the real heroine of the book." She came to personify "my own now hard decision that reality and reason (the one in literature, the other in philosophy) are my faiths." Accordingly, as he was rewriting, Fowles began to change "the relations between Nicholas and the 'magic.'" In the mid-1950s draft he had tried "to carry on the 'psychic' pretence far too long." Now he abandoned the game early on. "The audience knows the magician is tricking them," he wrote, "but they still watch."[55]

Just as Elizabeth Christy had come quietly and peripherally into John Fowles's life in 1952 and, once there, had completely reshaped it by her powerful presence, so in 1963, Elizabeth's avatar, Alison Kelly, slipped unexpectedly into the manuscript of *The Magus.* Once written in, she began to alter the text, overshadowing original characters, renaming the protagonist, reshaping the assumptions of the novel and how they were presented. It is one of the great coincidental ironies of Fowles's writing life that at the moment in the book's creation when the character based on Elizabeth was growing, balancing, and finally overcoming the influence of the character based on Sanchia, Sanchia herself should reappear and contact him.

After nine years Fowles left St. Godric's on April 10, feeling satisfaction at his work and affection for his students, but no sadness. Leaving the teaching profession to write was a radical and isolating act. Fowles understood he was abandoning the social mask he had worn for the past ten years. "Now," he declared, "I am a professional existentialist solitary." He recognized that he did not easily make friends. "They all bore me," he wrote regretfully, "even when I like them very much. . . . Their minds don't work like mine, they aren't 'free' or 'authentic' in the sense I use these words." The only people Fowles could now talk to openly were his wife and "very old friends."[56] He had dropped most of those too, and the ones that remained were seen only occasionally. Denys Sharrocks was teaching in Leeds but was soon to take a post in Nigeria. Fred Porter taught in North Oxford. Ronnie Payne lived in London but was often abroad on assignment. The familiar names of Fowles's St. G.'s colleagues had vanished from the diaries by mid-May.

Among those old friends whom Fowles had recently left behind, primarily out of boredom, was Roger Hendry, the New College friend with whom he had shared a staircase, a sense of humor, an intense love of Beethoven, and many delightful hours of orchid hunting. As Fowles embarked upon his new literary life in 1963, he learned that Hendry, married with three children, was dying of rapidly advancing multiple sclerosis. At Christmas 1962 Hendry had maneuvered his wheelchair to his upstairs bedroom window and thrown himself out. Although badly injured, he had survived to "carry on with his living death" and "the pretence of still earning his living" for some months more. When *The Collector* was published, Roger "bought and read your novel and was apparently very proud of you." No records indicate if Fowles saw Hendry again after he learned of his cruel illness, but he had "great waves of guilt" over his neglect of his first Oxford friend.[57] This guilt, some of the Roger Hendry memories, and the suicide attempt of a dying man resurfaced a decade later in the character of Anthony Mallory in *Daniel Martin*.

The Collector was published on April 23, and the first reviews appeared on May 5. The Sharrockses, holding the gift copy Fowles had sent them, waited for the newspapers in excitement.[58] John's sister, Hazel, thought in amazement, "My *brother* wrote this." John's father began what would be several scrapbooks, meticulously kept with all clippings and reviews of his son's work.[59] The reviews were raves. The *Sunday Times* welcomed "a new writer of real originality . . . who, with a single book, establishes himself as an artist of great imaginative power."[60] The *Sunday Telegraph* put the book "in the little masterpiece class," adding, "The creative spirit against the Philistine's, life against death—the theme of Mr. Fowles's astonishing little novel."[61] The *Evening Standard* declared, "[T]his is a horribly brilliant little first novel, extraordinarily assured and taut."[62] The *Observer*, somewhat tepidly, said the book was "an intriguing study in warped sexuality" and had "cunningly worked suspense."[63] Fowles was aware that the reviews were very positive, yet it disturbed him that so many professional readers missed his philosophical point.

When the former literary editor of the *New Statesman* (writing for the *Evening Standard*) focused entirely on the sensational aspects of *The Collector* plot, Fowles wrote that "it makes me feel ill. Precisely the people I hoped would understand the true theme of the novel, will not."[64] Periodicals like the *New Statesman,* Fowles's favorite, ignored the book.

Fowles had "no pleasure from reading the reviews" in the week that followed. He was jumpy and distracted.[65] When Elizabeth took him house hunting, he became so disoriented that he was left quaking with what he felt was "existentialist nausea." He wrote, "I could not feel less like someone who has written a successful book."[66] Ronnie and Betsa Payne mentioned going on holiday to Greece. On a wet afternoon, barely a fortnight after the publication of *The Collector,* John Fowles and Elizabeth suddenly decided to go off camping in that beloved country of which they had dreamed for the past ten years. The most celebrated new English author fled England.

They were gone more than two months, from May 29 to August 2, 1963. They lost themselves in every sense, leaving behind deal making and contract signing, the "nervous miasma" of "being an author in England."[67] In Fowles's 126-page diary for the journey, there are only two slim references to *The Collector* and one oblique reference to *The Magus.* For the first six weeks they had no books and only rarely an out-of-date newspaper. They all but rejected other human companionship, preferring their own company or brief encounters with peasants and other wayfarers. They disappeared into their own mythic landscape, into the private world they shared, and reemerged so strengthened in their basic values that they would not be lured away by the siren song of bestseller sales and celebrity. The journey allowed Fowles to slip the bounds of the conforming life he had lived for ten years and begin the transformation to being "a true isolate."[68] It renewed his sense of personal exile and allowed him to give vent, at least in the privacy of his diaries, to a bottled-up misanthropy. Fortunately, the trip also nourished the best in him, his affinity with the natural and wild world, his sense of romantic adventure, and his ability to evoke observed details in the rich language of narrative.

Arriving at Piraeus on June 1, John and Elizabeth felt "as if we were last there a year, instead of ten, ago." But much had altered in a decade. The hotel where they all had stayed had been pulled down; "a lot of the other old endearing shabbiness had gone, too, exterminated by neon lights, prestressed concrete and plate glass."⁶⁹ Tourists, John found to his abiding disgust, were now ubiquitous. He was "full of rage at this dreadful new thing: tourism, destroyer of all it touches," and had no sympathy for these "New People." He deliberately misdirected an American who mispronounced *Acropolis.* He loathed the middle-class, middle-aged single-women tourist, "ghastly child of feminine emancipation and the affluent society." The sleepy little villages of his memory were full of tourist shops and modern buzz. Delphi was worse: "dusty, chocked with charabancs, so used by tourism that I knew at once that it had gone, so completely and totally as some ancient cities have gone under sand."⁷⁰ His anger at the despoiling of the land he loved made him confrontationally rude. When "ordinary Greeks" eagerly asked his opinion of "the same wretched places—Delphi, Athens, Patras," he told them, "Athens stinks, and Delphi ought to be atom-bombed and Olympia bulldozed off the face of the map." Fowles called his remarks "my little contribution towards making them realize that their country is being raped by commerce."⁷¹

At ancient sites overrun with the despised tourists, they traveled for several friendly days with Ronnie and Betsa Payne. Betsa had always struck them as moody, but during this time of close proximity she was pronouncedly melancholic. Her tears were silent, sudden, and mysterious. They deeply sympathized with Ronnie, "whose patience and gentleness with her seem unlimited," but were truly fascinated by Betsa herself, "as if she turned into thin air, like someone in Alice in Wonderland. There's a voice, very occasionally, a faint smile, but no substance. . . ." Fowles was enthralled, finding her romantically, "interestingly deranged." He was arrested at the moments "when her wistful brown eyes looked at one and too calmly found words impossible."⁷² Betsa Payne's mysterious melancholia was eventually folded into Sarah Woodruff's character in Fowles's novel *The French Lieutenant's Woman.* The couples parted company at Patras, where the ruins had been engulfed by holiday camps offering barbed wire, bad food, fake Tahiti grass huts, and souvenir kiosks. On June 5 the Fowleses clambered onto a ramshackle bus full of Greek peasants and a priest, waved good-bye, and headed toward the Peloponnese.

There John and Elizabeth reentered the timeless Greece of their memories—rough, wild, empty—where kindness and hospitality had a rare humanity. As they hiked or bused from village to village, they were helped to food and shelter by the village headman, or priest, or school-master. Troops of solemn-eyed children followed them everywhere. Along the coast local boat captains carried them to the next destination. Alone in open land, they took wrong turnings, occasionally were lost—once all night in the hills, where they slept huddled against the slope, with Elizabeth terrified to tears. They were taken in at monasteries and explored ruined castles. They swam in pure streams and on deserted beaches covered with tar dumped by freighters. They lived rough. Each struggled with a forty-pound pack, including sleeping bag. They had their shoes reshod with pieces of old car tires. Between them, they suffered dysentery, heat stroke, mosquito attacks, dehydration, and the occasional emotional sourness of the "Aegean blues."

Like the simple and beautiful hillside room in which they slept in the village of Dimitsana, they lived, in Elizabeth's words, "life cut right down to the barest essentials. No ornaments, no fuss, nothing."[73] After several days of shaving in primitive facilities or in streams, John let his beard grow, first for convenience, then because he liked it. His face was to be partly hidden by the beard for the rest of his life. Time slowed and nearly stopped for them. As they turned away from the world, they turned in-ward, toward each other.

They wandered the western Peloponnese for a month, back and forth among Dimitsana, Karytena, Kalamata, Pylos, Methone, Korone. In blis-tering July heat, they spent days on the top of Monemvasia in south-eastern Lakonia, a desolate medieval citadel on a thousand-foot rock attached by causeway to the Peloponnese mainland. Afterward Fowles chose to set Nicholas Urfe's awakening after "detoxification" in its silent bleached-bone ruins and cavelike cisterns. At Kythera he dreamed for three nights running "of England, of a Constable-like English landscape of massive elms across meadows under heavy thunderclouds—green shot with sun and rain," and on July 25 they began their journey home.

Traveling third class on the overnight boat to Piraeus, they slept fit-fully on deck among the other passengers. At dawn on July 26 they awoke "to see a long low island north, which could only be Spetsai." Just as Fowles was reluctant to see Sanchia again, so he was determined not to revisit Spetsai. He had to look, however, and from a distance saw it un-changed, as he wanted it to be.[74]

By extraordinary irony, while John and Elizabeth strained their eyes to see Spetsai lying a few miles off, Roy Christy and his family, including twelve-year-old Anna and baby Adam, were on that island. Yanni Korkondilis, now a ship's captain, had turned up in London that spring, warmly urging Roy to come stay in the family house where he had lived with Elizabeth and their two-year-old daughter. Evangelakis ("a shade portly, respectable") still played his guitar in the summers there, but now it was in the many nightclubs that enlivened the booming tourist trade. Roy told Elizabeth ("a note of defence in his voice") that Spetsai was better now for development "than before when it was a oneyed dead old place."[75] The visit must have stirred up smoldering memories, for soon, with far-reaching consequences, Roy Christy would write a "Greek novel" of his own.

After a brief two-month stay in London, from September 14 to 21 John Fowles visited the United States for the first time on a publicity tour for Little, Brown, his American publishers. "Christ this is an experience," he wrote Elizabeth when he arrived in Boston, "and I'm filthy sorry you didn't come along."[76] British newspapers were filled with such anti-American tales that they both had been convinced it would be "ghastly." Elizabeth even wrote, "I'm bloody glad I'm not there. Horror and nightmare it all sounds to me."[77] So Fowles flew alone, with his "suitcase stuffed with a lifetime's prejudices against the place." When he returned a week later, he was "hopelessly in love."[78]

He expected in the United States, circa 1963, to find political cynicism, violence, and indifference. Instead, he discovered sincere engagement and thoughtfulness and "far more liberalism about than we give Americans credit for."[79] He expected American critics and readers to interpret *The Collector* as English critics had, as a suspense thriller or crime novel. Instead, his book was "a sort of 'in' book. . . . Everywhere I went I met people who wanted to argue about it, about what I meant." He was "staggered," he wrote to Elizabeth, to find that "people really do seem to feel that it's the novel of the year and are genuinely and deeply interested in the 'allegorical side.' The being reviewed in the crime columns business in England shocks them."[80] He thought Americans, compared with English interviewers, were more relaxed, "much less anxious to needle and much more anxious to find out what you really believe," although, he added wryly, "I have a job explaining existentialism."[81]

He expected to find cold, ultramodern cities of steel, glass, and plastic. Instead, Boston touched him with its "nice . . . human . . . tattiness . . . all the human failings of old civilization." The spaciousness of the New

England countryside, dotted with spare, painted wood frame houses and divided by old granite walls, was a delicious "shock." As the guest of Little, Brown Editor in Chief Larned G. Bradford and his wife, Pamela, Fowles succumbed to the "easy grace . . . and space" of their 1780 house on Cape Cod, "where no one ever locked windows and doors were unlocked by day." He was fascinated by American birds, by American oaks and maples as the leaves turned red in early fall. He liked drugstores, he discovered, and cranberry juice, liked the domestic architecture, liked, to his surprise, most Americans. Most of all, he liked Ned Bradford, his editor, "a quiet intellectual-executive type . . . glasses, spring-blue eyes,"[82] who filled Fowles "with a sort of quiet confidence; something neither Sheil nor Tom Maschler ever do."[83]

New York City wowed him. "The poetry of New York," he wrote, "under cloud, the skyscrapers losing their tops. Sunlight, the windowed cliffs floating in the blue sky, heavenly cities. The long vistas have an almost Claude-like peace. And the sunshafts catch little bits of green. New York is cool, zesty, young."[84] After an elegant Boston luncheon with the Arthur Thornhills, senior and junior, who headed Little, Brown, Fowles had been escorted by airplane to New York by Bob Fettridge, Little, Brown's chief publicist, who delivered him to the solid, old-fashioned comforts of the University Club on West Fifty-fourth Street and the ministrations of Naomi "Tommy" Thompson, LB's "publicity girl" for New York. Tommy's nurturing and gossiping sustained Fowles for the next week, as she escorted him to interviews, lunches, dinners, photo shoots, renowned jazz clubs, smoky Greenwich Village blues bars, Broadway theater, and expeditions to buy extra socks. Tommy was very tender about criticisms of America, and Fowles enjoyed teasing her by complaining about American inadequacies—no ink for a fountain pen, the heft of the Sunday *New York Times,* the huge gas-guzzling finned cars of 1963, the emptiness of a "consumer's paradise, where citizens have all and have nothing," and "the awful mixture of races" in the faces on a city street[85]—and by pontificating during broadcast interviews against such sacred cows as the British royal family.

The days flowed "in and out so fast that things seem to go by as in a dream." Fowles was simultaneously exhausted and exhilarated and found "the drinking pace . . . savage."[86] He was breakfasted, lunched, and dined at five-star restaurants by his American agent, Julian Bach, and by literary columnists and editors. He cooled his heels in the Columbia Pictures offices and did the rounds of eager magazine editors. He was interviewed by Norton Mockridge of the *World Telegram,* Lewis Nichols of the *New York Times,* Mitchel Krauss, Roger Smith, and Professor Warren Bower. In a hamburger joint at midnight Fowles argued with Roy Newquist in a conversation that yielded the first major John Fowles published interview. Fifteen million viewers watched as he appeared on the *Today* show, seated between Bobby Kennedy and the widow of Eero Saarinen, who was "a great fan of The Collector."[87]

Radio interviews were the funniest because any pretense of intellectual content was peppered with sponsor messages. The wonderful Arlene Francis, "a smart kooky girl with a deep-serious voice and a Donald-Duck voice and every other kind of voice," would just be able to query, "So death is a symbol of the defeat of the intelligent few?" in her "intellectual voice," before erupting into a raucous singsong, "'Maisy doats and lambsy divy say have you tried Ferguson's Tomayto, tomarto, what the hell, I'm talking about *joo-oo-oo-oce* and say men, have you tried Schick's new stainless steel blades, even Mr Fowles uses stainless steel blades, don't you Mr Fowles, boy what a lovely beard this man has, *music!*" After the jingle, she resumed solemnly: "And now, John Fowles, to return to your concept of existentialist authenticity. Would you say that . . . ?"[88]

At the insistent invitation of Gloria Vanderbilt, Fowles had champagne and conversation at the famed heiress's apartment, finding "Little Gloria" "just about the least affected and most secure person I met in New York."[89] He was invited, in his edgiest New York experience, to an intimate, jet set soiree to meet film director Roman Polanski, followed by a seductive, surreal evening during which wealthy, jaded women tried to "vamp" John and the other men. Fowles left, alone, "feeling corrupted," because as at Ashridge and Oxford, he found this café society deeply attractive. It was, he accused himself, "the old nostalgia for the court, the sort of thing one sees in Voltaire so clearly, a desire to live independent and to mix high." Fowles felt ashamed of his attraction, however, and rang up Elizabeth, just to hear her voice.[90]

The visit to America left its imprint on Fowles. He felt "deflated" coming home to England, as if the current of energy were "turned off suddenly." With the loss of energy, he also missed the sense of space. Elizabeth took him to see a small house in the Vale of Heath that unnerved him with "its whole invitation to a quiet, small life." After this first taste of the United States, he wrote, "I know now, deeply that I need openness, I need space . . . one has to probe a wider space . . . living closer to America, closer to power, to energy."[91]

In November 1963 Fowles was deep in *The Magus* (which now carried its final title), plunged into his "own unique world, one's own people, one's words." He reveled in both the "craft-joy" and the "emotional relationship" with his characters. "Conchis, Lily, Alison, Nicholas Urfe, they stand in the book and watch me," he wrote happily. "They are mine and yet I am theirs."[92] He had fallen under a new narrative influence that poured energy into what was the final draft. In November 1963 he noted reading, specifically for "the first time," a novel that made a profound impression on him, Alain-Fournier's *Le Grand Meaulnes*. Marking this diary passage with a large asterisk, he described the "strange experience" of "Crusoe-like seeing those footprints on the sand, knowing that after all one is not the first on this island." Alain-Fournier's book and his own had the same animating purpose, Fowles realized, "mystery, pure mystery." He was moved and excited by how "the marvelous" in Alain-Fournier's vision was "strictly enveloped in reality."[93] This stylistic idea inspired Fowles as he wrote his own final draft, and he stripped away some of Conchis's chicanery and didacticism, relying on the realistic texture to support the sense of wonder. Influenced by the dreamlike simplicity of Alain-Fournier's storytelling manner, Fowles "cut down the philosophy" in *The Magus,* slicing away all but pure narrative.[94] The personalized existentialist philosophy underlying the events of the novel was separated out into the manuscript of *The Aristos,* a book Fowles put on the shelf. He was scheduled to publish *The Magus* next and anticipated offering *The Aristos* at some undefined future date.

On November 22, 1963, however, U.S. President John F. Kennedy was assassinated. Shocked, Fowles felt the events confirmed so much of the philosophy he had struggled so long to express in *The Aristos*. It was capitalism, the "agora society" of greed, materialism, and lost individuality that was to blame, not the lone assassin. All the participants in the terrible international drama were driven by the *nemo,* the sense of not being, of no identity, to seek power, publicity, fame or notoriety. Fowles felt "a kind of mournful rage that I can't explain it all in public."[95] He believed his plainly stated philosophy, shared by publication, could assist the public to comprehend. He dropped what he was doing and, with a sense of urgent mission, furiously revised *The Aristos* for submission to publish.[96]

Into December, John and Elizabeth Fowles worked long hours to prepare the manuscript. Elizabeth, once again his first and most important editor, called the process *delousing,* "removing priggishnesses, pomposities, preachings . . . 'platforms.'" Fowles aimed for a "voice" that was "ageless, unvoguish . . . ," independent, and he was "prepared to risk accusations of pretentiousness to get it."[97] Of those accusations, he would have plenty. By the beginning of the next year, against all advice, he had submitted his "self-portrait in ideas" for publication.

In releasing *The Aristos,* Fowles was prepared to risk his newfound literary reputation to address the diseases and potential cures of postwar society. In continuing with the manuscript of *The Magus,* he was losing himself in the interior world of his imagination. Deeply as these works called to him, however, it would be *The Collector* that once more demanded his attention.

CHAPTER TWELVE

The Savage Eye

London, Hollywood: 1963–1965

> *. . . the permanent mystery of my life since The Collector; [is]
> that I don't feel (in any except one way) happier or more fulfilled.
> We have money enough now, freedom to live where we like and
> do what we like. I have one of the great blessings of life—no one
> is my master, I am completely my own. But I don't feel hap-
> pier . . . except in one way. . . . That is in writing—because I feel
> I am at last beginning to know clearly what I must write and (per-
> haps more important) how to write it. . . . The craving I used to
> have for the limelight, for a sort of publicity, has diminished a
> great deal. More and more I have a sense of immortality, of what
> will last and what won't, in contemporary literature.*

—JOHN FOWLES, *DIARIES*, SEPTEMBER 7, 1964

With the success of *The Collector* came the role of London literary lion, a part Fowles had longed to play for years. He scorned social celebrity per se, however. Just as his novel had been written as a parable of ideas, so Fowles thought that with public eminence his philosophies would be noted and he would have the opportunity to make a difference. His pub- lication of *The Aristos* was sincerely intended to offer a humane rational way of living in a troubled world and to stimulate public philosophic dis- course. He hoped the film of *The Collector* would more widely disperse his ideas, that the enlightened best in each ("the Few") was mercilessly exterminated by the ignorant, fearful worst in each ("the Many"). Fowles came to realize, however, that no one listened. He was beloved as a story- teller and reviled as a preacher. The sale of his work made him conventionally respectable, financially comfortable, and eventually rich. The same sales made the same work into a commodity, a commercial product to be marketed, even reshaped by other people. His writing against the "agora society," as he called it in *The Aristos,* took its public value less from its thoughtful content than from its place in the market economy. This frustrated, depressed, and at last deeply angered him.

At the beginning of October 1963, he was a panelist at the Cheltenham Literary Festival, with Frederic Raphael, Gabriel Fielding, J. B. Priestley, and Thomas Hinde. Eager to join in robust arguments and offer heated opinions, Fowles came "with the intention of attacking" several contemporary writers he believed overrated. However, seated next to him at the opening presentation ("The State of Literature Today") was famed novelist Iris Murdoch, the very writer Fowles wished to criticize. He found Murdoch "prim, rather schoolmarmishly precise," a "gentle creature, with a good clear mind," and "of course I couldn't attack her to her face." Fowles recalled Murdoch's husband, John Bayley, from Aix at Easter 1948, "a frail-looking, balding, myopic man with a stammer . . . the gentlest . . . solitary." Chairing the panel, J. B. Priestley imposed time limits and sanctioned discussing "other writers, or publishing, or reviewing," so that it was "all futile." No one attacked anything; "we just talked in vague generalizations."[1] To Fowles's disappointment, the festival was celebratory, where "nothing got defined . . . all very cold fish."[2] Socially, however, the Fowleses became friendly with writer Freddie Raphael ("a powerhouse of ideas"), their favorite young actress, Diana Rigg, and Guinness poetry prizewinner, Nathaniel Tarn ("Tall and quiet and slow to laugh. A sniff of the dandy about him, but this is pleasant").[3]

The simply social irritated Fowles. While he could be a charming conversationalist with one or two people, his shyness made him uncomfortable in larger social groups. The exclusive annual authors' party at Jonathan Cape was "names meeting names, and chitchatting." In Chelsea a film world party was "empty, void, because all the important people there were empty and void." Fowles was introduced to movie magnate Sam Spiegel, "the mogul of moguls," who briefly pronounced, "A great book you wrote." He was echoed by a "dwarf," "Mr. Spiegel thinks it a really great book," as Spiegel abruptly turned his back. Elizabeth thought the entire party "like a film set. Women, all in 'little black dress' showing much naked shoulder & bosom . . . unreal, yet familiar and conventional . . . not a notable evening. No one made me laugh."[4]

The film of *The Collector* was another ongoing source of distress. While Fowles had escaped to Greece in the summer of 1963, what was supposed to have been a "little black and white English film" became a major Hollywood project. Mike Frankovich, who had headed Columbia Pictures in Britain, was promoted to the head of studio for all of Columbia at its California headquarters. The modest English project under Frankovich's aegis—Blazer Film's *The Collector*—was moved to Hollywood. Now it would be filmed in Technicolor and have a major international director, William Wyler. Jud Kinberg slipped a disk in his back, and John Kohn, under pressure to produce a shooting script, brought in veteran scriptwriter Stanley Mann. Kohn and Mann gathered for script conferences around Kinberg's bed and argued loudly. The resulting script, however, appalled Fowles. Miranda's life was saved in a "happy" ending. The characters were "totally changed, motivations changed, most of all, my ideas changed."[5] The Englishness of the dialogue was distorted with Americanisms. It was all "implausible." Archie Ogden, the Sheil agency film agent, first dissuaded Fowles from sending the scorching letter of corrections he wrote when he saw the script, then convinced the writing trio that they "must have me in to clean things up."[6] Determined to keep control of his ideas and save his book, Fowles fought "the battle of the film-script" through August, putting in eighteen-hour days and arguing the results with Kinberg, Kohn, and Mann at 13 Wigmore Street. He called the process "on watching the rape of one's daughter."[7] Both Kinross and Maschler advised Fowles to keep out of the rewrite, especially because there were no firm financial terms. Fowles wouldn't listen: "I know I'm right. If they take only half the changes . . . then it's worth it."[8]

Fowles insisted on being involved in choosing locations and casting. He and Elizabeth spent days with Jud Kinberg photographing potential Hampstead locations for Wyler to choose from. Kinberg impressed Fowles as a well-balanced character, "an island of sanity in this world, with a nice Jewish sourness."[9] In casting for the lead roles, Fowles agreed readily with the choice for Clegg of Terence Stamp, whose star was rapidly rising after his portrayal of the stammering, doomed Billy Budd. Reading the galley proofs of *The Collector* as he rode the 73 bus through London, Stamp was so "hooked" that he missed his stop. When director William Wyler specifically asked for him, Stamp quickly accepted.[10]

Miranda was more difficult to cast. Kinberg and Kohn's first choice was Julie Christie, who had just appeared in *Billy Liar*. But Wyler rejected her in film clip after clip, explaining to the puzzled producers that she had "a thick lower lip." Diana Rigg was "just beautiful" but not sufficiently vulnerable. Susannah York and Sarah Miles were screen-tested. All along, however, Mike Frankovich insisted that Miranda would be played by Samantha Eggar. Fowles was convinced then and for the rest of his life that Samantha got the role because, he believed, she had been Frankovich's mistress. Wyler, who had the final say, accepted her because, as Kinberg recalled him saying, "I can get a performance out of her," a talent he was known for. Sometimes, Kinberg remembered, as he *"pushed* for a performance," Wyler "had a reputation for *bullying* his leading ladies."[11] Samantha Eggar, in any case, was not John Fowles's idea of Miranda. The author's objections were overruled, and he berated his "mistakes" and lamented: "The film is dead, before it's been born."[12]

Fowles tried to bring William Wyler around to his viewpoint on the film, arguing with him over the proposed happy ending and the "Americanization" of the story. He was surprised and slightly annoyed to discover that "Wyler himself is a bit too complex and untypical to be dismissable as just another Hollywood director-megalomaniac." He was in fact a very intuitive director, "one of these people who change their minds by some slow interior process . . . letting a decision grow turnip-slow in the field of his instinct."[13] Turning on Fowles his "creased face, and soft hazel eyes, lugubrious, probing," Wyler half moaned, "What's the girl die for? . . . that audience is just going to say—What happened, why'd she die?"[14] Frustrated, Fowles spent "sleepless nights traversed by fantasies in which cine moguls are subjected to every kind of Dr No type torture and beastly oriental (and occidental) humiliation." The film world "makes us so sick," he explained to apologize to the Sharrockses for boorish behavior during a visit, writing contritely, "As you have guessed, we are two very insecure people right now."[15]

To his surprise, however, Fowles was flown to Los Angeles, on March 16, 1964, for two weeks of script doctoring as Columbia Pictures prepared to shoot the interior scenes. Generally appalled by the Hollywood film industry, he viewed himself as "the Savage Eye . . . the only decent role here. Watch, record, and one day print."[16] Indeed, the fifty-five-hundred-word exposé he wrote after this experience ("Illusionsville: A Fortnight in Hollywood") was so "savage" that he ultimately suppressed it. First chronicled in letters to Elizabeth, Fowles emerges as a wide-eyed Candide marveling at the corruption and cynicism of this high-stakes industry of celluloid dreams. Yet in his first Hollywood adventure, Fowles was as much a meddler in "all this imbroglio" as an observer and recorder.[17] Less than a year after leaving his position as Head of the English Department at St. Godric's, John Fowles was making a movie—and a bit of mischief—in Hollywood.

In Hollywood Fowles did not limit himself to rewriting the script. Probably to Wyler's surprise, he involved himself in detailed arguments about sets, costumes, dialogue, and, especially, casting. The sets for the cellar and the Tudor house, surrealistically constructed in the middle of the huge factorylike studio, which sat in an "endless area of tall palms, parking lots and bizarrely exuberant cinemas and amusement places," gave him an "odd" feeling, "seeing one's words made so real." Fowles critiqued everything: floor coverings, graphics, electrical gear, and the flush toilet. ("'God, we can't use a camping stool,' says Jud. 'The audience will relate to shit!") He begged the carpenters to "distress" the house exterior because "it looks too damned new to be credible."[18] He complained about costuming, urging cardigans for Miranda and jackets without shoulder pads for Clegg. Maxwell Reed was Wyler's choice to play the artist George Paston, "supposed to be English . . . on the strength of having once been married to Joan Collins." Fowles "exploded" on the set when Reed read for the part. "I think I cooked Mr. Reed," Fowles exulted, and the part was eventually cut.[19]

"Mr. Jawn Fawles" was "luxuriously ensconced" in a hotel on the Sunset Strip that offered him a seductive night view over L.A., "a spill of endless jewels glittering in limpid air, or in clear oil."[20] The sound of swishing tires was a "perpetual . . . kind of boiling of rubber on concrete" sound in his room. Fires burned on the dry hills, the Santa Ana blew fine ash into his eyes, and people spoke of slipping their silver into their swimming pools for safety.[21] He dined at the Wylers' "palatial house" in Beverly Hills, surrounded by "four or five Utrillos . . . a fine Renoir, a Rivera, a Kisling, a Boudin" and couples like the Efrem Zimbalists and the George Axelrods.[22] Suzanne Kinberg drove him into the hills beyond the urban sprawl of L.A., where "like a thirsty man," he heard birds singing in the Greek-like Southern California landscape.[23]

Working on the script daily, Fowles allied himself with Jud Kinberg and John Kohn against the director and his "junta." He had always liked the two personally and now gained respect for their creative skill. Kohn had a knack for dramatic structure expressed in endless shouted energy.

Kinberg could be moody. Both loved melodrama, "wild ideas and flagrant corn," and "gimmicks," which Fowles countered with "realism." Working at Kohn's rented house, they "beat at the script, shouting and pleading and bellowing and walking away and let's-try-this-ing." Soon Fowles was freely included in their clowning insults and meaningless bad tempers—and he loved it. "I am the goddamn stupid moron who wrote that goddam crap novel," he wrote, obviously delighted. "When I solve a problem: 'God Jesus John, sometimes I think you oughter write a book.'"[24] He was disturbed, however, by the "sort of calculating machine feel" about script discussions, as scenes were shifted at great speed. Fowles thought it demonstrated "a complete dissociation from the characters and the story as a living organism."[25] Wyler shot down the team's best efforts anyway since long, unfamiliar words were forbidden and dialogue had to be "mishmashed to a smooth banality."[26]

On the set Fowles was thickest with Terence Stamp, the twenty-four-year-old English actor playing Freddie Clegg. With his brilliant blue eyes, hoarse Cockney voice, volcanic energy, and swaggering braggadocio, Terry charmed and dazzled Fowles from the first meeting. He was "splendid," said Fowles, "quick-thinking and highly articulate . . . sensitive and aggressive." Terry was like Hotspur, "a prince, the Cockney burst out of the class chrysalis."[27] Relishing their shared rapport, the reticent, thirty-nine-year-old English writer listened for delighted hours to Terry's lurid tales of his "incredible roll of bed-battle honours."[28] Stamp was also a polished and demanding actor. His Clegg, Kinberg remembered, was "chilling . . . you couldn't take your eyes off him." He was "letter-perfect," always prepared, and always in "absolute control of his voice."[29]

Beyond his genuine liking for Fowles, Terence Stamp loved having John as an admiring audience for his off-camera performances as the brilliant, charming "bad boy" of the company. On the set of *The Collector*, part of Stamp's comic holy terror persona was his contempt for Samantha Eggar in the role of Miranda. In this attitude Stamp was wholeheartedly joined by Fowles.

Indeed, Samantha Eggar—or Sam—began in over her head in the role. Jud Kinberg acknowledged years later that she hadn't the training for the part. But, he said, "of the two roles, the woman's role is the least grateful because she's whining all the time."[30] Sam had a bad time in rehearsals, forgot her lines, spoke them in a flat and "debby" voice, and quarreled with William Wyler on the set. Wyler, as he often did with his actresses, "bullied her." Viewing the first daily rushes of scenes depicting Miranda's illness and death, the audience laughed aloud. Terry didn't help. During one rehearsal he refused to look at Eggar and spoke all his lines to the script girl.[31] The "favourite sport on the Columbia lot," Fowles wrote, was "making fun of her behind her back."[32]

Fowles made the common error of confusing the actress with her role and was dismayed that Eggar was "so remote from my conception of Miranda." She hadn't Miranda's "vital spark" or "warm eagerness," and her early rehearsals eroded Fowles's small confidence.[33] He began taking her out to lunch, for a walk, to a Segovia concert in hopes of connecting her to the role. He begged her to ask him for help. But by the end of his first week in Hollywood Fowles was conspiring with his friends to have Sam removed from the picture.

Terry ignited the plot by "blowing his top" in the office where Fowles, Kinberg, and Kohn were working. Fowles suspected that the "magnificent fifteen minutes' solo performance of mingled rage, frustration and brilliant mimicry" of Sam had been rehearsed. "We're all in the fucking soup." Stamp exploded. "It's the film I've turned down a dozen fat Hollywood parts to do. It's the film that's going to make you boys [John and Jud]. It's *his* fucking first novel. I mean all this arsing about. It's fucking ridiculous. . . . There I am doing the big scene, shouting at her, doing my fucking nut, telling her she's never going to get out, and she's sitting there like a sow who's just had a full breakfast."[34]

They spent a weekend checking the availability of other actresses: Sarah Miles, Susannah York, and a new prospect, Yvette Mimieux. Fowles wrote a four-page "report for Wyler," criticizing all aspects of production, but especially "slamming Sam."[35] Wyler was so shocked he refused to speak with Fowles about any of it. The following week they conspired to undercut Sam. But watching her being snubbed on the set, Fowles pitied her as "a Renaissance princess among all the courtiers who know she's going to be poisoned for state reasons at dinner that night."[36] Mike Frankovich arrived the next day, and after a complicated, angry afternoon of meetings, Sam was let go. She was given "one more chance," but was off the picture by the twenty seventh. Meanwhile Fowles argued vehemently against her and then, guiltily, spent an evening coaching her. "That writer's a hypocrite," exploded Frankovich, "coaching the girl like that and then trying to get her the sack!"[37] Fowles wrote, "I suspect she thinks I'm terribly nice," while he saw himself as "the grey eminence of her downfall."[38] After her initial anguish, Samantha Eggar behaved with a dignity that impressed both Fowles and Jud Kinberg, waiting with "no tears, no tantrums, and surprisingly few recriminations."[39]

With three days until shooting was scheduled to begin, the question of who would play Miranda reached a crisis. "Don't worry," Wyler said to Kinberg, "I've sent the script to Audrey Hepburn. She'll play it. She owes me." After learning Miranda's age, the thirty-five-year old actress graciously declined.[40] Mike Frankovich, still fuming over Eggar's rejection, sent the script to Natalie Wood. Wood expressed interest, but her price made Columbia hesitate. Wyler's younger brother backed Jean Seberg. Rumors naming actresses flew around the lot: "Natalie Wood heads the stakes, but then there's Mimieux . . . Inge Stephens, Hope Lange, Susan Pleshette, wild talk of getting Sarah to break her contract with MGM, and many others whose names I've never heard of." Fowles left on Saturday, March 28, planning to stop in Boston to see editor Ned Bradford, without knowing who would play his heroine or even whether the production would continue. He said farewell to Sam by kissing her hand and telling her that "she was a brave girl, which I think she has been, by her lights."[41]

With John Fowles's departure, calm business as usual was restored. Wyler called Kinberg on Monday and said, "Well, you better get Samantha back." Said Kinberg: "And back she came. Sheer guts. The avidity every actress must have . . . it helped her in the role."[42] Terence Stamp returned from a weekend in New York. Everyone settled down and made the picture. Wyler "got his performance out of" Sam. Indeed, Samantha Eggar was nominated for Best Actress by the American Motion Picture Academy and won Best Actress at the Cannes Film Festival and the Golden Globes. A week after his return to England, Fowles read in a London newspaper how Miss Eggar "'had solved her difficulties with Columbia over the nude bath scene'" and was back on the set. [43]

Years of film watching from the dark front rows of the Everyman in Hampstead had nourished Fowles's ambition to reach millions of people through a cinematic immediacy with his stories and characters. In his dreams, however, he had written and controlled his own projects. But all filmmaking was a fractious collective endeavor, and Hollywood, in particular, was a money-driven industry producing commercial commodities.

Fowles came away from his first taste of Hollywood with "a tremendous love of the novel form and a tremendous hate of the film." Film was "bedevilled by the team" and a thousand other pressures. But the novel was "one man's work, or one man's and his wife's work."[44]

Fowles returned from the United States just in time for his sister's wedding to Daniel O'Sullivan. He had been home only long enough to collapse into bed ("total sex succeeded by total exhaustion") before his mother rang him to announce that his father had suffered a heart attack. John thought her voice gleamed with "a sort of madness. If Armageddon started tomorrow, she'd still see Hazel married in due pomp on Friday."[45] At Leigh, Gladys greeted John and Elizabeth by declaring, "He's putting on an act." Indeed, Robert Fowles, "in bed, muttering and grey-faced," seemed to his son to be enjoying himself.[46] So John put on a hired morning suit and on "the coldest April 3rd for a century" escorted his twenty-two-year-old sister down the aisle of Old Leigh Church. "You looked so bloody grim," laughed Elizabeth at the reception.[47]

If only by coincidence, Robert Fowles's collapse appears related to anxiety over the imminent release of *The Aristos*, which his son was correcting for publication. For John Fowles to publish a philosophical manifesto and self-definition was to measure himself by his father, a lifelong student of philosophy. Robert was "seriously fretting" over *The Aristos*, Elizabeth had written to John during his March absence in Hollywood. "He locks himself away with it every evening. Spread out on the dining room table. Your Mss. His reference books, piles of them. A huge wad of paper in which he makes copious notes . . . he is worried you will be condemned . . . the need for an index . . . worries him enormously." Nonetheless, Elizabeth "managed to pin him, to make him admit it was as a work, quite an achievement."[48] John Fowles had earned his father's approval, although indirectly bestowed and couched in contingency.

No reviewer of *The Aristos* would have the impact of Robert Fowles's opinion, but there were plenty of critics. Fowles's agent, Anthony Sheil, warned of the potential for obscurity by using Heracleitos and the special philosophical terminology. Fowles responded that he was aware of the dangers of the form, which "makes one sound more arrogant, more humourless, more obscure than one really is," but felt strongly that "the book must stand or fall as it is."[49] Tom Maschler feared the book would not "do his career, at that point, any good" but, knowing the importance of *The Aristos* to Fowles, wanted to support him. Maschler quietly sent it to writer/philosopher Frederic Raphael, who assured Maschler on the contents but commented, "There, but for the grace of God, go I." [50]

Fowles was discouraged by the "lukewarmedness" as he waited for American publication in 1964 and a June 1965 publication in Britain. He anticipated poor reviews attacking his philosophical arguments. He was not prepared for nasty personal slurs, however. The first advance review, by Virginia Kirkus in September 1964, set the tone of attacking the writer rather than the contents, calling Fowles a "poseur primping before his intellectual mirror."[51] The first English reviews of *The Aristos* appeared on June 13, 1965. While Julian Mitchell in the *Sunday Times* was perceptive, noting that the "self-portrait in ideas . . . is a fascinating gloss on . . . *The Collector*,"[52] most other reviews were sneeringly negative. The *Observer* was "malicious," dismissing the book with the summation "In tone, pretentious; in outlook, existentialist-socialist-humanist (ho-hum); in grammar, frequently lacking."[53] Nigel Dennis complained, "Mr. Fowles has no right to make himself unnecessarily unreadable. He deserves much better of himself."[54] In the *New Statesman,* John Mortimer sniffed: "The sad fact is that the meaning of life is not to be trapped in numbered paragraphs, even with the aid of Heraclitus, Teilhard de Chardin and the Latin word for no one."[55] Wounded, Fowles thought the reviews conspiratorial. "None of these reviews review the book; but the manner of it, or the writer. . . . Clearly the form is wrong." He felt isolated when old friends like Fred Porter read the poor reviews and refused comment.[56]

Fowles was also concerned by the contrast in American and English critical attitudes. That the Americans should hail his work puzzled him as much as he was disappointed that the English treated him coolly. English publications noted dismissively that Fowles had given up his job and "grown a fine, black beard" when his first novel was published or misquoted and garbled the writer's public remarks out of context.[57] But ordinary American readers wrote enthusiastic personal letters to him about their reactions to *The Collector,* and American scholars had begun requesting information on Fowles's literary intentions and biographical background by September 1964. He could not get articles published in British periodicals, while American magazines were eager for them.

John and Elizabeth went on assignment to Norway in June and July 1964 for the American magazine *Venture: The Traveler's World.*[58] Returning to Scandinavia for the first time since his university days, Fowles was so distressed by increased tourism that he worried lest his article contribute to the phenomenon he saw as a "blight."⁵⁹ Having traveled so far, however, Fowles was determined to return to Pasvik and the farm at Noatun where a seed of *The Magus* had been sown in 1949. Nursing bronchitis and exhaustion, Elizabeth drove "like a trouper over the pot-holed road," on and on through the tundra and ninety miles of forests, as the road became "lonelier and lonelier." Having reached Noatun with the midnight sun, they spent the short night in their blue secondhand Mini, supping on whiskey and cheese.⁶⁰

After fifteen years Fowles saw the farm again and was not disappointed. Now, writing the final draft of *The Magus,* he understood "why it has haunted me so long. . . . It is a private domaine, a secret one is glad to know. It inhabits one; one doesn't inhabit it." Noatun was a part of him, a mysterious "dream that remains a dream . . . even when awake, a last fragment of a better world."⁶¹ Of the hundreds of wild swans that had graced the lake at Noatun, only four remained. These became, in Fowles's *Venture* article, the symbol of the disappearance of wild Europe and of that better world.

This word *domaine* had entered Fowles's writing vocabulary only a few months earlier, as he read "for the first time" the haunting 1913 novel by Alain-Fournier (Henri-Alban Fournier) *Le Grand Meaulnes.* Narrated by the tender realist François Seurel, the novel tells of the romantic idealist Meaulnes, who, as a youth of seventeen, chances upon a *domaine perdu,* a spellbound lost landscape, and there falls instantly in love with an enchantingly beautiful girl, Yvonne de Galais. The *domaine* in this novel is a mysterious forest château where a festive wedding of children is being celebrated. After leaving, Meaulnes spends his life (and destroys the happiness of others) trying to recover the innocence and wonder of his few hours in the *domaine.* He finds and marries Yvonne, only to leave her after the wedding night, to wander on in his endless quest to find and restore the elements of his defining vision. In his absence, Yvonne gives birth and dies, attended by the faithful François. The tragically adolescent Meaulnes, as Fowles eventually wrote, strives "to maintain a constant state of yearning . . . eternally the mysterious house rising from among the distant trees, eternally the footsteps through the secret gate, eternally the ravishingly beautiful and unknown girl beside the secret lake."⁶² Irrecoverable, the *domaine perdu* is *le pays profond,* the inner landscape of youth and virginal perception.

This book so penetrated Fowles's bones that he became publicly associated with it, touring the sites of Henri-Alban Fournier's life, writing afterwords to both the 1972 and 1986 translations, opening an exhibition of paintings inspired by the novel, and championing all efforts to film it. In 1971 he suggested (and believed) that he had written the whole, rather than the final draft, of *The Magus* "very powerfully under its influence."[63] By 1985, without factual accuracy but in emotional sincerity, he could "remember . . . when I first read it as a schoolboy, many years ago."[64] The concept of the lost, secret place of childhood grace had been with him—unnamed—since his own adolescence in Devon. He had cherished for years the dream of slipping into a hidden place of wild nature, in which he met and fell in love with a mysterious young woman. Alain-Fournier gave him words to describe it. The *domaine perdu* of Alain-Fournier became the objective correlative of these imaginative elements for Fowles, suddenly imbuing them with clarity, form, a name, and great literary energy.

What Fowles felt at Noatun was in the starkest contrast with his life as an author in London. The "literary web rather tightens around us," wrote Elizabeth, adding that "sometimes one feels it is all rather a bad novel."[65] The Fowleses had been pulled into the London literary social scene. They dined out with Terry Stamp and his new girlfriend, supermodel Jean Shrimpton. They were frequent theater-goers with Ronnie and Betsa Payne. With Jud and Suzanne Kinberg, they went to deafening discotheques, like the fashionable Ad Lib Club, where Fowles described the dancers as "joylessly preoccupied . . . narcissistically shaking their bodies like trees, as if they must get the fruit off."[66] They joined sparkling artistic soirees at the Downshire Hill, Hampstead, home of Fred Uhlman, a painter and writer whom Fowles admired.[67] With Cape authors like Arnold Wesker, Honor Chapman, Edna O'Brien, and Nathaniel Tarn, they attended the publishers' annual parties, which Fowles grudgingly pronounced "better than last year."

At the center of this literary society was the Irish novelist Edna O'Brien, whom Fowles likened to "a favourite church . . . is visited by everyone."[68] Fowles thought O'Brien had "no intellect at all, only a brilliant intuitive feeling of what is central about people and things. . . . She would charm a stone to life."[69] She gathered "a microcosm of all Literary London" under her mother hen wings: "Rita Tushingham . . . the anti-actress, the anti-star . . . Kingsley Amis and Elizabeth Jane Howard and Mordecai Richler and Arnold Wesker and the film directors Clayton and Donner and Desmond Davies . . . this glitter of names; this demi-paradise of celebrity."[70] Elizabeth wrote that "the people she gathers at her house rather put one off her. It seems she is always surrounded by: The entire staff of the Newstatesman: All the leading writers of novel, film and stage, plus actors and directors of some aclaim too. And all at the same time." Edna O'Brien took up John and Elizabeth Fowles as well, including them in all her gatherings. Elizabeth wrote wistfully of how fond she felt toward Edna, and "she gives me the feeling she is fond of me, but I think she has the knack of being fond of a great number of people."[71]

The Fowleses were ambivalent participants in all this, a little awkward, a little shy. Elizabeth sent the Sharrockses amusing, wry reports of joking that "the 'Beatles' should be exterminated" and thereby offending Arnold Wesker, of exchanging flirty "looks" with Kingsley Amis and receiving "dirty looks" from "his lady wife," Elizabeth Jane Howard. "Here and there dotted all over the room," she went on, "are all the British film directors one admires. But hell what *do* you *say* to them?"[72] John Fowles was put off by talk that was "half vainly of one's own prospects, or half enviously of other people's. Who has an option on So-and-so's book— who will direct this, who will act in that." Everyone in that social world, he thought, was "driven frantically to destroy his or her nemo . . . to be in the limelight, in the okayest current of the age; where the cinema and the novel meet." Fowles distrusted this, he said, convinced "this must be inimical to good writing, let alone good living."[73]

Fowles felt himself a misfit in the greater society as well. As London became the trendy center of what was then called the swinging sixties, Fowles was less and less in sympathy with affluent English postwar culture. He wrote in September 1964 of how the past two or three years had "seen a strong conservative-fascist-selfish swing in the West; the decline of the intellectual approach to life and the rise of the visual; the predominance of . . . an amoral, . . . pragmatic attitude to living—enjoy it while you can, buy as many pleasures as the affluent society and you yourself can afford." He called it "immoral . . . blindly uncommitted to anything but selfishness." He felt "what many must have felt in the 1930s, a being swept in the direction I do not want to go."[74] He suffered "a deeper alienation," Fowles wrote to Denys Sharrocks. "Every time I go downtown I put on a sort of Dante mask—so this is hell and thank God I don't belong in it." He had an "insane dream," he wrote to his friend, "of an isolated country house with a large library and no telephone."[75]

Episodes like the fortnight in Hollywood, Fowles's tour of Norway for *Venture,* and the distractions of London's literary society interrupted the intense push to complete *The Magus* that occupied 1964 and the first half of 1965. In a new May 1964 contract with Little, Brown Fowles had agreed to deliver the manuscript by January 1, 1965. It required enormous physical effort, causing sleeplessness, stomach problems, assorted physical aches and pains, and a "collapse into flabbiness."[76] Fowles would wrestle for days with episodes like the "Eleutheria" massacre of chapter 53, then suddenly have the scene arrive so complete in his head that he could barely type fast enough.[77] By Saturday, November 7, he noted that the first draft was completed. Yet, only days later, he was "sunk in the rewriting" and on January 8, 1965 he was still working on it, writing to Denys Sharrocks that "it becomes more and more like a giant treadmill or a huge ill-built ship that keeps on springing new leaks." He hoped to be able "to beach the bloody thing" by March, adding, "Never will a place have been worked so thoroughly out of a system than Spetsai out of mine, when the glad day comes."[78] He and Elizabeth took the last part of the book to be typed on February 23, 1965, yet he admitted it was very far from finished.

As usual, Elizabeth thoroughly edited the typescript. She made suggestions for everything from individual words that sounded "odd" or "clumsy" to critiquing entire episodes, even to analyzing the character based on herself. Alison in chapters 38–42, for instance, should irritate Nicholas more. She should "row" with him rather than write him a letter. "People row more than they write letters," she noted. "One big love scene" should be used in place of several small ones. "My private opinion is hinted sexuality is much more exciting than the full treatment—see Thomas Hardy," Elizabeth offered, while slyly suggesting "some books you haven't read." John should cut "entirely unnecessary exchanges of dialogue . . . having nothing to do with the plot." She didn't like Conchis's "direct 'pinch' from 'aristos.'"[79] Fowles respected her opinions, and for the most part, incorporated them into his text. Together, they physically cut and pasted the manuscript for the typist, excising chunks with black crayon, inserting pieces typed on the reverse of script pages from *The*

Collector. "It is a great novel," wrote Elizabeth proudly to her friends. "I have always thought so."[80]

As they packed up the typescript in an old Hathaway shirt box, William Wyler arrived in London with an advance copy of *The Collector* on film. The delighted director was "in love with it."[81] When they saw the film, Fowles thought it "no better, and not much worse than I expected; technicoloured and glossied and blunted out of all contact with the book." He was genuinely surprised, however, by Samantha Eggar, who he thought gave "a moderate performance; but much better than I expected."[82] Elizabeth hated the film. "I think it stinks," she wrote. "I was bored into the ground second time around . . . and damn me if it isn't the USA entry at Cannes."[83] Worse than his wife's disappointment, however, was an entirely unexpected and unwelcome new development. As word of the upcoming film leaked out, along with the recent release of the paperback edition of the book, the lawsuits began.

In February 1965, Fowles received notice from his American agent that he was being sued for plagiarism for $2.5 million by a writer who claimed Fowles had stolen *The Collector* from him. The plaintiff, Johnson C. Montgomery, was a Hollywood lawyer and would-be scriptwriter who regularly brought this sort of suit. However, Montgomery had in 1962 indeed submitted an ugly two-page piece of soft pornography entitled "The Collector" to a trashy men's magazine titled *Mr.* Except for the butterfly-collecting metaphor, this snuff story bears no resemblance to Fowles's novel. Accustomed to attempted copyright attacks, Columbia treated the whole matter pragmatically. The studio assumed the legal costs of taking Fowles's deposition on August 31, 1965, in which he swore to the facts of the writing and sale of *The Collector*. Jud Kinberg shrugged off the suit as the usual nuisance of filmmaking and told John and Elizabeth to do likewise. Except for Elizabeth's divorce, however, the Fowleses had never been sued, and the situation left them unnerved.[84]

The next suit was not so easily shrugged off. In early March 1965 agents Anthony Sheil and Julian Bach and editors Tom Maschler and Ned Bradford received typescripts of *The Magus,* and by the last week of that month all were responding enthusiastically. Bradford telephoned in excitement that "he had never read anything like it before." Maschler telegraphed that he was "very very impressed."[85] But just as the congratulations were arriving on March 31, John Fowles's thirty-ninth birthday, notice of a libel suit was hand-delivered by bailiff to his paperback publisher, Pan Books Ltd. The plaintiff this time was no less than the Save the Children Fund.

On the final page of section 3 of *The Collector,* as the demented Clegg fantasizes committing suicide to join Miranda in death, he says: "There was the money, but I didn't care any more. Aunt Annie and Mabel would get it. Miranda talked about the Save the Children fund, but she was already half off her rocker. All those charities are run by crooks. Save the Trustees, more like."[86] The passage was clearly written to "give and giving a portrait of the mind of one Clegg which is utterly warped and crazed . . . a clear manifestation of insanity," as the defense later put it.[87] The real trustees of the Save the Children Fund, however, did not accept this argument. They required public apologies, retractions, withdrawal of the book, destruction of the offending passage, unspecified financial damages for slander and libel, and full payment of their legal costs. The individual officers of the fund also brought suit.

John and Elizabeth were stunned. They were already in a "raw stage of nerves," he in a "ludicrously tender state . . . nerves jangle," as he received specific criticisms and editing suggestions on *The Magus* manuscript from his editors and agents.[88] Feeling "utterly dazed," the couple "fled the country for sanity" for several weeks of driving in France. Letters from Fowles's solicitor reached them on April 8, 1965, at Avignon, informing them that while his counsel felt "quite strongly that taken within the context of the whole book this is not libellous and no Jury would find it so," it would be "a hard case to fight." Although there was a principle at stake, Fowles's publishers, with whom he carried a wide indemnity clause, were reluctant to defend the case, fearing huge damages ("settling is cheaper than fighting"). Fowles felt betrayed and heartsick.[89] Pan Books immediately pulped thousands of copies, the cost borne out of the author's royalties. The British reprint substituted an innocuous reference to unspecified "charities" for the name of the fund. To both the Fowleses, the timing seemed very suspicious. As Elizabeth wrote to the Sharrockses, "At the time when the paper-back is selling quite nicely, and when there is a bit of advance publicity about the film—right boys, we sue for slander. Clever isn't it? The hardback has been out for two years and now they sue."[90] Fowles's nervous solicitors argued him out of making similar angry statements in personal letters to the plaintiffs.

Jud Kinberg tried to help. First, he wrangled an invitation to the Cannes Film Festival "on the house" for John and Elizabeth. Then he cleverly rallied Columbia Pictures to Fowles's defense. Learning that the proceeds of Columbia charity premieres of *The Bridge on the River Kwai* and of *Lawrence of Arabia* had benefited the Save the Children Fund, Kinberg got Columbia Pictures to agree to offer a charity premiere of *The Collector* to the fund, on condition that they withdraw the complaint.[91] On June 7, the fund categorically and (Fowles said) ungraciously rejected this offer. So, through the summer of 1965, the case proceeded, and they lived, as Elizabeth put it, "with this impending kind of minor doom hanging over us."[92]

The Fowleses did attend the Cannes Film Festival during May 1965. It was pure glitz, but welcome. Elizabeth, at least, loved flying by jet, drinking champagne above the clouds, and staying in a first-class hotel on the beach. *The Collector* was nominated for Best Film, Terence Stamp for Best Actor, and Samantha Eggar for Best Actress. So on Wednesday night, May 20, Fowles put on a white tuxedo and braved the flashbulbs of an army of publicity journalists to attend the showing of *The Collector*. The film was favored to win first prize. "It is Columbia's favourite child of the moment," Fowles wrote. "Not that it is any better a film than it ever was . . . fatally soft at the edges artistically . . . but it seems remarkable by Hollywood standards."[93]

According to Jud Kinberg, William Wyler was particularly confident of the Best Film award because Olivia de Havilland was chairing the awards committee that year. Under Wyler's very pressured direction of *The Heiress*, de Havilland had won for Best Actress the 1950 Academy Award, the Golden Globe Award, and the New York Film Critics Circle Award. "Don't worry," Wyler assured the startled Kinberg, "Olivia owes me." Kinberg recalled sitting in front of the Carlton Hotel in Cannes with Wyler and other producing members of *The Collector* when their French press representative approached. "He said, 'You're not going to get it. You're not going to get Best Picture.' Willie said, 'What do you mean?' He said, 'Olivia de Havilland told the board that she would *die* before she would give that son-of-a-bitch Best Picture.' And Willie was *stunned*." The board was willing to give Samantha Eggar the Best Actress award, the rep went on. But Kinberg and Kohn insisted that they wanted that award only if Terence Stamp also received Best Actor. So, for the first time in the Cannes awards' history, Best Actress and Best Actor went to the same picture.[94]

While this politicking was going on, Fowles was observing the rites of

Cannes in his field naturalist fashion. He thought the real absurdity was how seriously everyone took "an evanescent medium . . . a world dominated by appearances. By images. By expendables." He compared it with Versailles: "An intense, incestuous interest in their world; none in any other. Endless intrigues. Vicious overspending on follies."[95] His comparisons of the glittering starlet hopefuls who decorated every Cannes event to the ageless "houris" of some mogul's harem were eventually published in *Holiday* magazine (1966) as "Gather Ye Starlets."[96]

Throughout the entire spring of 1965—the anxiety over the two lawsuits, the four April weeks spent driving in France, the anticipation of *The Aristos*'s publication, and the showing of *The Collector* at the Cannes Film Festival in May—Fowles was "making fairly big alterations" in *The Magus*.[97] It is testimony to his remarkable powers of submerging himself in the text he was writing that he was able to accomplish these substantial revisions so creatively and to push his worries aside.

CHAPTER THIRTEEN

The Fox at Bay

Highgate: 1964–1965

By this time we had abandoned hope of actually seeing a house we would want to buy, but then we arrived at Underhill Farm, near Lyme Regis, down a long unmade road. An ugly house, with a litter of chalets and chickenhouses lying about it; but beautifully set on the cliffs, three hundred yards from the sea, with its own field running down to the cliffedge and the water. The house is old, set uphill from a square highwalled garden. A figtree, strawberrybeds, the sea beyond. I have that strange feeling I wrote about in The Magus, of meeting oneself coming the other way in time. This is the place, something will be lost forever if one avoids the encounter.

—JOHN FOWLES, *DIARIES*, OCTOBER 10, 1965

Just as the literary life in London felt like a disappointing compromise to John Fowles, so their first house never did quite fit him. No. 44 Southwood Lane in Highgate was a small, pretty "peasant's cottage," just around the corner from Ronnie and Betsa Payne.[1] Narrow, small, and fronting directly on the street, the house nevertheless had the charm of a ground-floor garden room with an Adam fireplace and carved moldings and a narrow, sloping back garden between brick walls where forget-me-nots caught the morning sun. They moved in at the end of April 1964 and Fowles dug in to completing and revising *The Magus*. Though Elizabeth Fowles was delighted to have a house of her own to furnish, paint, and fit with new plumbing, John Fowles always seemed in temporary residence. He complained of noise, of close neighbors, and of new buildings and roads abutting his property. By the autumn of 1964 he and Elizabeth were making little tours of the west country, "vaguely . . . to prospect for a house."[2]

Fowles had created a vision of the "perfect house" in his imagination, and it was definitely not a city house. The country house of his quite specific dreams was either very modern or built between 1700 and 1830, secluded on an acre or so of ground, had water ("the sea or at least a stream"), an orchard, and a hilly landscape ("combes").[3] Ideally, it faced south and was sheltered by hills to the north. Elizabeth, who loved London, was willing to move to another city, perhaps Canterbury, but John was "hardening towards a house in the country."[4] On house hunting tours she tried to work up moods of "desperate spontaneity," but she truly dreaded the prospect of village life or rural isolation. The country houses rich in history over which her husband enthused made her panic, "suddenly overwhelmed and intimidated by this weight of years I stood in . . . this overpowering crumbling corpse of a manor house."[5]

Fowles lived in Highgate while finishing *The Magus* under great pressure. This was also the time when *The Collector* received the Hollywood treatment, when *The Aristos* was bloodied in the press, when Fowles was served with lawsuits, and when he grew more and more disaffected with London, the literary life, and the modern world in general. Through these months he worked stealthily on another book, a planned-for novel he began sketching out after his frustrated return from California in 1964 and kept up as a serious "next project" into the autumn of 1965, the precise period he lived at 44 Southwood.

The materials for this novel survive under the tentative title *The Fox*. Fowles called it by other prospective names, however: *The Shit, The Bugger, The Eliminator, The Philanderer, The Aristocrat,* and, most often, *The Fucker*.[6] This angry project was a psychologically secret place for Fowles to release the outrage and resentment he seldom expressed publicly. It served him as a safety valve, a hideout, an escape. He kept a file of random notes, scraps of dialogue, lists of words, rough outlines, and newspaper clippings on murders and class tensions. When he and Elizabeth toured the countryside, Fowles looked for settings, deciding, for example, that he would set a savage seduction scene "right in the heart of a very old England," among the tiny ancient villages of Dorset.[7]

The Fucker or *Fox* seems conceived as a companion piece to *The Collector*. In that 1963 novel in diary form, an uneducated, repressed member of the lower middle class (the "New People") imprisons and causes the death of a bright, educated girl of the upper middle class with the potential of being an "aristos," one of the best. In this 1964–1965 sketched-out, diary-structured novel, a full-blooded English country nobleman becomes a serial killer of the middle and lower classes. Here, as in *The Aristos*, the writer is dramatizing the difference between the "nominal aristocracy" of blood and birth and the "real aristocracy" of merit and sincerity. Preserved chunks of dialogue and description show the unnamed protagonist as a vicious character, deeply snobbish, repulsively selfish, cynical, and sadistic. He is a habitual adulterer, seducing his brother's wife, then their daughter, his niece. He has a military past and is an expert on china and ceramics, possibly an antiques dealer. Fowles also invested him with some of his own "'good' facets." The character is "a believer in the Green England," who enters "lonely English woods . . . as others go to church; to be in touch with something he cannot understand." An expert hunter, he "decides not to kill for sport any more—on the side of the animals, the wild, as symbols of the old order." Well read in the literature of the past, he looks back on the Renaissance as "a civilization that begins to sing" and once thought of becoming a novelist. "The F." certainly exceeds his creator, however, by acting on his murderous fantasies. He comes to regard murder "as a fine art . . . an expression of the man's hatred of his condition of the society." The other social classes become his hunter's prey. The bourgeoisie are the "real game . . . the noble stag," while the proletariat are "vermin," and are "to be poisoned"—(Fowles did not invent a method)—"to stop them encroaching on real game." After the F. shoots a stranger in a parked car, his violence escalates, and the Dorset police are plagued with a series of furtive, inexplicable murders.

Off and on for seventeen months, Fowles worked on this angry book. It perked along secretly under the surface of his otherwise courteous, considerate, hardworking life, like poison seeping through groundwater.

Life at Southwood Lane particularly suited Elizabeth, however, because she had at last established a close camaraderie with her daughter. Anna was now well aware that her "friend" Liz was actually her mother, and the young teenager was allowed to spend some weekends at the house in Highgate. Although Elizabeth complained laughingly that Anna, at fourteen, was "all sort of lithesome and energetic" and made her feel "frightfully ancient and rheumaticy," the two were boon companions. Together, they repeatedly strolled oh-so-casually past actor Peter O'Toole's Hampstead house in the hope of catching a glimpse of Anna's number one crush and, together, stood patiently waiting outside Covent Garden to brush against her number two crush, dancer Rudolf Nureyev. Together, they scouted out old churches to make brass rubbings. Elizabeth introduced Anna to some of the film people and writers she knew, including Terence Stamp. Annoyed to see Anna in her stepmother's castoffs, she bought her a few new clothes.[8] Beginning a lifelong passion for the dance, Anna was taking ballet lessons. Elizabeth, who loved dance herself, took Anna to a shop in the heart of London's theaterland to buy her daughter her first point shoes. In awe at the "pink satin gilt chairs and photos of famous ballerinas," Anna tried "very hard to convince myself I could be Cinderella and not an ugly sister."[9]

Roy Christy was "wild" with what Anna later understood to be jealousy of John Fowles's literary success and of Elizabeth's relationship with his teenaged daughter. Her attentions put him "into a Victorian paterfamilia fury," and he accused Elizabeth of giving Anna the wrong values. He wrote his former wife a scathing letter telling her that he would not have Anna "'lured by the superficial glamour of the Theatre, the Ballet, the Cinema, etc.'"—"his capitals," noted John—"and if she visits us she must devote her time to 'cooking, sewing and reading.'"[10] The effect of his rant was to make his own relationship with his daughter more estranged.

In the era of casual coupling of the swinging sixties and in stark contrast to the violence and mayhem of *The Fucker,* the Fowleses of Southwood Lane were a rock-solid, old-fashioned couple. In their marriage they maintained the absolute fidelity that Fowles had theorized while at Ashridge in 1953. Indeed, in all the years they were together, there is no evidence of any physical relationship with other people. Marriage, for Fowles, was more than a satisfying domestic arrangement. Fidelity in loving, he had written in 1953, was an act of "conscious creation," one of the few genuine opportunities for achieving an act of free will.[11] Marriage, as he had explored it in *The Aristos,* was the model for humane civilization, the example for modulating extremes of passion into harmonious, mutually nurturing living (although his life with Elizabeth clearly had its extremes of passion, both erotic and argumentative).

To many of his colleagues and friends, Fowles's adherence to this standard of marital fidelity (even in Elizabeth's absence) seemed corny and unsophisticated, and he often sounds sweetly abashed as he defends his position. Critiquing the manuscript of *The Aristos* in 1964, for example, agent Anthony Sheil found particular fault with Fowles's generalizations that in a marital relationship, "every adultery adulterates it, every infidelity betrays it, every cruelty clouds it," chiding these statements as being "unworthy of an existentialist." "Perhaps," Fowles shot back by return post, "but worthy of a happily married man."[12] During his fortnight in Hollywood, Fowles's notions of fidelity to a spouse six thousand miles away provoked incredulity. "You got a bit o' bird, John? What do you do for a fuck here?" Terence Stamp asked. Fowles explained his "theory of fidelity, which must be becoming as strange and incredible to Columbia [studio] ears as Einstein's theory in the 1920s was to the ordinary physicist." At the expression on Terry's face, Fowles added gently, "It's not about what happens outside, it's what happens inside."[13] To other studio scoffers Jud Kinberg vehemently defended his friend by shouting "incoherently" on John's behalf: "Fidelity was the most beautiful thing in the world, Eliz and I had a beautiful rich relationship!"[14]

That relationship was much more than domestic and sexual. Elizabeth Fowles was at this time her husband's professional support and confidante. She accompanied him to meetings with agents, publishers, and scriptwriters. She was his companion at literary festivals, film openings, and scouting expeditions for film locations. She was his driver, for John Fowles never learned to operate an automobile. While John was in America, she successfully read his poems at a public reading produced by the poet Nathaniel Tarn, although she had to swallow a tranquilizer to find the courage. As he produced manuscripts, she was Fowles's initial, and unsparing, editor, making challenging notes as first reader, then, working with him through many days and nights to cut, reassemble, and prepare the text for the typist. Though never a brilliant typist, she labored to type many of Fowles's early manuscripts and, with later texts, managed them through the typist and delivery to publishers. In the face of his doubts and suspicions about the motives of agents, publishers, and, most of all, reviewers, Elizabeth stood "like the rock of ages, telling me to have confidence, not to be shaken, to be patient. . . . That being a writer is really writing what you think fit, not what anyone else feels fit."[15] Elizabeth Fowles had become a professional "writer's wife," a role both of them accepted enthusiastically and in which John Fowles encouraged her. When they were not addressing each other by the slyly ribald nicknames, "Old

Boy" or "Old Cock," they referred to each other by the simple affectionate term "My friend." When Fowles wrote her from Hollywood—and repeated the phrase in his diary—that the novel was "one man's work, or
one man and his wife's work," he meant it.[16]

However, by defining herself entirely in terms of her husband and his
work—the conventional standards of the postwar period—Elizabeth
risked losing herself. When her talents were necessary to Fowles and she
was included in his life, she was happy and confident. When he was otherwise absorbed, she suffered. In the winter of 1964–1965 as, ironically,
John Fowles was overwhelmingly immersed in fully realizing Alison
Kelly's role in the final draft of *The Magus,* Elizabeth "had a kind of sensation of not really existing."[17] Fowles recorded her complaint as "loss of
identity." This was the time of the early stirrings of the feminist movement in America and England, and both John and Elizabeth had read
Betty Friedan's *The Feminine Mystique,* published in 1963. When they
quarreled on the subject, Fowles rebutted: "I don't believe all the feminist argument (Betty Friedan's) about unfulfilled women. There are just
as many unfulfilled men, because fulfilment is a comparative thing."
Fowles recognized, however, that his wife felt a loss of identity because
"she is looking at herself in the distorting mirror of me . . . this twisted
reflection. . . . All's E's complaints run on the 'Look at you and look at
me' line."[18]

Her self-esteem was often fragile. "I find myself at parties, increasingly," she wrote her friends, "with people who all DO something . . . at
Edna O'Briens house . . . two actors, rather nice young men actually,
thought I was being a bit affected when I said I don't Do anything." During the first few months of 1965 Elizabeth tried to address her need by
taking a job. Jonathan Cape editor Tom Maschler often used his authors'
wives as readers. He recruited Elizabeth Fowles, who became a Cape
reader of "all the Ms that pour into a publisher." With high expectations,
she read nine hours a day, sometimes four manuscripts a day, at the Bedford Square offices, thinking she would "discover a giant—read the most
interesting stuff. Also it meant POWER . . . to decide if the things were
worth publishing or not." She was rapidly disillusioned. "I was totally and
absolutely amazed," she wrote to the Sharrockses. "It was all the most incredible muck."[19] In her three or four months at Cape, Elizabeth Fowles
did not recommend a single manuscript. When John Fowles indicated
that he needed her editorial help on *The Magus,* Elizabeth was glad to

quit. It later became part of her "legend" that she had been so harsh in her judgment that Maschler fired her, but such was not the case. (In fact she continued for years to read, unpaid, the odd manuscript for Maschler.) What Elizabeth wanted to be was the essential and indispensable professional partner of the man she considered one of the great writers of the age, her husband.

Even while Fowles was resolutely committed to his ideal of marital fidelity, he was still sometimes attracted to other women. He had accepted that these attractions were mere romantic longings, however. Rather than act on his fantasies by pursuing affairs, Fowles had learned that feeding a fantasy while ignoring the real woman who inspired it could lead him into that imaginative world where his stories created themselves around him. He thought of this world as a secret, personal *domaine,* using the term he had borrowed from *Le Grand Meaulnes.* He thought of the fantasy girl with whom he imagined love as a key to this *domaine,* as Yvonne de Galais is in the Alain-Fournier novel. Later Fowles used the term *muse* to describe this anima figure.

John Fowles, happily married and in love with his wife, was now wise enough to know that he did not actually want the girls he encountered. He wanted the fantasy versions who would unlock the gates to the *domaine.* Just as he was reluctant to see Sanchia again in 1963, lest she spoil his version of his character Lily Montgomery, so the imaginative characters he summoned up were far too important to him for Fowles to risk a real involvement.

Elizabeth Fowles was surely aware of this aspect of her husband's process of inspiration. She was too bright and too intuitive, and she knew John Fowles too well to have been deceived about such an important issue. This was, after all, the woman who had written eloquently and intelligently about "dual loving" at the height of Fowles's confusion over Sanchia Humphreys in 1954 and had encouraged him to see that particular muse again when she contacted him in 1963. Elizabeth also had access to the diaries, and while she did not read them every day, she was familiar with the contents. Furthermore, Fowles regularly confided in her and chewed over his theories with her.

Occasionally Fowles described such muse attractions in his diary. For instance, at the Everyman Cinema in February 1961, Fowles was seated between Elizabeth and a strange girl "with red hair and a curious flat sunburned face . . . slim, tall, very upright . . . alone." The girl was only "half-glimpsed," for seldom did he look at these women straight on. He neither acknowledged nor spoke to her. Fowles found this nonencounter "intensely poetic and exciting, sitting between them; two opposites (with their secret complementarities, of course)." He felt some "mysterious current between this unknown girl and my mind."[20] When Fowles saw the same girl later that evening in a restaurant, alone, waiting, he wrote the poem "Never to Be." In it he observes this "red-haired grey-eyed sweetsour nineteen . . . wearing her loneliness like a scent" and wonders, "o God what pleasures might have been/if I had come ten years ago."[21] He categorized the incident as a "semi-sexual, semi-mythological . . . 'priestess in the dark grove'" encounter and wrote that such encounters "are strangely beautiful."[22] Episodes like this one are not recorded very often, though they were probably more frequent than Fowles documented. Perhaps he knew the limits to Elizabeth's tolerance.

Given that Fowles could recognize the "priestess in the dark grove" in the persons of nineteen-year-old strangers, it is not surprising to find that he occasionally encountered his own heroines on the street. While immersed in the character of Miranda at Columbia Studios and dismayed over Samantha Eggar's casting, he "saw" Miranda on a California street.[23] In June 1964 Fowles wrote "Heroine," a Pygmalion type of poem describing the evolution of a female character. The poem describes how a philosophical concept first becomes personified, then takes a female form. She begins like a doll on a shelf, "given an age, a shape, a look/Legs, arms, likings, tricks of the voice." With a name, however, she grows contrary, begins to speak for herself. "She says/ Things I do not want her to say,/Goes when I write stop, lingers/At exits, laughs at wrong moments." She contradicts her maker or yawns and refuses to appear. "One day she comes as I lie in bed/And undresses. Stands smiling." The poem ends with the creator glimpsing his character in the street and running after her. "Mistake." He sighs. "It is only some living girl/A little like her./But far less real."[24]

In the autumn of 1964, on the very day he wrote of Nicholas Urfe's final disillusionment with Lily in *The Magus*, he encountered "Lily" herself while browsing at Norman's bookshop. Alone in that quiet, windowless back room filled with old books, Fowles felt, rather than saw, the entrance of a pretty girl in a gray flannel suit. Although he avoided looking directly at her, Fowles was aware that the girl had very white-blond hair, an articulate way of speaking, and an upper-class accent. In her silent presence he began to experience "the feeling of fear, a vague anxiety," which he identified as "a fear that reality was getting out of hand." Experiencing "a strange wordless connection," Fowles felt that Lily was with him, that "this was a case of a character in a book almost springing to life . . . a sort of echo in reality." Unnerved, he expected the girl suddenly to turn and say, "I am Lily." He later wrote that it was "virtually a ghost experience." Interestingly, in his first conversation after this encounter, Fowles felt compelled to lie, as if inspired to storytelling by the girl in the bookshop.[25]

Fowles was obsessed by this chance encounter for days and decided (on no evidence) that the girl had seemed so familiar because she was Jennifer Hillary, an impressive young actress he and Elizabeth had recently seen in the play *A Scent of Flowers*. Fowles wrote to Hillary at the Duke of York Theatre to ask if she had been in a Hampstead bookshop on the afternoon of October 2, 1964. The actress was thrilled to write back to the author of *The Collector* (by coincidence, she had tried out for Miranda on the first casting call) but sorry to disappoint him. Fowles decided that Lily and this young actress were linked in his mind because Hillary had played the role of a girl who was dead and spoke from the dead about her past, exactly the role with which the Lily character began. "I now for the first time realize the significance of this," wrote Fowles in astonishment; "the dead-girl-in-the-past is of course my own nostalgia for incestuous relationship with my mother."[26]

When he wrote this in his diary, Fowles was engrossed in psychological study, seeking the patterns behind his compulsion to create fiction. He thought imagining fictive scenes was "analogous to remembering them," when memory was poor, as his was. Perhaps fiction, like dreams, tried to perfect the "imperfect basic material" of one's ordinary life. Objects in dreams and fiction were beautified, distinguished people were met, and one "cast oneself as more adventurous, heroic, pleasure-seeking than one really is."[27] The theory Fowles independently formulated at this time about his own work anticipated by over seven years the major Freudian critical approaches to his fiction. The impulse to dream and to write fiction, he believed, was "biologically attributable to the drive to recover the blissful primary stage (unseparated) of infancy, when all perhaps seemed perfect (or seems in recollection perfect)."[28]

In connection with these psychological studies, Fowles also completed an intense period of analysis of his dreams and those of his wife.[29] In his "method" he made the basic interpretation Freudian—that is, he wrote, "treat all imagery as illustration of pre-conscious traumas that have to do with (a) withdrawal of the breast—corruption of the pure mother-baby relationship (b) feelings about parents or the parent substitutes; Oedipus complex and the rest." Imagery, however, was to be interpreted using Jungian, Adlerian, and Hornerian methodologies. Lastly, he applied his own concept of polarity, or "the constant bifurcation of any given attitude before reality." He embarked on this analysis believing that "freedom, if it exists at all, can begin only beyond one's furthest knowledge of what motivates and haunts one's decisions."[30]

He found that Elizabeth had "a much 'richer' unconscious" than he did, for her color-filled dreams teemed with significant people and travels.[31] His were of familiar landscapes and familiar interests: china collecting, writing, birds and gardens, his bank. Sometimes too his matrix of Freudian interpretation led him to overlook the painfully obvious. Three times in less than one week Elizabeth dreamed of being given responsibility for a baby or an infantlike creature, of feeling delight, then of rejecting it and feeling terrible guilt and shame. On each occasion, applying his Freudian interpretation, Fowles analyzed his wife's dreams as relating to a childhood resentment of her sister's birth and the "trauma" of an interrupted relationship with their mother and father. The rejected baby figure, Fowles believed, was always Elizabeth's sister, Joanne, born when Elizabeth was fifteen. It seems not to have occurred to him, listening to his wife relate her dreams, that the rejected baby figure might be Elizabeth's own baby, her daughter, Anna, and that Elizabeth still was visited in her dreams by the sense of confusion and shame that had caused her such anguish ten years earlier. She broke off telling John her dreams at this point, saying, "This isn't doing me any good. It doesn't mean anything. . . . The more you discover the more reason I find to dislike myself."[32] Lost mythic mothers from infancy were more intriguing to Fowles than were the lost infants of real sorrowing mothers.

The editors and agents who read the manuscript of The Magus in March of 1965 didn't recognize Elizabeth in the Alison Kelly character. Even as editors and agents on both sides of the Atlantic reported enthusiastically about the novel (with "'rave' reports from the Americans"), there was plenty of missing the point. Stiffly, Anthony Sheil asked Fowles to chop the entire charades method of Conchis's "Godgame" and eliminate whole episodes, including the central episode of the German occupation (which Fowles kept) and an episode in which the "Furies" chase the lovers with whips (which Fowles discarded). Sheil complained that it was unrealistic for Nicholas Urfe to return to Alison.[33] Editor Tom Maschler also sighed at the "banality" of the relationship between Alison and Nicholas and asked for substantial cuts in those sections.[34] The readers had "still lots of doubts," Fowles noted. "I always underestimate the ability of people not to understand symbols. . . . Nobody seems clear what the two girls stand for. They are bewitched by Lily and Alison is a sort of intrusion, they can't believe in the ending."[35]

The ending was the major sticking point with all readers except, presumably, Elizabeth. Written in the autumn of 1964 and submitted with the February 1965 text, the original ending has Nicholas Urfe victimized by one last complicated "game" that reunites him with the lost Alison.[36] Back in London after being fired from his job in Greece, Nicholas learns Alison is alive and spends months seeking her through arcane Latin clues from Ovid's Orpheus and Eurydice legend. His final ordeal ("a real Walpurgis night") occurs on October 31 at midnight in London's Highgate Cemetery (near Fowles's house). The ornate 1838 funerary monuments called the Catacombs had struck him as architecturally like the royal tombs in Mycenae, where he had "tested" his fear of death. As Fowles had in 1952, Nicholas must enter a similar tomb to confront his notions of death and find them meaningless, then must prove himself worthy of Alison. Nicholas, a former commando, runs a veritable obstacle course of false suicides, skeletons, trapdoors, and creepy passageways until, at last, he finds Alison, locked in a barred, underground cell, from which his words must free her. In this version Alison must decide between her passionate love for Nicholas, who has hurt her, and the marriage offer of an older, professionally successful Australian architect (a Roy Christy figure) who respects her. Fowles's original intention was for a full, traditional resolution in the novel's conclusion. There is no ambiguity in this ending. In the finale, Alison passes Nicholas the key to her prison, and they embrace through the cold separating bars, "our eyes one, our beings one. . . . Mocking love; yet making it."

With admirable diplomacy, Tom Maschler advised Fowles to "rework" this "operatic and unnecessarily anti-climactic" ending. "Your reader," Maschler tactfully pointed out, "has now been held for more than 1000 pages, turn after turn, twist after twist—in my case, intrigued, surprised, and frequently delighted. . . . Conchis may well only be playing games with Nicholas at this point, but I think the reader has the right to be more demanding." He praised the "immensely enjoyable and readable book [also] a serious work of art" and urged Fowles "to bring Nicholas and Alison together under less melodramatic conditions."[37]

And so he did. In doing so, however, Fowles for the first time created an open-ended structure for his fiction, one that allowed for more than one possible outcome. This inventive approach was drawn from biographical experience. Fowles turned back to his 1953 memories of walking lovestruck with Elizabeth in Regent's Park as they worried over Roy and Anna. He also recalled the bitter late-October day in Kensington Park when Elizabeth parted from him to take her daughter to Birmingham and the lovers' future relationship hung undefined, clouded by multiple possibilities. Drawing on these memories Fowles wrote the 1965 conclusion in which Nicholas and Alison ambiguously enact a parting that might be a final separation or might be the prelude to their committed life as a couple. A final reference to the "architect" was eliminated at the last minute. Realistic, ordinary, and totally unmelodramatic, with Fowles even using Maschler's word *banal,* this innovative ending would ignite critical controversy, break hearts, and depart from the conventions of conclusive plot resolution. "I think the new ending is better," Fowles admitted.[38]

Fowles added a postscript when he submitted the revised manuscript for publication on June 16, 1965. His heart was so visible on his authorial sleeve that someone, probably wisely, must have told him to suppress the piece. He wrote of longing to name "the sole begetter . . . of this story . . . whom our common friends will know haunts every scene and every page." But she refused to allow him to do so. "All I can do is record my debt," he says, though he cannot hope she will ever "accept payment."[39] So Elizabeth's name did not appear in a dedication, but only as an inscription to the mysterious goddess by whose name Fowles sometimes described his wife's wisest expression: "To Astarte."[40]

It was nearly summer when John Fowles, at long, long last, sent the final revised typescript of *The Magus* to his publishers on June 16, 1965. He had no welcome sense of achievement, however, for he was reeling from the first English reviews of *The Aristos,* which had appeared on June 13. As *The Aristos* was "murdered" and *The Magus* was sent off, Fowles felt empty. "One goes through the motions of childbirth long after the baby's out," he wrote, "and nothing new has been conceived."[41]

In a stealthy way, however, Fowles was working on another book, *The Fucker,* and he took his ideas with him as he and Elizabeth set off on another house hunting tour.

By this time John and Elizabeth Fowles had been regularly house hunting for a year through rural England: East Anglia, the Midlands, Somerset, and, in particular "the West," Cornwall and the counties of Devon and Dorset, to which Fowles felt affinity. They moved slowly, in two-week loops, keeping to the narrow, hedge-lined lanes to avoid other people, stopping at every antiques shop to hunt for New Hall china. Dorset's "green valleys and straw-coloured downs" entranced Fowles. "There hangs over much of Southern Dorset a sort of very ancient magic of place," he wrote, "a patina of civilizations that believed in magic."[42]

As he traveled through this landscape, Fowles looked for settings for his planned novel. But the journey was also interpenetrated with his current reading, to the point where the physical landscape became a literary one. As Fowles imagined his angry aristocrat, "the F," awed by the green woodlands and countryside, it was *The French Lieutenant's Woman* that was beginning to form in the landscape of the writer's unconscious. The tours of summer 1965 are enfolded in Fowles's admiring rereading of Tennyson (especially "Maud") and of Joyce's *Ulysses* ("Joyce makes one re-think the whole problem of realism")[43] and his quarrelsome first reading of Alain Robbe-Grillet's *La Jalousie* and *Pour un Nouveau Roman.* "Heresy," he called the latter, "not a description of reality." Robbe-Grillet, Fowles fumed, "bans narrative, but mankind thinks, lives and normally recalls narratively. Life is a series of events that have happened chronologically, with relation to the individual. To deny causality, continuity, the suspense of development, in ordinary life is ridiculous. Then he bans character (personnage); . . . to deny that humanity can be truthfully characterized (is not biologically, by the process of evolution, polycharacterized) is ridiculous . . . to deny that we apprehend chronologically is worse than ridiculous."[44]

More than any other figure, the great nineteenth-century novelist Thomas Hardy loomed over Fowles's travels in the West. Traveling in October 1964 in a ten-day loop from Winchester and Salisbury throughout the south coast of Dorset and back to Avebury Circle, Fowles was intensely conscious of being in Thomas Hardy country. "I feel full of envy for Hardy, during our days round Dorchester," he wrote, "having such roots, such a rich humus of land and local history to suck from and retreat into."[45] Fowles felt that the "magic of place" reached back through Hardy, as he and Elizabeth drove through the Dorset countryside. Fowles stopped at Beaminster to talk to Stevens Cox, an ex-policeman who wrote monographs on Hardy. With "more than a touch of the mad sergeant" about him, Cox regaled Fowles, who loved gossip, especially literary, with "neurotic undertones" and "dirt" about Hardy that would be disputed by later scholars: "an incestuous love affaire with his illegitimate niece/cousin, Typhena, a 'buried child.' The first marriage . . . a disaster . . . the second . . . 'just Hardy being decent.' . . . all is rooted in Tryphena . . . the secrecy and the tragedy of Hardy's books, his poems, and his life."[46] Reading this precursor over the next few years, Fowles came to "feel very close to Hardy," knowing "exactly how his mind works, how he creates . . . because I have that same kind of mind, that adoration of personal myth, that ability to use and transmute it."[47]

On this journey Fowles was reading Hardy's novel *A Pair of Blue Eyes* and was impressed by the power of the narrative, even in a work so "immature."[48] He was still reading it when, on October 10, 1964, John and Elizabeth Fowles stopped for a night at a little town on the south Dorset coast called Lyme Regis. They were charmed, liking it best of all the seaside towns they had seen, "with its steep contours, old houses, the sea light, the beautiful harbour—the Cobb, the cliffs."[49]

John and Elizabeth were drawn back to Lyme Regis again in July 1965 after a long month of house hunting. They had looked at houses "remote . . . sad . . . lost" and "victorian parsonages which still smelt of cabbage-water and the village fetes of yesteryear." They saw "wrong houses with the right garden," houses "too bijou," ramshackle cottages, an Elizabethan manor house "run to rack and ruin," and old houses "Victorianized and dead."[50] They had abandoned hope of finding a house when they arrived at Underhill Farm.

The dwelling was a low farmhouse, surrounded by outbuildings and chicken houses and a garden full of figs and strawberries. The flagstones underfoot were studded with fossil ammonites, and a cool, slant-roofed, slate-paved dairy room ran the length of the rear of the cottage. The house stood on the sea side of a long, unpaved road that ran into the heavily wooded area called the Undercliff, a unique wilderness area west of the town of Lyme Regis. The fields of the farm ran right to cliff's edge overlooking the English Channel. Fowles felt instantly that he had arrived at his appointed place.

The couple who lived on the property ran it as a chicken farm, let out rooms, and served teas to walkers in the Undercliff. Elizabeth was appalled at such a prospect. Elizabeth saw a filthy and neglected dairy. John saw ammonites in the flagstones and a garden full of strawberries. Elizabeth heard dreary tales of keeping a remote bed-and-breakfast miles from town. John heard there was a ghost and that Jane Austen had come there to drink syllabub when she visited Lyme Regis in 1803 and 1804. Elizabeth learned that the house sat on England's most dangerous landslip area, that "the road may subside at any moment." John liked "the house being a Circe, a dangerous temptress . . . so literally on dangerous ground." Elizabeth veered "one way and then the next." John Fowles felt "the sort of certainty . . . one has only when one is in love." Elizabeth wept desperately through the night at the hotel. John, however, felt his "Cornish obstinacy as stiff as an iron stake inside me." So, said Fowles, "what with the ammonites, and Jane Austen drinking syllabub, and the figtree full of fat green figs, and the bullfinch I hear whistling at the garden-end, and the sound of the waves on the reefs below, and no house within two hundred yards, a private road, and nothing to the west but six miles of nature reserve, badgers everywhere, and the deer in winter, I know I have met my match."[51] By August 16, 1965, his bid on the farm had been accepted. By the end of September the sale was complete.

With the purchase of Underhill Farm, a secluded property that embodied all his dreams of a wild and mysterious *domaine*, Fowles very quickly lost interest in *The Fucker*. He abandoned the project in September 1965, explaining that "the implications of it are too black, in a way too frightening."[52] He toyed for a noncommittal three weeks with an idea for a novel inspired by his May 1965 Cannes experience, to be called *The Orgiasts* and to be set in Turkey. This was followed by the equally short-lived *The Accountant*. As Fowles engineered his genuine escape from all that had made him unhappy in his exposed urban environment, his nightmare fantasy of murder and complaint collapsed. The secret book, *The Fucker,* lost appeal, sinking invisibly into his psyche with all Fowles's months of preparation. "The F." was a persistent character, however. Fowles soon returned to writing about a confused aristocrat in a time of enormous social and class change, a young man who was most himself in the deep forest of an older "Green England." Lacking the rage, cruelty, and perversity of Fowles's abandoned protagonist, Charles Smithson would be the vehicle of Fowle's evolution as a novelist.

Denys and Monica Sharrocks were home on holiday from Nigeria, where Denys was serving with the British Council. Nigeria was not a happy posting. The country was politically unstable, and the Fowleses often worried about their friends. Fowles was disturbed to notice that eight months in that African country had "put grey in the hair of both of them."[53] When Denys returned, Monica remained in England to settle their son, Michael, into his new boarding school. Fowles had come to a tentative respect for his friend's wife. Characteristics that had irritated him, like Monica's independence and insistence on a life of her own, he now often viewed as "her courage really."[54] He begged her to join them in the first weeks of their move.

Elizabeth Fowles needed the support. She was profoundly anxious over the coming changes. Through the three months between the sale and the move, Fowles felt he lived "surrounded by a kind of resentment. . . . She has told me six hundred times that I am an egomaniac, I am self-actuated, I am full of romantic illusions, I think of no one but myself. . . . [I am] beginning to seem to her 'just a romantic novelist.' "[55] Fear of jeopardizing her relationship with Anna was part of Elizabeth's distress. When Anna was allowed to stay with them, Fowles felt Elizabeth "overmothers her, overloves her." They took the fifteen-year-old to see the farm. Elizabeth was "upset," but Anna was enthralled. "The miracle," wrote Fowles of his step-daughter, "is really that she is not in the least a problem child, has not turned into the neurotic guilt figure we all promised ourselves."[56]

While they prepared for the move, *The Magus* was shown in galleys to Twentieth Century-Fox. Jud Kinberg, then working for Sam Spiegel, was contacted from London by John Kohn. Reading the unpublished new book, Kinberg "was bowled over." But he telephoned Kohn, saying, "There's no way that we can make a movie of this!" Kohn replied, "We're going to have to. David Brown and Zanuck just made a deal for us to produce the film."[57] Fowles accepted Fox's handsome offer for the film option on October 17, two days before leaving London for Dorset. He now owned the Dorset farm, but the Highgate house would not sell, and there were financial worries from the Save the Children Fund lawsuit. Not until late March 1966, when 44 Southwood Lane was sold at a reduced price and his one-quarter portion of a five-hundred-guinea settlement to the fund was discharged, would Fowles be relatively solvent. So he was easily persuaded to become the project's screenwriter, adapting *The Magus* for film production. Fowles was a novice. To learn the format of a screenplay, he contacted an acquaintance, writer-director Robert Rossen, from whom he obtained a copy of Sidney Carroll and Rossen's script of *The Hustler*. Fowles used this screenplay as a template in writing his own first full script.

It was usually Elizabeth Fowles who suffered throat and chest infections, aggravated by her constant cigarette smoking and her sensitivity to cold and damp. John Fowles generally suffered stomach ailments, as he had as a boy and university student. On October 19, 1965, however, the day of the move to Undercliff Farm, a cold and sore throat he had been nursing for nearly a month flared up into acute pharyngitis. At the farm he was miserably confined to bed under a doctor's care for over a week, while Elizabeth and Monica managed the move in.

It was backbreaking work. In October 1965, the farmhouse was, Monica Sharrocks recalled with a laugh, *"extremely* primitive."[58] They unpacked boxes, scrubbed and cleaned, hauled ash and chopped and weeded in the garden in the mild autumn weather. As they clattered and chatted, John would suddenly scowl through a little window in the bedroom door and complain that they were as noisy as an entire convent of nuns. They laughed at him. For all the labor, the two women lived in "a fairytale" isolation and their friendship deepened profoundly. Elizabeth later recalled that they had floated among the strawberries at Underhill "in a ginfilleddaze."[59] Fowles wrote of Monica, "She has saved us, just by being here."[60] After her departure for Nigeria in November, Monica Sharrocks became Elizabeth's primary correspondent for the rest of her life. From her kitchen table, from the hairdressers, from the front seat of her automobile while she waited for Anna or John, from trips abroad, or over a drink in lonely evenings, Elizabeth poured out hundreds of pages of vivid, intimate, funny, and sad confidential letters documenting her life to the Sharrockses. On more than one occasion she joked that it was a "kind of therapy."[61]

In London, autumn came. *The Magus* was on its way to publication after fifteen tortured years of composition. *The Aristos* continued to garner poor reviews, when anyone noticed it at all. Lawsuits associated with *The Collector* wound their way through the legal process. The parties and literary soirees enlivened London society once more. John and Elizabeth Fowles, however, were no longer anxious participants. Slipping away from all pursuit, the fox had escaped. By late October they were gone.

CHAPTER FOURTEEN

The *Domaine*

Underhill Farm: 1965–1968

*a druid balm, a green sweetness over all . . . and such an infinity
of greens.*

—JOHN FOWLES, *THE FRENCH LIEUTENANT'S WOMAN,*
CHAPTER 29

After more than a decade of London life, they found themselves in a remote, extraordinary landscape, a unique wilderness created by the dynamic forces of time and nature. The Undercliff on the Dorset coast of
England encompasses almost eight hundred acres, stretching nearly six
miles along the south coast, between Lyme Regis and Axmouth. The
land beneath was laid down in layers over Triassic-era rocks during the
Cretaceous and Jurassic past, one hundred million to two hundred million years ago, when this part of the continent was a warm, shallow sea.
That primeval ocean was inhabited by prehistoric creatures that left their
bones, shells, and impressions of their softer parts fossilized in the various limestones, cherts, sandstones, and shales of the geological strata.
Their fossils wash onto the beach from the cliffs after rain and are turned
up by farmers plowing their fields.

This coastal region is well watered with springs, and softer strata are
eroded from deep within the earth, causing the land to subside without
warning, just as the sea and winter weather erode the exposed parts of
the cliffs and beaches. The Undercliff is one of the most geologically dynamic areas of England, prone to rockfalls, mud slides, landslides, and
"subsidence," the inward collapse of many acres of land. "The land

courts the sea here," Fowles's old neighbor growled when they met. " 'Tis sidling land."[1]

Erosion and landslips molded this small geological region into a startling landscape. "Very primeval and jungly," wrote Fowles happily. The cliffs, up to two hundred feet above sea level, tilting toward the south, plus the mild south coast climate, foster a sheltered, subtropical microclimate that nurtures plants unknown elsewhere in England. The habitats for bird, animal, and insect life are varied and protected, including thickly matted and dense woodland, freshwater ponds, sheer cliff faces, rocky scrublands, and seashore. Because the land is changeable and often dangerous, and building development impossible, the Undercliff is virtually a nonhuman environment, where other earthly occupants flourish safely. For unwary humans, it is an easy place to lose one's way, even deliberately. Fowles wrote with relish of the "two escaped German prisoners of war [who] survived there for three years during the war,"[2] of the religious Dissenters who met for secret worship in its sanctuary in the 1680s and 1690s, and of legendary poachers and smugglers who based their operations in this shoreline wilderness. The Undercliff was named a National Nature Reserve ten years before the Fowleses arrived.

To John Fowles, Underhill Farm was a daily miracle because of its impossibility. Geologic conditions meant that at any moment the whole farm could slip into the sea. Waking in the night, he could envision the "whole place slipping into chaos." Yet each dawn he and the farm remained, sitting "in its little cradle of land" where it scorned disaster.[3] He was filled with wonder. "We haven't as yet got used to living with half our horizon the sea," he wrote Denys Sharrocks. "It roars, pounds, hisses, mumbles on the reefs below our fields all day long, and then all night and gives a sort of voice to all those powers of nature that are exterminated almost everywhere else in England. . . . Green men could survive in those impenetrable thickets."[4]

Fowles thought of the farm "like a huge complex poem," "a book of hours, a symposium of all the springs that ever were and will be." He experienced his own life there as "poetry," as he wandered his fields "in a sort of trance," feeling an "immediacy of impression" that recalled his adolescence.[5] The light took his breath away, from earliest morning, when the mirrored light from the sea was reflected and magnified till it filled the bedroom through a single tiny window, to the night, when the image of the moon glimmered on the waters. Sheltered by encroaching forest, the farm was shielded from the wind and missed the winter snows. It was, he said, "a secret place."[6] The silence at night was profound, "no cars, no passers, nothing."[7] He was always aware of the sea, which he said "hushes and strishes on the reefs below."[8] He learned the creaks and murmurs of his house, the clicks of door latches and the boom of the furnace. Brown owls hooted around the house at night, "lovely cool sounds—mystic oboes."[9] Foxes yapped wildly in the darkness, "rather frantic and desperate; as if a dog has run off the edge of the world and is falling, falling through eternal space."[10] The sound of the foxes, he wrote to Michael Sharrocks, was like "five or six very small boys being murdered." Mike, in his first year of boarding school, also learned from John's letters how the shy roe deer sang at night ("they make a dreadful howling and groaning noise—actually their love 'song'—and you think the Lock Ness Monster must be out on the prowl") and of the badger and deer tracks he had discovered and of all the animal visitors to the garden.[11] Weasels danced wildly around the garden walls, and John madly chased off the rabbits from his lettuces. Deer remained close but usually invisible, as did the fat, old badgers who left their paw marks everywhere. Fowles allowed a flock of sheep to graze right up to the house to keep the grass down. Foxes sat watching the ewes in season, waiting for the lambs to drop. For Fowles, whose greatest pleasure since boyhood had been observing birdlife, the farm was "heaven." Swifts towered over the house; hawks hunted; nightingales sobbed in the darkness. As they had in Hampstead, blackbirds sang their hearts out at dawn. The air was so dense with song that Fowles began trying to transcribe them.

Fowles had longed for physical labor on his own land and worked to exhaustion. He spent weeks digging ditches to siphon off the many underground springs. He lifted potatoes, dug new beds in the garden, chopped wood, sawed logs, "and a thousand other things," he wrote. "It's the thousand-other-thing aspect [that] is one of its pleasantest, really. All days are too short, here."[12] When not laboring on the farm or writing, he walked. He walked miles along the deserted beach, picking up fossils scattered in the sand and watching the waves, "seaweed caught in them, swaled up, reddish-brown and sepia in the cool green aspic of the water."[13] He disappeared across the meadows and into the forest, leaving the paths and cutting his way into the dense undergrowth with secateurs. As in his Devon boyhood, he often failed to turn up for lunch and was gone until darkness fell. He soon knew "that little square mile between

David's Close and Pinhay better than anyone else in the world; every flower and every fossil."[14]

The Fowleses transformed Underhill Farm in the few years they lived there. They stripped off the ugly decorations of past owners, restored the beamed ceilings, painted the interiors white, modernized heating and plumbing systems, and sold off the chicken houses. They scouted auctions and secondhand shops for the orphaned furniture Elizabeth skillfully refinished and the paintings and prints with which John covered their walls. As a joke, Fowles posted a misspelled sign, NO CAMPING OR TEA'S, to ward off walkers expecting to stop at Underhill.[15] Fowles purchased the adjacent seaside fields in early 1966 and rebuilt the gardens with terraces. Through the first winter, however, they had no heat, and workmen were a constant invasive presence. Rats infested the house during renovations. For a month after Monica Sharrocks's November departure, the Fowleses had guests: architect Charlie Greenberg offering enthusiastic suggestions; Ronnie and Betsa Payne "enraptured" with the farm[16]; Fred Porter, "anti-peace, anti-country, anti-nature"[17]; and John's parents, in desperation of whose visit John and Elizabeth bought a television. Then, suddenly, the Fowleses were alone in their rural isolation. The fine weather turned to cold, pouring rain, and constant damp.

Fowles buckled down to work on the film treatment of *The Magus*, "a job that both bores and disgusts me."[18] The book was to be published in the United States on January 1, 1966, and on May 2 in Great Britain. The scripting, filming, and release of the movie correspond almost exactly to the Underhill Farm period in Fowles's life, interpenetrating his writing of *The French Lieutenant's Woman*. The film, and thus the story and characters of *The Magus*, were never far from Fowles's mind. He had converted one of the farm buildings to a study. It was a small two-story wooden cottage immediately adjacent to, but separate from, the western end of the farmhouse. Having combined the two upstairs rooms into one, he placed here his bulging bookshelves, his collection of New Hall china, his telescope, and his typewriter. He installed a telephone to connect him to Elizabeth's kitchen. It was "a dream workroom" with big plate glass windows and a superb, distracting view over the green fields to the sea. He longed to be outside on his land. He wrote Denys that "processing one's own novel really is paddling in one's own shit."[19] But he was "in a mess financially . . . the house in Highgate won't sell." So Fowles, with one best-selling novel behind him and another sold at a "vast sum of money," carried a large overdraft with his bank and periodically through March 1966 had to beg his banker to continue it.[20]

Elizabeth succumbed to melancholy and depression—"the blues," John Fowles called it, but it was much worse.[21] Isolated from the world, left alone while her husband worked, enduring the chaos of renovation and a cold, rainy, lonely winter, Elizabeth sank into the state she termed "personal disintegration."[22] She wept, slept long hours, lacked energy, and was generally despondent. She flew into terrible, black, accusatory rages. Once Fowles smashed plates in a quarrel with her and struck her. He wrote of her "terrible bitterness," of her determination "to destroy our life here."[23] These winter states of Elizabeth's became a pattern. She did consult a doctor, who offered neither treatment nor medication, only pieties about "outside interests and social work . . . hopelessly inadequate."[24]

Fowles said years later that his wife had suffered from SAD, or "seasonal affective disorder."[25] These mental states certainly were connected to the onset of dreary weather and lengthening darkness. Her letters in these times are needy and sad, with muffled, oppressed emotions. Sometimes she wrote several to the same correspondent, then destroyed them before posting. In contrast, the arrival of full spring or a trip to a sunnier climate quickly restored her. As fine weather returned and flowers bloomed, Elizabeth would wake early, filled with energy to tackle her furniture refinishing projects, and to garden, cook, and welcome constant crowds of guests. Her letters from these periods overflow with generous sympathy and droll humor, enlivened with keenly drawn sketches of people encountered and everyday domestic detail.

Yet her melancholia was not simply seasonal or connected with lack of light. After six weeks of despondency in the winter of 1965–1966, for example, Elizabeth came brilliantly back to sparkling life during a three-week promotional visit to the United States after the January 1 publication of *The Magus*. Initially nervous and overwhelmed, Elizabeth soon was invigorated. The United States was embroiled in the Vietnam War, and the newspapers were full of stories of urban violence. In spite of this, she loved "the sharpness and energy of the Yanks," found "a zest there, even the sharp, cold dry air makes one feel alarmingly alive."[26] They spent a happy week with Ned and Pam Bradford in "stuffy," lovable Boston and on Cape Cod, beautiful in snow, before heading to New York City (crippled by a rail strike) and a full-scale publicity barrage.

The newly published *Magus,* wrote Fowles to Denys Sharrocks (who, at his friend's request, was racing through the novel as a compulsive litigant in case of a libel action), "is getting lavishly overpraised and lavishly grilled, depending, as far as I can tell, on the bowelmovements of the respective reviewers. Telling the future by reading entrails."[27] Indeed, the responses ranged widely. In the *New York Times Book Review*, J. D. Scott rhapsodized that *The Magus* was "a sumptuous firework exhibition of fantasy upon themes of personal awareness . . . an extraordinary literary feat."[28] The curmudgeonly Marvin Mudrick in the *Hudson Review* complained that while "*The Magus* may well be, when it sticks to its job of mystification, one of the best 'mystery stories' ever written," he was annoyed at the "endless puzzle-chains, exploding cigars, flowers that metamorphose into octopi and squirt ink."[29] Fowles himself was not satisfied with *The Magus*. When he opened the first bound and printed copy, his eye fell on a sentence he wanted to change. He began editing in the margins from the day of publication, hoping someday to be able to publish a revised edition.

Through the entire publicity tour Elizabeth Fowles sat in control rooms watching in unvarnished admiration as her husband was interviewed on radio and television. She thought him "amazingly good at this publicity stunt . . . so smooth. . . . John is so pleasant and charming and serious and amusing with them all . . . some of the interviewers are as sharp as needles and the questions pretty penetrating too." There were "lunches galore with press or magazine people," smashing parties in the evenings, and a private dinner with Gloria Vanderbilt ("She was gorgeous—so sweet, so rich, a princess-woman. I loved her . . . her friends were awful"). They spent a whole Saturday in Greenwich Village, in and out of shops ("the wealth of the gorgeous and jolly things and people"), joining a party in an Italian restaurant, and singing along loudly with a pub piano player until two in the morning ("This was our best day here I think"). They sneaked off to the movies another day, having missed cinema for months. Holding hands, they ran down Broadway from movie house to movie house, watching films for seven hours straight.[30]

In the urban, highly social environment of New York City, radiant in her husband's company, Elizabeth Fowles sparkled with energy, laughter, and curiosity. Only days later, back in her damp, cold, isolated English farmhouse, she was again sunk in desperate emotional misery. Overnight, she wrote, they had "plunged" out of the twentieth century "into the heart of old England . . . pitched into dark, wet January . . . like we've returned to the Middle Ages."[31] Through the rest of the winter Elizabeth suffered a "period of ghastliness," punctuated with crushing depression and illnesses like bronchitis.[32] She seriously considered flying to Nigeria to see Monica Sharrocks. Yet with the return of spring and an Easter visit from Monica and young Michael, Elizabeth regained her balance.

Until mid-1966 John's sister, Hazel, lived with her husband, Dan O'Sullivan, and their baby son, Jonathan, in a flat in the Notting Hill Gate section of London. The tiny attic flat above them fell vacant in autumn 1965, and shortly after the move to Underhill Farm, the Fowleses took it. Originally a London flat was to be a base for John's business in the city. However, the various London flats became Elizabeth's emotional refuge. Often, particularly in January and February, the months she came to dread, Elizabeth would escape to the flat and leave John to write alone at the farm. This first little flat at 17 Pembridge Crescent, W 11 was austere: pale gray fitted carpet, painted white walls, two orange deck chairs, a plain galley kitchen, and a small room with a double bed. The simplicity deeply appealed to her, as well as to other women who had occasion to stay there. Monica Sharrocks occupied the flat for several months in summer 1967, preparing for the Sharrockses' 1968 return to England from Nigeria. Fred Porter's daughter, Cathy, assumed the lease when the Fowleses moved to 11 Hampstead High Street (Flat B) in October 1967. Indeed, for all John Fowles's frequent presence, the London flats assumed a feminine quality, as there Elizabeth spent days with Anna and her girlfriends, with her mother or sister, and with women friends. From the "brightness and cheerful warmth" of one "cozy" London flat, for example, she urged Monica to visit, saying it was "so restful and satisfactory being in the company of females. . . . It is a small female haven."[33]

Fowles needed a base in London in 1966–1967 for frequent script meetings for *The Magus* film. He had completed the treatment on December 3, 1965, had detoured from the January New York tour to Miami, Florida (which he christened "the painted arsehole of America"), for a script conference with Jud Kinberg and John Kohn, and was still working on rewrites through most of 1967.[34] "Getting the Magus off the ground filmwise will bring us all *under* the ground," wrote Elizabeth in exasperation. "We have the script writer—J. Fowles, the Director, the two producers endlessly chewing round the project. Endlessly flying from USA or

Spain, or toing and froing from Lyme to London, endless talk and counter-talk and ideas and counter ideas."[35]

London was also social, as the Fowleses joined the Kinbergs or the Paynes for dinners and theater outings. Through John's editor, Tom Maschler, with whom Fowles was developing a more personal relationship, they formed new close friendships with Tom and Malou Wiseman. Thomas Wiseman was another of Maschler's Cape writers, already the author of several successful novels. His wife, Malou, an Italian brought up in France, was beautiful, warm, and lively, with a penchant for quirky syntax that delighted Fowles, who called these expressions "malouisms" and her manner "malouantante." Wiseman said of Fowles that "friendship was important to him, but not socializing. He seldom initiated the move, you had to draw him out."[36] The Wisemans became regular guests in Lyme Regis. Their son, Boris, was soon one of the favorite children in Elizabeth's charmed circle.

In Lyme Regis, however, John and Elizabeth Fowles had few local friends in the early years. The fiftyish Leonora Smith, whom Fowles called "our one conversable neighbor," lived in a cottage up Ware Lane.[37] They met her while seeking a place to put out their dustbins in the first weeks at remote Underhill Farm. Leo, as this well-read lady and passionate gardener was always called, discovered that her new neighbor had written *The Collector* and invited the Fowleses to dinner. Of Leo's two daughters, Sarah Smith, the elder, was visiting at home and recalled seeing "two tall people, not Lyme people," walking across the field to their cottage.[38] Sarah Smith was then twenty-one, always a magical age to Fowles, with a pretty face and vivacious manner. She worked in London advertising and was immersed in the arts and photography. She had the sharp opinions and often barbed wit that always fascinated Fowles. Sarah must have intrigued him at that first meeting, for Elizabeth, just past her fortieth birthday, fell silent as drinks were offered, just as she had withdrawn into defensive silence when meeting John's friends in North Oxford in 1953. "Liz," said Leo Smith, "could take against somebody instantly. . . . She sort of froze up. She took against Sarah then. . . . She didn't speak the whole evening. Most embarrassing."[39] Later, Elizabeth grew friendly with both Smith daughters. In 1966 Leo Smith moved for some years to Oxford but visited the Fowleses often. The friendship lasted the rest of Elizabeth's life.

Aside from their fondness for Cecil Quick, or Quicky, who carried out all of Fowles's building projects for many years, and Jack Board, their laundryman while at Underhill, who later became their first gardener, the Fowleses had few local associations. John Fowles was happiest in isolation, tramping out into the Undercliff, working on his land, and writing in his secluded workroom. Elizabeth, advised by everyone to "take up something," was not one for the church and charitable good works of the middle-class ladies of Lyme.[40] She was lonely and frustrated.

Like some mythological earth deity, carried off to the dark regions for part of a year and reborn each spring, Elizabeth pined through the dreary, lonely winters. In the fine weather from Easter to mid-autumn, she was a fountain of loving generosity for all the Fowles friends and family. The summers at Underhill Farm were crowded with long visits from Elizabeth's mother and sister, from the growing O'Sullivan family, from Robert and Gladys Fowles. The Sharrockses came often. Fred Porter and Eileen Porter visited separately and together. Ronnie and Betsa Payne were regular guests. The Kinbergs combined film business with pleasure on long weekends. Architect Charlie Greenberg so liked the area that he and his wife purchased a weekend cottage nearby. Elizabeth cooked endless delicious meals, gaining a reputation for "more French than English" fresh fare.[41] She led expeditions through the fields and down the steep cliffs to picnics on the beach below. She introduced guests to Lyme's harborside shops and narrow lanes. She hosted rowdy birthday parties in the farmhouse for her friends' children.

With several hours of writing behind him each day, John was happy to join in. *His* walks were memorable, as he plunged into the woods, cutting his way off the path, secateurs in hand. He led friends out along the cliffs and left them bewildered, as he charged off to examine some discovery, moving quickly out of sight. Although he had written that he was pleased not to have children and was always visibly awkward with babies, he enjoyed young guests enormously. He loved sharing nature pursuits with Mike Sharrocks and, on discovering some new marvel in his woods or barn, could be heard to mutter, "*Wish* Mike was here!"[42] His sister's boys—Jonathan (born August 1965) and twins Simon and Tom (born late in 1967)—became very dear to him, especially as they grew old enough to play in his garden and go exploring with him.

The most welcome of all young guests was Anna Christy. After years of separation, broken only by short visits, nearly sixteen-year-old Anna arrived on July 22, 1966, to stay for an entire month. Elizabeth was very nervous. "What will the long spell with her be like, the first time since she was 3 years old?" she wrote anxiously.[43] But the visit proved to be "splendid." Anna found the ordinariness of daily life with her mother "*wonderful*" because she was included in the work of making Underhill Farm a home. The two cooked and made jam, harvested the garden, sewed clothes and curtains. Shopping was a "pioneering" effort in which they set out with rucksacks across the fields to bring home groceries. They explored up the coast ("safe walks, footpath stuff") and visited all the local churches to make brass rubbings. Fresh vegetables from the Fowles garden were a revelation to Anna in variety, textures, and flavors. It was Anna's first extended exposure to television as well. John Fowles had become "addicted" to watching televised sports, but Elizabeth steered her daughter to plays and cultural programming.[44]

"In a tenuous, artificial sort of way the three of us enter the father-mother-only-daughter situation," Fowles wrote. Anna was all "green sensuality," and "this business of my establishing a relationship with her is infinitely tentative." John's and Anna's shyness finally melted, however, before their shared excursions into the Undercliff, "when we went off into the wild." Fowles capitalized on Anna's interest in school geology. Rucksacks over their shoulders, teenager and once-distant stepfather hiked off together fossil hunting, and that "really hit it off for both of us."[45] Anna's visits over long school breaks became a regular pattern in the next few years. By the next summer Fowles could write that her presence diffused "a sort of warmth, perhaps a forgiveness of us."[46] On extended Dorset holidays the girl took up horseback riding ("a bit crazy on the horse riding at present," wrote Liz. "Bloody animals scare me to death"),[47] eventually working summers at the stable in nearby Chideock. She made local friends, even had boyfriends, and Fowles found himself in the unfamiliar situation of pacing and muttering, "What are they up to? What *do* they find to talk about all this time?" as his stepdaughter lingered in some pub or late at a party.[48]

The summer of 1966 was a major turning point for Anna Christy and Liz Fowles, the moment of restoration of their rightful relationship as mother and daughter. For the rest of her life Anna Christy would think of this green and golden season as the beginning of reconciliation. And it was. But even as the bonds between mother and child were reforged, unknown to Anna, a renewal of a sadder, darker story was taking place. In allowing his daughter to join her mother and Fowles for a month in

Dorset, Roy Christy gave cordial notice that he was about to publish a novel based on the Spetsai experience. Christy's publishers, aware of Fowles's new novel *The Magus*, had asked that Mr. and Mrs. Fowles read it and sign a release. "Like Charleys," wrote Fowles to Denys Sharrocks, "we said, Fine, so glad, we're sure it will be all right. Then we read the bloody thing." Indeed, while Anna and her mother chatted in the front seat on the drive to Dorset from the Christys' Fulham home, John sat in back reading Roy's novel. It was "a great (and undisguised) spewing-out of all his hatreds and (we now realize) his absolutely unassuaged determination to drink beakers of the bitter past—laced with our blood. It really was a terrible book—both as a bit of writing and in its vicious comminations of us. It was also sad. You know, the genius who never made it, and sees himself surrounded by people who have."[49]

Roy Christy's novel concerned the adulterous situation among three people on a Greek island where the two men were teachers. The Elizabeth character, called Meg, was "virtually a nymphomaniac," sleeping with the pupils of the Roy character, called (amazingly) John. She is "foul-mouthed," "lazy and sluttish," "drinks heavily," "is always exhibiting herself in the nude," and "forges cheques." Terribly and hurtfully, she is "a total bitch as regards children and child-bearing," with a "contempt for having children." The John Fowles character, called Philip, "engineers unjust dismissals," has "affaires in Paris," "despises the Greeks." He is "callous towards animals," beats his mistress, and "wriggles out of marriage." He takes the hero's wife away and "subsequently treats her in a manner that is a thousand times worse than the reality." Fowles wrote Denys Sharrocks that "dreadful fantasy scenes" were "interpolated in all the actual history—the Roy-figure reduces the me-figure to a cringing wreck in a fight scene . . . in another he has the Eliz-figure on her knees before him, begging to be taken back, but he sternly consigns her to the police-station (she's been forging cheques)." Elsewhere, a figure recognizably based on Denys Sharrocks and Eric Lyons, "by God . . . manoeuvres him out of a job."[50] There were libels against the Anargyrios School and even against Yanni Korkondilas. Fowles was sickened. "Only a man of not completely sound mind could have written it," he said; the book was "loathsome . . . must be stopped."[51]

They did stop it. John Fowles, representing himself and Elizabeth, wrote Roy Christy a long letter setting out their objections and their distress that Roy had created his "hideous wax caricatures" in such a way as

to make "absolutely certain that *only we* can be identified with your characters." Roy's "need for revenge" had cheapened all of them, John wrote.
But their "chief complaint against the book" was that it "would hurt Anna
deeply" and "might do her considerable harm." Indeed, Fowles's letter
was written in anguish and restraint, rather than in the boiling rage he
must have felt. He was reasonable in his arguments and mollifying in his
tone when threats would have been easier. He begged Christy to withdraw the book himself because "it is wrong to publish it" and "if it has to
be for someone's sake—then for Anna's."[52] A few years later this letter,
indeed the entire incident turned inside out, would model a similar letter
written by Anthony Mallory to Daniel Martin in the "Crimes and Punishments" chapter of that novel.[53]

John urged Roy to talk with them, to open "a door onto a better relationship among all of us." But by the new year there was "a ghastly new
schism . . . a total breakdown in communications." They had stopped
Roy's "masterpiece from appearing," Fowles reported to Denys Sharrocks,
and now had a new and "ultimate sin on our backs." Roy could forgive
them neither the past nor the present. He was writing another book now.
("Rather like knowing a vitriol-thrower's lurking in the woods up the
lane.")[54] Not until that second book was published in spring 1968 could
Roy speak to them civilly. Meanwhile Anna was "exchanged" at pubs or
picked up by arrangement. Anna Christy denied ever reading her father's
unpublished novel, but the Fowleses worried for years. Each time the
teenager was sulky or sullen, withdrawn or defiant, they wondered fear-
fully, Could it be that the girl had "read her father's monstrous book"?[55]

"Our past," wrote Fowles, "has suddenly come viciously back to life."[56]
Its resurrection, awakened by Roy's vengeful novel, deeply affected both
John and Elizabeth and took strange forms, out of which came a masterpiece, *The French Lieutenant's Woman*. Three days after sending his letter to Roy, after two years free from nightmares, Fowles began having
terrifying dreams. In the first, he entered a foreign boardinghouse with
another man, an Austrian. In a tiny room at the back of the top floor John
glanced into a mirror at his reflection. Back at him stared "a strange
sallow-faced woman . . . blank-eyed, Modigliani-like. . . . By my position
it could only be me." His entire being "screamed. . . . My heart stopped."
In daylight after the agony of a sleepless night, Fowles wrote, "I cannot
describe the horror of this dream, of this sudden total loss of personality."[57] Although he did not recognize it, Fowles's haunted woman and her

lover, the Austrian lieutenant, had returned. Their story, written into the third volume of *An Island and Greece,* had been the writer's response to his guilty love affair with Elizabeth, Fowles's own encrypted version of the events that Roy Christy's book had just churned up. Now, once again, this old, rejected tale began to float up through Fowles's unconscious to the surface. Through the autumn Fowles's dreams continued, many of them in the form of "mythopoeic stills," free-floating static images that drifted to him in the moments between waking and sleeping.[58]

In September 1966 the Fowleses traveled to Paris, France, to see actor-director Robert Hossien's staged version of *The Collector* ("Rather a mild hit," reported Elizabeth) and treated themselves to "three lovely rich days" in Paris.[59] They continued to Málaga, Spain, where John Kohn was on location for *Fathom,* for a script conference on *The Magus,* and were joined there by Jud Kinberg and the newly named director, Guy Green.

But once they were home in Dorset in October, reaction to the resurrection of the past overwhelmed Elizabeth. Coupled with her seasonal malaise about the rural isolation, she succumbed to "a sort of mute paralysis, like some animal trapped and now hopeless." Over and over she revisited the events of Spetsai and her loss of Anna. "Numb with rage," Fowles found concentration impossible.[60] He packed her off to the London flat. When he was alone, he went a little wild. He lived "like a hermit" in complete solitude for over a fortnight, speaking to no one, wearing filthy clothes, not bathing, forgetting to eat. He drifted around the fields, by day and by night, "and let them become parts of me, like the wild life," experiencing "this strange symbiosis with nature. . . . I mean I become an element of nature myself." It was sad, he thought, that not many more generations would know this experience. "Science and overpopulation must swamp nature." But he ached for his wife, missing her all the time, "as she was . . . not as she is." They talked for hours by telephone every day while Elizabeth rehearsed her misery over Anna, her own identity, her feelings of worthlessness, and her relationship with John. She sat alone in the half-furnished flat, Fowles wrote, "and relives the events of fifteen years ago."[61] Roy Christy had wrought a finer revenge than he knew. When Elizabeth returned to John on November 5, she was "haggard," her smile "contorted," "like someone who has been through a religious conversion."[62]

Other melancholy, lost, and guilty women were also on Fowles's mind through these months. Elizabeth had returned with tales of the misery of many of their London middle-aged women friends: mental breakdowns, psychoanalysis, late-life abortions, desertions by husbands, infidelities. They saw a good deal of Betsa Payne that autumn as well, both in London and, when the Paynes joined them for Christmas, at Underhill Farm. Elizabeth's bouts of sadness and confusion seemed well-balanced cheerfulness in contrast with the deep depression and neurotic behavior that Betsa now suffered. John felt sympathy for his old friend Ronnie, "preternaturally decent" in his unfailing care for his wife[63] ("A saint and a martyr," John wrote to Podge[64]). "Behind all these unhappy women is the same horror," wrote Fowles: "their loneliness, their unnecessity. The fault of society has been to emancipate women but to refuse to furnish (to train them for) their freedom."[65]

During Elizabeth's absence Fowles began a play on this theme, first called *Sensitivity,* then *The Swallow and the Scythe,* finally, simply *The Scythe.* The heroine was to be "a mixture of us both; and Betsa Payne, and Connie Ferrar."[66] Certain of his solution to the problems of modern women, he sped through several drafts in November 1966. But for all Fowles's understanding of the conflicts of women's emancipation, his solution was positively reactionary, a returning to some D. H. Lawrentian or Victorian view of feminine nature. "Woman has to retrace her steps to some of the parts of the contract that have been annulled," he wrote sincerely: "to loving the man more than the man loves her, to more domestic responsibility (the home as her province, not her millstone). . . . A woman is the port from which the ship sails, and to which it will return. She cannot fulfil this role, *and* try to be the joint captain of the ship."[67]

Elizabeth Fowles read *The Scythe* at the beginning of December 1966. She recognized the character and took it "all on herself." The result was an extremely bitter quarrel and Fowles's reluctant suppression of the play. "So that is banned," he wrote, "not to be gone on with except under the threat of her endless anger. She drives me now into a sort of silent rage that is new in my life."[68] Sometime later in the month, after the suffering female character of *The Scythe* had been suppressed, Fowles experienced one of his mythopoeic stills. In this one, famously, "a woman stands at the end of a deserted quay and stares out to sea." She wore black, turned her back reproachfully on the land, and was in some way an outcast. She haunted him. He "began to fall in love with her."[69]

One month later this haunting image became the the seed of *The French Lieutenant's Woman,* which he began writing on January 25, 1967.

Fowles named the woman in his waking dream Sarah Woodruff. As he speculated about her story and identity, the narrative that spun around her was a recognizable version of the melancholy and mysterious woman with a secret past love story that makes up volume 3 of *An Island and Greece*. Elizabeth Christy was the model for that heroine, the ill-fated Marie, making Elizabeth Fowles the ancestor of Sarah Woodruff. In the same way, Fowles double Kenneth Wilson, an unrealized young man awakened by love and nature, who loses his beloved, is in many ways the inspiration behind Charles Smithson. Ironically, Roy Christy, whose own terrible book of memory was now suppressed, had called these enduring literary characters into being.

Was Fowles aware that he was once again rewriting the oft-rejected *An Island and Greece*? There is no documentation, but he knew he was transmuting personal myth. Some years later he put out a theory that the black-clad female figure had been unconsciously inspired by memories of a favorite eighteenth-century French novel, *Ourika* by Claire de Duras.[70] If the image did originate in a text, however, it was his own text, which was in turn based on personal experience. Fowles's capacity for fertile forgetting was extraordinary. Facts and important incidents were often allowed, even encouraged to slip below the surface of his poor conscious memory into some unconscious but highly creative level of his being. Like this battered, buried first novel, they tended to send up shoots and reappear, blooming, unrecognized, years later.

The plot of *An Island and Greece* was a way of presenting the biographical events and discoveries of Fowles's experiences on Spetsai in 1951–1953. When the structure resurfaced in *The French Lieutenant's Woman,* it was as a vessel reshaped to contain the emotional essence of Fowles's life at Underhill Farm. The forbidden love affair between Charles Smithson and Sarah Woodruff spoke of the emotionally harrowing, but enduring passion between Fowles and his wife. The story contained John Fowles's rejection of London (in Charles's rejection of Ernestina and her money) as well as his mystical, sensuous rapture in the wilderness of the Undercliff, his experience of personal symbiosis with nature. The mysteriously suffering Sarah Woodruff dramatized Elizabeth's sense of guilt, isolation, and obliterating entrapment, as well as her intuitive longing for something better. Several key scenes in the novel are also emotionally supercharged by the mother-daughter reunion of Liz and Anna in 1966.

The book also gave Fowles a realm in which to speculate in mature and dramatic fashion on issues that had held his attention for decades: evolution and extinction, the inevitability of biological determinism, the myth of progress, existential philosophy, and the power of the past. He had become a self-conscious writer of fiction, operating at the height of his powers. This narrative became his experiment. It was a place to write a first-person novel about the creative process, disguised as a third-person Victorian romance. Simultaneously, Fowles brought himself into an intimate, emotionally filial relationship with novelist Thomas Hardy, while carrying on a lover's quarrel with modernists like Alain Robbe-Grillet and Roland Barthes, whose *Writing Degree Zero* he was reading and abandoned unfinished during the writing of the first draft of *The French Lieutenant's Woman*.[71]

Not only was Elizabeth Fowles the inspiration for the unforgettable story and character of Sarah Woodruff, but her editing actually altered the structure and published impact of the novel in very significant ways. She did not read the book until June 17, 1968, when Fowles was ready to make his third and final revision. Her typed and handwritten comments survive, with Fowles's note: "Comments of my sternest editor, otherwise my wife. They made me change the text considerably before it was sent out for professional reading. J.F. 1977."[72]

In fact, Elizabeth, whose editing always aimed for the economical, insisted that Fowles remove entire sections. He had written a comic episode in the manner of Lewis Carroll's *Alice in Wonderland* in which the intrusive writer/narrator appears as a notorious ax murderer escaping from the Exeter Asylum on the very day of Charles and Sarah's assignation. A dead ringer for this bearded maniac, Charles is prevented from returning to Sarah while detained by very Tweedle Dum–Tweedle Dee–like policemen. Riding the train to seek her in London, Charles meets his lunatic double, who threatens to chop him out of the story with a meat cleaver until recognizing him as his long-lost twin brother. Elizabeth wrote, "Positively *loath* maniac-author episode," so Fowles removed it. She also decided that Dr. Grogan's scenes echoed *The Magus* too much, that he was "getting too close to Conchis." She suggested subtle cuts that preserved the "authenticity." She made her husband peel away some of his interpolated explanations to preserve the story's ambiguity. Over one didactic speech she scrawled, "Give up lecture. Spoils magic."[73]

Elizabeth focused on Sarah Woodruff ("a brilliant creation," she assured him) and particularly on the novel's ending. Fowles's original ending reflected his view that a fulfilled woman would choose the traditional roles of wife and mother over pursuit of an independent destiny. It is a very limp, sentimental, conventional conclusion. After a twenty-month search Charles finds Sarah living in Clapham, presumably married. Denying she ever loved him, she sends him away. Leaving with bruised pride, Charles cynically sends flowers of farewell and learns from the seller that "Mrs. Smithson" lives alone, supporting her baby son by modeling at the Royal Academy of Art. Joyfully, Charles rushes to a tender reconciliation, to the promise of marriage and of another child.

"This is where you really throw it away," wrote Elizabeth of this conclusion. "NOT WORTHY of you." The mysterious melancholic creature had turned out, she said, "to be a shallow sort of Lily in the end," testing Charles with silly, pointless deceptions. It was Elizabeth's insight that making Sarah a mere model was placing her on "the rather tentative fringe" of the art world. "You should bang her somewhere into the centre," she insisted. "The mystery of Sarah," Elizabeth continued, "is not answered, wonder if it should be. . . . In fact to my way of thinking this novel should end with no answer but only an implied one of tragedy." Sarah, Elizabeth wrote, was "the *one* person who should come through strong as part of the 20th century condition of complicated male/female female intellect . . . should stand as the tragic figure in some way. Your inconclusive *modern* human being. . . . Therefore I do not think you can end with the ending you have. It is too pat."[74]

Many critics have floated scholarly theories on Fowles's celebrated "double ending," speculating on its postmodernity, its foreshadowing of deconstruction, and its philosophical implications. All these suggestions may be valid. However, only one scholar, Elizabeth Mansfield, ventured that Fowles was also responding to the intuitive wisdom of his wife.[75] Indeed, it was John Fowles who wrote the final chapter, but it was Elizabeth Fowles who determined what Sarah's destiny should be. In July 1968 Fowles wrote both a stronger version of the conventional "happy" ending and a new, "tragic" ending in which the couple part and Sarah continues, mysteriously, as "your inconclusive *modern* human being."

Fowles also followed Elizabeth's advice to "bang" Sarah into the center of the art world by making her the amanuensis to pre-Raphaelite artist Dante Gabriel Rossetti, living, working, and raising her child in his

Thames-side house. Yet even this choice was shadowed by the ghosts of Fowles's personal biography. Rossetti's Embankment house was in the same group of Chelsea houses as the flat occupied during the mid-1950s by Roy Christy, who, like Rossetti, was an artist. Fowles also rewrote Sarah's baby from a little boy to a little girl, one, indeed, who resembles Anna as a baby. So, as Charles and Sarah make their choice within the multiple possibilities of the novel's endings, they are haunted by the shades of those four real people trapped in their personal past—John, Elizabeth, Roy, little Anna—while they wrestle with their defining biographical situation and the consequences of their choices.

From January through October 1967, as Fowles wrote the first draft of *The French Lieutenant's Woman,* he struggled daily with the Sisyphean problems of the film production of *The Magus.* In January 1967 he announced to the Sharrockses with blithe cynicism: "All systems are go, for a really sensational splash in the mud." Shooting was scheduled to begin in Crete or Cyprus that summer. Fowles was already worried about the director, Guy Green, whom he thought "a nice man, but absolutely unsympathetic to the subject matter."[76] The English Green had made several notable films, including the prizewinning *The Angry Silence.* As this fine film shows, however, Green's talent lay in the gritty, understated, down-to-earth, and proletarian. In optimistic moments, Fowles was encouraged by Green's craftsmanship and uncompromising standards and his refusal to entertain the "bravura" Hollywood ideas of John Kohn and Jud Kinberg. But Fowles learned that Guy Green hated ambiguity, symbolism, and literary references, the very stuff of *The Magus.* "Deep down," he confessed, "GG frightens me." At one point Fowles found himself in agreement with Green, to Kohn's dismay, in wanting "to present the film as a kind of dream that Nicholas has." However, while Fowles welcomed this as a way to slip fanciful or psychologically powerful material effectively into the "too realistic medium" of cinema, Green wanted the dream idea because "nobody's going to believe that people like Conchis exist."[77]

As the months went on, Fowles found himself improbably allied with Green in the endless script conferences. Opposing them, Jud Kinberg and John Kohn worried over the lack of dramatic definition, Kinberg later saying that they never identified the "'categorical imperative' . . . what is it that the protagonist wants so much that he will sacrifice his life?"[78] As with *The Collector,* the film's ending posed the thorniest problems, with this controversial issue only resolved, poorly, in final editing. The two producers wanted a final resolution, which Fowles called "melodramatic and 'flamboyant.'" He and Green wanted a "quiet and emotional" ending.[79] Receiving his cut-up script "back from the boys in London" could send Fowles, Elizabeth wrote, "into a depressed fit . . . striding off across his fields."[80] He became convinced that he, John Fowles alone, should direct his own work. "I could certainly direct performance as well as the only other two directors I have seen at work (Wyler and Green)," he argued. "The technical knowledge needed doesn't seem very great. If one could only gain the autonomy one has in a novel I should be very tempted."[81]

Michael Caine, then the number two male box office draw in the world, had been cast as Nicholas Urfe. One of the worst pressures for Fowles was the fear of "alienating Mike Caine if he doesn't have a 'strong' last scene." To present Conchis as a teacher and, thereby, Nicholas "as someone who needs teaching" was "anathema." In the Hollywood jargon of script conferences, it "cuts Caine's balls off." So, throughout filming, they worked with an ending in which, Fowles said, in wild Western style the "goodie" gunned down the "baddie."[82]

Caine was the first person cast for the film, and he objected that the script made him "seem too much of a cad."[83] ("He's a natural bastard," mused Fowles, "so I suppose he's a sort of natural casting.") Caine's well-publicized reputation as a selfish Young Turk proved mostly publicity, however, and he impressed the Fowleses during filming as a "nice young man" with "exemplary" professionalism, though his performance disappointed.[84] Anthony Quinn, star of *Zorba the Greek* and a good friend and frequent colleague of Jud Kinberg's, was cast as Maurice Conchis. In fall 1966 "there was a dreadful brontosaurian clash of pea-brains and massive vanity" between the two stars over who got top billing.[85] Caine won. Quinn quit, although he returned the following spring. Persuading Tony Quinn to shave his head for the part was also a difficult issue, since he had what Fowles called "a Samson complex."[86] Caine and Quinn, Elizabeth commented to Monica: "Impossible to imagine any two less suitable in my humble opinion."[87]

Casting for the two girls, Anne (Alison renamed) and Lily, was delayed until almost the beginning of filming. "Now it's finding who will be least horrible," groaned Fowles.[88] European New Wave film star Anna Karina was, surprisingly, available and was lured to the role of Anne, a part Fowles had hoped would be played by Maggie Smith. For the mysterious Lily, Fowles yearned for Jean Shrimpton, Terence Stamp's supermodel girlfriend. Shrimpton could not act and had a kind of innocent and graceless simplicity off camera but her face, Fowles said, was "marvelous."[89] The part went to the beautiful but not-very-mysterious face of Candice Bergen, barely known in Europe, whose considerable, late-blooming talent was at that time undeveloped.

In an unforeseen catastrophe, on April 21, 1967, political unrest in Greece erupted into the military coup of "the Colonels" and seven ensuing years of fascist misrule. The film's art director, William Hutchinson, was on Crete, and for a terrible week everyone "thought we had lost him."[90] The location on Crete had to be abandoned because the insurers refused "to pay out for production delays caused by political unrest."[91] All concerned, including Fowles, also loathed the idea of supporting "the colonels' eagerness to get foreign money" with the film's three-million-dollar budget. Two film teams searched for a new location, one through Spain, the other "from the top to the bottom of Lebanon." In May 1967, Palma, Majorca, was selected, thus, wrote Fowles acidly to Fred Porter, "giving our 3 mill. to that famous old socialist Franco."[92]

John and Elizabeth Fowles joined the location filming in Majorca from September 6 to 20, 1967. On the first day Fowles was asked to appear in the opening scene of Nicholas Urfe's arrival on the island, playing the bit part of a gruff Greek sailor. Casting a line to the wharf, he jerks his head at the mysterious island and says tersely to Michael Caine, "Phraxos." Originally, First Assistant Director David Tringham was cast, but the young man didn't look Greek. John's acceptable performance in his film debut "broke the ice" for Fowles and Tringham. As Elizabeth took an interest in Annette Tringham and the couple's eighteen-month-old daughter, the four grew friendly.

Looking back on the filming of *The Magus,* David Tringham thought it was entirely miscast and misdirected. *The Magus* required "boldness, imagination, risk-taking," and a "broad brush" while Green's strength lay in quasi-documentary, realistic work. Fowles, in writing the script, had been "manoeuvred" by the director and producers into oversimplifying his rich, complex book, stripping away the mystery and ambiguity that were its essence. Tringham remembered so much tension between the director and the two producers, who lobbied for "more flamboyance," that Green had them barred from the set.[93]

Yet the shoot in Spain, Tringham also recalled, was a "golden dream of being on location, what you think being on location must be like and usually isn't." Scenes went well. Fowles laughed that there was no lack of seasoned German extras for the occupation scene, even to the ex-Wehrmacht man hired to train them. There were days spent swimming on the beach and spectacular weekend parties. The Tringhams held one festive party in their spacious rented house when the French-born Annette prepared a fruit concoction with a dozen bottles of Cointreau and a chicken Provençal from at least twenty chickens.[94] After two weeks Elizabeth was reluctant to leave. "I got to feel all part of the happy family atmosphere," she reminisced, "that feeling of being a part of the whole thing, everybody working hard at one project. I love it." John Fowles "fussed . . . to get back," insisting, "This is all time-wasting. He is right really. Damn him."[95]

Through the winter, optimistic news of the project drifted in. Anna Karina's "brilliant performance" was said to have stolen the picture. Quinn was said to be wonderful.[96] The producers believed "it just might be a great movie." Skeptically Elizabeth wrote, "They'll lose it some where along the way . . . will add up to lost opportunity."[97] Then, by the end of January 1968, there was worry: "It has gone all wrong somewhere. . . . All concerned with it are now trying to 'save' the film."[98] Shown a reedited rough cut at the end of February 1968, "Zanuck and the other 20th Century moguls" were "delighted." Guy Green's reward was to be signed for the summer's big picture, and Fowles was pleased that "the happy ending in London" of reunion and resolution had been cut, "as I've always wanted."[99] With cautious hope, he awaited the results.

Despite interruptions, Fowles had finished the first draft of *The French Lieutenant's Woman* by October 27, 1967, three weeks after returning from Spain. He let the manuscript lie for a few months. He amused himself in November by rescuing a book long out of print, *Mehalah: A Story of the Salt Marshes*, an 1880 novel by Sabine Baring-Gould.[100] It was the first of many forgotten novels that Fowles rehabilitated over the next twenty years. His zeal for the arcane research for this reprint edition was like his collecting of New Hall china, a substitute for hunting. In future, his dogged stalking of facts and details was to change both his writing and his relationship to the town of Lyme Regis.

In January 1968 Fowles reacted to the "third-person cerebrality of the FLW" by writing "a headlong love-and-mystery story."[101] Elizabeth was in

Norwich helping John's sister with her newborn twins. Alone at the farm, eating a meal a day standing over the kitchen sink and working sixteen-hour days, Fowles churned out a 110,000-word thriller in seventeen days flat. Elizabeth was astonished on her return, boasting to Monica that John had written two complete novels in less than half a year. "I feel he is rather good," she boasted "if a bit barmy."[102] The new book, *Somebody's Got to Do It,* was then shelved for many months.

By February 1968 Fowles was entangled in financial difficulties. He had reached a level of income where nearly half his earnings would go for taxes. He declared this was evidence of the general "rottenness of Britain" but felt "largely indifferent,"[103] although Elizabeth wrote that "a sense of defeat comes over him at times."[104] Many other authors lived abroad to avoid British taxes. Fowles, however, thought that if he could not keep his own earnings, he would like to benefit his loved ones: his sister's family, Elizabeth's daughter, Denys's wife and child, and other friends. At the suggestion of his accountant, he tried to set up a named beneficiary trust to which he would assign the copyright for *The French Lieutenant's Woman* to benefit those on his list. By February 1968, however, this scheme had been thoroughly debunked by the Lincoln's Inn barristers the Fowleses consulted. Indeed, with his various sources of income, in both Britain and the United States, it seemed that after a pre-publication valuation was made on *The French Lieutenant's Woman* (still in unfinished manuscript), Fowles would be taxed at the highest surtax rate, "that is, over 90% of my earnings will go to the ever-open maw."[105] Moreover, he could not use income from the new novel to pay what he owed but would have to find the money from other sources. "It took it out of John," wrote Elizabeth, "led finally to the conclusion that you pay up or leave the country . . . he went raging, I will not be *forced* into exile!"[106]

Returning home from the London meeting with the barristers on the Saturday night of February 24, 1968, Fowles peered wearily through the darkness and thought how odd it was that "the dying elm at the bottom of Batch [one of his oldest fields] didn't seem to be there."[107] The following morning Elizabeth sat reading the Sunday newspapers in her sunny kitchen when John came in from the garden, smiling strangely. "Well, you have got your wish," he said; "this place is done for."[108] He led his wife, eyes shut tightly, through the garden and over the wall, to show her how ten acres of the seaward fields of Underhill Farm had subsided in a huge landslip. It was "strangely beautiful in a chaos-creating sort of way; wild tilted tables of turf, naked faces of flint and greensand, like a golden dough, even the fences twisted flat." The sheep meadow was "ravaged and split," trees and bushes "turned somersault." In awe, sometimes laughing in disbelief, they wandered over the "total ravage of the land," marveling.[109]

They knew immediately that they had "lost the fifteen thousand pounds or so we have spent on buying the house and doing it up." But strangely, after the "stultifying" tax discussions in London, Fowles felt exhilarated and released.[110] He and Elizabeth opened a bottle of Scotch, "got tipsy and decided that all this was for the best." They would sell the property for whatever they could get, jettison their goods, leave the country, and embark on "a new phase of living . . . European travellers." They agreed that they were "too young to put down roots," owned too much, needed to live many "other ways of life."[111]

But they were miserable showing an estate agent around the house, fields, and barns. As the weeks went on, both were plagued with nightmares, and Fowles, characteristically, fell ill. "A weird sort of reversal" took place in their individual reactions.[112] In a classic case of denial Fowles was determined to live abroad, to finish his "living-in-the-country experience" without regret. He piled up justifications: He was eager to go. Relieved. Dorset had been "a dead end." He had become too immersed "in solitude and nature." He was becoming "too much of England. This attachment to an England of the past was morbid."[113] Elizabeth, on the other hand, wept and wrote, "Dearest Mon, I am scared, and wish to God you were here."[114] She was "all emotional or irrational," and grieved over "the threat of not seeing Anna so often, and the ending of the lovely school holidays she spends here with me."[115] Now she could not bear the thought of leaving Underhill Farm. While Fowles showed a stream of prospective buyers over the property in March, Elizabeth escaped to Hampstead. Alone, Fowles burned barn rubbish and some of his papers in a huge bonfire. In late April and early May she fled to help Monica move into the Sharrockses' first permanent home in rural Shropshire. By then John and Elizabeth could barely speak of the leaving to each other, living "on a day to day small talk basis."[116] Together, they planted the garden for summer vegetables.

Fowles's financial advisers were only too pleased to help him plan a life in exile, beyond the reach of British Inland Revenue. Every other week for months a new destination was put forth and a new strategy: a flat in Paris, a house in the Channel Islands, a rooftop apartment in Rome, a residence in Malta, especially on the nearby "allegedly unspoilt" island of Gozo.[117] Indeed, Fowles's accountant wanted them "to be on the move, resident nowhere, thus avoiding all tax liability," an idea that terrified Elizabeth.[118] Against the plans for exile abroad, a scheme was proposed in August that Fowles form a company and have it taken over and managed by Booker Brothers so that after five years he could receive 40 percent of his earnings instead of the 20 percent he could otherwise expect. Exile seemed better than this, until Fowles was informed that he would have to remain away from England for three years, actually residing on Malta for at least six months of the year. "He felt he couldn't face it," wrote Elizabeth in August.[119]

In 1968 the events of the outside world seemed to mirror the chaos and destruction of the landslip. In Greece the coup of the colonels had occurred in April 1967, followed that summer by the Arab-Israeli Six-Day War in the Middle East. In Britain the pound was devalued, and inflation was rampant. In 1968 there were race riots in Birmingham, England, and Enoch Powell made incendiary speeches. In the United States there were war protests, civil rights demonstrations, and student violence. In Memphis, Tennessee, American civil rights leader Martin Luther King, Jr., was slain in April 1968. In June Robert Kennedy was shot and killed in Los Angeles while campaigning for the presidency. Ironically, his assassination stopped the first public showing of *The Magus,* scheduled for that day in L.A. In May the Paris riots brought the capital of France to a standstill as students barricading the streets protested against their educational system, their culture, and the Vietnam War. Ronnie Payne covered the story for the *Daily Telegraph* and visited Underhill Farm afterward with hilariously told tales of his adventures during the street confrontations. In August the Soviets invaded Czechoslovakia, crushing the liberal reform movement of Alexander Dubček. The greater world was going to hell, it seemed. And the uglier it became, the more Underhill Farm seemed "the landscape of peace." Perhaps made bolder since the shared disaster of the landslip, wildlife once shy and invisible now accepted the inhabitants of the farmhouse. Hedgehogs played by the back door; roe deer lived openly in Fowles's fields, a pair of bats moved in under their roof. Fowles could directly approach birds and animals without frightening them. A vixen allowed him to sit close, watching newborn cubs sleeping by her burrow

Underhill Farm, Lyme Regis, Dorset, 1967. Fowles created the terraced garden. The white farmhouse is in the center. His workroom, where *The French Lieutenant's Woman* was written, is the building to the left.
Collection of John Fowles, by permission.

The Cobb at Lyme Regis, Dorset, from the air. The Undercliff begins at the left of the photograph; the town to the right. At the top of the hill, with a large, densely grown garden and western tower, sits Belmont House, the home the Fowleses bought in 1968.
Photograph by Bob Croxford/Atmosphere, by permission.

Anna Christy's summer of reunion, Underhill Farm, 1966.
Elizabeth Fowles, John Fowles, and Anna Christy.

Photograph by Fred Porter. Collections of Fred Porter and John Fowles, by permission.

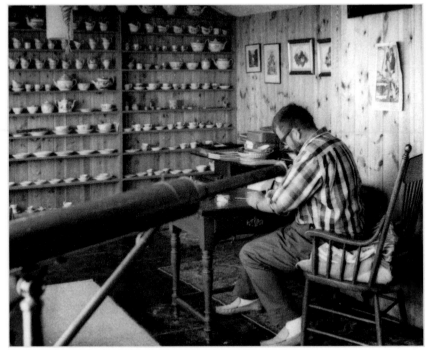

John Fowles in his workroom at Underhill Farm where *The French Lieutenant's Woman* was written, about 1966. Note his telescope and collection of New Hall china.

Collection of John Fowles, by permission.

Friends at Underhill Farm, about 1966. *Left to right:* Eileen Porter, Leonora Smith, Elizabeth Fowles, Anna Christy, and Fred Porter.

Collection of Fred Porter, by his permission and permission of John Fowles.

Fowles's editor at Little, Brown, Larned "Ned" Bradford and his wife, Pamela, on Cape Cod, Massachusetts, about 1967.

Collection of John Fowles, by permission.

The filming of *The Magus*, Majorca, 1967.
Collection of John Fowles, by permission.

Michael Caine as Nicholas and Anthony Quinn as Conchis in the film of *The Magus*.
The Magus © 1968 Twentieth Century-Fox. All rights reserved. Courtesy of Twentieth Century-Fox.

The extended family gathers at Belmont: Dan and Hazel O'Sullivan, one of the twins (Tom or Simon), Jonathan, and Joanne Whitton (later Collins), about 1973.

Collection of John Fowles, by permission.

John Fowles and his O'Sullivan nephews on the beach at Lyme Regis (Tom, Simon, and Jonathan), about 1973.

Collection of John Fowles, by permission.

Robert Fowles, a late harvest.
Collection of John Fowles, by permission.

Jud Kinberg's wedding to Monica Menell at the John Collier estate, France, August 1971. Documentary filmmaker Jo Menell (the bride's brother) and John Fowles were best men for film producer Jud Kinberg (*center*). The subjects always referred laughingly to this photograph as "the mafia picture."
Photograph by Steve Kinberg. Collection of Jud and Monica Kinberg, by permission.

John Fowles and Jonathan Cape editor Tom Maschler at Belmont in the 1970s.
Collection of Tom Maschler, by permission.

Elizabeth Fowles with director David Tringham on the set of *The Last Chapter*, July 1972.
Collections of David Tringham and John Fowles, by permission.

Anna Christy's wedding to Nick Homoky, July 20, 1974, Belmont. *In the foreground:*
Nick Homoky, Roy Christy, John Fowles, Anna Christy, Boris Wiseman, Elizabeth Fowles,
Ian Friend, and Fred Porter.

Collection of Anna Christy, by permission.

The beach at Lyme Regis, July 1974. *Left to right:* Annette Tringham, John Fowles, Malou Wiseman, and Tom Wiseman.

Photograph by David Tringham. Collection of David Tringham, by his permission and permission of John Fowles.

Little, Brown editor Ray Roberts and John Fowles squint into the morning sun on the terrace at Belmont, October 1983.

Photograph by Elizabeth Fowles. Collection of Ray A. Roberts, by permission.

Scriptwriter Harold Pinter, John Fowles, and director Karel Reisz on the set of
The French Lieutenant's Woman, Lyme Regis, 1980.
Collection of Ray A. Roberts, by permission.

Jeremy Irons as Charles and Meryl Streep as Sarah in the film of *The French
Lieutenant's Woman*.
The French Lieutenant's Woman © 1981 Juniper Films. All rights reserved. Courtesy of MGM Clip &
Still.

Anna with her children, Tess and
Will Homoky, 1981.
*Photograph by Nick Homoky, by his
permission.*

Will and Tess, Elizabeth Fowles's grandchildren.
Photograph by Nick Homoky, by his permission.

Scholars and museum staff gathered by the sea wall outside the Lyme Regis (Philpot) Museum for the John Fowles Symposium, July 1996.

Photograph by John B. Gurd, by his permission.

Dinner in the Belmont kitchen during the symposium, July 1996. *Clockwise from John Fowles:* Eileen Warburton, Anna Christy, Anna Peebles, Dianne Vipond, and Kirki Kefalea.

Photograph by Charles Glass, collection of the author.

Charles Glass and Anna Christy, Greece, 2001.
Photograph by Charles Glass, by his permission.

John Fowles interviewed on the portico of Yiasemine by Greek writer Nikos Dimou, Spetses, Greece, October 1996.
Photograph by the author.

John Fowles and his first biographer, Eileen Warburton, Pylos, Greece, November 1996.

Photograph by Kirki Kefalea, collection of the author.

John Fowles's wedding to Sarah Smith, September 3, 1998.
Photograph by Charles Glass, by his permission.

John and Sarah Fowles, September 4, 1998.
Photograph by Fred Porter, by his permission.

John Fowles in his garden at Belmont House, Lyme Regis, July 1996.
Photograph by the author.

near the house. Rabbits mated on the path in front of him. He caught a young pheasant in his hands. As Fowles signed for the sale of the house on June 1, he had never been more aware of "the intricacy of the web of wild life that has the house so closely enmeshed."[120]

With his beloved farm for sale and deep crevices from the landslip widening up to the garden wall, with the accountants demanding a decision and his wife full of anxiety, Fowles undertook the revisions of *The French Lieutenant's Woman,* completing the first on April 23, the second on June 17, and the third on August 25, 1968. In the same period he came to grips with the failure of the film of *The Magus.*

John and Elizabeth Fowles viewed the rough cut on March 8, 1968, with a crushing sense of disappointment. There was, Fowles mourned, "no poetry, no mystery." He blamed Guy Green. There was "just Caine, the bestpaid European filmstar, drifting through a role he doesn't understand."[121] The music was "banal" and the editing incomprehensible.[122] Under Green's unsympathetic direction, "all the dialogue is spoken at snail's pace and every meaningful line is atrociously overstressed, both in delivery and in the killing pause that precedes it." It was a terrible evening. At a restaurant afterward, the Fowleses were seated next to director Franco Zeffirelli and actors Vanessa Redgrave and Richard Harris. Harris turned, smiling, to say how much he had liked *The Collector.* Fowles could barely find his voice to answer. He suffered "a series of black and interwoven nightmares," trying to sleep in the Hampstead flat, agonizing over the film, the loss of his farm, his financial problems, the landslip, and worry about Anna.[123]

In July they endured a private showing of the final version of *The Magus* "with a host of film biz people and their glamourwives, who all look exactly the same shade of suntan and seem to get their clothes at the same shop." The Fowleses agreed it was "a disaster." Neither ever watched it again.[124] Fowles "couldn't pretend, afterwards," telling Jud Kinberg ("the one person I don't want to hurt") how "betrayed" he felt.[125] Wounded, Kinberg told Fowles that it was, after all, "his script."[126] Somehow their friendship survived their anger.

The film medium still called to Fowles, perhaps more seductively because *The Magus* under others' control was disappointing him. In April 1968 Kinberg had offered him a scriptwriting project. Paramount Pictures, just releasing the film of the best-selling novel *Rosemary's Baby,* assigned Kinberg to develop author Ira Levin's earlier play *Dr. Cook's Garden.* This thoughtful little thriller had premiered in New York the previous September, starring Burl Ives as old Doc and Keir Dullea as young physician Jim Tennyson. Set in a small "idyllic" New England town during the Vietnam War, the young man discovers that beloved Dr. Cook, his surrogate father, has created this "Eden" by medical murder, weeding out undesirables like a gardener.[127] Fowles welcomed the project as an opportunity to criticize what he saw as corrupt American values, writing to Fred Porter that he hoped the script would "end up as a small stick of gelignite . . . better an unjust anarchy than an unjust order."[128] Revising *The French Lieutenant's Woman* for the second and third times in summer 1968, Fowles also worked through three complete rewrites of this script. But the powerful *French Lieutenant's Woman* consumed the play. Through each rewrite the Vermont setting became more an English village like Lyme Regis, the dialogue less American. Most striking, Fowles extraneously introduced a dark, individualistic woman with a secret sorrow, a kind of outcast to the small town's conformist residents. So much derives from elements of his novel that his obsession is overwhelmingly evident. Paramount rejected the script in December as "not near enough to Rosemary's Baby, not exciting enough."[129] Kinberg blamed his own "ego" and desire to keep working with Fowles for the "failure" of not simply hiring a skilled scriptwriter.[130] The two, however, continued to try to develop filmscripts together.

Summer passed as Fowles revised. The family and friends visited as usual. The strawberries, marrow peas, and lettuces were abundant. By June 1, John and Elizabeth knew they would be leaving Underhill Farm on September 17. But "where we go, we dunno," wrote Elizabeth, announcing the sale and her feelings of "a most weird kind of anxiety and insecurity."[131] By August there was still no decision on living overseas. However, in an offhand way, almost as if they did not want to admit what they were doing, even to themselves, they were quietly looking at houses in Cornwall, Devon, Wiltshire, and Dorset. In Lyme Regis itself, a house called Belmont House, "a rather splendid Georgian affair," ten years vacant, had come on the market in late spring 1968. Fowles resisted the property from his conviction that he needed to leave Dorset, but the house "beckoned."[132]

Leaving the farm was "total madness," "a state of crisis," wrote Elizabeth after the September move, temporarily to the Hampstead flat. She was full of "heart-break and heartsearching," though she did not cry.[133]

Fowles finally admitted, privately, that losing Underhill Farm was "an amputation." He was unable to write about it. "Being stoic, that is silent," he confessed, "is the only way of living through it without tears."[134]

It was "all rather like a purge."[135] Furniture went into storage, with some things going to Hazel and Dan or to Monica and Denys. Fowles's rarest plants were temporarily placed in a local greenhouse. They dug up the strawberries for replanting. So many books went to the Lyme Regis hospital that the matron created a library for nurses and staff. The contents of bureaus and cupboards went to jumble sales by the carload.

In the midst of the chaos, on September 5, 1968, almost as if part of the general jettisoning of their lives, Fowles sent the manuscript of *The French Lieutenant's Woman* to Tom Maschler. "You won't like it," he said.[136] Two days later he made an offer for Belmont House.

CHAPTER FIFTEEN

Cast Out

Belmont House: 1969–1971

The poet has lost his rhyme
And that is the reason why
His cup of verse is dry.
But wait. Stay a while.
Chaste contemplation of your beauty
Will restore wisdom to his mind
(And strength to his legs and eyes)
And once again he'll versify your virtues.

—ROBERT J. FOWLES, 1970

Belmont House stands 200 feet above sea level, set back 230 yards from the easily visible English Channel, at the southeast corner of Pound Street and Cobb Road in Lyme Regis. Its grand Georgian property incorporates relics of dwellings from medieval and Renaissance times. The elegant façade dates from 1785, when Eleanor Coade, astute owner of the Coade Stone Manufactory in London, adorned the front of her summer villa with serenely classical, ceramic stone faces, samples of the company's fine Adam-style ornaments. John Fowles imagined Belmont as aristocratically feminine, though as they took possession of the house just after New Year's 1969, it was more like "an old whore, with its splendid façade and all the mess that lies behind."[1]

The house was in a perilous state. Occupied by Dr. Harry Joseph

Cooper from 1896 to 1959, it had then stood vacant. Oh, wrote Fowles to Fred Porter, "the folly of buying a house that's been empty for ten years!" Every inch of antiquated electrical wiring had to be replaced. There were "acres of floors," and most were rotted.[2] Damp seeped halfway up most walls. All the drains leaked. The stable and fences were collapsing. There was no central heating. The kitchen was defunct. Recent purchasers had been defeated by attempted renovations, but the Fowleses, who bought it from them, were not warned. Elizabeth groaned that the house had appealed to them "for all the wrong romantic reasons . . . what mad pretentiousness it all is!"[3]

Until May 4, 1969, when the main house was fit to live in, they occupied the small flat in the northwest corner of the ground floor. For those four months, supported by Mr. Quick and his crew (all part-time poachers and smugglers: "the whole thick underworld of Lyme; very rich, and unstudied"[4]), John and Elizabeth plunged into repairing and decorating. "Slog slog slog," moaned Liz at one of her lowest points. "None of that sort of rather crazy happy feeling of the Underhill house doing-up. . . . It has been almost as if there has been a curse on the place." They had no heat in the main house until March, and the cold was "so formidable."[5] Floors gave way ("a plank of sound wood becomes a kind of miracle"[6]). A ceiling, just repaired and painted, collapsed under the weight of snow on the roof. They were flooded during "the worst gales in Lyme's recent history." Trees blew over in the storms. They grew certain their furniture would "stay in store forever." Elizabeth, suffering (not surprisingly) from "despair and depression," was cheered, however, by the wallpapering and painting and by John's active interest ("he got quite carried away") in the "rather daring" color schemes of the rooms.[7]

In the southwest upstairs corner of the house, Fowles established his writing room, with his well-worn worktable, bookshelves, and space for his New Hall china. Looking seaward over the garden, French doors opened onto a south-facing balcony where vines eventually twined and birds alighted. The pounding of keys on his small portable typewriter thudded audibly through the house. The main bedroom was across the corridor. With a fireplace and adjacent bathroom, it was a wide, sunny, south-facing room, abutting a tower at the southwest corner of the house. The kitchen, beneath Fowles's study, opened onto the stone terrace and into the garden. It required complete renovation, but with its

Aga range, antique chests, and worn wooden table, it came to express more of Elizabeth's simple welcoming taste than any other room and was soon the center of domestic life.

The garden, which had attracted Fowles even more than the house, proved a constant, exciting surprise, "like a huge toy." In a wild "state of ruin," it spilled down the steep hillside toward the Lyme Regis seafront in a little over an acre, but seemed more like ten to Fowles. It was "full of terraces and lost corners," all thickly overgrown, as in a fairy tale, with "about thirty years of bramble." Just entering it was an "extraordinary . . . battle." It took him more than an hour to hack his way a mere twenty yards, "like going through a continuous jungle of barbed wire." Daily, however, he and Elizabeth discovered an amazing realm that repaid their back-breaking physical labor. They liberated "relics of its former grandeur": strange trees choked beneath the bramble, flights of stone steps descending the five terraces, a fishpond, the remnants of an orchard, old paths and walks, ancient cast-iron seats, even a two-story linhay. This garden infrastructure had been developed in the 1880s and 1890s by the owner, Dr. Richard Bangay, and been considered a notable sight of Lyme Regis in his day. After Bangay, Dr. Cooper had been a "seagoing doctor" who planted the sheltered, southerly acre with exotic plants from around the globe. As they forced their way in, the Fowleses found a magnificent palm tree, many rare old shrubs, and a huge spread of bamboo, over ten feet tall, with an entire colony of tiny dormice hibernating at the tops of the stalks. Everywhere Fowles dug there were bulbs: irises, daylilies, daffodils, and delicate ornamental onions. Many of the flowers that poured into bloom that spring were old-fashioned varieties with strange scents. By day he noted resident blackcaps, marsh tits, redwings, blackbirds, and a whitethroat, while a tawny owl took up residence in the magnolia each night.[8] For anyone else, putting to rights such a disastrously neglected garden would have been an exercise in misery. For Fowles, the immense labor gave him the purest pleasure. As years went by he further planted his acre with plants purchased and given but also surreptitiously cut or dug up on his travels in what he considered a game.[9] Retired laundryman Jack Board became Fowles's part-time gardener in April 1969.

Elizabeth Fowles emerged from her winter depression by Easter. As daffodils bloomed by the thousands, she bought "the best bargains" in furniture at a country house sale and found herself delighted with her newly renovated house.[10] From the arrival of Leo Smith, their first guest, in April until autumn, visiting family and friends filled Elizabeth's house and life, enthusing over Belmont, cooking with her in the new kitchen, enjoying the wild surprises of the garden. To increase her happiness, Anna's acceptance as a foundation art course student at the Exeter Art School for the fall meant she would join them for the summer and soon live nearby. Writing to Monica Sharrocks, Elizabeth admitted that depression had been deepened by her "terrible sense of loss" for Underhill Farm, "which I didn't face up to when we left there. A delayed action." John, she said, had not "suffered this remorse as much as me. Or at least hasn't allowed himself to indulge in it."[11]

It would be many years before John Fowles admitted the unhealed depth of his wound over losing Underhill Farm. Indeed, his denial of feeling became a kind of triumphant "told you so." When the road to the farm cracked and sank, when the neighboring cottage dropped two feet, when all his former fields split and subsided and all "the cliffs between Batch and Lyme poured mud, like brown lava," Fowles announced the events joyfully "like a man whose treble on the horses has just come up."[12] From the day he left his *domaine,* however, his mood darkened. By January 1969, as they moved into Belmont, Fowles was in as deep a depression as Elizabeth. Unlike Elizabeth, however, John's happiness did not return with spring weather and sunshine. Melancholy seeped permanently into his soul.

In the three weeks before the move to Belmont *The Magus* was released in the United States to mixed, but mostly poor, reviews. Fowles agreed with the worst. When Judith Crist pronounced the movie "one of the ten worst films of 1968," Fowles called it "fair" and a "truer judgement than that of the English-American publishers and agents' quartet of enthusiasm for the new book."[13] But the failure affected him. In the same week Paramount rejected the *Dr. Cook's Garden* script. Fowles still struggled with his financially complicated tax situation and the Belmont purchase. He was also, inexplicably, depressed over *The French Lieutenant's Woman,* a state that worsened each time his editors "overrated" him by their enthusiasm.[14]

For, to Fowles's surprise, Tom Maschler loved *The French Lieutenant's Woman.* "Magnificent!" he telegraphed. He offered Fowles an advance of eight thousand pounds, the highest Cape had ever paid "outside the Len Deighton and Ian Fleming thriller class."[15] Fowles, however,

began to feel very ambivalent toward his creation. The money and anticipated success distressed him. He was embarrassed telling his parents
and close friends of the advance. At the annual Jonathan Cape party in
1968, none of the directors but Tom spoke to the Fowleses and John
thought they blamed Maschler for the high advance. Although warmly
greeted by the Tarns, the Wisemans, and Kurt Maschler, Tom's father,
the Fowleses were also snubbed by several writer acquaintances, notably
Edna O'Brien, of whom Fowles wrote, "a treacherous woman . . . we are
evidently not on her list of knowable people any more."[16] A month later
Little, Brown offered a $125,000 advance, with generous royalties and a
paperback deal. Instead of exhilaration, however, Fowles felt depressed.
For the writer, "the two huge advances . . . have mysteriously devalued
it." He could not "believe the book is that good," felt himself "an im-
poster—almost, under the new consumer protection act, a criminal, asking an inflated price for a spurious product."[17] As his future books
became commercially successful commodities in the consumerist society Fowles so despised, he experienced this shame and depression at
each publication.

Fowles agreed to Maschler's editorial suggestion to switch the sequence of the two endings, placing the conventional ending of romantic
reunion before the tragic ending of parting. However, he resisted all suggestions to suppress the modern intrusive "author" figure and keep only
the single narrative line of the 1867 love story. It was the first indication
that such innovative elements as the diachronic narrative would be misunderstood.[18]

To Fowles's further surprise, Maschler proposed himself as the producer of a film of *The French Lieutenant's Woman*. He convincingly argued that the two previous films had disappointed. Together he and
Fowles should hold out for the very best director, script, and cast to fully
realize this novel as a great film. Warily Fowles agreed, and also agreed
that someone besides himself should write it. He felt betrayed by the entire disastrous experience of making *The Magus*, indeed, never entirely
got over it. Maschler's offer may have relieved Fowles of allowing his earlier partners to produce. He already trusted Maschler to do right by his
manuscripts. Perhaps as a film partner Tom could be a buffer, enjoying
the wheeling and dealing, while preserving Fowles's vision and rights of
veto. Fowles hoped Maschler could simplify the nightmare production
process of making the film, protecting Fowles's privacy and writing time.

Neither man dreamed at their October 1, 1968, meeting that the process of making this film would take nearly twelve years.[19]

Maschler's friend Karel Reisz declined to direct the film. Having recently completed *Isadora,* he balked at another costume drama. By December 1968 producer Oscar Lewenstein was involved. In quick succession, directors Ken Russell and Richard Lester declined offers. In spring 1969 director-designate Lindsay Anderson tried to suppress the author figure while creating "a voice-over commentary on the historical sidelights." As Maschler anticipated, the book's "diachronic" narrative of Victorian characters in the 1860s and an authorial perspective in the 1960s stymied potential directors for years. Novelist David Storey refused to write the script, saying there was no "strong enough male figure."[20] In addition to artistic concerns, Fowles's own film agent, Roger Burford, perhaps feeling pushed aside, made irritated queries about Maschler's role in arranging John Fowles's films. Fowles began to realize his hope of "a simpler way of doing things" was naïve.[21]

To address his messy tax situation, he incorporated J. R. Fowles Ltd., a company that owned his work and paid him a salary and expenses. He had turned down a Booker Brothers version of this scheme. However, the shelter arrangement pioneered by Booker Brothers helped provide funds for another of Tom Maschler's bold efforts, the establishment of the Booker Prize, the premier annual literary prize for British novels. By November 1968 J. R. Fowles Ltd. was managed by Equator and was able to keep about 48 percent of Fowles's immediate earnings. He still had to keep his overseas earnings abroad (in the United States or France, for example), owned by the company, not by him. He had to defer at least five years of income to avoid the 90 percent class. It all was very complicated and discouraging. Asked to project his future earnings over the coming decade, Fowles made a scrupulous effort but vastly underestimated the commercial success of his work.[22] In each of the next few years Fowles recorded in his diaries enormous six-figure sales in the United States and handsome sales in other countries. At the same time the income that came to his hand was annually about £29,500.[23]

The pressure to defer, in fact *not* to earn, undoubtedly contributed to Fowles's apathy about finishing work or publishing anything—and to his accompanying depression—over the next few years.[24] Writing to John Calley at Warner Brothers in December 1969, Fowles stressed that in any agreements "the one thing I don't want this year—and probably next—is more money."[25] Indeed, his accountant was peeved that *The French Lieu-tenant's Woman* would appear in spring 1969. "Most inconvenient," he sighed, "but if you *must*."[26]

Fowles had been emotionally insulated from political and social out-rage while living at Underhill Farm. At Belmont in early 1969 he was con-sumed with "depression," "bile," and "a kind of smouldering anger against the time." Observing what he considered foolish British trade and eco-nomic policies, he decided his country had "a death-wish, a longing for disaster." News from the United States about the Vietnam War and the in-auguration of Richard Nixon, Fowles found "frightening."[27] He felt alien-ated and distant from the rising generation too, though they were as disaffected as he felt at forty-five. He deplored how the young "rejected culture, book culture especially, and they embrace direct experience, doing your thing, finding your own scene and all the rest of the cant phrases."[28] It distressed him that eighteen-year-old Anna, developing into a sophisticated graphic and textile artist, was a "visual," less verbally artic-ulate than visually perceptive or that fifteen-year-old Michael Sharrocks was not, like both his parents, deeply part of a book culture.[29]

He worried over his father. Robert Fowles was able to visit Belmont with John's mother in 1969. The disciplined old gardener and relentless pruner was dismayed at the wildly unkempt new garden and thought his son's laissez-faire gardening philosophy was madness. Yet he blessed the Belmont folly with his gift of two cordon pear trees. Robert was now eighty, and his son noted how "he patters and potters with his little old man's trembling walk."[30] Later that year he went blind in one eye in an optic coronary and lost the last of his many sisters. Rob Fowles had out-lived all his siblings.

John Fowles worried about the welfare of his stepdaughter, Anna Christy. He had been financially supporting her for more than a year, al-though she remained with Roy and Judy Christy, studying for A-level ex-aminations and applying to art programs. Her keen involvement in a London amateur theater group helped motivate her through a difficult year. Her father's emotional state grew increasingly erratic. Roy still drank heavily, and signs appeared of what became manic depression. Re-peatedly, Roy kept Anna home from school and A-level studies to mind the younger children while he and his wife went off on short trips. Anna felt she had become "the nanny."[31] When the Fowleses fetched her for the summer and her move to Exeter, John wrote a heartfelt "She is ours now, thank goodness!"[32]

Roy Christy's jealous efforts to rival Fowles's success as a writer must have also affected his emotional state. After John and Elizabeth squelched his first novel in 1966, Roy wrote a second book, *The Nightingales Are Sobbing*. It was published in May 1968 by New Authors Ltd., a nonprofit publishing arm of Hutchinson of London, which aimed to launch new writers. Christy's book was comprised of two narratives. The first was a long short story based on his own working-class youth and the protagonist's tragicomic affair with an upper-class girl. The second piece, a novella, focused on old age and a surprising late love, which ends in tragedy. In both narratives, satirical blame for these failed lives is placed on the narrow moral restrictions of religions, both Protestant "chapel" denominations (like Roy's own Methodist family) and Roman Catholicism. Newspaper reviews were generally encouraging, calling *Nightingales* "funny, touching, and convincing."[33] Fowles, reading it, said it was "an egomaniac's book . . . full of a clipped gusto, that is as uncool as can be." He recognized Roy's book as "a lament for his own lost past" and wrote sadly, "It would have gotten attention twenty years ago."[34] The book sold only enough copies to convince Hutchinson's to publish the next novel under its regular imprint. *No Time Like the Past,* a somewhat confusing tale of adultery, inadvertent bigamy, unrecognized paternity, and a self-sacrificing friendship between two men who love the same woman, appeared in 1969.[35] Like its predecessor, this novel sank. While Fowles awaited publication of his own latest novel, he must have been conscious that Roy Christy was doing likewise. While Christy witnessed the failure of his literary ambitions, he must have been conscious of the tidal wave of commercial success that carried *The French Lieutenant's Woman* to ever-greater heights.

Publication days always made Fowles anxious and defensive, and the June 12, 1969, British release of *The French Lieutenant's Woman* was no exception. Fowles gave no publicity interviews and read few reviews. There was a "good" one in the *New Statesman* and a "bad" one in the *Times,* but, said Fowles, both were "full of misunderstanding, the voice of the literary establishment."[36] As reviews appeared in the following weeks, they seemed to be "bouquet-and-reservation."[37] The *Guardian* intoned: "Symbols and allegory stain almost every page of this long, puzzling book . . . characters fade to polemic . . . the mixture of sociology and fiction is now and again pretentious—but for all that I recommend. . . ."[38] An otherwise warm review in the *Observer* still admonished: "His presentation of himself as a novelist who feels the cooling draught of the *nouveau roman* and is no longer able to claim omniscience over or foreknowledge of his creations tends to diminish both him and them."[39] They were "all mean," griped Tom Maschler, disappointed.[40] Fowles labeled them all "irrelevant; praise or damnation in this poor sick culture— they alter nothing."[41] To Podge he wrote: "Some of the reviews have been pretty awful . . . how dare Mr Fowles tamper with trad Englit concepts of what the novel's about. . . . But who cares?"[42]

He cared. Fowles drifted in a blue mood for weeks after the publication of *The French Lieutenant's Woman,* complaining of malaise, aches and pains, nicotine addiction, and morbid apathy. Elizabeth, enjoying the splendid June sunshine, Anna's presence, visiting friends, and a rush of seasonal energy, laughed at her husband and wrote him a satirical poem on being "death-absorbed."[43] Day to day, he agreed, he enjoyed life, but on the larger scale, he had a persistent sense of failure. He began, on June 27, 1969, a novel with the working title *Futility*.

He considered calling it *The Two Englishmen*. "I want it to be the two sides of myself, two men, friends who have drifted apart, the outward success and the inward success. But over both of them, a sense of failure, of being defeated by their time. In the spirit of my own sickness."[44] Before published as *Daniel Martin* in 1977, this book was to have as fragmented a writing history as *The Magus*. As Fowles planned, started, and restarted this novel in the early 1970s, he was keenly sensitive to not only his own sense of futility but the middle-aged sense of failure or restlessness of many of his friends. Marriages broke up (the Paynes, the Porters, the Kinbergs, the Tarns), friends briefly questioned their career choices (Ronnie Payne, Denys Sharrocks, Podge Porter), several women friends were left stranded with neither husbands nor careers, three among his close acquaintance committed suicide, and his friend bookseller Francis Norman lost his only child in a terrible accident.

The character who would become Daniel Martin closely resembled Fowles himself in many ways. He began as "Tom Manning" in a first chapter written on June 27. Opening on a movie set in Los Angeles, Manning is a scriptwriter, "withdrawn" and reserved, who watches his scene being filmed like an unbeliever at a religious mass, an anthropologist studying a Neolithic tribe, or a zoologist observing animals.[45] The chapter's "angle" was wrong, Fowles thought, rejecting it, "like searching for a key among a forest of accidentals; a style." Conscious of critical misunderstanding of the stylistic experiments in *The French Lieutenant's Woman,* he was determined to "play no tricks this time; something classical, third-person and past tense."[46] Finally getting that chapter "right" was to take Fowles more than two years.

The other Englishman (eventually called Anthony Mallory), although "one of the two sides" of Fowles, would be a composite of a number of men that Fowles had loved and toward whom he felt some kind of guilt. This character had aspects of Roger Hendry, with whom John had shared music, laughter, and orchid hunting at Oxford and ignored just as Hendry, crippled and dying, needed him most. There are light touches of Denys Sharrocks, as the easy friend of his early working life. Robert Fowles, John's father, is also discernible in Anthony, the dying philosopher, aged by his illness to look like an old man, wasting before the hero's eyes. And in Anthony Mallory, the tormented Roman Catholic who marries the woman the hero loves, there is a lot of Roy Christy.

By autumn Fowles was further depressed by the English reception of *The French Lieutenant's Woman.* He thought that although better reviewed in Britain than his other two novels and "briefly on the bestseller list," it had "sunk for ever . . . like a stone in a rough sea." There hung over novel writing in England "a sort of twilight," he thought. "No one cares. I don't even care very much myself." Oddly, he partly drew this conclusion from the "total indifference of Lyme itself to the book." His writing, always his substitute for other forms of human connection, had failed to connect him to his own town, even when he set an entire novel there. The Lyme Regis community, which he had judged boring and unintellectual, had ignored him.[47]

He was not ignored by the American press, however. As the autumn U.S. publication date neared, interviewers arrived from the *New York Times* and *Time* magazine. Their questions required Fowles to analyze his intentions and meanings. He was embarrassed and bewildered. "What do I think of the break-up of the novel form? I think nothing. I write as it comes to me." He tried to explain how his writing was unconscious and organic but realized he was making up "a *fiction* about myself." His answers seemed merely "fortuitous," what happened to be in his mind at the time. Talking to the journalists, he felt like someone "from another planet."[48]

Fowles's depression was exacerbated by the first of many unsuccessful attempts to give up cigarettes, going overnight from chain-smoking three packs a day to nothing. Within weeks his mind seemed to stop, and Fowles lost ability to concentrate at the typewriter. He was easily irritated, more absentminded than usual, could not do simple sums, and found it difficult to open a tin. He poked at revising his thriller and worked without conviction on a novel entitled *Nugae,* about his month at Collioure in 1949. By November, for the first time in his adult life, Fowles was "blocked." In fact he was writing normally in his diary and revising on both novels. What eluded him was the creative experience of easily slipping into an imagined world. He wrote in circles. "I seem to be in a sort of multiple-possibility marsh. . . . I no sooner write a paragraph than I see improvements . . . intensely irritating and time-wasting, draft after draft after draft, in a sort of unimproving circle . . . in a state of constant partial error."[49]

Fowles felt weirdly dissociated from the hype as advance reviews arrived from the States on November 1, 1969. "Not that it isn't nice to be called 'the most brilliant of stars,' better than Bellow, Roth and Updike,' and the rest," he said, but the tone was "faintly hysterical," and the writers "mishandle the language so." He felt "forced out along a tightrope," as though everyone expected him to "get bigger and better and stranger and God knows what else." His little Collioure novel seemed "small," and he abandoned it.[50]

When John and Elizabeth Fowles made a three-week publicity tour of Boston, New York, Los Angeles, and San Francisco between November 9 and 28, 1969, Fowles was still battling depression, writer's block, nicotine withdrawal, and confusion over the public reception of *The French Lieutenant's Woman.* While an unqualified public relations success, the tour was a very sour experience for Fowles. Before he reached Boston, *The French Lieutenant's Woman* was in its third American printing, totaling a hundred thousand copies in its first week. It was a Literary Guild selection. The book remained on the *New York Times* and *Time* magazine best-seller lists for over a year. Before he had reached Los Angeles, the New American Library was offering $215,000 for the paperback rights. Every published review was positive. Journalists fought to interview him, and exhausted, he was scheduled back to back on television talk shows.

Fowles was puzzled by the contrast with the book's English reception, but it is not so difficult to understand. Aside from its enduring literary qualities, *The French Lieutenant's Woman* reverberated with a particular moment in American culture. Unlike postwar England, the United States had never abandoned Romanticism. Forbidden love trysts with mysterious dark strangers at the edge of a redeeming wilderness are a bred-in-the-bone theme of American literature. Fleeing the confinement of bourgeois conventions to "light out for the territories" and self-discovery is still the stuff of American dreams. In addition, however, Fowles's very personal novel with its Undercliff setting echoed the longings of the 1960s youth counterculture, the so-called Woodstock generation, for an Edenic return "to the garden."[51] The book was also revered because it dramatized youthful outsiders challenging a society's staid conventions. Even more, the myth-drenched character of Sarah Woodruff appeared in 1969, a watershed moment in the American feminist movement. There were at that time few women authors being commercially published who defined the personal and political self-consciousness of the women's liberation movement. Sarah's struggle to articulate her sense of social confinement, and then to create a new self in a new age, was hotly affirmed in the imaginations of thousands of women. Ironically, what many were responding to was Elizabeth Fowles's editorial insistence that Sarah's destiny be "inconclusive" and open to interpretation, rather than John Fowles's original matrimonial ending.

Although this brilliant bonfire of publishing success burned around him on the tour, John Fowles felt little exhilaration or satisfaction. He was saddened and outraged by private revelations, political events, and the general American cultural upheaval. Politically the United States in 1969 was far from a peaceable kingdom. The Vietnam conflict continued despite the Paris peace talks and Nixon's policy of Vietnamization. University campuses (including those Fowles visited) were rocked by protest and civil disobedience. While he was in San Francisco, militant Native Americans occupied the abandoned island of Alcatraz. There were riots in Chicago the month before Fowles arrived, and during his visit, on November 15, the largest anti–Vietnam War demonstration of all occurred in a massive march on Washington, D.C.

Privately, Fowles saw his friends in straits he thought were caused by the catastrophe of their culture. He and Elizabeth were deeply shaken to discover that two close friends had become virtually incapacitated with alcoholism. The requisite formal lunch at Little, Brown on Beacon Hill in Boston, which had been a pleasure for the visiting author on earlier tours, Fowles saw now as "a tyrannical ritual." Aging Arthur Thornhill, Sr., highly conscious of being "the Grand Old Man of American publishing," was stirring up, Fowles thought, "some kind of bitter battle . . . a jockeying for position, for the day when the Sun-king dies and the poor fish, his dauphin [Arthur Thornhill Junior] takes over."[52]

Whatever was actually happening on the tour, Fowles's descriptions are nightmarish. Alcohol and marijuana swirled around them, arousing his puritanism. He was "nauseated" by New York, by excess, gasoline stench, drunks, drugs, crowds, ugly people, bad food, and corrupt language.[53] Air-polluted, automobile-cursed Los Angeles was "a city of the damned . . . there can never have been such a repulsive city." American consumerism—the mass-produced food, the slick packaging, the ads in newspapers, and the "supermarketization of all basic products"—was an unmitigated evil. His repeated metaphor became "the big red apple"— eye-catching, mass-produced, and tasteless—which he contrasted with his own father's unbeautiful but uniquely flavorful fruits.[54]

Asked, repeatedly, what he "meant by" something he had written, Fowles began to "embroider, divagate, lie."[55] None of the California television interviewers had read his new book. Fowles was constantly congratulated for "putting down the sex novelists" like Harold Robbins and Jacqueline Susann, yet when they met on an interview, Robbins turned out to be one of the few who had read Fowles's books with intelligence. Fowles compared him (kindly) with a lizard basking in the sun of publicity and high sales and was pleased when Robbins generously offered them the use of his house, his car, and his office in Hollywood.[56]

Fowles was surprised by the warm student reception on college campuses. Yet as he was with their English counterparts, Fowles was ambivalent about the generation's values. For example, with the publication of *The French Lieutenant's Woman,* young people, correctly, saw Fowles as a "green" writer, whose passion for the natural world was in sympathy with growing concerns about the environment. Student interviewers kept asking what he would "'do' about ecology," a word popularized by Barry Commoner only the year before. Fowles, however, disapproved of their interest in doing "something active, not passive [which was an] abuse and destruction of natural environment." To respect nature, for Fowles, was to leave it alone. Visiting Muir Woods, he was scornful of its management as a nature reserve park. "I hate such gardening of nature—the labelling, the incorporation of the museum, the city park into what is of its essence wild," he wrote. The only solution to the threat to nature, he said, "is to reduce the population of the world drastically."[57]

When questioned by young people, especially in California, Fowles was disturbed to learn that some readers interpreted *The Magus* as a work of magic or drug-induced inspiration. "What were you writing 'under'?" he was asked, to his distress. His young interrogators assumed that the role-changing characters, the shape shifting, the charades of Conchis's "god-game" (psychological metaphors for the polymorphous imagination of the writer) were symbols for drug use and hallucination. Fowles neither used drugs nor approved of them (except alcohol and tobacco, the narcotics of his generation). Elizabeth Fowles was repelled by marijuana smoking.[58] Fowles, often asked his opinion of drug use for artistic inspiration, one day angrily wrote to an editor: "I am suspicious of much avowedly drug-influenced writing . . . I have not much time for this view of life. I certainly think alcohol can occasionally help, but permanent indulgence is, I think profoundly damaging. For every Rimbaud, there is a world of incomprehensible sots. . . . I have never used drugs."[59]

The sham magic trappings of *The Magus*—astrology, tarot cards, psychic predictions, and mysticism—were supposed to reveal Conchis as a trickster and send Nicholas back to "reality" and to the existential responsibility of creating his own life's meaning rather than adopting some religious interpretation. Fowles was dismayed at how many readers accepted the paraphernalia of superstition as the truth of the narrative. He saw "the childish obsession with astrology and 'magic'" among West Coast hippies as connected to the popularity of *The Magus*. When told, to his horror, that there was "some group in Missouri who re-enact rituals from the book," he uncharacteristically snarled, "And I'd fucking well like to catch them at it!"[60] Cheered by the "genuine love of the simple life and simple pleasures" of some hippie flower children he met in San Francisco, Fowles was sympathetic toward these young social dropouts.[61] Yet he was no advocate of what he judged "a flight from reason, refusal to face reality." He thought the "confused and politically null" hippies, "for all their present charm," were "really on the side of the fascists . . . both by nature and by default."[62]

During the late 1960s Fowles had become deeply disturbed by a growing sense that "freedom" in modern Western society had become selfish and self-destructive license. His November 1969 American tour pushed him into boiling rage and fantasies of destruction. In early January 1970 he began a critique of the United States called *America, I Weep for Thee*.[63] Originally intended as an article for the *Atlantic Monthly*, the essay in nine months grew to 139 typed pages, becoming a "pamphlet" and an "appendix" to *The Aristos*, which Fowles was concurrently revising for paperback publication by the New American Library. The new essay was now intended as a companion to *The Aristos*, continuing that book's "examination of human freedom—what constitutes it and what diminishes it." He discussed his concept of the *nemo* as the pervasive "root cancer of modern man." This "sense an individual has of his nothingness; his powerlessness; his failure" was manifested, Fowles believed, in all the individual selfishness and permissiveness of the late 1960s: in the acceptance of "the individual as 'the basic unit of society,'" in "drugs, alcohol, dropping out, overspending," and "all the other neurotic methods of avoiding reality." Like other unpublished works like *The Fucker* and *Sequence Four*, this pamphlet became one of those emotionally dark repositories for angry issues Fowles was exploring, themes that he eventually published in more positive forms.

While writing about the *nemo* in *America, I Weep for Thee*, Fowles penned a short story called "Zero." It dramatizes a failed poet so obsessed by his own nothingness that he defines himself through terrorism, the entirely random bombing of a cinema in New York. In its use of violence and obliteration as a kind of desperate "speech" for the *nemo*-driven, "Zero" is very similar to Fowles's 1954 short story "For a Casebook," indicating that the idea and structure had been with him for at least fifteen years.[64] Fowles and Jud Kinberg developed it as a screenplay in summer 1970. By October 17, 1970, when sold to producer Sidney Glazier, the script had become *Zip*.[65]

In *America, I Weep for Thee*, Fowles, once an outspoken advocate of isolated individual freedom, now argued for a restrained individualism, which ethically supported the good of the whole. The essay laid significant blame for rampant individualism on the "most essentially American philosophy of pragmatism" (the philosophy of Charles Sanders Peirce, William James, and John Dewey, who all struck Fowles as "anti-poetic"). "Debased pragmatism" underlay American tendencies to ask mechanistically, "How does it work?" and greedily, "What's in it for me?" It reduced to the profit motive all cultural evaluations of literature, art, music, and the general "poetry" of life. American pragmatism was to blame, Fowles thought, for the myth of progress; the pervasiveness of Madison Avenue advertising; the consumer society; the commercial exploitation of sex; lack of respect for the land, its resources, and its virtues; American imperialism (especially the Vietnam War); and the American political tendency to embrace local control rather than a sensible and effectively centralized federalism.

The essay also contains a long, shocking invective against Jewish control of the American film industry and the "immensely strong influence that Jewish feeling and taste has gained upon American cultural life." In a man with many professional associates and close personal friends who were Jews, this truly chilling diatribe argues a deep, angry disappointment and need to blame that Fowles could not otherwise express. Although his statements are indefensible, some of this bitterness must have grown from the caustic experience of filming his two novels, his ongoing discouragement over publishing industry values, and the continuing failure of *The French Lieutenant's Woman* film deal to gel. He maintained warm relations, both private and professional, with Jewish friends for the rest of his life, becoming godfather to one of Tom Maschler's daughters, for example, and acting as best man and witness to Jud Kinberg on his second marriage.

But this raging and "weeping" may have been directed at someone else. Many of the debated points in *America, I Weep for Thee* were those defended or challenged by John's father. Robert Fowles profoundly admired the American pragmatist philosophers. He always fiercely championed the United States in arguments with his son. It was Robert Fowles who furiously defended Jewish achievement and Jewish contributions to Western culture to his conventionally anti-Semitic neighbors, teaching his young son a rare degree of tolerance in the England of the 1930s. It was Robert Fowles whom John Fowles associated with the narrowness of suburban life and the rejection of the wild chaos of nature and the countryside. The younger Fowles came to associate his father with a "ghetto mentality" (indeed, of "Jewishness"): of admiration for intellectual achievement, of skill with "yield," of love of the virtuoso and sentimental in music and poetry, of "an almost total blindness to nature."[66] While in this vehement essay John Fowles was shedding verbal tears for America, it is also as if his younger self were still arguing with his father. Perhaps John was weeping too, for in 1970 Robert Fowles was dying.

John and Elizabeth rushed to Leigh on June 10 when told Robert Fowles had suffered a stroke and was on his deathbed. Robert rallied, however, and they took the parents to stay with them at Lyme Regis. For a fortnight's recuperation, John cared for his father, dressing and undressing him, assisting his moves from bed to chair, walking him around the garden, and watching cricket with him on television. In late August, back at 63 Fillebrook Avenue, the old man began refusing food, saying he wanted to die. "I don't know what's keeping him alive," John wrote in early September, "courage or convention. Not wanting to die or not knowing how to." Robert was moved to a nursing home, where "white-grizzled, sunkencheeked and bleary-eyed . . . in a kind of sleep coma," he murmured as if dreaming of his past.[67] John sat alone with him when his father began to mutter "an extraordinary poem-like, unpunctuated paragraph" from his memories of trench life in World War I: "Bobby Charles I sat beside him he was hit in the stomach I said you'll be all right Bobby he said I've seen too many like that too many out in No Man's Land." A few minutes later Robert woke and, groping for his son's hand, pleaded: "You must send me the bill for this. I want to pay the bill." John held his hand. "Yes, all right, I'll send you the bill."[68]

Gangrene developed in Robert's leg. Few had known the painful extent of the stoically dying man's circulatory disease. On September 16, while John Fowles vented his "black rage" at a God he professed not to believe in, the leg was amputated.[69] Again Robert Fowles rallied, so convinced that he was going home that he had his wife order bulbs and peat for the garden. But the gangrene spread. On October 26, while John Fowles lay in bed with a bad cold at Belmont, Robert Fowles died.

John Fowles declared himself relieved and showed no outward emotion. After the October 30 funeral, he quietly "abstracted" from the Fillebrook Avenue house his father's 1915–1918 paybook, some family letters, and several poems Robert Fowles had written during that year.[70] Under all their "total inadequacy" as poetry, wrote Fowles sadly, "is that mysterious drive: all his life he has scrawled on bits of paper." He recalled his father's "hopeless novel" as well, feeling "a sense of gigantic hereditary luck; that I am what he was always so afraid to be . . . beyond writing in secret. . . . He would never admit what he really loved and wanted."[71]

One of his father's poems made John Fowles "genuinely sad," both for its "badness" and "because he almost certainly never knew of Milton's agony in the same fire."[72] "Recompense" is about Robert's growing blindness; of how, formerly looking upon flowers and fruit in his sunny garden, "I saw them not." Yet in the "darkened world" of his blindness, he now sees ("in my mind") "more clearly/The beauty of things/I missed when sight was mine." Eight days after his father's funeral, apparently without making the connection, John Fowles began a novel about a blind man's learning to "see" through his heart and imagination. Once more, emotion Fowles denied was transformed at an unsconscious level and spilled out onto the page.[73]

John Fowles mourned by beginning *The Jesuit,* one of several fragmentary false starts to the *Daniel Martin* theme.[74] Two Roman Catholic brothers are somewhat estranged. The elder, Harold, lives in North Oxford with his non-Catholic wife and two small daughters. Under the conventional surface, his marriage is coming apart, and he is having an affair. The younger brother, Paul, is a Jesuit priest recently blinded. Recuperating in his brother's house, Paul begins to "see" the sensuous and emotional things he had missed before his blindness. The story is set up to unite Paul with his disaffected sister-in-law, Pauline. Unconvincing as a man who ever had a priestly vocation, Paul lacks substance. Yet in this failed beginning, abandoned after only three days, Fowles first enunciated the theme of finding "whole sight" that radiates through *Daniel Martin.* He did so in unconscious response to an aesthetically poor but heartfelt poem by his dead father.

Another biographical figure turns up as one of the little daughters in this fragment. For the 1969–1970 academic year Anna Christy lived in Exeter, Devon, an hour's journey from Lyme Regis. Several times she brought her housemate to visit, a single mother with two little girls who had an extraordinary effect on the childless Fowleses. Sophy, aged six, fastened herself to Elizabeth, while Emma, aged eight, attached herself to John. The little ones crawled into their bed in the morning, sat on their laps, held their hands, rode John's back. Elizabeth called them "just about the best kids I have ever known . . . they filled the house with love [and] I wished they were our children." Never sentimental about children, Fowles wrote that it was "headlong love at first sight between us." He and Emma effortlessly slipped into a private world, collecting fossils on the beach and spending hours in the garden. Emma made up little poems for him and was tenderly fascinated with his plants. He thought her "the only other person who has seen this garden quite as I see it, . . . still with the eyes of my own . . . childhood." When Emma left after the first visit, she sobbed all the way to the station. Afraid he would cry himself, Fowles did not accompany them. He still did not want children, he wrote; "I just wanted this one child." Emma haunted him, with her "strange direct . . . eyes, . . . a gay-grave, sensitive-bold, imperious-submissive child; with that . . . faint hint of sexuality . . . strange ghost of a first-class intelligence." Unable to have her in his real life, Fowles loved her and made her his own by writing her into his fiction. When she appears, often under her own name, Emma is the mythical girl in a garden, a hidden guarantor of some "right" value, or the active messenger of such values. Besides *The Jesuit,* Emma appears in short stories like "The Last Chapter" and "The Cloud" and in Fowles's thriller *The Device.* Under other names, she and her sister perhaps also stand behind the Mallory daughters in *Daniel Martin* and the daughters of David Williams in "The Ebony Tower." Fowles acknowledged that he owed the "strange experience" of Emma to Anna, even recognizing that in some ways Emma was a substitute for his missed relationship with Anna as a child.[75]

As Fowles partnered with Tom Maschler on *The French Lieutenant's Woman* film project, the Fowleses drew socially nearer to him and his fiancée, the darkly beautiful Fay Coventry, with whom Elizabeth became close friends. The dry-humored Fay was quietly deferential around Maschler's famous authors, all the while cooking exceptional meals that Fowles thought were "a web for [Tom] to fall into."[76] Their April 1970 wedding, attended by the full pantheon of Maschler's authors, took place in Wales. Fowles was much alarmed when Arnold Wesker, hosting the reception dinner, challenged each of these elite of English letters to toast Maschler in turn and "say what we all really feel about Tom." The awkward moment was "saved" by Doris Lessing ("placid-looking with closecombed hair, more from the Thirties than this decade"), who made a few gently noncommittal remarks, then raised her glass and quietly said, "We all know Tom can also be a bastard."[77]

A firm deal for *The French Lieutenant's Woman* continued to elude the partners. In February 1970 Michael Cacoyannis was keen to direct, with Vanessa Redgrave as Sarah Woodruff. The Greek Cacoyannis's doubts about filming in England, photographing "so much green," ended this association. By August 1970 Oscar Lewenstein's option had expired, while Warner Bros. and United Artists bid against each other. Maschler and Fowles elected to go with John Calley of Warner Bros., with Fowles insisting on consultation and veto on the director and the script. David Rudkin was hired as screenwriter and, to Fowles's approval, emphasized two major themes of the novel, evolution and adaptation to historical change. Rudkin was extremely respectful of Fowles's words, following the book faithfully. However, working in the author's point of view increasingly meant a "voice-over" narration. This doomed Rudkin's script, as it did scripts by later writers. Fowles once wrote an inquiring scholar that he had never liked the "voice off camera" solution to the "diachronic problem . . . as it turned everything into an illustrated history lecture."[78] When Warner Bros.' option expired in late 1971, Rudkin's script was rejected by the next potential producer.

While frustrated over *The French Lieutenant's Woman* and writing the scathing *Zip* for Jud Kinberg, Fowles began another film project with David Tringham. Wishing to direct his first picture and encouraged by John and Roy Boulton of British Lion Ltd., Tringham wrote Fowles in May 1970 to ask if he had available material. Fowles, eager to affect the public but unable to make any money, simply gave him outright an excellent unpublished short story. Fowles liked this thirty-year-old, although Tringham was too "nice . . . modest" and not enough of a "sacred monster" to become a powerful force in the "wretched industry."[79] He approved his January 1971 script, so faithful to the original. Ironically, Tringham's little 1972 movie of "The Last Chapter" became Fowles's most satisfying venture in filmmaking.

This nine-thousand-word 1970 short story was written in response to hearing James Bond author, Ian Fleming, "spitting on the muses."[80] Fowles felt a writer scorned at his peril the sort of inspiration symbolized by these nine classical goddesses. His protagonist was to be "a character like Ian Fleming," he explained in notes to David Tringham, "who has made an enormous success out of writing for the eternal adolescent in man and who needs to be reminded that that is not what serious writing is about. He's grown blind to the extent to which he's sold out; and tries to hide his fundamental artistic and spiritual bankruptcy under the mask of the machine-like efficiency with which he churns out his oeuvre."[81] However, "The Last Chapter" not only condemns lost creative focus and "selling out" in writers like Fleming but is also a reminder to Fowles himself, increasingly uncomfortable with his fame and the commercialization of his published work. The protagonist resembles Fowles in looks, age, and many work habits. While expressing scorn for writers like Fleming and Len Deighton, Fowles *did* read them, and he admired Raymond Chandler. He had a long love-hate relationship with the adventure thriller genre and was working earnestly on his own thriller as he wrote this short story.

"The Last Chapter" presents Robert Murray, a phenomenally successful writer of thrillers, completing the next in a series of the wildly popular, lurid, and violent adventures of superspy Moxon. He is interrupted by a surprise visit from a challenging eighteen-year-old girl, Emma. After he locks her out, he finds his text changing against his will as he writes it. The "two-dimensional cut-outs" of his characters become thoughtful and sad, old enemies grow tender toward one another; violence seems futile. Looking up, he sees Emma, stripped to the waist like a Minoan snake goddess, pressing her breasts and lipsticked mouth at him through the glass, mocking him at the window. Murray gives furious chase, only to be confronted by nine young women, all taunting and mocking him. Deeply shaken by this encounter with the "muses," the writer returns to his now transmogrifying book and out-of-control characters. Having reached the end of the page, he commits suicide.[82]

While criticizing the "adolescence" and "spiritual bankruptcy" of his own Robert Murray and the writers he was based on, Fowles was conscious that the thriller genre was, by its nature, a flight from reality. He defended writing his own thriller as "fun" and "entertainment," but the process was really an escape or a respite for him. He wrote the original draft of *The Device* at white heat at Underhill Farm in seventeen days in January 1968 while Elizabeth was in London and Norwich. He saw it as "a much needed relief from the Victorian past,"[83] "a reaction from the third-person cerebrality" of *The French Lieutenant's Woman*, which he was about to revise for the first time. "Not meant to be serious," he wrote, "just a headlong love-and-mystery story."[84] He went back to it in late winter of 1969 after the move to Belmont when he, and Elizabeth as well, suffered illness, cold, depression, and the enormous frustrations of the renovation of the old house. He sneaked into it when bored with duty writing, as he did when the revised *Zip* script was due.[85] He returned to it after *The French Lieutenant's Woman* had been reviewed in the United States, when his writing was blocked and he considered defying expectations by publishing the thriller next, "just to stop this higher-and-higher thing."[86] The thriller was his hideout, just as the Undercliff and the Belmont garden were.

The Device also grew to be huge: sixty complicated chapters and 531 pages long, longer than *The French Lieutenant's Woman* and only a bit short of *The Magus*. The "great spaghetti tangles of plot and motive that have to be unravelled" worried him only as he reached the finish.[87] In the book he made an effort to transcend the immaturity and violence of Fleming's and Deighton's work, trying to satisfy the requirements of the genre for male action and hot romance while simultaneously creating a larger social meaning. Indeed, in *The Device* Fowles is not so much writing a simple knockoff of a pulp action novel as he is attempting to redeem the whole thriller genre. It is an ambitious failure.

The Device, subtitled *Somebody's Got to Do It* (the original title), is, on the surface, a tale of weapons smuggling, international espionage, and romance.[88] The protagonist is a thirty-seven-year-old former Marine commando who owns an antiques business in Exeter, Devon. A John Fowles double, his name is a near anagram of the author's: Jeremy Simon Wolfe, or J. S. Wolfe. A little crooked, a little bitter, Simon is easily recruited as a courier in a shady operation off the Devon coast, where unknown international smugglers embed gold cores in lead weights attached to deepwater fishing nets. Simon suspects the gold smuggling operation to be a Zionist conspiracy headed by Leo Frend, former employer of his dead brilliant, homosexual brother Nicholas, but he is concerned only with what's in it for himself.

In twisty confrontations reminiscent of the convoluted plot of *The Magus,* in which polymorphous characters suddenly change names and roles, Simon is "tested" in seemingly random incidents. He falls in love with a young woman, Troy, who is a planted agent. The unwary Simon is kidnapped, interrogated, threatened, and finally recruited as a double agent by a mysterious group that seems to be the British Secret Service.

Its unit is called the Molehill, and all the operatives go by code names from *The Wind in the Willows:* Dr. Toad, Mr. Rat, Mr. Mole. The smuggling activities, they tell him, are actually part of a KGB operation to deliver nuclear timing devices. There is a bomb incident, an episode of vandalism, and enigmatic contacts hinting that his brother may not be dead and that Troy may be betraying him. A move against the alleged KGB cell is successful, and Simon passes one more mysterious test. When Troy brings Simon to a rendezvous deep in rural Devon, the entire arcane plot is revealed as a recruitment not to the British Secret Service, the Zionists, or the KGB but to a secret international brotherhood, the Wind. Formed immediately after the first New Mexico testing of the atomic bomb on July 16, 1945, all members are scientists and intellectuals committed to evading the restrictions of every government, media interest, and political system to disseminate information freely and keep the arms race in balance. All the members are also more or less blood relatives, and Simon is reunited with an interconnected family that includes all the players in the "game," including his still-living brother, Nicholas.

For all its "fun" and "ephemeral nonsense . . . for an Arabian Night,"[89] Fowles was serious about *The Device,* expecting it to "sell" and "make money."[90] Word leaked out that John Fowles was writing a spy thriller, and a buzz of anticipation erupted. Even Alfred Hitchcock cabled, asking "for a first look."[91] The unseen manuscript of *The Device* became a counter in the deal making surrounding negotiations of *The French Lieutenant's Woman* and *Zip.* When John Calley of Warner Bros. expressed his interest in *Zip* in June 1970, Fowles surmised, "What Calley really wants is to get a lien on the thriller—a first option."[92] When Calley optioned *The French Lieutenant's Woman* in September 1970, Fowles assured him that Warner Bros. had an inside track on the thriller.[93] Most important, when Fowles incorporated J.R. Fowles Ltd., he "gifted" the thriller he was writing to his wife, Elizabeth Fowles, expecting it to provide her an independent income.[94]

Fowles finished *The Device* on February 15, 1971, and collected it from the typist on March 29. For the first time in its three-year history, Elizabeth read part of the book. She was "grimly silent."[95] She had been suffering her usual winter blues, but contrary to pattern, even as spring arrived, Elizabeth had now "sunk into one of her old-hatred-of-Lyme moods." She stayed in bed mornings, wouldn't read, work in the garden, or help Fowles with his correspondence. She was clearly very troubled.[96]

On April 13, Fowles heard from Tom Maschler who, "behind a token noise of enthusiasm . . . obviously doesn't like it."[97] Maschler indeed was in the awkward predicament of rejecting a book by one of his most established authors and a valued friend. He "tried everything" to figure what could be done with the manuscript, but it was "unsalvageable." Maschler was very grateful, in fact, that Fowles "took it so well."[98] In reality, Maschler's rejection hurt Fowles very much. Agent Anthony Sheil agreed with the editor a few days later.[99]

After weeks of distressed silence, Elizabeth "at last says what she thinks: which is that she mostly hates it."[100] Months later Fowles called her expression an "outburst." It was clearly terribly wrenching and emotional for both of them. Inasmuch as the thriller was to be his gift to her, her rejection must have been doubly painful for Fowles. Afterward Elizabeth remained for two months more in a "profound depression—nothing new, but so deep this time that we live outwardly without rows or fighting. She calls it loss of identity, I call it inability to love." After Tom Maschler's decision on the manuscript, the editor immediately requested Fowles to do a translation of Perrault's *Cinderella.* Fowles wrote that the project was absurd; "our life has recently got so black and sour that it was . . . like having a picnic on a battlefield."[101]

By July 1971, in "one of her miraculous recoveries," Elizabeth was once again a cheerful "saint of briskness," and Fowles was scolding himself for doubting "her resilience."[102] But something vital had changed between them forever. John Fowles never again asked his wife to edit one of his fictions. Elizabeth remained John's domestic partner, lover, traveling companion, "best friend," deeply loyal admirer, and a profound influence on the female characters in his work. But she ceased to be the contributing literary partner she had always longed to be. She *had*, in fact, lost her most precious identity. Fifteen months after "her outburst over the thriller," Elizabeth still kept "total silence" about her husband's current writing projects. Fowles did not share his work in progress and ideas with her. "We have literally mentioned the subject not once," Fowles wrote defensively. "I'm glad it's treated as if it doesn't exist."[103] Asked by reviewers in 1977 why Elizabeth had not edited *Daniel Martin,* Fowles said, misleadingly, that he "just wanted to do things differently this time."[104] But asked in a 1997 interview why he had not asked for his wife's help on novels after *The French Lieutenant's Woman,* Fowles sighed heavily and answered with great sadness, "It was pique."[105]

In its way, this seismic shift in the literary relationship of John and Elizabeth Fowles changed the landscape of John Fowles's fiction as dramatically as the 1968 landslip at Underhill Farm had changed Fowles's private domain in the Undercliff. In years to come, Elizabeth did not cut the length of Fowles's novels or edit out parts she thought marred the whole. There would be more erotic description, for Elizabeth could no longer suggest delicacy. There would be greater didactic explication, for she would not write, "Give up lecture: Spoils magic," on his pages. Fowles's themes showed the rift as well. While he continued to write of two women who personified two different experiences of reality, there would be fictions like "The Ebony Tower" and *Mantissa,* in which the wife appears as a diminished, exterior figure. In "The Ebony Tower" this faded, distant woman even bears a version of Elizabeth's name. Most of all, John Fowles became more isolated as a creative writer, pursuing an imaginative path away from mundane reality into a seductive, solitary world of dreams where Elizabeth was barred from following.

CHAPTER SIXTEEN

The Hedgehog

Belmont House, 1970–1974

The experience is rare and in a very different category from the more or less normal feeling of moderate fertility characteristic of regular daily writing . . . often alarmingly disruptive and questioning . . . surrealistically allusive, fetching associations from personal experience, reading, the unconscious, that have nothing to do with the small forward leaps of ordinary literary invention . . . it can present hitherto undreamt-of scenes with a vividness and rapidity . . . that is sometimes very near to the supernatural. . . . It always gives me a not altogether pleasant sense of having inside me some power that is not me, but foreign and visiting.

—JOHN FOWLES "A PERSONAL CONFESSION," 1971
(SUPPRESSED)

Just before midnight during the early 1970s John Fowles often slipped out the back door of his kitchen with a bowl of bread and milk. He set it down by the Coadestone capstone and stepped back to wait for the hedgehogs. The old mother and two young ones shuffled out of the shadowy garden to the food. There were deer that visited that garden, boldly playful foxes, an occasional badger, the dormice, and many species of birds, but the hedgehogs gave Fowles special pleasure. They were totally useless animals, he wrote, scuffling about in the night. Stupid, selfish, gentle, small, and intent only on survival. The hedgehogs came to symbolize for Fowles the satisfaction of opting out of public duties and false responsibility simply to exist exactly as one truly was.[1]

Five years passed between the 1969 appearance of *The French Lieu-tenant's Woman* and the 1974 publication of *The Ebony Tower*. Aging from forty-three to forty-eight, John Fowles turned inward in his private life and ever inward in his fiction. Through this time his financial advisers discouraged him from major publishing endeavors. But unpublished projects laid foundations for works of the late 1970s and the 1980s. From 1969 to October 1971, when he finally began *Daniel Martin* in earnest, he was often distracted by domestic and family concerns, travel, professional obligations, and ongoing attempts to settle on a producer and film-script for *The French Lieutenant's Woman*. He experienced several sustained intervals of depression similar to that of June 1969 that seem connected to his sense of stark artistic isolation and "complete economic freedom." He wrote of "wallowing in this strange bath of aboulia and ac-cidie," of "indifference . . . towards what I 'ought' to be doing as a writer."[2]

His isolation as a writer was of his own making. He had removed him-self from London and the imposed discipline of a job. He and Elizabeth remained lifelong friends with writer/journalist Ronnie Payne, good friends with Tom and Fay Maschler, and on cordial terms with Cape writers like Arnold Wesker and Frederic Raphael. The only other novelist with whom Fowles socialized regularly, however, was Tom Wiseman. Having cut Elizabeth out of his editorial process, Fowles spoke to no one about what he was writing, nor did anyone dare ask—least of all his editors, his agent, or his wife. "Never a question do they seriously ask about John Fowles the novelist," he wrote about Maschler, Bradford, and Sheil during a spell of the deep blues in the summer of 1972. "'Are you writing?' is as senseless to me as 'Are you breathing?' It doesn't deserve a serious answer, and I don't give one."[3] What the foolish inquirer received, depending on Fowles's mood, was a charmingly affable red herring re-mark or a silent, icy stare. Yet although he claimed how well it suited him to be left alone, Fowles was petulant and wounded that his writing was "ignored" by Elizabeth and the rest of the Fowles family.[4] Although he occasionally fancied that this silence was a conspiracy, it was more likely a response to his attitude toward *them*.

For months at a stretch he insulated himself from "the alternating stupidity and spiteful coldness of English criticism [and] the total apathy about books in this country" by not reading the *TLS* ("it gives me nausea at the first paragraph") or the major transatlantic reviews.[5] But he was hurt by dismissive opinions, such as Alan Brien's May 21, 1971, article in the *Sunday Times* calling Fowles "a glass eye, a maker of soft-centred chocolates." Articles like this were "just one more nail in a coffin that already has enough."[6] The earliest serious academic criticism also caused Fowles's dismay. The first book, by Peter Wolfe, read in draft in November 1971, made his "skin crawl . . . not a good experience."[7] The 1972 issue of *Critique,* devoted to Fowles and to American novelist John Barth, "depressed" him. "The novel will die not for 'cultural' reasons, but of self-consciousness." He grew to loathe "anything that exposes the activity of writing to the public," and it was this intimate process of writing that more and more interested him.[8] He wrote an enormous amount, but his "sign," he said, was *"Publication is not for poets."*[9]

Fowle's published work of the very early 1970s was either previously produced material or occasional pieces. Daniel Halpern, young founder of a new North American creative review titled *Antaeus,* turned up in May of 1970 from a long stay with writer Paul Bowles in Tangier. Fowles gave Halpern an interview and some poems to publish. In August 1972, he allowed Halpern's Ecco Press to publish *Poems,* drawn from works of the 1950s and 1960s.[10] Fowles refused to review contemporary British authors (perhaps out of sympathy), but in 1973 he reviewed nature books for the *New Statesman.* His occasional pieces were mostly afterwords or forewords to new editions of long-dead writers. The afterwords for Lowell Blair's translation of *Le Grand Meaulnes* (1970)[11] and for Cape's new release of Arthur Conan Doyle's *The Hound of the Baskervilles* (1973)[12] are sharply penetrating. In 1972 Fowles proposed to *Sports Illustrated* an original article on cricket and wrote it straight from his heart. "Making a Pitch for Cricket," a warm article filled with loving youthful reminiscences,[13] outlined on pages of old Allen & Wright letterhead from Robert Fowles's business, is inhabited by the ghost of John's dead father.

What Fowles wrote and did not publish was another matter. Besides the suppressed thriller, fragments of fiction (*The Jesuit, Tom Manning*) served as failed experiments for his planned novel, *The Englishman.* There were short stories, like "Zip" and "The Last Chapter," that he reworked as filmscripts. In June of 1972, Fowles experienced a two-month spell of deep social disconnection, depression "with a strongly schizophrenic cast."[14] He stopped writing in the diary, answered no letters, and seldom left the house. During one of Elizabeth's London trips he did not step outside Belmont for two weeks. Instead, he wrote "a long erotic

poem . . . nearly a thousand quatrains, ballad-style" with an accompanying essay explaining why it was *not* obscene. Metaphorically, Fowles was
expressing "the parallels between the writing process and sexual pleasure" and how he had, "in sexual terms, a total interest in the foreplay
and a total lack of interest in ejaculation and consummation." He
needed to write, he stressed, but not to publish. Eroticism and creativity
occurred in the imagination, and the "parallel with what I feel about publishing is very close."[15] The erotic poem has not survived in its 1972 ballad
form but is probably the genesis of the controversial *Mantissa* (1982),
which Fowles told Donald Hall he had written rapidly, then set aside for
a decade.[16]

Mostly for pleasure, Fowles also translated from the French. By
chance, he reread *Ourika*, a forgotten 1824 best-seller by Claire de
Duras, unearthed a dozen years earlier in Norman's windowless backroom. Told as a first-person deathbed confession to a physician, *Ourika*
is a deceptively simple tale of an enslaved African woman, adopted at
age two into an aristocratic French family and educated as a lady. Genuinely loved by her foster mother and family, but alienated by her race,
Ourika is a psychological outcast in the only society she knows. When
she loses her beloved foster brother to a rival, she falls into life-
threatening melancholia. Helped to religious conversion, she becomes a
nun and dies in a convent just after the French Revolution.

Fowles became convinced that Ourika and her story had been "very active in my unconscious" as he was writing *The French Lieutenant's
Woman*.[17] The mythopoeic image that became Sarah Woodruff was clad
in black and loved a Charles. Was she related to black-skinned Ourika,
lover of another Charles? Fascinated by the possible psychological connection, Fowles translated the book in late 1970 or early 1971. His dream
image of a black-clad woman staring out to sea had acted as a magnetic
force pulling the events and characters of *The French Lieutenant's Woman*
into the vortex of his imagination. In the same way, the image of Ourika
focused Fowles's deepest concerns into an unpublished collection of
manuscript essays continuing his explorations of the relative freedom of
the self in society, philosophical concepts such as the *nemo*, and the inspiration of the creative artist. By the end of 1971 Fowles was writing *The
Prisoner*, a volume ordered around his translation of *Ourika*. It included
two long, overlapping essays, "Sensibility" and "The New Self," that show

Fowles wrestling with unresolved issues of self-containment and selfishness.[18]

In these two texts Fowles used the isolated black woman as a universal symbol of the human situation. Ourika's existentialist "despair of ever
attaining freedom in a determined and determining environment" was
"the case history of an outsider, of the eternal *étranger* in human society."
The essay "Sensibility" explored the European development of self-
consciousness rooted in "Feeling" as opposed to "Reason." Fowles saw
aesthetic and political history as an alternation between "ages of social,
political and artistic conservatism and ossification (Reason) followed by
disruptive and comparatively short-lasted periods typified by introspection, frustration (particularly in the arts) and neurosis, yet of great energy
and considerable achievement in evolutionary change." In an age of sensibility, a thoughtful person was *nemo*-driven, aware of his futility,
ephemerality, and virtual nothingness. In this anguish, a resentful, demanding "New Self" emerged, one centered on its own sense of unique-
ness, contingency, loneliness, and mortality, indifferent to "social
awareness," disinclined "to care, or to judge, or to participate, or to deter-
mine courses of action on altruistic grounds." From society's perspective,
it was "indistinguishable from selfishness."[19]

Exploring how a society of such new selves could survive, Fowles was
guiltily ambivalent. He was a prime example of this "new self." It was a
novelist's "duty to keep a sharp eye out on his society," but it was also his
"duty to have a profound love-affaire with the complexity of his own
mind." This inwardness, Fowles wrote, was "a main reason I feel myself
in exile from the society I live in. . . . I stare at non-artists and wonder
how on earth they can stand the work they do, with its brutal absence of
self-absorption, its unceasing demand for attention on other things,
other selves."[20] Yet such self-absorption, the defining characteristic of his
own personality, was if manifested in others, a danger to society. "Rampant obsession with feeling and self in our own age" could lead to nothing but "disaster." Fowles believed that "we are now not much more than
one generation out from hell; and sensibility is the wind behind our
tail."[21]

As with *The Aristos,* Fowles tried in this essay to balance the needs of
the individual with those of the society, sketching his own ideal civilization. The "best society," he wrote, would be the one to create a good "com-

promise between the ego and the demands of the species—or between personal enjoyment and public survival." Liberties to be curtailed were never of thought or time, but always of economic and material consumption. Writing during a period of fuel shortages, Fowles recommended something like wartime rationing. People would become "more fastidious about consumption," he argued, "if the rights to produce goods were more tightly licensed, the durability of manufactured goods was regulated more closely, and goods were replaced on a rationing system. Automobile ownership must be severely limited. England's population should be moved away from cities into rural villages, with the consequent removal of culture and entertainment facilities from the capital to the countryside. Education must be strengthened against the "brainwashing of children by the capitalist consumer industries."[22] Fowles, the freedom seeker of the 1950s, now endorsed a government of intervention.

Unnerved by the thought of academic criticism of this long, personal analysis of history, Fowles never published it. But in highly concentrated form the essay contains the seeds of much of his work through the 1970s and 1980s. Sensibility in modern writing was argued in *Daniel Martin*. Renewed interest in the *amour courtois* shaped translations of Marie de France and some of the stories in *The Ebony Tower*. A long-standing interest in dissident Protestantism energized *A Maggot*.

At the same time the uneasy interior argument between self and selfishness was unfolding in his unpublished writings, John Fowles was disentangling himself from the role of a "famous writer" in England in the 1970s. For all his natural love of isolation, he always partially remained the responsible Bedford School Head Boy who carried out his duty when asked. Indeed, his attitude through 1971 was summed up by the subtitle of his suppressed thriller, *Somebody's Got to Do It*. The public role made Fowles uncomfortable, but he faithfully spoke at literary festivals and universities, feeling it "futile" and writing how "appearing before a public is pandering to something bad in our . . . culture . . . a writer is someone who communicates through print."[23]

When he won the W.H. Smith Prize (1970) and the Silver PEN Award (1969) for *The French Lieutenant's Woman,* he was embarrassed. Returning from his 1969 American tour, Fowles was surprised to discover himself the prizewinner for the "English Circle of International PEN, whatever that is," since he had not known he was short-listed. Disapproving, on "principle," of literary prizes, he wanted to turn it down, but "Tom Maschler has already been to a dinner and accepted it for me."[24]

Now that he was Jonathan Cape's Managing Director, Fowles's editor and friend Tom Maschler was waging an energetic campaign to raise the status of fiction in England and direct benefits for writers. In the late 1960s and 1970s he turned to his most well-known authors, including Fowles, for support for his ideas.

Fowles was recruited in 1970 into the successful campaign for the Public Lending Right. The PLR scheme proposed that British lending libraries would be assessed a shilling each time a novel was loaned, the modest fee to be returned to the copyright owner. Fowles wrote a compelling essay, "Ordeal by Income," for a collection on the topic edited by Richard Findlater, who spearheaded the campaign.[25] On October 5, 1970, Fowles was asked by the PLR group to stand for Parliament as their candidate in the Marylebone by-election, scheduled for October 22. At the time his father remained in the hospital after his leg amputation and Fowles at first refused but was reluctantly persuaded to reconsider. When the group withdrew the candidacy, Fowles was very relieved.[26]

Of all of Tom Maschler's schemes for enhancing the prestige and sales of British books, none was as important and successful as the establishment of the Booker Prize. In 1968 Maschler publicly argued the need for a juried literary prize for British fiction that would be an English counterpart to the French Prix Goncourt. "French experience had shown choice by jury to be a disastrously dishonest method," objected John Fowles. "Things like that wouldn't happen in London," retorted Maschler.[27] Booker Brothers (also called Booker McConnell) had a successful authors' division representing writers like Agatha Christie, Georgette Heyer, and Harold Pinter. Booker had recently launched a tax-saving plan to help writers manage their income. Approaching Booker, Maschler frankly laid out the case for a British literary prize carrying the Booker name. Once it was well established, argued Maschler, "Booker might well find their sponsorship something they could be proud of."[28] The first award was made in 1969. In 1970 there was a minor argument about a collection of short stories by George Mackay Brown, and the rules were amended to read, in no less than three separate places, that the prize was for "the best full-length *novel*" published that year.[29]

When John Fowles was chosen as one of the 1971 judges, the Booker

Prize was still in its infancy, though attracting ever more attention. Fowles spent most of the summer reading laboriously through the forty-three entries submitted from the nation's publishing houses, breaking only for an August trip with Elizabeth to Grasse, France, to be best man and witness for Jud Kinberg at his wedding to Monica Mennel and to translate for the French rabbi.[30] Reading the Booker entries made him so bored and "tired of the novel . . . [and] with others' words [and] my own" that he ceased writing, including his diary, for two months.[31] Only three or four of the books interested him. His fellow judge Malcolm Muggeridge was so offended by the selections that he withdrew in mid-July, saying he was out of sympathy with such undistinguished "pornography" and it would be a long time, if ever, before he opened another contemporary novel. American novelist Saul Bellow (counted as a Canadian), whose *Mr. Sammler's Planet* had appeared the year before, held similar opinions but managed to honor his commitment anyway.

An impressive literary panel convened for the first meeting at London's St. James Hotel on September 14. Besides the best-selling Fowles, who had just won the first Silver PEN Award, and Philip Toynbee, working on a book about nuclear policy (1974), there was the chairman, John Gross, author of the 1969 *The Rise and Fall of the Man of Letters,* and Lady Antonia Fraser, biographer of *Mary, Queen of Scots* (1969) and at work on *Oliver Cromwell.* Bellow, teaching at the University of Chicago and Northwestern University, could only attend the final session a week later.

Hours of tight-smiling, diplomatic argument and "horse-trading" yielded "four certainties for the short list": Mordecai Richler's *St. Urbain's Horseman,* Doris Lessing's *Briefing for a Descent into Hell,* Elizabeth Taylor's *Mrs. Palfrey at the Claremont,* and the fourth candidate, V. S. Naipaul. His *In a Free State* is a collection bound together by themes of exile, prejudice, and loss of identity, consisting of a novella, two short stories, and a prologue and epilogue from the author's travel journals. The committee accepted it along with the other entries, all novels. Fowles and Toynbee favored Richler and Lessing, while Gross and Fraser argued for Naipaul and Taylor. Fowles "detected in Gross and A. Fraser a determination to get Naipaul the prize; a certain amount of smooth manipulation was going on."[32] Indeed, Fowles, backed by the memory of Marilyn Edwards, the attending representative from the Publishers Association, later recalled that both Gross and Fraser mentioned speaking directly to Naipaul about *In a Free State,* asking if he considered the book a "novel," and being assured that he did. Tom Maschler remembered Gross's saying something similar. Both Gross and Fraser adamantly denied these charges.

Fowles blamed the agony of a raging toothache for his inattention to the rules of the prize, specifically the eligibility clause stating that judges must consider only "full-length novels." Absent from the first meeting, Saul Bellow assumed that questions of eligibility had been fully answered, so despite unease over the Naipaul entry, he failed to raise objections. On the morning of the second and final meeting, Marilyn Edwards informed Tom Maschler that the committee was going to list a book of short stories, and Maschler telephoned both chairman John Gross and John Fowles to object that "the book isn't a novel." The committee took umbrage at Maschler's "interference" to the point where Philip Toynbee shouted, "To hell with Tom Maschler!" Fowles himself thought Maschler had overstepped but was suspiciously regarded, he believed, as "Maschler's man" by the others. "From that moment on," Fowles wrote that evening, "Naipaul had it virtually." The long meeting was "a chess game" in which the judges attacked one another's choices and sacrificed some of their own. Toynbee and Fowles stopped Bellow's first choice. Bellow and Fowles stopped Toynbee's first choice. Bellow and Toynbee stopped Fowles's first choice. Through all these feints and sacrifices, "the other two just sat and waited." Finally, "it came at last to Lessing and Naipaul, with Toynbee and I for her, Gross and Lady A. for Naipaul. Bellow therefore had the casting vote, and it went finally for Naipaul."[33]

Fresh from the dentist on the twenty-first, Fowles wrote to Tom Maschler, urging him to calm down. But Maschler's persuasive answer made Fowles take "a very belated look at the way things had been done." At the insistence of the permanent Publishers Association Committee, John Gross issued a justificatory statement for all the judges to sign. The document defines Naipaul's fictional collection as a novel, arguing that it is unified and coherent by theme and therefore a novel. Knowing he was walking into a hornets' nest, Fowles refused to sign. He wrote a long, eloquent letter setting out his memory of the meetings and his reasons for not supporting the decision. The Naipaul entry was not a "full-length novel" and, as a candidate for the prize, was *a borderline case at best,"* he declared. V. S. Naipaul's tremendous talent and the worthiness of his fiction were not in doubt, but this book's eligibility was. Gross's argument that the book was unified and coherent "by underlying theme alone" Fowles demolished by pointing out that "coherence can surely be granted to almost any great book of short stories one cares to mention" (himself mentioning *Dubliners* and *The Garden Party*). While the three stories of *In a Free State* "do interlock and reinforce each other thematically; so do all separate works by any serious writer. What is lacking is any narrative or character connection—or unity of place, for that matter." Fowles also expressed distress that this case had unfairly consumed discussion time that should have been apportioned to the other books.[34]

Between September 28 and October 4 highly defensive and diplomatically worded letters flew among John Gross, Lady Antonia Fraser, John Fowles, and Tom Maschler. All earnestly assured one another that everyone had acted honorably, that neither Gross nor Fraser had spoken to Naipaul, that there might be misunderstanding and honest doubts, but certainly no bad intentions, no, never. Wounded indignation was expressed, implications were intensely analyzed, and honeyed apologies exchanged. Fowles, with great courtesy and never ceasing to blame himself for his own lapses, stuck to his perceptions. As he wrote to Lady Antonia Fraser, "Nothing will ever persuade me that we looked properly at the matter; and everything, not least the anger I have provoked in you, makes me regret that we didn't. . . . The business of being fair to the other competitors, and how 'full-length novel' . . . can cover three stories without a semblance of continuity of narrative, or characters, or place, may be matters for disagreement."[35]

To resolve the worsening situation, the Publishers Association Committee upheld the judges' right to final decision but requested a revote on the eligibility of *In a Free State* as a "full-length novel." Fowles voted against, Gross and Fraser for. Saul Bellow joined Fowles, writing that he would vote anytime for Naipaul's talent, but that this book was not a full-length novel. Philip Toynbee, however, joined Fraser and Gross to uphold the judges' right to final decision. *In a Free State* was therefore awarded the Booker Prize for 1971.

"The Booker Prize Imbroglio," as he referred to it ever after, was Fowles's last foray into the world of high-stakes literary prizes, although he occasionally was judge or patron for school and civic competitions. He henceforth refused to allow his own books to be entered for any prizes. He refused to attend the Booker awards dinner and refused to cash the honorarium check sent him by the Booker committee for his services as a judge.

Curiously, as Fowles firmly shut the door on his public duties as a celebrated writer, the passageway to creative abundance opened once more. Three days after the conclusion of the Booker Prize imbroglio, Fowles was truly able to begin writing his long-planned *The Englishman* (eventually titled *Daniel Martin*). It had been two years since he had written "seriously," he said with immense satisfaction. Of course, during those two years Fowles had written a considerable amount, including diaries, a filmscript, short stories, revisions of the thriller, several fragments of novels, essays, translations, and reviews. But by "writing seriously," Fowles meant what happened to him when he entered the psychological state of inspiration in which his imagined "reality" became more powerful to him than factual, mundane reality. He became "possessed" by this alternative reality and the shape shifting of his own memory. "The experience is divine," he wrote; "there's no other word for it; exactly like the first week or two of a plant's growth—nothing in the future can ever equal these days." What enraptured Fowles was "the intense reality, and malleability of reality." It caught him by surprise. He had begun writing a first chapter set in Los Angeles, as he had always planned, "then suddenly switched back to Ipplepen in the war." The entire episode of the wartime harvest, completely forgotten until he began to "re-evoke" it in a single day's writing, came whole in an "unexplained intuition." In ten days in October, Fowles wrote the first five chapters of the novel, watched the "hero" take shape and "the two women (Jenny and Jane)" emerge.[36]

Fowles was still glowing with this experience ten days later, when by coincidence, he received a paper written by Gilbert Rose, a professor of psychiatry at Yale University, who had written "a Freudian psychoanalysis of The FLW."[37] This was *"The French Lieutenant's Woman:* The Unconscious Significance of a Novel to Its Author," published in 1972 in *American Imago,* an article that had a profound and lasting effect on Fowles.[38] From his Freudian perspective, Rose read Fowles's novel as an imaginative record of compulsive oedipal reunion with and separation from the novelist's mother. He buttressed his argument with "some rather absurd evidence he adduces from the text," which Fowles dismissed with a hearty laugh. The nine-month-long "gestation" of the first draft (which Rose suggested imitated pregnancy), for instance, had been determined by absences over the filming of *The Magus*. Rose's belief that the "*ninety* seconds I gave Charles and Sarah for making love is 'a prefiguration of the ensuing nine months' gestation, according to the well-known tendency of the Unconscious to play with numbers," was equally ludicrous, said Fowles. In yet another instance of the influence of Elizabeth Fowles on *The French Lieutenant's Woman*, "the ninety seconds were actually arrived at simply by calculating the fastest time for the actions described, stopwatch in hand."[39]

Fowles was fascinated, however, by Rose's explanation of artistic psychology, termed *irredentist*, a word referring to political advocacy for taking back territories of which a country has been deprived in order to reincorporate them into the nation's boundaries. "In the psychology of the artist," wrote Rose, "this lost territory is the original dual unity with the mother."[40] The irredentist theory, partially based on D. W. Winnicott's work, appealed to Fowles, because it "articulated what I always felt."[41] Just as reading Alain-Fournier's *Le Grand Meaulnes* in 1963 had given Fowles the words *domaine perdu* to articulate concretely his inner experience of a lost landscape, so Rose's article in 1971 gave him a vocabulary for describing the urgent need to recover that territory.

Soon, however, Fowles had discarded the notion of unity with the lost mother through completing a work of art. Instead, he favored the suggestion that artistic experience originates during the first two years when the "I" of a little child first begins to be organized. During this magical time, when the world is new and the sense of self is insecure but wonderful, the growth of sensual perception changes at such a rapid pace that the world is perpetually being re-created, reorganized, and renewed. This is not the period of total unity with the mother, but the period of early separation and return, where the categories of "self" and "other" ("I" and "thou") begin to be distinguished. Fowles's own compulsion for writing, he insisted, "centres in the processus," in the fluid, changeable, multiple experience of the actual process of writing, not in the finished (publishable) product.[42]

It is likely that Fowles would have been impressed by Gilbert Rose's article at any time. Only days before, however, while writing the first chapter of *The Englishman* (*Daniel Martin*), he had himself undergone just such an "irredentist" artistic experience as the psychiatrist described. Fowles was swept, amazed and elated, into the recovery of "The Harvest," a forgotten incident from his own childhood. Arriving when it did, Rose's article was a watershed for Fowles. It stayed with him and shaped his perceptions of his writing experience. He analyzed dreams by referring to it. He referred to the article often over the next twenty years. He immediately incorporated it into his "Sensibility" essay in an "ethnological" attempt to describe "the living behaviour . . . of the practising novelist" as he experienced rare bursts of rapid and very heightened "inspiration . . . a supranormal freedom of association," an experience "peculiarly oblique; and fairly obviously a form of instinctive self-therapy."[43]

The impact of "The Unconscious Significance of a Novel to Its Author" was at this time greatest on the emerging *Daniel Martin*. Fowles had begun the book "in the spirit of my own sickness,"[44] thinking to focus it on "futility," on "the failure of a generation as the failure of evolution—a temporary misadaptation."[45] He had rehearsed this theme in writings all the way back to the 1950s. But after the "divine" delights of an unforeseen recovery of a childhood memory through his writing and the revelation in Gilbert Rose's theory, *Daniel Martin* also became a book about recovering the past through the imagination. Indeed, as the two themes intertwined, *Daniel Martin* became a novel about how the imaginative recovery of the green past—childhood, parents, beloved landscapes, youthful friendships, and early romantic loves—could finally *redeem* the man of that futile generation from his heartsickness and sense of failure. Fowles, at work on the novel in 1974, hinted at this process in a letter to Gilbert Rose, saying "even when story and narrative method require a 'capturing' of the past, the dominant time sense [for the writer] is actually of a kind of futureness."[46] Time remembered, the past recovered, allowed a future of wholeness and authenticity to emerge.

Highly fluid and malleable in 1971, *Daniel Martin* was still a long way from the novel Fowles published in 1977. His notes[47] show that he intended far more emphasis on Dan's Hollywood career and connections. The early Jane was to be scornfully unsympathetic to the novel form. Most surprising is the presence in the notes of a character called "John Fowles." This "J.F." is a novelist and provincial bookseller. He is homosexual. He kept a detailed diary but burned it. His acquaintance with Daniel Martin (whose surname at one point is Smithson) dates to undergraduate years at New College, Oxford, where as Dan says to Barney Dillon, he was "not one of us, was he?" "J.F.'s father," also a bookseller,

grows apples and pears and discusses American philosophy with the protagonist. When Dan decides to leave Hollywood and write a novel, John
F. is an advising mentor. "Obviously you have a good dramatic sense.
That's half the battle," he tells Dan. But "hide yourself totally (keep personal biography out of it—because that's your powerhouse—must keep
it secret or loss of output); must not hurt those close to you." Dan asks if
the writer "must stick to what you know." J.F. responds: "Problem is rear-
ranging the known or the experienced—camoflage—building up the
known outlines." Using this John Fowles character made the real John
Fowles a bit nervous, however, for he wrote: "*must* also camoflage the fictional JF if used—that is, 'false' exterior, 'true' interior . . . F.U.F. urban,
queer, phys. different, etc." He eventually dropped the notion of using
John Fowles and gave these musings on the novel form directly to Daniel
Martin, having that character contemplate writing a novel about a protagonist called J. S. Wolfe, the anagrammed name of Fowles's hero in his
already written, emotionally charged but suppressed thriller.

Several important scenes from the novel do not figure in Fowles's
rough sketches of 1971 because they had not happened to him yet. In
fact the manuscript of *Daniel Martin* (like the stories of *The Ebony
Tower*) became a kind of repository for episodes from Fowles's life during the 1972–1975 writing period. In January 1972 he traveled to Egypt
with Elizabeth as that year's visiting writer at the American University in
Cairo. They spent the entire month enthusiastically touring, mirroring almost precisely the schedule kept by Daniel Martin and Jane Mallory in
the novel.[48] The trip provided Fowles with a perfect metaphor for the
film world of the Hollywood in which his hero, Daniel Martin, was a
screenwriter and a landscape to use in contrast with the green England
to which Daniel returns. From his first California experience during the
shooting of *The Collector,* Fowles had written that Hollywood was
"Egyptian" (always ancient pharaonic Egypt, not modern Egypt). To be
"Egyptian" or part of Hollywood was to be part of a decadent, death-
obsessed, fixed hierarchy, "totally unable to question rank, power, and
money."[49] Two other evocative landscapes from this journey were written
into *Daniel Martin,* almost exactly as John and Elizabeth experienced
them: Kitchener's Island ("green, shady, bird-haunted . . . I fall in love
with the place in five minutes"[50]), visited on the Nile tour, and Palmyra
("very stagy and strange, end-of-the-world . . . magic"[51]), the side trip that
ended the journey.

Fowles returned from Egypt brimming with Daniel Martin's story and his own renewed capacity to slip into the creative abundance of his uncanny states of inspiration. He no longer felt guilt about refusing the demands of the outer world to foster his inner world. The change in attitude was registered when, without thought of publication, he revised his thriller a final time. From its genesis in January 1969, when it was titled *Somebody's Got to Do It*, the book had been a tale of testing and recruitment leading to the hero's accepting a place in a universal organization, the Wind, dedicated to saving the planet from mankind's folly. In the February 1972 revision, Fowles changed the title to *The Hedgehog* and tacked on a new ending, in which J. Simon Wolfe *rejects* membership in the Wind. For all the courage and nobility of the secret group's enterprise, Simon recognizes, by watching a hedgehog, that someone in human society has to be like this little animal: have "some mysterious right to exist exactly" as it is; "have got to say no when everyone else says yes, not cooperate; not join the team, the party, the whatever it is." In a startling statement from the author of *The French Lieutenant's Woman* and the creator of the free spirit Sarah Woodruff, Simon also insists that his lover, Troy, must choose between life with him and her devotion to her cause. "So I'm to stop doing something I deeply believe in," she asks, "just for something you . . . happen to be? . . . you say you believe in freedom. Why can't I be free to be what I am?" Simon replies: "You can. But not under the same roof as me." Troy, in a clichéd (but not ambiguous) romantic ending, happily gives up her work and independence.[52]

More and more content with his decision to isolate himself, hedgehoglike, from the London literary scene, Fowles wrote more prolifically than ever. In the summer of 1972 he wrote the long erotic ballad that became *Mantissa*. By September he had begun the collection of fictions in *The Ebony Tower*. By May of 1973 he was remarking on his happiness in "now total isolation." Reading Quentin Bell's biography of Virginia Woolf, Fowles puzzled over the need of the Bloomsbury writers "to mob," writing letters to one another, socializing with one another. "I read and read," he mused, "I write, I think about writing; fire off the odd letter to some misguided American student. That is all. I am happy, the experience of reading and making is enough."[53]

Also out of the limelight, Fowles's young friend David Tringham had "got *The Last Chapter* off the ground" and filmed it in July 1972. Fowles found it ironic that while *The French Lieutenant's Woman* foundered "in serious doubt again" as yet another international producer and studio left them hanging, this small, unhailed short story had received support from John and Roy Boulton at British Lion and was smoothly proceeding. Tringham cast Denholm Elliott as the writer. Looking for his girl muse, he discovered Susan Penhaligon acting in a small play at the King's Head Theatre. The sets were secured "on the cheap" in a part of Shepperton Studios scheduled for demolition. Tringham got the abandoned gasworks for the Moxon scenes, for instance, for a "ten-quid tip" to the watchman. Tringham himself provided all transportation for the unit.[54]

John and Elizabeth joined the first read-through while having a well-lubricated lunch at Denholm Elliott's Camden Town house. There was no "monstrous show-biz glamour [or] contrived décor." Elliott, "an actor through and through," kept them laughing with his hilarious stage stories while Fowles rejoiced at how well the reading went.[55] Watching the "shoestring production" unfold on the set, he marveled how "the whole atmosphere has been jolly, so different from that of my two 'big' pictures."[56] When he and Elizabeth saw the finished film on November 13, he was pleased. "Not too bad for a first attempt," he wrote contentedly, "and I didn't have to put on a mask to say so to David."[57] Well reviewed and well received, *The Last Chapter* played in English cinemas as a thirty-minute opening short on a double bill in 1972 and 1973 and is still shown occasionally on British television.[58]

As Fowles disengaged himself from a high-profile literary life in London, he became more involved in Lyme Regis, the Dorset seacoast town in which he lived. The picturesque town is a very old English settlement, first mentioned in 774 and granted its royal charter in 1284. Through medieval and Renaissance times, it prospered as a vital trading port. By the mid-nineteenth century it had been discovered as a seaside spa. Because it is "built on and surrounded by some of the most unstable land in Britain . . . and exposed to the full fury of the sea," the town has not expanded or overbuilt. It therefore retains much of its historic character.[59] Its permanent population remains close to its medieval size (between three and four thousand), and its buildings are still clustered on steep streets and narrow lanes in and around the valley of the River Lym. The massive, ancient stone breakwater called the Cobb protects and frames the town's dramatic harbor.

Insensitive and (given the geological instability) potentially dangerous development threatened the town in 1971 and Fowles's help was recruited by Dr. Joan Walker, a member of the Lyme Regis Society. He supported the group's agitation against a proposed sewage plant in 1971 and a planned large apartment block in the spring of 1972. His interest in the history of Lyme Regis, first tasted while he wrote *The French Lieutenant's Woman* in 1967–1968, became a passion. He collected historical references to Belmont House and began researching other issues. He became friendly with Lyme's able amateur historian, Muriel Arber. The town also began at last to pay attention to its famous literary resident. In early 1974 Fowles's "A New Image for Lyme" was widely read in the *Festival News,* which opened the yearlong "1200 Celebration" of Lyme Regis. He pleaded for Lyme Regis, which competed with other seaside holiday towns for the lowest common denominator of tourism, to acquire "a radically new concept of itself—as a place that needs preserving as it is—not one scrambling after something it can never be and prostituting itself in the process."[60]

In spite of his local visibility, John and Elizabeth did not often associate with the "assembled upper middle class (in Lyme terms) of the town," finding it "the dullest and most abominably retarded community one can imagine." Fowles could always manage brief social encounters "by retreating into my ornithological self" and observing behaviors, but Elizabeth's feelings of nonassimilation contributed to her winter depressions.[61] They preferred the thatched Mason's Arms in Branscombe to Lyme restaurants and Axminster, Axmouth, and Exeter to Lyme's shops. Yet the couple established some local friendships among other culturally displaced Londoners.

Kenneth and Betty Allsop, for instance, lived in a converted millhouse in West Milton, Dorset, near Bridport. Kenneth Allsop was a noted journalist and conservation writer for the *Daily Mail* and *Sunday Times* who had gained prominence as the presenter for BBC television's *Tonight* and *24 Hours.* A popular and highly intelligent commentator, he gradually assumed a zealous leadership role in national conservation efforts, "willy-nilly," Fowles wrote, "becoming a kind of unofficial ombudsman for all Britain in the fight against the exploitation of nature."[62] With far more public fanfare than Fowles expended on his local projects, Allsop took on environmental "battles" against power companies, the Forestry Commission, and North American oil prospectors. Handsome and charismatic on camera, Allsop privately lived in constant pain, the result of a 1943

RAF training accident that had led to the amputation of his leg. Beyond mutual passion for nature and conservation, Ken Allsop and the six-years-younger John Fowles shared a range of other interests. Allsop was an authoritative print and radio commentator on literature, books, and jazz. He had published several novels, as well as books of nature observation. His personality, courage, interests, and environmental commitment were attractive to Fowles, and the two were warm friends from their first meeting in August 1970.

Much as he admired Ken Allsop, Fowles was always warily curious about the public "façade" the man was condemned to wear, "eternally genial, shrewd, wise, relaxed."[63] Fowles privately thought this conservation spokesman's attitude toward nature "outmoded," "irredeemably romantic," all "adoration of the purple-prose nature writers . . . too much winged freedom . . . too little hardheaded knowledge."[64] By late 1972 Fowles was feeling "sorry for him" as Allsop's television career unraveled and he was "a man facing retirement and obscurity of some kind." Fowles, now happily adjusted to self-imposed obscurity and writing *Daniel Martin,* felt "rather like a cat full of cream" compared with his "gloomy" friend.[65]

Through the Allsops and their circle John and Elizabeth also came to know the Maynes, playwright Ann Jellicoe and photographer Roger Mayne. Jellicoe taught and produced drama, and her play *The Knack* became a worldwide hit when filmed with Rita Tushingham in 1963 and won the Palme d'Or at Cannes. On meeting this couple, to Ann Jellicoe's irritation, Elizabeth Fowles had sighed, "*Must* we meet the locals?"[66] Both she and John Fowles became "quite chums" with them, however, with Fowles sharing his growing interest in local history. Elizabeth, who called Ann "a very jolly lifeful creature," was stimulated by Jellicoe's keen perceptions on theater and acting.[67] For several years the two households even shared the same cleaning woman, "Mrs. P."

As her husband turned inward or pursued interests that she did not share, Elizabeth Fowles often felt adrift. Fowles's total ability to retreat into his private imaginative world when family and friends visited infuriated her. She was aware that he frequently used his writing and total immersion in the garden as a "bulwark" against her moods.[68] She still suffered seasonal blues, though this cloud was almost always lifted by time spent at the London flat and she returned to Lyme as "her better self."[69] She resented that Fowles reported all their arguments in his diaries, complaining that he traduced everything in the journal, "never speak well of her in it, give only my point of view."[70]

None of this is apparent in her letters of this period or in his descriptions of their travels together. Indeed, he can complain in one passage of lack of affection and only a week later describe with relish how the two forty-six-year-olds found a hidden spot on one of their walks and "made love like teenagers under an oak-tree, with the green valleys below."[71] Their annual spring holidays in France were happily shared with little complaint, although Elizabeth drove for days on end. She was amused and patient as John stopped frequently to "botanize." While Elizabeth sat by her car reading *Time* magazine ("because the articles were short"[72]), John disappeared into the woods or fields, hunting for orchids and other flora. Hours could pass before he reappeared, often far down the road, gesturing to her to pick him up as he stood with his hands and pockets crammed with the contraband plants he had dug up and would smuggle home under the hood of the car.

Elizabeth's interests focused more than ever on her daughter, with whom she now shared an exceptionally close relationship. "They are like two pretty sisters," Fowles wrote during one of Anna's visits, "and make me purr."[73] Anna was shorter than her mother and had Roy's darker features, but she had her mother's mobile mouth and wide, sudden smile. As she walked or sat, her physical movements were uncannily like Elizabeth's. Fowles said once that all her faults and all her virtues had grown from being forced to be independent so young.[74] He called Anna "veiled" since he could not entirely read her emotions.[75] But she was simply cautious and aloof like her mother, wary of bestowing trust until certain her loyalty would be reciprocated.

After a year in the foundation art program at Exeter, Anna entered a graphics course at the West of England College of Art in Bristol in October 1970. She earned her degree in 1973 and her teaching credentials in 1974. By November 1971 she had a new boyfriend, Nick Homoky, a fellow student studying pottery. The son of a Hungarian refugee family, Nick was "a bloody good potter" (said Liz) with "great talent and common sense" (wrote John). Nick was "shy and not as worldly even as little Anna."[76] Fowles thought him culturally innocent in many ways, but liked him and found Nick's work impressive. They were completely delighted when Nick was accepted in 1973 for a competitive postgraduate course at the Royal College of Art and even more when Nick and Anna announced their engagement in August 1973.

Anna's student years coincided with the deterioration of her father's mental and emotional condition. Alternating with times of deep depression and alcoholism, Roy Christy fell into manic periods when he bought cars and furniture he couldn't afford, redecorated his house with pictures of Winston Churchill, drove in a manner that endangered his young children, and hid away in a bank the secret notes for a football novel that was to make him rich. He was unable to work and by August 1972 had to have electric shock therapy. The two young children, aged ten and seven, were sent to twenty-one-year-old Anna for a month. Roy had relapses into violence directed at Judy and Anna. He was eventually hospitalized.

Some of these people closest to John Fowles and the choices with which they struggled in 1972–1973 were reflected in the stories gathered into the volume published as *The Ebony Tower*. Composed in several prolonged pauses during the writing of *Daniel Martin*, each elegant short fiction articulates some failure or emptiness at the heart of success. Fowles titled them *Variations,* regarding them as variations on his previously published books. Tom Maschler and other Cape directors could not see the connection, however, and in January 1974 Fowles was pressed to change the title.[77]

The first story, "Poor Koko," began in an argument with an old sparring partner. In August 1972 John and Elizabeth visited Denys and Monica Sharrocks in Shropshire. They saw them occasionally in London, where Denys worked during the week, but this was John Fowles's first view of New House, an isolated, turn-of-the-twentieth-century stone house deep in unspoiled countryside near the Welsh Marches with "the feel of an ageless backwater." He had only recently observed sadly, in the company of the Maschlers, "how serious (or even intelligently humourous) discussion has now disappeared from the life of the successful intelligentsia."[78] Yet, living outside "the cynicism and contempt," his "old-fashioned," "provincial" friends the Sharrockses surprised him. "They belong to a group I often cannot believe really exists, interested students of the arts, who read." The couple's courtesy and respect toward each other's opinions "astounded" Fowles, who thought them "rather agreeable after everyone else we know."[79] This did not prevent him from clashing with the "puritanical-prickly" Monica, who at the age of forty-one, new teaching degree in hand, was about to take a post in a Stepney girls' school. Told that her job was "to 'culturize' the sixth formers," Monica prepared for her classes "full of fierce puritanical ideals about enlightening the under-privileged," which Fowles regarded as mostly hopeless.[80]

But the argument and the visit fed Fowles's imagination. Three weeks after the visit to Clun, he began writing a short story he titled "Poor Koko," finishing it on September 20, 1972.[81] When it was published two years later, Denys Sharrocks at once recognized Holly Cottage as New House. In the story a housebreaking member of "the classless British young" encounters the sixty-six-year-old narrator, a scholar of eighteenth-century literature, as the thief robs the remote cottage belonging to the writer's friends. Otherwise considerate of his hostage, the youth ties up the older man and burns his precious manuscript in front of his helpless, gagged face (actualizing Fowles's recurring fear of losing manuscripts to fire). The writer ultimately concludes that this pointed act of destruction occurred because the book represented "my generation's 'refusal' to hand down a kind of magic," a breakdown between the generations of the power of verbal and cultural literacy. In print, though not in person, Fowles was endorsing Monica Sharrocks's conviction that she could and should make a difference to these lost young people. "Koko," confesses the chastened narrator, "is a Japanese word and means correct filial behaviour, the proper attitude of son to father."

The next two stories, "The Cloud" (originally "The Picnic") and "The Enigma," were written the following summer. Through the latter part of May 1973 John and Elizabeth enjoyed one of their annual driving holidays through France. That spring their route took them through Brittany and south along the coast, where they picnicked by the wayside, walked through the forests, and explored villages and castles. On a fine afternoon, outside the château at La Rochefoucald beside the Forest of the Braconne they came upon a swift that had swallowed a fishhook and become entangled in overhead telephone wires. The bird struggled frantically, screaming in agony. "Oh, *do* something!" cried Elizabeth. But the tortured bird was impaled high over the river and the towering castle walls. Fowles thought how his friend Ken Allsop would share his dismay.[82]

On the same afternoon that John and Elizabeth stood helplessly watching the anguished death of the bird, the fifty-three-year-old Allsop

swallowed four times the lethal dose of barbiturates, washed down with
a bottle of red wine. His doctor did not show his long suicide letter to in-
vestigators, and the inquest returned an open verdict. Fowles forever associated Ken's suicide with the painful incident at the edge of a forest in
France.

Allsop's family blamed his despair on the pain of his amputated leg
and his dependence on painkillers, a recurrence of kidney tuberculosis,
and, most of all, his sense of hopelessness at the immensity of the struggle to save the natural environment and the degree that others depended
on his leadership. His death was a national shock in Great Britain, and
there was call for a suitable memorial, an effort in which John Fowles
was to take a leading role. Publicly Fowles supported the family's interpretation. In the privacy of his diary, however, he wondered over the
"mystery" of Ken's death. He suspected that Ken's sense of failure in his
highly visible public career was partly to blame. He noted that in the
manner of his suicide, "he wanted to hurt as he went, I think."[83] As for
Allsop's despair about saving nature, Fowles wrote privately, "In a way his
suicide is an example of the dangers of idealism . . . he did not really understand nature . . . never having hunted or shot wild animals . . . he
never realized how resilient nature is; how the death of species is part of
the system." Nature, for Fowles, was "a sanctuary, a buttress against the
possibility of suicide." Allsop's false conception of nature had failed him,
he thought. There was a "theme there," he wrote, "but it would hurt the
living too much to use it."[84]

Circumspectly, however, Fowles did use it. Three weeks after Kenneth Allsop's suicide, Fowles wrote "The Picnic," a haunting, impression-
istic story of friends picnicking at the edge of a forest in France.[85] The
men are television people and writers, and they all are staying at "the
mill." At some recent time a close friend, the husband of one of them,
had committed suicide. The wound of his sudden, inexplicable withdrawal from life is a key element of the story as Fowles draws portraits of
the others in the confusion of mid-life. There is the writer Paul, so clearly
Fowles himself, whose wife, Bel, recalls Elizabeth at her most earth-
motherish. They have two little girls, the younger named Emma. There is
the opportunistic Peter, a shallow television producer seeking the main
chance, his little boy, Tom, and his girlfriend, Sally, a young woman out
of her depth. Last is the bereaved, Catherine, a muse figure frozen into a
perpetual "now," whose inability to move past her husband's suicide gives

Fowles scope to dramatize the *nemo*-driven drift away from community. When published, this story was titled "The Cloud."

Two months later Fowles wrote "An Enigma," a detective/love story that questions why a highly successful public man with a family would one day simply choose to vanish.[86] In MP Marcus Fielding's disappearance from an outwardly satisfying life, maintained by the "leading principle . . . never, never, never show what you really feel," Fowles came as close as he dared to exploring the unanswerable mystery of who Ken Allsop might have been behind the public façade.

Fowles wrote the long story "The Ebony Tower" during the extended stay of Anna and her new fiancé, Nick Homoky, at Belmont through August and September 1973.[87] Anna's year was to be spent student teaching in Birmingham, while Nick began his postgraduate work at the Royal College of Art (RCA) in London. While the two couples played badminton by day on the wide green lawn behind the house and Monopoly and cards at night, Nick and John became admiring friends. At the RCA Nick was to be "shocked" by the unbalanced emphasis on "self-expression . . . everyone trying to be different, no interest in craft or functional values."[88] Fowles was aware of the difficulties for a young artist in trying to uphold his own standards, explore traditions, and follow his personal vision. For John Fowles, said Malou Wiseman, who often heard him speak of Anna's husband-to-be, "Nick was symbolically 'the young creator.'"[89] "The Ebony Tower" was, of course, heavily influenced by Marie de France's *Eliduc,* which Fowles translated in October 1973 as he revised this story. The tale also dramatizes Fowles's own creative situation as he turned away from the critically predictable to follow his personal vision. Yet the empathetic month with Nick Homoky, "the young creator" who was as close as Fowles ever came to having a son of his own, was also a major inspiration for this unsettling story.

Submitting the typed manuscript of *Variations* at the end of 1973 made John Fowles sad. Agent Sheil's praise was "guarded," though Tom Maschler admired the stories.[90] Elizabeth was silent reading "The Ebony Tower," a reaction probably caused by hurt at the portrayal of Beth, the wife in the tale. Fowles's gloom, however, stemmed from the "terrible sense of the pleasure being past" as he made the stories public.[91] In "Behind the Scenes," an essay intended for inclusion in the volume, Fowles had once more tried to express the "mysteriousness of the story-telling process," the distinction between the finished text in the hands of readers and the "main pleasures of the creative experience . . . ambiguity, malleability, fluidity." It was tempting to make fiction of the strangeness of "watching the process happen in one's own mind." But breaking the illusion and producing obscure, hermetic narrative were mistakes of the French deconstructionists and others who wished to "be considered fully contemporary." Failing to connect with the real humanity of the reader was the easy "downhill path to the ebony tower."[92] Fowles suppressed this essay at the insistence of Jonathan Cape's professional readers.

While *Variations,* now *The Ebony Tower,* was being prepared for publication, Anna Christy and Nick Homoky were married from Belmont House. Saturday, July 20, 1974, dawned "a peerless blue day." Fowles watched with deep affection as Anna emerged in "a pretty brown dress with old gold trimmings, a flowery straw hat." Into her bridal posy he tucked a single sprig of marjoram. Roy Christy appeared, trembling and haggard, to escort his daughter to the registry in Bridport. The reception afterward, which Elizabeth Fowles catered, was held on the green Belmont lawn, with the couple's college friends, the two extended families, and a few of the Fowleses' friends. It was a happy day.[93] By October the newlyweds had settled in a flat in Wandsworth, London, and Anna Homoky began teaching art at a comprehensive school in Battersea. The job was "nine parts riot control," wrote Fowles after his stepdaughter had been locked in a stockroom by her pupils during her first week.[94] But within the year, boasted Elizabeth, her daughter was "getting through to the kids."[95]

The Ebony Tower was published at the beginning of October 1974. The Americans loved the collection, while British critics gave it qualified approval. From the United States Ned Bradford praised "The Picnic" ("The Cloud") as "an absolute gem [that] unreels like a film."[96] Fowles turned down a half-million-dollar two-book deal with Little, Brown and Co., but the American publisher responded with a hefty offer for *The Ebony Tower* alone. By publication day the book had been sold to the New American Library and was a Literary Guild selection. By December it was on the *New York Times* best-seller list, where it stayed for six months. The book was on the English best-seller lists, but, wrote Fowles, "it cannot be thanks to the reviewers." Although fairly positive, few reviews were "more than a paragraph or two . . . all showing a ludicrous misunderstanding . . . downright errors of fact . . . not worth serious discussion."[97] Tom Maschler thought it was the "best sale of short stories since the war," exulted in the "turning point for Fowles in England," and ordered up twenty thousand copies ("sheer optimism," clucked Fowles).[98]

From the psychologically safe distance he had constructed, Fowles was moderately pleased by *The Ebony Tower*'s success. But praise or condemnation from reviewers had diminished in importance. Like Henry Breasley, the artist in "The Ebony Tower" who left Paris to dwell in the forest château of Coëtminais and paint from his personal vision, Fowles had retreated into the mythological forest of his own imagination. What was protected and flourishing there was his art. With relief he remarked as the reviews rolled out: "This time, publication hasn't stopped me going on with *Daniel Martin;* this hasn't happened before."[99] Indeed, nothing now could stop the writing of *Daniel Martin,* and John Fowles was about to enter one of his most prolific and creative periods.

CHAPTER SEVENTEEN

On the Island of *Daniel Martin*

Belmont and Other Islands: 1973–1977

> *I have always thought of my own novels as islands, or as is-*
> *landed. I remember being forcibly struck, on my very first visit to*
> *the Scillies, by the structural and emotional correspondences be-*
> *tween visiting the different islands and any fictional text: the al-*
> *ternation of duller passages . . . and the separate island quality*
> *of other key events and confrontations—an insight, the notion*
> *of islands in a sea of story, that I could not forsake now even if I*
> *tried. . . . The island remains where the magic (one's arrival at*
> *some truth or development one could not have logically pre-*
> *dicted or expected) takes place; and it rises strangely, out of*
> *nothingness, out of the onward dogwatches, mere journeying*
> *transit, in the writing.*
>
> —JOHN FOWLES, *ISLANDS*

New Mexico on Monday, November 25, 1974, was a "peerless" day, blue-skyed and cloudless, cool and dry. It was the final day of a surprise jour-ney John Fowles had sprung on his wife in Boston during the American publicity tour for *The Ebony Tower*. Feeling daring and nervous, Eliza-beth Fowles drove her rented Ford across desert and up and down moun-tain ranges. Santa Fe to Taos, through national parks and Indian pueblos, loving the food, the birdlife ("he had to get himself a whole new bird guide!"[1]), the relaxed welcome, the art and jewelry, the week was one of their happiest holidays. They had not experienced "quite such a fusion from a light and landscape for many years."[2] They chose to spend this last day at the ancient, abandoned pueblo of Tsankawi. Walking through pines to the cliff of cave dwellings, they passed age-old pictographs and rows of sockets for vanished roof beams and saw snowy mountains in the distance. Alone with "space, the soft wind, the ghosts," and Elizabeth, Fowles found the site evoked for him "a lost golden age; both intimate and remote." Haunting Tsankawi went on his personal "list" of emotionally defining landscapes.[3]

The day, the landscape, and the special quality of Tsankawi also went into the novel he was writing, *Daniel Martin*. There Fowles calls these places of retreat and healing solitude by different names: "the sacred combe," "la bonne vaux," "under the greenwood tree," "the orchard of the blessed," "the domain." Elsewhere in his works they are actually islands, remote from a mainland. All these settings join an exterior, physical retreat with an interior, emotional retreat into spiritually nourishing solitude: "secret places, where the unconscious grows conscious, where possibilities mushroom, where imagination never rests."[4] For Fowles, the writing of *Daniel Martin* itself was just such a retreat into a secure place of solitude and creative abundance, his own sheltering greenwood, his own remote island.

Daniel Martin, briefly, is the story of a successful English writer in exile, a forty-something screenwriter in Los Angeles, suddenly called home to repair a long-broken friendship from his youth before the friend dies. The suicide of this friend/brother figure, Anthony Mallory, sets in motion Daniel's reunion with his English past. Through a long, slow journey through the landscape of memory, Dan rediscovers his best self, including his relationship with Jane, his own great love and now Anthony's widow, and his own reborn vocation as a serious writer.

This vast ruminative book, salted with discursive examinations of John Fowles's social, political, and biological beliefs, was intended to be about self, Fowles's self. The only way to "historianize the personal past is through fiction," wrote Fowles, "by treating one's past self as a fictional situation . . . as a hypothesis." Fiction allows for making a clearer exploration of oneself, he stated, "even more widely than overt literary autobiography—which gives personal complexes too much power." Fowles wrote of "the way I am making Daniel Martin both 'marry' and diverge from myself."[5] As a fictional hypothesis of John Fowles's personal past, Dan was invested with fictionalized versions of many of Fowles's own biographical memories: his youth in Devon during the war, his undergraduate days at Oxford. He was given loves and friendships that recalled, though did not precisely repeat, people Fowles was close to. Daniel shared Fowles's regrets over lost possibilities, including regrets over a grown-up daughter not loved dearly enough in her childhood. He was a mouthpiece for Fowles's newly articulated beliefs about creativity as the urge to recapture the primal perceptions of infancy and for his old beliefs on the reassuring endurance of nature. "Daniel," said Fowles, was "my exteriorized imagination—imagination as substitute for biographical realization."[6]

By the time the book was about to be published in 1977, Fowles thought of Daniel and his story as "a symbolic representation of the ego" and of the book as "a hiding place" for that ego and how, upon publication, the hidden ego had "to be retrieved."[7] Thus, during the writing process the book was a *bonne vaux,* a secure, isolated place of creative solitude. During the five years that John Fowles remained in safe retreat within its shelter he was mostly happy, enormously productive, and able to manage setbacks with equanimity. Perhaps *Daniel Martin* is so long because its author did not want this writing experience to end.

Throughout the writing of this novel about a Hollywood screenwriter, Fowles was deeply immersed in what Elizabeth called filmbiz. Daniel's knowledge of and ultimate rejection of this world paralleled Fowles's own experience and his growing emotional distance from that medium. Valuable energy was wasted on the byzantine wheelings and dealings to get backing and production under way on a film of *The French Lieutenant's Woman,* on meetings, telephone calls, consultations, visits, script revisions, bidding by producers and directors, and long, anxious waits. "This endless talk of film business, meeting people I don't really want to meet, vile and endless fussing about nothing . . . my poor book, everything seems to want to tear me away from it," Fowles wrote.[8]

After director Karel Reisz turned down the project in 1969, Oscar Lewenstein held the option until 1970. John Calley of Warner Bros. took it up in fall 1970, allowing Tom Maschler to be the film's producer. In late November 1970 Maschler and Fowles, with Calley's approval, chose David Rudkin to write the script, riding over expressions of interest from Harold Pinter.

In April 1971, as the option expired, Warner Bros. rejected the Rudkin script, which Maschler and Fowles thought had bogged down in "illustrated history lesson" voice-overs. By November 1971 Fowles and

Maschler were negotiating with producer Lester Goldsmith and director Franklin Schaffner. Fowles felt uncomfortable with the secretive Goldsmith but sold him a year's option in May 1972. These two scouted locations in Lyme Regis with screenwriter James Goldman, insisting on hiking over the cliffs. Fowles marched them "through the jungle and along Pinhay Warren about the bay, then back to the path. In their dapper clothes," wrote Fowles, "they flop and wallow and fall about, get stung by nettles (what is that goddam plant?) and torn by brambles. It becomes sadistic."[9]

In November 1973 Fowles got a phone call from actress Sarah Miles, who desperately wanted the role of Sarah Woodruff. She had just been personally approached by twenty-four-year-old Prince Faisal Ibn Musaed, a nephew of the Saudi Arabian king, who claimed to own the film rights to *The French Lieutenant's Woman*. In Geneva in March 1973, Fowles learned, Prince Faisal had paid ninety-eight thousand pounds to a man named Goldsmith for the expiring option. Convinced it was an unrestricted right of grants and eager to make the film, the prince "had already 'booked' Robert Redford and Sarah Miles for the leading parts." Fowles was shocked by the "ludicrous and cold-blooded con trick," though Lester Goldsmith denied the scam.[10] Yet by April 1975 Fowles's film agent, Roger Burford, learned that Goldsmith had sold spurious "options" for *The French Lieutenant's Woman* to people in New York and California, skimming about two hundred thousand dollars altogether from the project. It was by then far too late to tell Prince Faisal, who was publicly beheaded in June 1975 for the assassination of his uncle, King Faisal, three months earlier.

From the time of David Rudkin's script in 1971, Fowles had grown convinced "that the book cannot be made into a good film." *The French Lieutenant's Woman* was "too complex for the medium, especially when it has to be put over in two hours."[11] He actually became cynically relaxed about it, "so sure of that now that I'm quite content to have it made."[12] In contrast with his deep involvement in the making of *The Collector* and *The Magus,* Fowles acted cheerfully indifferent to the filming of *The French Lieutenant's Woman,* ignoring the deal making when he could and being as genuinely helpful as possible when he was needed. He was not without interest, of course, retaining right of approval for director and casting and rigorously correcting scripts. His confidence in the film medium, however, was vanishing. "Writing *Daniel Martin* has cured me," he wrote in early 1975, of caring "a damn either way about *The FLW* being filmed."[13] He had in that very week reached the "Rain" chapter of *Daniel Martin*, the point of depicting "the first spring of feeling in the man" and Daniel's decision to leave the film world behind.[14] As Fowles had helped his character into a decision, so had he helped himself to a "cure."

Meeting the latest director, Fred Zinnemann, only a week later sparked feeling, however. Zinnemann, said Fowles, was "an impressive, humane man, and he fills me with hope; though much still remains to dash it."[15] By the end of April 1975, after two months of knocking on studio doors, Zinnemann had secured backing from Paramount Pictures, and the project was under way. Dennis Potter, novelist and successful, innovative television playwright, was secured as scriptwriter. The film was scheduled for location shooting in Lyme Regis for spring 1976. Actors were discussed and approached. Zinnemann favored Charlotte Rampling, Gemma Jones, Kate Nelligan, or Francesca Annis for the Sarah Woodruff role. Fowles wanted Helen Mirren. To Fowles's immense relief, Robert Redford was too expensive, although Zinnemann still insisted on casting an American in the Charles Smithson role because "the accent has to be mid-Atlantic" (this "depressed" Fowles).[16] By October 1975 actor Richard Chamberlain had been lined up for the part.

The film was poised for production when Dennis Potter's script was turned down. Conferences, revisions, and outright quarrels through autumn 1975 were of no avail when Paramount rejected the script in November. Sarah was "too mysterious," the ending too ambiguous, and the only character an American audience was thought able to identify with was the businessman Mr. Freeman.[17] Filming was "postponed" while James Costigan wrote an entirely new script. Paramount rejected that one as well in February 1976 and refused to put any more money into the project. Fred Zinnemann's "sincerely sad" voice on the telephone made Fowles sorry, for he liked and respected the director to the end. For the film, however, Fowles announced himself "unsurprised" and "indifferent."[18] "A pox on all of it!" he cried. "I went back to Daniel Martin. To the terrace over the Nile."[19]

The agony was still continuing a year later, on the very day *Daniel Martin* was handed in, January 17, 1977, when Saul Zaentz bought the option and, unsuccessfully, tried to put together a production for Fowles's novel.

Less extensive film projects were interwoven with the "filmbiz" time of *The French Lieutenant's Woman*. The *Zip* script circulated until March 1972. Also, David Tringham's 1972 success with *The Last Chapter* moved Fowles to work with him again. In November 1973 the Arab oil embargo created a serious energy crisis in the West that Fowles hailed as "a great warning bell . . . when the dream ended . . . and possibly when the end began."[20] As British Prime Minister Ted Heath announced controls and fuel rations, Fowles spent two days rapidly writing a macabre half-hour filmscript for David Tringham. Originally called *The Girl in Black,* the two worked on it through the spring of 1974 as *The Black Thumb.*[21] More visually dramatic than spoken, the story charts the travels of a Death figure, a mysterious GIRL in her early twenties who is erotic in a hard, scruffy way. By night she sleeps in an automobile junkyard ("piles of junked car-bodies, mechanical debris; no sign of life"). By day she hitchhikes around Cornwall. As in a medieval morality play, each person with whom she rides comes to a terrible automobile death. Fowles and Tringham spent months refining the script and plotting motorway locations. They never found production backing.

The sense of impending apocalypse underlying *The Black Thumb* was also reflected in a novel Fowles began and abandoned in October 1974. His notes give various titles: *The Mother Planet, The Final Account, A Last Account, The Survivor, Adam and Lupela,* and, at last, *The Screw.*[22] In the fictional fragments, Earth is completely devastated in a nuclear war in the year 2075. The narrator, a forty-five-year-old writer, is saved just before the catastrophe by the female voyagers of a spaceship from the planet Lupela. To the "Ladies, infinitely strange in form, infinitely kind of heart, my saviours," the earthman tries to explain his culture, the intricacies of human language, and the destruction of nature on his dying planet. The spaceship, "spherical . . . stationary and silent," and its wise feminine travelers are forerunners of the vessel and voyagers of the supernatural vision in *A Maggot*. Fowles was imaginatively at work on that book more than a decade before publishing it.

In spring 1975, at the time Zinnemann optioned *The French Lieutenant's Woman,* George Schaefer began eight years of attempts to produce "The Ebony Tower" as a feature film.[23] The project with Schaefer, to Fowles's disappointment, ended in 1983 with the final failure of a much-revised script by John Hopkins.[24]

While frustrated with the film industry, Fowles was being drawn to the live stage. In September 1975 he began an association with the National Theatre. The massive new, triple-stage complex on London's South Bank was under construction, and Peter Hall, artistic director since 1973, was planning the company's ambitious future productions. One of Hall's envisioned projects was a season devoted to the Don Juan legend, offering his own Glyndebourne production of Mozart's *Don Giovanni,* in repertoire with Shaw's *Man and Superman,* Odon von Horvath's *Don Juan Comes Back from the War,* and Molière's *Dom Juan.* Asked by the dramaturge John Russell Brown to provide the Molière, Fowles enthusiastically translated from an insight that "the play's real subject is the twin (though very different) traps of 'real' and 'artificial' language."[25] To his great disappointment, the *Dom Juan* was postponed in 1977, when Hall became embroiled in industrial actions over construction, a cash crisis, and public criticism.

Through years of "filmbiz" annoyance that produced little, Fowles worked on *Daniel Martin* in a state of gratified contentment. He enjoyed technical problems that once would have frustrated him. The book was his private retreat, shared with absolutely no one. A major theme was the hero's growing rejection of the film-producing world and a deepening commitment to writing novels.

During the writing years of *Daniel Martin,* as Fowles retreated to the private sanctuary of his manuscript, he also spent his energy and imagination on several island sanctuaries, beginning with his arrival on a rock nobody wanted, the island of Steep Holm. In the aftermath of Ken Allsop's untimely death in May 1973 Fowles was caught up in efforts to create a suitable memorial to that environmental crusader. Initial efforts were unsuccessfully directed toward purchasing Ken's favorite haunt, Eggardon Hill, overlooking Powerstock Common, a place Allsop had fought to save from oil speculators. By November 1973 the Allsop memorial committee, including both Fowleses, was looking at another conservation project as a monument.

Latitude 51 degrees 20.5 minutes north, longitude 3 degrees 6.5 minutes west, Steep Holm is an inhospitable fifty acres of rock and scrub in the middle of the Bristol Channel between Weston-super-Mare, England, and Penarth, Wales. Eight hundred meters long and 256 feet above sea level at its highest point, the island lies more than six miles off-shore in the open sea of one of the world's most challenging tidal estuaries. Leased and held by the Steep Holm Trust, it had been variously occupied through recorded history by "the Romans, the Danes, the Christians, the Coast Guard, and the Royal Artillery," none of whom found it "tractable."[26] Fowles, seeing it for the first time on November 4, 1973, called it "a very bizarre place," although ecologically "dull." Six thousand breeding pairs of herring gulls had driven everything else away, and the botany was not native. There were ruined fortifications from Victorian times on: "a dozen or more rusting cannon lying about, weird underground chambers, relics of ammunition railway . . . powder magazines." Buried in the undergrowth was a twelfth-century priory. Ruined cottages occupied the top of the cliffs. The sole habitable building was a dilapidated Victorian barracks. Steep Holm was desolate, remote, deserted, ecologically boring, climatically harsh, and extremely hard to get to. John Fowles fell in love at once. He called it "a very tempting toy to play with, as well as on," mused that the public should be let in and "the place used not for preserving the present ecology, but altering it."[27]

Only one other committee member shared Fowles's enthusiasm: Rodney Legg, the founder and "fierce little editor of the *Dorset County Magazine*." Legg was a scrappy proponent of all things Dorset, a keen explorer and naturalist, an investigative journalist with his hand in any number of projects, and a resourceful cutter of corners. Fowles, in one of his frequent animal images, thought of Legg as "a weasel . . . trusts no one and fears no one . . . formidably well equipped for the role he has assigned himself and his magazine—of attacking anything that attacks Dorset."[28] The two were acquainted, for Legg and his photographer/magazine partner Colin Graham had interviewed Fowles for a 1972 feature. Through the Allsop memorial committee, they became collaborators. Between them, they sold the idea of Steep Holm as the Allsop memorial to Ken's widow and the others. Because of John Fowles's outspoken advocacy, he was, reluctantly, drawn into becoming the leader of the effort, the chairman of the trust.

The myriad complications of legally acquiring the island and setting up the Kenneth Allsop Memorial Trust are thoroughly documented in Rodney Legg's *Steep Holm: Allsop Island*.[29] As they negotiated the 1974 lease and 1976 purchase of Steep Holm, established a charitable organization independent of other conservation agencies, and began to raise money, John Fowles was in the thick of it all. While he wrote *Daniel Martin* and the stories of *The Ebony Tower,* composed essays and reviews, pursued the scripting of *The French Lieutenant's Woman* and "The Ebony Tower," involved himself in David Tringham's smaller film projects, gardened, traveled, and saw to business, Fowles labored tirelessly on behalf of the trust. He wrote the appeal, chaired the committee, made the contacts, and helped raise the money. His own unspecified financial contributions were considerable. Rodney Legg always joked that the "ultimate secret" was "Did Elizabeth write the books?", for John Fowles seemed to him so busy with other projects.[30]

Appointed secretary of the trust, Legg led the physical, hands-on assault on the neglected habitat, becoming warden from 1975 until 1998. The immense task required decades of repairs, safety measures, path making, and management of plants and animals. It was agreed that the public should be allowed to visit, first because public education about the environment had been a priority for Allsop himself, second because it was the only solid source of income and volunteers. So visitors, from the vaguely curious to interested volunteers to troops of Boy Scouts, regularly made the wild and soaking journey from Weston-super-Mare out into the Bristol Channel to the island. Sometimes a landing was impossible. Sometimes, once landed, a return the same day was unfeasible, and visitors would be bunked down in primitive conditions in the Victorian barracks. "We never had an accident," recalled Rodney Legg, "which was utterly amazing."[31]

Part of the appeal of Steep Holm's remoteness for both Fowles and Legg was that despite an overseeing committee, they actually had free rein and little interference. They both were men of extremely independent mind, not to say downright perversity, and admired this quality in each other. In 1977, for instance, Rodney Legg, entirely on his own authority, introduced hedgehogs and muntjac deer to the island. Fowles was furious at first, mostly because *he* had not been consulted. He went to Legg's home at Sherborne to confront him but found "it's impossible to be angry with him . . . he lives in such a mess, cats, animals, two parrots in the lavatory, a shed with lemur-mongooses in the garden; and Rodney himself like some cross between a weasel and a pixie, enjoying the brouhaha."[32] He ultimately defended Legg's action to the more ecologically purist committee members. Fowles was very aware how hard Legg worked for so little return. After 1975, when Legg began selling antiquarian books, manuscripts, and prints, Fowles became his best customer. Although he loved the rare old volumes, Fowles also bought from Legg in great quantities to "thank him tacitly for all his work for the Trust."[33] Legg treasured a note Fowles enclosed with a payment: "Get thee behind me, thou Satan of Sherborne—decided last week to stop buying so many books, just never get round to reading most of them." However, he finished, "Cheque enclosed! . . . Have always wanted it in fact."[34]

Between 1974 and 1978 Fowles was a frequent visitor to the island. They crossed in the *Jane,* a low, open boat of perhaps twenty feet, registered for twelve passengers but often carrying as many as thirty. Rodney Legg remembered going into "horrendous seas" in "appalling conditions." While the *Jane* pounded and boomed into the waves, John and Rodney sat in the stern, drenched in heavy spray, taking turns operating the hand pump as water washed over the side and sloshed at their feet.[35] Elizabeth described one crossing when "the sea was bloody wild" and the waves smacked them broadside for an hour. "I was so scared—I hated it," she wrote. "I cursed the day that this damned island was ever suggested as a memorial to K. Allsop, and also felt he would have hated the damned getting to it as much as I did."[36] Elizabeth often stayed ashore at Weston, returning to pick up her husband at his journey's end.

Fowles himself was undeterred. On Steep Holm he invariably vanished for the day, off onto the cliffs or disappearing "underground, literally," into the tunnels that had once been arms magazines. Legg and Fowles both were explorers who cut their way off the beaten path with secateurs, but Legg would "generally get about 300 yards with him, and then we'd lost him." The "impossibility of doing a walk with John Fowles," recalled Legg, laughing, "is that doing a walk of just one mile could take days! He would disappear down the first scree slope and start turning over, literally, every stone." Fowles's path could be traced by the disturbed lichen-encrusted stones, the record of his careful examinations underneath for small insects and grubs. Wearing a filthy old macintosh with deep pockets, "tied together with a bit of baler twine," "Big John" ("we had a surfeit of Johns," said Legg) reappeared at the barracks in time for a late lunch and a drink. Standing there, "like Orson Welles, with this enormous presence that he brought with him," Fowles would say to Legg in his high, woeful voice, "I've brought you these." From one deep pocket he would extract a dozen purseweb spider (*Atypus*) tubes spotted with stored dead flies and other insects, gathered from under the rocks. From another he would pull out handfuls of colorful banded snails, from yet another, a collection of odd objects rescued from the nests of the herring gulls.[37] He also successfully nurtured Steep Holm wild peonies from seed in his garden at Belmont, a feat that, to his delight, Kew Gardens could not match.

Rodney Legg, like so many Fowles associates, appreciated Elizabeth's refreshing lack of reverence toward her famous husband and the way she punctured the solemnity of the "intense people," the "sycophants" who surrounded him in public. "Oh, Mr. Fowles," someone would breathe, "what is your *best* book?," to which Elizabeth would deadpan, "It's *Murder on the Orient Express,* isn't it, John?" His chuckle to this, Legg recalled, "nicely destroyed the attack." To a writer both "distracted" and "reclusive," she brought "a certain worldliness." Her irreverence extended to what she called the "bloody island" of Steep Holm.[38] Two elderly day-trippers to Steep Holm once asked her about the island's folklore. Straight-faced, Elizabeth concocted on the spot a lunatic tale of a "Headless Sea-Captain" who appeared from the sea each afternoon at three o'clock. Just before three, Legg encountered the two old ladies, looking expectantly down the beach for the apparition as promised by "a very cultured lady."[39] While John's attitude to the island was excited by the wild nature in isolation, Elizabeth's was buffered by outrageous humor. A BBC expedition to Steep Holm in June 1974 at first charmed Elizabeth and the television crew because hundreds of seagull chicks were hatching, scurrying and stumbling about before them. But the experience suddenly turned nasty and frightening when the group of watchers "had been shat upon by the parent birds and mobbed." It was typical of Elizabeth to shield the unpleasantness by declaring it "all very Monty Python" and carrying on for laughs with some of the BBC crew. She was later hurt to be "once again rapped over the knuckles by J.F. for finding it funny,"[40] since she had found "chums" among "sharp and cynical young men" of the kind Fowles detested.[41]

His work on Steep Holm led Fowles to other islands. He was looking for a way to direct proceeds from his published writing to the benefit of the trust when he first visited the Scilly Islands in February 1973. These austere and remote rocky isles off the western tip of Cornwall completely captivated the Fowleses, and they returned annually for years in the company of family or other couples. On a 1974 visit Fowles introduced Tom Maschler to some "splendid old photographs of ship-wrecks, all taken by a local family of photographers named Gibson."[42] Maschler enthusiastically proposed publishing a compilation of them with a text by John Fowles. This became *Shipwreck,* the first of Fowles's books to combine a collection of photographs with an evocative text.[43] Fowles learned that novelist Margaret Forster had discovered a legal technique for giving away a copyright, by donating it before writing a word ("then the copyright is between publisher and recipient").[44] Very pleased, Fowles assigned the copyright of *Shipwreck* to the Kenneth Allsop Memorial Trust. In a similar fundraising project, in 1978 he and Rodney Legg collaborated on *Steep Holm: A Case History in the Study of Evolution.*[45] The *Shipwreck* strategy of 1974 became Fowles's method of generating income for his projects.

Fowles's love for the Scilly Isles initiated a second photographic book. This time he wanted to interpret the landscape of islands in terms of their literary mythology, "to do a brief essay on the general charm of small islands, their *general* psychological and quasi-Jungian appeal."[46] He wanted to partner with a contemporary photographer capable of visually interpreting that same stark, archetypal quality that so moved him in these Cornish islands. In the summer of 1974 he met Fay Godwin, a photographer sent to do a series of publishers' headshot portraits of him and his wife. Fay Godwin was the widow of publisher Tony Godwin who had turned to photography after her husband died. She had a powerful sense of texture and form and a remarkable affinity for the elemental in landscape, for seeing through to the bones and essence of place. Although *Islands* did not appear until 1978, partly because of the cancer that Godwin battled and overcame in these years, Fowles had talked Tom Maschler into doing this innovative essay/photography volume by November 1975.

Also in 1975, Fowles returned in his imagination to another beloved island. Plans for a new British edition and several translations of *The Magus* moved Fowles to convince Maschler to allow a full revision of the 1966 novel. Fowles had never been completely happy with the novel on a line-by-line basis, and he was distressed at misinterpretations by some of his readers. Through the summer (July through mid-September 1975) he was "replunged in Greece," writing far, far into the night, "re-lost on Spetsai," even as he simultaneously wrote the last six Egyptian journey chapters of *Daniel Martin*. The experience was like "opium."[47] *The Magus* became "suddenly and miraculously all present and alive again, the book, and my past, and denying totally my theory that written books die for the writer."[48] He was humbled "to see how badly one wrote . . . how messy the plot in places." He was excited to feel "fixed situations melt, the characters live again, present new choices."[49]

In the fluidity of these new choices, Fowles felt free to alter the original *Magus*. He changed many scenes, mostly in the central Spetsai section, as well as the ending. He unmasked the mysteries earlier, thinking "Nicholas was made too gullible on those first visits; and the Conchis side of things too literal."[50] He strengthened the erotic element in the middle section, writing the kind of specific sexual descriptions against which Elizabeth had once cautioned him. Long, explanatory paragraphs analyzed the motives and callowness of Nicholas Urfe with the psychological vocabulary Fowles was using for *Daniel Martin*. Jungian archetypes are made explicit; writing theories about recapturing the eternal mother-child relationship are suggested.

Fowles was at pains in this revised version to recalibrate his definition of personal freedom. The revised Nicholas agonizes over his earlier notion of freedom as the selfish "freedom to satisfy personal desire, private ambition," as a representative of a generation "obsessed" with individuality, "our retreat from society, nation, into self." Against this definition, the revised Conchis sets "a freedom that must be responsible for its actions: something much older than the existentialist freedom . . . a moral imperative, an almost Christian concept."[51] This setting aside of existential individualism in favor of a traditional sense of obligation to the whole was a philosophical shift Fowles had hammered out in the pages of unpublished essays like *America, I Weep for Thee*, "The New Self," and "Sensibility." He was determined not to be misunderstood in *The Magus*, even if he erred on the side of didacticism.

Besides the obvious fact that Elizabeth Fowles did not edit *The Magus: A Revised Version*, economizing and excising the didactic parts as she once would have, the shift in the Fowleses' relationship is also reflected in the new edition. The first *Magus* dramatized an absolute choice between Lily, representing the romantic imagination, and Alison, cast as reality. This reflected the biographical choice Fowles had made in the 1950s, choosing Elizabeth and the hard road of poverty, fidelity, and obscurity over the life of fantasy and class privilege he had enjoyed at Ashridge, symbolized by Sanchia. By 1975, however, he had turned inward, away from the outward reality that Elizabeth/Alison symbolized. The inward "reality" he was exploring was, more than ever, represented by a young, erotic female figure. Variously, he called her "the muse," "the anima," "the original mother," and, soon, "the hag."

Originally a kind of fey ghost girl reflecting aspects of Sanchia and Monique, Lily becomes in the revised version a more substantial character and a real threat to Alison. Whereas, in the 1966 ending, Nicholas firmly makes his choice and voices his commitment, leaving Alison free to choose him or not by her own actions, the ending of the revised version finds him waffling. "If Lily walked down that path behind us and beckoned to me . . . I don't know. The fact that I don't know and never shall is what I want you to remember. And while you're about it, remember she isn't one girl, but a type of encounter."[52] In a conclusion even more obscure than the 1966 original, Fowles leaves himself and Nicholas room to follow their muse when she summons. Fowles also removed the emotionally charged original dedication "To Astarte."

When the revised *Magus* appeared in June 1977, Elizabeth sat in the sunshine of the Belmont garden and scribbled a quotation from poet John Keats to her friends: "I have a habitual feeling of my real life having passed, and that I am leading a posthumous existence."[53]

As he wrote *Daniel Martin,* John Fowles was aware that the character of Jane Mallory, like Alison before her, was largely patterned on Elizabeth Fowles. Not only did he draw many scenes directly and sometimes very closely from biographical incidents with Elizabeth, but he also recognized that "the outcome of the novel is a paradigm of what Eliz and I have created . . . the better conclusion to which we have come."[54] But although Elizabeth—her personality, her style, her instincts, her groping for a better sense of self, and John's deep feelings for her—was still an important part of what went *into* his work, she was no longer a part *of* his work process. This situation created a deepening divide.

Elizabeth was energized by other people and a life of relationships. Alone, especially in dreary weather, while John was completely absorbed in his writing, she collapsed emotionally, savagely expressing her "hatred" of huge Belmont House and Lyme Regis and her longing to move. When the house filled with people, she found herself very fond of it. She relished the "odd little dinner party, lunches for visiting TV producers, Time Inc. interviewers."[55] During school holidays she was apt to host family or friends with children for up to a week at a time. Christmases at Belmont were crammed, chaotic family affairs in which overflow guests might be bedded on lawn furniture in the laundry room and Elizabeth merrily cooked for a week. On summer days she could be found on the beach with various children belonging to Maschlers, Tringhams, Wisemans, or O'Sullivans. Through 1976 she and Fowles saw the Sharrockses two or three times a year, when they visited Belmont at half term holidays from their teaching posts in Shrewsbury. The four old friends walked miles in the countryside, stopping for "a mad Fowles picnic,"[56] and spent evenings in talk, food, drink, and clouds of tobacco smoke. When Denys Sharrocks was lured abroad for one last posting as Head of the British Council in Sweden, Fowles lectured at various universities there in 1977 ("bits about Rose's theory, Hardy, modernism and post-modernism; highly incoherent") so that the four could holiday together.[57] In 1977 John and Elizabeth also began yearly visits to the Wisemans' house in Grasse, France, where Fowles enjoyed boyish pleasures with young Boris, hiking the countryside or planting a dead grass snake in Malou's refrigerator.[58]

Elizabeth managed the couple's relationship with the "two old mums." Gladys Fowles moved to Yorkshire after Hazel did, buying a bungalow in 1974 in Great Ayton, where Dan now taught history and where John and Elizabeth loved walking on the moors with the O'Sullivan children. At seventy-five, still healthy and active, Gladys thoroughly enjoyed her new freedom to manage her own money, see Hazel frequently, and spoil the four grandchildren, who visited her weekly. At seventy-three Doris Whitton, with severely worsening arthritis, was not so well, though she continued working without complaint. Elizabeth regularly had both mums at Belmont. John Fowles, during these visits, managed well with his mother-in-law, a simple soul, "so gentle and still full of fun, makes no fuss." During fuel rationing, he, Elizabeth, and Doris huddled near the fireplace each evening, playing cards and board games.[59] He fled the company of his own mother, however. During one of Gladys's visits Elizabeth wrote in exasperation, "J.F. played the role of the totally occupied man, joining us for a meal in the evening—TV turned up loud so as to make sure there was no such thing as meaningless chitchat."[60] Ironically, this visit occurred as Fowles was writing the essay "Hardy and the Hag," in which he describes the novelist's obsessive need to recover "oneness with the original lost mother."

By the mid-1970s Elizabeth was spending much of the winter in short trips away, to assuage her seasonal depression and boredom with Lyme Regis. The "London pad" always restored her, and she returned serenely home as her "better self." She boasted in 1975 that she had "managed to survive another winter," even that it had been "rather jolly." London had been "a wow . . . an endless round of theatre, cinema, art exhibitions, people to visit, and people visiting me." John, she wrote, had remained in Lyme and "got relentlessly on with his book."[61] She had Anna and Nick in London, and she offered weekends at the Hampstead flat to her sister-in-law, as a break from a houseful of children. She gave weekends alone to the O'Sullivan nephews, crammed with movies and events, both in London and in Lyme Regis. Little Hannah Maschler ("the darling of my heart"[62]) sometimes stayed with her. She saw the Wisemans and Ronnie Payne and his new wife, journalist Celia Haddon.

Elizabeth was great friends with Fay Maschler. Having produced three children, Fay Maschler established herself as a formidable *Evening Standard* restaurant critic (writing "wittily" and "without mercy," said Fowles) and moved in rather fashionable circles.[63] In Fay's company, Elizabeth found herself gawping delightedly at trendy restaurant openings and exclusive parties, where she and Fay were apt to giggle in the ladies' loo like teenagers, spraying each other with expensive perfume and making up their eyes. She spent New Year's Eve 1976 dancing "wildly to loud modern music" with the Maschlers in an "extraordinary house of supreme modernity . . . like you see on telly. . . . Some people said where is John? I said back in Lyme Regis watching the Telly of course. As I flung across the room with my shoes off . . . Best New Year I have had in years."[64] To the fascinated Anna, she said, "I am fifty this year, and the pace seems to get wilder."[65] When Fowles joined Elizabeth in the city, he too made the social rounds of friends, restaurants, theater, cinema and, occasionally, going dancing with his wife. In London, said Malou Wiseman, Fowles always did what Elizabeth wanted to do.[66] He managed short doses well, although he was barbed about the Maschlers' lifestyle philosophy, which he labeled "Onlytheverybest."[67]

In Lyme, without Elizabeth, Fowles lived a life "so inward it is as if I am drugged." With his garden, bird-watching, and recorder playing, he often experienced "a most profound sense of harmony." He wrote contentedly, but his life was isolated, disorganized, and unhealthy. Chain-smoking cigarettes was an essential part of his writing concentration. The more he wrote, the more he smoked—and he wrote constantly. He had "permanent indigestion, malaise. I see no one, speak to no one."[68] He got no exercise and barely ate. Unable to break off from his text, he kept impossible hours. He rarely left the house and often felt "imprisoned" by his inability to drive a car.[69]

His complete immersion in the writing began to take a serious toll on his health. From his mid-forties, Fowles complained intermittently of breathlessness and pains in his lungs and chest. He was warned of potential ulcers. He began to be afflicted by problems in blood circulation, such as those that had plagued his father and that were to worsen later in his own life. In 1974 he developed varicose veins in his left leg. They throbbed and ached when he walked and gave "a queer impression of gurgling." He sometimes had "pins and needles in his left arm."[70] By 1977 his blood pressure was dangerously high. He experienced hearing loss during crowded receptions and, by the early 1980s, was hard-of-hearing in his right ear.

Both John and Elizabeth Fowles were highly conscious that their lives were diverging, that John's writing was carrying him inward and that Elizabeth was more absorbed in the domestic and social world than he could ever be. Because of their continuing love for each other, they were mutually distressed and actually shared a literary "myth" about a great writer and his wife that they applied to their own situation. The couple with whom they sympathetically identified was Thomas Hardy and his first wife, Emma. Fowles had often written of his feeling that Hardy was like "a brother," that he understood at a profound visceral level Hardy's "transmutation of a personal myth."[71] After quarreling with Elizabeth, he was apt to make an agonized comparison with Hardy's marriage: "What can prevent us sinking into the kind of misery that affected Hardy and Emma Lavinia? . . . the rage I feel that she will not admit that I live, economically as emotionally, by my imagination, her rage that I cannot see that I have 'reduced' her to a kitchen drudge."[72]

Elizabeth savored biographies, especially those of writers' wives like Vivienne Eliot, Jane Carlyle, Frieda Lawrence, Nora Joyce, and Emma Hardy, "a silly woman, but kindly," whom Hardy had treated "so badly."[73]

Like Elizabeth Fowles, Emma Hardy had begun her marriage as the right hand and editorial support of her husband, then been cut out of his writing process. In her later years Emma spent isolated days in a tiny furnished attic garret while Hardy wrote in his downstairs study. In the way that the Fowleses could often apply humor to a tender subject, John and Elizabeth developed a bedtime running joke about how Elizabeth "should go up to the attic."[74]

Though scholars had disproved it, Fowles clung to the creaky legend of Hardy's incestuous affair with his cousin Tryphena Sparks and their love child as the secret, obsessive, shaping myth behind all of Hardy's fiction. When Fowles published his "Hardy and the Hag" essay in 1977, he had an exchange of letters with Hardy biographer Robert Gittings, in which Fowles "discussed the Tryphena in his life, compared with the Tryphena in T. Hardy." Elizabeth was provoked ("Hello, I thought"). She was "on the rampage" in the kitchen when Fowles entered. "The sooner you get your bloody Tryphena in here to do the cooking and washing up the better pleased I will be," she snapped, to his laughter. A moment later she asked him to fetch a particular herb from the garden to add to her veal stew. "J.F. in his usual mood of literary and culinary confusion thought I had asked him to go and get some Tryphena." "What herb is that?" he asked. "And we fall against the Aga in giggles."[75]

Less comically, Elizabeth thought it "extraordinary . . . that Hardy created women in his novels with such tenderness. He was unable to love women except on paper." She hastened to add in her letter to the Sharrockses that John was still her "*very* best friend" and she was "not making any serious comparison." She was, however, nonplussed by "the endless flow of letters that come into this house from women who have read JF." That day there had been adoring letters from a French housewife and mother, an English nurse, and "not to mention the mad American ladies, too numerous to mention." The letters poured in, filled with life histories, thanking Fowles for his insight into their lives and the joy his works had given them, suggesting meetings. They "totally identify with his female creations," wrote Elizabeth. "They write . . . even longer letters than I do . . . some of them so nauseatingly personal, as to be quite unbelievable such people exist . . . I can see what drove Emma into her attic!"[76]

On the basis of his own intimate understanding, Fowles took up the theme of Thomas Hardy's "marital guilt" when he was asked in 1975 by editor Lance St. John Butler to contribute to the volume *Thomas Hardy After Fifty Years*.[77] "Hardy and the Hag," completed by August 1976 and published in September 1977, allowed him to apply his own version of Gilbert Rose's theory of the psychology of novel writing to Hardy's *The Well-Beloved*. Fowles describes the infant psyche of the future (male) novelist as one that retains such an obsessive memory of "the early one-ness with the mother" (a time of profound pleasure in "the fluid, polymorphic nature of the sensuous impressions, visual, tactile, auditory and the rest, that he receives") that he is fated forever to repeatedly "tamper with reality" to try to recover that lost world shared with "the original woman," the mother.[78] This essay was Fowles's clearest, most decisive statement of his theory. It was also the only nonfiction in which he acknowledges the novelist's "betrayal" of the real-life wife as he pursues this "original woman." In analyzing the tensions between Hardy's novel writing and his relationship with Emma (including "the additional problem of a childless marriage"), Fowles barely disguises—with his phrases: "I have no doubt," "I am sure that," "I am convinced that"—his own sadness and guilt over the "many years of feeling herself shuffled off" that Elizabeth (like Emma) endured. He also testifies that he could not, or would not, live without the obsession for pursuing the "original other woman."[79]

Around the time that Fowles agreed to write the Hardy essay, he received a letter from a young antiquarian bookseller and admirer in the United States. W. Thomas Taylor ran his small, highly personal business from his home near the University of Texas at Austin. Recognizing Fowles's love for old books and fine printing through an article, "Of Memoirs and Magpies," that appeared earlier that year in the *Atlantic Monthly*, Tom Taylor asked if Fowles would like to select a forgotten text for publication in Taylor's planned "Little Known Library."[80]

By May 1976 Fowles's translation of *Ourika* was in Tom Taylor's hands, and arrangements were under way for its printing on handmade paper by Henry Morris of Philadelphia. Taylor and probably Fowles wanted a private edition of 350 copies. Although a novice to publishing, Taylor was the kind of sincere enthusiast whom Fowles actually enjoyed dealing with. Though they never met face-to-face, their correspondence is warm, kindly, and trusting. Together they resisted pressure from Fowles's American publisher, Little, Brown, for a trade edition. The slim, elegantly set *Ourika,* carrying Fowles's signature, was published in a limited edition in June 1977, around the same time as *The Magus: A Revised Version* and only months before *Daniel Martin* appeared. It was the sole publication of The Little Known Library.[81]

Coincidentally, Fowles in September 1975 had made a gift of the typescript of *The Collector* to Amnesty International, from which Tom Taylor purchased it the following March for £750. During the *Ourika* correspondence, Taylor volunteered to help Fowles sell other manuscripts. In March 1977, Fowles took up his offer, sending him the final, and only existing, typescript of *The French Lieutenant's Woman,* including Elizabeth Fowles's notes and corrections. In May 1977, Thomas F. Staley, noted James Joyce scholar and bibliophile, Provost and Vice President for Academic Affairs at the University of Tulsa, in Oklahoma, and McFarlin Professor of Modern Literature, was surprised by the unannounced arrival of Tom Taylor in his office. The manuscript of *The French Lieutenant's Woman* was in the backseat of Taylor's car, parked outside. Would Staley be interested?[82] A Fowles admirer, Staley immediately purchased the typescript for the University of Tulsa, a bargain sweetened by Taylor's donation of *The Collector* typescript. Taylor refused any commission, and Fowles donated the ten-thousand-dollar purchase price to the charitable organization War on Want.

Despite his reclusiveness John Fowles had reached a certain eminence in Britain. The couple dined at 10 Downing Street in June 1975 with the Belgian ambassador. They attended 1976 opening festivities of the new National Theatre, both the first week's performance in March and the official ceremonies opened by Queen Elizabeth II in November, along with "all fashionable London . . . grousing and stabbing in the back".[83]

Fowles was also "now considered respectable" by the Oxford literary set, as he learned when he and Elizabeth were asked by strangers living nearby in Dorset to come to lunch in August 1977 at the invitation of Iris Murdoch and John Bayley. John and Elizabeth were quite surprised, having not encountered either since the 1963 Cheltenham Literary Festival, at which time, as Elizabeth recalled, Iris "seemed slim and very sharp and brushed me aside as if I were some playful puppy dog." Reconciling that memory to the "comfortable fat and smiling old Irish biddy . . . warmly planting kisses on our cheeks as if we were long-lost relations" was unsettling.[84] The Bayleys monopolized the Fowleses, "fussed and chatted over us both." John Bayley was so attentive with food, wine, and cigarettes, said Fowles gleefully, he rushed about "like a demented butler on holiday." Iris Murdoch engaged Fowles with questions about writing and religion:

> I.M.   Are you religious?
> J.F.   Not at all.
> I.M.   Nor am I.
> J.F.   in the normal sense of the word.
> I.M.   Ah. (long Pinter-like silence, contemplation of lawn outside.) I expect you have a nice intellectual circle at Lyme Regis?
> J.F.   Are you mad?[85]

The famous pair were touchingly kind and sympathetic, but John and Elizabeth had been so long outside the literary pall that they could be only "puzzled" at the personal attention paid to them.[86]

Literary glitter, however, had become for Fowles an "outer world that seems barren and dull." He lived his most engaged and genuine life in an "inner world . . . so much more enjoyable than the outer one . . . so much richer and . . . fertile." His two most intense interior experiences, nature and writing, he had come to view in terms of time—or rather, timelessness. The "Zen approach to nature," which Fowles now held as he lost himself in the Belmont garden, was not about categories and labels, "name-and-knowledge," but about immediate apprehension, "instantaneity, timelessness, inconsequentiality—seeing-now and thing-only."[87] Likewise, writing, increasingly, was the experience of an intense "plunge into the process of seeing (or making)." It was not, for Fowles, about polishing and distributing the finished artifact that "Society" valued and contemplated. Ruminating on time, he refined his theories so that Gilbert Rose's psychological explanations of creativity embraced the artist's apprehension of time remembered. The Freudian Rose had suggested that a novelist's psyche was mainly formed by environmental experiences dating from infancy. By 1975 Fowles had come to believe that "joy in fluid identity" sprang from "an innate special quirk in the key talent for perceiving time" and that "cultural triggering is a secondary matter." Always the biological naturalist, Fowles believed that what made the future novelist (or artist of any medium) was "a genetic or physiological 'golden flaw' in brain-structure," a "benign inability to see" spatial, visual, aural, tactile, and personal physical boundaries "in their temporal aspects." For the infant novelist, born biologically different, "in terms both of grammatical tense and space, his or her phenomena are all more *present* than the next child's."[88]

Fowles's beliefs about the nature of memory and the human apprehension of time shaped the structure of *Daniel Martin*. The chapters of the novel have names, not sequential numbers, and the hero's experiences move back and forth through Dan's present and his recalled past, arranged not by chronology but by Fowles's "view of the nature of memory—that it should properly be categorized by degree of emotion, personal significance, etc." Each chapter was a "discrete . . . fragment" in a design of "stained glass," as an overall order was seen "gradually forming out of chaos." In effect, this view of the past was "fluid . . . malleable," and the chapters could (at least theoretically) be rearranged. He endeavored to "synchronize varied pasts," making them "emotionally equipresent, structurally equipoised."[89] Like islands viewed equidistantly on a horizon of personal memory, the chapters floated independently in the sea of story.[90]

Fowles revised *Daniel Martin* through early 1976, until the working typescript became "a formidable pile . . . six inches or more high."[91] In November 1976, at Elizabeth's insistence, he hired a secretary to type up the final version. Mary Scriven, age thirty-two and newly married, had moved to Lyme that year. Ann Jellicoe, meeting Mary casually on the beach, had arranged an interview with Fowles. After a week of swollen wrists from trying to type the massive *Daniel Martin* on Fowles's portable manual typewriter, Scriven told Fowles (to his surprise at her temerity) that she would stay if he would rent her an electric typewriter. This reconditioned machine received such a workout on the 297,000-word text that it "blew up." Impressed, Fowles opted to buy her a new model, on which Mary Scriven completed the 1,108 typescript pages that Fowles delivered to his London agent on January 17, 1977.[92] Mary Scriven became so highly valued that she stayed with Fowles for ten years.

Fowles had safely inhabited *Daniel Martin* since 1972, and its shelter had granted him great emotional security to deal with the vagaries of his life and his career. His writing output had been prodigious, his outside interests focused and energetic, his private life reasonably balanced and good-humored. On the day the typescript left his hands, he became vulnerable and exposed. He once more had bouts of "growing depression;

emptiness, staleness, boredom." He felt it was like "a seven-year voyage ended . . . the sudden lack of onward motion is very like what a sailor feels when he is on land again; the voyage becomes a dream."[93] The financial trophies of his success once more felt undeserved and crushing. In February 1977 the publisher's advances for *Daniel Martin* and film options for *The French Lieutenant's Woman* totaled nearly "half a million dollars in one week." Painfully, Fowles wrote, "The gathering snowball . . . all I feel is that I am under it, and it begins an avalanche. Money is ice-cold to my touch; stifling in its descent."[94] The novel was selected as the October main choice for the Book-of-the-Month Club. A heated competition was waged for Canadian rights. The bid for American paperback rights was half a million dollars. Fowles could only gasp, "I feel like Midas; more exactly than most people could ever realize."[95] He was still paid a limited salary by "the company" and sometimes had to carry an overdraft at his bank.

Fowles escaped by going "junk shopping" with Elizabeth. Early in 1977 she had agreed to join her old friend Charlie Greenberg to create the Branscombe Gallery, an antiques shop in an old wheelwright's he had bought and renovated. Elizabeth had visions of selling antiques but also of devoting part of the shop to modern crafts—namely, Nick Homoky's pots and Anna Homoky's patchwork creations. She and Anna painted and designed the layout. She scoured the countryside for pewter mugs, Staffordshire pot dogs, tiles, old carpenters tools, and antique cooking utensils. It was great fun to buy from the dealers and bid at auctions, and Fowles joked that "even my suppers come with little price-stickers now."[96] Good-humored, he found accompanying Elizabeth a relief as the deals and money offers rolled in and the newspapers rang for interviews. While his agents enthused over international rights and options worth tens of thousands of pounds, Fowles gratefully sorted through bins and junk tables in secondhand shops throughout Dorset and Devon, Bristol and Somerset, making "doubly sure I can't be got at."[97] Elizabeth was thrilled and busy with preparations for the gallery, until it opened in April 1977. Then she rapidly found it "tedious."[98] Those who stopped in were tourists on holiday, usually asking for directions and ice lollies, not fine antiques. In early 1978 she bowed out.

In the summer of 1977 *The Magus: A Revised Version* was a best-seller, while the hype for *Daniel Martin* was building. Fowles thought the interviews for both British and American publications "something of a farce and imposture." No questioner understood "the unconscious element in writing; and that 'explaining it' is a very secondary aftermath." He felt compelled to give the "arranged answers of a performance; not the conflicting, blurred haphazard of the truth."[99] Elizabeth too felt like an impostor when Melvyn Bragg filmed an hourlong BBC program devoted to John Fowles. For a week in August an eight-man crew moved in with lights and equipment to follow John, and sometimes Elizabeth, through interviews, days of crab fishing with Quicky, exploring the landslip at Charmouth, "doing the JFowles botany bit, fossil-finding, etc.," even shopping in the Axminster market. Immediately afterward, the *Sunday Times* photographer and columnist Hunter Davies arrived for an interview. "I feel I have been posturing, playing a role, dressing up. . . . I lost my sense of humour," Elizabeth said, dismayed. "I felt I was taking part in a myth."[100]

This sense of disproportion continued for Elizabeth as they toured New York, Chicago, and Boston to promote *Daniel Martin* during September 1977. They were well received everywhere. The American reviews of *Daniel Martin* were largely generous and enthusiastic. John Gardner's now-famous review in the *Saturday Review* hailed Fowles as "the only novelist now writing in English whose works are likely to stand as literary classics—the only writer in English who has the power, range, knowledge, and wisdom of a Tolstoi or James."[101] Even Christopher Lehmann-Haupt of the *New York Times,* who thought parts of the book tedious, ended with a positive endorsement.[102]

But the autobiographical element of *Daniel Martin* put Elizabeth in the spotlight, and she found it difficult. "If you can't ask the writer what is biographical—you ask the wife!" she exclaimed. "Can you imagine the questions I am asked. . . . Who was the actress he had an affair with? Was I at Oxford. (a good question) . . . Women cluster around me and say, 'How interesting to meet the woman HE *is* ACTUALLY married to.'" The "whole ridiculous inflation of publicity in the USA" was aimed at "myth-making."[103]

Reassurance came from an unexpected source. The Maschlers gave them a welcome home dinner party on their October return to London, with guests who included "a very distinguished literary old lady from Chatto and Windus [and] Martin Amis and girl friend with uncovered bosoms." "Still in a state of rapport with the Yanks," Elizabeth was pleased to be seated beside the American novelist Philip Roth. Roth and

Elizabeth launched into a comic Cockney routine of how they would set up in the same bookshop on the day of Fowles's next book signing. "'I am not offering 50 p off, nor even 75 p off, But', he says, and slaps his watch on the table, 'a quid off plus this gold watch!' He and I think this a hell of a good joke." Their performance silenced the others: "Amis started on his Grass smoking. J.F. had got bored with the tits lady, and the others had long used up polite conversation . . . there was a hush . . . which we ignored." But under the giggles and stand-up routine, Philip Roth extended to Elizabeth the sympathy of having experienced what she was struggling with. As he recounted his own feelings reading reviews of *Portnoy's Complaint* and his life in the literary limelight, Elizabeth felt understood for the first time. "He was so nice," she wrote, "and had three wives and wondered why I had stuck it out with J.F." Roth cut the whole business of mythmaking "down to size," said Elizabeth. "It made being married to a writer—seem rather a lark." She called it "one of the best moments of my life. . . . For recently I have begun to feel I wish I was ordinary."[104]

CHAPTER EIGHTEEN

The Consolations of the Past

Lyme Regis: 1977–1981

*Time, properly understood, is not an irritatingly elusive enigma
of theoretical physics, is not a sadistic condition imposed on us
by some divinity hiding behind an equation, or a purposeless obstacle to some truth we should all be the happier for knowing;
but a greater potential consolation than all our gods, all our
philosophies and religions, all our arts and sciences.*

*That this necessity of death and its instrument, time, is be-
yond our personal comprehension seems to me a profound wisdom in things . . .*

—JOHN FOWLES, TO INTERNATIONAL SOCIETY FOR THE STUDY
OF TIME CONFERENCE ORGANIZERS, SEPTEMBER 1981

John Fowles's alter ego Daniel Martin finished his fictional journey
recommitted to writing fiction, to exploring the past, and to marrying
Jane Mallory, the great love of his youth. But the 1977 publication and reception of *Daniel Martin,* the novel, estranged its author from embracing
his own life as a novelist for the ensuing five years. He chose instead, like
Dan, to explore the historical past. The choice of this new direction,
however, further distanced him from the love of his youth, his wife Elizabeth.

The earliest British reviews of *Daniel Martin* crushed both Fowles
and his wife when they returned after the American tour. In The
Guardian Robert Nye wrote a snide, yawning analysis criticizing the
rhetorical style of the novel as "a little vulgar, a little tasteless, tactless"
and the ideas behind it as clichéd, "what gives this book its long lack of

depth."¹ Charles Nicholl in the *Daily Telegraph* was more perceptive but lukewarm, opining that the book delivered "not the instant masterpiece" it promised but a "*tour de force* of stamina and subtlety."² In the *Sunday Telegraph* Thomas Hinde took sideswipes at Fowles's earlier books of ideas, *The Collector, The Aristos,* and *The French Lieutenant's Woman,* while criticizing the inclusion of Fowles's philosophical message in a novel he characterized as "inflated" and "much, much too long."³ All seemed puzzled by the movements through memory that form the novel's structure. All of them were "a mealy mouther lot," Elizabeth howled angrily to Monica and Denys. "They have really been MEAN over J's book. It is the mean minded British one cannot help comparing with the serious and generous attitude the Yanks have towards a writer."⁴ Only Jacky Gillot in the *Times* praised *Daniel Martin* as "a work of imaginative energy and passionate honesty whose occasional flaws are immeasurably more fascinating than the small perfections of many another writer."⁵ It was more than a week before Christopher Booker's penetrating and enthusiastic psychological review appeared in the *Spectator*.⁶ The book's reception, Fowles wrote bitterly to Denys Sharrocks, was "one of the most spectacular English critical gang bangs in recent years." Part of the reaction, he guessed, was against "the generally very kind American reception and success . . . but I suspect not a very big part. I have somehow contrived to get across every[thing] dear to contemporary British fiction this time, at least in weekly reviewing terms."⁷

Elizabeth was prepared to defend both John and *Daniel Martin* against all comers. Passionately loyal about John and his books, she shared her private reservations about the novel only with the Sharrockses. She had found the book "a struggle to be perfectly frank." She had not been asked to edit it, "and if I had, it would have a lot cut." She thought the "switching from 1st to 3rd person . . . very literary . . . clever technique . . . a nice bit for the student studies . . . but hard going for the average reader." While the female characters were "OK to a large extent," she hated "those bloody cockney twins" and was "not terribly wild about the middleaged Jane with her varicose veins," since she herself had undergone surgery for that condition a few years earlier. Yet Elizabeth knew her husband was trying to do something completely new, and to achieve that, he was "being very self-indulgent in this opus. And he knows it."⁸

Something changed for John Fowles from the moment he reentered

England in October 1977 and the British reviewers battered *Daniel Martin*. The most startling indicator of this change is an unprecedented three-year silence in his diary. To be sure, this was an extraordinarily busy period. Yet Fowles had kept an astonishingly full schedule at other times over the previous thirty years and never sacrificed the inward examination and onward chronicle of his personal journal for longer than two months. Furthermore, when he resumed the diary on September 24, 1980, it had changed. It is less purposeful, full of gaps and catch-up entries. It is often sloppy in a chronological sense, as Fowles casually inserted things out of order. He continued to "jot down things to record" for the diary as he had always done, then found "no time, no inclination; no ego really . . . I have no will for this."[9]

Fowles was also greatly affected when, in spring 1979, his American editor, Ned Bradford, died. Professionally, Fowles was soon in good hands, as in late 1980 Little, Brown assigned as his editor Ray A. Roberts, a knowledgeable Fowles reader and collector and ardent admirer. Until Roberts's appointment, however, Fowles was in editorial limbo. Moreover, Bradford's death remained, for John and Elizabeth, an abiding personal sorrow.

In this vulnerable period, Fowles resolved not to publish fiction again. By October 1980 he could write of having "killed" the need to publish in himself. "What little of a 'literary person' I ever was, I have stopped being now," he wrote. "When I answer literary letters, or do interviews, it seems like someone else . . . another fiction." He had, however, "occasional accesses of fiction-writing," enjoyed "at least partly because I do not attach it to the notion of publishing."[10] In 1979 these accesses included the writing of *Mantissa* and the beginning of *A Maggot*.

For publication, Fowles wrote nonfiction. For instance, he agreed to review novels in the press for the first time, though not English novels, becoming the monthly reviewer for the *Irish Times* for 1978. In the early 1980s he reviewed history or nature books for the *Guardian*.[11] In his more personal nonfiction, however, there is a new elegiac note. In January 1978 he wrote the essay *Islands* to accompany Fay Godwin's stark and louring photographic studies of the Scilly Islands. It was published in December 1978 in Britain and appeared in the United States in June 1979. Writing of Shakespeare's *The Tempest,* he focused on Prospero, the exiled magician, who is, for Fowles, clearly the writer. He sees "a wise sadness seeping into the ritual happy ending . . . *Cui bono*, to what purpose? What will it change?" From his own experience, Fowles believes, the reader and audience gain little. "The truth is that the person who always benefits and learns most . . . is the inventor . . . that is, the artist-artificer himself."[12] John Fowles, who had begun writing in the conviction that his symbolic philosophical stories and essays could change his society, now believed that no one understood. No reader was changed. Writing was an inward voyage, a hermetic experience benefiting only the maker himself.

The following year Fowles journeyed further inward in his most autobiographical essay, *The Tree* (1979). While many of the themes were first explored in the suppressed, angry essays of the early 1970s (*America, I Weep for Thee,* "Sensibility," "The New Self"), spleen and indignation are radically transformed into quiet lyricism in this new piece. Long arguments are concentrated into distilled wisdom. Fowles's voice is calm, personal, and sincere.

Fowles had been inspired by photographer Frank Horvat's ravishing color studies of trees in France in 1978. They reflected his own growing recognition that his Belmont garden was "a part of me now, or a mirror, to a degree I conceal from everyone." Through his relationship with it, his sense of sanctuary within it, he had learned, nine years after the old man's death, to understand his father. "Getting in" his own abundant apples in the fall had become "a great pleasure" for John Fowles, one that even stimulated his writing. "The trees," he wrote, "are closer to me than most human beings. I understand at last what drove my father, with his."[13] In a spirit of reconciliation, Fowles wrote in *The Tree,* "As I grow older I see that the outwardly profound difference in our attitudes to nature—especially in the form of the tree—had a strange identity of purpose, a kind of joint root-system, an interlacing, a paradoxical pattern." In another partial reconciliation he asked Elizabeth to be the first reader.

Fowles wrote in *The Tree* how the condition of artistic creation was like a "green chaos," "a wood," where the walk is unplanned, haphazard, and immediate. Within the shifting green sunlight and gnarled branches of this unworldly woodland, he experiences and struggles to express "the namelessness, the green phosphorus of the tree," a silence that connects us to all nature.[14] His deep enchantment with the historical past was akin to this near-mystical experience of nature and the otherworldly reality he entered during the fiction-making process. He wrote of all three (writing, contact with nature, and working as a local historian) as offering him "the experience of timelessness; of all my present consciousness being in other time-scales (those of whatever world I am trying to recreate)." All three experiences had moments "in marked parenthesis from linear time." They were of a different reality from the mundane and linear.[15] Seeking this timelessness and the refuge of his other world, Fowles became immersed in the study of the historical past. Increasingly, this permeated his writing and influenced his professional choices.

In January 1978 Fowles was asked to become the co-curator of the Philpot Museum in Lyme Regis. Given to the borough in 1920 by Caroline Philpot, niece of its amateur paleontological founder, the museum was a dilapidated brick building on the seafront of Lyme Regis, housing a rich but ill-assorted, poorly labeled collection of fossils, civic artifacts, weapons, fishing and farm implements, and old photographs. Its permanent membership stood at thirty-four. Fowles had been involved with Lyme's local history almost from his arrival in Dorset in 1966, a fascination reflected in *The French Lieutenant's Woman*. He greatly admired the museum's collection of ichthyosaur fossils and was already involved in researching parish registers and tape recording oral histories of some of Lyme's oldest residents.

In 1977 the voluntary co-curators were the Maynes, photographer Roger Mayne and his wife, playwright Ann Jellicoe. Jellicoe and Fowles had worked on museum projects together, although she sometimes thought when speaking with him "that another, entirely different, conversation was going on in his head."[16] When Mayne was unable to continue in 1978, Jellicoe asked Fowles to join her. Within a month of his acceptance, she was pleading with Elizabeth Fowles to take over her role as co-curator. ("I refused point blank," said Liz emphatically.[17]) By the end of the year Jellicoe had resigned to focus all her energy on directing, playwriting, and managing the fast-growing community play movement she had launched: "one of the most amazing periods of my life," she wrote, "and certainly the most demanding and exhausting."[18] Mary Scriven agreed to continue as Fowles's secretary ("I'll do it, if you'll do it," he said).[19] He paid her salary out of pocket, and her efficient clerical skills supported his impressive gains of the next few years.

The museum in 1978 seemed a failing enterprise. The three-story building was handsome enough, a turn-of-the-twentieth-century pastiche of seventeenth-century Dutch architecture that complemented the adjoining Guildhall. Its condition, however, was extremely alarming. Permanent damp in the cellar had become standing water. Dry rot infested the cellar and ground floor. The iron girders supporting the ground floor were in danger of collapse. Stress cracks had appeared in the third-floor balcony that supported a historic iron bell. Part of a ceiling had fallen. Plaster and stonework were crumbling everywhere. The building was inadequately heated, and its proximity to the Gun Cliff meant it was shaken by heavy seas. Display cases were rife with fungus. Labeling was poor, and presentation unimaginative and without appeal to children. The history of Lyme was "not coherently shown at all." There was virtually no support from the town of Lyme Regis, either in money or volunteers, while the museum board had poor relations with the West Dorset District Council, which was, by the 1927 Foundation Agreement, technically responsible for the structural upkeep of the building but ignored it.[20]

Just as he had fallen for his "derelict farm" at Underhill, had loved on sight the chaotic, abandoned, and overgrown garden of Belmont, and had pursued the chance to preserve and nurture the deserted island of Steep Holm, Fowles went wading (sometimes literally) into the neglected, mismanaged mess that was the Philpot Museum. It became his special care, eclipsing any lingering sense of his identity as a literary figure. "I feel I am living with a working class chap now," laughed Elizabeth in March 1978; "he gets out of the house . . . just after breakfast . . . and up from under my feet." He kept reappearing, however, with "stuff" he found stashed in the museum's cupboards or languishing in the damp basement. He rescued photographs and jumbled manuscripts to bring home to his study. He dragged antique swords back to Belmont to strip off paint, left filthy old thatching tools in Elizabeth's kitchen to be cleaned. She found herself laundering fragile doll's clothes and polishing the brass helmets of long-dead firemen.[21]

As the "Honorary Curator" Fowles was not paid any fee or salary for what turned out to be ten years of extremely hard work. He never accepted the three-hundred-pound annual honorarium. In every other sense, Fowles was a hands-on curator trying to rescue and run the institution. He was involved in every aspect of the museum, either alone or supported by a small volunteer band of fellow history enthusiasts. He led the delegation to the West Dorset District Council in January 1979 that healed the administrative breach and began repairs to the building. He swept out floodwaters after storms, arranged display cases, and handwrote labels. He begged for acquisitions and sometimes purchased them for the museum with his own money. He established ties with other area museums and with fossil hunters and dealers. He worried about publicity, and he managed signage in the town. He located Lyme resources in other collections and visited other museums to learn about "display, labelling, finances."[22] He spoke at conferences. He hauled artifacts up the hill to Belmont and prepared them in his own kitchen. He handled all genealogical and family history inquiries personally and all correspondence with Mary Scriven. Mary, who lived directly opposite the museum, would often carry a cup of coffee across Bridge Street to find Fowles, standing on his feet for hours in his cramped office, working at the files. The curator who followed him remarked that Fowles had worked in "the tradition of the great 19th century learned societies." Administrative paperwork repelled him, but his great gift, "beyond rubies!," was his "intellectual standards. He put the museum back on its original path of scholarly inquiry which it had sadly drifted from."[23]

An early consulting expert was Jo Draper Chaplin, a historian and a ceramics specialist who worked on archaeological sites around Dorset. Draper began to refer to "the John Fowles factor" as little by little the Philpot Museum began to thrive. She meant more than the obvious fact that John Fowles's presence raised the museum's visibility. For Draper, "the John Fowles factor" referred to Fowles's ferocious and uncompromising standards in every matter having to do with Lyme Regis's history and the museum.[24] Just as he turned over every rock on his walks and scrutinized the smallest grubs and insects for the information he sought on natural history, so he left no historical stone unturned. Because Fowles really knew the history of Lyme Regis, as he knew the narrative of a subtly rich and complicated story, he understood what research needed to be done. Details, facts, objects that seemed to others—and particularly Elizabeth—insignificant and time-wasting fitted into the historical pattern of the story he carried in his head. He could envision and set project goals for himself and others in local historical research. He liked that it was all a jumble when he took it on. It made the enterprise seem a challenging puzzle, and Fowles was addicted to puzzles. He refused to accept the institution as forever condemned to a third-class existence. Always a tenacious man, in historical research he became absolutely dogged. Nothing was too small or too insignificant to escape his scrutiny. Draper reckoned he was in personal correspondence with more than forty Lyme families simultaneously. Museum members with genuine interest were glad to follow his lead. As his friend Muriel Arber wrote him in 1979, the museum's "luck" in getting John Fowles was "unbelievable."[25]

Fowles had always disdained the commercial world, but he plunged in, worrying about gate numbers, entry fees, and memberships. During his curatorship a museum gift shop was established. Walking tours of historic Lyme Regis were organized. While not an aggressive fund-raiser, Fowles was quick to express sincere gratitude for gifts from others. He was financially generous himself, but one of his greatest gifts was the contribution of his writing.

Once he became Honorary Curator, Fowles wrote local history pamphlets and assigned the copyrights to the Philpot Museum and, after 1981, to the Friends of the Lyme Regis Museum. By 1979 he had begun the published series of annual *Curator's Report by John Fowles, with Notes on Recent Discoveries, Research and New Acquisitions.* These booklets rapidly became collector's items.[26] After a 1979 pamphlet on Lyme's history, by 1981 he had filled the need for an overview of Lyme's history for the casual visitor with *A Brief History of Lyme.*[27] By 1982 these terse pages were augmented by the more interpreted and illustrated *A Short History of Lyme.*[28] In 1983 the Friends published *Lyme Regis: Three Town Walks,* which Fowles had written and developed with the help of his friends the Chaplins, Jo Draper creating the design and Christopher Chaplin, her husband, the maps. This was "packaged" with Fowles's very short *Thumbnail History of Lyme Regis.*[29, 30] His *Medieval Lyme Regis* was published in 1984.[31] When satisfied by accuracy, he encouraged the sales of works written by others by writing introductions, as he did for Geoffrey Chapman's and David West's *The Siege of Lyme Regis* in 1982.[32] Fowles's name sold all these works beyond expectations. More lucratively, in 1980 he assigned the copyright of the text of *The Enigma of Stonehenge* to the Philpot Museum.

The Stonehenge book was offered to Fowles in 1978 as the straightforward task of writing a companion essay to a series of evocative photographs of the ancient, mysterious monument by American photographer Barry Brukoff. Fowles's interest in this new format had first been awakened by *Shipwreck* and then sharpened by *Islands.* The essay with images hybrid allowed two creative artists, a photographer and a writer, to approach the same symbolic landscape intimately and independently yet to converge. Fowles took as his subject not only what scholars thought of the origins and purposes of Stonehenge but also, more important to him, the symbolic resonance of the monument through the centuries. How had Stonehenge been imagined? How did those who saw it use their vision of the past? He called these acts of imagination "the other Stonehenge, the dream-temple and polyvalent symbol of the scholars, poets, and artists."[33] He began *The Enigma of Stonehenge* in May 1979, right after *The Tree,* and finished it by mid-June.

Stonehenge research led Fowles to the antiquarian John Aubrey, the seventeenth-century chronicler of biography, court tattle, superstition, and science. In the matter of Stonehenge and the other nearby circle of stones, Avebury, Aubrey was, said Fowles, the most "important early investigator and first true archaeologist."[34] All of Aubrey's observations, measurements, research, and speculation on the antique monuments of Britain were amassed into his *Monumenta Britannica,* begun in 1654 and worked on until Aubrey's death in 1697. For more than three hundred years, the *Monumenta Britannica* had languished in the Bodleian Library at Oxford University as a chaotic, thousand-page manuscript jumble of Aubrey's notes. (Fowles called it, revealingly, a "wild undergrowth.") By coincidence, as Fowles researched Stonehenge, his fellow naturalist and amateur historian Rodney Legg was working to put into print a facsimile of this manuscript, which had defeated so many earlier scholars.

The most daunting aspect of the *Monumenta Britannica* manuscript for Legg was incorporating into the text Aubrey's sketchy working notes, three decades', Fowles said, "worth of notes, erasures, incomprehensible cross references, repetitions, classical quotations, insertions in other hands, blanks where Aubrey's memory failed him, illegible additions, and all the rest of it." Fascinated by the complicated editorial problem solving, Fowles asked Legg if he could crack the most complex examples from the *Monumenta.* Throughout 1979 and into 1980 Legg sent Fowles his daily transcripts of Aubrey's difficult handwriting. A selection could include "almost modernisms" for the seventeenth century "mixed with bits of Latin and medieval French and just about all of them abbreviated."[35]

Fowles found the task of teasing and deciphering this "incredible word cocktail" absolutely compelling. He made Aubrey's intriguing word puzzles his first duty each morning, his alternative to the *Guardian* crossword puzzles that had always started his day. He adored Aubrey's inventive language, his combination of the classical and the coffeehouse into some kind of lively seventeenth-century "pop-speak." Sometimes Fowles toyed over expressions for the rest of the day, even an entire week, but "invariably, he did crack them." The "puzzle aspect" was the stimulant. To anyone else, said Legg, this would have been "incredibly frustrating," but he ascribed Fowles's interest to "WORDS. His passion for words . . . doing a sort of spider and snail job with them . . . collecting these words." Fowles scrawled his answers on "any little recycled bit of paper that happened to be in front of him," including cigarette packets, sometimes folding a dead spider or snail into the scrap. Legg preserved several well-stuffed boxes of these quirky notes.[36]

Recognizing a kindred spirit across the centuries, Fowles came to "like Aubrey himself very much." He relished being inside "his chaotic mind," discovering "from the inside" what it was like "to be finding one's way, though often enough down cul-de-sacs and wrong turnings, towards a new vision of the past and a new scientific vision of the future."[37] One of the words a rival had scornfully used to describe him stuck with Fowles. Anthony Wood had written: "He was a shiftless person, roving and maggotie-headed, and sometimes a little better than crazed." In the seventeenth century, Fowles glossed, "a maggot was a whim, a crochet."[38] In February 1979 he contacted a musicologist to inquire about "musical Maggots," a seventeenth-century improvisational dance tune form.[39] *Maggot.* The word stayed in his repertoire and was added to the long lists of seventeenth-century phrases and words he was keeping. Off and on, Fowles was tinkering with a new novel.

Fowles liked the side of Rodney Legg "that has cocked a thumb and at least got the thing into print" but acknowledged the *Monumenta* enterprise was "absurd." They had "no right pretending to be authorities; only a team of qualified scholars could have done the thing properly." One major Aubrey scholar in fact had been turned away by Legg.[40] So Fowles, who thought he had only corrected "some of his countless reading errors," was surprised and dismayed when the first volume of *Monumenta Britannica* appeared from Legg's own Dorset Publishing Company in midsummer 1980 and he, John Fowles, was named on the cover as editor. "Rodney cheated in his usual fashion," he wrote in his diary; "there were many other things I would not have allowed, had I really been editor."[41] With his name at stake, Fowles was much more involved editorially when the time came to produce the second volume, which was published in

1981. His copyright for the 1982 one-volume American edition was as-signed to the Kenneth Allsop Memorial Trust to benefit Steep Holm.[42]

Elizabeth had no place in John Fowles's curatorial or historical work. When he first accepted the appointment to the museum, she felt proud of him, taking an interest in taped interviews of elderly Lyme residents and, with Anna, suggesting ways to make the displays appeal to children. But Fowles's enthusiasm for historical minutiae (the distinguishing char-acteristic of his research) completely eluded her. "Why does it matter who married who and where they were buried, and what property they owned, or lived in?" To Elizabeth it was "a naming of parts" lacking emo-tion, and "God knows it adds nothing to any feeling or sense."[43] Her daft sense of humor helped her cope for a while. In 1978, for instance, she followed Fowles as he slogged through "miserable church yards . . . on the most bleak muddy godawful wet days in villages of total dreary as-pect," tracking down his buried Cornish ancestors ("as if they were a sort of Cornish pest"). Elizabeth kept up a comic prattle, wittily observing the clerics of the churches, the other visitors, and mostly John himself.[44] Yet as Fowles grew more "deadly serious . . . quasi-academic" with the years, Elizabeth was closed out of a pursuit in which she had no interest.[45] Mu-seum people arrived unannounced at the house and took up Fowles's time with what she regarded as trivial matters. "The 'family history' brigade" that gathered around him was "totally and absolutely charm-less."[46] Leo Smith remembered that Elizabeth was criticized for not at-tending museum functions with her husband.[47]

Besides his worldwide readership, Fowles's published work was now attracting numerous scholars and academics who wrote to him or visited Belmont. Elizabeth took to some, welcoming their visits and even writing to them. American novelist Joyce Carol Oates, for example, won Eliza-beth's heart with her anxiety not to impose. Charlotte Rhodes, a literary trustee of the Ransom Center at the University of Texas, received chatty, sympathetic letters from Elizabeth when she was hospitalized.[48] Eliza-beth enjoyed meeting students and readers when Fowles lectured on tour. She liked defusing their "awe of us," reassuring them "that we are quite normal and simply quite vulnerable humans after all."[49] She was, of the two, the one happiest to sit at student dinners afterward and listen to "the problems of their lives. Literature . . . thrown to the wind."[50] But other visitors and critics felt to Elizabeth like invaders of her home and privacy. The daily post alone could take hours to open, and after *Daniel Martin*, Elizabeth noted, there was "a most extraordinary flow . . . from USA and England and Canada. The number of people who threaten to call is alarming." One man, to her complete disgust, wanted "to meet the 'Jane' in JF's life." When refused, he visited Lyme and "stood and gazed at her/our house. . . . What cheek!"[51] After the release of *The French Lieutenant's Woman* film, the invasion grew worse. People "simply arrive and knock the door," she said.[52] Mary Scriven remembered "a gaggle of people" gathering at the front gate and Fowles being "accosted in the garden while working."[53]

Elizabeth often wrote of "John's foolish USA female admirers" and resented his warmly attentive manner with some of the academic women who called. "Upstairs in JF's room there is the sound of hearty laughter," she wrote. "A lady visiting from some university." Elizabeth brought in tea and then was dismissed.[54] "The last one came from Singapore," she wrote another time. "A most beautiful creature with her tape machine sat curled up on my couch, sat there talking as I came in all hot (the middle of the summer it was) with a load of shopping. JF mesmerised with her deep questionings on the meanings of his books. I was given a compulsory wave and introduction and asked to make tea. I plonked down the shopping in the kitchen and banged on the kettle."[55] In interviews, Fowles often spoke of women as warmer, more liberal, tolerant, and intuitive than men, the harbingers of freedom in a society. "I can hardly believe my luck," wrote Elizabeth sarcastically, "in living with such a paragon of female sensitivities."[56] At one of Fowles's lectures, Elizabeth wrote Monica, "a student asked if he didn't have a Sexist notion of women. JF demanded a definition of 'Sexist.' When given it—he agreed. I was glad someone had asked the question."[57]

Elizabeth read a tremendous amount and was, even Fowles admitted, a severe critic. She had few friends nearby to share her love of books, but her written remarks are invariably perceptive. Yet Fowles was, said Tom Maschler, "extremely dismissive" of that part of her.[58] Monica Sharrocks, sleeping in the Fowleses' London flat on one occasion, was awakened by Elizabeth weeping after an argument when John had stormed out. Distraught, Liz sobbed that her husband had told everyone at the Wisemans' dinner party that *she* ("He called me 'she' as though I was the cat!") "never read anything."[59] She was touched and proud when Tom Maschler began bringing her manuscripts to read for him again or books he had bought in the United States and intended to publish. While Fowles remained isolated in his workroom, Maschler urged her to think of taking up more formal work for Cape. Elizabeth gratefully recalled his saying, "You ought to think about it, Liz, you are bloody good."[60] Similarly, when an article appeared in 1980 on her editing of *The French Lieutenant's Woman* and "my very words are quoted in full," she was staggered. "What a very lively and literary lady this Elizabeth Fowles," she wrote, amazed, "yet apart from the summers spent at Underhill, I remember the two winters spent in deep depression . . . so isolated and alienated from life." Bemusedly she called those days writing in the kitchen at Underhill Farm "probably my best creative period in the end. I doubt if much else of mine will be published."[61]

The widening distance between Fowles's interior creative life and his domestic reality with his wife is clearly represented in the one fiction he completed in 1979, *Mantissa*.[62] In this riff on a novel, an amnesiac writer, Miles Green, wakes in a gray padded, suspiciously brainlike hospital room (The Central), where two wise and seductive women, Dr. A. Delfi and Nurse Corey, use extraordinary erotic methods to help him recover his memory. Both are versions of the muse Erato, Green's companion in storytelling from his adolescence. What they help Miles recover are his interior memories of story variations with Erato, not his exterior life with his forgotten wife and children. Indeed, the anxious wife is brushed away and vanishes from the story.

In its nonmathematical sense, a mantissa, according to the dictionary, is "an addition of trivial importance, especially to a discourse." Fowles always represented *Mantissa* as a "minor work," although it was for him his clearest symbolic expression of what could go on in the brain of a writer possessed by the muse.[63] Probably derived from his long erotic poem of 1972, *Mantissa* was also inspired by Flann O'Brien's riotous comic novel *At Swim-Two-Birds* (1939), a favorite of Fowles's late friend Eileen Porter.[64] Reading in that book how the normal daily life of a struggling Irish writer is invaded and beset by his own willful characters, Fowles could always hear Eileen's droll delivery in his ear. Adopting this jokelike form allowed Fowles to eruditely send up everything, from his own notoriously fallible memory to fashionable literary theories like deconstruction.

Miles Green's muse is eternally his one most desirable woman and eternally in frustrating metamorphosis. It is likely that this erotic muse of Fowles's imagination required a real-life counterpart, a seductive woman who appealed to him, a flesh-and-blood temptress who stimulated romantic art rather than sexual relationship. Fowles's "Conditional," a 1978 poem written at the time of *Mantissa*, clearly reveals this "transmutation" of a flirty sexual attraction into the romantic beloved of Fowles's art, a muse held fast in "the net of words." A woman, "careless, open, young," arouses the poet, "old, reputed, closed." Beneath her "false culture" and "liberated sex," she has an "oddly gravid charm . . . both lithe and poised," and she is aware that she entices him ("you know you call"). With eyes that search his eyes, with "a hand, a hint, you would have stayed," with "wry, indifferent airs," the unnamed woman can "summon myths" of a weeping "succoured princess" and a "knight . . . drenched in dragon's blood." Silently she offers an affair. The poet, however, knows that "having kills." He wants no genuine sexual affair, but poetic inspiration. His poem is concerned with the "conditional," with possibilities dreamed about this young woman, with a relationship turned into literature, "imagined out; its pleasures printed . . . read long before you turned." While she dismisses his "cowardice" as "life aborted into verse," the poet knows that by his refraining from an affair in ordinary life, the desire stays alive in his art: "Once done is sere, undone stays green." There is no recorded trace of who inspired this poem, but Fowles valued it highly enough to have had it privately printed the following year in fine calligraphy in an exquisite broadside limited to 150 signed copies. [65] Elizabeth Fowles was well aware of this imaginative process in her husband. In the autumn of 1979, when "Conditional" was being so lovingly printed, she sat with Tom Maschler in the garden while Fowles remained "in his room on his own," and noted wryly, "He has his affairs up there."[66]

As he had done with "Conditional," Fowles thought to publish *Mantissa*, if at all, as a limited edition printed by "a very nice California small press."[67] But in March 1980 he was begged by editor Daniel Halpern for a piece of fiction from "the father of Daniel Martin" for the tenth anniversary of *Antaeus*.[68] Fowles complied with the opening chapter of *Mantissa*. After this appearance, an unheralded private printing was impossible, and both Jonathan Cape and Little, Brown insisted on treating the book as a major fiction event when it was published in 1982.

Although Elizabeth complained that as "the author's wife" she was "provider-comforter-car-driver-organiser for sick intellectuals" or "driver of motor car, valet, and general dogsbody,"[69] Fowles depended on her most to organize his personal life and build bridges to the world of family and friends. Fowles was always glad to see his friends but never thought to make social arrangements. He relied on Elizabeth for this. She telephoned John's mother, befriended his sister, orchestrated movie visits and walking tours with the nephews and niece. Her own mother's health was worsening, as Doris grew crippled with arthritis, was sometimes befuddled, and had difficulties with her heart and lungs. In 1983 Elizabeth and her sister moved her to the Abbeyfield Home at Colyton, Devon, midway between them.

Fowles depended on Mary Scriven to organize the professional side of his life, a task for which the patient, efficient young woman was well suited. She "could answer letters almost blindfold," said Elizabeth, and was a speedy typist with a "quick and easy way."[70] Museum tape transcriptions, reports, geological papers, his entire correspondence after he had opened and sorted it: Mary handled all of it. She proofread and typed final copies (always from his "clean and masterly" typescripts) of all his articles, manuscripts, and scripts and all his books from *Daniel Martin* (1977) through *A Maggot* (1985). She took Fowles's frequent absentmindedness in stride as his "being elsewhere." She also discovered the secret to his oft-changing handwriting—that it depended on which eyeglasses he happened to be wearing—and invented a method of tilting the page of an unreadable passage to put it in legible perspective.[71]

Mary was discreet and recognized Fowles's need for privacy. While he wrote upstairs in his workroom overlooking the garden and sea, she set up an office in the flat at the front of the house, slipped in and out without fuss, and, for the first year, went home for lunch. One stormy day, however, Elizabeth insisted she stay for lunch, and Mary, from that moment, was more or less adopted into the family. During Mary's first pregnancy, in 1978, Elizabeth took to driving her up the Broad Street hill to work. Mary brought her newborn daughter, Tanya, to her office, and later her son, Ben, both close in age to Anna's children. Elizabeth was glad to watch the children sometimes, so that Mary could work. Mary "sat with Doris . . . sat with Anna's kids, she looked in on the house when we were away." For Elizabeth, Mary was a companion. They could laugh together, and Elizabeth "loved it when she came into the house and we got a perspective on this life and author."[72] Mary was quite moved when Elizabeth said, "Oh Mary, I look on you as an older Anna."[73]

Mary treasured the "calm, artistic" atmosphere of Belmont, as Fowles wrote upstairs and Elizabeth wrote long letters to friends from her small desk tucked into the chimney corner of the front room. Having worked previously in a corporate environment, Mary delighted in the way Elizabeth would bring her a cup of tea or Fowles would leave a sprig of fresh jasmine on her desk. She was touched to see her famous employer brew a cup of tea for his gardener, Mr. Quick, or to see Fowles stretch and sigh each afternoon at four and go into his garden "to blow the cobwebs away." Fowles valued Mary highly and regarded her as "an intermediary with the town," who could bring him gossip from church, pub, and dramatic society. They could make each other laugh, and she found he had "a wicked, wonderful sense of humor."[74]

In his writing and his daily interests, the personal and historic past was Fowles's fascination and his consolation. Elizabeth's heart was in the present. Her first grandchild, a little girl named Tess, was born on December 13, 1977. Anna and Nick Homoky now lived in Penarth, Wales, just outside Cardiff, where Nick was an art lecturer at the college and pursued his pottery and Anna had a part-time teaching position in a small convent school. The birth was posterior, and Elizabeth imagined the worst through three sleepless nights while her daughter was in a difficult labor. When the good news came, Elizabeth fell upon John, kissing him over his morning coffee and newspaper ("Unusual at that hour for me, you might say . . ."). At that moment a lone female sparrow hawk landed on their terrace. ("A good omen, says J.")[75] Elizabeth, flying down the street to tell everyone she knew in Lyme that Anna had a daughter, looked up at a sunny sky: "Keep my girl safe I said to the trees and the sky, she likes it here."[76]

For Anna, having a girl was especially important for Liz's sake. Chubby and pink, with dark silky hair, Tess looked like Anna as a baby. Just days before Christmas, as she placed the baby in Liz's arms, Anna felt extremely proud. It was "*wonderful*, giving her this little baby daughter . . . it was definitely something that I had to do for Liz in a way." She told Rosie Jackson, "It was as if I was giving her back myself, giving back to her the years she had missed. . . . I know it was the best thing I could ever have done for her, and Tess was always so special for Liz."[77]

Tess's connection to Liz, which deepened as this quick and sunny-natured child grew older, was in many ways a restoration of something lost years before. This was both healing and distressing for Elizabeth. She took pride in the baby's closeness to her and could not go many weeks away from her. However, "having Tess, who looks amazingly like Anna at the same age," wrote Elizabeth in a self-revealing moment, "has re-aroused a most terrible sense of guilt." After a joyous visit with Tess she would again have her old "alarming dreams that I have a small child and I have lost it, or forgotten to feed it."[78] Anna was such "an intelligent and devoted Mum," she wrote, and "I didn't even stick to my own child for long." When she saw Anna and Tess, "beneath the surface of my joy of feeling for them both, I go through this awful process of past guilt, a wallow in self hate." She was self-aware enough to recognize how that self-hate turned into "a hate of my present," represented by John. She felt her sense of humor desert her and felt "physically ill" when she thought about it. She added, on this occasion, how a quarrel had been made up as John was "considerate, tender . . . and restored to humour . . . like old chums we go for walks, play badminton and work in this bloody garden till our backs break."[79]

Anna left teaching when the baby was born, while her husband became more engrossed in his work as artist and lecturer. Anna began making lengthy visits to Belmont while Nick remained at home at his wheel and kiln. Much like John Fowles, who liked and understood him, Nick was less present to his family when deep in his art. Gathered at Belmont, the little female circle of Liz, Anna, and Tess, and occasionally Doris, came to depend emotionally more and more on one another. After Tess's arrival, Elizabeth's life began to center on her daughter's family.

When Tess was a toddler, both Fowleses were "quite besotted" with her, with John "mad to buy her toys" and pick out dresses for her in France.[80] Much as he hated sitting on beaches, he was glad to explore Monmouth Beach with this "very precocious and pretty child," building her sand castles and catching small crabs in pools for her. He observed, fascinated, as Tess stared intently at a blossom in his garden or a spider weaving a web. "To my amazement, so much for genes . . . her most striking precocity is linguistic," he said (wondering if the genetic factor was Roy). He teased her by mispronouncing words just to hear her correct him, "very prim and schoolmarmish."[81]

In 1979 the Homokys moved back to Bristol, where Nick was appointed lecturer at his old college. He was established, noted Fowles with pleasure, "as a leading young potter; and seems to sell as much as he can produce."[82] On December 12, 1980, Anna gave birth to their second child, William Bela, always called Will. "Sort of lean and long, incredibly beautiful long fingers," enthused Liz, who stayed with them at the time of the birth. Baby William was "a fine looking chap," who was smothered with affection by his three-year-old sister.[83] Fowles never objected when Will was left with him while the others went off. When he saw Fowles on a visit, toddler Will would fall "all over John in delight."[84] As the little boy grew, he and his stepgrandfather would march off to the Cobb or along the beach quite content with each other's company. Fowles, ever strict about biological relationships, always referred to these children as his stepgrandchildren, but when they were little, the connection was as warm as if they were his own. Roy Christy, their grandfather, saw only Tess as a baby. By then he was living in a halfway house and just intermittently could hold a job. Judy Christy had legally separated from him, though he telephoned her "constantly." Anna had to keep her whereabouts from him. "It is tragic," said Elizabeth.[85]

In 1978, while Fowles in Lyme Regis grew more absorbed in his various forays into the past, Tom Maschler in London finally succeeded in giving the film of *The French Lieutenant's Woman* a future. Maschler lived only a few doors from film director Karel Reisz. Passing him in the street one September afternoon, Maschler asked what Reisz was working on. He had just completed *Who'll Stop the Rain,* Reisz said, and was now thinking of "doing something with Harold Pinter." Surprised, Maschler reminded Reisz that Pinter had twice considered writing a script for John Fowles's *The French Lieutenant's Woman*. Reisz expressed interest and said he might speak to Pinter about it. "Now," said Maschler, very excited, "why not speak to him *now*?" He turned his friend around and walked him back home, standing beside Reisz as he telephoned Pinter and the two arranged to meet that Sunday. Within two weeks Reisz and Pinter had resolved to make the film. John Calley of Warner Bros. ("a great John Fowles fan") immediately agreed to produce it, flying from California to England himself within four days to close the deal. Tom Maschler was named associate producer. Within another month, Karel Reisz had signed Meryl Streep, his first choice, for the part of Sarah Woodruff.[86]

Harold Pinter's screenplay hit on a workable solution to the plaguey problem of filming the diachronic (or twin-timed) narrative of *The French Lieutenant's Woman*. The final script presented a modern film company of contemporary actors who were shooting a movie of the Victorian romance told in the novel. Mike and Anna, the actors playing Charles (portrayed by Jeremy Irons) and Sarah (Meryl Streep), have a love affair. Their immersion in the fictive film characters of the past shapes and colors their contemporary involvement. The film moves back and forth between the Victorian story and the modern, centered in the complicated, dual relationship of the lovers. Fowles wrote that the script was not "a mere 'version' of my novel; but . . . the blueprint . . . of a brilliant metaphor for it."[87]

Although Fowles retained final oversight on the script, he was only called in to help on two romantic scenes. The proposal scene between Charles and Ernestina was "too curt and quick." Reisz told Fowles, "Harold says he'll do anything, but he simply can't write a happy scene." In Fowles's view, Pinter's first draft also failed to bring off the final scene, "when Charles and Sarah meet again (in Victorian terms); I think," said Fowles, "because he couldn't face the need for emotion." Pinter graciously made no argument when Fowles rewrote the scene "to put some of that back." Fowles believed that all such matters throughout the entire production were resolved "without any trouble or bad feeling, in a spirit of friendship and cooperation that must be rare in the cinema." For this "good spirit," he gave complete credit to Karel Reisz.[88]

"Neutral" about Reisz in the beginning, Fowles came to like him very much as the work went on. Reisz was "endlessly patient and optimistic . . . and funny." Watching a football match on television (Liverpool versus Aberdeen) with the famed director while their wives chatted comfortably over tea,[89] Fowles silently observed that in terms of their old-fashioned values and marriages, he and Elizabeth were "in philosophy and lifestyle . . . closer to" Karel and his wife, actress Betsy Blair, than to many of their other associates.[90]

Harold Pinter completely charmed Elizabeth Fowles ("we could, you might say, be buddies. Mind—does he need the booze") when they met in November 1978. He was "a dandy dresser," who earned Elizabeth's teasing by setting off to see the landslip beyond Underhill Farm in "sharp Saville Row suit and handmade delicate shoes, cuff links and tie." The "rough going" and steepness of the slope were too much, and Pinter turned back to the house to lie down. His profound vertigo was revealed when he was unable to stroll on the Upper Walk of the Cobb and had to walk below. Elizabeth was sorry she had mocked his "preciousness" as "a pose." For she was enthralled by Pinter's words and innate dramatic personality. "He is a pleasure to listen to," she wrote. "His words are chosen with marvellous precision and with great effect. And he is a glorious mimic. He touches one with a tenderness, his movements are elegant. He is in fact a poem. I quite loved him. He is not handsome. Anna said he had a perfect clown's face. His teeth are too wide apart, his eyebrows do not match his eyes. He self-mocks himself. Quite endearing." Harold Pinter also made Elizabeth comfortable, as she focused on the part of him that was "nice workingclass boy." Together they would put on a Cockney accent and burst in on the others in a routine they invented about going onstage in the West of England.[91] They were apt to be "rather silly" together, drinking and clowning in a London Chinese restaurant, for instance, while Fay Maschler lectured ("very sharp and schoolmisstry") on the proper way to eat Chinese food. Pinter gave Elizabeth his phone number and kissed and chatted with her toddler granddaughter.[92]

She was far from comfortable, however, with Pinter's new partner and soon-to-be wife. Lady Antonia Fraser and Fowles had "buried our Booker Prize hatchet" and talked seventeenth-century history together.[93] Elizabeth remarked sourly on their chumminess. After a quarrel with John, Elizabeth reported, "I was abused for my lack of many things and shortcomings and reminded that I might try to model myself upon the lady A. A person, so it seems, of *all* things to many men. . . . A certain blousey beauty, a good mind, a lack of interest in all things domestic (well who wouldn't with a house full of servants.) a breeder of interesting children. Amusing and aristocratic. Rich, and having entry into a fashionable and somewhat intellectual society." Elizabeth, now fifty-four, sighed. "As you might imagine I found the comparison—at my time of life—a teeny bit hurtfull."[94]

By the end of 1979 the finished script was universally applauded. "Brilliant. Fantastic!" John Calley telephoned Tom Maschler.[95] Intense preparations continued in anticipation of filming to commence in May 1980. Besides Meryl Streep and Jeremy Irons, Leo McKern had been cast as Dr. Grogan. Carl Davis was composing the musical score. The cooperation of Lyme Regis was negotiated, and complicated arrangements were made for dressing Broad Street as it would have appeared in 1866, including refronting the shops.

Without warning, in mid-January 1980, Maschler received a telegram from Calley. Warner Bros. was withdrawing. The film was "an art film." The budget was too big for an art film. The new head of studio had "just thrown it out." Furious, Maschler telephoned Calley in California. "You have known this from the beginning," he raged. "John Fowles, Harold Pinter, Karel Reisz, Meryl Streep . . . Of course it's an 'art film!' What do you want us to make of *The French Lieutenant's Woman*? A musical?"[96]

It was Meryl Streep's agent who saved the day, diplomatically negotiating the film contracts from Warner Bros. to United Artists in record time. The deal required that moneys be guaranteed back to the new studio in a "turn-around": Parts of the percentages contracted to Fowles, Pinter, Maschler, and Reisz had to be released to United Artists. Each of them, with their wives, hurriedly had to form a "company" to make this possible. The window was so tight that the documents received final signatures on June 5, 1980, when filming had actually begun on May 27.[97] The deal was a cliffhanger, and at least for Tom Maschler who had spent twelve years trying to make this film happen, the first day of filming was "very, very emotional."[98]

The earliest scenes were shot in Lyme Regis in May, before the start of the tourist season. Lyme residents were extras, the town being just far enough outside London to let union rules relax. The Victorianized streets with their dressed shopfronts were opened early in the morning for deliveries, then closed and resanded for the day's shooting, then opened in the evening for people to wander in. There was a great fuss about the very ugly bus shelter at Cobb Gate. The art department for the film created a permanent Victorian-style replacement that they thought handsome enough to be a kind of gift to the town. The council and Mayor Henry Broome refused, demanding the return and reconstruction of the ugly one.[99]

There was constant rain as filming continued through the summer in scenes in the Undercliff and outside the town. Meryl Streep's red wig disintegrated from the wet, and actors and crew were "wallowing about in mud" in the Undercliff. Ever positive, Karel Reisz built a staircase and cable slings for the brutes and camera down to the ilex grove. Outdoor scenes were rewritten for indoors or shot quickly between downpours. To his surprise, the foul weather provided the kind of rough sea that Fowles had assured Reisz would not arise until autumn, so the crew prepared to make the opening scene with Sarah at the end of the Cobb. Just as Meryl Streep was about to take her position, someone thought to phone United Artists. Under no circumstances, came the answer, was Miss Streep—a very expensive property—to stand exposed on that quay in the storm! So Terry Pritchard, one of the two art directors, pulled on "Sarah's" big black cape and tied himself to the Cobb with a stout rope around his waist while the waves crashed about him and cameras rolled.[100]

"The whole making of the thing was, internally, within the unit," Fowles recalled, "quite extraordinarily peaceful and unfraught; a model of how such things should be done, in a communal art."[101] There was all the *bonhomie* of a well-managed film location. Meryl Streep rented the Haye House for her stay and brought along her newborn daughter and a nanny so that she could continue feeding the baby while she worked. Karel and Betsy Reisz, with Jeremy Irons, rented Fowles's old house at Underhill Farm. One of the movie scenes was shot there. The Marine Parade surgery of Fowles's friend Dr. Joan Walker was dressed to become Dr. Grogan's. Long after midnight one night Jeremy Irons, unable to sleep, walked past and saw Walker's light. He visited, teasing her by hoarsely whispering from the shadows, "Have you got any speed?" and making her giggle. He sent flowers the next day.[102] Both Meryl Streep and Elizabeth Fowles entertained cast and crew. Many gathered each evening in the bowling alley at the back of the Red Lion Hotel for a glass of wine and the daily rushes.[103] Fowles seldom attended, feeling Reisz and Streep were "nervous as cats about my seeing anything." He suspected the end result would be "a brave effort; and not quite hang together."[104]

The filming of *The French Lieutenant's Woman* was book-ended by the making of two other Fowles films, which contributed to the mixed sense of excitement, anxiety, and exhaustion both John and Elizabeth felt. *Playhouse,* a program on BBC 2, produced a version of *The Ebony Tower* short story "The Enigma." The scriptwriter was the talented Malcolm Bradbury, a good friend of Fowles's, who annually brought Fowles to Cambridge for a summer seminar and often, fruitlessly, urged him to join his English literature department at the University of East Anglia, Norwich. Fowles retained script oversight and consulted with Bradbury before production, and he and Elizabeth were on location during at least one week of the fortnight's shooting (May 31–June 14, 1979) at Ealing Studios and on London streets. Directed by Robert Knights, produced by David Rose, and with Nigel Hawthorne, Philip Bowen, and Ursula Howells among the cast, the television version of "The Enigma" earned high critical reviews when broadcast on February 9, 1980.[105]

As the Lyme Regis filming of *The French Lieutenant's Woman* was wrapping at the end of summer 1980, shooting took place at Stonehenge for a BBC program called *Writers and Places,* produced by John Archer. With a script by Antony Rouse based on Fowles's just-published *The Enigma of Stonehenge,* filming at Stonehenge and Avebury commenced on August 26, 1980. The Fowleses were on site September 1–3, while John was filmed at Stonehenge and Elizabeth drove around the area, transporting museum artifacts to the shoot.[106]

Adding to the crush at that time, the lease of their Hampstead flat was not renewed. Late in 1980 Elizabeth persuaded John to purchase the eighty-four-year lease on the flat below Tom and Malou Wiseman in an aristocratic old house at 48 Regent's Park Road. She spent months cleaning and managing the conversion, to ready the flat by August 1981, just at the hectic time of the public release of *The French Lieutenant's Woman* film and as Fowles was finishing *Mantissa.* Suffering one of her frequent bronchial infections as she handled the move alone, Elizabeth, to John's terror, had a stress seizure severe enough to be mistaken for a heart attack and to put her in the hospital. Once in the new flat, they both had bouts of missing the "life and sympathetic side of Hampstead Village," where they had maintained a presence since 1953.[107] Eventually they adjusted. With "an excellent Greek eating house down the road [and] a good pub around the corner," 48a Regent's Park Road was convenient to the 74 bus, the West End theaters, and Primrose Hill. The spacious flat had their first extra bedroom, overlooking quiet gardens.[108] Best of all, while Tom and Boris Wiseman were good company, Malou was also a writer's wife. Elizabeth and Malou were constant and sympathetic companions in London.

The hype for the film of *The French Lieutenant's Woman* kept Fowles off-balance through 1981. When he and Elizabeth saw the final version in March, they were willing to rate it ("being very cruel and objective") as a beta plus, "far better than the wretched gammas and deltas I have had to suffer before." The others were far more enthusiastic. Fowles did think the photography beautiful and the major performances excellent.[109] In August, when the film premiered at the Odeon Haymarket, Fowles liked it a bit better. Yet he thought it failed "where it matters most, alas. It looks very good, but is somewhere empty at the heart." He wondered if it was Pinter's script or a fault of his book. The cinema audience was silent, "as if puzzled." The critics were mixed, with the popular press waxing enthusiastic and "the more egghead" damning the film.[110] A year later the film had "failed with both the Oscar and English Academy awards." Fowles and Elizabeth attended the latter and sat with Harold Pinter and Antonia Fraser and Jeremy Irons and his wife Sinead Cusack. It was a "sour evening" with "gloom at our table from Jeremy and Harold, while the rest of us rather enjoyed the vulgarity of it all."[111]

As Fowles was watching the public debut of *The French Lieutenant's Woman* in spring 1981, he was also in the final weeks of preparation for the National Theatre's long-delayed opening of *Dom Juan*. After four years the curtain rose on Fowles's Molière translation on April 7, 1981, in the Cottesloe Theatre, directed by Peter Gill. The production was well received, and critics generally liked Fowles's translation. Most agreed with Irving Wardle in the *Times* that the speeches took on "a powerful eloquence."[112] The *Telegraph*'s John Barber could not "recommend this fascinating play too highly."[113]

For Fowles, Molière's scandalous satire on seventeenth-century hypocrisy was about language, its use and abuse. No one knew better than Molière, Fowles said in an interview, "that double talk lies not only at the heart of all comedy, but of all social and political tyranny as well."[114] Don Juan he saw as "semiologist, a kind of early Roland Barthes . . . [with] an ear for the way people speak."[115] What ultimately damns this libertine as much as his real sins is his final use of "empty rhetoric and pious jargon" to hide them.[116]

After similar delays, Fowles's translation of Alfred de Musset's *Loren-zaccio* followed. Originally written, like *Dom Juan*, in 1978, *Lorenzaccio* was extensively reworked in 1980–1981 and was produced in 1983, directed by Michael Bogdanov. Never before produced in English from its original, *Lorenzaccio* ran 140 pages and required eighty speaking parts. Fowles ultimately cut this by one third, calling the textual problems "fiendish."[117] Still three intense hours long in performance, the play was a great success when it opened on March 15. Irving Wardle hailed "John Fowles's eloquent version" in the *Times* and the entire magnificent production as taking "to the Olivier stage like a heroic nineteenth-century painting."[118]

Musset's play dramatizes the assassination in 1537 of Duke Alessandro de Medici, cruel and corrupt despot of Florence, by his cousin Lorenzo. Lorenzo begins as a republican idealist who aspires, out of private ambition, to secure his destiny by assassinating the tyrant. Like Fowles's *Zip*, trying to overcome a sense of *nemo* by pointless violence, Lorenzo is determined to create an identity by doing political murder. He prepares for killing Alessandro by becoming the accomplice of that debauched ruler, thereby growing as morally corrupt as his victim.

Fowles's political views of this time were reflected in his translation. Like Musset, whose apathetic Florentine republicans fail to change their society when opportunity arises through the ducal assassination, Fowles believed there was "no hope for the Western World, it lies self-betrayed by its own stupidity and greed." His depression coincided with work on this play, as he blamed his own class of educated liberals as "traitors, the eternal clerks again. . . . Nine tenths or more of their ethics is based on self-perpetuation."[119] Elsewhere he wrote of such among his closest friends that "seem to me biologically *blind*, there is no other word for it. Their lives, their views, their judgements, are all dictated by a deep longing to maintain the social and political status quo—that is, a world where 'we' and our friends still maintain our absurdly privileged status. Which is of course maintained and propagated, 'down' from the elite, by all our media."[120]

Fowles remained active with the National Theatre until 1988, discovering that he thoroughly enjoyed translating and the collaborative energy of working with a director and live repertory company. Like his historical research, his work on Aubrey's *Monumenta Britannica,* and his forays into natural history, Fowles's dramatic translation gave him relief from writing original fiction and for much the same reasons. "I enjoy translation," he told John Higgins in the *Times,* "simply because it is much like a crossword puzzle . . . a number of pleasing problems to solve and your tool is language. You don't have the novelist's guilt of creating something out of blankness."[121]

In solving these problems, however, Fowles refocused his attention on dialogue and spoken language in ways that would affect his fiction. "Dialogue is magnetic," he wrote. "It pulls everything round it into the present. This is why play-texts are timeless, eternally present. And where all the 'presentness' of a novel . . . comes from."[122] In January 1977 Fowles had been nervous enough to show his *Dom Juan* script to Ann Jellicoe, who thought it "too academic and 'anxious' (didn't trust the actors enough)." Peter Hall at first thought "some of the lines unspeakable," but the actors proved him wrong. Fowles learned much from listening to actors speaking his words aloud and admitted that "novel dialogue is infinitely far from stage dialogue."[123] This new awareness was reflected not only in his future scripts but in the fictions written in the late 1970s. *Mantissa* is a playlike novel that may be read as entirely dialogue with some stage directions smoothing it out. Whole sections of *A Maggot* were written as unvarnished dialogue, incorporated into the text as legal deposition.

Beneath the well-managed surface of his demanding schedule, Fowles struggled with depression, of which he wrote frequently in 1981. The film and its publicity oppressed him; his career felt "like a millstone round my neck." He felt estranged culturally and politically from his contemporaries, even from his closest London friends. He recognized that he used "local history, old books, nature, etc. . . . to escape the present." Elizabeth called these his "drugs."[124] Exhaustion and worsening health caused loss of physical zest. Fowles still smoked three packs of cigarettes a day. He took poor care of himself when Elizabeth was in London or Bristol, as she often was in 1981.[125] His blood pressure and circulation problems grew worse, and medication for the blood pressure had side effects of agitation followed by lethargy and occasional impotence. Nearing his fifty-fifth birthday, Fowles complained wearily of "a kind of fatalistic numbness, the way old trees have dead branches, yet go on living. My dead branch is the creative (and sexual) side. It is not just Eliz, nothing stirs me in that way any more."[126] Yet it saddened Fowles terribly that "Eliz and I drift apart, without hatred or rows, by some process the reverse of osmosis."[127]

It was at this personal low that Fowles submitted *Mantissa* for publication. He felt "it wasn't really ready." The erotic, comic "mood it tries to present is totally contrary to everything I feel." He was unhappy to think "how Eliz will hate it, and countless others." He was unhappy to be publishing fiction at all, foreseeing only "punishment of one kind of another—both public and private."[128] Public disapproval he could endure, but private disapproval was much less bearable. Less than twenty years after rejoicing in the publication of *The Collector,* John Fowles faced the publication of his latest novel like a condemned man facing the scaffold.

CHAPTER NINETEEN

Here Be Dragons

1982–1990

eating an orange in front of the fire
watching its peel caught up in flame

I remember charcoal
oranges
Greek winter sun and a girlchild's name

I didn't know then that
alone
alone
is always the same

—ELIZABETH FOWLES, C. 1959,
REVISED SEPTEMBER 23, 1984

"At the end of May 1982," wrote Elizabeth Fowles on June 7, 1982, "I burnt my letters. Which I regret." She had sensed "that the relevance was lost," but "nothing is. Rooms and places I inhabited, jobs, emotions, possibilities, pleasures, sadness, extremes, poverty."[1]

Impulsive though it seems, Elizabeth's action was careful and specific. She burned her own letters from her love affair with John Fowles during 1953 and 1954. His letters to her survive, as do the letters from Roy Christy, her mother, old boyfriends, female friends, and her own letters from 1955 on. What Elizabeth tried to erase was the record of her own emotions, choices, guilt, and longings from that critical period of her life when she chose John Fowles, left Roy Christy, and lost her daughter,

Anna. Much of the destructiveness of the gesture was directed at herself.

The gesture was also directed at her husband and was calculated, unconsciously or consciously, to strike one of his most vulnerable spots. Fowles, after all, kept diaries over decades, saved every scrap of autobiographical documentation, tracked down his ancestors, spent countless hours acquiring and interpreting the details of strangers' lives, analyzed the minutiae of the past in town, county, country, and prehistory, and begged for the preservation of personal biographical documents about other writers' relationships. To destroy the intimate artifacts of their earliest relationship was to wound him. He wrote that he would never forgive her for it.[2]

The letters were also her own portrait of herself, her own written text. Burning her words was a rebellion. It was to slip away, to assert that her life and its evidence belonged to her, could not be used or captured.

Her action was also a plea for John's attention. "Now we sleep as far away as possible," her note continues, "talk of nothing remove ourselves entirely—touch not, communicate not." Remembering Sanchia Humphreys, her rival of 1954, Elizabeth wrote in parentheses, "S. may have been a better bet."

Ultimately she was heartsick and sorry she had done it. Tender memories of that time came flooding back and mixed with her anger and sadness as on her note she scribbled a little verse, "At Holly Hill," about the summer of 1954.

> *8 Holly Hill a small dark*
> *room with nothing in it*
> *was richer far more than*
> *this empty empty house of*
> *money and its fame*
> *Oh Holly Hill at number 8* [3]

While Elizabeth burned her letters, John Fowles was proofing the galleys of *Mantissa*, the book he was sure she would hate. She did not like the book much and was sorry, her friends whispered, that he had published it.[4] The first chapter's portrait of the wife, whose identity is completely forgotten by the amnesiac writer hero, could hardly have cheered her either.

Elizabeth was not the only detractor in Fowles's intimate circle. When *Mantissa* was published in September 1982, John and Elizabeth returned from a weeklong symposium at University of Liverpool via family visits in Yorkshire. Fowles had arranged to take an hour-and-a-half-long telephone interview with a "fancy New York journalist" at Gladys Fowles's tiny bungalow. Gladys was now rather deaf, and to keep her quiet while John spoke in the next room, Elizabeth sat her down with magazines on sewing and knitting. While Fowles, in Elizabeth's recounting, was "spouting on about the importance of loss and symbolic repair—the floating half conscious remembered Mother deliciousness of it all. And the MUSE . . . de dar de dar," Gladys suddenly "pounced" to give Elizabeth her opinion of her son's new novel. "Well," said the mother vehemently, "I think it is phonography!" In the background, said Elizabeth, "still, the booming voice of JF in high flown language over the lines and cables across the Atlantic to N. York," while Gladys went on, equally loudly, "Thank God his father is not alive. It is not JOHN—this sort of phonography—it is all totally phonographic."[5]

Fowles laughed as heartily as Elizabeth over that story, but the reviews of *Mantissa* were predictably negative or bewildered. Typical was John Walsh, who called *Mantissa* "an awful indulgence, a sterile joke" that "baffled many devoted fans."[6] "All the intellectual critics," wrote Fowles, gave "very bad reviews; only Malcolm Bradbury and David Lodge were faintly kind." Nonetheless, "*Mantissa* has done not too badly," he said.[7] The book remained on the best-seller lists only a month, from October into November.

Part of Fowles's time was absorbed by public performance. Public attention was still focused on *The French Lieutenant's Woman* film, nominated for Academy Awards in both Great Britain and the United States. There was a buildup to December rehearsals for *Lorenzaccio* at the National Theatre. Fowles was also in months of negotiation with writer John Mortimer and director Robert Knights, who ultimately persuaded Granada to finance a television production of *The Ebony Tower* and also persuaded Sir Lawrence Olivier to play the role of Henry Breasley. This was shot in France in 1983, with Roger Rees as David and Greta Scacchi as Diana. To please Olivier, almost all of Breasley's "blue language" was dropped, but Fowles found Mortimer's script "reasonably faithful and craftsmanlike."[8]

The greatest devourer of his time, however, was the museum. As he prepared *Mantissa* for publication and Elizabeth burned her letters, Fowles was embroiled in a long-simmering controversy that boiled over in 1982. For many years municipal authorities throughout Great Britain had wrestled with whether the collection of fossils from sites such as the Dorset cliffs around Lyme Regis should be forbidden to commercial amateur fossil hunters and allowed only to licensed semiacademic professionals. Fowles and his friends at the museum had always supported the amateurs, from commercial collectors to schoolchildren. In 1982 the West Dorset District Council tried to restrict fossil collection on the coastal cliffs between Lyme Regis and Golden Cap. Fowles successfully led the local opposition to defend amateur rights, banding with the Dorchester County Museum to insist on public inquiry.

Fowles took a highly visible, time-consuming role in other public controversies. In 1984 he and his friends fought a sewage treatment plant planned for an archaeologically sensitive area. From 1986 they fought to preserve the six-hundred-year old Town Mill and Malthouse from private development. Through these battles he came to know Liz-Anne Bawden, who had left an academic post at London's Slade School of Art to run the Portland Art Gallery in Broad Street, Lyme. Bawden, wrote Fowles, was "avis rarissima in Lyme," a "fiercely independent," activist town councillor, "Bull-terrierish" about her causes and an "aggressive democrat."⁹ Between 1982 and 1984 Fowles served on civic committees for the 1984 Charter 700 celebration in Lyme Regis and helped plan the museum's Charter 700 exhibition. He began a major address on amateur geologists at the British Association for the Advancement of Science in 1982 by saying, "I am pleased that today is given to the amateur in geology, because no one could be more amateur than I am." Indeed, said Jo Draper, Fowles was so incredibly busy with museum work in 1982 that she was amazed he could do anything else.¹⁰

However, by summer 1982, Fowles was also translating again for the National Theatre and had returned to the writing of his novel *A Maggot,* "three-quarters finished" and laid aside in 1979.¹¹ The writing and publication of this novel were threaded around not only the writing of successive translation drafts but also the entire period of production for all four of Fowles's contributions to the NT. The influence of these dramas carried into the fiction.

Fowles began translating Jean-Jacques Bernard's *Martine* in September 1982, though production was delayed until 1985.¹² Set just after World

War I, the play has a Chekhovian flavor. Beautiful and naïve, Martine is a peasant girl, wooed by Alfred, a stolid farmer. The aspiring Parisian journalist Julien meets Martine as he returns from the war and becomes infatuated with her. The magical week of romance is much more serious to Martine than to Julien, who carelessly returns to his witty, sophisticated fiancée. Although she continues to love Julien, Martine ultimately marries Alfred and is trapped into the role of provincial farmer's wife. The simple plot is driven by the suffering of the deeply feeling but mostly inarticulate Martine, whose inexpressible longings are trampled by the emotional carelessness of other characters. Essentially Martine and Julien are divided not by class but by language. His world is urban, a bit shallow, and verbally eloquent. Hers is traditional, sincere, and not easily put into words.

The play went up in the Lyttelton Theatre on April 20, 1985, with Peter Hall directing. Playing in the NT's repertoire through September 1985, *Martine* had limited commercial success. Critics raved, however, offering universal praise for Hall's subtle direction, Wendy Morgan's brilliantly affecting performance, and Fowles's delicate translation, in which the audience felt "a dialogue lying beneath the heard dialogue." John Barber in the *Daily Telegraph,* for example, hailed Hall's decision to place "this hushed French drama of nuance" into "the care of John Fowles . . . the great virtuoso of language, the daring experimentalist."[13]

Translating it, Fowles was fascinated by the playwright's emphasis on communication not through spoken dialogue but through silence. "The dramatic theory of Jean-Jacques Bernard (1888–1972) was centred on the idea that many things—moods, inner feelings, real motives—cannot be conveyed in (or are betrayed by) normal 'full' dialogue," Fowles wrote in his translation notes. "His texts constantly edge toward the broken sentence, the silences between people. . . . Theatre of the inexpressible' and 'theory of silence' were terms used to describe his method." Like Harold Pinter, whose similar methods were noted by both Fowles and the reviewers, meaning was conveyed in silence, pauses, and language "kept constantly plain, broken and tentative."[14]

As soon as he delivered the draft for *Martine,* Fowles turned to translating his favorite comedy from Oxford days, Marivaux's *Le Jeu de l'Amour et du Hasard* (1730) (produced as *The Lottery of Love*), which he worked on from November 1982 to May 26, 1983.[15] *Le Jeu* is an eighteenth-century French upstairs-downstairs romantic farce in which upper-class young people, matched by their families but strangers, switch places with their servants to test the perceptions of the would-be intended. Predictably, the true gentleman Richard and the young lady Sylvia fall in love through their disguises, as do the maid Louisa and the manservant Brass. Through the classic elements of comic timing, costume changes, and mistaken identities, Marivaux brings his young characters not only to loving each other but to greater understanding of their own natures. Fowles was deeply disappointed when it was staged only as a single Studio Workshop performance directed by Peter Gill on December 7, 1984.

By removing the action from the French social conventions of Marivaux's time to Regency England, Fowles liberated the dialogue. In Fowles's version the lovers' *marivaudage* is racy, sparkling, and flirtatious, revealing their attraction for each other and their own discomfiture at their emotion and desires. Unlike the broken, plain fragments of *Martine,* the discourse of *Le Jeu* is highly polished and witty. However, as in *Martine,* the dialogue of *Le Jeu* is more about indicating what is not said than it is about the actual words. Superficially different, in John Fowles's versions they both are plays about the indirection of language and about love existing in silences.

As he was completing *Martine* and writing *Le Jeu,* Fowles returned to writing *A Maggot,* a novel dramatizing much that is nonarticulated and inexpressible.[16] As in *Le Jeu,* characters are not what they seem. A company of travelers journey into the deserted southwest of England in 1736. They ride in silence and include the austere, secretive, and mostly silent Lord B. and his mute but highly intuitive servant. The two most conventional figures turn out to be actors, hired to play their parts. The modest, quiet young woman is revealed as a notorious prostitute. They travel toward a vision of something that transforms them but cannot be expressed in the language available to them. The experience must be translated, imperfectly, into approximations drawn from the religious and social framework of the time. Months after the "event," the driven, gifted leader has utterly vanished. The manservant is found hanged in a bizarre fashion. The actors have fled from suspicions of witchcraft and political heresy. And Rebecca, the prostitute with untapped emotional depths, has been reborn as a religious visionary, becoming the mother of the founder of a religious sect.

Fowles was conscious that his work for the National Theatre had affected this novel. Three-quarters of *A Maggot* was in the form of question and answer, like a trial, "'which means perhaps I am beginning to creep toward the theatre,' though novel and theatre dialogue are very different."[17] Except for the cinematic opening chapters, the novel is a collection of depositions and letters provided by the lawyer investigating the disappearance of the party's leader, the heretical, philosophical younger son of a great duke. Through the lawyer Ayscough's dry documents, Fowles provides many facts filtered through the class conventions of eighteenth-century English society but ultimately gives no answers. As in the plays he was translating, things are understood (if at all) by what is *not* said, rather than through the spoken dialogue.

A Maggot was inspired in the late 1970s when Fowles was completing *Daniel Martin*. The dreamlike image that begins the novel had come, he remembered years later, from the opening sequence of a 1953 Brazilian film, *O Cangaceiro*, ("The Bandit," released in dubbed English in 1962), directed by Lima Barreto.[18] "A small group of travelers, faceless, without apparent motive," he wrote in the 1985 prologue to *A Maggot,* rode horseback through a "deserted landscape . . . in my mind towards an event."[19] This was the "maggot," the queer, repetitive, undismissible idea, that haunted his imagination. Fowles fused to it both his 1974 apocalyptic vision of feminine voyagers traveling in a spherical vessel from a more enlightened planet and his fascination for the eighteenth-century apocalyptic sect the Shakers, to whose works and theology he had been introduced by Ned Bradford in 1977.

Fowles's interest in the Shakers did not come out of nowhere. For all his atheism, he had identified historically with religious Dissenters since at least the early 1960s. He was proud of his Nonconformist and Methodist ancestry through his mother's remote Cornish family. In his local history research he emphasized the dissenting traditions of Lyme Regis as the town's defining political and religious heritage. He even set Sarah Woodruff's "confession" of personal rebellion in *The French Lieutenant's Woman* in the hidden Undercliff grove where outlawed dissident Protestants had met in the 1780s.

The Dissenting figure who stalked Fowles's imagination through many years was John Wesley (1703–1791), the founder of Methodism. Wesley personified for Fowles the moment in the eighteenth century when "a repressive wall in many ordinary people" was breached and the emotional power of "sensibility" began to provoke tremendous change in English society. He longed to write a play or filmscript dramatizing

Wesley's famous open-air Kingswood preachings at Bristol in April 1739, "when his extraordinary power of releasing pent-up feelings was . . . first revealed." Beyond religious feeling, Fowles believed, the emotion awakened a sense of the individual self and therefore had the political and social "power to level." Sensibility, leading to individual self-consciousness, political revolution, the Romantic movement, and sensitivity to nature, Fowles traced to "various form[s] of dissident Protestantism," including "Quakerism and Methodism . . . religions of emotion rather than of reason."[20] Shakerism simply replaced Wesleyanism as Fowles's symbol of sensibility and spiritual self-awakening.

When he was introduced to the "brilliant simplicity" of Shaker design and theology while visiting Hancock, Massachusetts, in 1977, Fowles encountered the radical extreme of a dissident Protestantism that had challenged "reactionary, conservative" English society in the eighteenth century with an emphasis on emotional truth discovered within the individual self. Like the "mothers" from his imaginary planet Lupela, the Shakers, in Fowles's view, were "proleptic, future-looking" and feminist. In their fostering of the individual's salvation within an austere, disciplined, but nurturing collective, he thought them communist "in the purest, pre-Marxist sense." It also appealed to him that the "ultimate legacy" of Shaker vision was "not religious but artistic," of treating "material and form with such infallible instinct for their inherent nature." The new religious movement to which Rebecca Lee gives birth in A Maggot is, for Fowles, a fusion of the spiritual and the aesthetic. This artistic revelation is the event toward which his characters ride.[21]

When A Maggot appeared in September 1985, Fowles was braced for misunderstanding and sneering reviews. He refused nomination for the Booker Prize, saying he did not believe in literary prizes and his experience as a Booker judge had put him off. It is more likely he feared rejection. To his surprise, there were very few critical naysayers in England, and many formerly tepid reviewers published raves. Miranda Seymour called it "clever, ingenious and thoroughly engrossing . . . richly ambiguous . . . ambitious . . . a dramatisation of the war between faith and reason."[22] In the TLS Pat Rogers said, "Fowles's darting imagination skims across the landscape of two and a half centuries . . . produces compelling and passionate fiction."[23] "Three cheers . . . for A Maggot," cried John Walsh in Books and Bookmen, "a tour de force of enquiry into the true heart of things, carried out with its author's boldest strokes."[24] The

Times gasped that "the imaginative power of the novel is astounding, the technical virtuosity and structural daring equally so."[25] The *New States-man* urged people "with the strongest possible recommendation to read this book,"[26] while the usually denigrating Robert Nye of the *Guardian* wrote of "the new John Fowles" that it was "very nearly the best work to date of a highly talented and always interesting writer."[27] It is a bitter irony that this widespread critical praise for Fowles's novel came during a time of such personal pain that he could not enjoy it. It is equally sad that the critically successful *A Maggot* was to be his final published novel.

The reviewers were no longer the most influential opinion molders of Fowles's reputation anyway. In September 1983 a friend showed him an advertisement for a Manchester University course: "Is John Fowles a great novelist or not?" "Absurd," said Fowles. "The real question is whether John Fowles is still alive or not. Even to me he feels more and more a fiction of the past."[28] Through the 1980s John Fowles's literary reputation grew beyond the bestsellerdom of his millions of book sales to receive academic evaluation. There was a flood of published articles, books appeared, and Fowles's work became a subject for classroom study and doctoral dissertations around the world. Fowles was of two minds about academic attention. On the one hand, he welcomed it. He had long decided that the worth of his work would be weighed by its survival into the future. If his books were to endure, it would be because the sharpest professional literary analysts judged them on merits beyond their sales. Every literary scholar who interviewed him or sent him a manuscript could tell a story of Fowles's extremely courteous treatment and painstaking reading of their work. No one ever faulted his manners or kindness.

On the other hand, to be subjected to such close theoretical scrutiny was deeply unsettling for a man as private as Fowles. The process made him feel objectified and dead, "without feelings and without future." "No doubt how I look from the outside to the post-war generation," he wrote, "'Fowles' for students . . . some one to be dissected, and awarded a beta query." Reading the typescript of Simon Loveday's *The Romances of John Fowles* was painful. He could not "intellectually or morally" object to the "shrewd . . . structuralist, partly deconstructionist account of all my faults," he wrote, "but something here and there in the tone seems to me gratuitously diminishing and sneering, coldly reifying." Another symptom that he was an object was the denial that he was still in process himself, as an artist and as a man. In his late fifties and early sixties, he hated "the way things I said twenty years ago are produced as evidence of now."[29]

As he had written in "Hardy and the Hag," he also believed that reading too much analysis of his work was very bad for his creativity. He wrote Harold William Fawkner that he did not despise academic analysts but feared them "when they bring their gifts, as the Trojans did the Greeks." The result was "self-atomizing" and destroyed the "natural energy sources" of creation. He felt he already knew "too much . . . about what is going on when I write fiction; I mean in terms of structuralism, semiology, the various other fetish-disciplines since the war."[30]

Fowles himself was well up on these postwar "fetish-disciplines," although he always dismissed his knowledge. He had an intense "eternal tendency to roll up like a hedgehog before literary 'experts.'"[31] Public "talk, talk, talk about literature, about the state of the novel" made him feel "nauseous."[32] He read and understood the definitive treatises on deconstruction and semiology. He was familiar with the work of Barthes, Lacan, Lévi-Strauss, Derrida, and the rest. He was capable of judging the application of their theories in manuscripts sent to him. He was impressed, for example, by the doctoral thesis of Susana Onega as "very well up in all the latest French and American theory."[33] A Marxist theorist was "fine until the author denied 'the validity of personal taste as an artist's ultimate authority'—because such taste presupposes 'particular social and individual conditions' of formation." This was a "bone" he could not "swallow."[34] Fowles remained all his life committed to the "humanist view of life . . . tolerance, generosity, a classical observer role for the writer."[35] He believed that language referenced reality and that the writer was the originator of his own text. He was a long way from October 1967, when he joked to Denys Sharrocks that he had "given up the battle for Roland Barthes's great contribution to linguistics, [but] . . . If you have any really bright students who need keeping down I suggest you give them WRITING DEGREE ZERO."[36] However, when he was in Paris in 1981 for the French publication of *Daniel Martin*, Fowles was positively gleeful when told, with malicious amusement, that "structuralism, the *nouveau roman* and the rest, is (except among a die-hard minority) dead," while American and British academics were still exploiting these theories.[37]

He was scornful of the way that "particular languages destroy theo-

ries . . . the 'jargon' the theory-holders evolve to express themselves becomes a kind of cancer, a mortality. . . . What is it in theorists that makes
them wrap themselves in a language that only their fellow-believers can
understand?"[38] He was harsher still in July 1986 at the Cambridge Seminar, speaking against academics to the point of provoking an argument
with Terry Eagleton, the critical theoretician. "Surely," said Eagleton,
Fowles would agree "that criticism was as important as creative work, and
that we respected T. S. Eliot equally as critic and as poet?" Fowles gave
him "a rude answer both on the principle and his example." David Lodge,
novelist and critic, backed Fowles's view in more academic terms: "In
brief, that the Theory (i.e. structuralism, post-structuralism and deconstruction) was laying literature waste."[39]

What Fowles emphatically did not like was the scholarly assumption
that his work (or the work of any good novelist) originated in some cold,
intellectual decision to write a novel formed by *any* theory or technique.
If he experimented with form, as he had done in *The French Lieutenant's
Woman* and *Daniel Martin,* he had made those choices because his story
and philosophy demanded that shape, not so that he could prove some
theoretical point. When Martin Klopstock sent him a manuscript analyzing his theory of "aesthetics," Fowles shrugged, "a rather grand word for
what are feelings and instincts."[40] Fowles's emphasis was always, always
on the process of creative inspiration and writing, not on the product. He
wrote that even the best literary criticism missed what writing was actually about. "There is a ghostland between what books can be said to
mean in retrospect and what they are in experience . . . that seems to
have been left out of all critical account." Speaking of Jane Austen, he
wrote: "Inherent in literary criticism is some sort of false chain of cause
and effect—because Jane Austen wanted to state this, she took to writing novels; instead of, because she had to write novels, she took to stating
this. It is watching her having to write that needs attention, not watching
what she wrote."[41]

By the end of the 1980s, when books like *Critical Essays on John
Fowles* were appearing, Fowles was pleased to note "my arrival in
academe-worthy literature is accepted." He was grateful for the "much
kinder . . . general tone" of articles published on his work. But he was
still dismayed by the "awful seriousness of academics on writers, their
belief that we must believe in everything we say as heavily as peasant
Catholics in their creed. . . . Humour and irony forbidden."[42] His

ambivalence about "John Fowles scholarship" remained. Through the entire decade this anxiety about acceptance and exposure through academic "reification" contributed to his sense of disquiet and depression.

While at work on his own demanding projects, Fowles was generous with collaborations and support to advance the projects of his friends. Just as he often assigned copyrights to benefit cultural and charitable agencies, so he lent his full partnership, his name, or his publishing connections to lesser known people whose work he valued. In 1983 he collaborated with Jo Draper on a book project combining the Hermann Lea photographs of Thomas Hardy and the Dorset of his time with Draper's fact-crammed interpretive text. With Fowles's name on it the book was picked up by both Jonathan Cape and Little, Brown. Draper was gratefully aware that John's involvement had elevated the project.[43]

Like Draper, Fay Godwin was aware of the golden goose aspect of Fowles's 1984 introduction to Land, another of her photographic collections. Although he praises Godwin's scrupulous honesty as a photographer and her "subtle eye . . . and subtler human spirit," Fowles's essay is "a strange and crochety preamble" in which he declares his suspicion and dislike of the photographic image, the fixed landscape seen in time stopped through a lens instead of the actual experience of an intimate landscape unfolding in time.[44]

Fowles promoted the work of rising novelist Peter Benson as well, and the two became genuine friends. Benson, who lived in Lyme Regis, was writing his first novel, The Levels, when he introduced himself to Fowles in 1984.[45] Fowles encouraged Benson's work, reading drafts, contributing puffs of praise for the book jacket, occasionally floating a loan, and writing letters of support when Benson applied for grants. The Levels was enthusiastically reviewed and won the Guardian Fiction Prize for 1987. In 1988, when Mr. Quick retired from gardening and Fowles was very ill, Benson acted as Fowles's gardener for a time.

From 1985 to 1988 Fowles acted as encouraging editor to Robin Mackness, an old Bedfordian who had previously written him from a French prison, where he was detained under suspicion of smuggling gold. The gold had been part of a Nazi cache, and unraveling its provenance to defend himself had led Mackness to an explanation of the savage, but seemingly motiveless, 1944 Nazi massacre at Oradour, France. Fowles was fascinated by the tale that was set near his first overseas post at

Poitiers and had so many elements similar to his own thriller *The Device*. Astounding Mackness, Fowles essentially midwifed *Oradour* into being, correcting Mackness's drafts, making publishing contacts, and finally writing the introduction.[46]

Elizabeth was resentful that Fowles lavished his time and energy on strangers and their projects. She accepted Draper and Godwin but was initially suspicious of Peter Benson. Mackness she believed was "a CONMAN if ever I met one."[47] Fowles now seemed to say yes to everything. He committed himself to articles for newspapers, magazines, and book introductions. "Essays, I suppose one would name them. He commits himself to such things, but they take up days and days. Weeks and weeks."[48] Elizabeth spent "endless hours here on my own . . . JF relentlessly in his room. What he does there, I no longer ask."[49]

John Fowles himself was well aware that the manner in which he pursued his vocation was detrimental to his relationship with Elizabeth. That year, 1984, they saw *Tom and Viv,* a play by Michael Hastings about T. S. "Eliot's first marriage, and his less than decent behaviour towards Vivienne Haigh-Wood." Eliot, Fowles commented, "was almost as bad as Hardy." Could any writer "survive such examination" of his "private flaws"? he wondered. "Are they lesser writers because of all this dragging-out of their dirty linen and meanness? . . . the thing the play leaves out is the fact that Eliot was a great poet, despite his wrong principles and selfishness in human terms."[50] In a similar way, when he read Brenda Maddox's biography of Nora Joyce, Fowles thought James Joyce was to his family and wife "devious and unreliable, a 'bastard,' yet redeemed, now it's all over, by the splendid books." Nora, "with her flair for appearance, clothes, her quirkiness, her underlying constancy," reminded him of Elizabeth.[51] "'Writer destroys wife' may be nearly inevitable," he wrote in 1984, but the real disgrace was "the attempt to cover up . . . destroying the documentation (as Hardy did) or keeping it locked away (as the Eliot estate still does)."[52]

In response to John's coolness and distraction, Elizabeth's center of emotional attention shifted, symbolized by her travels. From the early 1980s Fowles's travels were almost entirely related to his professional commitments. Even when she enjoyed herself, Elizabeth felt like a fifth wheel, the driver and occasional companion to a famous writer. On their French driving holidays, she felt "lonely alienated" as she drove Fowles from place to place to see the flowers he knew would be blooming in one meadow, the birds he knew would be feeding at a particular lake. With his well-marked maps, he guided Elizabeth down lanes and over bridges, then left her with the car for hours as he splashed off through the rain in his Wellington boots to count orchids. "I have no such relation in terms of nature," she said, also berating herself for years of depending on him to speak the language for her, for not having learned French herself.[53] In Paris for the 1981 release of *Daniel Martin*, she felt isolated and panicky. Left by herself, she feared getting lost. "Allowed in on the meals, I sat there like a mute . . . mostly I felt awkward and ill at ease, lacking in confidence. Smoked too much."[54] At various symposiums and seminars, she would have begun a conversation with someone congenial when "JF staggers up to me white faced and eyes drawn and demands that we leave at once as he feels faint."[55] She wrote to her friends, "You see what I mean about holidays?"[56]

Anna Homoky also felt constricted by life with a husband with no interest beyond his work. In 1982 she and her mother booked a package holiday to Corfu, leaving baby Will with his father and taking four-year-old Tess with them. They stayed in simple, cheap lodgings, ate in tavernas, and sat in sunshine on the beach. Waking on the first morning to the pure Greek light and the calm, glittering Mediterranean was a revelation to them both. The following year they urged the husbands to join them, but neither was willing. So, taking both children, the two went to Crete. It became a pattern for them. Crete in 1983, Rhodes in 1984, Lesbos in 1984, Crete in 1985, Kynthos in 1985, Crete in 1986: Anna and Liz took the children to some quiet seaside village and made a simple life for themselves for a week or two. Husbands were invited but refused to break off their work. Renting a plain, small house, mother and daughter arranged it to suit themselves, joking how they were always making homes for each other. Content, Tess wrote and drew pictures, while Will looked for dragons and bottle tops for his collection ("he does make a poetry of his own for us").[57]

The sympathetic bond between the two women grew ever deeper through these escapes to Greece. Anna saw her mother in a context outside England and its class structure and outside her relationship with John. Where in England she "held back," in Greek villages Liz was quietly liberated of social artificiality. Delighting in the two little ones, the village women, when told that Liz was "the yaya," hooted with laughter "because they couldn't believe she was the grandmother."[58] Indeed, Fowles complained that "because of her passionate empathy with Anna," Elizabeth seemed twenty years younger than he was; there was "a kind of generation gap between us."[59] They missed John, said Elizabeth, because they could not recognize all the flowers and birds but were happiest just to be alone. They never tired of each other's company. "It is as if there is no fuss," Liz wrote, "and we have no real demands, nothing is expected of us, we do not have to measure up to some standard imposed. . . . It is all a bit of a let down when we return."

Anna's need to reestablish some space of her own was part of the long deterioration of her marriage with Nick Homoky. She had resumed her own art of landscapes created in textiles, her photography, and her long-neglected study of dance. She applied for divorce in the fall of 1985, and it was granted in April 1986. Fowles wrote that the marriage was "wrecked temperamentally" by the couple themselves. But Elizabeth felt cast, by Nick at least, in the role of "Anna's evil genius."[60] To Monica and Denys she wrote of painful "strain and soul searching . . . because I encouraged Anna out of her doll like role of wife and mother. Expecting Nick to be more intelligent than he is. (The wrong one does.) I have also, as I see it now perhaps tried to make up for my past."[61] Fowles wrote that "all her past guilt" over Anna was aroused. "The notion that she is now partly responsible for inflicting this on her beloved grandchildren . . . is too much to bear." He and Nick, he thought, paid "for what happened thirty years ago."[62]

Torn between Anna and Nick, Fowles also suffered. While realistic in assessing Nick's role in the separation, Fowles still sympathized with him, telling Elizabeth that *both* men envied and suspected the dependence of the two women for each other. They both were "difficult women," he told Nick.[63] He identified with Nick, he wrote, from his "own nightmare . . . both he and I will bear unhappiness at home if we are allowed to follow our respective arts. . . . If that becomes impossible . . . we are done for; we become unforgivable male chauvinists, totally selfish, to be . . . irrefutably blamed."[64]

In December 1985, after a six-month gap in the diary, Fowles wrote that he had "just passed the most unhappy six months of my life." He had moved numbly through the September publication of *A Maggot* and the American publicity tour "as in a bad dream, a sea-mist. The people unreal, and myself ("John Fowles") most unreal of all."[65] The disintegration of Nick and Anna's relationship threw into sharp relief the stresses of the Fowleses' marriage. As John took Nick's part and Elizabeth argued for Anna, they battled wearily about themselves. As Christmas approached, Elizabeth mourned, "I thought I had a family about me and all was normal. . . . What years one lives in a blinkered state."[66]

While the world hailed John Fowles as the author of an internationally best-selling, critically applauded novel, the Fowleses privately absorbed blow after blow. A few days before Christmas 1985 they returned from London to Lyme Regis to discover that Belmont House had been robbed and vandalized.[67] A month later one of Fowles's neighbors entered the Belmont garden by stealth and cut down several beloved fruit trees to improve his own view. At the same time the museum was "on top of" the "Hon. Curator," as always preceding spring opening, and Tom Gilbert, Fowles's friend and closest support in the daily operation of the institution, died. Unable to tap his overseas or "company money," Fowles also worried about finding the wherewithal in his regular income to buy a Bristol flat for Anna and her children.[68] He felt anguish over the "dreadful ambiance of hopelessness in Britain" and increasingly loathed "most of modern life and its ways, its endless, unstoppable violence."[69]

This stress took its toll. At the end of January 1986 Fowles was dictating to Mary Scriven when his head began swimming and his immediate memory disappeared. Words vanished as he spoke them, and he kept asking Mary to repeat his phrases. "Blood pressure," said Mary, and urged Fowles to lie on the floor until a doctor could be called. However, he felt "obliged" to try to write, discovering in consternation that the wrong letters appeared on the page or that the order of letters was scrambled in each word. He felt "not very ill, but ill in some horrid way."[70] The doctor, when summoned, diagnosed dangerously high blood pressure, lectured Fowles on exercise, smoking, and diet, and prescribed Adalat, a calcium channel blocker called nefedipine. The medication had nasty side effects: "no strength, mental or physical, no will. Garden, Museum, my literary life, all goes to pot. I also forget everything. It is rather like dying . . . in the sense that it is a gentle decline, or incline."[71] Fowles resigned from chairing the Allsop Trust. He longed to lay down the burden of the Lyme Regis Museum, but no one would relieve him.

At this nadir of emotional and mental stress, Fowles conceived his last novel. He had long stopped wanting to publish. But this would be a novel not only unpublished but almost entirely unwritten. It would be a book dreamed. It would be, like *Daniel Martin* and the rejected thriller, a place of psychological refuge where Fowles would find some safety and comfort through very difficult times.

In Hellugalia was a landscape that came to him "out of nowhere" a few days after the blood pressure incident. "A journey," Fowles noted, "through a huge, flat, marshy garrigue-like sort of landscape to a coastal town. A mysterious central character . . . vague notions, moods. An arrival in a hotel, two women playing tennis." Vaguely he saw "an old woman in a lonely sea cottage; irises; folk-musicians; a seduction; a cold anti-hero, no normal views or opinions." He tried to place it in the Balkans but realized immediately that "this strange country is somehow fiction itself, behind its oddly distinct exterior, in my imagination. That notion appeared within a page or two of the writing. This is a visit 'to where fiction happens, rather than life' . . . something like that."[72]

His travelers in *A Maggot* had journeyed toward an incomprehensible experience they could not adequately express. The characters of *In Hellugalia* emerged over several years as part of an entirely "imagined country" in a state of constant fluid process. Lady Dee, an upper-class Englishwoman, wife of the ambassador, is seduced by The Brock, part mountain brigand, part nobleman, a leader in some nameless civil war. As an old woman she tells to a young writer her tale of love in wartime and personal transformation. From rereading Samuel Johnson's *Rasselas,* Fowles gained "a great clue" for realizing Hellugalia, that it "no more needs to 'conform' to Albania, or the Balkans, to whatever vague real model I had in mind, than Rasselas did . . . to Ethiopia."[73] He felt entirely free to invent flora and fauna for his mythical country "where fiction happens," creating with delight not only new species of orchids and poisonous spiders but even a "vegetarian dinosaur like *Scelidosaurus.*"[74] He appropriated the character of real botanical artist Margaret Mee, who died in 1988, and merged her with his fictional Lady Dee.[75] Characteristically, he also invented bits of language, salvaging intriguing words and concepts from his wide reading through the centuries. On pure whim he introduced disparate cultural influences into Hellugalia, including a Catalan invasion, a version of Gaelic second sight, and a Minoan bull leaping.[76]

Although he wrote small fragments over several years, a great part of

Fowles's pleasure in *In Hellugalia* derived from the "fluidity" of its largely unwritten text. The malleable period of creation had always been his favorite part of writing. In the case of this new novel, the malleable period simply continued indefinitely. This fluidity and unwritability were also something he wanted the story to convey. It was related to the notion of freedom that had dominated Fowles's thinking throughout his life. Novels, cinema, television, he wrote, "freeze or fix." They all conveyed a sense that the story was "past, and 'written'; now is abolished." There was no freedom to intervene in a "pre-destined" world where "all has been chosen." For the book he dreamed and planned, he wrote, "I must attack this increased fixing of now—its instant relegation to the past. . . . This is why the 'hero' says 'I am a narrator.' Not a writer. Narrators can intervene as they 'tell,' not as they write. That is, they only are, are true narrators, when they bend or choose events—in no way when they tell orally or write them." He wondered, "How do you express this in a novel?"[77] The answer, of course, was that the novel must be in constant change and could never be fixed by writing or by publishing. *In Hellugalia* was Daniel Martin's novel that "can never be read, lies eternally in the future."[78] It was the "unwritable . . . unfinishable . . . unimaginable . . . endlessly revisable . . . text without words" longed for by Miles and his muse in *Mantissa*.[79] John Fowles's imagination had come to dwell within it.

Made nervous by illness and medication and feeling a new tenderness for Elizabeth, Fowles agreed to join his wife, Anna, and the children for an Easter 1986 trip to Crete, his first return since the 1950s, even overlapping the itinerary with the Sharrockses. While dismayed by tourism and ugly overbuilding along the coast, Fowles rejoiced to find his "wild Greece," the Crete of natural history, "remains largely untouched . . . only a short distance inland."[80] He spent the days around his sixtieth birthday exploring nearby Minoan ruins inhabited by warblers and rich in orchids. Seeking the sawfly orchid, Fowles climbed high in the foothills to find caches of this *Orphrys tenthredinifera* growing in wild profusion. "Why," he asked himself over and over, "have I denied myself this for so long . . . when I could so easily have afforded it?"[81] *Tenthredinifera* blooming in the high hills of Crete became Fowles's symbol for the natural world that again called to him to explore.

John's illness and Anna's divorce made Elizabeth feel "abandoned" and "uncomforted." Depression often lay on her heart like "a sort of stone."[82]

She had only two close companions nearby. One was Leo Smith, who had returned to the area, settling in an Axmouth cottage that Elizabeth had found for her. Doris Whitton's pluck and sympathy also kept her daughter going. "One thing about old Doris, she is always good for a laugh," Liz would say, rolling her mother out in the wheelchair. "I think, what shall I do when she is no longer there?"[83] She needed the laughter, for her sense of humor—always her greatest saving grace—was lost. Elizabeth still noted the same sort of quirky comic incidents but now found them more pitiful than funny. "I experience in isolation," she realized at last. "There is no shared joke."[84] Her days of "semi major/minor public functions . . . press, cameras, a speech," gave her a "sense of emptiness . . . of merely functioning."[85]

Throughout 1986 and 1987 she tried to convince Fowles to move from Belmont. They were in their sixties. The house required constant repair; the garden was chaotically overgrown. Elizabeth had no love for Lyme, overrun by tourists and beachgoers in the summer and culturally desolate in the winter. She felt the town exploited her husband, and she resented it. Fowles shared her hatred of the summer horde and Lyme's limitations but felt the history and cultural preservation of the town were his special responsibility. For Belmont he had, Elizabeth said in exasperation, "a sort of romantic notion of the edifice,"[86] and he could not be separated from his beloved garden, whose wild confusion was his joy. They looked at many smaller houses in the countryside, easier to manage and close to woods and fields. Fowles remained stubbornly in love with Belmont, his garden, and Lyme Regis.

Perhaps in compensation, Elizabeth rashly pushed her husband into buying a new London flat in July 1986. By November, however, with payments made, keys in hand, and eager buyers for 48a Regent's Park Road waiting, John and Elizabeth looked at their new flat and hated it. Fay Maschler intervened to tell Fowles he must renege, that Elizabeth was "intolerably depressed."[87] With embarrassment, but considerable relief, they backed out of the move, remaining at Regent's Park Road and selling the new flat the following spring.

In December 1986 they visited Spain, where Fowles was to speak at the university in Zaragoza and for the British Council in Madrid. In Barcelona, on the second day of the journey, they were mugged. Elizabeth, carrying all their cash, passports, tickets, credit cards, keys, and medications, was pushed and thrown violently against a wall, her handbag

slashed from her with a knife.[88] It was the last professional tour Elizabeth
was to make with Fowles. Back at Belmont, a January freeze had burst the
pipes. Water "poured down on us through the floors and ceiling and soaking all the millions of books and paintings and water colours," reported
Elizabeth bitterly. "And I could not give a damn."[89]

Easily the worst disaster of all these difficult months was Mary
Scriven's move from Lyme at the end of the summer of 1986. Elizabeth
felt "her loss enormously in a personal way," but Fowles was "totally and
utterly shattered."[90] He hired a hopeless replacement, who lasted only
three weeks. He tried sending manuscripts and dictated voice tapes to
Mary, but ceased when they went astray in the post office. For ten
months, until Fowles hired Jean Wellings to type, Elizabeth tried to fill in
but was overwhelmed. "The damned letters pour in from the academics
and the thesis writers," she exclaimed, trying to learn Mary's filing system
as she answered letters. "What is this one on about?" she asked John.
"Structure of language . . . your attitude to Adam and Eve . . . May I
quote you on this? . . . What is the influence on your writing of L.
Sterne? . . . Did you imagine the language of servants or was it a valid
language of the time?"[91] She handled his correspondence, trying "to stem
the flood of things or people he could get involved in/with," because
Fowles's blood pressure continued to rise, despite medication, and he
continued to agree to new obligations. He was caught in a "pattern" that
he would not see, "agreeing to do things and then everything gets out of
control . . . blood pressure pills . . . a total lack of energy . . . a down-
down mood . . . does not seem to understand a word I say."[92] She blamed
the museum as Fowles's "mad obsession . . . as if he is the entire memory
of the town and its history." Each spring, she wrote desperately, he struggled with "The Curator's Report . . . each year it is a plea, please get me
out from this burden and he gets ill and iller. Takes all so deadly seriously. . . . And who cares!"[93] They argued over Fowles's Russian translator, a woman with "a romantic fix on J.F.," whose plan to stay with them
while Fowles sponsored her emigration made Elizabeth feel "creepy."[94]
Burdened by anxiety for her husband, Elizabeth lay sleepless at night,
"extremely irritable, then caring and concerned by turn."[95]

Elizabeth managed to get John to the Greek Peloponnese for an
Easter holiday with Anna and children and all the O'Sullivans. Feeling
better in June 1987, he urged Elizabeth to take another holiday with
Anna, then was prescribed a doubled dose of Adalat. When he was alone

at Belmont, Fowles's mind went into chaos, had "patches of lucidity, then into walking darkness." Instead of telephoning his doctor or a neighbor, he spent days and sleepless nights "absolutely buggered, in misery," trying to write through the anguish, telling his distress to diary pages that, messy with wild typing and spellings, witness his confusion and fear.[96]

On August 24, 1987, Doris Whitton died in the small local hospital near Belmont House. Seeing her mother lying dead, Elizabeth cried out in despair, "Oh, Doris, Doris. What shall I do without you?" When she read Fowles's diary account of how he had touched Doris's hands and arranged her body "as Eliz could not," she was infuriated by the fiction.[97] In one of her rare interventions in the diary, Elizabeth scrawled angrily down the margin: "*I touched her hands I fondled her hands You see nothing You feel nothing All you see is how you see.*" For months she was inconsolable.

Fowles went alone to Paris in November 1987 for the publication of *Le Créature,* the French translation of *A Maggot,* which was a huge bestseller. Elizabeth refused to join him. Fowles enjoyed admiring interviews and the best reviews he had ever had in France. In January the book was selected as Le Meilleur Livre de l'Année, France's top book of the year, by the influential Bernard Pivot in *Lire* magazine. Fowles felt bitterly confused by the disparity between this literary success and the "mess, despair, bloodymindedness" of his private life.[98]

The project that absorbed Fowles's attention as he entered 1988 was a planned dramatization of the famous 1869 Huxley-Wilberforce debate on evolution for a British Association production at Oxford and possible filming by the BBC. He was excited by the prospect of writing the script and did research for months. But in February 1988 he panicked. He felt unable to master the scientific theory, wondered why the acknowledged experts had not been consulted, knew he was both ill and ill prepared. Fretting over how to extract himself from the commitment, he actually worried himself sick.

In the early morning of February 14, 1988, in the Regent's Park Road flat, John Fowles awoke and could not stand. His right leg collapsed under him. He had suffered a stroke affecting his right side. Rushing from upstairs, Tom and Malou Wiseman called their doctor and brought Fowles to the Royal Free Hospital in Hampstead. The Wisemans sat with their friends for four long hours before Fowles was admitted as patient No. 42885.[99] After a CAT scan, he was shown the image of his cerebellum. All the dead blood vessels were "like the dead rootlets of some storm-capsized tree . . . bizarrely fenestrated . . . the lacunae of my brain; the loss of memory I have talked vaguely of for some time now is not imaginary." He lay in the hospital bed, stunned with loss, repeating, "Tenthredinifera, tenthredinifera . . ." like a mantra, the symbol of all he thought he would never see again. He longed for Elizabeth, "just to hold her hand."[100]

Elizabeth wrote a common letter to all John's contacts, explaining the "minor stroke," extracting him from "commitments on the literary side of his life," and diplomatically apologizing.[101] Fowles was unable to script the Huxley-Wilberforce debate re-creation for Oxford. He dropped an introduction for a Thomas Hardy study. He was unable to write a stage version of Hardy's *Jude the Obscure* that the National Theatre had requested. There would be many difficult months before he could write at all.

"This has been," wrote Fowles to the Sharrockses in a profoundly sad letter a month after the stroke, "what the doctors call a transient is-chaemic episode—one of their little jokes I have decided, as it is neither transient nor just an episode; much more a life-altering trauma, and bru-tal shock."[102] His balance was affected. In the first weeks he could not read with any concentration and could not write very well, not even a let-ter or journal entry. He could not understand the crossword puzzles in the newspaper. He had difficulty following a conversation.

Fowles was deeply depressed and numbed by medication when al-lowed to go home on March 2. Mail was piled so high inside Belmont that they couldn't open the front door. Emotionally at his most vulnera-ble, he wrote often of his love and need for Elizabeth. To his friends, John admitted that he had acted like "a sort of zombie with her for sev-eral years now."[103] He now realized that she was the "redemption" for meaning in his life. "Eliz is my not nothing," he wrote. "This is not an in-tellectual thing, however badly I put it . . . a last bit of wood to a drown-ing sailor."[104] His happiest time was lying in bed next to her, needing human warmth and company. When Anna arrived to visit, he felt "ab-surdly grateful." When they saw friends like the Wisemans, the Paynes, or the Sharrockses, they both felt "bereft" on their departure.[105] He shocked himself by nearly weeping upon seeing Anthony Sheil, his agent.[106] Denys Sharrocks recalled a day trip the four friends made in the summer after the stroke. When the two men were alone, Fowles turned sorrowfully to Denys and spread his arms in despair. "Denys," he said in a "black . . . very moving" voice, "I'm sorry I'm such a *mess*."[107]

Elizabeth kept him on the daily routine that led him toward recovery. Every morning for more than a year she worked through the *Guardian* crossword puzzle with him, though it would be a long time before he could do the "difficult" one alone. Every day, no matter the weather, she went walking with him. In London they went to Regent's Park or climbed Primrose Hill. In Dorset they drove to another village or area of the countryside, then walked for several miles. Tess Homoky, age nine, wrote of being dragged out into the rain on "a very very boaring walk." The distress and false cheer of the adults are plain through the child's tedium, as Fowles distractedly searches for penknife and binoculars and Anna takes her daughter aside and says "in a solem voice I'll have a private talk with you later about why we have to do this."[108] The walks were not easy for either of them. John's leg still dragged, and balancing required real effort. To venture out on Ware Cliffs was a great accomplishment in early days, and he had to allow himself to slide or fall to descend the steep grades. Elizabeth was now constantly short of breath, suffering chest complaints like colds or bronchitis with increasing frequency.

In October 1988 Fowles was successfully operated on for prostate difficulties at the Royal Free Hospital in London. Settled after admission, he urged Elizabeth to go alone to an Old Vic preview of *The Tempest,* directed by Jonathan Miller. As the music rose, she realized it was composed by Carl Davis, who had written the music for *The French Lieutenant's Woman.* "What the hell am I doing?" she wondered, "with tears blinding me." Watching the play, with Max von Sydow as Prospero, she thought of the faraway days when "we did that play with those boys at Spetsia. We cut and rewrote the script and I trained the village girl to mouth Miranda . . . all such silly youthful unknowing fun." In tears, Elizabeth fled to the London flat, like Fowles, to write out her anguish. "So here I sit with a cheese sandwich (third) and a M and S bottle of wine (3.50 p) drunkenly typing. The vision . . . of dear old battered JF standing there as I left him . . . I needed old Doris. . . . And it was by chance my birthday. Sixtyfuckingthree."[109]

Though disengaged from his writing commitments, Fowles was still the curator of the museum. To his surprise and relief, Liz-Anne Bawden volunteered in March 1988 to take the position. Formerly an opinionated liberal town councillor, Bawden had her critics as well as allies. In the manner of provincial politics, there was controversy over her appointment to the museum curator's post, but Fowles, as much as health permitted, lent his support. "Liz-Anne may make mistakes," he wrote as he turned over the reins, "but they won't be of silly small-town intrigue and dishonesty."[110] With Jo Draper's help, Bawden retrieved the archive files of the museum from Fowles's study, relieving him of a decade's burden while diplomatically replacing the originals with copies for his Belmont files. Bawden gave him the title Honorary Archivist and welcomed Fowles's interest in research issues.[111]

His professional life as a writer halted for a time. An ongoing project that he truly cared about was the planned BBC production of *Daniel Martin.* Peter Prince had completed four scripts for a television miniseries about which both Fowles and producer Colin Rogers were enthusiastic. The surviving scripts are compelling, with excellent characterization and a true sense of the flow between past and present that distinguishes the book.[112] In March 1988, however, the new head of dramatic production dropped the option, citing financial reasons. In April there was "a nasty little piece in the *Sunday Times*: 'Many critics found it unreadable, now it has proved unfilmable.'" Fowles felt "numb and hurt, hopelessly wounded."[113]

At the time of the stroke, the examining neurologist at the Royal Free Hospital had said to Fowles, "You have lost your righting ability," meaning that the stroke had affected his ability to balance. Fowles heard, "You have lost your *writing* ability." Horrified, it was more than a day before he could ask what the man had meant. But he was to realize, grimly, that his imaginative capacity for fiction was gone. He no longer thought, he said, in constantly shifting alternative possibilities, but in simple straightforward situations.[114] Fowles had always written out of his own experience, and his fictions were largely about a displaced first person, a "John Fowles" character placed in a richly imaginative situation and transformed or disguised. From February 1988 Fowles is never disguised again in the writing. He wrote ever after in the first person, as an "I" offering direct personal anecdote and personal opinion.

By July 1988 Fowles was attempting to write again for publication. Picador was issuing a new paperback edition of *The Magus,* and Fowles was asked to write a guest column for the *Independent's* "Second Thoughts" feature. He contributed "Possessed by a Spell," a little memoir of his mistakes and feelings as he wrote the original *Magus,* then as he revised it ten years later. What he remembered, he wrote, was "the delicious and heady voyage of self-deception, the creating of the fiction, the unholy pleasure of playing god." A mere five hundred words, "Possessed by a Spell" cost Fowles at least five rambling drafts and pages of cramped notes.[115] He managed a little introduction to a collection of Don McCullin photographs, *Open Skies,* a month later. It was "just polite verbiage," but Fowles was encouraged. Elizabeth had helped him "cut some bad bits out; seldom to be faulted, her instincts here," he noted.[116] A year after his stroke he labored for weeks writing a review of William Golding's *Fire Down Below.* "Battle and struggle and write and rewrite," wrote Elizabeth sadly, "All for a piddling newspaper review. . . . Reading is all go, but then he has to get out 800 words." The effort brought on a severe attack of vertigo that left Fowles bedridden for days. "He is trying to prove something," she wrote sympathetically, "but mostly he is envious of Golding writing and he cannot."[117]

Only Fowles's diary was continued without terrible anguish of compositional effort. "I can write after a fashion here," he noted late in 1988; "indeed writing this, or keeping it, is my sole consolation these days."[118] As his daily walks exercised his body, so the diary was Fowles's exercise in words, difficult immediately after the stroke, but gaining in strength and suppleness as the months went on. For two years, however, the diary was more or less a record of observation, a cold eye on his daily life: walks, meals, shopping, health, minor travels, visitors, nature notes, times with Elizabeth. It recorded books, films, occasional notes for *In Hellugalia.* The voice is melancholy, vulnerable, and often despairing. With few exceptions, it is not the outpouring of the powerful, creative mind it had been since 1947 but is John Fowles's obstinate declaration that his life was still lived in words on the page.

Elizabeth had longed for John's attention. Now she struggled with his total dependence. Her entire life spun on the axis of keeping him going, and she could not leave him for more than a few hours at a time. Her fortnights alone in London with friends, her impulsive trips alone to Anna in Bristol were a thing of the past. The first time she left Fowles alone overnight was to attend the annual Jonathan Cape party in December 1988. They had agreed to go together, but Fowles had "flunked it" at the last minute. "I . . . wouldn't hear half of what was said," he wrote morosely. "I am too much of a literary wreck, a ghoul, to want to meet anyone, or imagine they should want to meet me. . . . I could not face other writers because I should be so envious. To command words, it is the impossible."[119] So Elizabeth, exhausted and worried, "did all the duty talks that JF should have, but did not. I found myself playing a role, John Fowles wife . . . talked to new authors, as if I were some old dowager. I felt old and yet still young . . . They get at him through me and hold my hand in affection and admiration."[120]

Elizabeth had some comfort, knowing that her daughter was in a positive relationship at last. In 1988 Anna Christy had met Charles Glass, a Bristol architect, also divorced with two children. "They are rather soppily in love, touching and hand-holding, all the rest," Fowles harrumphed, "but have an 'innocence' we find rather touching."[121] In her happiness, Anna asked Elizabeth and John to join them and the grandchildren for a holiday in Crete in May 1989. Fowles found his "wild Greece" once more but often felt self-exiled from the interests of his family. He was disappointed, but mistaken in his belief that none of the others shared his appreciation of the vast, the archetypal, and the unchanging in "the Crete I build from old memories."[122]

They often visited gardens in Devon and Dorset with Leonora Smith. Fowles and Leo shared a passionate interest in gardening, and Elizabeth remarked to Leo's daughter, Sarah, that her amusement on these excursions was listening to their rivalry. Sarah herself occasionally accompanied them. Now in her early forties and an advertising executive in London, the single and sophisticated Sarah Smith had recently returned from a year in India. Seeing her go in 1986, Fowles had commented, "She is a chic liberal, I'm afraid, paying for her long thraldom in the advertising world."[123] Irreverent in her opinions and smart in her manner, Sarah Smith amused Fowles, and he looked forward to her company. She often complained of hating her job and longing to relocate to Lyme Regis.

Elizabeth leaned heavily on Leo Smith, using the need to go to the markets near Axmouth as her excuse to visit this friend on her own. As the late-afternoon light faded in her cottage sitting room, Leo would hear a knock on the window and see "that tall figure outside," Elizabeth leaning down to look in. The two women would have a cup of tea by the fire, then a glass or two of whiskey and "a giggle together. (You can't giggle in the same way with John. Can't at all.)" Fowles, said Smith, "didn't like being on his own" and was annoyed that the two were drinking together. He would ring up to ask when his wife was coming home and how he would have his supper. "Tell him to put the potatoes on," Elizabeth would say, rising to go. She told Leo that John "would watch and wait" for her.[124] She said the same to her sister-in-law. It did not escape Hazel O'Sullivan that this was the very phrase her own mother had used to describe Robert Fowles's attitude to her in his old age.[125]

Fowles's "drift" and querulousness (so evident in his diary), his poor health, the provincial town, and "this half-life we lead" made Elizabeth feel more irritated and trapped.[126] Through 1989 she became ever more depressed, distant, and angry. She withdrew into sleep or books, occasionally writing letters through a sleepless night. "Eliz is in a poor state," Fowles complained in a typical comment, "very cross-tempered, totally indifferent to what I am doing." Her "total indifference to what she is, and what I am, is chilling. . . . She destroys all warmth."[127] Others who loved her also worried. Even Anna said later that throughout this year Liz "had not been herself."[128] Through the final six months of 1989 John Fowles was ill, exhausted, and critical of nearly everything he observed. Elizabeth Fowles was ill, fatigued, and angry. In their concern over John's health, everyone but Anna seems to have missed the signs that Elizabeth was failing. Fowles wrote: "She is difficult these days, like a bad-tempered, frightened cat, so quick to the spitting and the claws. . . . I sound angry in defense, sometimes before she even speaks."[129]

Through the diary Fowles, by his words and his perceptions, controlled the record of their life together. One late November afternoon Elizabeth edited that record with an impetuous wrath similar to her letter-burning incident in 1982. On the pages from September through November, she scrawled furious marginal comments beside those of Fowles's entries that judged her, presumed to record her opinions, or criticized those she loved. These enraged notations seem a desperate effort to escape an entrapping text in which her husband had pinned her. "You say *we*," she fumed. "*We* did not. . . . I am not a *we*." . . . "You assume my rejection. Your silence is rejection. Always you presume. Always you say nothing. But presume." On October 7, he had not only ignored her sixty-fourth birthday but spent an outing with Leo Smith, lecturing them both on a book and writer Elizabeth had read and he had not. "You performed on a book you hadn't even read," she wrote in fury, "You shout over your opinion. . . . And my not even existing. . . . I was discounted, criticized, put down." He sarcastically judged the cottage of an artist couple for their modernist work and "chic décor." She wailed back: "We create nothing. We never move on we remain static. They totally rebuild & enlarge a tiny cottage. We live in a dead dying house & garden now too large and unnecessary for us. It had a life once. Now it is gone." When he was sharp about her grandchildren, saying they acted bored or insufficiently grateful, Elizabeth exploded in gasping fragments: "You did not. Did not want. And can't imagine. You were and always will be dead about living reality of children . . . you understand nothing of graceless impatience in children. You know nothing about children. You are theory and non-life. Pretend 'Nature' is all." When he condemned others' purchases as part of some "bourgeois capitalist corruption," Elizabeth asked, "Question. Why your buying in the 60's 70's was not corrupt we have evidence standing about dust collecting pots. Volumes . . . Why did you buy and barter for objects in auctions . . . Teapots, cups, and plates . . . We are crippled with possessions." When he discounted the lives of Londoners he saw walking in Regent's Park as "such unfree worlds of repression," she snarled: "You walk with your feeling of freedom in a park. And criticize people for not living in the country. You do not live in the country. You potter about your garden and a seaside town." Now, she raged, "you become the Censorous critic. You lived once. You do not anymore. . . . What poetry do you express in anything? It has long since died."[130]

How, Fowles wondered, could Elizabeth not understand "how destructive to both of us is her resentment of everything in Lyme and my life?" He loved her "with a kind of hopelessness."[131] She told him she no longer wanted to live.[132]

They spent Christmas 1989 in Grasse, France, with Tom and Malou Wiseman, grateful to be with affectionate old friends. Malou was shocked at Elizabeth's emphysema, shortness of breath, and inability to walk any distance. She recalled Fowles's urging Elizabeth to give up cigarettes, saying he would quit if she would.[133]

In January 1990 the disease that had been Elizabeth's shadow companion of the past months became impossible to ignore. She had agonizing pains in her back and stomach. Insomnia. Nosebleeds. No appetite. Doctors who saw her in January scheduled tests into mid-February. When on Tuesday, February 20, she was finally able to see a chest specialist, he was so shocked at her wasted appearance that he bullied the hospital in Exeter into finding a bed for her. The next day he took blood platelet counts, then a bone marrow sample. Elizabeth, he told John Fowles, was riddled with advanced cancer, ultimately diagnosed as pancreatic cancer, one of the swiftest and most deadly forms. Lungs, stomach, liver, uterus, and bone marrow all were infected. She probably had a fortnight to live, he said. He was wrong. It was nine days.

Anna Christy arrived at Belmont and dreamed that night of her mother, walking toward her "very drawn and terribly old."[134] Filled with dread on the drive home from the hospital on Wednesday, she pulled over by the roadside, and Fowles told his stepdaughter the searing news. They wept together. Leo Smith was at Belmont when they arrived, watching Tess, who had become sick in the night. "I shall never, *never* forget poor Anna's face," Leo recalled, "and I flung my arms around her . . . and tried to comfort her." But Fowles, she thought, had "the most extraordinary . . . sort of a smile on his face."[135] He immediately went up to his workroom. Within minutes they could hear the thudding sound of the typewriter as Fowles wrote in the diary, registering the harsh reality in his own way.

On Friday, John Fowles, with Anna beside him, told Elizabeth that she was dying. Only Elizabeth did not break down. She laughed a little. "I won't go to Corfu," she said. "What about the children?" and "I can't believe it, this isn't real, it's not happening."[136]

Elizabeth Fowles was brought home to Belmont House by ambulance on Saturday, February 24. A nursing service was secured. Anna's children returned to Bristol with their father, and Charles Glass arrived to support Anna. John felt helpless, "hopeless and useless."[137] He was physically unable to share the labor of caring for his wife. Anna could hear him weeping in the night, a horrible keening wail. He wrote his way through the experience, sometimes noting details that he would assign to the Lady Dee character of *In Hellugalia*. He received kind, supportive daily visits from a local friend, Dr. Michael Hudson, who helped him understand what was happening. The speed of events bewildered Fowles, and sometimes he continued to hope that there would be some remission from a short course of chemotherapy his wife had received.

Neither Elizabeth nor Anna had any such illusions. Anna, clearheaded and accepting, took over her mother's medication and care and was always grateful that the two had shared those final days. As they had done in Greece on their holidays, Anna "made a home" for Liz. They joked about it while Anna cleaned the bedroom windows to let in light and the view, adjusted the furniture, and sealed any cracks from drafts. They had their small rituals. Liz could barely manage food but would say with comic archness, "I will have my little bit of porridge now." Fowles noted that she had "flashes of her old humour, pawky dryness" that pierced his numbness.[138] Liz read an article aloud to Anna from the *Spectator* "about February being the month for dying, and the food one serves, and so on . . . oh, it made us laugh." Liz wondered about an afterlife and tried, in an oblique way, to tell Anna of her terrible guilt at having left her when she was a child, "that she'd made such a mess, so-called, of my life." "That doesn't matter," said Anna. "What we've got now is greater than anything that we could have had earlier. She would live in me and in my children and in my memories of her." Anna also assuaged her worries over what would happen to John Fowles: "I was sure we would find a way."[139]

From Sunday to Wednesday Elizabeth weakened as the cancer moved rapidly through her system. The nurses taught Anna how to lift her mother and how to help her take a slow walk around the bedroom. To be handled, even gently, left bruises on Elizabeth's arms and back. Her beautiful face was so wasted that Leo Smith, briefly making her daily morning visit on Wednesday, could barely look at her. What would happen to John? Elizabeth asked her friend. Leo could not answer.[140]

Watching her mother waste and weaken, Anna concluded that their time would be brief. On Wednesday night, February 28, she laid a table at the foot of Liz's bed and brought John in to have supper beside her. "I didn't say to him at the time, 'This might be your last evening with her,' but I felt it strongly."[141] Anna lay in the bed beside her mother through the last night, with the nurse keeping watch outside. Elizabeth was in great pain. On the morning of Thursday, March 1, she spoke a little with John and Anna. Around noon she was given morphine intravenously, and within an hour, with John and Anna beside her, she had slipped into the deep final sleep and hoarse, rasping breathing induced by the morphine.

Fowles had telephoned Monica and Denys Sharrocks the night before, but Elizabeth was past speech or recognition when they arrived. Fowles said numbly, "We cannot take them up."[142] Monica simply walked in and kissed her dying friend. Through the afternoon, each watcher took a turn beside the brass bed where Elizabeth lay. Around five o'clock Denys was moved to see John kneeling by his wife, speaking urgently, smoothing her face.[143] Just before seven Denys went to keep the vigil while the others prepared a meal. Denys talked to Elizabeth. There was a lot to remember. When he said, ". . . and we love you," her terrible rasping breathing ceased.

When Denys came and stood in the kitchen door, the other three could not speak or move. He said, "I think you ought to go up. . . . Her breathing has changed. . . . I don't know. . . ." It was a long moment before anyone moved. Then John climbed the stairs, with Anna behind him, and Monica and Denys following. They saw John then, half crouched in the bedroom doorway, his hands held "like paws in front of his face."[144]

He howled.

CHAPTER TWENTY

Tendresse

Domaine perdu *and Afterward: 1990–2000*

I had never comprehended this, the absoluteness *of never.*

—JOHN FOWLES, *DIARIES,* MARCH 9, 1990

The *Times* of March 6, 1990, carried the obituary notice: "Fowles, Eliza-beth . . . mother of Anna and wife of John."[1] It touched Anna Christy that John Fowles named her first. Roy Christy wrote to his old rival, "Tough luck, old man. Now neither of us has got her."[2]

On the day the notice appeared, Fowles was staggered by a telephone call from Sanchia Humphreys. In her "rather elegant, successful, edu-cated" voice, she improbably queried Fowles about the disposal of the letters he had written her in 1954. Fowles was pushed "out of my depth" by this call from the "ghost" of "that 'other' life refused . . . so many years ago."

He was confused by Elizabeth's absence. "Boyzo," he would call ab-sentmindedly, "where's my . . . where's the . . . ?" Each time the tele-phone rang, he felt for an instant that Elizabeth "had got through." He wept over recordings of Django's "Les Billets Doux" or Billie Holiday singing "Easy to Love" or "No Regrets."[3] In the garden he listened for the jangle of the bell his wife had used to call him "when she wanted me and I was lost in some corner." The echoes of Elizabeth's being and the fact of her not being harrowed John Fowles for years.

Elizabeth Fowles's memorial service was held at 2:00 P.M. on Friday, March 9, 1990, at the Exeter Crematorium. Twenty-two mourners gath-ered at the nonreligious, humanist service. Britten's *War Requiem* was performed. Readings included Elizabeth's Greek winter poem and John's "By the Appian Way." The passage from *The Magus* in which Nicholas contemplates and mourns Alison's presumed death ("a shovelful of ashes . . . remembering her, remembering her") was read, those present had always known that Elizabeth was Alison. Fowles had also selected a passage about "the writer's wife" from *Nora,* Brenda Maddox's biography of Nora Joyce, one of the last books Elizabeth had read: "Theirs was a constant companionship based on love and congenial understanding. . . . Unless one had seen them together one would not realize how much he depended on her. . . . It was Nora . . . who held them together with her courage and rock-firm common sense. . . . Her grandson said 'She was a rock. He would have done none of it, written not one of his books without her.'"[4]

Ronnie Payne spoke on behalf of the "fortunate circle who knew them well," of "Elizabeth and John . . . John and Elizabeth." Payne remembered her sizing him up at first meeting, his relief at passing "the test," and her last words to him, an embrace and "I do like a good hug." He spoke of sharing with Elizabeth "a sense of wonder" at starting from humble beginnings to "become citizens of a different world," of how she had left Walsall to be "transformed into an elegant, beautiful and intelligent lady equally at home in Athens, New York, Paris and the West End." He spoke—through tears—of Elizabeth's love, loyalty, and pride for John, even of her occasional exasperation with him; of her deep love and pride for Anna, "as an artist and as a woman." He added, "Amazed to find herself a grandmother, and never successful at looking like one, she was devoted to her grandchildren. . . . It is hard to believe that she is gone."[5]

Beyond the terrible loneliness, Fowles was scalded by memories of the past few years when he and Elizabeth had been estranged in many ways. Each evening, as the light faded, he was overcome by "bitter waves of being alone" and recalled "the awful frigidity of our lives together in those last two or three years, ever since the dread sexlessness struck."[6] Writing of "the grimnesses of solitude" to Anna, he at last understood Elizabeth's "hatred of this town and our life in it." "Eliz's memory-ghost stands there with a dry light in her eyes," he wrote her daughter; "now I know why she always so loathed the small, the provincial, the not-London."[7] "The horror that it happened as it did, that we should have been such fools with time, somehow believing in 'always,' . . . keeps returning to me in waves, like nausea. . . . The silences we sat in . . . oh God . . . from the voice one should have treasured most, silence, silence, silence."[8]

People did their best. Anna visited often. Leo Smith called in frequently. Fowles's friends from the museum dropped by: Jo Draper and Chris Chaplin, Joan Walker, and Liz-Anne Bawden. Mike and Anne Hudson visited often. Peter Benson came several days a week. There was little professional life to distract him, and Fowles could not find the will or energy to begin a new project. He worked off and on writing captions for *Lyme Regis Camera,* a collection of vintage photographs of the historic town and its people that he had long wanted to make more accessible. Jo Draper helped him make the selection, and the book was published late in 1990, copyrighted to the museum. Working on a project for the museum, Jo Draper stayed a night each week at Belmont. Her down-to-earth kindness was a solid support for Fowles in his loneliest time.

In April Fowles went to Andros, Greece, with Anna and her children and Charles Glass. After her mother's funeral Anna had revealed that Charles had quietly proposed marriage during the week of Liz's last illness at Belmont. Their wedding was planned for mid-September in Bristol, and they would honeymoon on Spetsai. In Greece, Fowles felt Elizabeth constantly, "here and not here." Her "total goneness . . . haunts me every day." He could not exchange knowing looks with her and had no one with whom to be intimate. "Far less for what that may seem to entail or mean physically; but the letting one's mind, one's persona, both outward and inner, be naked."[9] He found, there as in his garden at home, "that things seen by one person are somehow not seen, how seeing is a shared, joint experience if it is fully real. Seeing alone becomes a kind of blindness."[10] In his diaries, Fowles realized that "even here I write as if she were reading, she will read it one day. . . . It is *never* being able to say what is in the heart, what one truly is."[11]

Fowles could not manage his solitary life at Belmont. Anna had discussed this with him during Elizabeth's final illness and suggested that since Sarah Smith constantly complained of her job and wanted to relocate to Lyme Regis, perhaps she would make a temporary arrangement with him.[12] Fowles, to Leo Smith's dismay, had wasted no time. Telephoning Leo on the evening of Elizabeth's death, he asked her to come over the next day. When she arrived after the mortician's van departed,

Fowles drew her apart into the garden. Did she think, Fowles asked Leo, that her daughter Sarah would be willing to leave London for Lyme Regis, live in the Belmont flat, and "housekeep" for him? Leo was shocked, thinking, "How extraordinary! At *this* time to be thinking of yourself." She thought her daughter might be bored, she said, but he would have to ask for himself.[13] After the funeral Fowles asked Sarah. She considered. Ultimately, however, she turned him down in a letter that spoke of the things she still envisioned for her life—both in her profession and in returns to India.[14] In April, Fowles asked Ann Jellicoe to recommend someone suitable to housekeep for him. He assured her that there would be "no funny business, 'I'm well past that,' he said."[15]

Fowles was quite attracted to Sarah Smith, though admitting he hardly knew her. He thought her like "a robin" in her bright energy, her start-and-stop conversation.[16] She was slight, "faintly boyish . . . very pretty," with "red-brown hair."[17] He noted her "delicate, bare sandalled feet, the toenails bright red, a coral anklet round one of them." She tinkled with wrist and ankle jewelry, made him hold her rings when they went to the beach with Anna and Leo.[18] Embarrassed by his "folly of suggesting she might come and 'companion' me," Fowles still felt "tempted" to touch her. He dreamed of holding her. He disliked her "ad-agency world" but thought her "bright and independent,"[19] speaking "the same language" as he did. Sarah guarded that independence, however, and there was "something suspicious, wary" in her attitude to him.[20]

He often longed to hold Anna as well, though this was associated with Elizabeth, whom she so resembled. Sometimes, sitting with Anna in the evening out of doors, it felt to John that "Eliz joins us," that they sat "in Eliz's aura." He feared Anna would not understand if he touched her. "I do not even take her hand. I read."[21]

Fowles came to define his yearning to be close to women by the French word *tendresse*. Existing in the nostalgic consciousness of the loss of sexual desire, these were "feelings which a certain kind of woman inspires in me; they are my *tendresses*. I dream far less of a truly sexual intimacy, than of a human closeness." He went on: "Yes, it involves being alone with the object (though making her a subject, another I); alone with her, in that self-fictional world—myself in a dream world, an imagined one—that seems the only reality left me."[22] In the summer after Elizabeth's death, John Fowles met such a girl.

Elena van Lieshout was twenty-one when she arrived at the door of

Belmont, an undergraduate about to enter her final year reading English at St. Hilda's College, Oxford. Welsh on her mother's side, Dutch on her father's, Elena had grown up, their only child, in the North Wales village of Bala. She was a talented pianist with ambitions for the concert stage. Her parents struggled to give her the necessary training, sending her to music school in Manchester as a teenager. Entering Oxford University, she abandoned music for literature. Lyme Regis had become a kind of bolt-hole for her by that time, inspired by an interest in John Fowles and *The French Lieutenant's Woman.* She had been coming to Lyme alone, for solace when unhappy, since 1985, when she was sixteen. In late May 1990 she arrived to arrange a summer job as a waitress at the Bell Cliff restaurant. Her landlady remarked sadly that Mr. Fowles had recently lost his wife to cancer. Elena slipped a note of condolence through the letter slot at Belmont. Fowles returned a note of thanks, adding that the next time she visited Lyme she should come to see him.[23]

On July 6, facing a weekend without Anna or other visitors, Fowles wrote in his diary of "the black aftermath" of Elizabeth's death, how waves of solitude "flood back, blocking all present life out, crushing it like a roller." He felt perpetually ill and exhausted, unable to work, and will-less. "I miss her, I miss her," he repeated, "as a child its mother; which she always accused me of, that I sought a mother in her, not what she was or saw herself as."[24] On July 9, 1990, Elena van Lieshout came to tea.

Fowles told Denys Sharrocks that Elena's coming was "like a visitation."[25] She was, in his eyes, the composite of all his adored muses since Monique, since Sanchia, genuinely a visitation from the *domaine perdu* of his imagination. That afternoon Elena stood on the doorstep like "a demure Welsh princess." She was slender, "a slight body, in a print dress." Her long dark hair gleamed with the red lights of henna; her eyes were "beautifully grave and dark brown . . . sepia pools; a timid child's eyes." She had a "pretty face," a warm, shy smile. Her whispery, little-girl voice held "only a trace of an accent, the occasional Welsh lilt." When Elena left three hours later, Fowles upbraided himself for not asking "her to come and live here and housekeep during her long vac. . . . the idea of sharing this house for a month or two with what seems a bright girl."[26] When, on the twenty-fifth, she returned a book he had lent her, Fowles asked her to "come and Cinderella for me here."[27] By July 30, 1990, Elena had moved in: to Fowles's house, his bed, his life. He was sixty-four years old. Incapable of living in the world of bereavement and loneliness, Fowles entered his "other" world, the kingdom apart with its muse princess, its solitary pleasures, its romantic code of chivalric language. "Life imitating art," said his friends.[28]

"Some little miracle of good fortune, like a delicious gust of spring rain, has swept over my dry self," Fowles wrote in grateful disbelief. "Its name is Elena." He was overwhelmed that "anyone of her age, 21, feminine, pretty, in her second year at Oxford, should have a moment's patience with me."[29] For two months, until Elena returned to Oxford, the two dwelt in a private, romantic world in Lyme Regis and in London. It was an intensely "literary" world, and Fowles regarded it as a "situation from a novel."[30] Indeed, the entire relationship was rendered, for Fowles at least, in literary metaphors. Elena was John's "Cinderella," cooking and keeping house for him ("she's an awful housekeeper," he admitted[31]). She was also "Morgan le Fay," the dark enchantress of the King Arthur stories who spirits the old king away to the isle of Avalon. In this mode, said Fowles, Elena was "grave enchantment, and I am bewitched; the way we have wreathed tentacles around each other's souls, got to know each other, is *marvellous,* in all the old sense of that word . . . and the modern ones also. In another, darker, world I sense I am out of my depth, I'm not sure what is really happening."[32] He was, he said, like the victim "in all those old Celtic folk-tales," someone "almost wilfully bewitched." She was like the *princesse lointaine* who "so entranced Marie de France and her audiences."[33] He was "Ulysses unbound, the sirens' prey. All wisdom, all reason, regulation, normality, is washed away, as in a flash flood."[34] As if to seal the role she played for him, Fowles gave Elena one of the rare 1979 broadside copies of his beautifully printed 1978 poem, *Conditional,* in which the teasing muse figure becomes the poet's inspiration *because* they do not consummate their desire. Fowles was keenly aware of the forty-three-year gap between them and wrote and spoke daily of his impotence. But he speculated, as if writing fiction, what it would have been like to win and marry this girl, indeed, even what their children would have been like.

Elena also made his own books live, as Fowles was aware. The girl was self-consciously inspired by Sarah Woodruff in *The French Lieutenant's Woman,* seeing herself as rebellious and determined to live entirely on her own terms. In early August, Fowles took her to the spot in the Undercliff where his character had made her fictional "confession" in the twentieth chapter of the novel. They sat on "the bough of a collapsed tree on the knap leading to the spring, beneath Chimney Rock" by "a bed of enchanter's nightshade, *Circaea,* still in flower; always a faintly magical plant for me." Leaning back against Fowles, in a blue sheath dress with a short skirt, she spoke "in little spurts of confession . . . not quite unconsciously repeating the role of Sarah in *The FLW* (she is to do a paper on me for her degree); the outwardly demure but inwardly self-consumed woman, obsessed by her own freedom and how she may achieve it, all that spirit in the book."[35] He recognized that the scene of an older man dwelling in isolation in an enchanted place with a much younger woman echoed throughout his fiction. Friends noted parallels to Fowles's story "The Ebony Tower." Peter Benson, for example, told of arriving at Belmont on an August day when Anna was visiting. Benson saw Fowles sitting in the garden, with two young, beautiful women in two-piece bathing suits lounging on chairs on either side of him. "It was so much like that story of his," said Benson, "that I was taken aback."[36]

Literary or not, the erotically charged relationship was not easy for many to accept. The gossiping tongues of Lyme Regis wagged, but Fowles did not care. "I am half-soppy about her," he declared. "I don't care what they think in Lyme or who sees us."[37] Anna Christy struggled to understand at first but soon despised Elena nearly as much as Elena despised her. Beyond John's attitude to this girl, it was difficult to watch—only six months after Liz's death—a determined undergraduate take possession of her mother's house, her mother's bed, even her mother's favorite ring, which Fowles had given her. Anna refused to have Elena at her September 15 wedding to Charles Glass, and Fowles attended with Leo Smith and Sarah Smith, who was Anna's witness. Elena was bitter and John was angry that Anna was "shocked and obtuse."[38] He was angrier still about Leo Smith. He had introduced Elena to Leo, then seventy-five, and Leo judged the girl an opportunist, a "hanger-on for money." Leo was very embarrassed by the "fuss" Fowles made of Elena in public and thought him "totally and utterly enthralled."[39] Some weeks after Anna's wedding, Fowles visited Leo and tried to explain. Her "conventional" viewpoint ("so much the old vicar's daughter") made him so angry that they did not communicate again for two and a half years.[40] "I am not forgiven for seeming to have forgotten Eliz. I have not and shall not. Our schism is really between my total atheism and their variously lingering Christianity."[41] There were those who accepted the situation, like Ronnie Payne and Celia Haddon, who saw John return to life and interest after the harrowing solitude of losing Elizabeth, or like Fowles's secretary, Jean Wellings, who tended to have a sensible, pragmatic tolerance for all of Fowles's behavior. Visiting almost daily, Peter Benson was fascinated by the unfolding situation and liked Elena, even giving her driving lessons in Fowles's car.

After her winter term at Oxford, with its stolen weekends and nightly phone calls, Fowles was determined to marry the girl. At this, she turned away suddenly and fiercely. To keep her in his life, Fowles accepted that they would be only "friends" and offered to hire her as his "assistant" when she finished at the university. For Elena's use, he bought a flat over-looking the sea in Lyme, which she occupied from June 1991 until November 1992. He turned over his car to her and bought himself another. "She has two almost diametrically opposed faces," he wrote as he knew her better, "one soft and sweet, the other as hard, as callous as a diamond or a razor."[42] He had fallen for the first persona in the summer of 1990; he became intimately acquainted with the second during the next two years.

Elena experienced wild mood swings and veered unpredictably in her intentions and ambitions. During her time in Lyme Regis she nurtured fantasies of becoming a novelist, then an actress, then once more a concert pianist. Nothing was to stand in the way of her success, which was to happen speedily. In her hometown newspaper Elena's mother boasted that her daughter was to be—at age twenty-two—"Fowles's full-time editor and researcher . . . [with] full power to edit and rewrite some of his novels . . . given a free hand."[43] However, as she nominally worked as Fowles's assistant, Elena was absent or late or wrote her own stories or letters to her friends ("what a bad joke she is as any kind of secretary or assistant"[44]). Fowles was trying to revise *Tesserae,* his novel from 1959, to show to Tom Maschler. Elena decided that she disliked it and refused to type it. She could turn suddenly vitriolic, with a temper that scorched Fowles. In such moods she became "Medusa [with] her beady, staring eyes"[45] or the Eumenides, the classical furies. In one of their ugliest battles, she accused him of being "no better than the man in *The Collector*."[46]

Her sweet moods and kisses were dear to Fowles, and dear they cost him. He paid for her bank overdrafts, her clothes, her jewelry, her parking fines, her hefty telephone bills. He threw her and her friends a party at Belmont when she finished at Oxford and took her to literary events among such old friends and colleagues as Margaret Drabble, Michael

Holroyd, Doris Lessing, and Rose Tremain. He paid for her to travel alone in Europe and for her parents to have a holiday in Vienna. He paid her way on trips to the Scilly Islands, Portugal, and the United States, all occasions on which she behaved remorselessly toward him, setting up his expectations, abandoning him, quarreling with him in front of hosts. He bought a Broad Street flat in historic Pyne House for her use and gave her 50 percent more salary than he had originally offered when she declared, "I'm an Oxford graduate now!"[47] She had use of his car, and she wrecked it. He bought her a piano, paid for London piano lessons and her travel to and fro. He paid for her application to the Royal Academy of Dramatic Art and was prepared to pay her tuition had she been accepted. He paid for her application to the Royal Academy of Music and was prepared to pay her tuition had she been accepted. "She uses me?" wrote Fowles. "Very well, all right, she does. Even if true, what am I to do? Refuse to be used—and join the dead?" He likened her calculations in her overall feelings for him as "no more than Sycorax' and Prospero's magic . . . deeply better that than none."[48] She was his "muse . . . or whatever it is that enchants and tortures, that inspires and twists one."[49]

However, if Elena was Fowles's muse (thereby the Erato of *Mantissa*), she did not inspire works of fiction or poems or any serious creative writing. She inspired two and a half years of intense adoration in the pages of his diaries. Until November 1992 Fowles was only rarely interested in anything beyond describing Elena's physical attributes and behavior and his feelings for her. Just as he had formerly been immersed in the trivia of local history or the fine nuances of language in fiction, now he was immersed in the tiniest details of Elena. Like his earlier muses, Elena is the world Fowles observes in page after page of descriptive nouns and adjectives about her physical characteristics, her dress, and her actions. She is electricity, alcohol, lightning, a can of petrol to his match. Wholly mercurial. She is Satanic, perverse, massively egotistical. She is intoxicatingly innocent and natural . . . asleep, defenseless and childlike. She is vicious, venomous, vengeful, spiteful, a heartlessly cold and calculating vampire. She is dazzling in her seductiveness, sexy, gauguinesque. She is a small girl, a lost child. She is radiant. She is greedy, grasping, hard, foreign, an inhuman little tramp. Unique, incomparable. A meteor. She is green life. And so on, for roughly six hundred pages, in five and a half volumes.

Fowles's obsession with Elena cut him off from many of those who had shaped the life he had shared with Elizabeth. He refused to see Leo Smith. Sarah Smith returned to India for a year. Anna Christy stayed with Leo when she visited the area and managed to maintain her friendship with John by not mentioning Elena. Denys Sharrocks met Elena for five minutes. Fred Porter, after years of estrangement, suddenly turned up at Belmont and resumed their relationship as if there had been no break at all. Instead of his old friends, Fowles became completely enmeshed in the convoluted cast of characters of Elena's life, the other men with whom she became involved while working for Fowles (the serious lovers, the hangers-on, and the ambitious fantasy crushes) and her Oxford women friends with their hapless love lives. He felt this generation kept him young. Fowles developed a peculiar relationship with Elena's parents, making a third older person endlessly discussing the girl, then battling with them over control of her. By 1992 he regularly referred to Elena as "the daughter I never had."[50] Often, by 1992, she called him "Dad."[51] "Morgan le Fay," he repeated, ruefully, "something unholy about it, finally."[52] "Even at her worst, she enchants me."[53]

One of the things the Elena enchantment did give Fowles was renewed health. His friends commented that he looked very well; his doctor was amazed to see him so fit.[54] He had energy to travel abroad, to lecture at universities, and to be sociable in Lyme. His handwriting was firmer, his typing strong and clear. Even when he was miserable, he was never bored. Elena had "saved" his life, he often said.[55] He may have been correct.

People thought John had forgotten Elizabeth. Not so. The intensity of his clinging to Elena was actually an indicator of how he still felt his wife's loss. In his diary he wrote of her constantly, mourning and missing her. Her memory and presence were "a sort of magmatic heat underlying all."[56] It was important to him to imagine that Elizabeth would have liked Elena. "If she had been alive, yes, she might have been furious. . . . When she lived I betrayed her with no one, nor wanted to, nor would have ever done so if she had survived."[57] But Elizabeth was gone, and loving Elena "simply makes it possible to stand the vividness of its pain, the reality of her death. I have had to live that, its totality, this last year. I couldn't have done it without Elena."[58] So Fowles imagined how his lost wife "would have put her arm round her . . . would have understood what a confused little waif she was, or one part of her was, would have sympathized with her."[59] He likened Elizabeth's aloofness and impulsiveness to this girl's. He often imagined Elizabeth shaking her head over him. He often sensed "Eliz's grey eyes on me."[60]

The affair had gone irredeemably sour by November 1992. Elena was ready to depart but decided to accompany Fowles on a speaking tour in the eastern United States. By North Carolina she had reached such a state of cold fury ("black ice") that she would not speak to him. They parted at London's Heathrow Airport. "You become Persephone," he wrote her, "sink into the night."[61] She took the piano, the clothes, and the jewelry. When he deposited the key to the flat with the solicitor next door, she threatened by solicitor's letter to sue him for access to her things. She married in 1993, divorced in 1995. By 1995 she had joined the police force. But like Persephone, Elena occasionally reappeared, turning up briefly as Fowles's friend over the next few years. She usually had some pressing expenses. He was always kind.

In January 1993 John Fowles set sail on the *Sea Princess* on a four-month cruise to Australia and New Zealand. His intention, reserving the two cabins, had been to travel with Elena. Since she had moved on, Fowles asked Jean Wellings, his secretary, to keep him company. Jean, a kindly, pragmatic sixty-five-year old, who had never left England before, had "the trip of a lifetime!"[62] His fellow passengers were, wrote Fowles, "an unholy mixture of the last dregs of the old Raj . . . and a ripe old collection of Scottish & Northcountry mums & dads who've made their little piles." They made him feel "so politically incorrect I wonder I haven't jumped overboard."[63] But Fowles the natural historian was excited by the unfamiliar flora and fauna, and the landscape affected him. He wrote his friends how in the Red Centre of Australia he experienced a kind of "metamorphosis . . . some odd little changes of angle."[64] Everything personal and individual seemed "an absurd farce" in the presence of "the vastness, the emptiness, the *age* of this *planet*."[65] But he scarcely elaborated this insight in his diaries. Although he constantly made copious notes in the palm-size notebooks he always carried, he barely wrote them up. As Elena disappeared from Fowles's life, so did his will to maintain the diaries. He continued sporadic entries while at home, but his travels, from this point, went largely unchronicled.

Other women became part of Fowles's daily life on Elena's departure. Fowles had arranged for Jean Wellings to move into the Belmont flat in spring 1991. Her homey presence made the large house feel less abandoned. Eventually a friend of her daughter's came in as a regular cook and helper. Fowles resumed his friendship with Leo Smith and her daughters, Charlotte and Sarah. Anna Christy visited regularly once more. There was also a new academic friend, Jan Relf.

In June 1990 Fowles's personal archives were sought by the Harry Ransom Humanities Research Center at the University of Texas at Austin (HRC). The director was Thomas F. Staley, the same modernist scholar who had purchased the typescripts of *The French Lieutenant's Woman* and *The Collector* for the University of Tulsa in 1977. Fowles was made profoundly uncomfortable by his sense of being a commodity. Yet the depth and quality of this very distinguished American collection impressed him. Fowles's papers would be in the company of manuscripts by James Joyce, D. H. Lawrence, Virginia Woolf, Samuel Beckett, Graham Greene, Ernest Hemingway, T. S. Eliot, Carson McCullers, Isaac Bashevis Singer, Tennessee Williams, Anne Sexton, Edith Wharton, George Bernard Shaw, Evelyn Waugh, and many other seminal figures of twentieth-century letters. By spring 1991 Fowles had agreed to sell his papers, including drafts, unpublished manuscripts, much correspondence, and the diaries for $150,000.[66]

They agreed to an arrangement whereby the HRC would own the diaries, but the originals would be securely archived at the University of Exeter while Fowles continued to work on them. He had begun rereading them to answer some of Elena's questions and was amazed by his own forgotten past. ("What a prig I was! . . . the awful stuffy young Englishman."[67]) Fowles intended, as he wrote Thomas Staley, to transcribe the "illegible manuscript originals . . . to help if anyone else tries to tackle the deciphering of them [while] scrupulously . . . *not* correcting . . . any of the obvious errors and infelicities." Fowles remained adamant that "the value of past records must lie in the writer's honesty about what he was, not what he is. I don't want to cosmeticize the corpse of my own past."[68] He was convinced that the modern trend in autobiography "to dress oneself up as if you were already in the past what you have now become" was "dishonest."[69] Fowles set this arrangement in motion early in 1991 by telephoning his only contact at Exeter, Jan Relf.

Relf had interviewed Fowles in 1985, while writing her doctoral thesis on his work, and Fowles had also met her in 1983, when the University of Exeter awarded him an honorary doctorate. When she arranged with University of Exeter officials for Fowles's diaries to be archived, she soon became his confidante. She was fifty, divorced and remarried, a mother and grandmother. He liked her serious intellect and her rejection of the "sentimental" and "the 'follies' and excesses of the Romantics." Talking with Jan, Fowles felt he entered "a quiet, ordered, rational oasis" in contrast with "the hectic fever" of Elena.[70] Slender, gray-haired Jan reminded him a little of Elizabeth in her "dryness" and in being "very free, herself without fuss."[71] Both personally and academically, Relf was a feminist. She told Fowles with amusement that he was "unreconstructed" and corrected his constant use of "girl" for "woman." She told him, when he talked of his impotence, that there was no male aggression at Belmont and she liked the "safe" atmosphere.[72] She supplied him with a new label to describe his feelings for mysterious young women, "nympholepsy . . . a perverse but persistent condition of desire for the unattainable."[73]

In May 1991, at the suggestion of her colleagues, Relf asked Fowles if she could write his biography.[74] Fowles agreed, offering her "free run of the diaries." To his own surprise, he looked forward to it, "not from vanity, nor from fear of having revealed too much about myself," but from curiosity to know if the journals would interest others.[75] For several years the biography project remained agreed but not contractually begun. In January 1994 Relf withdrew, choosing instead to work as Fowles's editor on a collection of his published nonfictional essays.[76]

Not until October 1995 did Fowles begin to have his illegible diaries transcribed for future publication and scholarly use. He hired a second secretary, one capable of organizing the manuscripts and reading and typing the unreadable. Karen Daw was thirty, formerly a union organizer and a recent M.A. from the University of Birmingham with plans for a Ph.D. Receiving her credentials, Fowles interviewed her under the guise of filling a position for "a friend." However, when he learned that she was from Thomas Hardy's Puddletown, where both "her father and grandfather had been cobblers; like that cousin of Hardy," he asked her to begin work immediately.[77] Karen's cropped blond hair, short skirts, and big eyes set off the gossips of Lyme Regis. But she was smart enough and cautious enough to remain friends with Fowles without becoming a *tendresse*. He liked how she reminded him of Elizabeth in her determination "to educate and better herself," to "reach higher [than] the world she was born into."[78] While there was not the romantic connection between them the gossips imagined, Fowles did feel that he was "making myself naked beside her." What he meant was that he was "'undressed' beside her because she types my 1951 Greek diary, which suddenly takes on mysterious life."[79] For Fowles, this intimacy of sharing his revealing words with a woman in some ways transcended the physical. Karen, seated at Elizabeth's old escritoire at John's suggestion, was always aware that she was entrusted with Fowles's essential self.

When he returned from his antipodean cruise in April 1993, Fowles became for several years the companion of Anna Peebles, a recent divorcée in her early fifties. Her roots in Lyme Regis were deep, as her family had summered there for generations. Her father, Zdzislaw Ruszkowski (1907–1991), had been a Polish artist whose paintings of Lyme greatly appealed to Fowles. During the week, Anna Peebles studied art and taught primary school in Winchester, living in a small house overflowing with books, paintings, two dogs, four adolescent children, and a rose-crammed garden, where she taught primary school and studied art. Most weekends she drove to Lyme Regis, where she and Fowles attended local events or dined out with friends. They traveled abroad together in Europe and the United States. She had energy, good humor, kindness, and little use for Fowles's habitual cynicism. He wrote of "her marvellous tact and practicality and patience. She is truly of gold."[80] It was not, however, a relationship imagined in romantic literary terms, the way Fowles thought of his muses, his *tendresses*. The sympathetic friendship drifted into the ever more casual until sometime in 1997.

During this time Fowles was increasingly harassed by circulatory problems similar to those his father had suffered. His circulatory system developed painful "counter-flow," in which the blood pooled in his legs, throbbing and burning.[81] Between spring 1993 and summer 1994 Fowles developed ulcers on his feet and legs that refused to heal. He was forced to cancel lecture tours in Australia and Spain and a much-anticipated tour of India. His veins were operated on, and the right foot improved. The left, however, would not heal, and in July 1994 Fowles was advised that the left leg should be amputated. His old friend Fred Porter intervened. In 1992 Porter had been advised to have both legs amputated. One leg was taken, but during delays for the second operation, the other leg improved. Porter refused the second amputation and continued actively through his mideighties, able to drive, play in music ensembles, take

courses, and travel. Hearing the prognosis for Fowles in 1994, he telephoned urgently: "Don't let them do it!"[82] Anna Christy and Charles
Glass also intervened, taking Fowles to a London specialist. After six
weeks in the Edward VII Hospital for Officers, the amputation was
averted. However, he continued to suffer the bouts of pain and immobil-
ity caused by a failing circulatory system.

Although Fowles continued to publish occasional reviews or introductions, his writing output decreased. Indeed, his stroke in 1988 and Elizabeth's death in 1990 mark an end to any published or publishable fiction.
In 1993 he barely corresponded or kept the diary. Fowles still spoke of his
dream novel *In Hellugalia* to many people as a genuine work in progress.
Tom Maschler finally stopped believing it was real, recalling that Fowles
had never talked about any other novels as he worked on them ("They
just appeared on my desk.").[83] Fowles still made notes for *In Hellugalia*,
however, sometimes finding himself writing about Elizabeth, even when
he thought he was writing about a character. In the January 12, 1994,
poem "Je Fable," for example, he wrote of Lady Dee, describing how she
walked "decades behind reality/Yet made the dullest tat flash sudden
all." He recalled the intensity of lovemaking ("how close you clung/Such
fevers, driving love to cries . . .") and her excitement "when you glimpsed
a sudden first/(Look oh look oh Christ oh look)." "The truth you had,"
Fowles wrote, and realized that he was remembering Elizabeth. He
called her "the ultimate *revenante* in my green life, forever unable to
leave each now."[84]

In 1994 Fowles wrote two filmscripts, under contract to John Calley
of Paramount. The first was a script for *Daniel Martin*. Fowles wrote one
version and Peter Benson wrote a second script. Neither was adopted by
the studio, and the option lapsed. Fowles and Benson also collaborated
on an idea for an uncompleted script, *The Manager,* a story about a successful man who absconds from his life, thematically similar to "The
Enigma" in *The Ebony Tower*. Fowles was more excited to write a script
for *Le Grand Meaulnes* for Paramount, which he completed. This project
sank, beyond Fowles's control, from a lack of cooperation between the
producing parties. In 1997 there was further interest in *Daniel Martin*.
The option was sold once more, and novelist Rose Tremain became the
writer for a hoped-for film.

As Fowles's active life as a writer diminished, scholarly interest in his
work matured and grew enormously. Not only did works of which he ap-

proved appear in the early 1990s, but Fowles also began to enjoy the friendship of scholars who studied him. Among them were even a few new *tendresses*. Romantic and unattainable, such physically distant literary friendships energized Fowles. Of one he sighed: "Everything pales beside her (or more my fabricated image of her)." Of another he was inspired to "meditate an essay which I shall call *Tendresses*: on how men of my age can develop strange sour-sweet relationships with intelligent young women of hers."[85] He continued to dismiss academic or journalistic interviews as "the usual rhubarb" but liked giving them. Convinced of "the intrinsic slipperiness and ambiguity of words," he was still not ready to accept the "fetish-disciplines" of postmodernism.[86] He likened the state of literature since deconstruction, for example, to "the scene ten minutes after the Titanic sank—frightened lifeboats in a cold sea, no one believing it's happened, with panic-stricken shouts in the darkness. Are you there? Who's still alive?"[87]

Rising scholarly interest in his work, as well as Fowles's own friendships among academics, led to a wave of events that consolidated and celebrated his reputation as a major literary figure. The year of his seventieth birthday, 1996, was a series of personally satisfying occasions for Fowles, beginning with the March publication of a John Fowles special issue of the American critical journal *Twentieth Century Literature*, edited by James R. Baker and Dianne Vipond.[88] At the time *TCL*, "42.1" appeared, Fowles's last great essay was also published. Very much in the tradition of *Islands* and *The Tree*, "The Nature of Nature" is Fowles's intimate, personal statement on his long love affair with *Le Sauvage*, the wild nature that had captivated him from childhood and on how nature's constant renewal nourished an optimism that belied all the writer's pessimism about the state of the world and his human condition in it. Fowles had long admired the fine hand press–printed work of James Robertson, the California publisher of the Yolla Bolly Press. "The Nature of Nature" was published by Yolla Bolly in 1995, paired with "The Tree," in a very limited edition with woodcuts by Aaron Johnson, and reprinted as a solo essay in 1996, in a limited printing of 275.[89]

In conjunction with these publications, Fowles toured the West and East coasts of the United States in May 1996. It was a sentimental journey to friends that he called "The Meander." Tom Maschler had pledged to publish a promised narrative account, but Fowles never wrote up his notes. However, he spoke in Portland and Seattle, was interviewed in

San Francisco, and lectured at universities from Stanford to Long Beach. Scholar Dianne Vipond helped Fowles revisit his past in Southern California, where he reminisced with his old Hollywood friends at a garden party given by Barbara Kohn.[90] Academic friends on the East Coast took him on tours to several islands of New England.[91]

From July 10 to 12, 1996, an international scholarly symposium was held on John Fowles's work under the aegis of the Lyme Regis Philpot Museum. The museum had prospered under the direction of Liz-Anne Bawden, Fowles's choice as Honorary Curator in 1988. By the mid-1990s she had achieved the museum's independence from the West Dorset District Council, managed the arduous task of having it registered with the Museums and Galleries Commission, won grants enabling a complete reconstruction of the building and the redesign of the collection display, and overseen the first stages of the rebuilding project. By the time Bawden retired in 2000, she had overseen the entire rebuilding and Jo Draper's redesign of the entire collection. In 1999 the museum that Fowles had returned to its scholarly mission from 1978 to 1988 and Bawden had rebuilt from 1988 to 1999 won the South West Museum of the Year Award, was short-listed for National Museum of the Year (winning a special award for design), and was awarded the Gulbenkian Prize, which was presented by HRH Prince Charles.[92]

"John Fowles: Love, Loss, and Landscape" was the museum's opportunity to honor and thank John Fowles and to celebrate its own success. For academic help in organizing the event, Bawden turned to James Aubrey, Professor of English at the Metropolitan State College of Denver, in Colorado, author of *John Fowles: A Reference Companion*.[93] Sixty scholars attended the sessions, the dinners, the guided walk through the Undercliff, and the Strawberry Tea in the garden at Belmont. Twenty-eight gave papers in the Masonic Hall overlooking the sea and the rooftops of Lyme. Fowles had awaited the arrival of this academic contingent with considerable anxiety. It was soon obvious, however, that these people regarded him with enormous affection. His house was filled with his friends, and he basked in the presence of enthusiastic readers and speakers from all over the world. He attended all the sessions, listening affably from front-row center where he could hear.

In the autumn of 1996 Fowles's past continued to haunt him. First, in early September, Sanchia Humphreys came to visit him in Lyme Regis. Recalling his fascination for her in 1954, Fowles was dismayed to find that the woman, at over sixty, was not the mysterious young girl of his memories. "Alas, all her freshness, her twentyishness, is staled; every thing that made me create the essence of Julie in the Magus seems almost a bad joke." Sanchia had never married, and Fowles thought her very snobbish, "so admiring of 'nice people,' the best people . . . still lives as if the last century never happened and we all still inhabit quasi-Victorian times."[94] Sanchia had spent a career "on the fringes of both the louche aristocratic and the film world," and had managed residences for mid-rank nobility or kept house for stars like Marlon Brando on film locations. She had a rich store of film gossip and also recalled many funny stories from their days at Ashridge that Fowles had forgotten.[95] Through her professional life and wide travels she had become an extraordinary cook as well and, on her several visits over the next two years, tempted Fowles with jugged hare, grouse, and exotic dishes from Africa or Iran. On a visit in 1997 Sanchia returned the "fragments" of Fowles's letters and poems to her from 1954. He felt bewildered reading them once more.[96]

In October 1996, Fowles reclaimed his past in Greece, returning to Spetsai after an absence of forty-three years. The occasion was the publication of *E Ellenike Empeiria* ("John Fowles and the Greek Experience"), a compilation volume of his poems, short pieces, and diary excerpts on Greece translated into Greek and edited by Kirki Kefalea.[97] Anna Christy, whose work was then being shown in an Athenian gallery, and I (recently accepted as Fowles's biographer) joined them in Athens for Fowles's speech at Athens University and events sponsored by Estia, his Greek publisher. Nicos Dimou, a well-known writer, handsomely arranged for a private yacht to transport Fowles and his party through the Saronic Gulf to Spetsai. The island buzzed with rumors of John Fowles's arrival. As in some legendary return of a king, Fowles and his group were made welcome at the villa Yiasemine by the Botassi family. People from all over Greece attended the grand reception when Fowles came ashore. Susie Botassi, whom Fowles had glimpsed when she was a child, was now the mother of filmmaker Lilette Botassi and grandmother to Alkis. In his quiet happiness, Fowles was like a delighted child himself. "This is *our* kind of place," he sighed to Anna Christy. He spent evenings and mornings on the colonnade of the villa enshrined in *The Magus*. He explored wild glades blooming with cyclamen, the beaches and bays of which he had written, and the empty buildings of the Anargyrios School. There was a taverna evening for Fowles's party and the Botassi family with Greek music, endless dishes of food and bottles of wine. "Oh," said Fowles, saddened suddenly amid the gaiety, "I wish my wife was here. She would have loved this."[98] He felt on Spetsai "an unexpected sanction . . . it reeked of freedom," he wrote, "and then the cyclamen, the pines, the sea, the silence, the ineffable view. Some returns and the kindness of the people who make them possible make one weep."[99] After Spetsai, he continued to Monemvasia, the Mani, and places along the Adriatic he had explored with Elizabeth in the fifties and sixties, staying with the director of the British Council, meeting the legendary hero of the Resistance, the writer Patrick Leigh Fermor. As before, Fowles did not fashion his copious notes into the diary narrative he had promised himself and others that he would write. The journey itself, however, allowed Fowles to reclaim emotionally in his present life the Greece of his memories. He returned several times in the following years.

Fowles's relationship with Anna Christy, his stepdaughter, had reached a place where he respected her as his closest family, while never referring to her as his daughter. Anna and her husband, Charles Glass, came frequently to Belmont from their new home in Bristol, and Anna occasionally traveled with Fowles. Both of Elizabeth's grandchildren aspired to professional careers. Tess Christy attended Cambridge, studying English and Art History, and then trained as a teacher. Will Homoky, a seasoned veteran of mountain climbing and research expeditions in the Arctic, studied Geology at the University of Leeds.

Fowles and Jan Relf worked through the collection of his nonfiction essays, finishing the editing in spring 1997. She pushed Fowles to keep to schedule, edited the essays, tied them together thematically, and introduced the book. Real alterations were "minor." Relf suggested some "'edits' (effectively cuts)," which Fowles rejected. "It's very seldom," he said, "I totally disclaim or deny what I once wrote."[100] At Peter Benson's suggestion, Fowles called the collection *Wormholes,* alluding to the holes in space that theoretically connect widely separated galaxies to one another.[101] Fowles's essays, differing in theme and treatment, had just such underlying connections. The word also played on the notion of the humble garden earthworm, dear to Fowles, whose unseen movement underground turns and enriches the soil and makes it fertile. The allusion to Fowle's last novel, *A Maggot,* also pleased him.

In the months before this work appeared in 1998, Fowles was again hospitalized by circulatory problems in his leg and had to cancel travel plans to Spain and Greece. He wrote that his life lay "in shards . . . in endless chaos, like a shattered mirror."[102] The fragments all seemed to be feminine. His house was full of women: caring for him, cooking for him, typing and transcribing him, editing him, writing about him, interviewing him, tempting him, amusing him, visiting him. The only male in his household was his Scottish gardener, Neil Reid, who lived in the old house at Underhill Farm and seemed perpetually, quietly amused by Fowles's circle of women. The universal joke developed that John Fowles kept a "harem." Fowles himself believed, and wrote frequently, that he understood women in his present circumstances far better than he had in his younger life. He thought of himself, under Jan Relf's influence, as a "feminist," though his tone was invariably patriarchal and patronizing in a kindly avuncular way.

Fowles still generalized all members of the genders into traditional categories that he believed were biologically determined. When his mother, Gladys Fowles, died in August 1992, he felt "next to nothing." "Tedious" bonds of family were "obstructive of my natural male-aggressive needs for power, I want nothing to do with them." The "part emotional, part ritualistic importance of maintaining bonds, supporting the clanlet, the family group" was a female prerogative, "feminine instinct, very primitive historically." Elizabeth had had this "primitive" sensitivity toward family. "I put all that aside, in the usual indifferent male way." (He assumed that *all* males behave this way.) For Fowles, these gender characteristics still defined what, biologically, made an artist. "The marked male escape into art (the need to write music and poetry)" grew from "the escape" into solitude. "Man uses his instinct to evade all familial and tribal bonds to strengthen his power both in and through art; will therefore be cruel to the women, such as mothers, that surround him. I've been guilty of this; put simply, no cruelty, no art."[103]

Nonetheless, Fowles now defined himself as "much more feminist. In any case," he wrote, "[I] truly despise most of my own gender and much of my own past behaviour towards women; recognize their complex virtues and goodnesses as I never fully managed before. . . . In virtually every way I am glad now I'm impotent; since at last it enables me to *see* women."[104] He thought of women as "a nice, sympathetic sex." Still, his sympathy for particular women was almost always determined by their physical attributes, and he felt he "must resist their little tyrannies."[105]

By 1996 the "head woman" of this so-called harem was Sarah Smith.

"We always joke and tease about my being a pasha and having a harem," he wrote of her.[106] He called her "the begum," which he defined as "the head woman in an Indian harem, who says 'Do this,' 'Don't do that,' and drops a drop of poison when necessary to take care of difficulties. . . . I need that, I need that."[107] He felt "very close to Sarah," was "always *conscious* of her, understand her feelings, even when I don't quite (or at all) agree with them."[108] Where Fowles loved the eighteenth century and loathed the modern, Sarah loved her advertising work and "adore[d] the Nicolsons, Wood, Gill, Spencer *et al.*"[109] She had a "usual not quite-as-happy-as-she-ought-to-be self; somehow a shade too sceptical and too thin and high-strung not to frighten any man," yet these qualities greatly appealed to Fowles. He loved too her "quirky sense of humour" with which his "English self [felt] so frequently in accord." She indulged and understood the "schoolboy Fowles's" little nicknames, mostly derogatory, with which he labeled even those he was fond of.[110] He remarked that she was different from his other women friends, that together they "made fun of everybody."[111] Yet she was often sympathetic and anxious to help him when his health was difficult and was immensely practical as well as caring. Beyond her smart fashion sense and "London chicness," they shared a love of the countryside. He loved her "innocence" of it, yet her "eagerness."[112] She was tolerant and amused that Fowles could pick up secateurs and wander off to prune his garden while important visitors waited for him. After selling the Regent's Road flat at the end of 1994, Fowles always stayed at Sarah's on his rare trips to the capital. He sensed himself "on the brink."[113]

In June 1997 Sarah Smith bought a small Lyme Regis cottage up the hill from Belmont. Fowles saw only its "post-war suburbanness and pokiness."[114] Sarah, however, planned and accomplished a handsome refurbishment, including opening the cottage up to garden and sea with an avant-garde greenhouse design, "a sort of Mies [van der Rohe]."[115] She arranged her hours of work so that she could commute to London for three days each week and spend long weekends in Lyme Regis with her mother, her two cats, and John Fowles.

Sarah Smith also was an important early supporter of Fowles's plans for the ultimate fate of Belmont House. He had been concerned since at least 1995 lest after his death it would be sold and converted into yet another Lyme Regis hotel. He feared that his beloved garden would be destroyed. He looked for ways to create a trust that would establish

Belmont as a student writing center, nature research center, and conference facility, under the aegis of an institution of higher learning. Many
of his friends in Great Britain and the United States made contacts with
their universities in hopes of discovering an interest. Ultimately Fowles's
longtime friend Christopher Bigsby, of the University of East Anglia in
Norwich, agreed to accept Belmont as a conference and study site, in association with other interested agencies and educational institutions. A
registered John Fowles Literary Trust was planned in 1998 to map out
Belmont's future and secure funding. Sarah Smith was one of the first
that Fowles asked to sit on the board of that trust. At the initial meeting,
January 10, 1998, at Belmont in Lyme Regis, Fowles introduced Sarah to
the distinguished gathering, taking her hand tenderly and declaring that
she knew his wishes and desires better than anyone.

For the publication of *Wormholes,* Fowles was invited to tour in the
United States. After spending several weeks with Kirki Kefalea and Anna
Christy in Greece, however, he faced the American journey with major
health problems, including a developing heart condition. Determined,
however, he traveled to North America in May 1998. He began in
Toronto with his friend paleontologist Christopher McGowan. He ex-
plored the Maine wilderness with Fowles scholar Katherine Tarbox.
Spending an evening with her University of New Hampshire students,
Fowles was asked what an aspiring writer should do to prepare himself.
"Kill your parents," said Fowles, "kill your Professors, kill your lovers.
Above all else have courage and patience or the only other option may be
a bullet in the brain."[116] After Sarah Smith joined him in Newport, Rhode
Island, he took the same message on to New York City. He appeared at a
sellout evening on May 19 at the Poetry Center of the 92nd Street Y, interviewed by Dianne Vipond. "Kill your wife," he told the audience, "kill
your parents." When he had reached California to tour, to speak, and to
see friends, John Fowles asked Sarah Smith to "be an idiot and marry
me. She said, If you must."[117]

Sarah and John kept their engagement a secret from everyone during
the summer of 1998. In August they sent out a poem that one of Katherine Tarbox's students, the poet "Sturgis," had fashioned from his impressions of meeting Fowles on May 9, 1998. Sarah had set it in Didot, and
Fowles added his notes, which ended with the news of their promise to
marry. That August, Sarah Smith took John Fowles and Belmont in
hand. She wrote letters to some of his women friends, asking them not to

contact Fowles in future. She changed some of the Belmont staff. During the interim she retained Sanchia Humphreys to come to Belmont to cook and housekeep. She supported Fowles during medical treatments to treat him for a broken ankle and when he was hospitalized for a pacemaker operation.

The wedding guests learned of the Thursday, September 3, wedding date just a week before the ceremony. Fowles had absentmindedly triple-booked his calendar. Besides his wedding, he was scheduled to sign copies of *Wormholes* in Lyme Regis and had arranged for Karen Daw to come and type for the day. When Daw telephoned on the second to confirm, Sanchia Humphreys informed her that John Fowles was being married the next day, and "all the staff are invited, except you, you poor girl." Karen Daw never saw or heard from Fowles again.[118] Kirki Kefalea, telephoning from Athens the day before and the day after the wedding, was not told of the wedding or of Fowles's hospital stays. Of Fowles's old friends, only Fred Porter was invited. It was a quiet, intimate celebration among immediate family, Lyme friends, and a few of Sarah's London friends. Anna Christy was asked to be John Fowles's witness at the small civil ceremony in a pretty sunny room overlooking the sea at the registry office. At the end of a day of friendship, saffron wedding cake, and champagne, Anna watched Sanchia Humphreys as she left Belmont, pausing a moment to stand and look up at the house before being driven away.

Sarah Fowles made John Fowles happy and content. He was delighted enough to proclaim his love even to journalists. Interviews in the months after the wedding depict the couple teasing and holding hands, with Sarah ruffling his hair and calling him "John Robert" or "His Nibs." She was realistic about him: "Seriously creative people, which he obviously is, are a rare species . . . demanding beyond belief . . . all loners and possessive through insecurity," she told a journalist, but "I can't tell you how much John makes me laugh and smile. I am so lucky."[119] Another interviewer observed, "She seems to ward off self-pity and confusion."[120] Sarah organized her husband's life, while not giving up her own. She arranged for live-in housekeepers and caregivers for the three days a week she continued to work in London and created a work environment for Fowles to encourage his writing. Through her practical arrangements, he continued his ongoing interests in local history and preservation projects. His health, never good, was well managed through his wife's loving, sensible attention.

Sarah Fowles kept her little Lyme Regis house up the hill, although she stayed her long weekends in Belmont, the house that was placed in her name. On occasional weekends, when one of her old friends visited, Sarah stayed at her cottage and Anna and Charles came to Belmont to be with John.

So it was, that on a sunny May afternoon in 2000, ten years after her death, John Fowles and Anna Christy decided to scatter Elizabeth's ashes in the garden.[121] They sat together on a bench built around a great tree, as Anna, in a calm, natural, graceful gesture, sifted her mother's ashes through her fingers over the earth.

For a long time there was silence. Then, from the dense undergrowth, a blackbird burst into song.

NOTES

SOURCES AND ABBREVIATIONS

THE JOHN FOWLES DIARIES: ABBREVIATED IN NOTES AS JFD

Basic citation form for diary entries is as follows: JFD, volume number (original diaries in manuscript [MS] or typescript [TS]) in Roman numerals, date of entry. E.g., JFD, III, 30 Nov. 1952.

Amended citations occur when Fowles writes a travel diary and does not provide specific dates: JFD, "section title," volume number, approximate date or page number. E.g., JFD, "Hollywood," X, 12.

A FEW WORDS ABOUT THE DIARIES

The John Fowles Diaries encompass Fowles's personal journals beginning in late 1948, although evidence exists of earlier diaries. The originals of volumes I–XVII (1–17, from 1948 to March 31, 1990) are archived at the Harry Ransom Center for Humanities Research, University of Texas, Austin, the principal repository for the bulk of Fowles's papers. Photocopies are also archived at the University of Exeter, Exeter, Devon, the library that kept the originals secure from 1992 to 1998. The first eight handwritten manuscript volumes were transcribed into a legible typescript by John Fowles and his diary secretary, Karen Daw, between 1995 and 1996, greatly enhancing accessibility. However, for reasons unknown, Fowles renumbered these newly typed volumes so that the volume numbers of the original versions and the transcribed versions do not correspond. For example, volume V of the manuscript originals is a straightforward record from March 1953 to February 1958. Volume 5 of the 1995–1996 typescript, however, is a collection of assorted pieces from the 1950s, including unpublished poems and uncollected diary entries. To avoid confusion, the notes to this biography consistently cite the original manuscript or original typescript volumes (not the typed 1995–1996 transcribed version).

Within the original volumes, issues of dating and citation also arise. Volume I (1948–1950) is actually a compilation of pieces, including three numbered notebooks, titled by John Fowles the "disjoints." So I have cited I (for volume 1), followed by the particular disjoint notebook. Fowles also kept separate diaries when he traveled, sometimes incorporating these narratives into his regular diary later, sometimes gathering them into independent volumes. His travel diaries are often dated more generally than the specifically dated regular diaries. When dates are missing, I have tried to supply the closest approximation, using internal clues. Sometimes I have had to indicate a citation by page number. Regrettably, these page numbers have often been assigned by me using simple hand counting and do not appear on the original pages.

To the best of my knowledge, volumes XXII–XXXII (April 22–23, 1990, to mid-1997) remain privately in John Fowles's hands. (There are no volumes 18 through 21.) Fowles made Volumes XXII–XXXII available to me in photocopy in 1997, personally placing the folders on the passenger seat of my hired car.

JOHN FOWLES DIARIES (JFD) CONTENTS BY ORIGINAL VOLUME

Vol. 1	Beating Book	MS
	Late 1948–May 1950 (disjoints 1, 2, 3)	MS
	Scandinavia 1949	TS
Vol. 2	May 1950–June 1951	MS
Vol. 3	July 5, 1951–March 9, 1953	MS
Vol. 4	September 1951–July 1952 (overlaps vol. 3)	MS
Vol. 5	March 1953–February 1958 plus	MS
Vol. 6	March 3, 1958–January 9, 1959	MS
	France, August 1958	TS
Vol. 7	1959–1962	MS
Vol. 8	1962–1965	MS
Vol. 9	June–July 1963, Greece	TS
	September 1963, New York	TS
Vol. 10	March 1964, Hollywood	TS
	June–July 1964, Norway	TS
Vol. 11	1965–1970	TS
Vol. 12	May 4, 1970–April 1977	TS
Vol. 13	February 1977–June 1984 (slightly overlaps vol. 12)	TS
Vol. 14	December 1985–February 1988	TS
Vol. 15	February 13, 1988–November 20, 1988	TS
Vol. 16	November 1988–August 1989	TS
Vol. 17	July 20, 1989–March 31, 1990	TS
Vols. 22–32	April 1990–mid-1997	TS

ABBREVIATIONS FOR SOURCES AND NOTES: CORRESPONDENTS

L-AB	Liz-Anne Bawden
PB	Peter Benson
AC	Anna Christy, also Anna Homoky
RC	Roy Christy
EC	Elizabeth Christy, former married name of Elizabeth Fowles
JC	Joanne Collins, also Joanne Whitton
KD	Karen Daw
JD	Jo Draper
EF	Elizabeth Fowles, also Betty Whitton or Elizabeth Christy (see Elizabeth Christy) or Liz Fowles
GF	Gladys Fowles
JF	John Fowles, also John Robert Fowles
RJF	Robert J. Fowles
SF	Sarah Fowles, also Sarah Smith
FG	Fay Godwin
CH	Celia Haddon
SH	Sanchia Humphreys
AJ	Ann Jellicoe

JKinberg	Jud Kinberg
JKohn	John Kohn
RL	Rodney Legg
TM	Tom Maschler
AMcC	Angus McCallum, also Mac McCallum
AM	Anne Mitchell, also Anne Manning
HO'S	Hazel O'Sullivan, also Hazel Fowles
DO'S	Daniel O'Sullivan
RSP	Ronald S. Payne, also Ronnie Payne
FP	Fred Porter, also Podge Porter
JR	Jan Relf
MScriven	Mary Scriven
AS	Anthony Sheil
DS	Denys Sharrocks
MSh	Monica Sharrocks
LS	Leonora Smith, also Leo Smith
DT	David Tringham
EvL	Elena van Lieshout
JW	Jean Wellings
DW	Doris Whitton
WW	William Wilcox

INTERVIEWS WITH THE AUTHOR CITED IN NOTES AS "NAME (OR ABBREVIATION), DAY, MONTH, YEAR"

John Fowles, interviews with the author, tape recordings:
January 12, 1981, Lyme Regis, Dorset
January 21, 1997, New York
March 5, 1997, Lyme Regis
March 8, 1997, Lyme Regis
April 12, 1997, Lyme Regis
October 30, 1997, Lyme Regis
November 11, 1997, Lyme Regis
November 13, 1997, Lyme Regis
November 17, 1997, Lyme Regis

John Fowles, cited personal conversations with the author:
May 22, 1996, Newport, Rhode Island
January 22, 1997, New York
October 30, 1997, Lyme Regis
March 9, 1998, telephone, Lyme Regis to Newport

Other correspondents: interviews with the author, tape recordings:
Liz-Anne Bawden, May 29, 1999, Lyme Regis, Dorset
Peter Benson, October 28, 1997, Lyme Regis
Anna Christy, March 15, 1997, Bristol
Joanne Collins, June 6, 1999, Totnes, Devon
Jo Draper, October 31, 1997, Lyme Regis
Sarah Fowles, June 6, 1999, Lyme Regis
Fay Godwin, June 15, 1999, Pett Level, near Hastings, East Sussex
Ann Jellicoe and Roger Mayne, May 29, 1999, Lyme Regis
Jud Kinberg, October 29, 1999, New York
John Kohn, October 26, 2000, Los Angeles
Rodney Legg, June 8, 1999, Wincanton, Somerset

Tom Maschler, April 29, 1997, London
    November 9, 1997, London
Daniel O'Sullivan, November 4, 1997, Great Ayton, Yorkshire
Hazel Fowles O'Sullivan, November 4, 1997, Great Ayton
Ronald Payne, also Celia Haddon, April 1, 1997, Minster Lovell, Oxford
Fred Porter, April 1, 1997, New College, Oxford
Jan Relf, November 15, 1997, Bradford-on-Avon, Wiltshire
Mary Scriven, May 3, 1999, Goring-on-Thames, Oxford
Denys Sharrocks, March 31, 1997, Clun, Shropshire
    November 3, 1997, Clun
Monica Sharrocks, March 31, 1997, Clun
    November 3, 1997, Clun
Leonora Smith, October 31, 1997, Axmouth, Devon
David Tringham, April 30, 1999, London
Elena van Lieshout, November 16, 1998, Bradley Stoke, Bristol
Jean Wellings, June 7, 1999, Lyme Regis
Tom and Malou Wiseman, May 1, 1999, London

Interviews with the author:
Anna Christy, May 31, 1999, Bristol
Karen Daw, June 9, 1999, Exeter, Devon
Denys and Monica Sharrocks, June 1, 1999, Clun
Thomas F. Staley, January 20, 1999, Austin, Texas
John Sylvester, April 29, 1999, Bedford, Bedfordshire
John Wilcox, May 5, 1999, telephone
William Wilcox, May 4, 1999, Westcliff-on-Sea, Essex

Letters are cited in the following format: correspondent to recipient, date. Collections are assumed to be privately held by recipients, unless otherwise cited. (E.g., EF to MSh, 10 Oct. 1989 = Elizabeth Fowles, letter to Monica Sharrocks, October 10, 1989. Sharrocks Collection.) Correspondence among John Fowles, Roy Christy, and Elizabeth Christy (later Elizabeth Fowles) for the years 1952–1956 is in the John Fowles Papers, University of Exeter.

ABBREVIATIONS OF COLLECTIONS AND RESOURCES

HRC	John Fowles Papers. Harry Ransom Center for the Humanities, University of Texas, Austin (citation form: HRC Box/Folder, page)
Tulsa	John Fowles Papers. Special Collections, McFarlin Library, University of Tulsa, Tulsa, Oklahoma (citation form: Tulsa Box/Folder, page)
Exeter	John Fowles Papers. Rare Books, University of Exeter Library, University of Exeter, Exeter, Devon
LRM	Lyme Regis (Philpot) Museum Archives
JF Col.	Private collection of John Fowles, Lyme Regis, Dorset
AC Col.	Private collection of Anna Christy, Bristol
Sharrocks Col.	Private collection of Denys and Monica Sharrocks, Clun, Shropshire
FP Col.	Private collection of Fred Porter, Oxford
JFD	John Fowles Diaries

INTRODUCTION

1. JF, "A Personal Confession," Foreword to *The Prisoner (Ourika),* 21C–21G, HRC 32/14. Epigraph to the Introduction from JF, letter to Jo Jones, 15 Sept. 1980. Pasted into JFD, XIII, 15 Sept. 1980.

CHAPTER 1: VOICES IN THE GARDEN

1. In addition to citations noted below, information in chapter 1 was obtained through interviews with John Fowles in March 1997 and November 1997, and with his sister, Hazel O'Sullivan, in November 1997. Family tree of the Pascoe-Richards family was researched and written by John Fowles in 1979 and of the Fowles family in 1980 by Hazel O'Sullivan (JF Col). Historical and statistical information about Leigh-on-Sea, Essex, was obtained from various sources, including but not limited to: A. C. Edwards, *A History of Essex* (London: Phillimore, 1978), and *A History of Essex with Maps and Pictures* (London: Darwen Finlayson, 1962); P. H. Reaney, *Essex* (Yorkshire: S. R. Publishers County History Reprints, 1970); J. R. Smith, *Southend Past* (Chelmsford: Essex County Council, 1979). Further information was obtained through the Essex Record Office, Southend Branch, General Registry Office, Southport, Merseyside, and the Office for National Statistics, London.
2. JFD, XIV, 7 Dec. 1986, 46.
3. JF, 8 March 1997.
4. DO'S, 4 Nov. 1997.
5. JFD, XI, 23 Dec. 1969.
6. HO'S, 4 Nov. 1997.
7. HO'S and DO'S, 4 Nov. 1997.
8. JFD, III, 29 Aug. 1951.
9. HO'S, 4 Nov. 1997.
10. JFD, XII, 25 March 1971, 53.
11. HO'S, 4 Nov. 1997.
12. JFD, XII, 25 March 1971, 53.
13. HO'S, 4 Nov. 1997.
14. JF, 5 March 1997.
15. The original address was 37 Fillebrook Avenue, Westcliff-on-Sea. It was renumbered 63 when reassigned to Leigh-on-Sea in 1930.
16. JF, in *Playground Memories,* Nick Gammage ed. (Amersham, Bucks: Elangeni Middle School, privately printed, 1996), 32–33.
17. JF and Frank Horvat, (London: Auram Press, 1979), *The Tree,* 2–3. Rep. (without preface or photographs (New York: Ecco Press, 1983), 6.
18. JF, 8 March 1997.
19. JFD, III, 29 Aug. 1951.
20. JF and Horvat, *Tree,* 4.
21. JFD, III, 29 Aug. 1951.
22. RJF, letter to Humfrey Grose-Hodge, 4 Aug. 1944, HRC 51/12.
23. WW, 4 May 1999.
24. Alleyn Court School reports of John Fowles, 1939, HRC 51/12.
25. JF, "Vain Memories," *Quick Singles,* ed. Christopher Martin-Jenkins (London: JM Dent, 1986), 119. Essex CC lists D. R. Wilcox as "joint-captain" 1933–39.
26. Ibid., 118–19.
27. JF, *Tree,* 11.
28. Ibid., 10.
29. Ibid.
30. DO'S, 4 Nov. 1997.
31. JF, *Tree,* 5.
32. HO'S, DO'S, 4 Nov. 1997.
33. JF, *Tree,* 5.
34. JFD, II, 17 Jan. 1951.
35. JFD, V, 27 Sept. 1953, 75.
36. John Fowles showed me this notebook in November 1997, pulling it from a file drawer in his writing room at Belmont House, Lyme Regis. He allowed me to handle it and briefly look through it, but not to make copies or take notes. "My poor father," said Fowles with a little chuckle, "he did all this." Hazel O'Sullivan also confirmed seeing such a notebook in conversation, 4 Nov. 1997.
37. JF, *Tree,* 10.
38. JFD, II, 17 Jan. 1951.
39. JFD, V, 27 Sept. 1953.
40. JF, *Tree,* 6. The antiquated language and old-fashioned story were confirmed by the O'Sullivans, 4 Nov. 1997.
41. HO'S, 4 Nov. 1997.
42. John Wilcox, telephone interview, 5 May 99.
43. JF, "The Nature of Nature," in *"The Tree" and "The Nature of Nature"* (Cov-

elo, CA: Yolla Bolly Press, 1995), 79. Rep. in *Wormholes,* 348.

44. JFD, IV, 5 Apr. 1952.

45. JF, "Nature of Nature," ix, 99.

46. Fowles, JR, and DL Erwood, "Entomology for the Schoolboy," in *Alleyn Court* magazine 9.2 (1938), 11.

47. JF, "Pervasive Fear of the Unknown." Review of *Bright Paradise: Victorian Scientific Travellers,* by P. Raby, *The Spectator* (September 28, 1996), 50.

48. Fowles read *Le Grand Meaulnes* for the first time in November 1963 but claimed in "A Modern Writer's France," in *Studies in Anglo-French Cultural Relations,* ed. Ceri Crossley and Ian Small (London: Mochillan, 1988); rep. in *Wormholes,* ed. Jan Relf (New York: Henry Holt, 1998), 53, that he had read this deeply haunting novel "countless times" in his "schoolboy days." He read *The Wind in the Willows* for the first time in 1948.

49. JFD, XXIII, 27 Oct. 1990.

50. Richard Jeffries, *Bevis: The Story of a Boy,* reprint of 1882 ed. (Ware, Hertfordshire: Wordsworth Classics, 1995).

CHAPTER 2: THE GREENNESS AT THE HEART OF OUR GROWTH

1. Records of the Bedford School between 1939 and 1944, including registry and full run of the *Ousel,* were generously made available to me by John Sylvester, on behalf of the Old Bedfordians. Information on Bedford School's history was obtained from school publications, notably M. E. Barlan, M. P. Stambach, and D. P. C. Stileman, *Bedford School and the Great Fire* (London: Quiller Press, 1984). For the school's history during World War II, I owe a great debt to Angus McCallum's *To Be a Kiwi: The Autobiography of Angus McCallum,* vol. 1 (Masterton, NZ.: privately printed, 1991). The epigraph for chapter 2 originally appeared in the *Texas Quarterly,* vol. 7 (1964), 154–62.

2. Anon., "The School at War," *Ousel,* vol. 43, no. 706 (October 25, 1939).

3. JF, letter to Michael Sharrocks, n.d. Sept. 1965.

4. Ibid.

5. AMcC, *Kiwi,* 33.

6. RSP, 1 Apr. 1997.

7. JF, 8 March 1997.

8. H. Boys-Stone, school reports of John Fowles, 1939–1945, December 1939, HRC 51/12.

9. V. Fisher, ibid.

10. RSP, 1 Apr. 1997.

11. A. H. Cobby, school reports of John Fowles, 1939–1945, Easter 1940, HRC 51/12.

12. Mark Amory, "Tales out of School," *Sunday Times Magazine* (September 22, 1974), 33–34, 36.

13. May 13, 1940.

14. AMcC, *Kiwi,* 40.

15. HO'S, 4 Nov. 1997.

16. Anon., *Ousel,* vol. 44 (October 1940).

17. Tallied by author from the *Ousel,* 1939–1945.

18. WW, 4 May 1999.

19. JFD, XXIII, 25 Oct. 1990, 18.

20. HO'S, 4 Nov. 1997. The physician was Margaret Frye, M.D.

21. JF, 8 March 1997.

22. JFD, V, i, 13–22 Aug. 1956, 1–2. Fowles's descriptive memories of Ipplepen are taken from his diary of a 1956 August holiday in Ipplepen with Elizabeth Christy (later Fowles). The holiday diary forms a separate part of vol. V, 1950s "Diary for August Holiday at Ipplepen."

23. JF, 8 March 1997.

24. AMcC, *Kiwi,* 42–44.

25. Ibid., 53–55.

26. JF, 5 March 1997.

27. O. V. Bevan, school reports of John Fowles, 1939–1945, Summer 1941, HRC 51/12.

28. Humfrey Grose-Hodge, school reports of John Fowles, 1939–1945, Summer 1941, HRC 51/12.

29. A. G. A. Hodges, school reports of John Fowles, 1939–1945, December 1941, HRC 51/12.

30. A. Goderic A. Hodges, *Memoirs of an Old Balloonatic* (London: William Kimber, 1972).

31. JF, "AGAH, A Hodges at Bedford School," 1954, 3–7, HRC 1/2.

32. JF, 8 March 1997.

33. AMcC, *Kiwi,* 47.
34. JF, "AGAH," 1954, 3–7.
35. Ibid.
36. RSP, 1 Apr. 1997.
37. JF, "AGAH," 1954, 3–7.
38. Joan Allen, interview by James R. Aubrey, June 20, 1988, J. R. Aubrey, *John Fowles: A Reference Companion* (Westport, Conn.: Greenwood Press, 1991), 9.
39. Ibid.
40. JFD, V, i, 13–22 Aug. 1956, 2.
41. JF, "Nota Natura Res," HRC 51/3.
42. JF, HRC 51/3.
43. JFD, I, 2 Apr. 1950.
44. JFD, II, 23 July 1950.
45. JFD, I, 16 Dec. 1949.
46. JFD, III, 20 Aug. 1951.
47. JFD, VIII, 1 Apr. 1963.
48. JFD, II, 13 March 1951.
49. JFD, V, 14 May 1956.
50. JFD, V, i, 17 Aug. 1956, 8.
51. JF, *Up-Shot,* 1942–1951, HRC 51/4.
52. JF, "Weeds, Bugs, Americans," *Sports Illustrated* (December 21, 1970), 95.
53. A. G. A. Hodges, school reports of John Fowles, 1939–1945, Summer 1942, HRC 51/12.
54. James G. P. Crowden, letter to author, 22 Sept. 1998.
55. (Rev.) Peter Pickett, letter to author, 6 March 2000.
56. Anon., "First XI Characters," *Ousel,* vol. 47, no. 730 (July 1943), 86–87. Today a swerve bowler is called a swing bowler.
57. Humfrey Grose-Hodge, school reports of John Fowles, 1939–1945, Summer 1943, HRC 51/12.
58. JF, "Vain Memories," 121.
59. RSP, 1 Apr. 1997.
60. Ibid.
61. Anon., "Cricket Review," *Ousel,* vol. 47, no. 729 (May 15, 1943).
62. JF, "AGAH."
63. AMcC, *Kiwi,* 51.
64. Patricia McCallum, AMcC, letter to author, 10 Dec. 1999.
65. AMcC, *Kiwi,* 52.
66. J. R. Fowles, "Angus Bruce McCallum," *Ousel,* vol. 48, no. 734 (June 28, 1944), 52.
67. Patricia McCallum, AMcC, letter to author, 30 Nov. 1999.
68. Ibid., 10 Dec. 1999.
69. Mark Amory, 22 Sept. 1974, 33.
70. JF, 8 March 1997.
71. JFD, "Beating Book, 1944" in vol. I.
72. Humfrey Grose-Hodge, school reports of John Fowles, 1939–1945, December 1943, HRC 51/12.
73. A. G. A. Hodges, school reports of John Fowles, 1939–1945, December 1943, HRC 51/12.
74. AMcM, *Kiwi,* 55.
75. Patricia McCallum, AMcC, letter to author, 30 Nov. 1999.
76. JF, "AGAH."
77. A. G. A. Hodges, school reports of John Fowles, 1939–1945, Summer 1944, HRC 51/12.
78. Humfrey Grose-Hodge, letter to RJF, July 1999. HRC 51/12.
79. A. G. A. Hodges, school reports of John Fowles, 1939–1945, Summer 1944, HRC 51/12.
80. C. W. Edwards, "School Notes," *Ousel* (June 1944), 95–96.
81. Humfrey Grose-Hodge, letter to RJF, July 1944. HRC 51/12.
82. RJF, letter to Humfrey Grose-Hodge, 4 Aug. 1944. HRC 51/12.
83. Certificate of Merit for John Fowles, University of Edinburgh, HRC 51/12.
84. JF, 8 March 1997.
85. JFD, XII, 30 Jan. 1973, 140.
86. JF, "AGAH."
87. JF, 8 March 1997.
88. JF, *Nature Notes* and *Up-Shot,* HRC 51/2 and 4. Fowles's nature notebooks track his activities and locations during 1945 and 1946.
89. JF, 8 March 1997.
90. JF, "Conan Doyle," in *The Hound of the Baskervilles,* by Arthur Conan Doyle (London: J. Murray : Cape, 1974), 7–11.
91. JF, 8 March 1997.
92. JFD, V, 27 Sept. 1953, 76–77.
93. JF, "AGAH."
94. JFD, XII, 16 Feb. 1973, 144.
95. JF, *"Nature Notes,"* HRC 51/4.

CHAPTER 3: A LARGER WORLD

1. In addition to the JF Diaries, descriptions of student life at Oxford University in the late 1940s were enriched by

the memories of Ronald S. Payne and
Fred Porter, by interview on April 1,
1997, and by subsequent conversations.
Epigraph to chapter 3 is preserved in
JFD, VIII, 50.

2. RSP, 1 Apr. 1997.
3. James R. Baker, "John Fowles: The Art
of Fiction CIX: An Interview with John
Fowles," in *Conversations with John
Fowles,* ed. Dianne L. Vipond (Jackson:
University of Mississippi Press, 1999),
182.
4. JF, 8 March 1997.
5. JF, "A Modern Writer's France," in
*Studies in Anglo-French Cultural Rela-
tions,* ed. Ceri Crossley and Ian Small,
(London: Macmillan, 1988). Rep. in
Wormholes, ed. Jan Relf (New York:
Henry Holt, 1998), 47.
6. JF, MS notes, 10, HRC 32/14.
7. JF, 12 Jan. 1981.
8. JFD, III, 12 May 1951.
9. JFD, VII, 8 Dec. 1961.
10. JFD, I, disjoint 2, 6 Oct. 1949.
11. JFD, II, 15 Feb. 1951.
12. JF, "Vain Memories," 121.
13. JFD, II, disjoint 3, 1 May 1950.
14. JFD, II, disjoint 3, 24 Nov. 1949.
15. JFD, II, disjoint 3, II, 18 Apr. 1950.
16. JFD, II, 15 Feb. 1951.
17. JFD, II, 3 June 1950.
18. RSP, 1 Apr. 1997.
19. JFD, I, disjoint 3, 4 Apr. 1950.
20. JFD, note to "Paris 1949" I, 25 Nov.
1992.
21. FP, 1 Apr. 1997.
22. JFD, I, disjoint 1, 29 May 1949.
23. JFD, I, disjoint 1, 5 June 1949.
24. JFD, I, disjoint 1, 3 Apr. 1949.
25. JFD, I, disjoint 2, 30 Sept. 1949.
26. JFD, I, disjoint 2, 9 July 1949.
27. HO'S, 4 Nov. 1997.
28. JFD, I, disjoint 2, 24 Sept. 1949.
29. JFD, I, disjoint 3, 3 Apr. 1950.
30. HO'S, 4 Nov. 1997.
31. JFD, I, disjoint 3, Dec. 1949.
32. Ibid.
33. RSP, letter to author, 30 Sept. 1999, E-
mail.
34. Fowles's memories of Easter 1948 in
Aix-en-Provence, as well as this poem,
are preserved in "Collioure, 1948,"
140–69, in JFD, II, 15–21 March 1951.

35. RSP, 1 Apr. 1997.
36. JFD, XXXII, 28 Sept. 1997.
37. JFD, "Collioure, 1948," II, 15 Feb. 1951.
38. RSP to author, 30 Sept. 1999, E-mail.
39. JF, "A Modern Writer's France," 49.
40. Ibid., 49.
41. JFD, I, disjoint 2, 31 July 1949.
42. JF, 5 March 1997.
43. Kaja Juhl, letter to JF, 7 Nov. 1953, Exeter.
44. JF, 5 March 1997.
45. JFD, I, disjoint 1, autumn 1948, 10.
46. The following discussion of Fowles's
struggles to understand and accept existentialism at Oxford is drawn from JFD,
I. This volume is partly composed of
three fragmentary disjoints (1, 2, and 3),
written from autumn 1948 to June 1949.
47. JFD, I, disjoint 3, Dec. 1949.
48. All quotes are drawn from JFD, "Scandinavia 1949," I.
49. JF, *The Magus* (Boston: Little, Brown,
1965 and London: Jonathan Cape,
1966), 284.
50. FP, 1 Apr. 1997.
51. JFD, I, disjoint 3, 3 May 1950.
52. JFD, II, 24 June 1950.
53. JFD, I, disjoint 3, 12 Nov. 1949.
54. JFD, I, disjoint 3, 12 Feb. 1950.
55. JFD, I, disjoint 2, 5 Nov. 1949.
56. JFD, I, disjoint 3, 12 Nov. 1949.
57. Ibid.
58. JFD, I, disjoint 3, 9 March 1950.
59. JFD, I, disjoint 3, n.d. Jan.–Feb. 1950.
All quotes of five-week stay in nursing
home drawn from this section.
60. JFD, I, disjoint 3, 9 March 1950.
61. JFD, I, disjoint 3, 5 March 1950.
62. JFD, I, disjoint 3, 4 Apr. 1950.
63. JFD, I, disjoint 3, 9 Apr. 1950.
64. JFD, I, disjoint 3, 12 Apr. 1950.
65. JFD, II, 18 May 1950.
66. JFD, II, 28 May 1950.
67. JFD, II, 15 May 1950.
68. JFD, I, disjoint 3, 10 May 1950.
69. JF, letter to FP and Eileen Porter, 26
July 1950.
70. JFD, II, 8 June 1950.
71. JFD, II, 14 May 1950.
72. JFD, "Cold Brayfield," II, 28 June to 30
July 1950. (All quotes from these dates.)
73. JF, letter to FP and Eileen Porter, 26
July 1950.

74. JFD, II, 26 July 1950.
75. JFD, II, 30 July 1950.

CHAPTER 4: IN THE LAND OF
ILLUSIONS INFANTILES

1. JFD, II, 25 Sept. 1950.
2. JFD, II, 2 Oct. 1950.
3. JFD, II, 2 Sept. 1950.
4. JFD, II, 2 Oct. 1950.
5. JFD, II, 11 Oct., 15 Oct. 1950.
6. JFD, II, 25 Oct. 1950.
7. JFD, II, 12 Sept. 1950.
8. JFD, II, 23 Sept. 1950.
9. JFD, II, 25 Sept. 1950.
10. John Fowles, "The Blinded Eye," in *Animals,* vol. 13, no. 9 (January 1971), 260, rep. in *Wormholes.* A much-embellished version of this tale was told to me on March 5, 1997.
11. JFD, III, 6 Dec. 1951.
12. JFD, II, 7 Nov. 1950.
13. JFD, II, 28 Oct. 1950.
14. JFD, II, 2 Nov. 1950.
15. Ibid.
16. JFD, II, 7 Nov. 1950.
17. JFD, II, 11 Oct. 1950.
18. JFD, II, 13 Nov. 1950.
19. JFD, II, 17 Nov. 1950.
20. JF, *Magus,* 13.
21. JFD, II, 8 Dec. 1950.
22. Ibid.
23. JFD, II, 1 Jan. 1951.
24. JFD, II, 2 May 1951.
25. Ibid.
26. JFD, II, 17 Nov. 1950.
27. JFD, II, 1 Dec. 1950.
28. JFD, II, 20 Aug. 1951.
29. JFD, II, 14 Jan. 1951.
30. JFD, II, 31 Jan. 1951.
31. JFD, II, 1 Feb. 1951.
32. JFD, II, 14 Jan. 1951.
33. JFD, II, 17 Nov. 1950.
34. JFD, II, 26 Nov. 1950.
35. JFD, II, 25 March 1951.
36. JFD, II, 17 Dec. 1950.
37. JFD, II, 17 Jan. 1951.
38. JFD, II, 7 Jan. 1951.
39. JFD, II, 16 March 1951.
40. JFD, II, 13 March 1951.
41. JFD, II, 28 Feb. 1951.
42. JF to EC, 29 Oct. 1953.
43. JFD, III, 10 July 1951.
44. JFD, II, 13 March 1951.
45. JFD, II, 2 May 1951.
46. JFD, II, 13 June 1951.
47. JFD, II, 14 may 1951.
48. JFD, II, 27 March 1951.
49. JFD, II, 2 March 1951.
50. JFD, II, 12 Apr. 1951.
51. JFD, II, 3 Apr. 1951.
52. JFD, II, first week June 1951.
53. JFD, II, 8 June 1951.
54. JF, 5 March 97. JF translated both Ginette Marcailloux's letters aloud during this interview: 11 June 1983 and n.d., late June or early July 1983.
55. JFD, II, 8 June 1951.
56. JFD, II, first week June 1951.
57. HO'S, 4 Nov. 1997.
58. JFD, II, 17 June 1951.
59. JFD, III, 20 Aug. 1951.
60. JFD, III, 3 Aug. 1951.
61. JFD, III, 8 Aug. 1951.
62. JFD, III, 18–22 Aug. 1951.
63. JFD, III, 20 Aug. 1951.
64. JFD, III, 14 Aug. 1951.
65. JFD, III, 20 Aug. 1951.
66. JFD, III, 18 Aug. 1951.
67. JFD, III, 22 Aug. 1951.
68. JFD, III, 14 Oct. 1951.
69. JFD, III, 20 Oct. 1951.
70. JFD, III, 6 Dec. 1951.
71. JFD, III, 26 Dec. 1951.
72. JFD, III, 20 Oct. 1951.
73. JFD, III, 26 Dec. 1951.
74. JFD, III, 29 Aug. 1951.
75. JFD, III, 1 Oct. 1951.
76. Kenneth Pringle, letter to JF, n.d. Dec. 1951, Spetsai, Greece.
77. JFD, III, 26 Dec. 1951.

CHAPTER 5: AN ISLAND AND GREECE

1. Denys Sharrocks, interview by author, tape recording, March 31, 1997, Clun, Shropshire. Description of life on Spetsai in the early 1950s was enriched by this interview, a second interview November 3, 1997, and subsequent letters and conversations between Denys and Monica Sharrocks and the author. Epigraph for chapter 5 from *Magus,* ch. 7, 46.
2. JFD, IV, 6 Jan. 1952
3. JFD, IV, 8 Jan. 1952.

4. Students, Fowles assignments, Anargyrios College, HRC 50/1.
5. JFD, XII, 7 Jan. 1972.
6. JFD, IV, 3 Feb 1952.
7. JFD, IV, 11 June 1952.
8. Ibid.
9. DS, 31 March 1997.
10. JFD, IV, 12 Jan. 1952.
11. JFD, IV, 12 Jan., 6 Feb. 1952.
12. DS, 31 March 1997.
13. JFD, IV, 18 Jan. 1952.
14. JFD, IV, 12 Jan. 1952.
15. DS, 31 March and 3 Nov. 1997.
16. DS, 31 March 1997.
17. JFD, IV, 18 Jan. 1952.
18. JFD, IV, 22 June 1952.
19. JFD, IV, 18 Jan. 1952.
20. JF, An Island and Greece, vol. II, 159A, HRC 17/6.
21. JFD, IV, 18 Jan. 1952.
22. JFD, IV, 11 Feb. 1952.
23. JFD, IV, 12 Jan. 1952.
24. JFD, IV, 11 May 1952.
25. JFD, IV, 15 Apr. 1952.
26. DS, 3 Nov. 1997.
27. JF, vol. I., A Journey to Athens, 1–136, HRC 17/4–5.
28. Ibid, ch. 11, 41–42, HRC 17/5.
29. JFD, IV, 8 Jan. 1952. Published in "Behind The Magus," (London: Colophon Press, 1994), rep. in Wormholes, 56–66.
30. In 1993, for a planned biography by Jan Relf, JF annotated the typed transcript of this entry: "Jan, I think we may call this early January entry above the genesis of The Magus!" In my own view, inspiration for the novel dates to Fowles's experience on the Pasvik River in Norway in August 1949 and, possibly, to his sojourn in the south of France in September 1948. The idea of sudden moments of inspiration always appealed to Fowles, but the evidence shows each of his works developing in slow, organic fashion over many years.
31. JFD, IV, 18 Jan. 1952.
32. JFD, III, 6 Oct. 1952, 118.
33. JF, An Island and Greece, vol. III, 250, HRC 17/7.
34. JF, notebook containing bird notes, Spetsai, Greece, 1951–1952, HRC 51/5.
35. JFD, IV, 8 Jan. 1952.
36. DS, 3 Nov. 1997. Denys Sharrocks's joke about this lifelong accusation from Fowles was that his own epitaph would someday read: "He said there were no birds on the island."
37. JFD, III, 30 Nov. 1952.
38. JF, "Behind The Magus," 22.
39. JFD, IV, 15–30 Apr. 1952, 94. Entries of "1952 Cretan Journey" are not dated, 87–118.
40. DS, 31 March 1997.
41. JFD, IV, 15–30 Apr. 1952, 112.
42. Ibid., 106–07.
43. JFD, IV, 5 Apr. 1952.
44. JFD, IV, 4 June, 5 Apr. 1952.
45. Kenneth Matthews, Aleko (London: Peter Davies, 1934).
46. JFD, IV, 21 June 1952.
47. JFD, IV, 5 Apr. 1952.
48. Ibid.
49. JFD, IV, 10 June 1952.
50. JFD, IV, 1–16 July 1952, 27–74. Some parts out of sequence.
51. JFD, IV, 2 July 1952.
52. JFD, IV, 4 July 1952.
53. JFD, III, 23 July 1952.
54. JFD, III, 25 July to 24 Aug. 1952. Entries of "Spain–Morocco Journey, July–August 1952" not dated, 52–104.
55. Ibid., 57.
56. Ibid., 57, 64, 75, 99, 100, 108–109.
57. Ibid., 104.
58. Ibid., 63.
59. Ibid., 101–102.
60. Ibid., 74.
61. Ibid., 68.
62. Ibid., 98.
63. Ibid., 68.
64. Ibid., 49.
65. The dates of this tour are 25–31 Aug. 1952. Fowles wrote up the episode in early October, when he had returned to Spetsai. JFD, III, MS 117–19.
66. JFD, III, 6 Oct. 1952, 118.
67. JFD, III, 3 Oct. 1952, 106–108.
68. JFD, III, 2 Sept. 1952.
69. JFD, III, 17 Sept. 1952.

CHAPTER 6: ELIZABETH AND ROY

1. For information on the Whitton family I am indebted to Elizabeth Fowles's sister, Joanne Whitton Collins, interviewed on June 6, 1999, and to Anne

Mitchell and Anna Christy, as well as the Office of National Statistics (ONS) and Elizabeth Fowles's letters. A most interesting source of information is the record of "Dream Analysis 1964," densely annotated with autobiographical notes by both John and Elizabeth Fowles, HRC 50/7. Biographical information on Roy Christy was partly provided by his daughter, Anna Christy, and by Anne Mitchell, Denys Sharrocks, John Fowles's diaries, and the ONS. Epigraph to chapter 6 is from JFD, V, 15 June 1953.

2. JC, 6 June 1999.
3. MSh to author, conversation, 3 Nov. 1997.
4. JC, 6 June 1999.
5. JF, "Dream Analysis, 1964," 14–20 Sept; further notes 3 Oct., HRC 50/7.
6. Ibid.
7. Ibid.
8. Ibid.
9. Ibid.
10. EF to MS, 10 Oct. 1989.
11. JF, "Dream Analysis, 1964," HRC 50/7.
12. JF, 5 March 1997.
13. Alan's surname is never mentioned. It is assumed that as the brother of Betty Pace he had the same name. His letters are in Exeter.
14. DW to EC, n.d., c. 6 March 1950, Exeter.
15. Peter's surname is unknown. His letters are in Exeter.
16. JC, 6 June 1999.
17. RC to EC, 24 Aug. 1953, Exeter.
18. AM to author, 20 Jan. 2000.
19. AM to JF, 16 Feb. 1992.
20. AM to author, 20 Jan. 2000.
21. JC, 6 June 1999.
22. AM to JF, 16 Feb. 1992.
23. JF to EC, 29 Oct. 1953. Fowles uses the word *affaire* to describe this relationship, but *affaire* for him can mean anything from a serious flirtation to cohabitation. Nevertheless, in this case there seems to have been sexual involvement.
24. AM to author, 20 Jan. 2000.
25. JF, letter to Exeter University Library, 27 Aug. 1992. Typed biographical notes to letters and diaries placed at Exeter.

JF preserves information from conversations with DS and responds to AM's Feb. 1992 letter.
26. AC, 15 March 1997.
27. DS, 31 March 1997.
28. AM to JF, 16 Feb. 1992.
29. Ibid.
30. JF to Exeter, 27 Aug. 1992.
31. DS, 31 March 1997.
32. RC, letter to *New Statesman*, n.d. Oct. 1950. Unpublished. An angry response to a review of Berdyaev's autobiography by Dr. Joad, JF Col.
33. AM to JF, 16 Feb. 1992.
34. DW, n.d., c. 6 March 1950.
35. AM to JF, 16 Feb. 1992.
36. AM to author, 20 Jan. 2000.
37. JF, "Dream Analysis, 1964," 14 Sept. 1964, HRC 50/7.
38. AM to JF, 16 Feb. 1992.
39. DS, 31 March 1997. Roy Christy knew of the Anargyrios School from other sources. The second husband of his first wife was teaching on Spetsai at the time of DS's arrival in the late 1940s. They all had known one another at university. "All very incestuous," laughed Denys Sharrocks.
40. RC to EC, spring 1952, Exeter.
41. RC to EC, 24 Aug. 1953, Exeter.
42. AM to JF, 16 Feb. 1992.
43. Ibid.
44. JFD, III, 8–14 Oct. 1952.
45. JFD, III, 11 Nov 1952.
46. AC, 15 March 1997.
47. JFD, III, early Dec. 1952, 132.
48. JFD, V, 1 May 1953.
49. JFD, III, 25 Feb. 1953.
50. JFD, III, 18 Jan. 1953.
51. JFD, III, 30 Nov. 1952.
52. Ibid.
53. JF, "Nature Notebook, 1952–53," HRC 51/6.
54. JFD, III, 26 Dec. 1952.
55. JFD, III, 25 Feb. 1953.
56. Ibid.
57. JFD, III, 26 Dec. 1952.
58. JFD, III, 18 Jan. 25 Feb. 11 Feb. 1953.
59. JFD, V, 26 May 1953.
60. JFD, V, 24 May 1953.
61. JFD, III, 25 Feb. 1953.
62. JFD, III, 18 Jan. 1953.
63. JFD, III, 25 Feb. 1953.

64. JFD, III, early Dec. 1952, 130.
65. JFD, III, 18 Jan. 1953.
66. JFD, IV, 15–30 Apr. 1952, 87.
67. JFD, III, 25 Feb. 1953.
68. AM to JF, 16 Feb. 1992.
69. JFD, III, 25 Feb. 1953.
70. JFD, III, 26 Dec. 1952.
71. JFD, V, 1–14 Apr. 1953, 3.
72. JFD, III, 11 Feb. 1953.
73. JFD, III, early Dec. 1952, 130.
74. JFD, V, 1–14 Apr. 1953, 3–5.
75. Ibid., 2.
76. Ibid., 11.
77. Ibid., 13.
78. JFD, V, 20 Apr. 1953.
79. William Shakespeare, *The Tempest*, 3.1.89.
80. JFD, V, n.d. May 1953, 39.
81. JFD, V, 11 June 1953.
82. JFD, V, 17 May 1953.
83. JFD, V, late May 1953, 46–48.
84. JFD, V, 11 June 1953.
85. JFD, V, 24 May 1953.
86. JFD, V, 9 June 1953.
87. JFD, V, n.d., June 1953, 50.
88. Ibid., 51.
89. Ibid., 52.
90. George Sotiriou, President of the Anargyrios and Corgialenios School of Spetsai and Academic Professor of the Athens University, letter to JF, 24 June 1953, Exeter. Legends arose on Spetsai about the dismissals of John Fowles and Roy Christy. In October 1996 on Spetsai I was informed in English that the two masters had been suspected of spying and of homosexuality. A Greek colleague, Dr. Marianne Betitoubi, was told emphatically in Greek that Fowles and Christy *were* spies and they *were* homosexuals.
91. JFD, V, n.d. June 1953, 53.
92. Ibid., 54.
93. JFD, V, 28 July 1953, 62.
94. JFD, V, n.d. June 1953, 55–56.
95. Ibid., 56.
96. AC, 15 March 1997.
97. JF to the author, conversation, 22 May 1996.
98. JFD, V, n.d. June 1953, 57.
99. Ibid., 55.
100. JFD, V, 28 July 1953, 58.

101. Ibid., 62.
102. Ibid., 59.
103. Ibid., 63.

CHAPTER 7: ANNA

1. JFD, V, 31 July 1953.
2. JFD, V, 7 Aug. 1953.
3. JFD, V, 31 July 1953.
4. JFD, V, 7 Aug. 1953.
5. JFD, V, 27 Sept. 1953, 67.
6. Ibid., 68.
7. Ibid., 69.
8. Ibid.
9. Ibid., 70.
10. Ibid., 71.
11. Ibid., 73–74.
12. Ibid.
13. FP, 1 Apr. 1997.
14. DW to EC, 8 Sept. 1953, Exeter.
15. RC to EC, 24 Aug. 1953.
16. RC to EC, 4 Nov. 1953.
17. JFD, V, 27 Oct. 1953, 78.
18. Ibid., 79.
19. Ibid., 80.
20. JF to EC, 24 Oct. 1953 (mislabeled 27 Oct.).
21. JC, 6 June 1999.
22. RC to EC, 26 Oct. 1953.
23. AM to JF, 16 Feb. 1992. Other information from JC and AC.
24. JF to EC, 27 Oct. 1953 (mislabeled 24 Oct.).
25. JF to EC, n.d., c. 3 Oct. 1953.
26. JFD, V, 27 Oct. 1953, 83.
27. JF to EC, 27 Oct. 1953 (mislabeled 24 Oct.).
28. JF, *An Island and Greece*, vol. 2, Oct. 1953–June 1962, 119–243, HRC 17/6.
29. Douglas Coult, *A Prospect of Ashridge* (London: Phillimore, 1980). Other information on Ashridge from Alan Bryant, Kay Sanecki, and Richard Wheeler, *The Garden at Ashridge* (Ashridge Bonar Law Memorial Trust, 1989), 20. Also Douglas Coult, *Ashridge: A Short Guide* (Ashridge Management College, 1991, rev. 1994), 17.
30. JFD, V, 27 Oct. 1953, 81.
31. JF to EC, 27 Nov. 1953.
32. JF, 27 Oct. 1953 (mislabeled 24 Oct.).
33. JFD, V, 27 Oct. 1953, 81.

34. JFD, V, 5 Nov. 1953.
35. JFD, V, 9 Nov. 1953.
36. FP to JF, n.d. Nov. 1953.
37. JF to EC, 11 Nov. 1953.
38. JF's economical habit of typing the drafts of his fictions on the reverse of pages "cadged" from his workplace has preserved much information about Ashridge in HRC 17/5, 6, and 7 and HRC 26/6, 7, and 8.
39. JF to EC, 27 Nov. 1953.
40. Ibid.
41. JF to EC, 3 Dec. 1953.
42. Ibid.
43. JF to EC, 18 Nov. 1953.
44. JFD, V, 20 Dec. 1953.
45. JF to EC, 13 Nov. 1953.
46. JFD, V, 28 Nov. 1953.
47. JF to EC, 27 Nov. 1953.
48. JF to EC, 3 Dec. 1953.
49. JF to EC, 10 Nov. 1953.
50. JF to EC, 27 Nov. 1953.
51. JF to EC, 26 Nov. 1953.
52. JF to EC, 11 Nov. 1953.
53. JF to EC, 13 Nov. 1953.
54. JF to EC, 27 Nov. 1953.
55. JF to EC, 11 Nov. 1953.
56. JF to EC, 12 Nov. 1953.
57. JF to EC, 5 Dec. 1953.
58. RC to EC, 16 Nov. 1953.
59. JF to EC, 10 Nov. 1953.
60. JF to EC, 13 Nov. 1953.
61. JF to EC, 18 Nov. 1953.
62. JF to EC, 30 Nov. 1953.
63. JF to EC, 4 Dec. 1953.
64. JFD, V, 20 Dec. 1953.
65. Ibid.
66. JFD, V, 29 Dec. 1953.
67. JFD, V, 4 Jan. 1954.
68. Ibid.
69. JFD, V, 21 Jan. 1954.
70. JFD, V, 4 Jan. 1954.
71. JFD, V, 20 Dec. 1953.
72. JFD, V, 29 Dec. 1953.
73. JF to EC, 14 Dec. 1953.
74. JFD, 5 Dec. 1953.
75. JF, An Island and Greece, vol. 3, 250, HRC 17/7.
76. DS, 31 March 1997.
77. EC, letter to "Inga," n.d., c. 1 Feb. 1954, "RC to EF Letters," Exeter.
78. MSh to author, 4 Nov. 1997.

CHAPTER 8: THE LILY AND THE ROSE

1. JFD, V, 16 Nov. 1953.
2. JF to EC, 27 Nov. 1953.
3. JF to EC, 12 Nov. 1953.
4. JFD, V, 7 Dec. 1953.
5. JFD, V, 26 Feb. 1954.
6. JFD, V, 20 Dec. 1953.
7. Ibid.
8. JFD, V, 27 June 1954.
9. JFD, V, 20 Dec. 1953.
10. JFD, V, 29 Dec. 1953.
11. JFD, V, 20 Dec. 1953.
12. JF to EC, 14 Dec. 1953.
13. JFD, V, 14 Jan. 1954.
14. JF to EC, 17 Jan. 1954.
15. JFD, V, 21 Jan. 1954.
16. JF to EC, 1 Feb. 1954.
17. JFD, V, 9 Feb. 1954.
18. JFD, V, 12 Feb. 1954.
19. JFD, V, 3 Feb. 1954.
20. JFD, V, 12 Feb. 1954.
21. JFD, V, 26 Feb. 1954.
22. Ibid.
23. JFD, V, 22 Feb. 1954.
24. JF to EC, 26 Feb. 1954.
25. JFD, V, 1 March 1954.
26. JFD, V, 31 March 1954.
27. JFD, V, 1 Apr. 1954.
28. JFD, V, 9 Feb. 1954.
29. JFD, V, 6 Jan. 1954.
30. JFD, V, 3 June 1954.
31. JFD, V, 29 Jan. 1954.
32. JFD, V, 4 Apr. 1954.
33. JFD, V, 31 March 1954.
34. JFD, V, 12 Feb. 1954.
35. JFD, V, 20 March 1954.
36. JFD, V, 22 May 1954.
37. JFD, V, 20 March 1954.
38. JFD, V, 29 March 1954.
39. JFD, V, 6 Apr. 1954.
40. EF, personal note, 7 June 1982. AC Col. and JF Col.
41. JFD, V, 12 Feb. 1954.
42. EC to JF, n.d., c. late March 1954.
43. JF to EC, 12 Feb. 1954.
44. JF to EC, 1 Feb. 1954.
45. JF to EC, 9 Apr. 1954.
46. JF to EC, 1 Apr. 1954.
47. JF to EC, 12 Feb. 1954.
48. RC to EC, 1 March 1954.
49. RC to EC, 12 Apr. 1954.
50. RC to EC, 26 Apr. 1954.

51. RC to EC, 25 Apr. 1954.
52. JF, *The Magus,* ch. 51, 362.
53. JFD, V, May 1954, insert MS 125.
54. Ibid.
55. JFD, V, 10 May 1954.
56. JFD, V, 3 June 1954.
57. JFD, V, May 1954, insert MS 125.
58. JF to EC, 10 May 1954.
59. JFD, V, 13 June 1954.
60. JF to EC, 18 May 1954.
61. JFD, V, 20 March 1954.
62. JF to EC, 20 May 1954.
63. JFD, V, 15 May 1954.
64. JF to EC, 21 May 1954.
65. JF to EC, 20 May 1954.
66. JFD, V, 13 June 1954.
67. JFD, V, 3 June 1954.
68. JF to EC, 5 June 1954.
69. JF to EC, 22 June 1954.
70. JF to EC, 23 June 1954.
71. JF to EC, 10 July 1954.
72. JFD, V, 2 Aug. 1954.
73. JF to EC, 5 June 1954.
74. JFD, V, 27 June 1954.
75. JFD, V, 2 July 1954.
76. JFD, V, 27 June 1954.
77. JFD, V, 26 July 1954.
78. JFD, V, 20 July 1954.
79. JFD, V, 2 July 1954.
80. JFD, V, 16 July 1954.
81. JFD, V, 28 July 1954.
82. JFD, V, 27 June 1954.
83. JFD, V, 27 July 1954.
84. JFD, V, 28 July 1954.
85. JFD, V, 20 July 1954.
86. JFD, V, 10 July 1954.
87. JFD, V, 2 July 1954.
88. JFD, V, 10 July 1954.
89. JFD, V, 20 July 1954.
90. JFD, V, 16 July 1954.
91. JFD, V, 27 July 1954.
92. JFD, V, 27 June 1954.
93. JFD, V, 1 July 1954.
94. JFD, V, 25 July 1954.
95. JFD, V, 1 July 1954.
96. JFD, V, 5 July 1954.
97. JFD, V, 12 July 1954.
98. JFD, V, 9 Aug. 1954.
99. JFD, V, 5 July 1954.
100. JFD, V, 2 July 1954.
101. JFD, V, 12 July 1954.
102. JFD, V, 27 July 1954.

103. JFD, V, 25 July 1954.
104. JF to EC, n.d., c. late Sept./early Oct. 1953.
105. JFD, V, 13 June 1954.
106. JFD, V, 2 July 1954.
107. JFD, TS vol. 5. Not to be confused with MS vol. 5. This typed "volume" is a mixed collection of short pieces, including poems through the 1940s and 1950s. No page numbers.
108. JF to EC, n.d., c. late Sept./early Oct. 1953.
109. JFD, V, 25 July 1954.
110. JFD, V, 5 July 1954.
111. JFD, V, 12 July 1954.
112. JF to EC, 16 July 1954.
113. JF to EC, 17 July 1954.
114. JF to EC, 16 July 1954.
115. JFD, V, 24 July 1954.
116. JFD, V, 16 July 1954.
117. JFD, V, 25 July 1954.
118. JFD, V, 24 July 1954.
119. JFD, V, 28 July 1954.
120. JFD, V, 9 Aug. 1954.
121. Ibid.
122. EC to JF, 15 Aug. 1954.
123. JFD, V, 12 Aug. 1954.
124. JFD, V, 5 Sept. 1954.
125. EC to JF, 15 Aug. 1954.
126. JFD, V, 4 Sept. 1954.
127. JF to SH, 3 Sept. 1954. JF Col., gathered in TS vol. 5, not to be confused with MS vol. 5.
128. JFD, V, 14 Sept. 1954.
129. JF, *Magus,* ch. 78, 605.

CHAPTER 9: THE WAITING ROOM

1. JFD, V, 9 Oct. 1954.
2. JFD, V, 25 Sept. 1954.
3. EF to MSh, 25 May 1976.
4. HO'S, 4 Nov. 1997.
5. JFD, V, 20 Oct. 1954.
6. JFD, V, 22 Feb. 1955.
7. JFD, V, 17 Sept. 1954.
8. JFD, V, 1 Nov. 1954.
9. JFD, V, 22 Sept. 1954.
10. JFD, V, 1 Nov. 1954.
11. JFD, V, 22 Sept. 1954.
12. JFD, V, 13 Oct. 1954. As with his economies at Ashridge, JF's thrift in writing his drafts on the reverse of his

workplace papers has preserved ample classroom and administrative materials from his teaching career at St. Godric's. The best group of preserved documents is in HRC 26/6 and 7, drafts of *The Magos,* parts 1 and 2. Dates on these communications are also very helpful in accurately dating Fowles's works in progress.

13. JFD, V, 6 July 1955.
14. JFD, V, 14 March 1955.
15. JF, "The Functioning of the English Department," HRC 26/7.
16. JF, various St. Godric's materials, HRC 26/6 and 7.
17. JFD, V, 10 Oct. 1955.
18. Ibid.
19. JFD, V, 15 Oct. 1955.
20. JFD, V, 13 Oct. 1954.
21. JFD, V, 13 Nov. 1954.
22. JFD, V, 20 Dec. 1956.
23. JFD, V, 9 Oct. 1955.
24. JFD, V, 20 Oct. 1954.
25. JFD, V, 12 Jan. 1955.
26. JFD, V, 17 Sept. 1954.
27. JFD, V, 10 March 1955.
28. JFD, V, 25 Oct. 1955.
29. JFD, V, 6 Nov. 1954.
30. JFD, V, 1 Feb. 1955.
31. JFD, V, 14 Sept. 1954.
32. JFD, V, 1 Feb. 1955.
33. JFD, V, 23 Nov. 1954.
34. JFD, V, 12 Dec. 1954.
35. JFD, V, 1 Aug. 1955.
36. JFD, V, 12 Dec. 1954.
37. JFD, V, 18 Nov. 1954.
38. JFD, V, 23 Nov. 1954.
39. JFD, V, 1 Feb. 1955.
40. JFD, V, 23 Nov. 1954.
41. JFD, V, 12 Dec. 1954.
42. JFD, V, 7 Sept. 1955.
43. JFD, V, 1 Feb. 1955.
44. JFD, V, 10 March 1955.
45. JFD, V, 25 Oct. 1955.
46. JFD, V, 8 Nov. 1955.
47. JFD, V, 19 May 1955.
48. JFD, V, 8 Feb. 1956.
49. JFD, V, 12 Dec. 1956.
50. JFD, V, 20 Dec. 1956.
51. JFD, V, 10 Feb. 1957.
52. JFD, V, 28 Jan. 1956.
53. JFD, V, 8 May 1956.
54. JFD, V, 22 Sept. 1954.
55. JFD, V, 18 Nov. 1954.
56. JFD, V, 22 Sept. 1954.
57. JFD, V, 18 Nov. 1954.
58. JFD, V, 29 Nov. 1954.
59. JF to Exeter University Library, 1993. Biographical notes appended to correspondence.
60. FP, 1 Apr. 1997.
61. JF to EC, 10 Nov. 1953.
62. JFD, V, 11 Dec. 1955.
63. JFD, V, n.d., July 1957.
64. JFD, V, 14 July 1956.
65. JFD, V, 22 Nov. 1954.
66. JFD, V, 6 May 1955.
67. JFD. V, 9 May 1955.
68. JFD, V, 25 Nov. 1955.
69. JFD, V, 9 Oct. 1955.
70. JFD, V, 21 May 1956.
71. JFD, VIII, 11 Apr. 1963.
72. JFD, V, 12 Nov. 1955.
73. JFD, V, 25 Feb. 1955.
74. JF, "For a Casebook," HRC 14/9.
75. JFD, V, 18 Aug. 1956.
76. JF to TM, pasted in JFD, VIII, 8 July 1963.
77. JFD, V, n.d., May 1955, insert, MS 126.
78. JFD, V, 9 Sept. 1955.
79. JFD, V, 9 Oct. 1955.
80. JFD, V, 28 Jan. 1956.
81. JFD, V, 12 Sept. 1956.
82. JFD, V, 20 Dec. 1956.
83. JF, "A Modern Writer's France," 51.
84. JFD, V, 20 Dec. 1956.
85. JFD, V, 10 Feb. 1957.
86. JFD, V, 27 Dec. 1956.
87. Ibid.
88. JFD, V, 10 Feb. 1957.
89. JFD, V, 15 Feb. 1957.
90. Ibid.
91. JFD, V, 15 June 1956.
92. JFD, V, 10 Jan. 1956.
93. JFD, V, 10 Feb. 1956.
94. JFD, V, 31 March 1956.
95. JF, "Seidevaare," HRC 28/4.
96. JFD, V, 14 May 1956.
97. Ibid.
98. JFD V, 9 Oct. 1956.
99. JF, "Dream Analysis, 1964." 19 Sept. 1964, HRC 50/7.
100. EF to DS, MSh, 1 May 1965.

101. JF, "May, 1956," unpublished poem, in JFD, TS vol. 5, not to be confused with MS vol. V.
102. JFD, V, 27 Feb. 1957.
103. JFD, V, 2 March 1957.
104. JFD, V, 31 March 1957.
105. JFD, V, 2 Apr. 1957.
106. JF, "Epithalamion," 2 Apr. 1957, unpublished poem in JFD, TS vol.5.

CHAPTER 10: A WRITER UNPUBLISHED

1. JFD, VI, n.d.c. 2 Aug. 1958, epigraph for ch. 10 in HRC 26/6 and 7.
2. JFD, VII, 3 June 1963.
3. JFD, V, 1 Sept. 1956.
4. JFD, VII, 20 March 1960.
5. JFD, V, 30 Dec. 1957.
6. JFD V, n.d., Dec. 1957.
7. JFD, V, 3 Nov. 1957.
8. JFD, VI, 2 Apr. 1958.
9. JFD, VII, 2 Jan. 1961.
10. EF to JF, 18 Dec. 1961. In JFD VII, 18 Dec. 1961.
11. JFD, V, Whitsun, June 1957.
12. JFD, VII, 29 Dec. 1961.
13. JFD, VI, 3 March 1958.
14. JFD, VII, 2 Jan. 1961.
15. JFD, VI, 3 March 1958.
16. JFD, VI, 1 March 1959.
17. JFD, VI, 3 March 1958.
18. EF to JF, 18 Dec. 1961. In JFD VII, 18 Dec. 1961.
19. HO'S, 4 Nov. 1997.
20. JFD, VII, 25 Oct. 1960.
21. JFD, VI, 5 Sept. 1958.
22. JFD VII, 25 Oct. 1960.
23. JF, *Poems* (New York: Ecco Press, 1973), 58–59.
24. JFD, VII, 28 Sept. 1959.
25. JFD, VII, 1 Sept. 1959.
26. JFD, VII, 28 Sept. 1959.
27. JFD, VII, 1 Sept. 1959.
28. JF, "The Functioning of the English Department," HRC 26/7.
29. JFD, VII, 9 May 1961.
30. EF to DS, MSh, 23 Oct. 1962.
31. JFD, VII, 8 Apr. 1960.
32. JFD, VII, 7 Jan. 1962.
33. JFD, VII, 13 Apr. 1962.
34. JFD, VII, 25 Oct. 60.
35. JFD, VII, 8 Apr. 60.
36. JFD, VII, 3 Aug. 1959.

37. FD, VII, 19 Jan. 1959.
38. FD, VII, 6 July 1959. In 1959, JF began translating the Roman poets, especially Martial, Juvenal, Horace, and Catullus.
39. EF to DS, 1 Sept. 1959.
40. JFD, V, 29 June 1957.
41. JFD, VII, 29 June 1961.
42. JFD, VII, 9 May 1961.
43. JF to DS, 2 Sept. 1959.
44. JF to DS, 21 Feb. 1958.
45. JF to DS, 2 Sept. 1959.
46. JFD, VII, 23 May 1961.
47. Ibid.
48. JFD, VII, 7 Aug. 1961.
49. JFD, VIII, 11 Apr. 1963.
50. JFD, VII, 28 Aug. 1960.
51. JFD, VII, 4 May 1962.
52. JFD, VII, 12 Feb. 1959.
53. JFD, VII, 13 Apr. 1959.
54. JFD, VII, 22 Apr. 1962.
55. EF to DS, 1 Sept. 1959.
56. JFD, V, 27 July 1957. The Hampstead potter was "Hilda."
57. EF to DS, 18 June 1958.
58. AC, 15 March 1997.
59. Ibid.
60. JFD, V, 3 Nov. 1957.
61. JFD, VI, 2 Apr. 1958.
62. Ibid.
63. EF to DS, 1 Sept. 1959.
64. Ibid.
65. Ibid.
66. Rosie Jackson, *Women Who Leave: Behind the Myth of Women Without Their Children* (London: HarperCollins [Pandora]), 1994), 265. Interview with Anna Christy, May 24, 1993. Information also in AC, 15 March 1997.
67. AC, 15 March 1997.
68. Ibid.
69. JFD, VII, 17 Dec. 1960.
70. JFD, VII, 9 July 1961.
71. AC, 15 March 1997.
72. EF to DS, 1 Sept. 1959. Edgar Whitton's death and funeral described in EF to DS, 21 Feb. 1958.
73. JFD, VII, 3 Aug. 1959.
74. JFD, VII, 1 March 1961.
75. JFD, VII, 9 May 1961. I am grateful to James C. Gedney, M.D., who researched information about this surgical procedure for me. Salpingostomy is

seldom performed now. The reconstructive surgical procedure sometimes used for this condition is fimbrioplasty. See C. P. Wheelers, Jr., *Atlas of Pelvic Surgery* (Baltimore: William & Wilkens, 1997).

76. JFD, VII, 1 March 1961.
77. JFD, VII, 9 May 1961.
78. JFD, VII, 24 Nov. 1961.
79. EF, inserted in JFD, VII, 22 Nov. 1961, 194–99. At JF's urging, EF wrote her own description of the events of November 1961.
80. EF to Charlotte Rhodes, 19 June 1983, HRC 52/3.
81. JFD, VII, 28 Nov. 1961.
82. JFD, VII, 4 Dec. 1961.
83. Richard Boston, "John Fowles, Alone but Not Lonely," *New York Times Book Review* (Nov. 9, 1969), 53.
84. JF, *Poitiers Novel*, HRC 33/1, "unfinished novel."
85. JF, 12 Jan. 1981.
86. JFD, VII, 24 March 1962.
87. JFD, I, disjoint 3, 4 Apr. 1950.
88. JFD, VII, 19 Nov. 1960.
89. JFD, VII, 2 Dec. 1960.
90. JF to TM, 8 July 1963, pasted into JFD, VII, 8 July 1963.
91. JFD, "THE COLLECTOR: Some Notes," 18 Apr. 1963, HRC 19/5. Written in "diary" form, 2 Dec. 1960–18 Apr. 1963. First draft of "I Write, Therefore I Am" (1964), in *Wormholes*, 5–12.
92. JFD, VIII, 3 Feb. 1963.
93. JF, "COLLECTOR: Some Notes," HRC 19/5.
94. JFD, VII, 2 Dec. 1960.
95. JF, "COLLECTOR: Some Notes," HRC 19/5.
96. JFD, VIII, 16 Apr. 1963.
97. JFD, VII, 31 March 1961.
98. JF, "COLLECTOR: Some Notes," HRC 19/5.
99. Ibid.
100. JFD, VII, 31 March 1962.
101. James Kinross to JF, 15 May 1962, copied by JF into JFD, VII, 15 May 1962.
102. JFD, VII, 18 May 1962.
103. JFD, VII, 20 May 1962.
104. JFD, VII, 4 July 1962.

CHAPTER 11: STRAIGHT TO THE TOP OF PARNASSUS

1. TM, 11 Nov. 1997.
2. James Kinross to JF, 4 July 1962, copied by JF into JFD, VII, 15 May 1962.
3. TM, 11 Nov. 1997.
4. JFD, VII, 6 July 1962.
5. TM, 11 Nov. 1997.
6. JF to TM, 8 July 1962, copied into JFD, VII, 8 July 1962.
7. JF to TM, 11 July 1962, copied into JFD, VII, 11 July 1962.
8. JFD, VII, 14 July 1962.
9. RJF to JF, 2 Jan. 1963, pasted into JFD, VIII, 10 Jan. 1963.
10. JFD, VII, 21 July 1962.
11. DS, 31 March 1997.
12. JFD, "Rome, 1962" VII, 31 July–6 Sept., 265. Insert, n.d., MS. 260–278.
13. JFD, "Rome 1962," MS 274.
14. DS, 31 March 1997.
15. MSh, conversation with author, March 31, 1997.
16. JFD, "Rome 1962," MS 270.
17. Ibid., 271. In MSh's memory of this event, the swimmers did not swim nude, as do the characters in *Daniel Martin*.
18. JFD, VIII, 10 Oct. 1962.
19. JFD, VIII, 25 Sept. 1962.
20. James Kinross to JF, 31 Oct. 1962, copied by JF into JFD, VII, 15 May 1962.
21. JF to DS, MSh, 6 Nov. 1962.
22. JFD, VIII, 16 Oct. 1962.
23. JFD, VIII, 18 Jan. 1963.
24. JFD, VIII, 24 Oct. 1962.
25. EF to DS, MSh, 23 Oct. 1962.
26. JFD, VIII, 24 Oct. 1962.
27. EF to DS, MSh, 23 Oct. 1962.
28. JFD, VIII, 24 Oct. 1962.
29. JFD, VIII, 3 Oct. 1962.
30. JFD, VIII, 4 Oct. 1962.
31. John Fowles, "'The Rain Took the Road This Winter,'" in *Poems*.
32. EF to DS, MSh, 23 Oct. 1962.
33. JFD, VIII, 24 Oct. 1962.
34. John Fowles, *Sequence Four*, HRC 34/12.
35. JF, "The Woman in the Reeds," *Michigan Quarterly Review* No. 4, 131–45.
36. JF, 12 Jan. 1981.
37. JKinberg, 29 Oct. 1999.

480   Notes

38. JKohn, 26 Oct. 2000. Also JKinberg, 29 Oct. 1999.
39. JF, *The Temptation of Anthony*, HRC 34/18, unfinished play.
40. Most important of Fowles's Anthonys is Anthony Mallory of *Daniel Martin*, who succumbs to the temptation of institutional piety, thereby (in Fowles's view) sinning against much of his better nature. In early drafts of *The Magus* (c. 1959–1963), the priest who was to be called John Leverrier, one of Nicholas's predecessors at the Lord Byron School, appears as Anthony, a priest sexually tempted by Lily and religiously tempted by Conchis, who withdraws to an Italian monastery.
41. JFD, VIII, 27 Jan. 1963.
42. JFD, VIII, 11 May 1963.
43. JFD, VIII, 10 Jan. 1963.
44. JFD, VIII, 2 May 1963.
45. JFD, VIII, 9–11 May 1963.
46. JFD, VIII, 1 Apr. 1963.
47. JFD, VIII, 10 Apr. 1963.
48. SH to JF, n.d. March 1963, copied by JF into JFD, VIII, 28 March 1963.
49. EF, "There's a Sting in the Tail," pasted into JFD, VIII, 28 March 1963.
50. JFD, VIII, 28 March 1963.
51. JFD, VIII, 19 Apr. 1963.
52. JFD, VIII, 19 Apr. 1963.
53. JFD, VIII, 23 Apr. 1963.
54. JF to SH, n.d., c. late 1964 (internal dating). In this note JF promises an advance copy of *The Magus*, "newminted from the Boston presses. I think you'll understand it rather better than anyone else in the world, and perhaps dislike it rather more. It's about masks. A sort of long letter that was never written. And I began it at Ashridge. It's all in metaphors, so don't worry—I mean about identification; not comprehension." JF Col., returned by SH in 1997.
55. JFD, VIII, 7 Sept. 1964.
56. JFD, VIII, 10 Apr. 1963.
57. EF to JF, 18 Sept. 1963. Also JFD, IX-A, MS 17.
58. DS, 31 March 1997.
59. HO'S, 4 Nov. 1997.
60. Julian Jebb, "A Brilliant Revelation," *Sunday Times* (May 5, 1963).

61. Elizabeth Coxhead, "Lovingly Walled Up," *Sunday Telegraph* (May 5, 1963).
62. Richard Lister, "One Girl and a Study in Terror," *Evening Standard* (May 7, 1963).
63. Simon Raven, *Observer* (May 5, 1963).
64. JFD, VIII, 7 May 1963.
65. JFD, VIII, 9–11 May 1963.
66. JFD, VIII, 17 May 1963.
67. JFD, VIII, 28 May 1963.
68. JFD, VIII, 10 Apr. 1963.
69. JFD, "Greece," 1963 IX-A, insert, n.d., 4–5.
70. JFD, IX-A, 7.
71. JFD, IX-A, 81.
72. JFD, IX-A, 10–11. RSP recognized attributes of his second wife in Sarah Woodruff when he read *The French Lieutenant's Woman*. Fowles admitted this to me March 1997.
73. JFD, IX-A, 6.
74. JFD, IX-A, 120–21.
75. EF to JF, 16 Sept. 1963.
76. EF to JF, n.d., c. 18 Sept. 1963.
77. EF to JF, 16 Sept. 1963.
78. JFD, "Success Bit, New York, September 1963," IX-B insert, 1–22, 1.
79. JFD, IX-B, 2.
80. JF to EF, n.d., c. 20 Sept. 1963.
81. JFD, IX-B, 4.
82. JFD, IX-B, 1.
83. JFD, "Hollywood," X, 32.
84. JFD, IX-B, 6.
85. JFD, IX-B, 12.
86. JF to EF, n.d., c. 20 Sept. 1963.
87. JFD, IX-B, 8.
88. JFD, IX-B, 9.
89. JFD, IX-B, 14.
90. JFD IX-B, 18–19.
91. JFD, IX-B, 22.
92. JFD, VIII, 9 Nov. 1963.
93. JFD, VIII, 29 Nov. 1963.
94. JFD, VIII, 9 Nov. 1963.
95. JFD, VIII, 26 Nov. 1963.
96. JFD, VIII, 29 Nov. 1963.
97. JFD, VIII, 3 Dec. 1963.

CHAPTER 12: THE SAVAGE EYE

1. JFD, "Cheltenham, October 1963," VIII, 3–6 Oct. 1963, 98 typed insert n.d., TS 98–103.

2. JFD, VIII, 99.
3. JFD, VIII, 102.
4. JF, EF to DS, MSh, 18 Nov. 1963.
5. JFD, VIII, 6 Aug. 1963.
6. JFD, VIII, 9 Aug. 1963.
7. JFD, VIII, 18 Nov. 1963.
8. JFD, VIII, 20 Aug. 1963.
9. JFD, VIII, 19 Nov. 1963.
10. Terence Stamp, *Double Feature,* vol. 2, (London: Bloomsbury, 1989), 111–12.
11. JKinberg, 29 Oct. 1999.
12. JFD, VIII, 19 Nov. 1963.
13. JFD, "Hollywood, March 1964," X, n.d., 16–29 March 1964, 12. Contains JFD, X, pp. 1–32; also "Illusionsville: A Fortnight in Hollywood" (unpublished article), pp. 1–17; also "For Mr. Wyler—Comments from John Fowles, pp. 1–4.
14. JFD, VIII, 28 Jan. 1964.
15. JF to DS, MSh, 18 Nov. 1963. Fowles also expressed these fantasies in an unfinished, untitled play, a savage, anti-Semitic satire on the American movie business, HRC 34/8.
16. JFD, "Hollywood" X, 12.
17. Ibid., 17.
18. Ibid., 4, 17.
19. Ibid., 13.
20. Ibid., 2, 4.
21. Ibid., 14.
22. Ibid., 11.
23. Ibid., 29.
24. Ibid., 16.
25. Ibid., 9.
26. Ibid., 7.
27. Ibid., 4, 5, 27.
28. Ibid., 24.
29. JKinberg, 29 Oct. 1999.
30. Ibid.
31. JFD, "Hollywood," X, 17–19.
32. Ibid., 14.
33. Ibid., 3–5.
34. Ibid., 13.
35. Ibid., 17. Also "For Mr. Wyler—Comments from John Fowles."
36. JFD, "Hollywood" X, 17.
37. Ibid., 22.
38. Ibid., 20.
39. JKinberg, 29 Oct. 1999.
40. Ibid.
41. JFD, "Hollywood," X, 27.
42. JKinberg, 29 Oct. 1999.
43. JFD, "Illusionsville: A Fortnight in Hollywood," X, 7.
44. JFD, "Hollywood," X, 25, originally written in letter to EF, 25–29 March 1964.
45. JFD, VIII, 1 Apr. 1964.
46. JFD, VIII, 2 Apr. 1964.
47. JFD, VIII, 3 Apr. 1964.
48. EF to JF, 22 March 1964.
49. JF to AS, 13 Feb. 1964, pasted into JFD, VIII, 13 Feb. 1964.
50. TM, 29 Apr. 1999.
51. JFD, VIII, 9 Sept. 1964, JF responding to *Kirkus Review,* September 1964.
52. Julian Mitchell, "The Aristos: Review," *Sunday Times* (June 13, 1965).
53. Francis Hope, "Pensees Manquees," *Observer* (June 13, 1965).
54. Nigel Dennis, "Mr. Superman," *Sunday Telegraph* (June 13, 1965).
55. John Mortimer, "Contra Clegg," *New Statesman* (July 2, 1965).
56. JFD, VIII, n.d., c. 5 July, 1965.
57. JFD, VIII, n.d., c. 10 Jan. 1964. JF responding to Harold Nicolson in *Books and Bookmen,* January 1964, and *British Books,* December 1963.
58. JF, "Swan Song of the European Wild," *Venture: The Traveler's World* (October 1964), 134–143.
59. JFD, "Norway, June–July 1964," X, 25 June 26–July 1964, 2. n.d.
60. Ibid., 28.
61. Ibid., 28–31.
62. JF, "Afterword," in *The Wanderer, or The End of Youth (Le Grand Meaulnes)* by Alain-Fournier (New York: New American Library, 1971), 208–33, 209.
63. Ibid., 208.
64. JFD, "A Modern Writer's France," in *Studies in Anglo-French Cultural Relations,* ed. Ceri Crossley and Ian Small (London: Macmillan, 1988), 53.
65. EF to DS, MSh, 1 May 1965.
66. JFD, VIII, 10 Jan. 1965.
67. JFD, VIII, 28 Jan. 1964.
68. JFD, VIII, 29 Nov. 1964.
69. JF to DS, 8 Jan. 1965.
70. JFD, VIII, 15 March 1964.
71. EF to DS, MSh, 1 May 1965.
72. Ibid.
73. JFD, VIII, 15 March 1964.

74. JFD, VIII, 7 Sept. 1964.
75. JF to DS, 8 Jan. 1965.
76. JFD, VIII, 23 Aug. 1964.
77. JFD, VIII, 12 Sept. 1964.
78. JF to DS, 8 Jan. 1965.
79. EF, critical comments on final draft of *The Magus,* 1965, HRC 26/8.
80. EF to DS, MSh, 1 May 1965.
81. JFD, VIII, 23 Feb. 1965.
82. JFD, VIII, 25 Feb. 1965.
83. EF to DS, MSh, 1 may 1965.
84. JF Papers, HRC 50/8.
85. JFD, VIII, 26 March 1965.
86. JF, *The Collector,* 1960–1962. Tulsa 1/1–6. TS draft novel; typed on verso of mimeographed sheets, 284 pages.
87. JF Papers, HRC 50/8.
88. JFD, VIII, 15 March 1965.
89. JFD, VIII, 7 May 1965.
90. EF to DS, MSh, 1 May 1965.
91. JKinberg to JF, 19 May 1965. HRC 50/8.
92. EF to DS, MSh, 1 May 1965.
93. JFD, VIII, 19 May 1965.
94. JKinberg, 29 Oct. 1999.
95. JFD, VIII, 21 May 1965.
96. JF, "Gather Ye Starlets," *Holiday* (June 1966), rep. in *Wormholes,* 89–99.
97. JFD, VIII, n.d., early May 1965.

CHAPTER 13: THE FOX AT BAY

1. JFD, VIII, 18 Oct. 1964.
2. JFD, VIII, 14 Oct. 1964.
3. JFD, VIII, 11 May 1963, 14 Oct. 1964.
4. JFD, VIII, 11 Oct. 1963.
5. EF, "A Day in the Country," (Unpublished: n.d., c. 1964), AC Col.
6. John Fowles, *The Fox,* HRC 14/19, unfinished novel.
7. JFD, "Tour of the West," VIII, 6–15 Oct 1964, 175.
8. EF to DS, MSh, 1 May 1965.
9. AC to author, 17 June 2001, E-mail.
10. JF to DS, MSh, 8 Jan 1965.
11. JFD, V, 9 Nov 1953.
12. JFD, VIII, 12 Feb. 1964.
13. JFD, "Hollywood," X, 24.
14. Ibid., 10.
15. JFD, VIII, 23 Feb 1965.
16. JFD, "Hollywood," X, 25. Also JF to EF, 29 Oct. 1964.

17. EF to DS, MSh, 1 May 1965.
18. JFD, VIII, 17 Sept. 1965.
19. EF to DS, MSh, 1 May 1965.
20. JFD, VII, n.d. early 1961, 117–18.
21. JF, *Poems,* 66.
22. JFD, VII, n.d., early 1961, 117–118.
23. "Meeting Miranda in Hollywood" has not survived.
24. JFD, "Heroine, June 1964," VIII, 20 Oct. 1964.
25. JFD, VIII, 20 Oct. 1964.
26. JFD, VIII, 2 Oct. 1964.
27. JFD, VIII, 15 Sept. 1964.
28. JFD, VIII, 18 Sept. 1964.
29. JF, "Dream Analysis, 1964," 14–20 Sept., further notes 3 Oct. 1964, HRC 50/7.
30. JFD, "Dream Analysis," 14 Sept. 1964, HRC 50/7.
31. Ibid.
32. JFD, XIII, 22 Dec. 1982.
33. Anthony Shield to JF, 24 March 1965. HRC 28/5.
34. TM to JF, 31 March 1965. HRC 28/5.
35. JFD, VIII, 7 May 1965.
36. JF, "First ending of *The Magus*" 1132–45, HRC 28/4.
37. TM to JF, 31 March 1965. HRC 28/5.
38. JFD, VIII, 16 June 1965.
39. JF, drafts of *The Magus,* June 1965, HRC 28/4.
40. JF, *Magus,* 5.
41. JFD, VIII, n.d., c. 17 June 1965.
42. JFD, "Tour of the West," VIII, 6–15 Oct. 1965, 176.
43. JFD, VIII, 23 July 1965.
44. JFD, VIII, 8 July 1965.
45. JFD, VIII, c. 7 Oct. 1965, 175.
46. JFD, VIII, 10 Oct. 1965, 177.
47. JFD, XI, 29 Oct. 1968.
48. JFD, VIII, 15 Oct. 1965, 179.
49. JFD, VIII, 10 Oct. 1965, 177.
50. JFD, VIII, 26 July and 3 Aug. 1965.
51. JFD, VIII, c. 30 July 1965, 217.
52. JFD, VIII, 10 Sept. 1965.
53. JFD, VIII, 17–22 Aug 1965.
54. JFD, VIII, 17 Sept. 1965.
55. Ibid.
56. JFD, VIII, 29 Aug–5 Sept. 1965.
57. JKinberg, 29 Oct. 1999.
58. MSh to author, 3 Nov. 1997.
59. EF to MSh, 18 June 1974.
60. JFD, VIII, 5 Nov. 1965.

61. EF to DS, MSh, 1 May 1965, 10 June 1983.

CHAPTER 14: THE *DOMAINE*

1. JFD, VIII, 10 Nov. 1965.
2. JF to DS, 8 Nov. 1965.
3. JFD, VIII, 27 Nov. 1965.
4. JF to DS, 8 Nov. 1965.
5. JFD, XI, 16 March 1966.
6. JFD, VIII, 5 Nov. 1965.
7. JFD, VIII, 20 Oct. 1965.
8. JFD, VIII, 23 Oct. 1965.
9. JFD, VIII, 20 Oct. 1965.
10. JFD, VIII, 23 Oct. 1965.
11. JF, letter to Michael Sharrocks, 1 March 1966.
12. JFD, VIII, 26 Oct. 1965.
13. JFD, VIII, 5 Nov. 1965.
14. JFD, XI, 2 Apr. 1969.
15. MSh to author, 3 Nov. 1997.
16. EF to MSh, 25 Nov. 1965.
17. JFD, VIII, 5 Dec. 1965.
18. JFD, VIII, 27 Nov. 1965.
19. JF to DS, 8 Nov. 1965.
20. JFD, VIII, 27 Nov. 1965.
21. JF to DS, MSh, 1 Jan. 1966.
22. EF to MSh, 8 July 1966.
23. JFD, XI, 18 Dec. 1965.
24. JFD, XI, 16 March 1966.
25. JF to author, 22 May 1996.
26. EF to MSh, 25 Jan. 1966.
27. JF to DS, MSh, 17 Jan. 1966.
28. J. D. Scott, "Seeing Things on Phraxos," *New York Times Book Review* (January 9, 1966), 4–5.
29. Marvin Mudrick, "Evelyn, Get the Horseradish," *Hudson Review* (1966), 305–7.
30. EF to DS, MSh, 17 Jan. 1966.
31. EF to MSh, 25 Jan. 1966.
32. EF to MSh, 1 Apr. 1966.
33. EF to MSh, 30 Jan. 1968.
34. JFD, XI, 22 Jan. 1966. JKohn, more courteously, remembered this nickname as "the painted toenail of America" on 26 October 2000.
35. EF to MSh, 2 Dec. 1966.
36. Tom Wiseman, Malou Wiseman, 1 May 1999.
37. JF to FP, 15 May 1966.
38. SF, 6 June 1999.
39. LS, 31 Oct. 1997.

40. EF to MSh, 2 Dec. 1966.
41. EF to MSh, 28 June 1967.
42. EF to MSh, 19 March 1968.
43. EF to MSh, 8 July 1966.
44. AC, 15 March 1997.
45. Ibid.
46. JFD, XI, 8 Aug. 1967.
47. JFD, XI, 20 July 1966.
48. EF to MSh, 30 Jan. 1968.
49. JF to DS, MSh, 3 Jan. 1967.
50. Ibid.
51. JFD, XI, 8 Aug. 1966.
52. JF to RC, 5 Aug. 1966, in JFD, XI, 5 Aug. 1966.
53. JF, *Daniel Martin* (Boston: Little, Brown, 1977), 164–65.
54. JF to DS, MSh, 3 Jan. 1967.
55. JFD, XI, 6 Jan. 1967.
56. JFD, XI, 8 Aug. 1966.
57. JFD, XI, 9 Aug. 1966.
58. JF, "On Writing a Novel," *Cornhill* (Summer 1969), 281–95. Rep. in *Wormholes*, 13–26. Also in JFD, XI, 16 May 1967.
59. EF to MSh, 2 Dec. 1966.
60. JFD, XI, 20 Oct. 1966.
61. JFD, XI, 30 Oct. 1966.
62. JFD, XI, 5 Nov. 1966.
63. JFD, XI, 27 Dec. 1966.
64. JF to FP, 5 Aug. 1969.
65. JFD, XI, 5 Nov. 1966.
66. JFD, XI, 20 Oct. 1966.
67. JFD, XI, 6 Nov. 1966.
68. JFD, XI, 1 Dec. 1966.
69. JF, "On Writing a Novel."
70. Claire de Durfort Duras, *Ourika, Introduction and Epilogue by John Fowles* (Austin, TX: W. Thomas Taylor, 1977).
71. JF to DS, 10 Oct. 1967.
72. JF, *The French Lieutenant's Woman*, 1977, Tulsa 2/4. TMTS draft.
73. EF, critique of *The French Lieutenant's Woman*, June 1968, Tulsa 2/4.
74. Ibid.
75. Elizabeth Mansfield, "A Sequence of Endings: The Manuscripts of *The French Lieutenant's Woman*," *Journal of Modern Literature*, No. 8, (1980–1981), 275–86.
76. JF to DS, MSh, 3 Jan. 1967.
77. JFD, XI, 1 Dec. 1966.
78. JKinberg, 29 Oct. 1999.
79. JFD, XI, 11 Feb. 1967.

80. EF to MSh, 17 Aug. 1967.
81. JFD, XI, 16 May 1967.
82. JFD, XI, 22 Jul. 1967.
83. EF to MSh, 29 Apr. 1967.
84. JFD, "Shooting *The Magus* in Majorca" XI, 6–20 Sept. 72.
85. JF to DS, MSh, 3 Jan. 1967.
86. JF to DS, 10 Oct. 1967.
87. Ef to MSh, 29 Apr. 1967.
88. JFD, XI, 3–8 June 1967.
89. JFD, XI, 16 May 1967.
90. EF to MSh, 29 Apr. 1967.
91. JFD, XI, n.d. May 1967.
92. JF to FP, 1 July 1967.
93. DT, 30 Apr. 1999.
94. Ibid.
95. EF to MSh, 11 Oct. 1967.
96. JFD, XI, 8 Dec. 1967.
97. EF to MSh, 20 Nov. 1967.
98. EF to MSh, 30 Jan. 1968.
99. JFD, XI, 5 March 1968.
100. JF, "Introduction to *Mehelah*," HRC 16/15; major correspondence for *Mehelah*, Tulsa 1/1.
101. JFD, XI, 8–23 Jan. 1968.
102. EF to MSh, 30 Jan. 1968.
103. JFD, XI, 31 Dec. 1967.
104. EF to MSh, 9 Feb. 1968.
105. JFD, XI, 21 Feb. 1968.
106. EF to MSh, 27 Feb. 1968.
107. JFD, XI, 25 Feb. 1968.
108. EF to MSh, 27 Feb. 1968.
109. JFD, XI, 25 Feb. 1968.
110. Ibid.
111. EF to MSh, 27 Feb. 1968.
112. JFD, XI, 2 March 1968.
113. JFD, XI, 26 Feb. 1968.
114. EF to MSh, 27 Feb. 1968.
115. EF to MSh, 9 April 1968.
116. Ibid.
117. JFD, XI, 18 Aug. 1968.
118. JFD, XI, 2 March 1968.
119. EF to MSh, 14 Aug. 1968.
120. JFD, XI, 18 Aug. 1968.
121. JFD, XI, 7–9 March 1968.
122. JFD, XI, 23 July 1968.
123. JFD, XI, 7–9 March 1968.
124. EF to MSh, 14 Aug. 1968.
125. JFD, XI, 23 July 1968.
126. JKinberg, 29 Oct. 1999.
127. JF, *Dr. Cook's Garden* or *The Guardian*, HRC 10/1, 2, Drafts of filmscript of play by Ira Levin.
128. JF to FP, 17 June 1968.
129. JFD, XI, 25 Dec. 1968.
130. JKinberg, 29 Oct. 1999.
131. EF to MSh, 8 June 1968.
132. EF to MSh, 23 Sept. 1968.
133. EF to MSh, 14 Aug. 1968.
134. JFD, XI, 18 Aug. 1968.
135. EF to MSh, 23 Sept. 1968.
136. TM, 29 Apr. 1999.

CHAPTER 15: CAST OUT

1. JFD, XI, 1 Dec. 1968.
2. JF to FP, 28 Jan. 1969.
3. EF to MSh, 6 March 1969.
4. JFD, XI, 9 Dec. 1968.
5. EF to MSh, 6 March 1969.
6. JF to FP, 28 Jan. 1969.
7. EF to MSh, 6 March 1969.
8. JFD, XI, 1 Dec. 1968. Also, XI, 4 and 9 Dec. 1968; EF to MSh, 6 March 1969; XII, 6 Oct. 1971.
9. JFD, XII, 5 Feb. 1973.
10. EF to MSh, 18 April 1969.
11. EF to MSh, 6 March 1969.
12. JFD, XI, 2 Apr. 1969 and 15 Apr. 1970.
13. JFD, XI, 12 Jan. 1969.
14. JFD, XI, 15 June 1969.
15. JFD, XI, 2 Oct. 1968.
16. JFD, XI, 29 Oct. 1968.
17. JFD, XI, 15 Jan. 1969 and 2 Oct. 1968.
18. JFD, XI, 1 Oct. 1968. The term *diachronic* is used to mean occurring in two interwoven time frames in the same narrative.
19. TM, 29 Apr. 1999. Also, JFD, XI, 1 Oct. 1968.
20. JFD, XI, 24 Apr. 1969.
21. JFD, XI, 8 Dec. 1968.
22. JFD, XI, 24 Nov. 1968 and 23 Feb. 1969.
23. JFD, XII, 23 March 1971.
24. JFD, XII, 22 June 1970.
25. JF to John Calley, Dec. 1969, HRC 35/19.
26. JF to FP, 28 Jan. 1969.
27. JFD, XI, 15 Jan. 1969.
28. JFD, XI, 3–11 Oct. 1969.
29. JFD, XII, 15 July 1970.
30. JFD, XI, 3 Oct. 1968.
31. AC, 15 March 97.
32. JFD, XI, 21 June 1969.
33. Roy Christy, *The Nightingales Are Sob-*

bing. New Authors, Ltd., vol. 68 (London: Hutchinson, 1968). Book jacket quote from the *New Statesman.*

34. JFD, XI, 29 Oct 1968. Denys Sharrocks characterized the novel as "a poor man's *Lucky Jim,*" 31 March 1997.
35. Roy Christy, *No Time Like the Past* (London: Hutchinson, 1969).
36. JFD, XI, 12 June 1969.
37. JFD, XI, 15 June 1969.
38. William Trevor, "Conjuring with Ghosts," *Guardian* (June 12, 1969), 9.
39. Stephen Wall, "In Hardy's Footsteps," *Observer Review* (15 June 1969), 29.
40. JFD, XI, 15 June 1969.
41. JFD, XI, 12 June 1969.
42. JF to FP, 22 June 1969.
43. JFD, XI, 27 June 1969.
44. Ibid.
45. JF, *Tom Manning,* HRC 2/7, draft.
46. JFD, XI, 27 June 1969.
47. JFD, XI, 15 Sept. 1969.
48. JFD, XI, 16 Oct. 1969.
49. JFD, XI, 19 Dec. 1969.
50. JFD, XI, 1 Nov. 1969.
51. Joni Mitchell, "Woodstock," Siquomb, BMI, in *So Far,* Crosby, Stills, Nash, and Young (New York: Atlantic, 1974).
52. JFD, XI, 10 Nov. 1969.
53. JFD, XI, 11–12 Nov. 1969.
54. JFD, XI, 14 Nov. 1969.
55. JFD, XI, 17 Nov. 1969.
56. JFD, XI, 10 Nov. 1969.
57. JFD, XI, 23 Nov. 1969.
58. EF to MSh, DS, 14 Nov. 1979. In this typical letter, EF writes of her "dislike and, indeed, horror" when marijuana is smoked at a dinner party and how she finds pot smoking "intolerable."
59. JF to Doug Balding, editor of *Arete,* 1990, HRC 51/13.
60. JFD, XI, 16 Nov. 1969.
61. JFD, XI, 23 Nov. 1969.
62. JFD, XI, 16 Nov. 1969.
63. JF, *America, I Weep for Thee: A Pamphlet,* 139, HRC 1/3.
64. JF, "For a Casebook," HRC 14/9, unpublished short story.
65. JF, *Zip,* a screenplay, HRC 35/17–19.
66. JF, with photographs by Frank Horvat, *The Tree* (London: Aurum Press, 1979), 12–30.

67. JFD, XII, 6 Sept. 1970.
68. JFD, XII, 7 Sept. 1970.
69. JFD, XII, 16 Sept. 1970.
70. JFD, XII, 30 Oct. 1970.
71. JFD, XII, 8 Sept. 1970. RJF's poems are copied into JFD on this date. They are: "Lost," "What Goethe Found," and "Recompense."
72. Ibid.
73. JFD, XII, 8, no 70.
74. JF, *The Jesuit,* HRC 19/9, abandoned novel, 9 Nov. 1970.
75. JFD, XII, 9 Feb. 1970.
76. JFD, XI, 15–18 Aug. 1969.
77. JFD, XI, 24 Apr. 1970.
78. JF to Volker Behrens, 5 Oct. 1987, HRC 40/4.
79. JFD, XII, 7 Nov. 1970.
80. JF, notes for "The Last Chapter" ("The Final Chapter," "Chapter 16"), HRC 19/14, unpublished short story.
81. JF to DT, 8 July 1971.
82. This version of the theme of a man pursued to his destruction by the muses is remarkably similar to Fowles's 1962 poem "Myth," part of the *Sequence Four* cycle, HRC 34/12.
83. JF, "Forword to *The Device,*" HRC 6/5.
84. JFD, XI, 8–23 Jan. 1968.
85. JFD, XII, 20 Jan. 1971.
86. JFD, XI, 1 Nov. 1969.
87. JFD, XII, 15 Feb. 1971.
88. JF, *The Device (Somebody's Got to Do It,* also *The Hedgehog),* HRC 6/5–8, 7/1–6, 8/1–6, and 9/1, 2, unpublished novel.
89. JFD, XII, 29 March 1971.
90. JFD, XI, 15 Sept. 1969.
91. JFD, XI, 22 June 1969.
92. Ibid.
93. JF to John Calley, Sept. 1970, HRC 35/19.
94. JFD, XI, 23 Feb. 1969.
95. JFD, XII, 29 March 1971.
96. JFD, XII, 3 Apr. 1971.
97. JFD, XII, 13 Apr. 1971.
98. TM, 29 Apr. 1999.
99. JFD, XII, 20 Apr. 1971.
100. JFD, XII, 13 Apr. 1971.
101. JFD, XII, 23 Apr. 1971.
102. JFD, XII, 22 Aug. 1971.
103. JFD, XII, 2 July 1972, 117.
104. JF, interview by Bob Cromie,

"*Daniel Martin* by John Fowles," *Book Beat*. Prod. Pat Downey. PBS WTTW, Chicago, Broadcast WHYY Philadelphia-Wilmington, 4 Jan. 1978.

105. JF to author, private conversation, 30 Oct. 1997.

CHAPTER 16: THE HEDGEHOG

1. JFD, XII, 25 July 1970, 1 Nov. 1971, 22 June 1973.
2. JFD, XII, 2 July 1972, 117.
3. Ibid., 117.
4. JFD, XII, 22 Nov. 1971.
5. JFD, XII, 2 July 1972, 117.
6. JFD, XII, 21 May 1971. Fowles evened this score by using Alan Brien as the model for the hollow man Fleet Street journalist Barney Dillon in *Daniel Martin*. Tempted after a January 17, 1974, argument to use his old friend Ronnie Payne, Fowles resisted and used Brien instead. As *DM* went to press, Fowles was introduced to Brien at a party by Ronnie Payne. "Author meets character in his yet unpublished book. I quite enjoyed it, not least because he proved he deserves what I give him in Barney Dillon," wrote Fowles. JFD, XII, 9 March 1977.
7. JFD, XII, 5 Nov. 1971. Peter Wolfe, *John Fowles: Magus and Moralist* (1976), 2d ed. (Lewisburg, Pa.: Bucknell University Press, 1979).
8. JFD, XII, 22 July 1972, 117. *Critique* 13.3 (1972).
9. JFD, XII, 2 July 1972, 116.
10. JF, *Poems*.
11. JF, Afterword, in *The Wanderer*, 208–23.
12. JF, "Conan Doyle," 7–11.
13. JF, "Making a Pitch for Cricket," correspondence in HRC 29/3.
14. JFD, XII, 2 July 1972, 116.
15. JFD, XII, 2 July 1972, 117.
16. Donald Hall, "John Fowles's Gardens," *Esquire* (October 1982), 99.
17. Claire de Durfort Duras, *Ourika, Translation, Introduction and Epilogue by John Fowles* (Austin, TX: W. Thomas Taylor, 1977), xxix. JF's unpublished drafts of introduction, HRC 32/14.
18. JF, "*Sensibility*" (also titled "*The New Self*"), HRC 34/11, unpublished.
19. Ibid., 60X, HRC 34/11.
20. Ibid., 39, HRC 34/11.
21. Ibid., 70X, HRC 34/11.
22. Ibid., 47, HRC 34/11.
23. JFD, XII, 9 Nov. 1970.
24. JFD, XI, 17 Dec. 1968.
25. John Fowles, "Ordeal by Income," in *Public Lending Right: A Matter of Justice*, ed. Richard Findlater (London: Andre Deutsch in association with Penguin Books, 1971), 99–108. Also HRC 32/12.
26. JFD, XII, n.d., 6–16 Oct. 1970.
27. JF to TM, 30 Sept. 1971, HRC 50/61.
28. "About the Prize," 19 Aug. 2002, Internet Web site, bookerprize.co.uk.
29. JF, "The Booker Prize Imbroglio," HRC 50/6, correspondence and clippings resulting from Fowles's participation as a Booker Prize panel member. "The Rules" were published January 1971.
30. JFD, XII, 29 Aug. 1971.
31. JFD, XII, 22 Aug. 1971.
32. JFD, XII, 14 Sept. 1971.
33. JFD, XII, 20 Sept. 1971.
34. JF to John Gross, 28 Sept. 1971, HRC 50/61.
35. JF to Antonia Fraser, 2 Oct. 1971, HRC 50/61.
36. JFD, XII, 20 Oct. 1971.
37. JFD, XII, 1 Nov. 1971.
38. Gilbert Rose, "*The French Lieutenant's Woman*: The Unconscious Significance of a Novel to its Author," *American Imago*, vol. 29 (1972), 165–76.
39. JF, "Sensibility," 48, HRC 34/11.
40. Rose, "*The French Lieutenant's Woman*," 173.
41. JFD, XII, 20 Nov. 1971.
42. JF to Gilbert Rose, 13 July 1974, copy in author's possession, courtesy of Dr. Rose.
43. JF, "A Personal Confession," foreword to *The Prisoner* (*Ourika*), HRC 32/14, unpublished essay.
44. JFD, XI, 27 June 1969.
45. JF, *Daniel Martin* memo book, HRC 2/6.
46. JF to Gilbert Rose, 13 July 1974.
47. JF, notes for *Daniel Martin*, HRC 2/7.
48. EF to MSh, 14 May 1972. Also JFD, "Egyptian Journey," XII, Jan. 1972.

49. JFD, VIII, 24 Oct. 1963.

50. JFD, "Egyptian Journey," 1972, XII, n.d., c. 16 Jan. 1972, 100.

51. Ibid. 24 Jan 1972, 108.

52. JF, *The Device (Somebody's Got to Do It,* also *The Hedgehog),* ch. 60, HRC 9/2.

53. JFD, XII, 2 May 1973.

54. DT, 30 Apr. 1999.

55. JFD, XII, 4 July 1972.

56. JFD, XII, 7 July 1972.

57. JFD, XII, 13 Nov. 1972.

58. JF, *The Last Chapter,* 1972, directed by David Tringham (London: Ltd. Cassius Film Production, 13 November 1972), with Denholm Elliott and Susan Penhaligon, 35-minute film.

59. JF, *A Short History of Lyme Regis* (New York: Little, Brown, 1982), 10–11.

60. JF, "A New Image for Lyme," HRC 32/7, published in *Festival News,* 1974.

61. JFD, XII, 6 June 1970.

62. JF, "Kenneth Allsop," HRC 19/11, published as "The Man and the Island" in *Steep Holm: A Case History in the Study of Evolution,* ed. JF (Sherborne: Dorset Publishing Co., 1978).

63. JFD, XII, 28 Aug. 1970.

64. JFD, XII, 4 July 1973.

65. JFD, XII, 10 Nov. 1972.

66. Ann Jellicoe and Roger Mayne, 29 May 1999. "Mrs. P." was Mrs. Pettis.

67. EF to MSh, 14 May 1972.

68. JFD, XII, 20 Nov. 1971.

69. JFD, XII, 3 Sept. 1974.

70. JFD, XII, 18 June 1975.

71. JFD, XII, 19 Aug. 1972.

72. MSh to author, 3 November 1997.

73. JFD, XII, 22 July 1972.

74. JFD, XIV, 10 Apr. 1986.

75. JFD, XXXII, 28 Sept. 1997.

76. EF to MSh, 14 May 1972. Also JFD, XII, 16 Oct. 1972.

77. JFD, XII, 24 Jan 1974.

78. JFD, XII, 22 July 1972.

79. JFD, XII, 15 Aug. 1972.

80. JFD, XII, 19 Aug. 1972.

81. JF, "Poor Koko," 13–20 Sept. 1972, HRC 10/7, original MS.

82. JFD, XII, 23 May 1973.

83. JFD, XII, 4 June 1973.

84. JFD, XII, 4 July 1973.

85. JF, "The Picnic" (also "The Cloud"), 14–20 June 1973, HRC 10/6. Original MS.

86. JF, "An Enigma," 13–17 Aug 1973, HRC 10/6, original MS.

87. JF, "The Ebony Tower" (also "The Parallel"), Aug–Sept. 1973, revised Oct. 1973, HRC 10/7, original MS.

88. JFD, XII, 13 Nov. 1973.

89. Tom Wiseman and Malou Wiseman, 1 May 1999.

90. JFD, XII, 1 Jan 1974.

91. JFD, XII, 8–12 Nov 1973.

92. JF, "Behind the Scenes," Nov., Dec. 1973, HRC 10/6, in *Variations,* unpublished.

93. JFD, XII, 20 July 1974.

94. JF to DS, MSh, 25 Sept. 1974.

95. EF to MSh, 11 March 1976.

96. JFD, XII, 17 Jan. 1974.

97. JFD, XII, 27 Oct. 1974.

98. JFD, XII, 3 Oct. 1974.

99. Ibid.

CHAPTER 17: ON THE ISLAND OF *DANIEL MARTIN*

1. EF to DS, MSh, 13 Dec. 1974.

2. EF to DS, MSh, 19 Nov. 1974. Postcard.

3. JFD, XII, 25 Nov. 1974, 238–39.

4. JF, with photographs by Fay Godwin, *Islands* (London: Jonathan Cape, 1978), 28, epigraph to ch. 17, 30.

5. JFD, XII, 16 March 1975.

6. JFD, XII, 5 Dec. 1975.

7. JFD, XIII, 26 Aug. 1977.

8. JFD, XII, 15 Apr. 1975.

9. JFD, XII, 21 May 1972.

10. JFD, XII, 13 Nov. 1973.

11. JFD, XII, 11 Feb. 1976. David Rudkin's script, HRC 39/4.

12. JFD, XII, 30 Nov. 1971.

13. JFD, XII, 3 March 1975.

14. JFD, XII, 26 Feb. 1975.

15. JFD, XII, 11 March 1975.

16. JFD, XII, 12 Apr. 1975.

17. JFD, XII, 1 and 18 Nov. 1975. D. Potter's script, HRC 39/2.

18. JFD, XII, 11 Feb. 1976.

19. JFD, XII, 20 Nov. 1975.

20. JFD, XII, 13 Nov. 1973.

21. John Fowles, *The Black Thumb,* HRC 1/13–14. Copy of screenplay and other information, DT, 30 Apr. 1999.

22. JF, *The Screw* and abandoned science-fiction fragments, Oct. 1974, HRC 34/9.
23. JFD, XII, 3 May 1975.
24. JF, *The Ebony Tower,* film correspondence and contracts (1975–1981), HRC 36/8.
25. JFD, XII, 7 Nov. 1975.
26. Rodney Legg, *Steep Holm: Allsop Island* (Wincanton, Somerset: Wincanton Press, 1992), 5.
27. JFD, XII, 4 Nov. 1973.
28. JFD, XII, 29 July 1973.
29. RL, *Steep Holm.*
30. RL, 8 June 1999.
31. Ibid.
32. JFD, XII, 25 Feb. 1977.
33. JFD, XII, 20 Feb. 1977.
34. RL, 8 June 1999.
35. Ibid.
36. EF to MSh, 18 June 1974.
37. RL, 8 June 1999.
38. Ibid.
39. RL, *Steep Holm,* 19.
40. EF to MSh, 18 June 1974.
41. JFD, XII, 11 June 1974.
42. JFD, XII, 26 Feb. 1974.
43. JF, *Shipwreck,* Photographs by the Gibsons of Scilly (London: Jonathan Cape, 1974).
44. JFD, XII, 15 Apr. 1974.
45. JF, *Steep Holm.*
46. JF to Fay Godwin, 2 Feb. 1976.
47. JFD, XII, 16 July 1975.
48. JFD, XII, 12 Aug. 1975.
49. JFD, XII, 3 Aug. 1975.
50. JFD, XII, 16 July 1975.
51. JF, *The Magus: A Revised Version* (London: Jonathan Cape, 1977), 440–41.
52. Ibid., 653.
53. EF to DS, MSh, 10 July 1977.
54. JFD, XII, 5 Dec. 1975.
55. EF to MSh, 21 Feb. 1975.
56. EF to DS, MSh, 24 Apr. 1976.
57. JFD, XIII, 1 May 1977.
58. JFD, XIII, 24 June 1977.
59. JFD, XII, 17 Nov. 1973. Also, EF to MSh, 18 Oct. 1978.
60. EF to DS, MSh, 21–22 Oct. 1976.
61. EF to MSh, 21 Feb. 1975.
62. EF to DS, MSh, 26 Jan. 1976.
63. JFD, XII, 25 March 1973.
64. EF to DS, MSh, 26 Jan. 1976.
65. EF to MSh, 9 June 1975.
66. Tom Wiseman and Malou Wiseman, 1 May 1999.
67. JFD, XII, 6 May 1974.
68. JFD, XII, 14 Jan. 1976.
69. JFD, XII, 31 May 1977.
70. JFD, XIII, 10 Sept. 1977.
71. JFD, XI, 31 Oct. 1968.
72. JFD, XII, 2 Dec. 1974.
73. EF to DS, MSh, 20 March 1978.
74. Ibid.
75. EF to DS, MSh, 15 Oct. 1977.
76. EF to DS, MSh, 20 March 1978.
77. John Fowles, "Hardy and the Hag," in *Thomas Hardy After Fifty Years,* ed. Lance St. John Butler, (Totowa, N.J.: Rowman & Littlefield, 1977), 28–42.
78. Ibid., 31.
79. Ibid., 38–39.
80. W. Thomas Taylor, letter to JF, 24 Nov. 1975, HRC 32/14.
81. Duras, *Ourika,* limited to 350 copies, $90 each.
82. Thomas F. Staley, 20 Jan. 1999.
83. JFD, XII, 18 Jan. 1977.
84. EF to DS, MSh, 22 Aug. 1978.
85. JF to DS, MSh, 22 Aug. 1978, postscript.
86. JFD, XIII, 18 Aug. 1977.
87. JFD, XII, 2 July 1972.
88. JFD, XII, 16 March 1975.
89. JF, letter to Harold William Fawkner, 12 May 1981, insert in JFD, XIII, 25.
90. JF, letter to Stephen Van Damme, 22 Sept. 1980, insert in JFD, XIII.
91. JFD, XII, 5 Dec. 1975.
92. JFD, XII, 17 Jan. 1977.
93. JFD, XIII, 4 Feb. 1977.
94. JFD, XIII, 24 March 1977.
95. JFD, XIII, 11 Feb. 1977.
96. JF to DS, 5 Apr. 1977.
97. JFD, XIII, 8 Apr. 1977.
98. EF to MSh, 10 July 1977.
99. JFD, XII, 24 Aug. 74.
100. EF to DS, MSh, 22 Aug. 1977.
101. John Gardner, "In Defense of the Real," *Saturday Review* (October 1, 1977), 22–24.
102. Christopher Lehmann-Haupt, "Un-Inventing the Novel," *New York Times* (September 13, 1977), 29.

103. EF to DS, MSh, 11 Oct 1977.
104. Ibid.

CHAPTER 18: THE CONSOLATIONS OF THE PAST

1. Robert Nye, "Tasteless, Tactless," *Guardian Books* (6 Oct. 1977), 9.
2. Charles Nicholl, "A Fowles Captive," *Daily Telegraph* (October 6, 1977), 14.
3. Thomas Hinde, "Heads in the Sand?," *Sunday Telegraph* (October 9, 1977), 16.
4. EF to DS, MSh, 11 Oct 1977.
5. Jacky Gillot, "Home to Make Peace," *Times* (October 6, 1977), 20.
6. Christopher Booker, "Psychonundrum," *Spectator* (October 15, 1977).
7. JF to DS, MSh, 21 Oct. 1977.
8. EF to DS, MSh, 8 Feb. 1978.
9. JFD, XIII, 1 March 1981.
10. JFD, XIII, 31 Oct. 1980.
11. JF, reviews, 1970–1978, HRC 33/2–50; 34/1–3, 6, 7.
12. JF, *Islands,* 98.
13. JFD, XIII, 24 Sept. 1980.
14. JF, *The Tree,* 12, 121.
15. JF, "A Subjective View: Letter to Conference organizers" (September 1981). Bellagio, Italy, Conference on Scientific Concepts of Time in Humanistic and Social Perspectives, July 1981. In JFD, XIII, 74. Epigraph to chapter 18 is also from this letter.
16. AJ, 29 May 1999.
17. EF to DS, MSh, 8 Feb. 1978.
18. Ann Jellicoe, *Community Plays: How to Put Them On* (London: Methuen, 1987), 3.
19. MScriven, 3 May 1999.
20. JF, *Curator's Report, 1978* (Lyme Regis: Philpot Museum, 1979). Courtesy of Nigel Cozens, Lymelight Books.
21. EF to DS, MSh, 1 March 1978.
22. JFD, XIII, 13 Oct. 1980.
23. L-AB, 29 May 1999.
24. JD, 31 Oct. 1997.
25. Muriel Arber, letter to John Fowles, 25 Feb. 1979, LRM.
26. Lyme Regis Museum and JF, *Curator's Report: With Notes on Recent Discoveries and New Acquisitions* (Lyme Regis: Lyme Regis (Philpot) Museum, 1980–1988). *Curator's Report 1987–88* was coauthored by Liz-Anne Bawden and copyrighted by the Friends of the Lyme Regis (Philpot) Museum, 1989.
27. JF, *A Brief History of Lyme* (Lyme Regis, Dorset: Friends of the Lyme Regis Museum, 1981).
28. JF, *A Short History of Lyme Regis* (New York: Little, Brown, 1982).
29. JF and Friends of the Lyme Regis Museum, *Lyme Regis: Three Town Walks* (Lyme Regis: Friends of the Lyme Regis Museum, 1983).
30. JF, *Thumbnail History of Lyme Regis* (Lyme Regis: Friends of the Lyme Regis Museum, 1981).
31. JF, *Medieval Lyme Regis* (Lyme Regis: Lyme Regis [Philpot] Museum, 1984).
32. Geoffrey Chapman, JF, and David West, *The Siege of Lyme Regis* (Lyme Regis, Serendip Books, 1982).
33. JF, with photographs by Barry Brukoff, *The Enigma of Stonehenge* (New York: Summit Books, 1981), 88.
34. Ibid., 92.
35. RL, 8 June 1999.
36. Ibid.
37. JFD, XIII, 7 Nov. 1980.
38. JF, *Stonehenge,* 92.
39. Marie Broxall to JF, 5 Feb. 1979, HRC 26/3.
40. JF, correspondence (1978–1981), Dr. Michael Hunter, Dept. of History, University of London, Birkbeck College, author of *John Aubrey and the Realm of Learning* (New York: Science History Publications, 1975), HRC 32/2.
41. JFD, XIII, 7 Nov. 1980.
42. John Aubrey, *Monumenta Britannica,* ed. JF and annotated Rodney Legg, (Sherborne: Dorset Publishing Co., 1980–1981). In United States, subtitled *A Miscellany of British Antiquities,* 1 vol. (Boston: Little, Brown, 1982). HRC 32/2, 3, 4.
43. EF to DS, MSh, Aug. 1985.
44. EF to DS, MSh, 20 March 1978.
45. EF to DS, MSh, 10 June 1983.
46. EF to DS, MSh, Aug. 1985, 28 Nov. 1986.
47. LS, 31 Oct. 1997.

48. EF to Charlotte Rhoades, 19 June 1983. HRC 52/1.
49. EF to DS, MSh, 10 Oct. 1986.
50. EF to DS, MSh, 14 March 1986.
51. EF to DS, MSh, 8 Feb. 1979.
52. EF to author, conversation, September 1982, Lyme Regis.
53. MSh, 3 May 1999.
54. EF to DS, MSh, 29 Aug. 1980.
55. EF to DS, MSh, 31 Oct. 1983.
56. EF to MSh, 1 Oct. 1979.
57. EF to MSh, 16 Oct. 1980.
58. TM, 29 Apr. 1999.
59. MSh, letter to author, 4 Nov. 1997.
60. EF to MSh, 1 Oct. 1979.
61. EF to MSh, 15 Jan. 1980.
62. JF, *Mantissa* (London: Jonathan Cape, 1982). U.S. edition: Boston: Little, Brown, 1982.
63. Eileen Warburton, "Fowles Takes a Risk for 'Minor' Work," *Los Angeles Times* (September 29, 1982).
64. Flann O'Brien, *At Swim-Two-Birds* (*1939*) (Normal: Dalkey Archive Press, Illinois State University, 1998). Eileen Porter died of cancer on October 10, 1975.
65. JF, *Conditional* (Northridge, CA: Lord John Press, 1979). Broadside, designed and printed by William Everson and Richard Bigus for the Lord John Press. Calligraphy by M. Carey. Limited to 150 copies. Courtesy of Nigel Cozens, Lymelight Books.
66. EF to MSh, 1 Oct. 1979.
67. Warburton, "Risk for 'Minor' Work."
68. Daniel Halpern, letter to JF, 24 Apr. 1980, HRC 29/7.
69. EF to DS, MSh, 16 Oct. 1980, 10 Aug. 1979, 7 July 1986.
70. EF to DS, MSh, 22 Oct. 1986.
71. MScriven, 3 May 1999.
72. EF to DS, MSh, 22 Oct. 1986.
73. Ibid.
74. Ibid.
75. EF to DS, MSh, 15 Dec. 1977.
76. EF to AC (Anna Homoky), 13 Dec. 1977.
77. Rosie Jackson, *Women Who Leave: Behind the Myth of Women Without Their Children* (London: HarperCollins [Pandora], 1994), 267. Interview with Anna Christy, May 24, 1993.
78. EF to DS, MSh, 10 Nov. 1978.
79. EF to DS, MSh, 1 Sept. 1978.
80. EF to MSh, 1 Oct. 1979.
81. JFD, XIII, 24 Sept. 1980.
82. Ibid.
83. EF to DS, MSh, 22 Dec. 1980.
84. EF to DS, MSh, 22 Sept. 1982.
85. EF to MSh, 1 Oct. 1979.
86. TM, 29 Apr. 1999.
87. JF, "Foreword," xii, in Harold Pinter, *The French Lieutenant's Woman: A Screenplay* (Boston: Little, Brown, 1981).
88. JFD, XIII, 24 Oct. 1980, 69.
89. Ibid.
90. JFD, XIII, 7 March 1981.
91. EF to DS, MSh, 10 Nov. 1978.
92. EF to DS, MSh, 10 Aug. 1979.
93. JFD, XIII, 24 Oct. 1980.
94. EF to MSh, 16 Oct. 1980.
95. TM, 29 Apr. 1999.
96. Ibid.
97. JF, film agreements, *The French Lieutenant's Woman*, HRC 38–40.
98. TM, 29 Apr. 1999.
99. MScriven, 3 May 1999. Mary Scriven served as assistant location manager during the Lyme Regis filming. I am grateful for her many colorful and amusing memories of this episode.
100. JFD, XIII, 24 Oct. 1980.
101. JFD, XIII, 7 March 1981.
102. Joan Walker to JF, 27 Nov. 1981, LRM.
103. MScriven, 3 May 1999.
104. JFD, XIII, 24 Oct. 1980.
105. Malcolm Bradbury, *The Enigma, A Screenplay*; from a story by John Fowles, 1980, BBC-TV, HRC 13/4, 37/6.
106. Antony Rouse, *The Enigma of Stonehenge*, from the book by John Fowles, 1981, BBC-TV, HRC 37/7.
107. JFD, XIII, 1 March 1981.
108. EF to DS, MSh, 23 Sept. 1984.
109. JFD, XIII, 7 March 1981.
110. JFD, XIII, Aug. 1981, 86.
111. JFD, XIII, 22 Dec. 1982.
112. Irving Wardle, "Preview Review of *Dom Juan*," *Times* (April 6, 1981).
113. John Barber, *Telegraph* (April 6, 1981).
114. JF, "A Source of Sedition," program

notes for *Dom Juan*, HRC 9/8.

115. John Higgins, "A Fresh Mind on Molière's 'Odd Man Out'," *Times* (April 6, 1981). HRC 9/9.

116. JF, "A Source of Sedition," HRC 9/8.

117. JF, "The Background to Lorenzaccio," introduction, and "Background Notes for Teachers and Pupils," 1983, HRC 20/6.

118. Irving Wardle, *Times* (March 14 1983). HRC 20/6.

119. JFD, XIII, 4 Nov. 1980.

120. JFD, XIII, 26 Oct. 1981.

121. John Higgins, 6 Apr. 1981.

122. JFD, XIII, Aug. 1981, 85.

123. JFD, XII, 18 Jan. 1977.

124. JFD, XIII, 26 Oct. 1981.

125. JFD, XIII, Aug. 1981, 86.

126. JFD, XIII, 1 March 1981.

127. JFD, XIII, 26 Oct. 1981.

128. JFD, XIII, Aug. 1981 86.

CHAPTER 19: HERE BE DRAGONS

1. EF, personal note, 7 June 1982. JF Col., AC Col.

2. JF to DS, MSh, 5 Aug. 1992.

3. EF, personal note, 7 June 1982. JF Col., AC Col.

4. JFD, XIII, 14 June 1984. Here JF argues against H. W. Fawkner and EF, who unsuccessfully demanded "an explanation of why *Mantissa* was written." During interviews for this biography, many of EF's friends also murmured (with the tape recorder off) that she had disliked the book.

5. EF to DS, MSh, 22 Sept. 1982.

6. John Walsh, "The Strand Man," *Books and Bookmen* (September 1985).

7. JFD, XIII, 22 Dec. 1982.

8. JFD, XIII, 17 June 1983.

9. JFD, XIV, 9 Aug. 1987. XV, 9 March 1988.

10. JD, 31 Oct. 1997.

11. Warburton, "Risk for 'Minor' Work," *Los Angeles Times* (September 29, 1982).

12. JF, *Martine* working documents, HRC 31/1, 4–10.

13. John Barber, "Between the Lines,"

Daily Telegraph (April 15, 1985), 12.

14. JF, "The Value of the Unspoken," program, HRC 319. Earlier version, "Translator's Notes, 26 aug 82," HRC 315.

15. JF, *Le Jeu de l'Amour et du Hasard,* by Marivaux, translation and working documents, HRC 21/1–4.

16. JF, *A Maggot* (London: Jonathan Cape, 1985). Also: Boston, Little, Brown, 1985.

17. Barber, "Between the Lines."

18. L-AB, 29 May 1999.

19. JF, *A Maggot,* "Prologue," v.

20. JF, "Sensibility," 24, HRC 3411.

21. JFD, XIII, 21 Sept. 1977.

22. Miranda Seymour, "The War Between Faith and Reason," *Books and Bookmen* (September 1985).

23. Pat Rogers, "Left Lobe and Right," *TLS* (September 20, 1985), 1027.

24. John Walsh, "The Strand Man," *Books and Bookmen* (September 1985).

25. Stuart Evans, "Shaking History and Mysticism," *Times* (September 19, 1985).

26. Anne Smith, "Naught for Your Comfort," *New Statesman* (September 20, 1985), 30.

27. Robert Nye, "Magus's Maggot," *Guardian* (September 1985), 10.

28. JFD, XIII, n.d. Sept. 1983, 102.

29. Ibid., 102.

30. JF to Harold William Fawkner, 12 May 1981, in JFD, XIII.

31. JFD, XIV, c. 14 Dec. 1986.

32. JFD, XII, 9 Nov. 1970.

33. JFD, XIV, 16 Dec. 1986.

34. JFD, XII, 2 Jan. 1971.

35. JFD, XIII, 23 March 1983.

36. JF to DS, 10 Oct. 1967.

37. JFD, XIII, Apr. 1981.

38. JFD, XIII, 22 Dec. 1982.

39. JFD, "Cambridge Seminar," XIV, 9–13 July 1986, 32. JF was angry enough to mix up his predators, calling Terry Eagleton "Terry Hawk" in this entry.

40. JFD, XIII, 14 June 1983.

41. JFD, XII, 16 Aug. 1972.

42. JFD, XIV, 26 Jan. 1987.

43. Jo Draper and JF, *Thomas Hardy's England* (London: Jonathan Cape, 1984).

Correspondence and documents, HRC 17/2.

44. Fay Godwin and JF, *Land* (London: Heinemann, 1985), ix–xii. Correspondence and documents, HRC 19/12.

45. Peter Benson, *The Levels* (London: Constable & Penguin, 1987).

46. Robin Mackness, *Oradour: Massacre & Aftermath* (London: Bloomsbury, 1988).

47. EF to DS, MSh, 22 Oct. 1986.

48. EF to DS, MSh, Aug. 1985.

49. EF to DS, MSh, 6 June 1984.

50. JFD, XIII, 11 Feb. 1984.

51. JFD, XVII, 2 Sept. 1989.

52. JFD, XIII, 11 Feb. 1984.

53. EF to DS, MSh, 10 June 1983.

54. EF to DS, MSh, 27 June 1981.

55. EF to DS, MSh, 21 Nov. 1982.

56. EF to DS, MSh, 10 June 1983.

57. EF to DS, MSh, 6 June 1984.

58. AC, 15 March 1997.

59. JFD, XIV, 27 Dec. 1985.

60. Ibid.

61. EF to DS, MSh, Aug. 1985.

62. JFD, XIV, 27 Dec. 1985.

63. EF to DS, MSh, Aug. 1985.

64. JFD, XIV, 8 Dec. 1985.

65. Ibid.

66. EF to DS, MSh, 28 Nov. 1985.

67. EF to DS, MSh, 28 Jan. 1986. JFD, XIV, 19 Dec. 1985.

68. JFD, XIV, 9 Feb. 1986.

69. JFD, XIV, 9 May 1986.

70. JFD, XIV, 24 Jan. 1986.

71. JFD, XIV, 4 June 1986.

72. JFD, XIV, 31 Jan. 1986.

73. JFD, XV, 29 Nov. 1989.

74. JFD, XIV, 24 May 1987.

75. JF to DS, 25 Feb. 1988.

76. JFD, XIV, 18 Dec., 21 Nov. 1986.

77. JFD, XIV, 20 Jan. 1987.

78. JF, *Daniel Martin,* 629.

79. JF, *Mantissa,* 161.

80. JFD, XIV, 25 March 1986.

81. JFD, XIV, 8 Apr. 1986.

82. EF to DS, MSh, 5 March 1986.

83. EF to DS, MSh, 28 Nov. 1985.

84. EF to DS, MSh, 14 March 1986.

85. EF to DS, MSh, 27 June 1986.

86. EF to DS, MSh, 18 March 1987.

87. JFD, XIV, 10 Nov. 1986.

88. JFD, XIV, 12 Dec. 1986.

89. EF to DS, MSh, mid-Jan. 1987.

90. EF to DS, MSh, 22 Oct. 1986.

91. EF to DS, MSh, n.d. Feb. 1987.

92. EF to DS, MSh, 25 Feb. 1987.

93. EF to DS, MSh, 18 March 1987.

94. JFD, V, 27 July 1954.

95. JFD, V, 27 June 1954.

96. JFD, XIV, 6 June 1987.

97. EF, JFD, XIV, 24 Aug. 1987, margin, 73.

98. JFD, XIV, 13–14 Feb. 1988.

99. Tom Wiseman and Malou Wiseman, 1 May 1999.

100. JFD, XV, 17 Feb. 1988.

101. EF, letter to "friends," 20 Feb. 1988. JFD, XIV.

102. JF to DS, MSh, 17 March 1988.

103. Ibid.

104. JFD, XV, 17 Feb. 1988.

105. JFD, XV, 19 March 1988.

106. JFD, XV, 29 Apr. 1988.

107. DS, 3 Nov. 1997.

108. Tess Homoky, "A Very Boaring Walk," HRC 9/9.

109. EF to DS, MSh, 7 Oct. 1988.

110. JFD, XV, 9 March 1988.

111. L-AB, 29 May 1999.

112. Peter Prince, *Daniel Martin,* filmscript, HRC 365.

113. JFD, XV, 15 Apr. 1988.

114. James R. Baker, "The Art of Fiction, CIX, *Paris Review* III, Summer 1989," in *Conversations with John Fowles,* ed. Dianne L. Vipond, (Jackson: University Press, Mississippi, 1999), 195–96. Also David Streitfeld, "A Writer Blocked" in *Washington Post* (May 6, 1996), D-1.

115. JF, "Possessed by a Spell," HRC 33/2.

116. JFD, XV, 23 Aug. 1988.

117. EF to DS, MSh, 7 March 1989.

118. JFD, XV, 13 Dec. 1988.

119. Ibid.

120. EF to DS, MSh, 20 Dec. 1988.

121. JFD, XVI, 8 Jan. 1989. Anna resumed the surname Christy after her divorce.

122. JFD, XVI, 23 May 1989.

123. JFD, XIV, 8 Oct. 1986.

124. LS, 31 Oct. 1997.

125. HO'S, 4 Nov. 1997.

126. JFD, XVI, 22 Jan. 1989.

127. JFD, XVI, 24 March 1989.

128. AC, 15 March 1997.

129. JFD, XVII, 15 Dec. 1989.
130. EF, JFD, XVII, Sept.–Nov. 1989, margins: 26, 28, 35, 41, 43, 49, 51, 53, 58, 66, 70. All EF comments written 26 Nov. 1989.
131. JFD, XVII, 24 Nov. 1989.
132. JFD, XVII, 26 Nov. 1989.
133. Malou Wiseman, 1 May 1999.
134. AC, 15 March 1997.
135. LS, 31 Oct. 1997.
136. AC, 15 March 1997. Also, JFD, XVII, 22 Feb. 1990.
137. JFD, XVII, 24 Feb. 1990.
138. Ibid.
139. AC, 15 March 1997.
140. LS, 31 Oct. 1997.
141. AC, 15 March 1997.
142. JFD, XVII, 1 March 1990.
143. DS to author, conversation, 1 June 1999.
144. MSh, *The Moment,* unpublished essay, Sept. 1990.

CHAPTER 20: *TENDRESSE*

1. Obituary, "Elizabeth Fowles," *Times* (March 6, 1990).
2. AC, 15 March 1997.
3. JFD, XVII, 3 March 1990.
4. Brenda Maddox, *Nora: The Real Life of Molly Bloom* (Boston: Houghton Mifflin, 1988), 375–76. The "quote" used for EF's funeral is an edited-down version of assessments of Nora Barnacle Joyce by Arthur Powers and by her grandson, Stephen Joyce.
5. RSP, "Funeral Address," 9 March 1990.
6. JFD, XVII, 29 March 1990.
7. JF to AC, 28 June 1990.
8. JFD, XVII, 24 March 1990.
9. JFD, XXIV, 4 March 1991.
10. JFD, XXIII, 13 Dec. 1990.
11. JFD, XXII, 10 May 1990.
12. AC to author, conversation, May 31, 1999.
13. LS, 31 Oct. 1997.
14. SF, 6 June 1999.
15. AJ to author, conversation, May 29, 1999.
16. JFD, XXX, 23 March 1996.
17. JFD, XXII, 27 May 1990.
18. JFD, XXII, 21 July 1990.
19. JFD, XXII, 27 May 1990.
20. JFD, XXIV, 28 May 1991.
21. JFD, XXII, 21 July 1990.
22. JFD, XXVIII, 25 Sept. 1994.
23. EvL, 16 Nov. 1997. EvL to JF, 30 May 1990.
24. JFD, XXII, 6 July 1990.
25. DS, 31 March 1997.
26. JFD, XXII, 9 July 1990.
27. JFD, XXII, 31 July 1990.
28. "Life imitating art." At some point in interviews (with recorder off), most of Fowles's male friends (Peter Benson, Denys Sharrocks, Tom Wiseman, Ronnie Payne, Tom Maschler) used the same phrase about JF's relationship with EvL.
29. JFD, XXII, 31 July 1990.
30. JF to DS, MS, 22 Jan. 1991.
31. JFD, XXII, 23 Sept. 1990.
32. JFD, XXII, 31 July 1990.
33. JFD, XXII, 9 Aug 1990.
34. JFD, XXII, 17 Aug. 1990.
35. JFD, XXII, 31 July 1990.
36. PB, 28 Oct. 1997.
37. JFD, XXII, 9 Aug. 1990.
38. JFD, XXII, 8 Sept. 1990.
39. LS, 31 Oct. 1997.
40. JFD, XXIII, 5 Oct. 1990.
41. JFD, XXII, 8 Sept. 1990.
42. JFD, XXII, 12 Sept. 1990.
43. JFD, "A New Chapter Begins for Elinor's Career," XXV, pasted in July 1991.
44. JFD, XXV, 2 Sept. 1991.
45. JFD, XXV, 2 Oct. 1991.
46. JFD, XXV, 4 Sept. 1991.
47. JFD, XXV, 9 June 1991.
48. JFD, XXIII, 2 Jan. 1991.
49. JFD, XXVI, 22 Nov. 1991.
50. JFD, XXIV, 1 Apr. 1991. XXVI, 16 Apr. 1992; XXV, 17 July 1991.
51. JFD, XXVI, 3 Apr. 1992.
52. JFD, XXII, 12 Sept. 1990.
53. JFD, XXVI, 6 March 1992.
54. JFD, XXIII, 6 Dec. 1990.
55. JFD, XXIV, 29 March 1991. Many other examples. Also to author, Jan. 1992.
56. JFD, XXIX, 1 March 1995.
57. JFD, XXV, 10 Aug. 1991.
58. JFD, XXIV, 27 Feb. 1991.
59. JFD, XXIV, 29 March 1991.
60. JFD, XXVI, 3 Nov. 1991.
61. JF to EvL, 19 Nov. 1992, JFD, XXVII.

62. JW, 7 June 1999.
63. JF to DS, MS, 5 Feb. 1993.
64. JF to Anthony Sheil, 2 Nov. 1993, JFD, XXVII.
65. JFD, XXVII, 13 Oct. 1993.
66. Thomas F. Staley, letter to JF, 19 May 1991, Courtesy of Dr. Staley and HRC.
67. JFD, XXIV, 10 March 1991.
68. JF to Thomas F. Staley, 16 Nov. 1993.
69. JFD, XXIV, 10 March 1991.
70. JFD, XXV, 26 July 1991.
71. JFD, XXVI, 22 March 1992.
72. JFD, XXVII, 13 Oct. 1992.
73. Relf, Introduction, *Wormholes*, xxvii. Fowles himself defined the term "in the older sense, 'a frenzy of desire caused by something unattainable, a passion for an ideal.'" JFD, XXV, 9 June 1991.
74. JR, 15 Nov. 1997.
75. JFD, XXIV, 5 May 1991.
76. JR to JF, 19 Jan. 1994, JFD, XXIX.
77. JFD, XXX, 28 Oct. 1995.
78. JFD, XXX, 24 Nov. 1995.
79. JFD, XXX, 25 Nov. 1995.
80. JFD, XXVII, 13 Oct. 1993.
81. JFD, XXVIII, 4 Apr. 1994.
82. FP, 1 Apr. 1997.
83. TM, 29 Apr. 1999.
84. JF, "Two Poems by John Fowles," *Twentieth Century Literature: John Fowles Issue*, vol. 42, no. 1 (Spring 1996), 8–9. ed. James R. Baker and Dianne L. Vipond.
85. JFD, XXVIII, 22 Feb. 1994.
86. JFD, XXVIII, 27 Oct. 1994.
87. JFD, XXVII, 27 Oct. 1993.
88. Baker and Vipond, eds., *Twentieth Century Literature: John Fowles Issue*.
89. JF, "The Nature of Nature," in *The Tree; The Nature of Nature*: Two Essays Accompanied by Eight Woodcuts by Aaron Johnson and Published by Carolyn and James Robertson (Covelo, CA: Yolla Bolly Press, 1995), and *The Nature of Nature* (Covelo, CA: Yolla Bolly Press, 1996).
90. Kohn, 26 Oct. 2000.
91. Katherine Tarbox to Monhegan Island, Maine, and Eileen Warburton to Aquidneck Island, Rhode Island.
92. L-AB, 29 May 1999. Also letter to author, 4 Aug. 2000.
93. James R. Aubrey, *John Fowles: A Reference Companion* (Westport, CT: Greenwood Press, 1991).
94. JFD, XXXII, 20 Sept. 1997.
95. JFD, XXXI, 12 Sept. 1996.
96. JFD, XXXI, 22 Feb. 1997.
97. Kirki Kefalea, ed., *H Ellenike Empeiria* [John Fowles and the *Greek Experience*]. (Athens, Greece: Olkos, 1996).
98. AC, letter to author, 3 Dec. 1996.
99. JF, "Greece, 1996," in *Wormholes,* 71–72. First published in *H Ellenike Empeiria,* transl. by John Fowles.
100. JFD, XXXII, 12 May 1997.
101. PB, 28 Oct. 1997.
102. JFD, XXXI, 18 March 1997.
103. JFD, XXVI, 6 Aug. 1991.
104. JFD, XXIX, 13 Oct. 1993.
105. JFD, XXX, 1 Jan. 1996.
106. JFD, XXXII, 21 June 1997.
107. JF to author, telephone, 9 March 1998.
108. JFD, XXXII, 12 May 1997.
109. JFD, XXIX, 29 Jan. 1995.
110. JFD, XXXII, 21 June 1997.
111. JF to author, conversation, January 21, 1997.
112. JFD, XXX, 14 Apr. 1996.
113. JFD, XXXII, 21 June 1997.
114. Ibid.
115. JFD, XXXI, 9 Sept. 1996.
116. Sturgis, "Coëtminais, Sanford, Ninth of May 1998. Henry Breasley, Magus, John Fowles. Lives Changed by a Difference."
117. Ibid.
118. KD, 9 June 1999.
119. Kim Willsher, "The French Lieutenant's New Woman," *Mail on Sunday* (November 22, 1998), 42–43.
120. Melissa Denes, "Fowles on a Fair Day," *Sunday Telegraph Magazine* Novembe 22, 1998, 29–32.
121. Charles Glass to author, E-mail, May 11, 2000.